MEDITERRANEAN
500 CLASSIC RECIPES

MEDITERRANEAN
500 CLASSIC RECIPES

A FABULOUS COLLECTION OF TIMELESS, SUN-KISSED RECIPES, FROM APPETIZERS AND SIDE DISHES TO MEAT, FISH AND VEGETARIAN MEALS, ALL DESCRIBED STEP-BY-STEP, WITH 500 PHOTOGRAPHS

TRADITIONAL, BEST-LOVED REGIONAL DISHES FROM MOROCCO, SPAIN, TURKEY, GREECE, FRANCE AND ITALY PROVIDE INSPIRATION FOR WONDERFUL FOOD TO SUIT ANY OCCASION

EDITOR: BEVERLEY JOLLANDS

This edition is published by Southwater, an imprint of Anness Publishing Ltd,
108 Great Russell Street, London WC1B 3NA; info@anness.com

www.southwaterbooks.com; www.annesspublishing.com; twitter: @Anness_Books

If you like the images in this book and would like to investigate using them for publishing, promotions or advertising, please visit our website www.practicalpictures.com for more information.

Publisher: Joanna Lorenz
Editorial Director: Helen Sudell
Project Editor: Rosie Gordon
Jacket Design: Jonathan Davison
Production Controller: Rosanna Anness

A CIP catalogue record for this book is available from the British Library.

COOK'S NOTES
Bracketed terms are intended for American readers.
For all recipes, quantities are given in both metric and imperial measures and, where appropriate, in standard cups and spoons. Follow one set of measures, but not a mixture, because they are not interchangeable.
Standard spoon and cup measures are level. 1 tsp = 5ml, 1 tbsp = 15ml, 1 cup = 250ml/8fl oz.
Australian standard tablespoons are 20ml. Australian readers should use 3 tsp in place of 1 tbsp for measuring small quantities.
American pints are 16fl oz/2 cups. American readers should use 20fl oz/2.5 cups in place of 1 pint when measuring liquids.
Electric oven temperatures in this book are for conventional ovens.
When using a fan oven, the temperature will probably need to be reduced by about 10–20°C/20–40°F.
Since ovens vary, you should check with your manufacturer's instruction book for guidance.
The nutritional analysis given for each recipe is calculated per portion (i.e. serving or item), unless otherwise stated.
If the recipe gives a range, such as Serves 4–6, then the nutritional analysis will be for the smaller portion size, i.e. 6 servings.
The analysis does not include optional ingredients, such as salt added to taste.
Medium (US large) eggs are used unless otherwise stated.

Main front cover image shows Grilled Skewered Lamb – for recipe, see page 35.

PUBLISHER'S NOTE
Although the advice and information in this book are believed to be accurate and true at the time of going to press, neither the authors nor the publisher can accept any legal responsibility or liability for any errors or omissions that may have been made nor for any inaccuracies nor for any loss, harm or injury that comes about from following instructions or advice in this book.

Contents

Numerous nations and communities live around the Mediterranean's rocky coast and on its islands, and all have distinctive and thriving culinary traditions. In a region that brings together the diverse cultures of Europe, Africa and Asia, and where every village seems to boast its own speciality, it seems surprising that the food of the region as a whole can be so easily characterized as "Mediterranean". Yet there are strong themes that unite all the different local styles of cooking, and they are dictated by the land itself.

The Mediterranean region is often described as coinciding with the limit of the olive tree's distribution, and olives and olive oil are of course staples of Mediterranean cooking. The vine is another signature crop of the region, and the two plants grow so well there because they are perfectly suited to the climate and the terrain. Their long roots push down through the stony soil to find water in seasons of drought, at the same time anchoring the plants safely to resist the wind. They cling to the land with a tenacity like that of the people who grow them. For many centuries, Mediterranean farmers and smallholders have eked a living from a region where small patches of cultivated land are scattered between mountains, forest and shore. The soil is stony and shallow, the weather hot and dry in summer, stormy and unpredictable in winter. But while it has always been difficult to grow arable crops on a large scale or to provide sufficient rich pasture for cattle, fruit trees and vegetables thrive, providing crops that are unrivalled anywhere in the world.

The "Mediterranean diet", which is now hailed as a key to good health and long life, stems from a traditional reliance on the area's abundance of vegetables, fruit, pulses, herbs, nuts and grains, together with a wide variety of fish fresh from the sea, and with relatively little meat and dairy produce. Mediterranean cooks are frugal, but the flavours they create are generous and memorable. Meat and fish are grilled over charcoal or wood, vegetables are stewed in olive oil, salads are laced with garlicky dressings, and everything is fragrant with herbs and spices. Summer visitors to the region have their senses awakened by its dazzling light and colour, and the intense flavours of its food have a comparable effect, which can be quite addictive.

The lands of the Mediterranean have been repeatedly invaded and colonized since Phoenician traders criss-crossed the sea 3,000 years ago, carrying foodstuffs, cooking techniques and recipes from port to port. The whole area was at the heart of the Roman Empire, and was later dominated by

the Byzantine Empire. In the 8th century it came under Islamic influence, and the Arabs, who remained in Spain until the 14th century, established orchards and gardens, introduced irrigation technology, and planted many crops new to Europe, including rice, sugar cane, oranges, spinach and dates. Other ingredients that are now considered staples of Mediterranean cooking, such as tomatoes, peppers and chillies, came from the New World.

Successive incomers stamped their own styles of cooking on the region, and ideas spread along the trade routes they set up. As a result, similar dishes can often be found in the cuisines of different countries: fish soups, pizzas and tarts, vegetable stews and nut-thickened sauces and dips occur in many guises but are recognizable as variations on ancient and well-loved themes.

This book brings together a huge selection of recipes collected from all over the Mediterranean, ranging from simple snacks and ideas for quick family meals to full-on festive feasts. Many are faithful versions of traditional dishes, carefully adapted where necessary for today's kitchens and ingredients. Others are modern recipes, though still just as authentic, because despite its respect for tradition, the cooking of the region is constantly evolving.

There are many tantalizing pictures of the finished dishes and ingredients to inspire you and whet your appetite. An important part of the attraction of Mediterranean food is its visual impact. Its colours are as sparkling as its flavours, and its vivid reds, greens and yellows are drawn from the same bright palette as the deep blue of the summer sky and the clear turquoise of the sea.

Finally, all the recipes have been analysed by a nutritionist, and the energy, fat, carbohydrate and protein count, and levels of fibre, calcium and sodium, are detailed under each entry. This information helps you to plan meals that are both delicious and nutritious.

Anchovy and Caper Bites

These miniature skewers are very popular in Spain, where they are called *pinchos*, which literally means "stuck on a thorn". Taste, colour and shape guide the choice of ingredients that are speared together on cocktail sticks. The selection may also include pieces of cold or cured meat, pickled tuna, salted fish or even hard-boiled eggs. In the south of the country, piquant pickled vegetables are the most popular combination. In that region, the resemblance of the little sticks to a bullfighter's dart was noticed and so the dish was renamed.

Serves 4

12 small capers
12 canned anchovy fillets in oil, drained
12 stoned (pitted) black olives
12 cornichons or small gherkins
12 silverskin pickled onions

1 Using your fingers, place a caper at the thicker end of each anchovy fillet and carefully roll it up, so that the caper is completely enclosed.

2 Thread one caper-filled anchovy, one olive, one cornichon or gherkin and one pickled onion on to each of 12 cocktail sticks (toothpicks). Chill and serve.

Cook's Tip

If the anchovies you are using are extremely salty, try soaking them in a little milk before using them. Salted capers should also be rinsed before use.

Variations

- *Add a chunk of canned tuna in oil to each stick.*
- *You can vary the ingredients if you like, using slices of cold meats, chunks of cheese and pickled vegetables. Choose a selection of 3–4 ingredients to give contrasting textures, flavours and colours.*

Prosciutto and Pepper Crostini

The delicious flavours of these quick and easy Italian appetizers are hard to beat. Quickly put together on chunky slices of ciabatta, they look like mini-pizzas and are just as popular. Eat them in your fingers as a snack with drinks or, for a first course, serve with mixed salad greens and sliced plum tomatoes.

Makes 4

½ ciabatta loaf
1 red (bell) pepper, roasted, peeled
1 yellow (bell) pepper, roasted, peeled
4 thin slices prosciutto, cut into thick strips
50g/2oz reduced-fat mozzarella cheese
freshly ground black pepper
fresh basil leaves, to garnish

1 Preheat the grill (broiler) to high. Cut the ciabatta bread diagonally into four thick slices and toast until crisp and golden on both sides.

2 Cut the roasted red and yellow pepper flesh into thick strips and arrange them on the toasted bread slices. Top with the strips of prosciutto.

3 Thinly slice the mozzarella and arrange on top, then season with plenty of black pepper. Grill (broil) for 2–3 minutes, or until the cheese is melting.

4 Sprinkle the basil leaves on top to garnish and serve the crostini immediately.

Cook's Tips

- *To prepare the peppers, grill (broil) under a high heat, turning frequently, until the skins are charred on all sides. Put the hot peppers into a plastic food bag for a few minutes to allow the steam to loosen the skins. When they are cool enough to handle, strip off the skin and remove the seeds.*
- *For an extra healthy version, use wholemeal (whole-wheat) toast instead of a ciabatta loaf.*
- *Try dolcelatte instead of mozzarella for a tangy flavour.*

Anchovy and Caper Bites: *Energy 41kcal/169kJ; Protein 2.8g; Carbohydrate 2.2g, of which sugars 1.6g; Fat 2.4g, of which saturates 0.4g; Cholesterol 6mg; Calcium 44mg; Fibre 0.8g; Sodium 636mg.*
Crostini: *Energy 202kcal/854kJ; Protein 9.5g; Carbohydrate 31.7g, of which sugars 7g; Fat 5g, of which saturates 2.2g; Cholesterol 11mg; Calcium 113mg; Fibre 2.6g; Sodium 397mg.*

Crostini with Tomato, Red Pepper and Mozzarella Toppings

This Italian hors d'oeuvre was originally a way of using up an over-abundance of tomatoes at harvest time.

Makes 16

1 ciabatta loaf

For the tomato, pepper and anchovy topping

400g/14oz can or bottle Italian roasted red (bell) peppers and tomatoes, in vinegar or brine
50g/2oz can anchovy fillets
15ml/1 tbsp extra virgin olive oil
15–30ml/1–2 tbsp balsamic vinegar
1 garlic clove
25ml/1½ tbsp red pesto
30ml/2 tbsp chopped fresh chives, oregano or sage, to garnish
15ml/1 tbsp capers, to garnish

For the mozzarella and tomato topping

25ml/1½ tbsp green pesto
120ml/4fl oz/½ cup thick home made or bottled tomato sauce
75g/3oz reduced-fat mozzarella cheese, cut into 8 thin slices
2–3 ripe plum tomatoes, seeded and cut into strips
fresh basil leaves, to garnish

1 Preheat the grill (broiler) to high. Cut the ciabatta into 16 slices. Toast until golden on both sides. Cool on a wire rack.

2 For the tomato, pepper and anchovy topping, drain the tomatoes and peppers and wipe dry with kitchen paper. Cut into 1cm/½ in strips and place in a shallow dish. Rinse and dry the anchovy fillets and add to the peppers and tomatoes. Drizzle with the olive oil and sprinkle with the balsamic vinegar.

3 Using a sharp knife, peel and halve the garlic clove. Rub 8 toasts with the cut edge of the clove and lightly brush the toasts with a little red pesto. Arrange the tomatoes, peppers and anchovies decoratively on the toasts and sprinkle with chopped herbs and capers.

4 For the mozzarella and tomato topping, lightly brush the remaining toasts with the green pesto and spoon on some tomato sauce. Arrange a slice of mozzarella on each and cover with the tomato strips. Garnish with basil leaves.

Tomato and Mozzarella Toasts

These small toasts made from a slim Italian loaf resemble tiny pizzas and are good with drinks before a dinner party. You can prepare them several hours in advance and pop them in the oven just as your guests arrive to bring out while the cheese is hot and bubbling.

Serves 6–8

3 sfilatini (thin ciabatta)
about 250ml/8fl oz/1 cup sun-dried tomato paste
3 × 150g/5oz packets mozzarella cheese, drained
about 10ml/2 tsp dried oregano or mixed herbs
30–45ml/2–3 tbsp olive oil
ground black pepper

1 Cut each sfilatino on the diagonal into 12–15 slices, discarding the ends of the loaves. Toast the slices lightly on both sides until just coloured.

2 Preheat the oven to 220°C/425°F/Gas 7. Spread sun-dried tomato paste on one side of each slice of toast. Chop the mozzarella cheese into small pieces and arrange them over the tomato paste.

3 Put the toasts on baking sheets, sprinkle with herbs and pepper to taste and drizzle with oil. Bake for 5 minutes or until the mozzarella has melted and is bubbling. Leave the toasts to settle for a few minutes before serving.

Variations

Use red or green pesto instead of the sun-dried tomato paste – a combination of colours is especially effective if the toasts are served on a large platter. Halved olives can be pressed into the cheese, or criss-crossed strips of anchovy.

Cook's Tip

Mozzarella has an elastic texture and stretches into long strings when melted. Cutting it into small pieces before cooking will make the toasts easier for your guests to eat.

Crostini: *Energy 116kcal/488kJ; Protein 4.8g; Carbohydrate 15.9g, of which sugars 3.2g; Fat 4.1g, of which saturates 1g; Cholesterol 5mg; Calcium 60mg; Fibre 1.3g; Sodium 301mg.*
Toasts: *Energy 227kcal/947kJ; Protein 13.3g; Carbohydrate 10.9g, of which sugars 4.8g; Fat 14.8g, of which saturates 8.2g; Cholesterol 33mg; Calcium 230mg; Fibre 1.2g; Sodium 365mg.*

Cannellini Bean and Sun-Dried Tomato Bruschetta

This traditional Italian dish is a sophisticated version of beans on toast. The beans make these appetizers filling and substantial, but they are low in fat.

Serves 6

150g/5oz/¾ cup dried cannellini beans
5 tomatoes
10ml/2 tsp olive oil
2 sun-dried tomatoes in oil, drained and finely chopped
2 garlic cloves
30ml/2 tbsp chopped fresh rosemary
12 slices Italian-style bread, such as ciabatta
salt and freshly ground black pepper
fresh basil leaves, to garnish

1 Soak the beans in water overnight. Drain, rinse, place in a pan and cover with water. Boil rapidly for 10 minutes then reduce the heat and simmer for 50–60 minutes. Drain.

2 Meanwhile, place the tomatoes in a bowl, cover with boiling water, leave for 30 seconds, then refresh in cold water. Skin, seed and chop the flesh.

3 Heat the oil in a pan and add the fresh and sun-dried tomatoes. Crush 1 garlic clove and add with the rosemary. Cook for 2 minutes. Add the mixture to the cooked cannellini beans, season to taste with salt and ground black pepper, and mix well. Heat through gently.

4 Preheat the grill (broiler) to high. Cut the remaining garlic clove in half and rub the bread slices with it. Toast the bread lightly on both sides. Spoon the cannellini bean mixture on top of the toast. Garnish with basil leaves and serve immediately.

Variation
Canned beans can be used instead of dried; use 275g/10oz/2 cups drained, canned beans, rinse well, drain and add to the tomato mixture in step 4.

Buñuelos

The name of these cheese puffs literally means "puffballs". In Spain, they are usually deep-fried, but baking is easier when you are entertaining, and it gives wonderful results. The dough is made in the same way as French choux pastry, and the *buñuelos* should be eaten within a few hours of baking.

Serves 4

50g/2oz/¼ cup butter, diced
1.5ml/¼ tsp salt
250ml/8fl oz/1 cup water
115g/4oz/1 cup plain (all-purpose) flour
2 whole eggs, plus 1 yolk
2.5ml/½ tsp Dijon mustard
2.5ml/½ tsp cayenne pepper
50g/2oz/1/2 cup finely grated Manchego, Gruyère or Cheddar cheese

1 Preheat the oven to 220°C/425°F/Gas 7. Place the butter and salt in a pan, then add the water. Bring the liquid to the boil. Meanwhile, sift the flour on to a sheet of baking parchment or greaseproof (waxed) paper.

2 Working quickly, tip the flour into the pan of boiling liquid in one go and stir it in immediately.

3 Beat the mixture vigorously with a wooden spoon until it forms a thick paste that binds together and leaves the sides of the pan clean. Remove the pan from the heat.

4 Gradually beat the eggs and yolk into the mixture, then add the mustard, cayenne pepper and cheese.

5 Place teaspoonfuls of mixture on a non-stick baking sheet and bake for 10 minutes. Reduce the temperature to 180°C/350°F/Gas 4. Cook for 15 minutes until well browned. Serve hot or cold.

Cook's Tip
Manchego is a semi-hard Spanish cheese made with sheep's milk. It has a firm, creamy texture and a nutty, piquant flavour that is very distinctive.

Bruschetta: *Energy 284kcal/1203kJ; Protein 12.7g; Carbohydrate 49.7g, of which sugars 5.3g; Fat 5g, of which saturates 0.7g; Cholesterol 0mg; Calcium 127mg; Fibre 5.1g; Sodium 376mg.*
Buñuelos: *Energy 296kcal/1237kJ; Protein 9.9g; Carbohydrate 22.5g, of which sugars 0.6g; Fat 19g, of which saturates 10.5g; Cholesterol 185mg; Calcium 156mg; Fibre 0.9g; Sodium 223mg.*

Half-Moon Cheese Pies

These delicious small Greek pies, which are called *skaltsounakia*, always dazzle people and are a favourite at every meze table. In Crete, where they are very popular, there are several variations, including one with a filling of sautéed wild greens. Serve them freshly baked, hot from the oven or while still warm.

Makes 12–14

1 egg, plus 1 egg yolk for glazing
150g/5oz feta cheese, chopped and crumbled
30ml/2 tbsp milk
30ml/2 tbsp chopped fresh mint leaves
15ml/1 tbsp raisins
15ml/1 tbsp pine nuts, lightly toasted
a little vegetable oil, for greasing
a few sprigs of fresh mint, to garnish

For the pastry

225g/8oz/2 cups self-raising (self-rising) flour
45ml/3 tbsp extra virgin olive oil
15g/½oz/1 tbsp butter, melted
90g/3½oz/scant ½ cup Greek (US strained) yogurt

1 To make the pastry, put the flour in a bowl and mix in the oil, butter and yogurt by hand. Cover and rest in the refrigerator for 15 minutes.

2 Meanwhile, make the filling. Beat the egg lightly in a bowl. Crumble in the cheese, then mix in the milk, mint, raisins and pine nuts.

3 Preheat the oven to 190°C/375°F/Gas 5. Cut the pastry into two pieces and cover one with clear film (plastic wrap) or a dish towel. Thinly roll out the remaining piece of pastry and cut out 7.5cm/3in rounds.

4 Place a heaped teaspoonful of filling on each round and fold the pastry over to make a half-moon shape. Press the edges to seal, then place the pies on a greased baking sheet. Repeat with the remaining pastry.

5 Brush the pies with egg yolk and bake for 20 minutes, or until golden. Serve hot.

Pimiento Tartlets

These pretty Spanish tartlets are filled with strips of roasted sweet peppers and a creamy, cheesy custard. They make a perfect snack to serve with drinks.

Serves 4

1 red (bell) pepper
1 yellow (bell) pepper
175g/6oz/1½ cups plain (all-purpose) flour
75g/3oz/6 tbsp chilled butter, diced
30–45ml/2–3 tbsp cold water
60ml/4 tbsp double (heavy) cream
1 egg
15ml/1 tbsp grated Parmesan cheese
salt and ground black pepper

1 Preheat the oven to 200°C/400°F/Gas 6, and heat the grill (broiler). Place the peppers on a baking sheet and grill for 10 minutes, turning occasionally, until blackened. Cover with a dish towel and leave for 5 minutes. Peel away the skin, then discard the seeds and cut the flesh into very thin strips.

2 Sift the flour and a pinch of salt into a bowl. Add the butter and rub it in until the mixture resembles fine breadcrumbs. Stir in enough of the water to make a firm, not sticky, dough.

3 Roll the dough out thinly on a lightly floured surface and line 12 individual moulds or a 12-hole tartlet tin (muffin pan). Prick the bases with a fork and fill the pastry cases with crumpled foil. Bake for 10 minutes, then remove the foil and divide the pepper strips among the pastry cases.

4 Whisk the cream and egg in a bowl. Season and pour over the peppers. Sprinkle each tartlet with Parmesan and bake for 15–20 minutes until firm. Cool for 2 minutes, then remove from the moulds and transfer to a wire rack. Serve warm or cold.

Variation

Use strips of grilled aubergine (eggplant) mixed with sun-dried tomatoes in place of the roasted peppers.

Half-Moon Pies: *Energy 160Kcal/669kJ; Protein 5g; Carbohydrate 16.4g, of which sugars 2.5g; Fat 8.8g, of which saturates 3.4g; Cholesterol 31mg; Calcium 129mg; Fibre 0.7g; Sodium 270mg.*
Tartlets: *Energy 427kcal/1778kJ; Protein 8.4g; Carbohydrate 40g, of which sugars 6.4g; Fat 27g, of which saturates 16.1g; Cholesterol 112mg; Calcium 131mg; Fibre 2.8g; Sodium 180mg.*

Olive and Anchovy Bites

These little melt-in-the-mouth morsels are very moreish, and are perfect accompaniments for drinks. They are made from two ingredients that are forever associated with tapas and are included in many traditional recipes – olives and anchovies. The reason for this is that both contain plenty of salt, which helps to stimulate thirst and therefore drinking.

Makes 40–45

115g/4oz/1 cup plain (all-purpose) flour
115g/4oz/½ cup chilled butter, diced
115g/4oz/1 cup finely grated Manchego, mature (sharp) Cheddar or Gruyère cheese
50g/2oz can anchovy fillets in oil, drained and roughly chopped
50g/2oz/½ cup stoned (pitted) black olives, roughly chopped
2.5ml/½ tsp cayenne pepper
sea salt, to serve

1 Place the flour, butter, cheese, anchovies, olives and cayenne pepper in a food processor and process to a firm dough.

2 Wrap the dough loosely in clear film (plastic wrap). Chill for 20 minutes.

3 Preheat the oven to 200°C/400°F/Gas 6. Roll out the dough thinly on a lightly floured surface.

4 Cut the dough into 5cm/2in wide strips, then cut across each strip in alternate directions, to make triangles. Transfer to baking sheets and bake for 8–10 minutes until golden. Cool on a wire rack. Sprinkle with sea salt.

Variations

- *To add a little extra spice, dust the olive and anchovy bites lightly with cayenne pepper before baking.*
- *Crisp little nibbles set off most drinks. Serve these bites alongside little bowls of seeds and nuts such as sunflower seeds and pistachios. These come in the shell, the opening of which provides a diversion while chatting and gossiping. Toasted chickpeas are another popular tapas snack.*

Feta Pastries

Known as *börek* in Turkey, these crisp, cheese-filled pastries are a common feature of street food throughout much of the Mediterranean, where they are often eaten with aperitifs. They are quite easy to make at home, though they require a little time and patience.

Makes 10

250g/9oz feta cheese, crumbled
2.5ml/½ tsp freshly grated nutmeg
30ml/2 tbsp each chopped fresh parsley, dill and mint
10 filo pastry sheets, each about 30 x 18cm/12 × 7in, thawed
75g/3oz/6 tbsp melted butter or 90ml/6 tbsp olive oil
ground black pepper

1 Preheat the oven to 190°C/375°F/Gas 5. Mix the feta cheese, nutmeg and fresh herbs in a bowl. Add pepper to taste and mix.

2 Brush a sheet of filo pastry lightly with butter or oil, place another on top of it and brush that too.

3 Cut the buttered sheets in half lengthways to make 10 strips, each 30 × 9cm/12 × 3½in. Place 5ml/1 tsp of the cheese filling at the base of a long strip, fold the corners in diagonally to enclose it, then roll the pastry up into a cigar shape.

4 Brush the end with a little butter or oil to seal, then place join-side down on a non-stick baking sheet. Repeat with the remaining pastry and filling. Brush the pastries with more butter or oil and bake for 20 minutes, or until crisp and golden. Cool on a wire rack.

Cook's Tip

When using filo pastry, it is important to keep the sheets from drying out. Cover the pile with a damp dish towel, and take out one sheet at a time to brush with butter. The quantities for filo pastry in this recipe are approximate, as the size of filo sheets varies. Any unused pastry will keep in the refrigerator for a week or so, if it is well wrapped.

Bites: Energy 145Kcal/602kJ; Protein 4.7g; Carbohydrate 6.3g, of which sugars 0.6g; Fat 11.4g, of which saturates 7.4g; Cholesterol 33mg; Calcium 108mg; Fibre 0.4g; Sodium 407mg.
Feta Pastries: Energy 171kcal/713kJ; Protein 5.5g; Carbohydrate 12.2g, of which sugars 0.8g; Fat 11.5g, of which saturates 7.4g; Cholesterol 33mg; Calcium 121mg; Fibre 0.7g; Sodium 407mg.

Spinach Empanadillas

Little pies like these are part of the Moorish tradition in Spain. The Arabs brought spinach to Europe, and pine nuts and raisins are typical Arab flavourings.

Makes 20

25g/1oz/¼ cup raisins
25ml/1½ tbsp olive oil
450g/1lb fresh spinach leaves, washed, drained and chopped
6 canned anchovies, drained and chopped
2 garlic cloves, finely chopped
25g/1oz/¼ cup pine nuts, roughly chopped
350g/12oz puff pastry
1 egg, beaten
salt and ground black pepper

1 To make the filling, soak the raisins in a little warm water for 10 minutes. Drain well, then chop roughly.

2 Heat the olive oil in a large pan, add the spinach, stir, then cover and cook over a low heat for about 2 minutes until the spinach starts to wilt. Remove the lid, turn up the heat and cook until any liquid has evaporated.

3 Add the chopped anchovies, garlic and seasoning to the spinach and cook, stirring, for about 1 minute.

4 Remove the pan from the heat, then stir in the soaked raisins and pine nuts, and set aside to cool.

5 Meanwhile, preheat the oven to 180°C/350°F/Gas 4. Roll out the pastry on a lightly floured surface to a 3mm/⅛ in thickness.

6 Using a 7.5cm/3in pastry cutter, cut the pastry into 20 rounds, re-rolling any scraps if necessary. Place about 10ml/2 tsp filling in the middle of each round, then brush the edges with a little water.

7 Bring up the sides of the pastry and seal well. Press the edges together with the back of a fork. Brush with egg.

8 Place the pies, slightly apart, on a lightly greased baking sheet and bake for about 15 minutes, until puffed and golden brown. Transfer to a wire rack to cool and serve warm.

Filo Cigars Filled with Feta, Parsley, Mint and Dill

These classic cigar-shaped Turkish pastries are popular snack and meze food, and they are also good as nibbles with drinks. In this version they are filled with cheese and herbs, but other popular fillings include aromatic minced meat, baked aubergine (eggplant) and cheese, or mashed pumpkin, cheese and dill. The filo pastry can be folded into triangles, but cigars are the most traditional shape. They can be prepared in advance and kept under a damp dish towel in the refrigerator until you are ready to fry them at the last minute.

Serves 3–4

225g/8oz feta cheese
1 egg, lightly beaten
1 small bunch each of fresh flat leaf parsley, mint and dill, finely chopped
4–5 sheets of filo pastry
sunflower oil, for deep-frying
dill fronds, to garnish (optional)

1 In a bowl, mash the feta with a fork. Beat in the egg and fold in the herbs. Working with one sheet at a time, cut the filo into strips about 10–13cm/4–5in wide, and pile them on top of each other. Keep the strips covered with a damp dish towel.

2 Place a heaped teaspoon of the cheese filling along one of the short ends of a strip. Roll the end over the filling, quite tightly to keep it in place, then tuck in the sides to seal in the filling and continue to roll until you get to the other end.

3 Brush the tip with a little water to help seal the roll. Place the filled cigar, join-side down, on a plate and cover with a damp dish towel to keep it moist. Continue with the remaining sheets of filo and filling.

4 Heat enough oil for deep-frying in a wok or other deep-sided pan, and deep-fry the filo cigars in batches for 5–6 minutes until crisp and golden brown. Lift out of the oil with a slotted spoon and drain on kitchen paper. Serve immediately, garnished with dill fronds if you like.

Empanadillas: *Energy 95kcal/396kJ; Protein 2.4g; Carbohydrate 7.8g, of which sugars 1.5g; Fat 6.4g, of which saturates 0.3g; Cholesterol 10mg; Calcium 53mg; Fibre 0.5g; Sodium 125mg.*
Filo Cigars: *Energy 311kcal/1291kJ; Protein 12.4g; Carbohydrate 11.2g, of which sugars 1.6g; Fat 24.4g, of which saturates 9.5g; Cholesterol 92mg; Calcium 278mg; Fibre 1.7g; Sodium 838mg.*

Potato Tortilla

The classic tortilla can be found in every tapas bar in Spain. The size of a large cake, it is dense and very satisfying. It can be eaten in wedges with a fork – a meal in itself with salad – or cut up into chunks and speared, to be enjoyed as a snack with drinks.

Serves 6

450g/1lb small waxy potatoes, peeled
1 Spanish onion
45ml/3 tbsp vegetable oil
4 large eggs
salt and ground black pepper
fresh flat leaf parsley or tomato wedges, to garnish

1 Using a sharp knife, cut the potatoes into thin slices and slice the onion into thin rings. Heat 30ml/2 tbsp of the oil in a 20cm/8in heavy frying pan.

2 Add the potatoes and the onions to the pan and cook over a low heat for 20 minutes, or until the potato slices are just tender. Stir from time to time to prevent the potatoes sticking. Remove from the heat.

3 In a large bowl, beat together the eggs with a little salt and pepper. When the cooked potatoes and onion have cooled a little, stir them into the eggs.

4 Clean the frying pan with kitchen paper then heat the remaining oil and pour in the potato mixture. Cook very gently for 5–8 minutes until set underneath. During cooking, lift the edges of the tortilla with a spatula, and allow any uncooked egg to run underneath. Shake the pan from side to side, to prevent sticking.

5 Place a large heatproof plate upside-down over the pan, invert the tortilla on to the plate and then slide it back into the pan. Cook for 2–3 minutes more, until the underside of the tortilla is golden brown.

6 Cut the tortilla into wedges and serve immediately or leave until warm or cold. Serve garnished with fresh flat leaf parsley or tomato wedges.

Yogurt Cheese in Olive Oil

Sheep's milk is widely used in cheese-making in the eastern Mediterranean, particularly in Greece where sheep's yogurt is hung in muslin to drain off the whey before patting into balls of soft cheese. Here it's bottled in extra virgin olive oil with chilli and herbs – an appropriate gift for a friend who enjoys Greek cuisine.

Fills two 450g/1lb jars

750g/1oz/1¼ cups Greek sheep's yogurt
2.5ml/½ tsp salt
10ml/2 tsp crushed dried chillies or chilli powder
15ml/1 tbsp chopped fresh rosemary
15ml/1 tbsp chopped fresh thyme or oregano
about 300ml/½ pint/1¼ cups olive oil, preferably garlic flavoured

1 Sterilize a 30cm/12in square of muslin (cheesecloth) by steeping it in boiling water. Drain and lay over a large plate.

2 Mix the yogurt with the salt and tip on to the centre of the muslin. Bring up the sides of the muslin and tie firmly with string. Hang the bag of yogurt over a large bowl to catch the whey and leave in a cool place for 2–3 days, or until the whey stops dripping.

3 Wash thoroughly and dry two 450g/1lb glass preserving jars or jam jars. Sterilize them by heating them in an oven preheated to 150°C/300°F/Gas 2 for 15 minutes.

4 Mix together the chilli and herbs. Take teaspoonfuls of the cheese and roll into balls with your hands. Lower into the jars, sprinkling each layer with the herb mixture.

5 Pour the olive oil over the soft cheese balls until they are completely covered. Mix gently with the handle end of a wooden spoon in order to blend the flavourings through the olive oil, making sure that you do not break up the cheese balls. Store in the refrigerator for up to 3 weeks.

6 To serve the cheese, spoon out of the jars with a little of the flavoured olive oil and spread on to lightly toasted bread.

Tortilla: Energy 163kcal/681kJ; Protein 5.8g; Carbohydrate 14.7g, of which sugars 2.9g; Fat 9.5g, of which saturates 1.9g; Cholesterol 127mg; Calcium 32mg; Fibre 1.2g; Sodium 56mg.
Yogurt Cheese: Energy 1331kcal/5488kJ; Protein 24g; Carbohydrate 7.5g, of which sugars 7.5g; Fat 138.2g, of which saturates 33.8g; Cholesterol 0mg; Calcium 563mg; Fibre 0g; Sodium 758mg.

Marinated Pimientos

Pimiento is simply another word for sweet peppers, which in this recipe are cooked and skinned, then marinated in a garlicky oil and vinegar dressing that goes well with their smoky flavour. You can buy preserved peppers in cans or jars, but they are very much tastier when homemade. They create a delicious, healthy appetizer, on their own or with other antipasti, and can also be used to top crostini or mini-pizzas.

Serves 4
3 red (bell) peppers
2 small garlic cloves, crushed
45ml/3 tbsp chopped fresh parsley
15ml/1 tbsp sherry vinegar
25ml/1½ tbsp olive oil
salt, to taste

1 Preheat the grill (broiler) to high. Place the peppers on a baking sheet and grill (broil) for 8–12 minutes, turning occasionally, until the skins have blistered and blackened. Remove the peppers from the heat, cover them with a clean dish towel or place in a plastic bag and leave for 5 minutes so that the steam softens the skin and makes it easier to peel.

2 Make a small cut in the bottom of each pepper and squeeze out the juice into a bowl. Peel away the skin and cut the peppers in half. Remove and discard the core and seeds.

3 Using a sharp knife, cut each pepper in half lengthways into 1cm/½in-wide strips. Place them in a bowl.

4 Whisk the garlic, parsley, vinegar and oil into the pepper juices. Add salt to taste. Pour over the pepper strips and toss well. Cover and chill, but, if possible, bring the peppers back to room temperature before serving.

Cook's Tip
The marinated pimientos can be stored in the refrigerator for up to 2 weeks covered in olive oil in a screw-top jar. The flavours will blend and improve with keeping.

Aubergine, Garlic and Red Pepper Pâté

Serve this Italian-style chunky, garlicky pâté of smoky baked aubergine and red peppers, on a bed of salad, accompanied by crisp toasts. Baking the ingredients imparts a wonderful smoky flavour.

Serves 4
3 aubergines (eggplants)
2 (bell) red peppers
5 garlic cloves
7.5ml/1½ tsp pink peppercorns in brine, drained and crushed
30ml/2 tbsp chopped fresh coriander (cilantro)

1 Preheat the oven to 200°C/400°F/Gas 6. Arrange the whole aubergines, peppers and garlic cloves on a baking sheet. Bake for 10 minutes, then remove the garlic cloves and set aside. Turn over the aubergines and peppers, return to the oven and bake for a further 20 minutes.

2 Meanwhile, peel the garlic cloves and place them in a blender or food processor.

3 Remove the charred peppers from the oven and place in a plastic food bag. Set aside to cool. Return the aubergines to the oven and bake for a further 10 minutes.

4 Split each aubergine in half and scoop out the flesh into a sieve (strainer) placed over a bowl. Discard the skin. Press the flesh with a spoon to remove the bitter juices. Discard the juices. Add the aubergine to the garlic in the blender or food processor and process until smooth. Put the mixture in a bowl.

5 Skin, core and seed the red peppers and finely chop the flesh; stir into the aubergine mixture. Mix in the peppercorns and chopped coriander until thoroughly combined. Spoon into a serving dish and serve immediately.

Variation
Use orange or yellow (bell) peppers in place of the red ones.

Pimientos: Energy 84kcal/349kJ; Protein 1.7g; Carbohydrate 8.7g, of which sugars 8.3g; Fat 4.9g, of which saturates 0.8g; Cholesterol 0mg; Calcium 33mg; Fibre 2.7g; Sodium 9mg.
Pâté: Energy 69kcal/292kJ; Protein 3.5g; Carbohydrate 11.8g, of which sugars 10g; Fat 1.3g, of which saturates 0.3g; Cholesterol 0mg; Calcium 31mg; Fibre 6.2g; Sodium 8mg.

Smoked Aubergine and Yogurt Purée

One of the most popular Turkish meze dishes, this garlic-flavoured purée varies from house to house and from region to region. It is sometimes made with a heavy hand of garlic, with a kick of chilli, or with the fresh taste of dill, mint or parsley. The purée is heavenly when it is freshly made, served with chunks of warm crusty bread for scooping it up.

Serves 4

2 large, plump aubergines (eggplants)
30ml/2 tbsp olive oil, plus extra for drizzling
juice of 1 lemon
2–3 garlic cloves, crushed
225g/8oz/1 cup thick natural (plain) yogurt
salt and freshly ground black pepper
a few fresh dill fronds, to garnish
lemon wedges, to serve

1 Put the aubergines directly on the gas flame on top of the stove, or under a conventional grill (broiler), and turn them from time to time until the skin is charred on all sides and the flesh feels soft.

2 Place the aubergines in a plastic bag and leave for a few minutes to soften the skin.

3 Hold each aubergine by the stalk under cold running water and gently peel off the charred skin until you are left with just the smooth bulbous flesh. Squeeze the flesh between your hands to get rid of any excess water and place it on a chopping board.

4 Chop the aubergine flesh to a pulp, discarding the stalks. Put the flesh in a bowl and add 30ml/2 tbsp oil, the lemon juice and garlic. Beat well to mix, then beat in the yogurt and season with salt and pepper.

5 Transfer the mixture to a bowl, drizzle with olive oil and garnish with dill. Serve at room temperature, with lemon wedges for squeezing.

Chilli Aubergine Peppers

This is a lovely Turkish dish of smoked aubergine and peppers with a refreshing lemony tang. Its Arabic name is Acvar, and it is traditionally served warm with lemon wedges to squeeze over it as part of a meze. Here the dish is accompanied by toasted pitta with which to scoop it up, but you could increase the quantities and serve it as a main dish with yogurt and bread, or as a side dish with barbecued chicken, lamb or fish.

Serves 4

2 red (bell) peppers
1 fat aubergine (eggplant)
30–45ml/2–3 tbsp olive oil
1 red onion, cut in half lengthways and finely sliced along the grain
1 fresh red chilli, seeded and finely sliced
2 garlic cloves, chopped
5–10ml/1–2 tsp sugar
juice of 1 lemon
dash of white wine vinegar
a large handful of fresh flat leaf parsley, roughly chopped
salt and ground black pepper
lemon wedges and toasted pitta bread, to serve

1 Place the peppers and aubergine under a conventional grill (broiler), or on a rack over the hot coals of a barbecue. Turn them from time to time until the skin is charred on all sides and the flesh feels soft. Place them in a plastic bag and leave for a few minutes to soften the skin.

2 One at a time, hold the charred vegetables under cold running water and peel off the skins.

3 Place the vegetables on a chopping board and remove the stalks. Halve the peppers lengthways and scoop out the seeds, then chop the flesh to a pulp. Chop the aubergine flesh to a pulp too.

4 Put the oil into a wide, heavy pan and toss in the onion, chilli, garlic and sugar. Cook over a medium heat for 2–3 minutes, until they begin to colour.

5 Toss in the pulped peppers and aubergine, stir in the lemon juice and vinegar and season with salt and pepper. Toss in the parsley and serve with lemon wedges and toasted pitta bread.

Purée: *Energy 103kcal/431kJ; Protein 4.4g; Carbohydrate 7.7g, of which sugars 6.4g; Fat 6.5g, of which saturates 1.2g; Cholesterol 1mg; Calcium 118mg; Fibre 2.3g; Sodium 49mg.*
Aubergine Peppers: *Energy 102kcal/425kJ; Protein 1.8g; Carbohydrate 10.5g, of which sugars 9.8g; Fat 6.2g, of which saturates 1g; Cholesterol 0mg; Calcium 19mg; Fibre 3.1g; Sodium 6mg.*

Poached Eggs with Garlic Yogurt

This dish of poached eggs on a bed of garlic-flavoured yogurt is surprisingly delicious. It is called Cilbur in Turkey, where it is served as a meze dish or snack, but it works equally well for supper with a green salad. Hen's or duck's eggs can be used, and you can poach or fry them. Spiked with Turkish red pepper or paprika, and served with ciabatta or flat bread, it is simple and satisfying.

Serves 2

500g/1¼lb/2¼ cups thick natural (plain) yogurt
2 garlic cloves, crushed
30–45ml/2–3 tbsp white wine vinegar
4 large (US extra large) eggs
15–30ml/1–2 tbsp butter
5ml/1 tsp Turkish red pepper or paprika
a few dried sage leaves, crumbled
salt and ground black pepper

1 Beat the yogurt with the garlic and seasoning. Spoon into a serving dish or on to individual plates, spreading it flat to create a thick bed for the eggs.

2 Fill a pan with water, add the vinegar to seal the egg whites, and bring to a rolling boil. Stir the water with a spoon to create a whirlpool and crack in the first egg. As the egg spins and the white sets around the yolk, stir the water for the next one. Poach the eggs for 2–3 minutes so the yolks are still soft.

3 Lift the eggs out of the water with a slotted spoon and place them on the yogurt bed.

4 Quickly melt the butter in a small pan. Stir in the red pepper or paprika and sage leaves, then spoon the mixture over the eggs. Eat immediately.

Cook's Tip

Leave the yogurt at room temperature to form a contrast with the hot eggs, or heat it by placing the dish in a cool oven, or by sitting it in a covered pan of hot water.

Stuffed Vine Leaves

This popular Greek dish keeps moist when cooked slowly in a casserole or clay pot. Fresh vine leaves are best, but preserved or canned will also work well.

Serves 4

12 fresh vine leaves
30ml/2 tbsp olive oil
1 small onion, chopped
30ml/2 tbsp pine nuts
1 garlic clove, crushed
115g/4oz/1 cup cooked long grain rice
2 tomatoes, skinned, seeded and finely chopped
15ml/1 tbsp chopped fresh mint
1 lemon, sliced
150ml/¼ pint/⅔ cup dry white wine
200ml/7fl oz/scant 1 cup vegetable stock
salt and ground black pepper
extra virgin olive oil, lemon wedges and mint sprigs, to garnish

1 Soak the clay pot in cold water for 20 minutes, then drain. Blanch the vine leaves in a pan of boiling water for about 2 minutes or until they darken and soften. Rinse the leaves under cold running water and leave to drain.

2 Heat the olive oil and fry the onion for 5–6 minutes, stirring frequently, until softened. Add the pine nuts and crushed garlic and cook, stirring, until the onions and pine nuts are golden. Stir the onion mixture into the rice, then add and stir in the chopped tomatoes and fresh mint. Season to taste with salt and freshly ground black pepper.

3 Place a dessertspoonful of the rice mixture at the stalk end of each vine leaf. Fold the sides of the leaf in over the filling and roll up tightly. Place the stuffed vine leaves close together, seam side down, in the clay pot. Place the lemon slices on top and in between the stuffed vine leaves. Pour over the white wine and sufficient stock just to cover the rolls and lemon slices.

4 Cover the dish and place in an unheated oven. Set the oven to 200°C/400°F/Gas 6 and cook for 30 minutes. Reduce to 160°C/325°F/Gas 3 and cook for a further 30 minutes. Serve hot or cold as a starter or as part of a meze table, drizzled with fruity extra virgin olive oil and garnished with lemon wedges and a few sprigs of fresh mint.

Poached Eggs: *Energy 345kcal/1438kJ; Protein 25.4g; Carbohydrate 19.1g, of which sugars 19.1g; Fat 19.8g, of which saturates 8.3g; Cholesterol 400mg; Calcium 534mg; Fibre 0.1g; Sodium 393mg.*
Vine Leaves: *Energy 188Kcal/782kJ; Protein 2.9g; Carbohydrate 13.6g, of which sugars 4.1g; Fat 11.3g, of which saturates 1.3g; Cholesterol 0mg; Calcium 37mg; Fibre 1.4g; Sodium 9mg.*

Courgette Rissoles

This is an ingenious way of transforming courgettes into a sharply appetizing dish.

Serves 6

500g/1¼lb courgettes (zucchini)
120ml/4fl oz/½ cup extra virgin olive oil
1 large onion, finely chopped
2 spring onions (scallions), green and white parts finely chopped
1 garlic clove, crushed
3 medium slices of bread (not from a pre-sliced loaf)
2 eggs, lightly beaten
200g/7oz feta cheese, crumbled
50g/2oz/½ cup freshly grated Greek Graviera or Italian Parmesan cheese
45–60ml/3–4 tbsp finely chopped fresh dill or 5ml/1 tsp dried oregano
50g/2oz/½ cup plain (all-purpose) flour
salt and ground black pepper
Lemon wedges, to serve

1 Bring a pan of lightly salted water to the boil. Slice the courgettes into 4cm/1½in lengths and add them to the pan. Cover and cook for about 10 minutes. Drain and cool.

2 Heat 45ml/3 tbsp of the olive oil in a pan, add the onion and spring onions and sauté until translucent. Add the garlic and as soon as it becomes aromatic remove the pan from the heat.

3 Squeeze the courgettes to extract as much water as possible, then place them in a large bowl. Add the fried onion and garlic mixture and mix well.

4 Toast the bread, discard the crusts, then break up the toast and crumb it in a food processor. Add to the courgette mixture, with the eggs, feta and Graviera or Parmesan cheese. Stir in the dill or oregano and add salt and pepper to taste. If the mixture seems too wet, add a little flour.

5 Take a heaped tablespoon of the courgette mixture, roll it into a ball, using your hands, and press it lightly to make a rissole shape. Make more rissoles in the same way. Coat them lightly in the flour. Heat the remaining extra virgin olive oil in a large, non-stick frying pan, then fry the rissoles in batches until they are crisp and brown, turning them over once. Drain on kitchen paper and serve with the lemon wedges.

Chickpea Rissoles

This is one of the classic meze dishes that are typically found on a Greek table. It is an inexpensive dish, but very appetizing.

Serves 4

300g/11oz/scant 1½ cups chickpeas, soaked overnight in water to cover
105ml/7 tbsp extra virgin olive oil
2 large onions, chopped
15ml/1 tbsp ground cumin
2 garlic cloves, crushed
3–4 fresh sage leaves, chopped
45ml/3 tbsp chopped flat leaf parsley
1 egg, lightly beaten
45ml/3 tbsp self-raising (self-rising) flour
50g/2oz/½ cup plain (all-purpose) flour
salt and ground black pepper
radishes, rocket (arugula) and olives, to serve

1 Drain the chickpeas, rinse under cold water and drain again. Tip them into a large pan, cover with plenty of fresh cold water and bring them to the boil. Skim the froth from the surface of the water with a slotted spoon until the liquid is clear.

2 Cover the pan and cook for 1¼–1½ hours, or until the chickpeas are very soft. Set aside a few tablespoons of cooking liquid, then strain the chickpeas, discarding the rest of the liquid. Transfer them to a food processor, add 30–45ml/2–3 tbsp of the reserved liquid and process to a velvety mash.

3 Heat 45ml/3 tbsp of the olive oil in a large frying pan, add the onions, and sauté until they are light golden. Add the cumin and the garlic and stir for a few seconds until their aroma rises. Stir in the chopped sage leaves and the parsley, and set aside.

4 Scrape the chickpea mash into a large bowl and add the egg, the self-raising flour, and the fried onion and herb mixture. Season and mix well. Take large walnut-size pieces and flatten them so that they look like thick, round mini-hamburgers.

5 Coat the rissoles lightly in the plain flour. Heat the remaining olive oil in a large frying pan and fry them in batches until they are crisp and golden on both sides. Drain on kitchen paper and serve hot with the radishes, rocket and olives.

Courgette Rissoles: *Energy 343Kcal/1,424kJ; Protein 14.7g; Carbohydrate 18.5g, of which sugars 4.9g; Fat 23.9g, of which saturates 8.6g; Cholesterol 95mg; Calcium 301mg; Fibre 2.2g; Sodium 668mg.*
Chickpea Rissoles: *Energy 532Kcal/2231kJ; Protein 19.7g; Carbohydrate 63.6g, of which sugars 8.1g; Fat 23.9g, of which saturates 3.2g; Cholesterol 0mg; Calcium 222mg; Fibre 10.7g; Sodium 77mg.*

Marinated Vegetable Antipasto

Antipasto means "before the meal" and traditionally consists of a selection of marinated vegetable dishes served with good Italian salami and thin slices of Parma ham. Serve in attractive bowls, with plenty of fresh crusty bread.

Serves 4

For the peppers

3 red peppers
3 yellow peppers
4 garlic cloves, sliced
handful fresh basil, plus extra to garnish
extra virgin olive oil
salt and ground black pepper

For the mushrooms

450g/1lb open cap mushrooms
60ml/4 tbsp extra virgin olive oil
1 large garlic clove, crushed
15ml/1 tbsp chopped fresh rosemary
250ml/8fl oz/1 cup dry white wine
fresh rosemary sprigs, to garnish

For the olives

1 dried red chilli, crushed
grated rind of 1 lemon
120ml/4fl oz/½ cup extra virgin olive oil
225g/8oz/1⅓ cups Italian black olives
30ml/2 tbsp chopped fresh flat leaf parsley
1 lemon wedge, to serve

1 Grill (broil) the peppers, turning occasionally, until they are blackened and blistered all over, then place in a large plastic bag. When cool, remove the skin and seeds. Cut the flesh into strips lengthways and place in a bowl with the garlic and basil. Add salt to taste, cover with oil and marinate for 3–4 hours, tossing occasionally. When serving, garnish with more basil leaves.

2 Thickly slice the mushrooms and place in a large bowl. Heat the oil and add the garlic, rosemary and wine. Bring to the boil, then lower the heat and simmer for 3 minutes. Season to taste and pour over the mushrooms. Mix well and leave until cool, stirring occasionally. Cover and marinate overnight. Serve at room temperature, garnished with rosemary sprigs.

3 To prepare the olives, place the chilli and lemon rind in a small pan with the oil. Heat gently for about 3 minutes. Add the olives and heat for 1 minute more. Tip into a bowl and leave overnight. Sprinkle with parsley and serve with a lemon wedge.

Aubergine Fritters

The aubergine is popular all over the Mediterranean and appears in many recipes. These simple and delicious fritters make a superb starter or a vegetarian supper dish.

Serves 4

1 large aubergine (eggplant), about 675g/1½lb, cut into 1cm/½in thick slices
30ml/2 tbsp olive oil
1 egg, lightly beaten
60ml/4 tbsp chopped fresh parsley
2 garlic cloves, crushed
130g/4½oz/2¼ cups fresh white breadcrumbs
90g/3½oz/generous 1 cup grated Parmesan cheese
90g/3½oz/generous 1 cup feta cheese, crumbled
45ml/3tbsp plain (all-purpose) flour
sunflower oil, for shallow frying
salt and ground black pepper

To serve

natural yogurt, flavoured with fried red chillies and cumin seeds
lime wedges

1 Preheat the oven to 190°C/375°F/Gas 5. Brush the aubergine slices with the olive oil, then place them on a baking sheet and bake for about 20 minutes until golden and tender. Chop the slices finely and place them in a bowl with the egg, parsley, garlic, breadcrumbs, Parmesan and feta. Add salt and pepper to taste, and mix well. Leave the mixture to rest for about 20 minutes. If the mixture looks very sloppy, add some more breadcrumbs.

2 Divide the mixture into eight balls and flatten them slightly. Place the flour on a plate and season with salt and pepper. Coat the fritters in the flour, shaking off any excess. Shallow-fry in batches for 1 minute on each side, until the fritters are golden brown. Drain on kitchen paper and serve with the flavoured yogurt and lime wedges.

Cook's Tip

Large aubergines can sometimes be bitter. To avoid this, sprinkle the slices with salt and leave to drain for an hour, then rinse and squeeze or pat dry before cooking.

Vegetable Antipasto: *Energy 449kcal/1857kJ; Protein 5.6g; Carbohydrate 18g, of which sugars 16.9g; Fat 35.4g, of which saturates 5.3g; Cholesterol 0mg; Calcium 93mg; Fibre 7.7g; Sodium 1289mg.*
Aubergine Fritters: *Energy 508kcal/2122kJ; Protein 20.7g; Carbohydrate 38.3g, of which sugars 5g; Fat 31.4g, of which saturates 10.4g; Cholesterol 86mg; Calcium 458mg; Fibre 5.1g; Sodium 842mg.*

Grilled Aubergine in Honey and Spices

Hot, spicy, sweet and fruity flavours are a classic combination in this delicious Moroccan dish. Many different kinds of aubergine are grown in the Mediterranean, in all sizes and ranging from white to purple and black. Baby ones are effective for this recipe as you can slice them in half lengthways and hold them by their stalks to eat.

Serves 4

2 aubergines (eggplants), thickly sliced, or 8 baby aubergines, halved lengthways
25ml/1½ tbsp olive oil
2–3 garlic cloves, crushed
5cm/2in piece fresh root ginger, peeled and grated
5ml/1 tsp ground cumin
5ml/1 tsp harissa
75ml/5 tbsp clear honey
juice of 1 lemon
salt, to taste

1 Preheat the grill (broiler) or a griddle. Lightly brush each aubergine slice with olive oil and cook under the grill or in a griddle pan. Turn the slices during cooking so that they are lightly browned on both sides.

2 In a wide non-stick frying pan, fry the garlic in the remaining oil for a few seconds, then stir in the ginger, cumin, harissa, honey and lemon juice. Add enough water to cover the pan's base and to thin the mixture, then lay the aubergine slices in the pan. Cook the aubergines gently for about 10 minutes, or until they have absorbed all the sauce.

3 Add a little extra water, if necessary, season to taste with salt, and serve at room temperature, with chunks of fresh bread to mop up the juices.

Variation
If you want to make a feature out of this sumptuous dish, serve it on a platter accompanied by other grilled (broiled) vegetables and fruit, such as (bell) peppers, chillies, tomatoes, oranges, pineapples and mangoes.

Mozzarella Skewers

These crunchy appetizers have stacks of flavour and contrasting textures – layers of oven-baked mozzarella, tomatoes, basil and bread infused with fruity olive oil.

Serves 4

12 slices white bread (not from a pre-sliced loaf), each about 1cm/½in thick
45ml/3 tbsp olive oil
225g/8oz mozzarella cheese, cut into 5mm/¼in slices
3 plum tomatoes, cut into 5mm/¼in slices
15g/½oz/½ cup fresh basil leaves, plus extra to garnish
salt and ground black pepper
30ml/2 tbsp chopped fresh flat leaf parsley, to garnish

1 Preheat the oven to 220°C/425°F/Gas 7. Trim the crusts from the bread and cut each slice into four equal squares. Arrange on a baking sheet and brush on one side (or both sides) with half the olive oil. Bake for 3–5 minutes until the squares are pale gold.

2 Remove from the oven and place the bread squares on a board with the other ingredients.

3 Make 16 stacks, each starting with a square of bread, then a slice of mozzarella topped with a slice of tomato and a basil leaf. Sprinkle with salt and pepper, then repeat, ending with a square of bread.

4 Push a skewer through each stack and place on the baking sheet. Drizzle with the remaining oil and bake for 10–15 minutes until the cheese begins to melt. Garnish the stacks with fresh basil leaves and serve scattered with chopped fresh flat leaf parsley.

Cook's Tips
- *If you use wooden skewers, soak them in water first, to prevent them scorching in the oven.*
- *Use country bread with a full flavour and an open texture. Day-old bread will crisp more quickly.*

Grilled Aubergine: *Energy 151kcal/631kJ; Protein 1.4g; Carbohydrate 17.6g, of which sugars 17.3g; Fat 8.9g, of which saturates 1.3g; Cholesterol 0mg; Calcium 16mg; Fibre 3g; Sodium 5mg.*
Mozzarella Skewers: *Energy 1693kcal/7107kJ; Protein 71.6g; Carbohydrate 169.4g, of which sugars 18.1g; Fat 85.9g, of which saturates 36g; Cholesterol 131mg; Calcium 1222mg; Fibre 8.6g; Sodium 2606mg.*

Stuffed Roast Peppers with Pesto

For a delectable first course, serve these scallop- and pesto-filled sweet red peppers with plenty of warm Italian bread, such as ciabatta or focaccia, to mop up the garlicky juices.

Serves 4

4 squat, even-sized red (bell) peppers
2 large garlic cloves, cut into thin slivers
60ml/4 tbsp olive oil
4 shelled scallops
45ml/3 tbsp pesto
salt and freshly ground black pepper
freshly grated Parmesan cheese, to serve
salad leaves and fresh basil sprigs, to garnish

1 Preheat the oven to 180°C/350°F/Gas 4. Cut the peppers in half lengthways, through their stalks. Scrape out and discard the cores and seeds, leaving the stalks attached. Wash the pepper shells and pat dry.

2 Put the peppers, cut-side up, in an oiled roasting pan. Divide the slivers of garlic equally among them and sprinkle with salt and pepper to taste. Spoon the oil into the peppers, then roast for 40 minutes.

3 Cut each of the shelled scallops in half horizontally to make two flat discs. Remove the peppers from the oven and place a scallop half in each pepper half. Top with pesto.

4 Return the pan to the oven and roast for 10 minutes more. Transfer the peppers to individual serving plates, sprinkle with grated Parmesan and garnish each plate with a few salad leaves and fresh basil sprigs. Serve warm.

Cook's Tip

Scallops are available from most fishmongers and supermarkets with fresh fish counters. The flesh should be firm and creamy-white with a sweet aroma. They need very little cooking: Never cook them for longer than the time stated in the recipe or they will be tough and rubbery.

Roast Pepper Terrine

This terrine is perfect for a dinner party because it tastes better if made ahead. Prepare the salsa a few hours before serving. Serve with hot Italian bread.

Serves 8

8 (bell) peppers
675g/1½lb/3 cups mascarpone or ricotta cheese
3 eggs, separated
30ml/2 tbsp each roughly chopped flat leaf parsley and shredded basil
2 large garlic cloves, chopped
2 red, yellow or orange (bell) peppers, chopped
30ml/2 tbsp extra virgin olive oil
10ml/2 tsp balsamic vinegar
a few basil sprigs
pinch of sugar
salt and freshly ground black pepper

1 Place the peppers under a hot grill (broiler) for 8–10 minutes, turning frequently until charred and blistered on all sides. Put the peppers in plastic bags and leave to cool. Rub off the skins and remove the seeds, then cut 7 of the peppers lengthways into thin, even-sized strips.

2 Put the mascarpone cheese in a bowl with the egg yolks, herbs and half the garlic. Add salt and pepper to taste and beat well. In a separate bowl, whisk the egg whites to a soft peak, then fold into the cheese mixture until evenly incorporated.

3 Preheat the oven to 180°C/350°F/Gas 4. Line the base of a lightly oiled 900g/2lb loaf tin (pan). Put one-third of the cheese in the tin and spread level. Arrange half the pepper strips on top and repeat until all the cheese and peppers are used. Cover with foil and place in a roasting pan. Pour in boiling water to come halfway up the sides. Bake for 1 hour. Leave to cool in the water bath, then lift out and chill overnight.

4 To make the salsa, place the remaining roast pepper and fresh peppers in a food processor. Add the remaining garlic, oil, vinegar and basil, keeping a few leaves for garnishing. Process until finely chopped. Add salt and pepper to taste and mix well. Tip into a bowl, cover and chill until ready to serve. Turn out the terrine, peel off the paper and slice thickly. Garnish with the basil leaves and serve cold, with the salsa.

Roast Peppers with Pesto: *Energy 233kcal/965kJ; Protein 9.4g; Carbohydrate 12g, of which sugars 10.8g; Fat 16.6g, of which saturates 3.3g; Cholesterol 16mg; Calcium 95mg; Fibre 2.9g; Sodium 111mg.*
Roast Pepper Terrine: *Energy 276kcal/1145kJ; Protein 12.5g; Carbohydrate 16.8g, of which sugars 16.1g; Fat 18g, of which saturates 8.9g; Cholesterol 107mg; Calcium 41mg; Fibre 3.8g; Sodium 37mg.*

Grilled Vegetable Terrine

Serve this colourful terrine with hot crusty bread or pittas, and feta cheese or grilled halloumi.

Serves 6

4 red and yellow (bell) peppers, quartered
1 large aubergine (eggplant), sliced lengthways
2 large courgettes (zucchini), sliced lengthways
90ml/6 tbsp olive oil
1 large red onion, thinly sliced
75g/3oz/½ cup raisins
15ml/1 tbsp tomato purée (paste)
15ml/1 tbsp red wine vinegar
400ml/14fl oz/1⅔ cups tomato juice
15g/½oz/2 tbsp powdered gelatine
fresh basil leaves, to garnish

For the dressing

90ml/6 tbsp extra virgin olive oil
30ml/2 tbsp red wine vinegar
salt and ground black pepper

1 Place the peppers skin-side up under a hot grill (broiler) until the skins are blackened. Place them in a large plastic bag and leave to cool. Brush the aubergine and courgette slices with oil and cook under the grill, turning occasionally, until tender and golden. Heat the remaining olive oil in a pan and add the onion, raisins, tomato purée and red wine vinegar. Cook gently until soft and syrupy. Set aside to cool in the pan.

2 Pour half the tomato juice into a pan, and sprinkle with the gelatine. Stir the mixture over a low heat until dissolved.

3 Lightly oil a 1.75 litre/3 pint/7½ cup terrine and line it with clear film (plastic wrap). Place a layer of red peppers in the bottom and pour in enough of the tomato juice and gelatine mixture to cover. Continue layering the aubergine, courgettes, yellow peppers and onion mixture, finishing with another layer of red peppers. Pour tomato juice over each layer of vegetables. Add the remaining tomato juice to any juices left in the pan, and pour into the terrine. Cover and chill until set.

4 To make the dressing, whisk together the oil and vinegar, and season with salt and pepper. Turn out the terrine and remove the clear film. Serve in thick slices, drizzled with dressing. Garnish with a few fresh basil leaves.

Chickpea Pasta Parcels

Somewhere between a dumpling and pasta, this is a popular Turkish snack.

Serves 4–6

450g/1lb/4 cups plain (all-purpose) flour
2.5ml/½ tsp salt
1 egg, beaten with 1 egg yolk
salt and ground black pepper

For the filling

400g/14oz can chickpeas, drained and thoroughly rinsed
5ml/1 tsp cumin seeds, crushed
5ml/1 tsp paprika

For the yogurt

about 90ml/6 tbsp thick natural (plain) yogurt
2–3 garlic cloves, crushed

For the sauce

15ml/1 tbsp olive oil
15ml/1 tbsp butter
1 onion, finely chopped
2 garlic cloves, finely chopped
5ml/1 tsp Turkish red pepper, or 1 fresh red chilli, seeded and finely chopped
5–10ml/1–2 tsp granulated sugar
5–10ml/1–2 tsp dried mint
400g/14oz can chopped tomatoes, drained
600ml/1 pint/2½ cups vegetable or chicken stock
1 small bunch each of fresh flat leaf parsley and coriander (cilantro), roughly chopped

1 To make the dough, sift the flour and salt into a wide bowl and make a well in the middle. Pour in the beaten egg and 50ml/2fl oz/¼ cup water. Using your fingers, draw the flour into the liquid and mix to a dough. Knead the dough for 10 minutes, then cover the bowl with a damp dish towel and leave to rest for 1 hour.

2 Meanwhile, prepare the filling and yogurt. In a bowl, mash the chickpeas with a fork. Beat in the cumin, red pepper or paprika and seasoning. In another bowl, beat the yogurt with the garlic and season with salt and pepper.

3 To make the sauce, heat the oil and butter in a heavy pan and fry the onion and garlic until softened. Add the red pepper or chilli, sugar and mint, then stir in the tomatoes and cook gently for about 15 minutes. Season and remove from the heat.

4 Preheat the oven to 200°C/400°F/ Gas 6. Roll out the dough as thinly as possible on a lightly floured surface. Using a sharp knife, cut the dough into small squares (roughly 2.5cm/1in).

5 Spoon a little chickpea mixture into the middle of each square and bunch the corners together to form a little pouch. Place the filled pasta parcels in a greased ovenproof dish, stacking them next to each other. Bake, uncovered, for 15–20 minutes, until golden brown.

6 Pour the stock into a pan and bring to the boil. Take the pasta parcels out of the oven and pour the stock over them. Return the dish to the oven and bake for a further 15–20 minutes, until almost all the stock has been absorbed. Meanwhile, reheat the tomato sauce.

7 Transfer to a serving dish and spoon the yogurt over them. Top the cool yogurt with the hot tomato sauce and sprinkle with the chopped herbs.

Vegetable Terrine: *Energy 205Kcal/853kJ; Protein 3.8g; Carbohydrate 21.7g, of which sugars 20.9g; Fat 12g, of which saturates 1.8g; Cholesterol 0mg; Calcium 47mg; Fibre 4.1g; Sodium 173mg.*
Chickpea Pasta Parcels: *Energy 416kcal/1760kJ; Protein 14.8g; Carbohydrate 73.7g, of which sugars 5.9g; Fat 9g, of which saturates 2.6g; Cholesterol 71mg; Calcium 179mg; Fibre 5.9g; Sodium 360mg.*

Tzatsiki with Courgettes and Aubergines

Tzatsiki is a cool dip made with yogurt, cucumber and mint, which is extremely well suited to the heat of the summer. It can be served with all kinds of grilled meats and roasts, but is also perfect with freshly fried slices of courgettes and aubergines.

Serves 4

3 courgettes (zucchini)
1 aubergine (eggplant)
25g/1oz/¼ cup plain (all-purpose) flour
sunflower oil, for frying
salt and ground black pepper

For the tzatsiki

15cm/6in piece of cucumber
200g/7oz Greek (US strained) yogurt
1 or 2 garlic cloves, crushed
15ml/1 tbsp extra virgin olive oil
30ml/2 tbsp thinly sliced fresh mint leaves, plus extra to garnish

1 Start by making the tzatsiki. Peel the cucumber, grate it coarsely into a colander, and press out most of the liquid. Add to the yogurt with the garlic, olive oil and mint. Stir in salt to taste, cover and chill.

2 Trim the courgettes and aubergine, rinse and pat dry. Cut them lengthways into long, thin slices and coat lightly with flour.

3 Heat the oil in a large frying pan and add as many courgette slices as it will hold in one layer. Cook for 1–2 minutes, then turn over and brown the other side. Lift the slices out, drain them on kitchen paper and keep them hot while cooking the remaining courgettes and then the aubergines.

4 Pile the fried slices in a warmed bowl, season and serve immediately with the chilled tzatsiki garnished with mint leaves.

Cook's Tip

If you are making the tzatsiki several hours before serving, don't add the salt until later, as it will make the yogurt watery.

Salad of Puréed Aubergines

In the heat of high summer, *melitzanosalata* makes a surprisingly refreshing meze. To be strictly authentic, the aubergines should be grilled over charcoal, but baking them gives a very satisfactory result.

Serves 4

3 large aubergines (eggplants), total weight about 900g/2lb
15ml/1 tbsp chopped onion
2 garlic cloves, crushed
juice of ½ lemon, or a little more
90–105ml/6–7 tbsp extra virgin olive oil
1 ripe tomato, peeled, seeded and finely diced
salt and ground black pepper
finely chopped fresh flat leaf parsley, to garnish
chicory (Belgian endive), and black and green olives, to serve

1 Preheat the oven to 180°C/350°F/Gas 4. Prick the aubergines and lay them directly on the oven shelves. Roast them for 1 hour, or until soft, turning them over twice.

2 When the aubergines are cool enough to handle, cut them in half. Spoon the flesh into a food processor and add the onion, garlic and lemon juice. Season with salt and ground black pepper and process until smooth.

3 With the processor motor running, gradually drizzle in the olive oil through the feeder tube, until the mixture forms a smooth, light paste. Taste the mixture and adjust the seasoning if necessary, then spoon the purée into a bowl and stir in the diced tomato.

4 Cover and chill for 1 hour before serving. Garnish with chopped fresh flat leaf parsley and serve with fresh, washed chicory leaves and bowls of black and green olives.

Cook's Tip

If you wish to barbecue the aubergines instead of using the oven, prick them and barbecue over a low to medium heat for at least 1 hour.

Tzatsiki: Energy 247Kcal/1,020kJ; Protein 7.6g; Carbohydrate 11g, of which sugars 5.5g; Fat 19.9g, of which saturates 4.6g; Cholesterol 0mg; Calcium 149mg; Fibre 3.2g; Sodium 41mg.
Puréed Aubergines: Energy 190Kcal/788kJ; Protein 2.3g; Carbohydrate 6.7g, of which sugars 5.9g; Fat 17.5g, of which saturates 2.6g; Cholesterol 0mg; Calcium 28mg; Fibre 4.9g; Sodium 7mg.

Taramasalata

This delicious speciality makes an excellent start to any meal, accompanied by fruity black olives and warm pitta bread. One of the most famous Greek dips, and a central part of any meze table, homemade taramasalata is incomparably better than the versions sold in supermarkets.

Serves 4

115g/4oz smoked mullet roe or smoked cod's roe
2 garlic cloves, crushed
30ml/2 tbsp grated onion
60ml/4 tbsp olive oil
4 slices white bread, crusts removed
juice of 2 lemons
30ml/2 tbsp milk or water
ground black pepper
warm pitta bread, to serve

1 Place the smoked fish roe, garlic, grated onion, oil, bread and lemon juice in a blender or food processor and process until the mixture is smooth.

2 Scrape down the edges of the food processor or blender to ensure that all the ingredients are properly incorporated. Blend quickly again.

3 Add the milk or water and process again for a few seconds. (This will give the taramasalata a creamier texture.)

4 Pour the taramasalata into a serving bowl, cover with clear film (plastic wrap) and chill for 1–2 hours before serving. Sprinkle the dip with black pepper and serve with warm pitta bread.

Cook's Tip
The smoked roe of grey mullet is traditionally used for taramasalata, but it is expensive and can be difficult to obtain. Smoked cod's roe is often used instead to make this dish. It varies in colour and may be paler than the burnt-orange colour of mullet roe, but is still very good. When buying smoked cod's roe, make sure that it is not overcooked as this makes it hard and prevents it blending well.

Feta and Roast Pepper Dip with Chillies

This is a familiar meze in Greece, called *htipiti* and often served as a snack with a glass of ouzo. Its Greek name means "that which is beaten" and it has a tart, spicy flavour. If you chill the mixture before serving the texture will become firmer.

Serves 4

1 yellow or green elongated or bell-shaped pepper
1–2 fresh green chillies
200g/7oz feta cheese, cubed
60ml/4 tbsp extra virgin olive oil
juice of 1 lemon
45–60ml/3–4 tbsp milk
ground black pepper
finely chopped fresh flat leaf parsley, to garnish
slices of toast or toasted pitta bread, to serve

1 Scorch the pepper and chillies by threading them on to metal skewers and turning them over a flame or under the grill (broiler), until blackened and blistered all over.

2 Put the pepper and chillies into a plastic bag to loosen the skin and set aside until cool enough to handle.

3 Peel off as much of the skins as possible and wipe off the blackened parts with kitchen paper. Slit the pepper and chillies and discard the seeds and stems.

4 Put the pepper and chilli flesh into a food processor. Add the feta cheese, olive oil, lemon juice and milk, and blend well. Add a little more milk if the mixture is too stiff, and season with black pepper. Spread the dip on slices of toast, sprinkle a little fresh parsley over the top and serve.

Variation
The dip is also excellent served with a selection of vegetable crudités, such as carrot, cauliflower, green or red (bell) pepper and celery.

Taramasalata: *Energy 185Kcal/770kJ; Protein 8.4g; Carbohydrate 11.4g, of which sugars 1.7g; Fat 12.1g, of which saturates 1.8g; Cholesterol 95mg; Calcium 38mg; Fibre 0.5g; Sodium 139mg.*
Roast Pepper Dip: *Energy 245Kcal/1,014kJ; Protein 8.7g; Carbohydrate 4.5g, of which sugars 4.3g; Fat 21.5g, of which saturates 8.6g; Cholesterol 36mg; Calcium 198mg; Fibre 0.8g; Sodium 727mg.*

Roast Garlic with Goat's Cheese, Walnut and Herb Pâté

This mellow combination of flavours works beautifully.

Serves 4

4 large garlic bulbs
4 fresh rosemary sprigs
8 fresh thyme sprigs
60ml/4 tbsp olive oil
sea salt and ground black pepper

For the pâté

200g/7oz soft goat's cheese
5ml/1 tsp finely chopped thyme
15ml/1 tbsp chopped parsley
50g/2oz shelled walnuts, chopped
15ml/1 tbsp walnut oil (optional)
fresh thyme, to garnish

4–8 slices of sourdough bread
shelled walnuts, to serve

1 Preheat the oven to 180°C/350°F/Gas 4. Strip the papery skin from the garlic bulbs. Place them in an ovenproof dish that fits them snugly with the rosemary, thyme, oil and seasoning. Cover with foil and bake for 50–60 minutes, basting once. Leave to cool. Preheat the grill.

2 Cream the cheese with the thyme, parsley and walnuts; beat in 15ml/1 tbsp of oil from the garlic and season to taste. Drizzle walnut oil over the paté, if using, and a grind of black pepper.

3 Brush the bread with oil from the garlic pan and toast under the grill. Serve a bulb of garlic, toasts and a spoonful of pâté on each plate, garnished with walnuts and thyme.

Baked Chickpea Purée

Hot, oven-baked hummus is an eastern Turkish speciality.

Serves 4

225g/8oz/1¼ cups dried chickpeas, soaked in cold water for at least 6 hours
about 50ml/2fl oz/¼ cup olive oil
juice of 2 lemons
3–4 garlic cloves, crushed
10ml/2 tsp cumin seeds, crushed
30–45ml/2–3 tbsp light sesame paste (tahini)
45–60ml/3–4 tbsp thick natural (plain) yogurt
30–45ml/2–3 tbsp pine nuts
40g/1 1/2oz/3 tbsp butter or ghee
5–10ml/1–2 tsp roasted Turkish red pepper or paprika
salt and ground black pepper

1 Drain the chickpeas and put them in a pan with plenty of cold water. Boil for 1 minute, then lower the heat and simmer for about 1 hour, or until they are easy to mash. Drain, rinse well under cold running water and remove any loose skins.

2 Preheat the oven to 200°C/400°F/Gas 6. Pound the chickpeas with the oil, lemon juice, garlic and cumin with a pestle and mortar, or use a food processor. Beat in the sesame paste, then the yogurt. Season to taste. Transfer to an ovenproof dish and smooth the top.

3 Dry-roast the pine nuts over a medium heat. Lower the heat, melt the butter, then stir in the red pepper or paprika.

4 Pour the mixture over the hummus and bake for about 25 minutes, until it has risen slightly and the butter has been absorbed. Serve straight from the oven.

Spicy Walnut Dip

This popular, spicy walnut dip, called Muhammara in Arabic, is usually served with toasted flat bread or crusty bread. It can also be served as a dip for raw vegetables and as an accompaniment to grilled, broiled or barbecued meats. The ingredients vary a little – mashed chickpeas or carrots may be used instead of bread, grated feta or yogurt may be added for a creamy texture, and garlic may be included in liberal quantities – but the general aim is to create a fiery dip spiked with Turkish red pepper or chillies. The dip is traditionally made with pomegranate syrup, but contemporary recipes often use lemon juice instead. The parsley leaves at the end help to cut the heat, so add more if you like.

Serves 4–6

175g/6oz/1 cup broken shelled walnuts
5ml/1 tsp cumin seeds, dry-roasted and ground
5–10ml/1–2 tsp Turkish red pepper, or 1–2 fresh red chillies, seeded and finely chopped, or 5ml/1 tsp chilli powder
1–2 garlic cloves (optional)
1 slice of day-old white bread, sprinkled with water and left for a few minutes, then squeezed dry
15–30ml/1–2 tbsp tomato purée (paste)
5–10ml/1–2 tsp granulated sugar
30ml/2 tbsp pomegranate syrup or juice of 1 lemon
120ml/4fl oz/½ cup olive or sunflower oil, plus extra for serving
salt and ground black pepper
a few sprigs of fresh flat leaf parsley, to garnish
strips of pitta bread, to serve

1 Using a mortar and pestle, pound the walnuts with the cumin seeds, red pepper or chilli and garlic (if using). Add the soaked bread and pound to a paste, then beat in the tomato purée, sugar and pomegranate syrup.

2 Now slowly drizzle in 120ml/4fl oz/½ cup oil, beating all the time until the paste is thick and light. Season with salt and pepper, and spoon into a bowl. Splash a little olive oil over the top to keep it moist, and garnish with parsley leaves. Serve at room temperature.

Roast Garlic with Pâté: Energy 371Kcal/153kJ; Protein 18.52g; Carbohydrate 5.1g, of which sugars3.7g; Fat 32.7g, of which saturates 11.3g; Cholesterol; Calcium 192mg; Fibre 1.7g
Chickpea Purée: Energy 433kcal/1803kJ; Protein 15g; Carbohydrate 29.5g, of which sugars 3g; Fat 29.2g, of which saturates 7.7g; Cholesterol 21mg; Calcium 160mg; Fibre 6.8g; Sodium 91mg.
Spicy Walnut Dip: Energy 339kcal/1399kJ; Protein 4.8g; Carbohydrate 5.1g, of which sugars 2.8g; Fat 33.4g, of which saturates 3.5g; Cholesterol 0mg; Calcium 34mg; Fibre 1.2g; Sodium 32mg.

Cannellini Bean Purée with Grilled Chicory

The slightly bitter flavours of chicory and radicchio make a wonderful marriage with the creamy bean purée to create this low-fat appetizer or snack.

Serves 4

400g/14oz can cannellini beans
45ml/3 tbsp sour cream
finely grated rind and juice of 1 large orange
15ml/1 tbsp finely chopped fresh rosemary
4 heads of chicory (Belgian endive)
2 heads of radicchio
10ml/2 tsp walnut oil
longer shreds of orange rind, to garnish (optional)

1 Drain the beans, then rinse and drain them again. Place the beans in a blender or food processor with the sour cream, orange rind and juice and chopped rosemary and process until smooth and well mixed. Set aside.

2 Cut the heads of the chicory in half lengthways. Cut each radicchio head into 8 even wedges using a sharp knife. Preheat the grill (broiler) to medium.

3 Lay the chicory and radicchio on a baking sheet and brush lightly with the walnut oil. Grill (broil) for 2–3 minutes. Serve with the bean purée and garnish with orange shreds, if using.

Variation
Serve the dip with olives and pitta or as part of a meze table.

Cook's Tip
The dip can be made using dried cannellini beans, which must first be soaked in cold water for 5–6 hours. Place the drained beans in a pan, cover with fresh water and boil briskly for 10 minutes, then lower the heat and simmer for 1–1½ hours until tender. Drain and cool a little before puréeing.

Hummus

This classic chickpea dip from the eastern Mediterranean is a firm favourite everywhere. It is flavoured with garlic and tahini – sesame seed paste. For extra flavour, a little ground cumin can be added, and olive oil can also be stirred in to enrich the hummus, if you like. It is lovely served with wedges of toasted pitta or with crudités as a delicious dip.

Serves 4-6

400g/14oz can chickpeas, drained
60ml/4 tbsp tahini
2–3 garlic cloves, chopped
juice of ½–1 lemon
salt and ground black pepper
a few whole chickpeas reserved, to garnish

1 Reserving a few for garnish, coarsely mash the chickpeas in a mixing bowl with a fork. If you like a smoother purée, process the chickpeas in a food processor or blender until a smooth paste is formed.

2 Mix the tahini into the bowl of chickpeas, then stir in the chopped garlic cloves and lemon juice. Season to taste and garnish the top with the reserved chickpeas. Serve the hummus at room temperature.

Variations

- *Process 2 roasted red (bell) peppers with the chickpeas, then continue as above. Serve sprinkled with lightly toasted pine nuts and paprika mixed with a little extra virgin olive oil.*
- *Add a pinch of cayenne to the mixture.*
- *Instead of chickpeas, top with a drizzle of olive oil and a dusting of paprika.*

Cook's Tip
Add more lemon juice to taste if necessary when seasoning.

Purée: *Energy 129kcal/542kJ; Protein 6.8g; Carbohydrate 17.3g, of which sugars 3.3g; Fat 4.9g, of which saturates 1.9g; Cholesterol 7mg; Calcium 48mg; Fibre 5.5g; Sodium 427mg.*
Hummus: *Energy 210Kcal/880kJ; Protein 10.3g; Carbohydrate 16.9g, of which sugars 0.6g; Fat 11.8g, of which saturates 1.6g; Cholesterol 0mg; Calcium 146mg; Fibre 5.5g; Sodium 223mg.*

Fresh Vegetable Medley

This Turkish meze dish is a refreshing and colourful mixture of chopped fresh vegetables. Along with cubes of honey-sweet melon and feta, or plump, juicy olives spiked with red pepper and oregano, this is meze at its simplest and best. Popular in kebab houses, it dish makes a tasty snack or appetizer, and is good served with chunks of warm, crusty bread or toasted pitta.

Serves 4

2 large tomatoes, skinned, seeded and finely chopped
2 Turkish green peppers or 1 green (bell) pepper, finely chopped
1 onion, finely chopped
1 green chilli, seeded and finely chopped
1 small bunch of fresh flat leaf parsley, finely chopped
a few fresh mint leaves, finely chopped
15–30ml/1–2 tbsp olive oil
salt and ground black pepper

1 Put all the finely chopped ingredients in a bowl and mix well together.

2 Toss the mixture with the olive oil to bind the ingredients, and season to taste with salt and pepper.

3 Leave the dish to sit for a short time for the flavours to blend. Serve at room temperature, in individual bowls or one large dish.

Variations

- *The salad can be turned into a paste. When you bind the chopped vegetables with the olive oil, add 15–30ml/1–2 tbsp tomato purée (paste) with a little extra chilli and 5–10ml/1–2 tsp sugar. The mixture will become a tangy paste to spread on fresh, crusty bread or toasted pitta, and it can also be used as a sauce for grilled (broiled), roasted or barbecued meats.*
- *Add other salad vegetables to the mixture, such as chopped cucumber and spring onions (scallions).*

Pea Purée

This fresh-tasting spicy dip is similar to guacamole, but uses peas instead of avocados. It's a really fresh tasting and unusual dip to serve as tapas. Serve with crisp fruit and vegetable crudités.

Serves 6

350g/12oz/3 cups frozen peas, thawed
1 garlic clove, crushed
2 spring onions (scallions), trimmed and chopped
5ml/1 tsp finely grated lime rind
juice of 1 lime
2.5ml/½ tsp ground cumin
dash of Tabasco sauce
15ml/1 tbsp reduced-calorie mayonnaise
30ml/2 tbsp chopped fresh coriander (cilantro)
salt and ground black pepper
pinch of paprika and lime slices, to garnish

For the crudités

6 baby carrots
2 celery sticks
1 red-skinned eating apple
1 pear
15ml/1 tbsp lemon or lime juice
6 baby corn

1 Put the peas, garlic clove, spring onions, lime rind and juice, cumin, Tabasco sauce, mayonnaise and salt and ground black pepper in a blender or food processor and process for a few minuts, or until smooth.

2 Add the coriander and process for a few seconds. Spoon the mixture into a serving bowl, cover with clear film (plastic wrap) and refrigerate for 30 minutes, to let the flavours develop.

3 For the crudités, trim and peel the carrots. Halve the celery sticks lengthways and trim into sticks the same length as the carrots. Quarter, core and thickly slice the apple and pear, then dip into the lemon or lime juice to prevent discolouration. Arrange with the baby corn on a serving platter. Sprinkle the paprika over the purée and serve garnished with slices of fresh lime.

Variation

Use ground coriander in place of ground cumin, if you like.

Fresh Vegetable Medley: *Energy 101kcal/420kJ; Protein 2.3g; Carbohydrate 9.3g, of which sugars 8g; Fat 6.3g, of which saturates 0.9g; Cholesterol 0mg; Calcium 66mg; Fibre 2.7g; Sodium 15mg.*
Pea Purée: *Energy 93kcal/386kJ; Protein 5.2g; Carbohydrate 14.7g, of which sugars 9g; Fat 1.9g, of which saturates 0.3g; Cholesterol 1mg; Calcium 41mg; Fibre 5.1g; Sodium 232mg.*

Carrot and Caraway Purée with Yogurt

Long, thin carrots that are orange, yellow, red and purple are a colourful feature in vegetable markets throughout Turkey. Used mainly in salads, lentil dishes and stews, they are also married with garlic-flavoured yogurt for meze – sliced and deep-fried, drizzled with yogurt, grated and folded in, or steamed and puréed, then served with the yogurt in the middle, as in this recipe.

Try serving the carrot purée while it is still warm, with chunks of crusty bread or warm pitta to scoop it up.

Serves 4

6 large carrots, thickly sliced
5ml/1 tsp caraway seeds
30–45ml/2–3 tbsp olive oil
juice of 1 lemon
225g/8oz/1 cup thick natural (plain) yogurt
1–2 garlic cloves, crushed
salt and ground black pepper
a few fresh mint leaves, to garnish

1 Steam the carrots for about 25 minutes, until they are very soft. While they are still warm, mash them to a smooth purée, or whizz them in a blender.

2 Beat the caraway seeds into the carrot purée, followed by the oil and lemon juice. Season to taste with salt and ground black pepper.

3 In a separate bowl, beat the yogurt with the garlic and season with salt and pepper. Spoon the warm carrot purée around the edge of a serving dish, or pile into a mound and make a well in the middle. Spoon the yogurt into the middle, and garnish with mint.

Cook's Tip
It is always better to steam, rather than boil, vegetables, so that they retain more of their taste, texture and goodness. This purée would not taste nearly as good if the carrots were boiled and watery.

Sesame and Lemon Dip

This delightful little dip comes from Turkey, where it is often served in outdoor cafés and restaurants as a meze dish on its own – a sort of whetting of the appetite while you wait for the assortment of exciting dishes to come. Sometimes you will see groups of old men drinking rakı or refreshing tea, sharing a plate of *tahin tarama* or a bowl of roasted chickpeas while they play cards or backgammon. The dip is sweet and tangy, and is delicious mopped up with chunks of crusty bread or toasted pitta bread.

Serves 2

45ml/3 tbsp light sesame paste (tahin)
juice of 1 lemon
15–30ml/1–2 tbsp clear honey
5–10ml/1–2 tsp dried mint
lemon wedges, to serve

1 Beat the sesame paste and lemon juice together in a bowl.

2 Add the honey and mint and beat again until thick and creamy, then spoon into a small dish.

3 Serve at room temperature, with lemon wedges for squeezing.

Cook's Tip
Tahin or tahini, made from ground sesame seeds, is available "hulled" or "unhulled". The latter is made with the whole seed and is more nutritious, but can be bitter.

Variation
Popular in Turkey for breakfast or as a sweet snack is tahin pekmez. *Combine 30–45ml/2–3 tbsp tahini with 30ml/2 tbsp grape molasses* (pekmez) *to form a sweet paste, then scoop it up with chunks of bread. If you can't find pekmez, substitute date syrup, from Middle Eastern and health food stores.*

Carrot Purée: *Energy 157Kcal/651kJ; Protein 4.2g; Carbohydrate 15.3g, of which sugars 13.6g; Fat 9.2g, of which saturates 1.6g; Cholesterol 1mg; Calcium 140mg; Fibre 3.3g; Sodium 78mg.*
Sesame and Lemon Dip: *Energy 160kcal/664kJ; Protein 4.3g; Carbohydrate 6.4g, of which sugars 6.2g; Fat 13.3g, of which saturates 1.9g; Cholesterol 0mg; Calcium 155mg; Fibre 1.8g; Sodium 6mg.*

King Prawns in Crispy Batter

A huge range of prawns is enjoyed in Spain, each with its appropriate cooking method. Langostinos are deep-water prawns, often with tiger stripes, and can be among the largest. The best way to enjoy them is dipped in a simple batter and deep fried.

Serves 4

120ml/4fl oz/1/2 cup water
1 large (US extra large) egg
115/4oz/1 cup plain (all-purpose) flour
5ml/1 tsp cayenne pepper
12 raw king prawns (jumbo shrimp), in the shell
vegetable oil, for deep-frying
flat leaf parsley, to garnish
lemon wedges, to serve

1 In a large bowl, whisk together the water and the egg. Whisk in the flour and cayenne pepper until smooth.

2 Peel the prawns, leaving just the tails intact. Make a shallow cut down the back of each prawn.

3 Using the tip of the knife, pull out and discard the dark intestinal tract.

4 Heat the oil in a large pan or deep-fat fryer, until a cube of bread dropped into the oil browns in 1 minute.

5 Holding the prawns by tails, dip them into the batter, one at a time, shaking off any excess. Carefully drop each prawn into the oil and fry for 2–3 minutes until crisp and golden. Drain on kitchen paper, garnish with parsley and serve with lemon wedges, if you like.

Octopus Salad

Baby octopus makes a delicious salad, ever popular in Greece.

Serves 4–6

900g/2lb small octopus or squid, skinned and cleaned
175ml/6fl oz/¾ cup olive oil
30ml/2 tbsp white wine vinegar
30ml/2 tbsp chopped fresh parsley or coriander (cilantro)
12 black olives, stoned (pitted)
2 shallots, thinly sliced
1 red onion, thinly sliced
salt and ground black pepper
sprigs of coriander, to garnish
8–12 cos or romaine lettuce leaves and lemon wedges

1 Boil the octopus or squid in salted water for 20–25 minutes, or until just soft. Do not overcook it, as it can become rubbery. Drain and leave to cool completely before covering and chilling for 45 minutes.

2 Lay the octopus out on a chopping board. Cut the tentacles from the body. Chop all the flesh into even pieces, slicing across the thick part of the tentacles and following the direction of the suckers. If using squid, chop into even rings.

3 In a bowl, combine the oil and vinegar. Add the herbs, olives, shallots, octopus and red onion. Season to taste and toss well.

4 Arrange the octopus on a bed of lettuce, garnish with coriander and serve with lemon wedges.

Butterflied Prawns in Chocolate

There is a tradition in Spain, which originates in Mexico, of cooking savoury dishes with chocolate – and this extends far beyond the classic chilli con carne. This dish is just the kind of culinary adventure that Spanish chefs love.

Serves 4

8 large raw prawns (shrimp), in the shell
15ml/1 tbsp seasoned plain (all-purpose) flour
15ml/1 tbsp pale dry sherry
juice of 1 large orange
15g/½oz dark (bittersweet) chocolate, chopped
30ml/2 tbsp olive oil
2 garlic cloves, finely chopped
2.5cm/1in piece fresh root ginger, finely chopped
1 small dried chilli, seeded and chopped
salt and ground black pepper

1 Peel the prawns, leaving just the tail sections intact. Make a shallow cut down the back of each one and carefully pull out and discard the dark intestinal tract.

2 Turn the prawns over so that the undersides are uppermost, and then carefully slit them open from tail to top, using a small sharp knife, cutting them almost, but not quite, through to the central back line.

3 Press the prawns down firmly to flatten them out. Coat with the seasoned flour and set aside.

4 Gently heat the sherry and orange juice in a small pan. When warm, remove from the heat and stir in the chopped chocolate until melted.

5 Heat the oil in a frying pan. Add the garlic, ginger and chilli and cook for 2 minutes until golden. Remove with a slotted spoon and reserve. Add the prawns, cut side down and cook for 2–3 minutes until golden brown with pink edges. Turn the prawns and cook for a further 2 minutes.

6 Return the garlic mixture to the pan and pour the chocolate sauce over. Cook for 1 minute, turning the prawns to coat them in the glossy sauce. Season to taste and serve hot.

King Prawns: Energy 253kcal/1061kJ; Protein 13.1g; Carbohydrate 22.4g, of which sugars 0.4g; Fat 13.1g, of which saturates 1.8g; Cholesterol 145mg; Calcium 87mg; Fibre 0.9g; Sodium 113mg.
Octopus Salad: Energy 320kcal/1334kJ; Protein 23.5g; Carbohydrate 2.9g, of which sugars 0.8g; Fat 24g, of which saturates 3.7g; Cholesterol 338mg; Calcium 37mg; Fibre 0.6g; Sodium 280mg.
Butterflied Prawns: Energy 125kcal/520kJ; Protein 8.5g; Carbohydrate 6.5g, of which sugars 3.6g; Fat 6.9g, of which saturates 1.5g; Cholesterol 88mg; Calcium 44mg; Fibre 0.2g; Sodium 88mg.

Flash-Fried Squid with Paprika and Garlic

Fried squid are part of every tapas bar selection, but this recipe is unusual in that it uses fresh chillies. Serve the dish with dry sherry as a tapas dish or with salad leaves and bread, for a substantial first course to serve four.

Serves 6–8

500g/1¼lb very small squid, cleaned
90ml/6 tbsp olive oil, plus extra
1 fresh red chilli, seeded and finely chopped
10ml/2 tsp Spanish mild smoked paprika
30ml/2 tbsp plain (all-purpose) flour
2 garlic cloves, finely chopped
15ml/1 tbsp sherry vinegar
5ml/1 tsp grated lemon rind
30–45ml/2–3 tbsp finely chopped fresh parsley
salt and ground black pepper

1 Using a sharp knife, cut the squid body sacs into rings and cut the tentacles into bitesize pieces.

2 Place the squid in a bowl and pour over 30ml/2 tbsp of the olive oil, half the chilli and the paprika. Season with a little salt and some pepper, cover with clear film (plastic wrap), place in the refrigerator and leave to marinate for 2–4 hours.

3 Toss the squid in the flour. Heat the remaining oil in a wok or deep frying pan over a high heat until very hot. Add half the squid and quickly stir-fry for 1–2 minutes, or until it becomes opaque and the tentacles curl. Add half the garlic. Stir, then turn out into a bowl. Repeat with the remaining squid and garlic, adding more oil if needed.

4 Sprinkle with the sherry vinegar, lemon rind, remaining chilli and parsley. Season and serve hot or cool.

Cook's Tip
Smoked paprika has a wonderful, subtle flavour, but if you cannot find it, you can use mild paprika instead.

Marinated Anchovies

The Spanish term for marinated anchovies is *boquerones*, while *anchoas* is their word for the canned and salted varieties, which are much used as a flavouring in many parts of the Mediterranean region.

Serves 4

225g/8oz fresh anchovies, heads and tails removed, and split open along the belly
juice of 3 lemons
30ml/2 tbsp extra virgin olive oil
2 garlic cloves, finely chopped
15ml/1 tbsp chopped fresh parsley
flaked sea salt

1 Turn the anchovies on to their bellies, and press down with your thumb.

2 Using the tip of a small, sharp knife, carefully remove the backbones from the flattened fish, and arrange the anchovies skin side down in a single layer on a large plate.

3 Squeeze two-thirds of the lemon juice over the fish and sprinkle them with the salt. Cover and leave to stand for 1–24 hours, basting occasionally with the juices, until the flesh is white and no longer translucent.

4 Transfer the anchovies to a serving plate and drizzle with the olive oil and the remaining lemon juice. Scatter the fish with the chopped garlic and parsley, then cover with clear film (plastic wrap) and chill until ready to serve.

Salted and Grilled Sardines

Grilled sardines are classic Mediterranean beach food.

Serves 4-8

8 sardines, about 800g/1¾lb total weight, scaled and gutted
50g/2oz/¼ cup salt
oil, for brushing
focaccia, to serve

For the herb salsa

5ml/1 tsp sea salt flakes
60ml/4 tbsp chopped fresh tarragon leaves
40g/1½oz/generous 1 cup chopped flat leaf parsley
1 small red onion, very finely chopped
105ml/7 tbsp extra virgin olive oil
60ml/4 tbsp lemon juice

1 Make the herb salsa by grinding the salt in a mortar and adding the other salsa ingredients one at a time.

2 Wash the sardines inside and out. Pat dry with kitchen paper and rub them inside and out with salt. Cover and put in a cool place for 30–45 minutes. Meanwhile, prepare the barbecue.

3 Rinse the salt off the sardines. Pat them dry with kitchen paper, then leave to air-dry for 15 minutes.

4 When the coals have a thick coating of ash, brush the fish with olive oil and cook directly on the oiled grill.

5 Cook for about 3 minutes on one side and about 2½ minutes on the other. Serve with the herb salsa and toast.

Flash-fried Squid: *Energy 139kcal/580kJ; Protein 10.1g; Carbohydrate 3.8g, of which sugars 0.1g; Fat 9.4g, of which saturates 1.4g; Cholesterol 141mg; Calcium 21mg; Fibre 0.3g; Sodium 70mg.*
Marinated Anchovies: *Energy 108kcal/449kJ; Protein 14.2g; Carbohydrate 0g, of which sugars 0g; Fat 5.6g, of which saturates 0.9g; Cholesterol 35mg; Calcium 169mg; Fibre 0g; Sodium 221mg.*
Sardines: *Energy 423Kcal/1,754kJ; Protein 31.5g; Carbohydrate 1.8g, of which sugars 1.4g; Fat 32.1g, of which saturates 6.4g; Cholesterol 0mg; Calcium 187mg; Fibre 1g; Sodium 667mg.*

Fried Whitebait with Sherry Salsa

Small freshly fried fish are offered on the counter of every tapas bar in Spain. Black-backed anchovies are the best, but they need to be cooked within a day of catching. Tiny *chanquetes*, or whitebait, are also popular, though their sale has now been banned in Spain as the stocks are depleted and so many juvenile fish of other species were being caught in the small nets used to catch them. The term "whitebait" refers to different species in different regions, but all are delicious fried, and go well with this lovely salsa. Serve with lemon wedges to squeeze over the fish.

Serves 4

225g/8oz whitebait
30ml/2 tbsp seasoned plain (all-purpose) flour
60ml/4 tbsp olive oil
60ml/4 tbsp sunflower oil

For the salsa

1 shallot, finely chopped
2 garlic cloves, finely chopped
4 ripe tomatoes, roughly chopped
1 small red chilli, seeded and finely chopped
30ml/2 tbsp olive oil
60ml/4 tbsp sweet oloroso sherry
30–45ml/2–3 tbsp chopped mixed fresh herbs, such as parsley or basil
25g/1oz/½ cup stale white breadcrumbs
salt and ground black pepper

1 To make the salsa, heat the olive oil in a frying pan over a low heat and add the chopped shallot, garlic, tomatoes and chilli. Cover the pan with a lid and cook the ingredients gently for about 10 minutes.

2 Pour the sherry into the pan and season with salt and pepper to taste. Stir in the herbs and breadcrumbs, then cover the pan and keep the salsa hot until the whitebait are ready.

3 Preheat the oven to 150°C/300°F/Gas 2. Wash the whitebait thoroughly, drain well and dry on kitchen paper, then dust in the seasoned flour.

4 Heat the oils together in a heavy frying pan and cook the fish in batches until crisp and golden. Drain on kitchen paper and keep warm until all the fish are cooked. Serve at once with the salsa.

Spanish Pizza with Onion and Anchovy Topping

Called Cocas in Spain, these have a similar tradition to Italian pizza. Fresh bread dough is baked with a variety of savoury toppings, often including salt fish.

Serves 6-8

400g/14oz/3½ cups strong white bread flour
2.5ml/½ tsp salt
15g/½oz easy-blend (rapid-rise) dried yeast
120ml/4fl oz/½ cup olive oil
150ml/¼ pint/⅔ cup milk and water, in equal quantities, mixed
3 large onions, thinly sliced
50g/2oz can anchovies, drained and roughly chopped
30ml/2 tbsp pine nuts
30ml/2 tbsp Muscatel raisins or sultanas (golden raisins), soaked
5ml/1 tsp dried chilli flakes or powder
salt and ground black pepper

1 Put the flour and salt into a food processor with the yeast. Process, gradually working in 60ml/4 tbsp oil and a little of the milk and water. Gradually add the remaining milk and water. Turn the dough into a bowl, cover with a dish towel, then leave in a warm place for about 1 hour to rise.

2 Preheat the oven to 240°C/475°F/Gas 9. Heat the remaining oil in a large pan, add the onions, and cook gently until soft.

3 Return the dough to the food processor and knead it. On a lightly floured surface roll out the dough to a rectangle about 30 × 38cm/12 × 15in. Place on an oiled baking sheet.

4 Cover the dough with the onions. Scatter with the anchovies, pine nuts, raisins or sultanas and chilli flakes or powder and season. Bake for about 10 minutes, until puffed up and beginning to brown at the edges. Serve hot, cut into wedges.

Variation

You can eat cocas with a wide range of different toppings. Try spinach sautéed with garlic or sweet red (bell) peppers.

Fried Whitebait: *Energy 407kcal/1689kJ; Protein 13g; Carbohydrate 13.1g, of which sugars 5.1g; Fat 32.8g, of which saturates 3.4g; Cholesterol 0mg; Calcium 526mg; Fibre 2g; Sodium 191mg.*
Spanish Pizza: *Energy 335kcal/1407kJ; Protein 7.8g; Carbohydrate 47.5g, of which sugars 7.7g; Fat 14g, of which saturates 1.8g; Cholesterol 4mg; Calcium 110mg; Fibre 2.8g; Sodium 252mg.*

Spiced Clams

Spanish clams tend to be much larger than clams found elsewhere, and have more succulent flesh. This modern recipe uses Arab spicing to make a hot dip or sauce. Serve with plenty of fresh bread to mop up the delicious juices.

Serves 3–4

1 small onion, finely chopped
1 celery stick, sliced
2 garlic cloves, finely chopped
2.5cm/1in piece fresh root ginger, grated
30ml/2 tbsp olive oil
1.5ml/¼ tsp chilli powder
5ml/1 tsp ground turmeric
30ml/2 tbsp chopped fresh parsley
500g/1¼lb small clams, in the shell
30ml/2 tbsp dry white wine
salt and ground black pepper
celery leaves, to garnish
fresh bread, to serve

1 Place the onion, celery, garlic and ginger in a large pan, add the olive oil, spices and chopped parsley and stir-fry for about 5 minutes.

2 Add the clams to the pan and cook for 2 minutes. Add the wine, then cover and cook gently for 2–3 minutes, shaking the pan occasionally. Season. Discard any clams whose shells remain closed.

3 Serve, garnished with celery leaves and accompanied by fresh, crusty bread.

Cook's Tip

- *There are many different varieties of clam fished off the coast of Spain. One of the best is the* almeja fina *(the carpet shell clam), which is perfect used in this dish. It has a grooved brown shell with a yellow lattice pattern, which gives it its English name. In France it is known as the* palourde *and in Italy as the* vongola.
- *Before cooking the clams, check that all the shells are closed and discard any that are not. Any clams that do not open during cooking should also be discarded.*

Deep-Fried Mussels in Beer

In Turkey, fried mussels are skewered on sticks and eaten with a garlicky *tarator* sauce made with walnuts, almonds or pine nuts.

Serves 4–5

sunflower oil, for deep-frying
about 50 fresh mussels, cleaned, shelled and patted dry

For the batter

115g/4oz/1 cup plain (all-purpose) flour
5ml/1 tsp salt
2.5ml/½ tsp bicarbonate of soda (baking soda)
2 egg yolks
175–250ml/6–8fl oz/¾–1 cup light beer or lager

For the sauce

75g/3oz/½ cup broken shelled walnuts
2 slices of day-old bread, sprinkled with water and left for a few minutes, then squeezed dry
2–3 garlic cloves, crushed
45–60ml/3–4 tbsp olive oil
juice of 1 lemon
dash of white wine vinegar
salt and ground black pepper

1 Make the batter. Sift the flour, salt and soda into a bowl. Make a well in the middle and drop in the egg yolks. Using a wooden spoon, slowly beat in the beer and draw in the flour from the sides of the well until a smooth, thick batter is formed. Set aside for 30 minutes.

2 Meanwhile, make the sauce. Pound the walnuts to a paste using a mortar and pestle, or whizz them in a blender. Add the bread and garlic, and pound again to a paste. Drizzle in the olive oil, stirring all the time, and beat in the lemon juice and vinegar. The sauce should be smooth, with the consistency of thick double (heavy) cream – if it is too dry, stir in a little water. Season with salt and pepper and set aside.

3 Heat enough sunflower oil for deep-frying in a wok or other deep pan. Dip each mussel into the batter and drop into the hot oil. Fry in batches for a minute or two until golden brown. Lift out with a slotted spoon and drain on kitchen paper.

4 Thread the mussels on wooden skewers, or spear them individually, and serve hot, accompanied by the dipping sauce.

Spiced Clams: Energy 92kcal/381kJ; Protein 6.5g; Carbohydrate 2.2g, of which sugars 1.1g; Fat 5.9g, of which saturates 0.9g; Cholesterol 25mg; Calcium 50mg; Fibre 0.7g; Sodium 458mg.
Mussels in Beer: Energy 439kcal/1827kJ; Protein 10.6g; Carbohydrate 24.6g, of which sugars 1.9g; Fat 33g, of which saturates 4g; Cholesterol 89mg; Calcium 115mg; Fibre 1.5g; Sodium 502mg.

Leek, Saffron and Mussel Tartlets

Serve these vividly coloured little tarts with cherry tomatoes and salad leaves.

Makes 12
4 large yellow (bell) peppers, halved
2kg/4½lb mussels, scrubbed and beards removed
large pinch of saffron threads
30ml/2 tbsp hot water
4 large leeks, sliced
60ml/4 tbsp olive oil
4 large (US extra large) eggs
600ml/1 pint/2½ cups single (light) cream
60ml/4 tbsp chopped fresh parsley
salt and ground black pepper

For the pastry
450g/1lb/4 cups plain (all-purpose) flour
5ml/1 tsp salt
250g/8oz/1 cup butter, diced
30–45ml/2–3 tbsp water

1 To make the pastry, mix together the flour and salt and rub in the butter. Mix in the water and knead lightly. Wrap the dough in clear film (plastic wrap) and chill for 30 minutes.

2 Grill (broil) the pepper halves, skin sides uppermost, until blackened. Place them in a plastic bag and leave for 10 minutes, then peel and cut the flesh into thin strips.

3 Preheat the oven to 190°C/375°F/Gas 5. Use the pastry to line 12 × 10cm/4in tartlet tins (muffin pans), 2.5cm/1in deep. Prick the bases and line with foil. Bake for 10 minutes. Remove the foil and bake for another 5–8 minutes, or until lightly coloured. Reduce the oven temperature to 180°C/350°F/Gas 4.

4 Soak the saffron in the hot water for 10 minutes. Fry the leeks in the oil for 6–8 minutes until beginning to brown. Add the pepper strips and cook for another 2 minutes.

5 Put the mussels in a large pan, discard any open mussels that do not shut when tapped sharply. Cover and cook, shaking the pan occasionally, for 3–4 minutes, or until the mussels open. Discard any mussels that do not open. Shell the remainder. Beat the eggs, cream, saffron liquid and parsley together and season. Arrange the leeks, peppers and mussels in the pastry, add the egg mixture and bake for 20–25 minutes, until just firm.

Mussels with a Parsley Crust

Spain produces some of the best mussels in the world. Known as *mejillones* in Spain, they grow to an enormous size in a very short time, without becoming tough. Here they are grilled with a deliciously fragrant topping of Parmesan cheese, garlic and parsley, which helps to prevent the mussels from becoming overcooked.

Serves 4
450g/1lb fresh mussels
45ml/3 tbsp water
15ml/1 tbsp melted butter
15ml/1 tbsp olive oil
45ml/3 tbsp freshly grated Parmesan cheese
30ml/2 tbsp chopped fresh parsley
2 garlic cloves, finely chopped
2.5ml/½ tsp coarsely ground black pepper
crusty bread, to serve

1 Scrub the mussels thoroughly, scraping off any barnacles with a round-bladed knife and pulling out the gritty beards. Sharply tap any open mussels and discard any that fail to close or whose shells are broken.

2 Place the mussels in a large pan and add the water. Cover the pan with a lid and steam for about 5 minutes, or until the mussel shells have opened.

3 Drain the mussels well and discard any that remain closed. Carefully snap off the top shell from each mussel, leaving the actual flesh still attached to the bottom shell. Balance the shells in a flameproof dish, packing them closely together to make sure that they stay level.

4 Preheat the grill (broiler) to high. Put the melted butter, olive oil, grated Parmesan cheese, parsley, garlic and black pepper in a small bowl and mix well to combine.

5 Spoon a small amount of the cheese and garlic mixture on each mussel and gently press down with the back of the spoon.

6 Grill (broil) the mussels for about 2 minutes, or until they are sizzling and golden. Serve the mussels in their shells, with plenty of bread to mop up the delicious juices.

Leek Tartlets: *Energy 506kcal/2112kJ; Protein 17.2g; Carbohydrate 35.1g, of which sugars 6.1g; Fat 34.1g, of which saturates 18.3g; Cholesterol 155mg; Calcium 221mg; Fibre 2.8g; Sodium 273mg.*
Mussels with Parsley: *Energy 110kcal/456kJ; Protein 5.4g; Carbohydrate 0.3g, of which sugars 0.3g; Fat 9.7g, of which saturates 4.7g; Cholesterol 21mg; Calcium 165mg; Fibre 0.6g; Sodium 156mg.*

Mini Saffron Fish Cakes

A scented cucumber salad makes a superbly refreshing accompaniment for these fish cakes. Both the fish cakes and salad include sweet and spicy flavours. If you can't buy fresh fish, tuna canned in spring water or brine (drained) is a good substitute.

Serves 6

450g/1lb white fish fillets, such as sea bass, ling or haddock, skinned and cut into chunks
10ml/2 tsp harissa
rind of ½ preserved lemon, finely chopped
small bunch of fresh coriander (cilantro), finely chopped
1 egg
5ml/1 tsp clear honey
pinch of saffron threads, soaked in 5ml/1 tsp hot water
15ml/1 tbsp sunflower oil
salt and ground black pepper

For the salad

2 cucumbers, peeled and grated
juice of 1 orange
juice of ½ lemon
15–30ml/1–2 tbsp orange flower water
15–20ml/3–4 tsp caster (superfine) sugar
2.5ml/½ tsp ground cinnamon

1 Make the salad in advance so that it has time to chill. Place the cucumber in a colander over a bowl and sprinkle with salt. Leave to drain for about 10 minutes. Squeeze out the excess liquid and place the cucumber in a bowl. To make the dressing, combine the orange and lemon juice, orange flower water and sugar and pour over the cucumber. Toss well to mix, sprinkle with cinnamon and chill for at least 1 hour.

2 To make the fish cakes, put the fish in a food processor. Add the harissa, preserved lemon, chopped coriander, egg, honey, saffron with its soaking water, and seasoning, and whizz until smooth. Divide the mixture into 18 equal portions. Wet your hands under cold water to prevent the mixture from sticking to them, then roll each portion into a ball and flatten in the palm of your hand.

3 Heat the oil in a large non-stick frying pan and fry the fish cakes in batches, until golden brown on each side. Drain on kitchen paper and keep hot until all the fish cakes are cooked. Serve with the chilled cucumber salad.

Chorizo in Olive Oil

Spanish chorizo sausage is robustly seasoned with garlic, chilli and paprika. Serve this simple dish with bread to mop up the flavoured oil. For real authenticity use a fruity virgin Spanish olive oil to cook the sausage. The dish tastes superb when complemented with a glass of chilled Spanish fino or manzanilla sherry.

Serves 4

350g/12oz chorizo sausage
75ml/5 tbsp olive oil
1 large onion, thinly sliced
roughly chopped flat leaf parsley, to garnish

1 Skin the chorizo and slice it diagonally into thick chunks.

2 Heat the oil and fry the chorizo over a high heat until the edges are beginning to colour. Remove from the pan with a slotted spoon.

3 Add the onion to the pan and fry until coloured. Return the chorizo to the pan for 1 minute to heat through.

4 Transfer the mixture to a warmed serving dish and sprinkle with freshly chopped parsley.

Cook's Tips

- *Chorizo is a Spanish dry-cured sausage, made in various shapes and sizes. that derives its characteristic colour and taste from pimenton, or Spanish paprika. The sausages vary in the blend of hot, sweet and smoked paprikas used to flavour them, but are generally spicy and gutsy.*
- *When you are preparing tapas, simple dishes such as this one can be made in advance and kept warm, then garnished as you serve them. This approach will allow you to serve several hot tapas dishes and spend time with your guests.*
- *Try the multi-seeded loaf on page 246 with this recipe.*

Saffron Fish Cakes: *Energy 115kcal/481kJ; Protein 15.6g; Carbohydrate 5.6g, of which sugars 5.5g; Fat 3.5g, of which saturates 0.6g; Cholesterol 66mg; Calcium 42mg; Fibre 0.8g; Sodium 63mg.*
Chorizo: *Energy 408kcal/1689kJ; Protein 9.2g; Carbohydrate 15.2g, of which sugars 5.1g; Fat 35g, of which saturates 10.7g; Cholesterol 35mg; Calcium 58mg; Fibre 1.3g; Sodium 711mg.*

Lamb and Potato Cakes

An unusual dish, these minced lamb triangles are easy to serve hot for a buffet, or they can be eaten cold as a snack. They are also excellent for picnics.

Makes 12–15

450g/1lb new or small, firm potatoes
3 eggs
1 onion, grated
30ml/2 tbsp chopped fresh flat leaf parsley
450g/1lb/2 cups finely minced (ground) lean lamb
115g/4oz/2 cups fresh breadcrumbs
vegetable oil, for frying
salt and ground black pepper
a few sprigs of fresh mint, to garnish
toasted pitta bread and herby green salad, to serve

1 Cook the potatoes in boiling salted water for 20 minutes, or until tender, then drain and leave to one side to cool.

2 Beat the eggs in a large bowl. Add the grated onion, parsley and seasoning and beat together.

3 When the potatoes are cold, grate them coarsely and stir into the egg mixture. Then add the minced lamb and stir in, using your hands to blend the mixture fully. Knead for 3–4 minutes, or until the ingredients are thoroughly blended.

4 Take a handful of the lamb and potato mixture and roll it into a ball, about the size of a golf ball. Repeat this process until all is used.

5 Roll the balls in the breadcrumbs and then mould them into thin triangular shapes, about 13cm/5in long. Coat them in the breadcrumbs again on both sides.

6 Heat a 1cm/½in layer of oil in a frying pan over a medium heat. When the oil is hot, fry the cakes for 8–12 minutes, or until golden brown on both sides, turning occasionally. Drain well on a plate covered with a few layers of kitchen paper, changing the paper when necessary. Serve hot, garnished with a few sprigs of fresh mint and accompanied by freshly toasted pitta bread and a green salad.

Grilled Skewered Lamb

This dish, *souvlakia*, is classic Greek street food, and is eaten daily for lunch or as a snack, stuffed into pitta bread with some salad. There is nothing to match the succulence and flavour of barbecued lamb, though it has now largely been replaced by pork, which is considerably cheaper. Souvlakia are at their best served with tzatziki, a large tomato salad and barbecued bread.

Serves 4

1 small shoulder of lamb, boned and with most of the fat removed
2–3 onions, preferably red onions, quartered
2 red or green (bell) peppers, quartered
75ml/5 tbsp extra virgin olive oil
juice of 1 lemon
2 garlic cloves, crushed
5ml/1 tsp dried oregano
2.5ml/½ tsp dried thyme or some sprigs of fresh thyme
salt and ground black pepper

1 Ask your butcher to trim the meat and cut it into 4cm/1½in cubes. A little fat is desirable with souvlakia, as it keeps them moist and succulent during cooking. Separate the onion quarters into pieces, each composed of two or three layers, and slice each pepper quarter in half widthways.

2 Put the oil, lemon juice, garlic and herbs in a large bowl. Season with salt and pepper and whisk well to combine. Add the meat cubes, stirring to coat them in the mixture. Cover the bowl tightly and leave to marinate for 4–8 hours in the refrigerator, stirring several times.

3 Lift out the meat, reserving the marinade, and thread it on long metal skewers, alternating each cube of meat with a piece of pepper and a chunk of onion. Lay them across a grill pan or baking tray and brush them with the reserved marinade.

4 Preheat a grill (broiler) until hot or prepare a barbecue. Cook the souvlakia under a medium to high heat or over the hot coals for 10 minutes, until they start to scorch. Turn the skewers over, brush them again with the marinade (or a little olive oil) and cook them for 10–15 minutes more. They should be served immediately.

Lamb Cakes: *Energy 181Kcal/760kJ; Protein 10.8g; Carbohydrate 13.9g, of which sugars 1.1g; Fat 9.6g, of which saturates 2.8g; Cholesterol 76mg; Calcium 31mg; Fibre 0.8g; Sodium 128mg.*
Skewered Lamb: *Energy 358kcal/1486kJ; Protein 21.4g; Carbohydrate 11.5g, of which sugars 9.5g; Fat 25.4g, of which saturates 7.3g; Cholesterol 76mg; Calcium 34mg; Fibre 2.5g; Sodium 92mg.*

Marinated Pork Kebabs

The Moors introduced both skewers and the idea of marinating meat to Spain. These little yellow kebabs, called Pinchitos Moruños are a favourite in Andalusia. The Arab versions used lamb, but pork is now preferred as the spicing suits it so perfectly.

Serves 4

2.5ml/½ tsp cumin seeds
2.5ml/½ tsp coriander seeds
2 garlic cloves, finely chopped
5ml/1 tsp paprika
2.5ml/½ tsp dried oregano
15ml/1 tbsp lemon juice
45ml/3 tbsp olive oil
500g/1¼ lb lean cubed pork
salt and freshly ground black pepper

1 Starting a couple of hours in advance, grind the cumin and coriander seeds in a mortar and work in the garlic with a pinch of salt. Add the paprika and oregano and mix in the lemon juice. Stir in the olive oil.

2 Cut the pork into small cubes, then skewer them, three or four at a time, on to cocktail sticks (toothpicks).

3 Put the skewered meat in a shallow dish, and pour over the marinade. Spoon the marinade back over the meat to ensure it is well coated. Leave to marinate in a cool place for 2 hours.

4 Preheat the grill (broiler) to high, and line the grill pan with foil. Spread the kebabs out in a row and place them under the grill, close to the heat. Cook for about 3 minutes on each side, spooning the juices over when you turn them, until the meat is cooked through. Sprinkle with a little salt and pepper, and serve at once.

Cook's Tip
Leaving the meat in a marinade allows the flavours of the spices to penetrate and also results in tender, juicier meat. If it is convenient, you can assemble the kebabs and put them into the marinade earlier in the day, or the day before you need to cook them.

Crispy Pork Crackling

The Spanish eat everything that comes from the pig, and even the humble rind goes to make this delicious little salted, piquant snack. This crispy, crunchy pork crackling is the perfect accompaniment for a glass of wine or chilled beer.

Serves 4

115g/4oz pork rind
vegetable oil, for frying
paprika and coarse sea salt, for sprinkling

1 Using a sharp knife, cut the pork rind into strips. There is no need to be too precise, but try to make the strips roughly 1cm/½in wide and 2.5cm/1in long.

2 Pour the vegetable oil to a depth of 2.5cm/1in in a deep heavy frying pan. Heat the oil and check that it has reached the correct temperature by dropping in a cube of bread, which should brown in 1 minute.

3 Cook the strips of rind in the oil for 1–2 minutes, until they are puffed up and golden brown. Remove with a slotted spoon and drain on kitchen paper.

4 Sprinkle the chicharrones with paprika and salt to taste. Serve them hot or cold. Although they are at their best 1–2 days after cooking, they will keep reasonably well for up to 2 weeks in an airtight container.

Cook's Tips
- *Make these cracklings spicier, if you wish. Paprika is the pepper of Spain, and any kitchen may well have one sweet variety, one smoked and one hot – hot chilli powder, cayenne and Tabasco sauce can all be substituted.*
- *Strips of streaky (fatty) belly can be used instead of pork rind. Cut the strips into the same lengths, removing any bones. Cook them until all the fat has run out, and they look like crisp honeycombs. They are known as* torreznos.

Marinated Pork Kebabs: *Energy 233kcal/970kJ; Protein 27g; Carbohydrate 0.7g, of which sugars 0g; Fat 13.5g, of which saturates 2.9g; Cholesterol 79mg; Calcium 25mg; Fibre 0.6g; Sodium 99mg.*
Crispy Pork Crackling: *Energy 247kcal/1018kJ; Protein 4.1g; Carbohydrate 0g, of which sugars 0g; Fat 25g, of which saturates 6.4g; Cholesterol 28mg; Calcium 3mg; Fibre 0g; Sodium 20mg.*

Chicken Croquettes

Croquetas are very popular tapas fare and there are many different variations. The filling of this version is based on a thick béchamel sauce, which is perfect for taking on different flavours such as ham or chopped peppers, or in this case chicken. The croquettes are best fried just before serving so that they are piping hot and the crisp, crunchy coating contrasts beautifully with the creamy filling.

Serves 4
25g/1oz/2 tbsp butter
25g/1oz/¼ cup plain (all-purpose) flour
150ml/¼ pint/⅔ cup milk
15ml/1 tbsp olive oil
oil for deep-frying
1 boneless chicken breast with skin, diced
1 garlic clove, finely chopped
1 small egg, beaten
50g/2oz/1 cup stale white breadcrumbs
salt and ground black pepper
fresh flat leaf parsley, to garnish
lemon wedges, to serve

1 Melt the butter in a pan. Add the flour and cook gently, stirring, for 1 minute. Gradually stir in the milk and cook until smooth and thick. Cover and set aside.

2 Heat the oil in a frying pan and fry the chicken and garlic for 5 minutes.

3 When the chicken is lightly browned and cooked through, tip the contents of the frying pan into a food processor and process until finely chopped. Tip the mixture into the sauce and stir to combine. Season with plenty of salt and pepper to taste, then set aside to cool completely.

4 Once cooled and firm, shape the mixture into eight small sausage shapes. Dip each one in beaten egg, then roll in breadcrumbs to coat.

5 Heat the oil in a large pan, until a cube of bread dropped in the oil browns in 1 minute. Lower the croquettes into the oil and cook for 4 minutes until crisp and golden. Lift out using a slotted spoon and drain on kitchen paper. Serve with lemon wedges and garnish with fresh flat leaf parsley.

Chicken Livers in Sherry

Higadillas con jerez is very popular, and is made with traditional Spanish ingredients. It makes a delicious little tapas dish and is particularly good eaten with bread or on toast.

Serves 4
225g/8oz chicken livers, thawed if frozen, trimmed
15ml/1 tbsp olive oil
1 small onion, finely chopped
2 small garlic cloves, finely chopped
5ml/1 tsp fresh thyme leaves
30ml/2 tbsp sweet oloroso sherry
30ml/2 tbsp crème fraîche or double (heavy) cream
2.5ml/½ tsp paprika
salt and ground black pepper
fresh thyme, to garnish

1 Trim any green spots and sinews from the chicken livers. Heat the oil in a frying pan and fry the onion, garlic, chicken livers and thyme for 3 minutes.

2 Stir the sherry into the livers, then add the cream and cook briefly. Season with salt, pepper and paprika, garnish with thyme and serve immediately.

Cook's Tip
Don't overcook the chicken livers: they should be just cooked through and soft and pink inside. If they are very large, cut them into even, bitesize pieces.

Chicken Croquettes: *Energy 286kcal/1195kJ; Protein 13.9g; Carbohydrate 16.4g, of which sugars 2.2g; Fat 18.9g, of which saturates 5.8g; Cholesterol 89mg; Calcium 80mg; Fibre 0.5g; Sodium 189mg.*
Chicken Livers: *Energy 131kcal/545kJ; Protein 10.4g; Carbohydrate 2.1g, of which sugars 1.5g; Fat 8.2g, of which saturates 3.3g; Cholesterol 224mg; Calcium 14mg; Fibre 0.2g; Sodium 46mg.*

Gazpacho

This classic chilled Spanish soup is deeply rooted in Andalusia. The soothing blend of tomatoes, sweet peppers and garlic is sharpened with sherry vinegar, and enriched with olive oil. Serving it with a selection of of garnishes has virtually become a tradition. In Spain, very ripe tomatoes are used: if necessary, add a pinch of sugar to sweeten the soup slightly.

Serves 4

1.3–1.6kg/3–3½lb ripe tomatoes
1 green (bell) pepper, roughly chopped
2 garlic cloves, finely chopped
2 slices stale bread, crusts removed
60ml/4 tbsp extra virgin olive oil
60ml/4 tbsp sherry vinegar
150ml/¼ pint/⅔ cup tomato juice
300ml/½ pint/1¼ cups iced water
salt and ground black pepper
ice cubes, to serve (optional)

For the garnishes

30ml/2 tbsp olive oil
2–3 slices stale bread, diced
1 small cucumber, peeled and finely diced
1 small onion, finely chopped
1 red (bell) and 1 green (bell) pepper, finely diced
2 hard-boiled eggs, chopped

1 Skin the tomatoes, then quarter them and remove the cores and seeds, saving the juices. Put the pepper in a food processor and process for a few seconds. Add the tomatoes, reserved juices, garlic, bread, oil and vinegar and process. Add the tomato juice and blend to combine.

2 Season the soup, then pour into a large bowl, cover with clear film (plastic wrap) and chill for at least 12 hours.

3 Prepare the garnishes. Heat the olive oil in a frying pan and fry the bread cubes for 4–5 minutes until golden brown and crisp. Drain well on kitchen paper, then arrange in a small dish. Place each of the remaining garnishes in separate small dishes.

4 Just before serving, dilute the soup with the ice-cold water. The consistency should be thick but not too stodgy. If you like, stir a few ice cubes into the soup, then spoon into serving bowls and serve with the garnishes.

Chilled Avocado Soup with Cumin

Andalusia is home to both avocados and gazpacho, so it is not surprising that this chilled avocado soup, also known as green gazpacho, was invented there.

Serves 4

3 ripe avocados
1 bunch spring onions (scallions), white parts only, trimmed and roughly chopped
2 garlic cloves, chopped
juice of 1 lemon
1.5ml/¼ tsp ground cumin
1.5ml/¼ tsp paprika
450ml/¾ pint/scant 2 cups fresh chicken stock, cooled, and all fat skimmed off
300ml/½ pint/1¼ cups iced water
salt and freshly ground black pepper
roughly chopped fresh flat leaf parsley, to serve

1 Starting several hours ahead, put the flesh of one avocado in a food processor or blender. Add the spring onions, garlic and lemon juice and purée until smooth.

2 Add the second avocado and purée, then the third, with the spices and seasoning. Purée until smooth.

3 Gradually add the chicken stock. Pour the soup into a metal bowl and chill.

4 To serve, stir in the iced water, then season to taste with plenty of salt and black pepper. Garnish with chopped parsley and serve immediately.

Cook's Tips

- *Hass avocados, with bumpy skin that turns purplish black when ripe, generally have the best flavour. They should be perfectly ripe for this recipe.*
- *Avocado flesh blackens when exposed to air, but the lemon juice in this recipe preserves the colour of the soup.*

Gazpacho: *Energy 356kcal/1494kJ; Protein 7.6g; Carbohydrate 41.9g, of which sugars 21.5g; Fat 18.8g, of which saturates 2.9g; Cholesterol 0mg; Calcium 90mg; Fibre 6.7g; Sodium 346mg.*
Avocado Soup: *Energy 151kcal/623kJ; Protein 2.1g; Carbohydrate 2.6g, of which sugars 1.1g; Fat 14.6g, of which saturates 3.1g; Cholesterol 0mg; Calcium 19mg; Fibre 3g; Sodium 6mg.*

Yogurt and Cucumber Soup

Yogurt is frequently used in Greek cookery, and it is usually made at home. Sometimes it is added at the end of cooking a dish, to prevent it from curdling, but in this cold soup the yogurt is one of the basic ingredients. It makes a cool and refreshing first course for a hot summer's day.

Serves 4

1 large cucumber, peeled
300ml/½ pint/1¼ cups single (light) cream
150ml/¼ pint/⅔ cup natural (plain) yogurt
2 garlic cloves, crushed
30ml/2 tbsp white wine vinegar
15ml/1 tbsp chopped fresh mint
salt and ground black pepper
sprigs of fresh mint, to garnish

1 Grate the cucumber coarsely. This can be done in a food processor or blender, or you can do it by hand using the coarse side of a grater.

2 Stir it into the cream, yogurt, garlic, vinegar and mint. Season to taste. Chill for at least 2 hours. Stir before serving and garnish with mint.

Cook's Tip

In Greece, a rich and creamy yogurt is made from sheep's milk. This soup is equally good made with low-fat or whole milk varieties of yogurt.

Chilled Almond Soup with Grapes

Called *ajo blanco* – white garlic soup – this is a Moorish recipe of ancient origin. It is a perfect balance of crushed almonds, garlic and vinegar in a smooth purée enriched with oil.

Serves 6

115g/4oz stale white bread
115g/4oz/1 cup blanched almonds
2 garlic cloves, sliced
75ml/5 tbsp olive oil
25ml/1½ tbsp sherry vinegar
salt and ground black pepper

For the garnish

toasted flaked almonds
green and black grapes, halved and seeded
chopped fresh chives

1 Break the bread into a bowl and pour in 150ml/¼ pint/⅔ cup cold water. Leave to soak for about 5 minutes, then squeeze the bread dry.

2 Put the almonds and garlic in a food processor or blender and process until very finely ground. Add the soaked white bread and process again until thoroughly combined.

3 Continue to process, gradually adding the oil until the mixture forms a smooth paste. Add the sherry vinegar, followed by 600ml/1 pint/2½ cups cold water and process until the mixture is smooth.

4 Transfer the soup to a bowl and season with salt and pepper, adding a little more water if the soup is very thick. Cover with clear film (plastic wrap) and chill for 2 hours or more.

5 Ladle the soup into bowls. Scatter the almonds, halved grapes and chopped chives over to garnish.

Cook's Tip

To accentuate the flavour of the almonds, dry-roast them in a frying pan until they are lightly browned before grinding them. This will produce a slightly darker soup.

Yogurt and Cucumber Soup: *Energy 77kcal/322kJ; Protein 6.9g; Carbohydrate 10.3g, of which sugars 10.1g; Fat 1.3g, of which saturates 0.6g; Cholesterol 2mg; Calcium 255mg; Fibre 0.3g; Sodium 106mg.*
Almond Soup: *Energy 165kcal/683kJ; Protein 3.9g; Carbohydrate 7.4g, of which sugars 0.9g; Fat 13.5g, of which saturates 1.5g; Cholesterol 0mg; Calcium 45mg; Fibre 1.2g; Sodium 68mg.*

Avgolemono

This egg and lemon soup is a great favourite in Greece, and it is a fine example of how a few ingredients can make a marvellous dish if they are carefully chosen and cooked. It is essential to use a well-flavoured chicken stock: a stock cube won't give you a satisfactory result. Add as little or as much rice as you like, depending on how thick you want the soup to be.

Serves 4

900ml/1 ½ pints/3¾ cups chicken stock, preferably homemade
50g/2oz/generous ⅓ cup long grain rice
3 egg yolks
30–60ml/2–4 tbsp lemon juice
30ml/2 tbsp finely chopped fresh parsley
salt and freshly ground black pepper
lemon slices and parsley sprigs, to garnish

1 Pour the stock into a pan, bring to simmering point, then add the drained rice. Half cover and cook for about 12 minutes until the rice is just tender. Season with salt and pepper.

2 Whisk the egg yolks in a bowl, then add about 30ml/2 tbsp of the lemon juice, whisking constantly until the mixture is smooth and bubbly. Add a ladleful of soup and whisk again.

3 Remove the soup from the heat and slowly add the egg mixture, whisking all the time. The soup will turn a pretty lemon colour and will thicken slightly.

4 Taste and add more lemon juice if necessary. Stir in the parsley. Serve at once, without reheating, garnished with lemon slices and parsley sprigs.

Cook's Tip
The trick here is to add the egg mixture to the soup without it curdling. Avoid whisking the mixture into boiling liquid. It is safest to remove the soup from the heat entirely and then whisk in the mixture in a slow but steady stream. Do not reheat, as curdling would be almost inevitable.

Sherried Onion Soup with Saffron

The Spanish combination of onions, sherry and saffron gives this soup a beguiling flavour that is perfect for the opening course of a meal. The addition of ground almonds to thicken the soup gives it a wonderful texture and flavour.

Serves 4

40g/1 ½ oz/3 tbsp butter
2 large yellow onions, thinly sliced
1 small garlic clove, chopped
pinch of saffron threads
50g/2oz blanched almonds, toasted and finely ground
750ml/1 ¼ pints/3 cups chicken or vegetable stock
45ml/3 tbsp fino sherry
2.5ml/½ tsp paprika
salt and ground black pepper

To garnish

30ml/2 tbsp flaked or slivered almonds, toasted
chopped fresh parsley

1 Melt the butter in a heavy pan over a low heat. Add the onions and garlic, stirring to ensure that they are thoroughly coated in the melted butter, then cover the pan and cook very gently, stirring frequently, for about 20 minutes, or until the onions are soft and golden yellow.

2 Add the saffron threads to the pan and cook, uncovered, for 3–4 minutes, then add the finely ground almonds and cook, stirring the ingredients constantly, for a further 2–3 minutes, until the almonds are golden.

3 Pour in the chicken or vegetable stock and sherry into the pan and stir in 5ml/1 tsp salt and the paprika. Season with plenty of black pepper. Bring to the boil, then lower the heat and simmer gently for about 10 minutes.

4 Pour the soup into a food processor and process until smooth, then return it to the rinsed-out pan. Reheat slowly, stirring occasionally, without allowing the soup to boil. Taste for seasoning, adding more salt and pepper if required.

5 Ladle the soup into heated bowls, garnish with the toasted flaked or slivered almonds and a little chopped fresh parsley and serve immediately.

Avgolemono: *Energy 104kcal/438kJ; Protein 5.5g; Carbohydrate 14.3g, of which sugars 0.7g; Fat 3.2g, of which saturates 0.8g; Cholesterol 95mg; Calcium 20mg; Fibre 0.6g; Sodium 117mg.*
Sherried Onion Soup: *Energy 246kcal/1017kJ; Protein 5.5g; Carbohydrate 9.5g, of which sugars 6.7g; Fat 19.6g, of which saturates 6.1g; Cholesterol 21mg; Calcium 76mg; Fibre 2.9g; Sodium 68mg.*

French Onion Soup

In France, this standard bistro fare is served so frequently, it is simply referred to as *gratinée.* The onions need to be cooked slowly so that they caramelize and give the soup its beautiful brown colour and rich flavour.

Serves 6–8

15g/½oz/1 tbsp butter
30ml/2 tbsp olive oil
4 large onions (about 675g/1½lb), thinly sliced
2–4 garlic cloves, finely chopped
5ml/1 tsp sugar
2.5ml/½ tsp dried thyme
30ml/2 tbsp plain (all-purpose) flour
125ml/4fl oz/½ cup dry white wine
2 litres/3⅓ pints/8 cups chicken or beef stock
30ml/2 tbsp brandy (optional)
6–8 thick slices French bread, toasted
1 garlic clove
340g/12oz Gruyère or Emmenthal cheese, grated

1 In a large, heavy-based pan or flameproof casserole, heat the butter and oil over a medium heat. Add the sliced onions and cook for 10–12 minutes until they have softened and are beginning to brown.

2 Add the garlic, sugar and thyme and continue cooking over a medium heat for 30–35 minutes until the onions are well browned, stirring frequently.

3 Sprinkle over the flour and stir until well blended. Stir in the white wine and stock and bring to the boil. Skim off any foam that rises to the surface, then reduce the heat and simmer gently for 45 minutes. Stir in the brandy, if using.

4 Preheat the grill (broiler). Rub each slice of toasted French bread with the garlic clove. Place six or eight ovenproof soup bowls on a baking sheet and fill about three-quarters full with the onion soup.

5 Float a piece of toast in each bowl. Top with the grated cheese, dividing it evenly, and grill (broil) about 15cm/6in from the heat for about 3–4 minutes until the cheese begins to melt and bubble. Serve immediately.

Italian Onion Soup

This warming winter soup comes from Umbria, where it is sometimes thickened with beaten eggs and lots of grated Parmesan cheese. It is then served on top of hot toasted croûtes – rather like savoury scrambled eggs. Even without eggs it still makes a substantial dish.

Serves 4

115g/4oz pancetta rashers, any rinds removed, roughly chopped
30ml/2 tbsp olive oil
15g/½oz/1 tbsp butter
675g/1½lb onions, thinly sliced
10ml/2 tsp granulated sugar
about 1.2 litres/2 pints/5 cups chicken stock
350g/12oz ripe Italian plum tomatoes, peeled and roughly chopped
a few basil leaves, shredded
salt and freshly ground black pepper
freshly grated Parmesan cheese to serve

1 Put the chopped pancetta in a large saucepan and heat gently, stirring constantly, until the fat runs. Increase the heat to medium, add the oil, butter, onions and sugar and mix well.

2 Half cover the pan and cook the onions gently for about 20 minutes until golden. Stir frequently to prevent them browning too much and lower the heat if necessary.

3 Add the stock, tomatoes and salt and pepper and bring to the boil, stirring. Lower the heat, half cover the pan and simmer, stirring occasionally, for about 30 minutes.

4 Check the consistency of the soup and add a little more stock or water if it is too thick.

5 Just before serving, stir in most of the basil and taste for seasoning. Serve hot, garnished with the remaining shredded basil. Hand round the freshly grated Parmesan separately.

Cook's Tip

Look for Vidalia onions to make this soup. They have a very sweet flavour and attractive yellowish flesh.

French Onion Soup: *Energy 311kcal/1309kJ; Protein 9.8g; Carbohydrate 46.2g, of which sugars 9.5g; Fat 10.6g, of which saturates 5.1g; Cholesterol 19mg; Calcium 180mg; Fibre 3.1g; Sodium 767mg.*
Italian Onion Soup: *Energy 232kcal/963kJ; Protein 7.2g; Carbohydrate 16.1g, of which sugars 12.2g; Fat 16g, of which saturates 5.2g; Cholesterol 27mg; Calcium 51mg; Fibre 3.2g; Sodium 398mg.*

Leek Soup with Feta, Dill and Paprika

Creamy leek soup is a popular home-cooked dish in Turkey. Flavoured with dill and topped with crumbled white cheese, this one is warming and satisfying. The saltiness of feta is good in this soup, but you could just as well use Roquefort or Parmesan, both of which are equally salty, and you could substitute croûtons for the cheese. Serve with chunks of fresh, crusty bread.

Serves 3–4

30ml/2 tbsp olive or sunflower oil
3 leeks, trimmed, roughly chopped and washed
1 onion, chopped
5ml/1 tsp sugar
1 bunch of fresh dill, chopped, with a few fronds reserved for the garnish
300ml/½ pint/1¼ cups milk
15ml/1 tbsp butter (optional)
115g/4oz feta cheese, crumbled
salt and ground black pepper
paprika, to garnish

1 Heat the oil in a heavy pan and stir in the chopped leeks and onion. Cook for about 10 minutes, or until the vegetables are soft but not coloured.

2 Add the sugar and dill, and pour in 600ml/1 pint/2½ cups water. Bring to the boil, lower the heat and simmer for about 15 minutes.

3 Leave the liquid to cool a little, then process in a blender until smooth.

4 Return the puréed soup to the pan, pour in the milk and stir over a gentle heat until it is hot (don't let it come to the boil or the texture will be spoiled).

5 Season with salt and pepper, bearing in mind that the feta is salty. If using the butter, drop it onto the surface of the soup and let it melt.

6 Ladle the soup into warmed bowls and top with the crumbled feta. Serve immediately, garnished with a little paprika and the dill fronds.

Broad Bean and Potato Soup

In Spain, *habas* are fresh broad beans, and are a great deal nicer than the dried variety, known as *favas*. The latter word has now vanished from the Spanish dictionary and the rather indigestible dried bean has all but disappeared from Spanish cookery as well. This fresh soup uses a modern herb, too – coriander is not a common Spanish ingredient, but it adds a delicious flavour.

Serves 4

30ml/2 tbsp olive oil
2 onions, chopped
3 large floury potatoes, peeled and diced
450g/1lb fresh shelled broad (fava) beans
1.75 litres/3 pints/7½ cups vegetable stock
1 bunch fresh coriander (cilantro), roughly chopped
150ml/¼ pint/⅔ cup single (light) cream, plus a little extra, to garnish
salt and ground black pepper

1 Heat the oil in a large pan and fry the onions, stirring, for 5 minutes until soft.

2 Add the potatoes, most of the beans (reserving a few to garnish the soup) and the stock, and bring to the boil. Simmer for 5 minutes, then add the coriander and simmer for a further 10 minutes.

3 Blend the soup in batches in a food processor or blender, then return to the rinsed pan.

4 Stir in the cream, season, and bring to a simmer. Serve garnished with coriander, beans and cream.

Cook's Tip

The broad bean is the native European bean, and was an important staple food for centuries before the arrival of the haricot bean from America. Very young broad beans are often eaten raw, especially in Italy. It would be best to make this soup in early summer before the beans toughen and get over-large, but you could alternatively use frozen beans.

Leek Soup: *Energy 203kcal/844kJ; Protein 10g; Carbohydrate 10.9g, of which sugars 9.4g; Fat 13.5g, of which saturates 5.7g; Cholesterol 25mg; Calcium 259mg; Fibre 4.1g; Sodium 454mg.*
Broad Bean Soup: *Energy 263kcal/1113kJ; Protein 13.9g; Carbohydrate 47g, of which sugars 10.8g; Fat 3.5g, of which saturates 0.9g; Cholesterol 2mg; Calcium 142mg; Fibre 10.2g; Sodium 45mg.*

Italian Cabbage and Bean Soup

Cavolo nero is a dark green cabbage with a nutty flavour, which comes from southern Italy. It is ideal for this traditional recipe. It is available in most large supermarkets, but if you can't get it, use Savoy cabbage instead. Serve this hearty soup with warm crusty bread.

Serves 4

2 × 400g/14oz cans chopped tomatoes with herbs
250g/9oz cavolo nero leaves, rinsed and drained
400g/14oz can cannellini beans
20ml/4 tsp extra virgin olive oil
salt and ground black pepper

1 Pour the tomatoes into a large pan and add a can of cold water. Season with salt and pepper and bring to the boil, then reduce the heat to a simmer.

2 Roughly shred the cabbage leaves and add them to the pan. Partially cover the pan and simmer gently, stirring occasionally, for about 15 minutes, or until the cabbage is tender.

3 Drain and rinse the cannellini beans, add to the pan and warm through for a few minutes.

4 Check and adjust the seasoning, then ladle the soup into warmed bowls. Drizzle each portion with a little olive oil and serve immediately.

Pasta, Bean and Vegetable Soup

This is a Calabrian speciality and by tradition anything edible can go into it: use whatever beans and vegetables are to hand.

Serves 6

75g/3oz/scant ½ cup dried brown lentils
15g/½oz/¼ cup dried mushrooms
15ml/1 tbsp olive oil
1 carrot, diced
1 celery stick, diced
1 onion, finely chopped
1 garlic clove, finely chopped
a little chopped fresh flat leaf parsley
a good pinch of crushed red chillies (optional)
1.5 litres/2½ pints/6¼ cups vegetable stock
150g/5oz/1 cup each canned red kidney beans, cannellini beans and chickpeas, rinsed and drained
115g/4oz/1 cup dried small pasta shapes, such as rigatoni, penne or penne rigate
salt and ground black pepper
chopped flat leaf parsley, to garnish
freshly grated Pecorino cheese, to serve (optional)

1 Put the lentils in a pan, add 475ml/16fl oz/2 cups water and bring to the boil. Reduce the heat and simmer gently, stirring occasionally, for 15–20 minutes, or until tender. Soak the dried mushrooms in 175ml/6fl oz/¾ cup warm water for 20 minutes.

2 Drain the lentils, then rinse under cold water. Drain the soaked mushrooms and reserve the soaking liquid. Finely chop the mushrooms and set aside.

3 Heat the oil in a large saucepan and add the carrot, celery, onion, garlic, chopped parsley and chillies, if using. Cook over a low heat, stirring constantly, for 5–7 minutes. Add the stock, then the mushrooms and their soaking liquid. Bring to the boil, then add the beans, chickpeas and lentils, with salt and pepper to taste. Cover, and simmer gently for 20 minutes.

4 Add the pasta and bring the soup back to the boil, stirring. Simmer, stirring frequently, for 7–8 minutes or until the pasta is *al dente*. Season, then serve hot in soup bowls, garnished with chopped parsley. Sprinkle with grated Pecorino, if you like.

Cabbage and Bean Soup: *Energy 155kcal/655kJ; Protein 8.2g; Carbohydrate 22.3g, of which sugars 10.4g; Fat 4.2g, of which saturates 0.7g; Cholesterol 0mg; Calcium 60mg; Fibre 7.9g; Sodium 443mg.*
Pasta Soup: *Energy 206kcal/874kJ; Protein 10.7g; Carbohydrate 36.7g, of which sugars 5g; Fat 2.9g, of which saturates 0.4g; Cholesterol 0mg; Calcium 72mg; Fibre 6.4g; Sodium 306mg.*

Bean Soup with Tomatoes

This Italian soup is rather like minestrone. It is based on tomatoes, but is made with beans instead of pasta. In Italy it is traditionally ladled over a chunk of bread and a green vegetable.

Serves 8

350g/12oz well-flavoured tomatoes, preferably plum tomatoes
15ml/1 tbsp extra virgin olive oil or sunflower oil
2 onions, chopped
2 carrots, sliced
4 garlic cloves, crushed
2 celery sticks, thinly sliced
1 fennel bulb, chopped
2 large courgettes (zucchini), thinly sliced
400g/14oz can chopped tomatoes
15ml/1 tbsp pesto sauce
900ml/1½ pints/3¾ cups vegetable stock
400g/14oz can haricot (navy) or borlotti beans, drained
salt and ground black pepper

To finish

10ml/2 tsp extra virgin olive oil
450g/1lb fresh young spinach
8 small slices white bread
Parmesan or Pecorino cheese shavings, to serve (optional)

1 To skin the tomatoes, plunge them into boiling water for 30 seconds, then refresh in cold water. Drain the tomatoes, then peel off and discard the skins. Chop the tomato flesh and set it aside.

2 Heat the oil in a large non-stick pan. Add the onions, carrots, garlic, celery and fennel and cook gently for 10 minutes. Add the courgettes and cook for a further 2 minutes.

3 Stir in the chopped fresh and canned tomatoes, pesto, stock and beans, and bring to the boil. Reduce the heat, cover the pan and simmer gently for 25–30 minutes, or until the vegetables are completely tender and the stock is full of flavour. Season the soup with salt and pepper to taste.

4 To finish, heat the oil in a non-stick frying pan and cook the spinach for 2 minutes, or until wilted. Place a slice of bread in each serving bowl, top with the spinach and then ladle the soup over the spinach. Serve with a little Parmesan or Pecorino cheese to sprinkle on top, if you like.

Tuscan Bean Soup

There are lots of versions of this wonderful and very substantial soup, which makes a meal in itself. This one uses cannellini beans, leeks, cabbage and good olive oil. It's a good idea to make it in advance of the meal, as it tastes even better when reheated.

Serves 4

45ml/3 tbsp extra virgin olive oil
1 onion, roughly chopped
2 leeks, roughly chopped
1 large potato, peeled and diced
2 garlic cloves, finely chopped
1.2 litres/2 pints/5 cups vegetable stock
400g/14oz can cannellini beans, drained, liquid reserved
175g/6oz Savoy cabbage, shredded
45ml/3 tbsp chopped fresh flat leaf parsley
30ml/2 tbsp chopped fresh oregano
75g/3oz/1 cup Parmesan cheese, shaved
salt and ground black pepper

For the garlic toasts

30–45ml/2–3 tbsp extra virgin olive oil
6 thick slices country bread
1 garlic clove, peeled and bruised

1 Heat the oil in a large saucepan and gently cook the onion, leeks, potato and garlic for 4–5 minutes.

2 Pour on the stock and liquid from the beans. Cover and simmer for 15 minutes.

3 Stir in the cabbage and beans with half the herbs, season and cook for 10 minutes more. Spoon about one-third of the soup into a food processor or blender and process until fairly smooth. Return to the soup in the pan, taste for seasoning and heat through for 5 minutes.

4 Meanwhile make the garlic toasts. Drizzle a little oil over the slices of bread, then rub both sides of each slice with the garlic. Toast until browned on both sides.

5 Ladle the soup into bowls. Sprinkle with the remaining herbs and the Parmesan shavings. Add a drizzle of olive oil and serve with the toasts.

Bean Soup with Tomatoes: *Energy 183kcal/770kJ; Protein 8.7g; Carbohydrate 28.5g, of which sugars 9.3g; Fat 4.5g, of which saturates 0.6g; Cholesterol 0mg; Calcium 188mg; Fibre 7.1g; Sodium 426mg.*
Tuscan Bean Soup: *Energy 445kcal/1863kJ; Protein 18.9g; Carbohydrate 45.8g, of which sugars 9.3g; Fat 21.8g, of which saturates 6g; Cholesterol 19mg; Calcium 391mg; Fibre 9.1g; Sodium 707mg.*

Chickpea and Parsley Soup

Thick, tasty and comforting, this low-fat soup is perfect for wintry evenings, or when storecupboard ingredients are all you've got.

Serves 6

225g/8oz/1 ⅓ cups dried chickpeas, soaked overnight
1 small onion
1 bunch fresh parsley (about 40g/1 ½oz)
1.2 litres/2 pints/5 cups vegetable or chicken stock
juice of ½ lemon
salt and ground black pepper
lemon wedges and finely pared strips of rind, to garnish
crusty bread, to serve (optional)

1 Drain the chickpeas and rinse them under cold water. Cook them in a pan of rapidly boiling water for 10 minutes, then reduce the heat and simmer for 1–1 ½ hours, or until just tender. Drain.

2 Place the onion and parsley in a blender or food processor and process until finely chopped.

3 In a large saucepan or flameproof casserole cook the onion and parsley mixture gently for 5 minutes, or until the onion is slightly softened.

4 Add the chickpeas, cook gently with the onion and parsley for 1–2 minutes, then add the vegetable or chicken stock. Season well with salt and pepper. Bring the soup to the boil, then reduce the heat, cover and simmer for 20 minutes, or until the chickpeas are soft.

5 Allow the soup to cool a little. Purée most of the soup in a blender or food processor, reserving a portion and stirring it in so that the soup is thick and still has plenty of texture. Alternatively, simply mash the chickpeas fairly roughly with a fork or a vegetable masher in the pan.

6 Return the soup to a clean pan, add the lemon juice and adjust the seasoning, if necessary. Reheat gently and then serve, garnished with lemon wedges and finely pared lemon rind. Serve with crusty bread, if you like.

Lentil Soup with Tomatoes

A classic rustic Italian soup flavoured with rosemary, this is delicious served with crusty bread. You could use fresh tomatoes if you have an abundance of very ripe ones, but canned tomatoes are full of flavour and are often preferable.

Serves 4

225g/8oz/1 cup dried green or brown lentils
10ml/2 tsp extra virgin olive oil
2 rindless lean back bacon rashers (strips), diced
1 onion, finely chopped
2 celery sticks, finely chopped
2 carrots, finely diced
2 rosemary sprigs, finely chopped
2 bay leaves
400g/14oz can chopped plum tomatoes
1.75 litres/3 pints/7 ½ cups vegetable stock
salt and ground black pepper
bay leaves and rosemary sprigs, to garnish

1 Place the lentils in a bowl and cover with cold water. Leave to soak for 2 hours. Rinse and drain well.

2 Heat the oil in a pan. Add the bacon and cook for 3 minutes, then add the onion and cook gently for 5 minutes, or until softened, stirring occasionally.

3 Stir in the celery, carrots, rosemary, bay leaves and lentils and toss over the heat for 1 minute.

4 Add the tomatoes and the stock and bring to the boil. Reduce the heat, partially cover the pan and simmer, stirring occasionally, for about 1 hour, or until the lentils are tender.

5 Remove and discard the bay leaves, add salt and pepper to taste and serve with a garnish of fresh bay leaves and small rosemary sprigs.

Cook's Tip

If you can buy it, use 50g/2oz diced pancetta (Italian salt belly pork) instead of the bacon to give the soup a more authentic Italian flavour.

Chickpea and Parsley Soup: *Energy 159kcal/668kJ; Protein 8.3g; Carbohydrate 19.6g, of which sugars 1.7g; Fat 5.8g, of which saturates 0.6g; Cholesterol 0mg; Calcium 76mg; Fibre 4.5g; Sodium 17mg.*
Lentil Soup: *Energy 339kcal/1425kJ; Protein 18.6g; Carbohydrate 38.1g, of which sugars 7.3g; Fat 13.5g, of which saturates 3g; Cholesterol 13mg; Calcium 53mg; Fibre 4.7g; Sodium 430mg.*

Spicy Red Lentil Soup with Onion and Parsley

In Istanbul and Izmir, Turkish lentil soups are light and subtly spiced, and served as an appetizer or as a snack. In Anatolia, lentil and bean soups are made with chunks of mutton and flavoured with tomato and spices, and are usually served as a meal on their own.

Serves 4–6

30–45ml/2–3 tbsp olive or sunflower oil
1 large onion, finely chopped
2 garlic cloves, finely chopped
1 fresh red chilli, seeded and finely chopped
5–10ml/1–2 tsp cumin seeds
5–10ml/1–2 tsp coriander seeds
1 carrot, finely chopped
scant 5ml/1 tsp ground fenugreek
5ml/1 tsp sugar
15ml/1 tbsp tomato purée (paste)
250g/9oz/generous 1 cup split red lentils
1.75 litres/3 pints/7½ cups chicken stock
salt and ground black pepper

To serve

1 small red onion, finely chopped
1 large bunch of fresh flat leaf parsley, finely chopped
4–6 lemon wedges

1 Heat the oil in a heavy pan and stir in the onion, garlic, chilli, cumin and coriander seeds. When the onion begins to colour, toss in the carrot and cook for 2–3 minutes. Add the fenugreek, sugar and tomato purée and stir in the lentils.

2 Pour in the stock, stir well and bring to the boil. Lower the heat, partially cover the pan and simmer for 30–40 minutes, until the lentils have broken up.

3 If the soup is too thick, thin it down with a little water. Season with salt and pepper to taste.

4 Serve the soup straight from the pan or, if you prefer a smooth texture, whizz it in a blender, then reheat if necessary.

5 Ladle the soup into bowls and sprinkle liberally with the chopped onion and parsley. Serve with a wedge of lemon to squeeze over the soup.

Cream of Courgette Soup

The colour of this soup is beautifully delicate, and really suits its rich and creamy texture and subtle taste. If you prefer a more pronounced cheese flavour, you can use Gorgonzola instead of Dolcelatte.

Serves 4–6

30ml/2 tbsp olive oil
15g/½oz/1 tbsp butter
1 medium onion, roughly chopped
900g/2lb courgettes (zucchini), trimmed and sliced
5ml/1 tsp dried oregano
about 600ml/1 pint/2½ cups vegetable or chicken stock
115g/4oz Dolcelatte cheese, rind removed, diced
300ml/½ pint/1¼ cups single (light) cream
salt and freshly ground black pepper
fresh oregano and extra Dolcelatte, to garnish

1 Heat the oil and butter in a large saucepan until foaming. Add the onion and cook gently for about 5 minutes, stirring frequently, until softened but not brown.

2 Add the courgettes, oregano, and salt and pepper to taste. Cook over a medium heat for 10 minutes, stirring frequently.

3 Pour in the stock and bring to the boil, stirring. Lower the heat, half cover the pan and simmer gently, stirring occasionally, for about 30 minutes. Stir in the diced Dolcelatte until melted.

4 Process the soup in a blender or food processor until smooth, then press through a sieve into a clean pan.

5 Add two-thirds of the cream and stir over a low heat until hot, but not boiling. Check the consistency and add more stock if the soup is too thick. Taste for seasoning, then pour into heated bowls. Swirl in the remaining cream. Garnish with oregano and extra cheese and serve.

Cook's Tip

To save time, trim off and discard the ends of the courgettes, cut them into thirds, then chop in a food processor.

Spicy Lentil Soup: Energy 203kcal/856kJ; Protein 11.1g; Carbohydrate 31.8g, of which sugars 7.3g; Fat 4.4g, of which saturates 0.6g; Cholesterol 0mg; Calcium 45mg; Fibre 3.5g; Sodium 26mg.
Courgette Soup: Energy 248kcal/1024kJ; Protein 8.5g; Carbohydrate 5.4g, of which sugars 4.8g; Fat 21.5g, of which saturates 11.7g; Cholesterol 47mg; Calcium 181mg; Fibre 1.6g; Sodium 266mg.

Spanish Garlic Soup

This rich, dark garlic soup, from central Spain, divides people into two groups: they either love it or hate it, so it's probably best to try this recipe when feeding people you know really well. The soup has harsh, strong flavours to match the often merciless heat of the climate. Poaching a whole egg in each bowl just before serving transforms the soup into a complete meal.

Serves 4

30ml/2 tbsp olive oil
4 large garlic cloves, peeled
4 thick slices stale country bread
20ml/4 tbsp paprika
1 litre/1¾ pints/4 cups beef stock
1.5ml/¼ tsp ground cumin
4 large eggs
salt and ground black pepper
chopped fresh parsley, to garnish

1 Preheat the oven to 230°C/450°F/Gas 8. Heat the olive oil in a large pan. Add the whole peeled garlic cloves and cook until they are golden, then remove and set aside.

2 Fry the slices of bread in the oil until golden, then set these aside.

3 Add 15ml/1 tbsp of the paprika to the pan, and fry for a few seconds. Stir in the beef stock, cumin and remaining paprika, then add the reserved garlic, crushing the cloves with the back of a wooden spoon. Season to taste, then cook for about 5 minutes.

4 Break up the slices of fried bread into bitesize pieces and stir them into the soup. Immediately after this, ladle the soup into four ovenproof bowls. Carefully break an egg into each bowl of soup and place in the hot oven for about 3 minutes, or until the eggs are set (but soft). Sprinkle the soup with chopped fresh parsley and serve immediately.

Variation
If you prefer, you can simply whisk the eggs into the hot soup.

Roasted Vegetable Soup

A fusion of flavours from the sunny Greek islands creates this fabulous soup, which is served with tzatziki. Use a good-quality olive oil, as it enhances the richness of the roasted vegetables.

Serves 4

2 large aubergines (eggplant)
4 large courgettes (zucchini)
1 onion, roughly chopped
4 garlic cloves, roughly chopped
45ml/3 tbsp extra virgin olive oil
1.2 litres/2 pints/5 cups vegetable stock
15ml/1 tbsp chopped fresh oregano
salt and ground black pepper
mint sprigs, to garnish

For the tzatziki

1 cucumber, peeled, seeded and diced
10ml/2 tsp salt
2 garlic cloves, crushed
5ml/1 tsp white wine vinegar
225g/8oz/1 cup Greek natural (plain) yogurt
small bunch of fresh mint leaves, chopped

1 Preheat the oven to 200°C/400°F/Gas 6. Cut the aubergines and courgettes into large dice and place in a roasting pan. Add the onion and garlic, drizzle the oil over and spread out the vegetables in an even layer. Roast for 35 minutes, turning once, until tender and slightly charred.

2 To make the *tzatziki*, place the cucumber in a colander and sprinkle with the salt. Place on a plate and leave for 30 minutes. Mix the garlic with the vinegar and stir carefully into the yogurt. Pat the cucumber dry with kitchen paper and fold it gently into the yogurt mixture. Season to taste and stir in the mint. Chill.

3 Place half the roasted vegetables in a food processor or blender. Add the stock and process until almost smooth. Then pour into a large pan and add the remaining vegetables.

4 Bring the soup slowly to the boil, then reduce the heat and simmer gently for a few minutes. Season well with salt and pepper, then stir in the chopped oregano. Ladle the soup into four bowls. Garnish with mint sprigs and serve immediately. Hand round the bowl of *tzatziki* so that your guests can add a dollop or two to their soup, swirling it around the top layer.

Spanish Garlic Soup: *Energy 200kcal/836kJ; Protein 9.8g; Carbohydrate 15.6g, of which sugars 0.9g; Fat 11.8g, of which saturates 2.4g; Cholesterol 190mg; Calcium 62mg; Fibre 0.9g; Sodium 396mg.*
Vegetable Soup: *Energy 222Kcal/920kJ; Protein 9.7g; Carbohydrate 12.7g, of which sugars 11g; Fat 15.7g, of which saturates 4.5g; Cholesterol 0mg; Calcium 192mg; Fibre 6.3g; Sodium 1034mg.*

Mediterranean Vegetables with Eggs

This is Turkish street food, known as Menemen. Cooked everywhere on makeshift stoves – at ports, stations and rest houses – it makes a satisfying snack or a complete meal. Depending on the cook, the eggs are either stirred into the tomato and pepper ragoût to scramble them, or they are cracked on top and cooked in the steam under a domed lid until just set.

Serves 4

15ml/1 tbsp olive oil
15ml/1 tbsp butter
2 red onions, cut in half and sliced along the grain
1 red or green (bell) pepper, sliced lengthways
2 garlic cloves, roughly chopped
5–10ml/1–2 tsp Turkish red pepper, or 1 fresh red chilli, seeded and sliced
400g/14oz can chopped tomatoes
5–10ml/1–2 tsp sugar
4 large (US extra large) eggs
salt and freshly ground black pepper

To serve

90ml/6 tbsp thick natural (plain) yogurt
1–2 garlic cloves, crushed
a handful of fresh flat leaf parsley, roughly chopped

1 Heat the oil and butter in a heavy frying pan. Stir in the onions, sliced pepper, garlic and Turkish red pepper or chilli and cook until they begin to soften.

2 Add the chopped tomatoes and sugar and mix them in thoroughly. Cook for about 10 minutes, or until the liquid has reduced and the mixture is quite saucy, then season with salt and pepper.

3 Crack the eggs over the top of the tomato mixture, cover the pan with a lid and simmer gently for 2–3 minutes, or until the eggs are just done.

4 Meanwhile, beat the yogurt with the garlic in a bowl and season with salt and pepper.

5 Ladle the soup into bowls and serve hot, topped with parsley and dollops of garlic-flavoured yogurt

Spicy Pumpkin Soup

Pumpkin is popular all over the Mediterranean and it's an important ingredient in Middle Eastern cooking. Ginger and cumin give the soup its spicy flavour.

Serves 4

900g/2lb pumpkin, peeled and seeds removed
10ml/2 tsp olive oil
2 leeks, trimmed and sliced
1 garlic clove, crushed
5ml/1 tsp ground ginger
5ml/1 tsp ground cumin
900ml/1½ pints/3¾ cups chicken or vegetable stock
salt and ground black pepper
fresh coriander (cilantro) leaves, to garnish
60ml/4 tbsp natural (plain) yogurt, to serve

1 Cut the pumpkin into chunks. Heat the oil in a large pan and add the leeks and garlic. Cook gently until softened.

2 Add the ginger and cumin and cook, stirring, for a further minute. Add the pumpkin chunks and the stock and season with salt and pepper. Bring to the boil, then reduce the heat and simmer for 30 minutes, or until the pumpkin is tender. Cool slightly, then process the soup, in batches if necessary, in a blender or food processor.

3 Gently reheat the soup in the rinsed out pan, then serve in warmed soup bowls, with a swirl of yogurt and a garnish of coriander leaves.

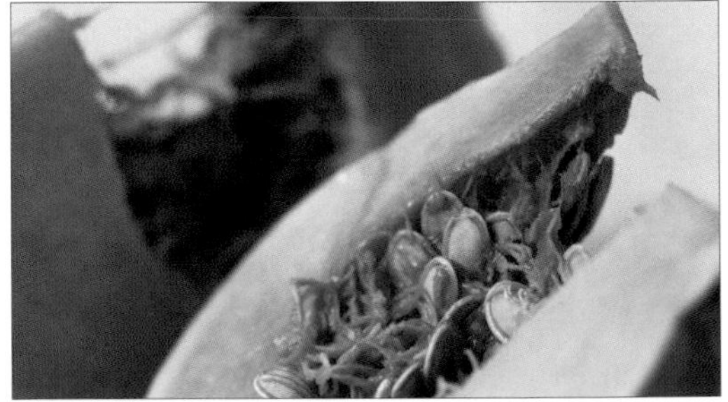

Mediterranean Vegetables: *Energy 190kcal/790kJ; Protein 8.6g; Carbohydrate 14.9g, of which sugars 12.4g; Fat 11.2g, of which saturates 3.5g; Cholesterol 196mg; Calcium 65mg; Fibre 3.1g; Sodium 101mg.*
Pumpkin Soup: *Energy 105kcal/441kJ; Protein 2.3g; Carbohydrate 12.5g, of which sugars 7.9g; Fat 3.6g, of which saturates 0.6g, Cholesterol 0mg; Calcium 27mg; Fibre 2.3g; Sodium 61mg.*

Roasted Garlic and Butternut Squash Soup with Tomato Salsa

This is a richly flavoured soup, given bite by the spicy tomato salsa served with it. It makes a fabulous soup for an autumn lunch.

Serves 6

2 garlic bulbs, outer papery skin removed
a few fresh thyme sprigs
15ml/1 tbsp olive oil
1 large butternut squash, halved
2 onions, chopped
5ml/1 tsp ground coriander
1.2 litres/2 pints/5 cups vegetable or chicken stock
30–45ml/2–3 tbsp chopped fresh oregano or marjoram
salt and ground black pepper

For the salsa

4 large ripe tomatoes, halved and seeded
1 red (bell) pepper
1 large fresh red chilli, seeded
15ml/1 tbsp extra virgin olive oil
15ml/1 tbsp balsamic vinegar
pinch of caster (superfine) sugar

1 Preheat the oven to 220°C/425°F/Gas 7. Wrap the garlic bulbs in foil with the thyme and 7.5ml/1½ tsp of the oil. Put the parcel on a baking sheet with the squash and the tomatoes, pepper and fresh chilli for the salsa. Brush the squash with 10ml/2 tsp of the remaining oil. Roast the vegetables for 25 minutes, then remove the tomatoes, pepper and chilli. Reduce the oven temperature to 190°C/375°F/Gas 5 and roast the squash and garlic for a further 20–25 minutes, or until tender.

2 Heat the remaining oil in a large non-stick pan and cook the onions and ground coriander gently for about 10 minutes.

3 Meanwhile, skin the pepper and chilli, then process them with the tomatoes and the oil for the salsa. Stir in the vinegar and seasoning to taste, adding a pinch of sugar if necessary.

4 Squeeze the roasted garlic out of its skin into the onions and add the squash, scooped out of its skin. Add the stock, season with salt and pepper, and simmer for 10 minutes. Stir in half the chopped fresh herbs then process or sieve (strain) the soup. Reheat and taste for seasoning. Serve in warmed bowls topped with a spoonful of salsa and sprinkled with the remaining herbs.

Tomato and Fresh Basil Soup

This is a good soup to make in late summer, when wonderful fresh tomatoes are at their most flavoursome and abundant.

Serves 4–6

15ml/1 tbsp olive oil
25g/1oz/2 tbsp butter
1 medium onion, finely chopped
900g/2lb ripe Italian plum tomatoes, roughly chopped
1 garlic clove, roughly chopped
750 ml/1¼ pints/3 cups chicken or vegetable stock
120ml/4fl oz/½ cup dry white wine
30ml/2 tbsp sun-dried tomato paste
30ml/2 tbsp shredded fresh basil, plus a few whole leaves, to garnish
150ml/¼ pint/⅔ cup double (heavy) cream
salt and ground black pepper

1 Heat the oil and butter together in a large saucepan until the butter starts to foam. Add the chopped onion and cook gently for about 5 minutes, stirring frequently, until softened but not beginning to brown.

2 Stir in the chopped tomatoes and garlic, then add the stock, white wine and sun-dried tomato paste, with salt and pepper to taste. Bring to the boil, then lower the heat, half cover the pan and simmer gently for 20 minutes, stirring occasionally to stop the tomatoes sticking to the base of the pan.

3 Process the soup with the basil in a blender or food processor, then press through a sieve (strainer) into a clean pan.

4 Add the double cream and heat through, stirring. Do not allow the soup to approach boiling point. Check the consistency and add more stock if necessary and then taste for seasoning. Pour into heated bowls and garnish with a few sprigs of fresh basil.

Variation
The soup can also be served chilled. Pour it into a container after sieving and chill for at least 4 hours. Serve in chilled bowls.

Garlic and Squash Soup: *Energy 238kcal/986kJ; Protein 2.9g; Carbohydrate 11.9g, of which sugars 10.3g; Fat 20.2g, of which saturates 3.1g; Cholesterol 0mg; Calcium 79mg; Fibre 4.1g; Sodium 11mg.*
Tomato and Basil Soup: *Energy 97kcal/409kJ; Protein 2.4g; Carbohydrate 9.6g, of which sugars 9.2g; Fat 3.7g, of which saturates 1.4g; Cholesterol 4mg; Calcium 32mg; Fibre 2.7g; Sodium 42mg.10mg.*

Roasted Pepper Soup

Grilling intensifies the flavour of sweet red and yellow peppers and helps this low-fat soup to keep its stunning colour and delicious flavour.

Serves 4

3 red (bell) peppers
1 yellow (bell) pepper
1 onion, chopped
1 garlic clove, crushed
750ml/1¼ pints/3 cups vegetable stock
15ml/1 tbsp plain (all-purpose) flour
salt and ground black pepper
red and yellow (bell) peppers, diced, to garnish

1 Preheat the grill (broiler) to high. Halve the peppers lengthways, then remove and discard their stalks, cores and seeds.

2 Line a grill (broiling) pan with foil and arrange the pepper halves skin side up in a single layer. Grill (broil) until the skins have blackened and blistered.

3 Transfer the peppers to a plastic bag and leave until cool, then peel away and discard the charred skins. Roughly chop the pepper flesh and set aside.

4 Put the onion, garlic clove and 150ml/¼ pint/⅔ cup stock into a large pan. Bring to the boil on a high heat and boil for about 5 minutes, or until the stock has reduced in volume. Reduce the heat and stir until the onion is softened and just beginning to colour.

5 Sprinkle the flour over the onion, then gradually stir in the remaining stock. Stir in the chopped, roasted pepper flesh and bring to the boil. Cover and simmer for a further 5 minutes.

6 Remove the pan from the heat and leave to cool slightly, then purée the mixture in a blender or food processor until smooth. Season to taste with salt and pepper. Return the soup to the pan and reheat gently until it is piping hot. Ladle into four soup bowls and garnish each with a sprinkling of diced peppers to serve.

Summer Tomato Soup

The success of this soup depends on having really ripe, full-flavoured tomatoes, such as the oval plum variety, so make it when the tomato season is at its peak.

Serves 4

15ml/1 tbsp olive oil
1 large onion, chopped
1 carrot, chopped
1kg/2¼lb ripe tomatoes, cored and quartered
2 garlic cloves, chopped
5 thyme sprigs, or 1.5ml/¼ tsp dried thyme
4–5 marjoram sprigs, or 1.5ml/¼ tsp dried marjoram
1 bay leaf
45ml/3 tbsp crème fraîche, sour cream or yogurt, plus a little extra to garnish
salt and ground black pepper

1 Heat the olive oil in a large, preferably stainless-steel, pan or flameproof casserole.

2 Add the onion and carrot and cook over a medium heat for 3–4 minutes, until just softened, stirring occasionally.

3 Add the tomatoes, garlic and herbs. Reduce the heat and simmer, covered, for 30 minutes.

4 Pass the soup through a food mill or press through a sieve (strainer) into the pan. Stir in the cream or yogurt and season. Reheat gently and serve with a spoonful of cream or yogurt and a sprig of marjoram.

Variation
This soup is also delicious served cold. Make it a few hours in advance, omitting the cream or yogurt, and cool, then chill.

Cook's Tip
Plum tomatoes have relatively few seeds, firm flesh and an intense flavour, making them the best type for cooking.

Pepper Soup: *Energy 79kcal/330kJ; Protein 2.4g; Carbohydrate 16.3g, of which sugars 11.6g; Fat 0.8g, of which saturates 0.2g; Cholesterol 0mg; Calcium 25mg; Fibre 3.2g; Sodium 8mg.*
Summer Tomato Soup: *Energy 138kcal/576kJ; Protein 3g; Carbohydrate 13.7g, of which sugars 12.4g; Fat 8.3g, of which saturates 3.7g; Cholesterol 13mg; Calcium 61mg; Fibre 4.2g; Sodium 35mg.*

Wild Mushroom Soup

In France, many people pick their own wild mushrooms, taking them to a pharmacy to be checked before using them in all sorts of delicious dishes. Dried mushrooms add an earthy flavour to this soup, but use 175g/6oz fresh wild mushrooms instead when available.

Serves 6–8

25g/1oz dried wild mushrooms, such as morels, ceps or porcini
1.5 litres/2½ pints/6 cups chicken stock
25g/1oz/2 tbsp butter
2 onions, coarsely chopped
2 garlic cloves, chopped
900g/2lb button or other cultivated mushrooms, trimmed and sliced
2.5ml/½ tsp dried thyme
1.5ml/¼ tsp freshly grated nutmeg
30–45ml/2–3 tbsp plain (all-purpose) flour
125ml/4fl oz/½ cup Madeira or dry sherry
125ml/4fl oz/½ cup crème fraîche or sour cream
salt and ground black pepper
chopped fresh chives, to garnish

1 Put the dried mushrooms in a sieve (strainer) and rinse them well under cold running water. Place them in a pan with 250ml/8fl oz/1 cup of the stock and bring to the boil. Remove the pan from the heat and set aside for 30–40 minutes to soak.

2 Meanwhile, in a large, heavy pan, melt the butter over a medium-high heat. Add the onions and cook for 5–7 minutes until they are softened and just golden. Stir in the garlic and fresh mushrooms and cook for 4–5 minutes until they begin to soften, then add the salt and pepper, thyme and nutmeg and sprinkle over the flour. Cook for 3–5 minutes, stirring frequently.

3 Add the Madeira or sherry, the remaining chicken stock, the dried mushrooms and their soaking liquid and cook, covered, over a medium heat for 30–40 minutes until the mushrooms are very tender.

4 Purée the soup in batches in a blender or food processor. Strain it back into the pan, pressing firmly to force the purée through. Stir in the crème fraîche or soured cream and sprinkle with the chopped chives just before serving.

Variation

If you are a vegetarian or prefer not to use chicken stock, this may be substituted with vegetable stock. If making your own stock, add half a bulb of fennel and a teaspoon of pink peppercorns to give it more depth of flavour. Strain and cool the stock before using it.

Cook's Tip

The combination of mushrooms and tangy blue cheese is excellent, so if you are serving this soup as a lunch main course then serve a very fresh baguette or rustic bread and some French Roquefort or Italian Gorgonzola cheese with it. If you plan to serve the soup as a starter then simply offer crisp melba toasts or slices of baguette and butter.

Spanish Potato and Garlic Soup

Served in earthenware dishes, this classic Spanish soup really is one to savour.

Serves 6

15ml/1 tbsp olive oil
1 large onion, thinly sliced
4 garlic cloves, crushed
1 large potato, halved and cut into thin slices
5ml/1 tsp paprika
400g/14oz can chopped tomatoes, drained
5ml/1 tsp chopped fresh thyme leaves
900ml/1½ pints/3¾ cups vegetable stock
5ml/1 tsp cornflour (cornstarch)
salt and freshly ground black pepper
chopped fresh thyme leaves, to garnish

1 Heat the oil in a large pan. Add the onions, garlic, potato and paprika and cook for 5 minutes, or until the onions are softened, but not browned.

2 Add the tomatoes, thyme and stock. Bring to the boil, reduce the heat and simmer for 15–20 minutes until tender.

3 Blend the cornflour with a little water in a small bowl to form a paste, then stir into the soup. Simmer for 5 minutes, stirring, until the soup is thickened.

4 Break the potatoes up slightly. Season to taste. Sprinkle with the chopped thyme leaves to garnish.

Wild Mushroom Soup: *Energy 153kcal/638kJ; Protein 3.2g; Carbohydrate 9.3g, of which sugars 0.5g; Fat 11.8g, of which saturates 7.2g; Cholesterol 29mg; Calcium 26mg; Fibre 1.6g; Sodium 82mg.*
Spanish Potato Soup: *Energy 74kcal/313kJ; Protein 1.6g; Carbohydrate 12.8g, of which sugars 4.8g; Fat 2.2g, of which saturates 0.4g; Cholesterol 0mg; Calcium 17mg; Fibre 1.6g; Sodium 12mg.*

Mediterranean Farmhouse Soup

Root vegetables form the base of this flavourful, chunky, minestrone-style soup. You can vary the vegetables according to what you have to hand.

Serves 6

15ml/1 tbsp olive oil
1 onion, roughly chopped
3 carrots, cut into large chunks
175–200g/6–7oz turnips, cut into large chunks
about 175g/6oz swede (rutabaga), cut into large chunks
400g/14oz can chopped Italian tomatoes
15ml/1 tbsp tomato purée (paste)
5ml/1 tsp dried mixed herbs
5ml/1 tsp dried oregano
50g/2oz/½ cup dried peppers, washed and thinly sliced
1.5 litres/2½ pints/6¼ cups vegetable stock or water
50g/2oz/½ cup dried small macaroni or conchiglie
400g/14oz can red kidney beans, rinsed and drained
30ml/2 tbsp chopped fresh flat leaf parsley
salt and ground black pepper
freshly grated Parmesan cheese, to serve (optional)

1 Heat the oil in a large non-stick pan, add the onion and cook gently for 5 minutes until softened. Add the fresh vegetables, tomatoes, tomato purée, herbs and dried peppers. Season. Stir in the stock or water and bring to the boil. Cover, reduce the heat and simmer for 30 minutes, stirring occasionally.

2 Add the pasta and bring to the boil, stirring. Reduce the heat and simmer uncovered, stirring frequently, for about 5 minutes or until the pasta is only just al *dente*.

3 Stir in the beans. Heat through for 2–3 minutes, then remove from the heat and stir in the chopped parsley. Taste the soup for seasoning. Serve hot in warmed soup bowls, with grated Parmesan handed around separately, if you like.

Cook's Tip
Packets of dried Italian peppers are sold in supermarkets and delicatessens. They are piquant and firm with a "meaty" bite to them, which makes them ideal for adding to vegetarian soups.

Quick Pistou Soup

A delicious chunky vegetable soup served with tomato pesto. Serve in small portions as an appetizer, or in larger bowls with crusty bread as a filling lunch.

Serves 6

1 courgette (zucchini), diced
1 small potato, diced
1 shallot, chopped
1 carrot, diced
400g/14oz can chopped tomatoes
1.2 litres/2 pints/5 cups vegetable stock
50g/2oz green beans, cut into 1cm/½in lengths
50g/2oz/½ cup frozen petits pois (baby peas)
50g/2oz/½ cup small pasta shapes
30ml/2 tbsp pesto sauce
10ml/2 tsp tomato purée (paste)
salt and ground black pepper
freshly grated Parmesan or Pecorino cheese, to serve

1 Place the courgette, potato, shallot, carrot and tomatoes in a large pan. Add the vegetable stock and season with salt and plenty of black pepper. Bring to the boil over a medium heat, then reduce the heat, cover the pan and simmer for 20 minutes.

2 Add the green beans and petits pois to the pan and bring the soup back to the boil. Boil the mixture briefly for about a minute.

3 Add the pasta. Simmer the soup for a further 10 minutes, or until the pasta is tender. Taste and adjust the seasoning.

4 Ladle the soup into bowls. Mix together the pesto and tomato purée; stir a little into each serving and sprinkle with grated cheese.

Variations
- *To strengthen the tomato flavour, try using tomato-flavoured spaghetti, broken into small lengths, instead of pasta shapes.*
- *Sun-dried tomato purée (paste) can be used instead of the regular kind if you prefer.*

Farmhouse Soup: *Energy 154kcal/651kJ; Protein 7g; Carbohydrate 26.6g, of which sugars 10.3g; Fat 2.9g, of which saturates 0.4g; Cholesterol 0mg; Calcium 106mg; Fibre 7.2g; Sodium 282mg.*
Quick Pistou Soup: *Energy 96kcal/406kJ; Protein 4.1g; Carbohydrate 15g, of which sugars 5.3g; Fat 2.7g, of which saturates 0.7g; Cholesterol 2mg; Calcium 47mg; Fibre 2.5g; Sodium 37mg.*

Provençal Vegetable Soup

This satisfying soup captures all the flavours of a summer in Provence. The basil and garlic purée, *pistou*, is an essential part of the soup.

Serves 6–8

275g/10oz/1 ½ cups fresh broad (fava) beans, shelled, or 175g/6oz/¾ cup dried haricot (navy) beans, soaked overnight
2.5ml/½ tsp dried herbes de Provence
2 garlic cloves, finely chopped
15ml/1 tbsp olive oil
1 onion, finely chopped
2 small leeks, finely sliced
1 celery stick, finely sliced
2 carrots, finely diced
2 small potatoes, finely diced
120g/4oz green beans
1.2 litres/2 pints/5 cups water
120g/4oz/1 cup shelled garden peas, fresh or frozen
2 small courgettes (zucchini), finely chopped
3 medium tomatoes, peeled, seeded and finely chopped
handful of spinach leaves, cut into thin ribbons
sprigs of fresh basil, to garnish

For the pistou

1 or 2 garlic cloves, finely chopped
15g/½oz/½ cup (packed) basil leaves
60ml/4 tbsp grated Parmesan cheese
60 ml/4 tbsp extra virgin olive oil

1 To make the *pistou*, put the garlic, basil and Parmesan cheese in a food processor and process until smooth, scraping down the sides once. With the machine running, slowly add the olive oil through the feed tube. Or, alternatively, pound the garlic, basil and cheese in a mortar and pestle and stir in the oil.

2 To make the soup, if using dried haricot beans, place them in a pan and cover with water. Boil vigorously for 10 minutes and drain. Place the parboiled beans, or fresh beans if using, in a pan with the *herbes de Provence* and one of the garlic cloves. Add water to cover by 2.5cm/1in. Bring to the boil, reduce the heat and simmer over a medium-low heat until tender, about 10 minutes for fresh beans and about 1 hour for dried beans. Set aside in the cooking liquid.

3 Heat the oil in a large pan or flameproof casserole. Add the onion and leeks, and cook for 5 minutes, stirring occasionally, until the onion just softens.

4 Add the celery, carrots and the other garlic clove and cook, covered, for 10 minutes, stirring. Add the potatoes, green beans and water, then season lightly with salt and pepper. Bring to the boil, skimming any foam that rises to the surface, then reduce the heat, cover and simmer gently for 10 minutes.

5 Add the courgettes, tomatoes and peas together with the reserved beans and their cooking liquid and simmer for 25–30 minutes, or until all the vegetables are tender. Add the spinach and simmer for 5 minutes. Season the soup and swirl a spoonful of *pistou* into each bowl. Garnish with basil and serve.

Cook's Tip

Both the pistou and the soup can be made one or two days in advance and chilled. To serve, reheat the soup gently, stirring occasionally.

Summer Minestrone

This brightly coloured, fresh-tasting soup is low in fat and makes the most of intensely flavoured summer vegetables.

Serves 4

10ml/2 tsp olive oil
1 large onion, finely chopped
15ml/1 tbsp sun-dried tomato purée (paste)
450g/1lb ripe Italian plum tomatoes, peeled and finely chopped
225g/8oz green courgettes (zucchini), trimmed and roughly chopped
225g/8oz yellow courgettes (zucchini), trimmed and roughly chopped
3 waxy new potatoes, diced
2 garlic cloves, crushed
about 1.2 litres/2 pints/5 cups vegetable stock or water
60ml/4 tbsp shredded fresh basil
25g/1oz/¼ cup finely grated fresh Parmesan cheese
salt and ground black pepper

1 Heat the olive oil in a large saucepan, add the chopped onion and cook gently, stirring constantly, for about 5 minutes, or until softened.

2 Stir in the sun-dried tomato purée, chopped tomatoes, courgettes, potatoes and garlic. Mix well and cook gently for 10 minutes, uncovered, shaking the pan frequently to stop the vegetables sticking to the base.

3 Add the stock or water. Bring to the boil, reduce the heat, partially cover the pan and simmer gently for 15 minutes, or until the vegetables are just tender. Add a little more stock or water if necessary.

4 Remove the pan from the heat and stir in the basil and half the cheese. Taste for seasoning. Serve hot, sprinkled with the remaining cheese.

Cook's Tip

Classic recipes for minestrone usually include either pasta or rice to make a thick, substantial soup, but this is a lighter summer version.

Vegetable Soup: *Energy 126kcal/525kJ; Protein 6.1g; Carbohydrate 8.7g, of which sugars 3.3g; Fat 7.6g, of which saturates 2g; Cholesterol 6mg; Calcium 102mg; Fibre 3.6g; Sodium 72mg.*
Minestrone: *Energy 228kcal/951kJ; Protein 9.2g; Carbohydrate 18.8g, of which sugars 7.2g; Fat 13.4g, of which saturates 4.1g; Cholesterol 13mg; Calcium 194mg; Fibre 3.1g; Sodium 156mg.*

Meadow Yogurt Soup with Rice and Mint

In every soup house, bus station and roadside café throughout Turkey you will come across yogurt soup. Based on well-flavoured stock and yogurt, it usually contains a little rice, bulgur, chickpeas or barley, depending on which region you are in, and occasionally it is coloured with saffron or sprinkled with paprika. When it is flavoured with dried mint, it is called *yayla çorbası*, or meadow soup.

Serves 4

15ml/1 tbsp butter or sunflower oil
1 large onion, finely chopped
scant 15ml/1 tbsp plain (all-purpose) flour
1.2 litres/2 pints/5 cups lamb or chicken stock
75g/3oz/scant ½ cup long grain rice (wild or plain), well rinsed
15–30ml/1–2 tbsp dried mint
400ml/14fl oz/1⅔ cups strained natural (plain) yogurt
salt and ground black pepper

1 Melt the butter in a heavy pan, add the onion and cook until soft. Off the heat, stir in the flour, then the stock. Return the pan to the heat and bring to the boil, stirring constantly.

2 Stir in the rice and most of the mint, reserving a little for the garnish. Lower the heat, cover the pan and simmer for about 20 minutes, until the rice is cooked. Season to taste.

3 Beat the yogurt until smooth, then spoon almost all of it into the soup. Keep the heat low and stir vigorously to make sure the yogurt remains smooth and creamy and is well blended. Ladle the soup into bowls, swirl in the remaining yogurt, and garnish with the remaining mint.

Cook's Tip
If you can't buy strained yogurt you can make it yourself. Line a sieve (strainer) with a piece of muslin (cheesecloth) and spoon thick and creamy plain yogurt into it. Allow the excess liquid to drip through the muslin, then tip the yogurt into a bowl.

Spinach and Rice Soup

This light and fresh-tasting soup is based on two key foodstuffs introduced to the Mediterranean by the Arabs. Rice is grown in the marshland areas and is a characteristic ingredient of dishes of the whole region.

Serves 4

675g/1½lb fresh spinach, washed
45ml/3 tbsp extra virgin olive oil
1 small onion, finely chopped
2 garlic cloves, finely chopped
1 small fresh red chilli, seeded and finely chopped
115g/4oz/generous 1 cup risotto rice
1.2litres/2 pints/5 cups vegetable stock
60ml/4 tbsp grated Pecorino cheese
salt and ground black pepper

1 Place the spinach in a large pan with just the water that clings to its leaves after washing. Add a large pinch of salt. Heat gently until the spinach has wilted, then remove from the heat and drain, reserving any liquid.

2 Either chop the spinach finely using a large knife or place in a food processor and process to a fairly coarse purée.

3 Heat the oil in a large saucepan and gently cook the onion, garlic and chilli for 4–5 minutes until softened.

4 Stir in the rice until well coated, then pour in the stock and reserved spinach liquid. Bring to the boil, lower the heat and simmer for 10 minutes.

5 Add the spinach, with salt and pepper to taste. Cook for another 5–7 minutes, until the rice is tender.

Cook's Tip
Spinach is a very versatile vegetable, delicious served as an accompaniment to meat and fish dishes, but also widely used in fillings for pasta and pies, in egg dishes and in sauces. Use very fresh, young spinach leaves to prepare this light and fresh-tasting soup.

Meadow Yogurt Soup: *Energy 187kcal/781kJ; Protein 7.6g; Carbohydrate 30.3g, of which sugars 11.1g; Fat 4.4g, of which saturates 2.5g; Cholesterol 9mg; Calcium 215mg; Fibre 1g; Sodium 108mg.*
Spinach and Rice Soup: *Energy 324kcal/1346kJ; Protein 9.1g; Carbohydrate 48.8g, of which sugars 3.4g; Fat 9.9g, of which saturates 1.4g; Cholesterol 0mg; Calcium 301mg; Fibre 3.8g; Sodium 237mg.*

Pomegranate Broth

With its origins in Persia and Azerbaijan, this fresh-tasting delicate soup, known in Turkey as *narlı çorba*, is perhaps the best way of appreciating sour pomegranates, as it is pleasing both to the eye and the palate. Clear and refreshing, it is served as a sophisticated palate cleanser between courses, or as a light appetizer to a meal. Sour pomegranates are available in Middle Eastern stores, but if you can only find sweet pomegranates, add some lemon juice.

Serves 4

1.2 litres/2 pints/5 cups clear chicken stock
150ml/¼ pint/⅔ cup sour pomegranate juice (see below)
seeds of 1 sweet pomegranate
salt and ground black pepper
fresh mint leaves, to garnish

1 Pour the stock into a pan and bring to the boil. Lower the heat, stir in the pomegranate juice, together with the lemon juice if you are using sweet pomegranates, then bring the stock back to the boil.

2 Lower the heat again and stir in half the pomegranate seeds, then season and turn off the heat.

3 Ladle the hot broth into warmed bowls. Sprinkle the remaining pomegranate seeds over the top and garnish with mint leaves.

Cook's Tip

The ruby-red grains of sweet pomegranates are eaten fresh, while the sour fruits are used in soups, marinades, dressings and syrups. For 150ml/¼ pint/⅔ cup juice, you will need 5–6 sour pomegranates. Cut the pomegranates in half crossways and squeeze them with a stainless steel, glass or wooden lemon squeezer to extract the juice. Do not use any metal other than stainless steel for squeezing or it will react with the astringent juice of the pomegranates, causing the juice to discolour and taste unpleasant.

Spanish Seafood Soup

This hearty seafood soup is substantial enough to serve as a main course, but can also be thinned with white wine and water to make an elegant appetizer for six.

Serves 4

675g/1½lb raw prawns (shrimp), in the shell
900ml/1½ pints/3¾ cups water
1 onion, chopped
1 celery stick, chopped
1 bay leaf
45ml/3 tbsp olive oil
2 slices stale bread, crusts removed
1 small onion, finely chopped
1 large garlic clove, chopped
2 large tomatoes, seeded and chopped
½ large green (bell) pepper, finely chopped
500g/1¼lb cockles (small clams) or mussels, cleaned
juice of 1 lemon
45ml/3 tbsp chopped fresh parsley
5ml/1 tsp paprika
salt and ground black pepper

1 Pull the heads off the prawns and put them in a pan with the water. Add the onion, celery and bay leaf and simmer for 20–25 minutes. Meanwhile, peel the prawns, adding the shells to the stock as you go along.

2 Heat the oil in a wide, deep flameproof casserole and fry the bread slices quickly, then reserve. Fry the onion until soft, adding the garlic towards the end. Add the tomatoes and the green pepper and fry briefly, stirring occasionally.

3 Strain the stock into the casserole and bring to the boil. Check over the cockles or mussels, discarding any that are open or damaged. Add half the shellfish to the stock. When open, use a slotted spoon to transfer them to a plate. Discard any that have failed to open during cooking. Remove and discard about half of the shells. Meanwhile, repeat the process to cook the remaining cockles or mussels.

4 Return the cockles or mussels to the soup and add the prawns. Add the bread, torn into little pieces, and the lemon juice and chopped parsley. Season to taste with paprika, salt and pepper and stir gently to dissolve the bread. Serve at once in soup bowls, providing a plate for the empty shells.

Pomegranate Broth: Energy 62kcal/260kJ; Protein 2g; Carbohydrate 3.9g, of which sugars 2.3g; Fat 4.4g, of which saturates 0.4g; Cholesterol 0mg; Calcium 14mg; Fibre 0.6g; Sodium 205mg.
Spanish Seafood Soup: Energy 301kcal/1266kJ; Protein 39.5g; Carbohydrate 13.5g, of which sugars 6.3g; Fat 10.3g, of which saturates 1.6g; Cholesterol 362mg; Calcium 223mg; Fibre 1.9g; Sodium 709mg.

Asparagus Soup with Crab

The French name for this dish, *Crème d'Argenteuil au Crabe*, refers to the town of Argenteuil in north central France that is particularly famed for this superb seasonal delicacy. However, asparagus is also grown in the western Mediterranean and the species can be found growing wild in sandy coastal areas.

Serves 6–8

1.3kg/3lb fresh asparagus
25g/1oz/2 tbsp butter
1.5 litres/2½ pints/6 cups chicken stock
30ml/2 tbsp cornflour (cornstarch)
125ml/4fl oz/½ cup whipping cream
salt and ground black pepper
175–200g/6–7oz white crab meat, to garnish

1 Trim the woody ends from the bottom of the asparagus spears and cut the spears into 2.5cm/1in pieces.

2 Melt the butter in a heavy pan or flameproof casserole over a medium-high heat. Add the asparagus and cook for 5–6 minutes, stirring frequently, until they are bright green, but not browned.

3 Add the stock and bring to the boil over a high heat, skimming off any foam that rises to the surface. Simmer over a medium heat for 3–5 minutes until the asparagus is tender, yet crisp. Reserve 12–16 of the asparagus tips for garnishing. Season with salt and pepper, cover and continue cooking for about 15–20 minutes until very tender.

4 Purée the soup in a blender or food processor and pass the mixture through the fine blade of a food mill back into the pan. Bring the soup back to the boil over a medium-high heat. Blend the cornflour with 30–45ml/2–3 tbsp cold water and whisk into the boiling soup to thicken, then stir in the cream. Adjust the seasoning.

5 To serve, ladle the soup into bowls and top each with a spoonful of the crab meat and a few of the reserved asparagus tips.

Spiced Mussel Soup

Chunky and colourful, this Turkish fish soup is like a chowder in its consistency. It is flavoured with harissa sauce, an ingredient that is more familiar in North African cooking.

Serves 6

1.3–1.6kg/3–3½lb fresh mussels, in their shells
150ml/¼ pint/⅔ cup white wine
3 tomatoes
15ml/1 tbsp olive oil
1 onion, finely chopped
2 garlic cloves, crushed
2 celery sticks, thinly sliced
bunch of spring onions (scallions), thinly sliced
1 potato, diced
7.5ml/1½ tsp harissa
45ml/3 tbsp chopped fresh parsley
ground black pepper, to taste
thick natural (plain) yogurt, to serve

1 Scrub and debeard the mussels, discarding any that are damaged or any open shells that do not close when tapped with a knife.

2 Bring the wine to the boil in a pan. Add the mussels and cover with a lid. Cook for 4–5 minutes, or until the mussels have opened wide. Discard any that remain closed. Drain, reserving the cooking liquid. Set aside a few mussels for garnish, then shell the rest.

3 Skin the tomatoes and dice the flesh. Set aside. Heat the oil in a pan and cook the onion, garlic, celery and spring onions for 5 minutes. Add the mussels, reserved liquid, potato, harissa and tomatoes. Bring to the boil, then reduce the heat, cover and simmer gently for 25 minutes, until the potatoes break up.

4 Stir in the parsley and pepper and add the reserved mussels in their shells. Heat through for 1 minute. Serve hot with a spoonful of yogurt.

Variation
Use 3–4 shallots if you have them, finely chopped, in place of the standard onion.

Asparagus Soup: *Energy 157kcal/652kJ; Protein 9.7g; Carbohydrate 7.6g, of which sugars 4g; Fat 9.9g, of which saturates 5.6g; Cholesterol 38mg; Calcium 87mg; Fibre 3.2g; Sodium 147mg.*
Spiced Mussel Soup: *Energy 153kcal/644kJ; Protein 14.5g; Carbohydrate 7.8g, of which sugars 3.2g; Fat 5.6g, of which saturates 0.9g; Cholesterol 30mg; Calcium 178mg; Fibre 1.5g; Sodium 175mg.*

Saffron Mussel Soup

This is one of France's most delicious seafood soups – serve it with plenty of French bread.

Serves 4–6

40g/1½oz/3 tbsp unsalted butter
8 shallots, finely chopped
1 bouquet garni
5ml/1 tsp black peppercorns
350ml/12fl oz/1½ cups dry white wine
1kg/2¼lb mussels, scrubbed and debearded
2 medium leeks, trimmed and finely chopped
1 fennel bulb, finely chopped
1 carrot, finely chopped
several saffron strands
1 litre/1⅔ pints/4 cups fish or chicken stock
30–45ml/2–3 tbsp cornflour (cornstarch), blended with 45ml/3 tbsp cold water
125ml/4fl oz/½ cup whipping cream
1 medium tomato, peeled, seeded and finely chopped
30ml/2 tbsp Pernod (optional)
salt and ground black pepper

1 In a large heavy pan, melt half the butter over a medium-high heat. Add half the shallots and cook for 1–2 minutes until softened. Add the bouquet garni, peppercorns and white wine and bring to the boil. Add the mussels, cover tightly and cook over a high heat for 3–5 minutes, shaking the pan occasionally, until the mussels have opened. Transfer them to a bowl with a slotted spoon. Strain the cooking liquid through a sieve (strainer) lined with muslin (cheesecloth) and reserve. Remove most of the mussels from their shells, adding any extra juices to the reserved liquid. Discard any closed mussels.

2 Rinse the pan and melt the remaining butter over a medium heat. Add the remaining shallots and cook for 1–2 minutes. Add the leeks, fennel, carrot and saffron and cook for 3–5 minutes. Stir in the reserved cooking liquid, bring to the boil and cook for 5 minutes. Add the stock and bring to the boil, skimming any foam that rises to the surface. Season with salt, if needed, and black pepper and cook for a further 5 minutes.

3 Stir in the blended cornflour and simmer for 2–3 minutes to thicken slightly, then add the cream, mussels and tomato. Stir in Pernod, if using, and cook for 1–2 minutes until hot, then serve.

Prawn Bisque

The classic French method for making a bisque requires pushing the shellfish through a *tamis*, or drum sieve. This is much simpler and the result is just as smooth.

Serves 6–8

675g/1½lb medium cooked prawns (shrimp) in the shell
25ml/1½ tbsp vegetable oil
2 onions, halved and sliced
1 large carrot, sliced
2 celery sticks, sliced
2 litres/3⅓ pints/8 cups water
a few drops of lemon juice
30ml/2 tbsp tomato purée (paste)
bouquet garni
50g/2oz/4 tbsp butter
50g/2oz/⅓ cup plain (all-purpose) flour
45–60ml/3–4 tbsp brandy
150ml/¼ pint/⅔ cup whipping cream
salt and white pepper

1 Remove the heads from the prawns and peel away the shells, reserving the heads and shells. Chill the peeled prawns.

2 Heat the oil in a large pan, add the prawn heads and shells and cook over a high heat, stirring frequently, until they start to brown. Reduce the heat to medium, add the onions, carrot and celery and fry gently, stirring occasionally, for about 5 minutes until the onions start to soften.

3 Add the water, lemon juice, tomato purée and bouquet garni. Bring the stock to the boil, then reduce the heat, cover and simmer gently for 25 minutes. Strain the stock through a sieve (strainer).

4 Melt the butter in a heavy pan over a medium heat. Stir in the flour and cook until just golden, stirring occasionally. Add the brandy and gradually pour in about half of the prawn stock, whisking vigorously until smooth, then whisk in the remaining liquid. Season with salt, if necessary, and white pepper. Reduce the heat, cover and simmer for 5 minutes, stirring frequently.

5 Strain the soup into a clean pan. Add the cream and a little extra lemon juice to taste, then add most of the reserved prawns. Cook over a medium heat, stirring frequently, until hot. Serve immediately, garnished with the reserved prawns.

Saffron Mussel Soup: Energy 441kcal/1825kJ; Protein 9.6g; Carbohydrate 3.1g, of which sugars 3.1g; Fat 39.1g, of which saturates 23.9g; Cholesterol 116mg; Calcium 137mg; Fibre 0.6g; Sodium 156mg.
Shrimp Bisque: Energy 269kcal/1121kJ; Protein 9.3g; Carbohydrate 18.5g, of which sugars 7.5g; Fat 18g, of which saturates 8.9g; Cholesterol 63mg; Calcium 158mg; Fibre 0.9g; Sodium 1026mg.

Provençal Fish Soup

The addition of rice makes this a substantial soup.

Serves 6

450g/1lb mussels
about 250ml/8fl oz/1 cup dry white wine
675–900g/1½–2lb mixed white fish fillets such as monkfish, plaice, flounder, cod or haddock
6 large fresh scallops
15ml/1 tbsp olive oil
3 leeks, chopped
1 garlic clove, crushed
1 red (bell) pepper, cut into 2.5cm/1in pieces
1 yellow (bell) pepper, cut into 2.5cm/1in pieces
175g/6oz fennel bulb, cut into 4cm/1½in pieces
400g/14oz can chopped tomatoes
150ml/¼ pint/⅔ cup passata (bottled strained tomatoes)
about 1 litre/1¾ pints/4 cups well-flavoured fish stock
generous pinch of saffron threads, soaked in 15ml/1 tbsp hot water
175g/6oz/scant 1 cup basmati rice, soaked
8 large fresh raw prawns (shrimp), peeled and deveined
salt and ground black pepper
30–45ml/2–3 tbsp fresh dill, to garnish

1 Clean the mussels, discarding any that do not close when tapped with a knife. Place them in a heavy pan. Add 90ml/6 tbsp of the wine, cover and cook for about 3 minutes to open the mussels. Strain, reserving the liquid, and discard any mussels that have not opened. Set aside half the mussels in their shells for the garnish; shell the rest and put them in a bowl.

2 Cut the fish into 2.5cm/1in cubes. Detach the scallop corals and slice the white flesh into three or four pieces. Add the scallops to the fish and the corals to the shelled mussels.

3 Heat the oil in a non-stick pan and cook the leeks and garlic for 3–4 minutes. Add the peppers and fennel, and cook for a further 2 minutes. Add the tomatoes, passata, stock, saffron water, mussel liquid and wine. Season and cook for 5 minutes. Stir in the rice, cover and simmer for 10 minutes. Add the white fish and cook gently for 5 minutes. Add the prawns, cook for 2 minutes, then add the scallop corals and shelled mussels and cook for a further 2–3 minutes. Serve in warmed bowls, topped with the mussels in their shells and a little chopped dill.

Mediterranean Leek and Fish Soup

This chunky soup makes a robust and wonderfully aromatic dish, perfect for a lingering al fresco summer lunch or a light supper with friends. Serve it with crisp-baked croûtons or fresh crusty bread dunked in warm olive oil.

Serves 6

2 large thick leeks
15ml/1 tbsp olive oil
5ml/1 tsp crushed coriander seeds
pinch of dried red chilli flakes
300g/11oz small salad potatoes, peeled and thickly sliced
400g/14oz can chopped tomatoes
600ml/1 pint/2½ cups fish stock
150ml/¼ pint/⅔ cup white wine
1 fresh bay leaf
1 star anise
strip of pared orange rind
good pinch of saffron threads
450g/1lb white fish fillets, such as monkfish, sea bass, cod or haddock
450g/1lb small squid, cleaned
250g/9oz fresh raw peeled prawns (shrimp)
30–45ml/2–3 tbsp chopped fresh flat leaf parsley
salt and ground black pepper

1 Slice the leeks, keeping the green and white parts separate. Wash the leek slices thoroughly and drain them well. Set the white slices aside for later.

2 Heat the oil in a heavy pan and add the green leek slices, crushed coriander seeds and dried red chilli flakes. Cook gently, stirring occasionally, for 5 minutes.

3 Add the potatoes and tomatoes, and pour in the stock and wine. Add the bay leaf, star anise, orange rind and saffron. Bring to the boil, then reduce the heat and partially cover the pan. Simmer for 20 minutes, or until the potatoes are tender. Taste and adjust the seasoning.

4 Cut the white fish into chunks. Cut the squid sacs into rectangles and score in a criss-cross pattern. Add the fish to the soup and cook gently for 4 minutes. Add the prawns and cook for 1 minute. Add the squid and the reserved sliced white part of the leeks and cook, stirring occasionally, for a further 2 minutes. Finally, stir in the chopped parsley and serve at once.

Provençal Fish Soup: Energy 352kcal/1481kJ; Protein 37.9g; Carbohydrate 33.3g, of which sugars 8.6g; Fat 4.6g, of which saturates 0.8g; Cholesterol 117mg; Calcium 129mg; Fibre 4.5g; Sodium 208mg.
Mediterranean Fish Soup: Energy 249kcal/1051kJ; Protein 35.2g; Carbohydrate 13.3g, of which sugars 4.5g; Fat 4.7g, of which saturates 0.9g; Cholesterol 285mg; Calcium 90mg; Fibre 3g; Sodium 223mg.

Fish Soup with Orange

The old Spanish name for this soup is *sopa cachorreña* – Seville orange soup – and it is good served just after Christmas, when bitter Seville oranges (the kind used for making marmalade) have their short season. Their clear, sharp flavour is very welcome after a lot of rich festive food. At other times of year add lemon to sharpen the flavour of sweet oranges. The fish normally used is small hake, but any white fish is suitable.

Serves 6

1kg/2¼lb small hake or whiting, whole but cleaned
1.2 litres/2 pints/5 cups water
4 bitter oranges, or 4 sweet oranges and 2 lemons
30ml/2 tbsp olive oil
5 garlic cloves, unpeeled
1 large onion, finely chopped
1 tomato, peeled, seeded and chopped
4 small potatoes, cut into rounds
5ml/1 tsp paprika
salt and ground black pepper
15–30ml/1–2 tbsp finely chopped fresh parsley, to garnish

1 Fillet the fish and cut each fillet into three, reserving all the trimmings. Put the fillets on a plate, salt lightly and chill.

2 Put the fish trimmings in a pan, add the water and a spiral of orange rind. Bring to a simmer, skim, then cover and cook gently for 30 minutes.

3 Heat the oil in a large flameproof casserole over a high heat. Smash the garlic cloves with the flat of a knife and fry until they are well-coloured. Discard the garlic and turn down the heat. Fry the onion gently until it is softened, adding the tomato halfway through.

4 Strain in the hot fish stock (adding the orange spiral as well if you wish) and bring back to the boil. Add the potatoes to the pan and cook them for about 5 minutes.

5 Add the fish pieces to the soup, a few at a time, without letting it go off the boil. Cook for about 15 minutes. Add the squeezed orange juice and lemon juice, if using, and the paprika, with salt and pepper to taste. Serve in bowls, garnished with a little parsley.

Turkish Wedding Soup

Düğün çorbası is the soup that is served at Turkish weddings. Steeped in tradition, it varies little throughout the country, the only difference being the inclusion of cinnamon in some areas to flavour the stock. It is made with lamb stock and contains chunks of lamb, stewed slowly so that it is extremely tender. The soup has a slightly sour flavour, from the classic liaison of lemon, egg and yogurt.

Serves 4–6

500g/1¼lb lamb on the bone – neck, leg or shoulder
2 carrots, roughly chopped
2 potatoes, roughly chopped
1 cinnamon stick
45ml/3 tbsp strained plain (natural) yogurt
45ml/3 tbsp plain (all-purpose) flour
1 egg yolk
juice of ½ lemon
30ml/2 tbsp butter
5ml/1 tsp Turkish red pepper or paprika
salt and ground black pepper

1 Place the lamb in a deep pan with the carrots, potatoes and cinnamon. Pour in 2 litres/3½ pints/8 cups water and bring to the boil, then skim any scum off the surface and lower the heat. Cover and simmer for about 1½ hours, until the meat is so tender that it almost falls off the bone. Lift the lamb out of the pan and place it on a chopping board.

2 Remove the meat from the bone and chop it into small pieces. Strain the stock and discard the carrots and potatoes. Pour the stock back into the pan, season and bring to the boil.

3 In a deep bowl, beat the yogurt with the flour. Add the egg yolk and lemon juice and beat well again, then pour in about 250ml/8fl oz/1 cup of the hot stock, beating all the time.

4 Lower the heat under the pan and pour the yogurt mixture into the stock, beating constantly so that it is well blended. Add the meat and heat through.

5 Melt the butter in a small pan and stir in the red pepper or paprika. Ladle the soup into bowls and drizzle the pepper butter over the top.

Fish Soup with Orange: *Energy 245kcal/1028kJ; Protein 26.7g; Carbohydrate 19.7g, of which sugars 11.1g; Fat 7.1g, of which saturates 1.1g; Cholesterol 30mg; Calcium 89mg; Fibre 3.1g; Sodium 155mg.*
Turkish Wedding Soup: *Energy 281kcal/1178kJ; Protein 19.3g; Carbohydrate 18.8g, of which sugars 2.8g; Fat 14.9g, of which saturates 7.4g; Cholesterol 108mg; Calcium 46mg; Fibre 1.3g; Sodium 122mg.*

Lamb Meatball Soup with Vegetables

A variety of vegetables makes a tasty base for the meatballs in this soup, which will make a hearty meal served with crusty bread.

Serves 4

1 litre/1¾ pints/4 cups lamb stock
1 onion, finely chopped
2 carrots, finely sliced
½ celeriac, finely diced
75g/3oz/¾ cup frozen peas
50g/2oz green beans, cut into 2.5cm/1in pieces
3 tomatoes, seeded and chopped
1 red (bell) pepper, diced
1 potato, coarsely diced
2 lemons, sliced
salt and freshly ground black pepper
crusty bread, to serve

For the meatballs

225g/8oz/1 cup very lean minced (ground) lamb
40g/1½oz/¼ cup short-grain rice
30ml/2 tbsp chopped fresh parsley
plain (all-purpose) flour, to coat

1 Put the stock in a large pan over a medium heat. Add the onion, carrot, celeriac and peas, and gently stir in.

2 Add the beans, tomatoes, red pepper and potato with the slices of lemon. Add a little salt and freshly ground black pepper and bring the mixture to the boil. Once it is boiling strongly, reduce the heat and simmer for 15–20 minutes.

3 Meanwhile, prepare the meatballs. Mix the minced meat, rice and parsley together in a bowl and season well. It can be easiest to use your hands to combine the ingredients, using a kneading action.

4 Take out a rounded teaspoon of the mixture and roll it into a small ball, roughly the size of a walnut. Toss it in the flour and repeat until you have finished the mixture.

5 One by one, drop the meatballs into the soup and simmer gently for 25–30 minutes, stirring occasionally, to prevent the meatballs from sticking. Adjust the seasoning and serve in warmed serving bowls, accompanied by crusty bread.

Salt Pork and Bean Soup

This classic Galician soup features salt pork and beans with young turnip tops, although purple sprouting broccoli makes a very pretty substitute. Make the soup ahead of time so that the flavours have a chance to blend. You will need to start making the soup at least a day in advance.

Serves 6

150g/5oz/⅔ cup haricot beans, soaked overnight in cold water and drained
1kg/2¼lb smoked gammon (cured or smoked ham) hock
3 potatoes, quartered
3 small turnips, sliced in rounds
150g/5oz purple sprouting broccoli
salt and ground black pepper

1 Put the drained beans and gammon into a casserole and cover with 2 litres/3½ pints/8 cups water. Slowly bring to the boil, skim off any scum, then turn down the heat and cook gently, covered, for about 1¼ hours.

2 Drain, reserving the broth. Return the broth to the casserole and add the potatoes, turnips and drained beans.

3 Meanwhile, strip all the gammon off the bone and return the bone to the broth. Discard the rind, fat and gristle and chop half the meat coarsely. Reserve the remaining meat for another recipe (see tip below).

4 Add the chopped meat to the casserole. Discard the hard stalks from the broccoli and add the leaves and florets to the broth. Simmer for 10 minutes. Season generously with pepper, then remove the bone and leave the soup to stand for at least half a day.

5 To serve, reheat the soup, add a little more seasoning if necessary, and ladle into soup bowls.

Cook's Tip

The leftover gammon can be chopped into bitesize pieces and added to rice or vegetable dishes, or tortillas.

Meatball Soup: *Energy 226kcal/948kJ; Protein 15.7g; Carbohydrate 25.1g, of which sugars 11.4g; Fat 7.7g, of which saturates 3.2g; Cholesterol 43mg; Calcium 75mg; Fibre 5.2g; Sodium 102mg.*
Salt Pork Soup: *Energy 363kcal/1522kJ; Protein 37.5g; Carbohydrate 24.4g, of which sugars 4g; Fat 13.4g, of which saturates 4.4g; Cholesterol 38mg; Calcium 73mg; Fibre 4.4g; Sodium 1486mg.*

Chicken Soup with Eggs and Lemon

The much-loved Greek chicken and lemon soup has to be one of the most delicious and nourishing soups in the world.

Serves 4–6

I chicken, about 1.6kg/3½lb
1.75 litres/3 pints/7½ cups water
2 onions, halved
2 carrots
3 celery sticks, each sliced into 3–4 pieces
a few sprigs of flat leaf parsley
3–4 black peppercorns
50g/2oz/generous ⅓ cup short grain rice
salt
lemon wedges, to serve

For the egg and lemon sauce

5ml/1 tsp cornflour (cornstarch)
2 eggs, at room temperature
juice of 1–2 lemons

1 Place the chicken in a large pan with the water. Bring to the boil and skim off any scum using a slotted spoon. Add the vegetables, parsley and peppercorns, season with salt and bring to the boil. Lower the heat, then cover the pan and cook for 1 hour until the chicken is very tender.

2 Carefully lift out the chicken and put it on a board. Strain the stock and set it aside, discarding the vegetables. Pull away the chicken breasts and legs, skin them and dice the flesh. Pour the stock back into the pan and add the chicken meat.

3 Shortly before serving, heat the stock and diced chicken. When the stock boils, add the rice. Cover the pan and cook for about 8 minutes, until the rice is soft. Take the pan off the heat and let the soup cool a little before adding the sauce.

4 Mix the cornflour to a paste with a little water. Beat the eggs in a separate bowl, add the lemon juice and the cornflour mixture and beat together until smooth. Gradually beat a ladleful of the chicken stock into the egg mixture, then continue to beat for 1 minute. Add a second ladleful in the same way, then pour the sauce slowly into the soup, stirring vigorously. Warm the soup over a gentle heat for no more than 1–2 minutes to avoid curdling the eggs. Serve immediately in warmed bowls, accompanied by lemon wedges.

Minestrone with Pancetta

This classic minestrone from Lombardy includes pancetta for a pleasant touch of saltiness. Italian cooks vary the recipe according to what ingredients they have to hand, and you can do the same.

Serves 4

45ml/3 tbsp olive oil
115g/4oz pancetta, any rinds removed, roughly chopped
2–3 celery sticks, finely chopped
3 medium carrots, finely chopped
1 medium onion, finely chopped
1–2 garlic cloves, crushed
2 × 400g/14oz cans chopped tomatoes
about 1 litre/1¾ pints/4 cups chicken stock
400g/14oz can cannellini beans, drained and rinsed
50g/2oz/½ cup short-cut macaroni
30–60ml/2–4 tbsp chopped flat leaf parsley, to taste
salt and freshly ground black pepper
shaved Parmesan cheese, to serve

1 Heat the oil in a large pan. Add the pancetta, celery, carrots and onion and cook over a low heat for 5 minutes, stirring constantly, until the vegetables are softened.

2 Add the garlic and tomatoes, breaking them up well with a wooden spoon. Pour in the stock. Add salt and pepper to taste and bring to the boil. Half cover the pan, lower the heat and simmer for about 20 minutes, until the vegetables are soft.

3 Drain the beans and add them to the pan with the macaroni. Bring to the boil again. Cover, lower the heat and continue to simmer for about 20 minutes more. Check the consistency and add more stock if necessary. Stir in the parsley and taste for seasoning.

4 Serve hot, sprinkled with Parmesan cheese. This makes a meal in itself if served with chunks of crusty Italian bread.

Variation
Use long-grain rice instead of the pasta, and borlotti beans instead of cannellini.

Chicken Soup: *Energy 599kcal/2489kJ; Protein 53.5g; Carbohydrate 8.5g, of which sugars 3g; Fat 39.1g, of which saturates 10.8g; Cholesterol 359mg; Calcium 50mg; Fibre 1.2g; Sodium 236mg.*
Minestrone: *Energy 324kcal/1356kJ; Protein 13.4g; Carbohydrate 32.3g, of which sugars 12.3g; Fat 16.6g, of which saturates 3.9g; Cholesterol 19mg; Calcium 111mg; Fibre 8.5g; Sodium 696mg.*

Sea Bass in a Salt Crust

Baking fish in a crust of sea salt keeps in the flavours, enhancing the natural taste of the fish. It is a popular way of cooking fish on the Greek islands, where large outside ovens are used to prevent the inside of buildings becoming too hot. Any firm fish can be cooked with a salt crust. Break it open at the table to release the glorious aroma.

Serves 4

1 sea bass, about 1kg/2¼lb, cleaned and scaled
1 sprig fresh fennel
1 sprig fresh rosemary
1 sprig fresh thyme
2kg/4½lb coarse sea salt
mixed peppercorns
seaweed or samphire, blanched, to garnish
lemon slices, to serve

1 Preheat the oven to 240°C/475°F/Gas 9. Spread half the salt on a shallow baking tray (ideally oval or rectangular).

2 Wash out the sea bass and dry any excess moisture with kitchen paper. Open the fish and lightly season the insides with salt and freshly ground black pepper, then fill the cavity of the fish with all the fresh herbs. Do not worry if the fish does not close properly as the herbs will become much more compact as soon as they have been heated through and cooked.

3 Lay the sea bass on the salt. Cover the fish with a 1cm/½in layer of salt, pressing it down firmly. Moisten the salt lightly by spraying with water from an atomizer. Bake the fish in the hot oven for 30–40 minutes, or until the salt crust is just beginning to colour.

4 Garnish the dish with seaweed or samphire and use a sharp knife to break open the salt crust at the table. Serve with lemon slices.

Cook's Tip
Make sure that you leave enough time for the oven to heat up properly, as a cooler oven will not be able to set the salt crust.

Grilled Sea Bass with Fennel

Fennel grows wild in Greece and flavours many fish dishes. Here, pastis adds extra warmth and richness.

Serves 6–8

1 sea bass, weighing 1.8kg/4–4½lb, cleaned
60–90ml/4–6 tbsp olive oil
10–15ml/2–3 tsp fennel seeds
2 large fennel bulbs, trimmed and thinly sliced (reserving any fronds for the garnish)
60ml/4 tbsp pastis (such as Pernod or Ricard)
salt and ground black pepper

1 With a sharp knife, make three or four deep cuts in both sides of the fish. Brush the fish with olive oil and season with salt and freshly ground black pepper, both inside and outside. Sprinkle the fennel seeds into the stomach cavity and push deep down into each of the cuts. Cover loosely and set aside in a cool place while you prepare and cook the fennel.

2 Preheat the grill (broiler) to a medium heat. Put the slices of fennel in a flameproof dish or on the grill rack and brush with olive oil. Grill (broil) for 4 minutes on each side until tender. Transfer to a platter and spread evenly to cover the base, loosely cover to keep warm and set aside.

3 Place the fish on the grill rack and position about 10–13cm/4–5in away from a medium heat. Grill for 10–12 minutes on each side, brushing occasionally with olive oil. Transfer the fish to the platter, on top of the fennel. Garnish with fennel fronds.

4 Heat the pastis in a small pan, light it and pour it, still flaming, over the fish. Serve immediately.

Variation
If you have access to it, use traditional Greek ouzo instead of pastis. It has a similar aniseed flavour and is frequently used in Greek cooking to enhance the taste of fish and shellfish. You can buy it in Greek stores and it is sometimes also available in Turkish stores.

Sea Bass in a Salt Crust: Energy 83kcal/351kJ; Protein 16.1g; Carbohydrate 0g, of which sugars 0g; Fat 2.1g, of which saturates 0.3g; Cholesterol 67mg; Calcium 109mg; Fibre 0g; Sodium 2021mg.
Sea Bass with Fennel: Energy 296kcal/1241kJ; Protein 38.7g; Carbohydrate 12.3g, of which sugars 11.8g; Fat 10.5g, of which saturates 1.6g; Cholesterol 144mg; Calcium 308mg; Fibre 7.2g; Sodium 391mg.

Sea Bass Wrapped in Vine Leaves

Prepare this easy dish in advance and keep the wraps chilled and ready to pop on to the barbecue. The wraps are delicious served with a piquant salsa and cooling cucumber salad.

Serves 8

90g/3 1/2oz/½ cup Chinese black rice
400ml/14fl oz/1⅔ cups boiling water
45ml/3 tbsp extra virgin olive oil
1 small onion, chopped
1 fresh mild chilli, seeded and finely chopped
8 sea bass fillets, about 75g/3oz each, with skin
16 large fresh vine leaves
salt and ground black pepper

1 Place the rice in a large pan. Add the measured boiling water and simmer for 15 minutes. Add a little salt to taste and simmer for a further 10 minutes, or until tender. Drain well and tip into a bowl.

2 Meanwhile, heat half the oil in a frying pan. Fry the onion gently for 5 minutes until softened but not browned. Add the chilli. Stir into the rice and season with salt and pepper according to taste. Cool the rice completely and cover and chill until needed.

3 Season the sea bass fillets. Wash the vine leaves in water, then pat dry with kitchen paper. Lay each leaf in the centre of a double layer of foil. Top with a sea bass fillet. Divie the rice mixture among the fillets, spooning it towards one end. Fold the fillet over the rice, trickle over the remaining oil, lay the second vine leaf on top and bring the foil up around the fish. Scrunch it together to seal. Chill the packages for up to 3 hours, or until needed.

4 Take the fish out of the refrigerator and prepare the barbecue. Position a lightly oiled grill rack over the hot coals. Cook the wraps for 5 minutes over high heat, turning them around by 90 degrees halfway through. Open up the top of the foil a little and cook for 2 minutes more. Gently remove from the foil and transfer the vine parcels to individual plates. Serve immediately.

Salt Cod in Spicy Tomato with Potatoes

Salt cod is a popular ingredient in Spain, not just a Lenten necessity. Look out for a loin piece, which has very little waste; if you can't find one, buy a larger piece to ensure you have enough once any very dry bits have been removed.

Serves 4

400g/14oz salt cod loin, soaked in cold water for 24 hours
30ml/2 tbsp olive oil
1 large onion, chopped
2 garlic cloves, finely chopped
1½ green (bell) peppers, chopped
500g/1¼lb ripe tomatoes, peeled and chopped, or a 400g/14oz can tomatoes
15ml/1 tbsp tomato purée (paste)
15ml/1 tbsp clear honey
1.5ml/¼ tsp dried thyme
2.5ml/½ tsp cayenne pepper
juice of ½ lemon
2 potatoes
45ml/3 tbsp stale breadcrumbs
30ml/2 tbsp finely chopped fresh parsley
salt and ground black pepper

1 Drain the salt cod and place in a pan. Cover generously with water and bring to the boil. Remove the pan from the heat as soon as the water boils, then set aside until cold.

2 Heat the oil in a medium pan. Fry the onion, and add the garlic after 5 minutes. Add the chopped peppers and tomatoes, and cook gently. Stir in the tomato purée, honey, dried thyme, cayenne, black pepper, a little salt and lemon juice to taste.

3 Halve the potatoes lengthways and cut them into slices just thicker than a coin. Drain the fish, reserving the cooking water. Preheat the grill (broiler) to medium with a shelf 15cm/6in below it. Bring the reserved fish cooking water to the boil and cook the potatoes for about 8 minutes. Do not add extra salt.

4 Remove the skin and bones and flake the fish. Spoon one-third of the tomato sauce into a flameproof casserole, top with the potatoes, fish and remaining sauce. Combine the breadcrumbs and parsley and sprinkle over. Heat the dish through under a grill for 10 minutes.

Sea Bass in Vine Leaves: *Energy 180kcal/750kJ; Protein 19.9g; carbohydrate 1.2g, of which sugars 1.1g; Fat 8.1g, of which saturates 1.2g; Cholesterol 80mg; calcium 146mg; Fibre 1.6g; Sodium 76mg.*
Salt Cod with Potatoes: *Energy 321kcal/1358kJ; Protein 36.6g; Carbohydrate 28.6g, of which sugars 12.3g; Fat 7.5g, of which saturates 1.2g; Cholesterol 59mg; Calcium 73mg; Fibre 3.5g; Sodium 517mg.*

Baked Salt Cod with Potatoes and Olives

Salt cod has been a winter staple in Greece for generations. It is also popular during the period of Lent, and is often on the menu at restaurants on Fridays during this time.

Serves 4

675g/1½lb salt cod
800g/1¾lb potatoes, cut into wedges
1 large onion, finely chopped
2 or 3 garlic cloves, chopped
leaves from 1 fresh rosemary sprig
30ml/2 tbsp chopped fresh parsley
120ml/4fl oz/½ cup olive oil
400g/14oz can chopped tomatoes
15ml/1 tbsp tomato purée (paste)
300ml/½ pint/1¼ cups hot water
5ml/1 tsp dried oregano
12 black olives
ground black pepper

1 Soak the cod in cold water overnight, changing the water as often as possible during the evening and morning. The cod does not have to be skinned for this dish, but you may prefer to remove the skin, especially if there is a lot of it on the fish. You should also remove any obvious fins or bones. After soaking, drain the cod and cut it into 7cm/2¾in squares.

2 Preheat the oven to 180°C/350°F/Gas 4. Mix the potatoes, onion, garlic, rosemary and parsley in a large roasting pan with plenty of black pepper. Add the olive oil and toss until coated.

3 Arrange the pieces of cod between the coated vegetables and spread the tomatoes over the surface. Stir the tomato purée into the hot water until dissolved, then pour the mixture over the contents of the pan. Sprinkle the oregano on top. Bake for 1 hour, basting the fish and potatoes occasionally with the pan juices.

4 Remove the roasting pan from the oven, sprinkle the olives on top, and then cook for 30 minutes more, adding a little more hot water if the mixture seems to be drying out. Garnish with fresh parsley. Serve hot or cold.

Baked Cod with Garlic Mayonnaise

In the Mediterranean, cooks use a variety of firm, white fish for this dish. The mayonnaise is a version of aioli, the ever-popular sauce from Provence, which is traditionally served with fish stew as well as vegetables and crudités.

Serves 4

4 anchovy fillets
45ml/3 tbsp finely chopped fresh parsley
coarsely ground black pepper
90ml/6 tbsp olive oil
4 cod fillets, about 675g/1½lb total, skinned
30ml/2tbsp plain breadcrumbs

For the mayonnaise

2 garlic cloves, finely chopped
1 egg yolk
5ml/1 tsp Dijon mustard
150ml/6fl oz/¾ cup vegetable oil
salt and ground black pepper

1 To make the mayonnaise, mash the garlic to a paste using a pestle and mortar, then beat it with the egg yolk and mustard in a medium bowl. Add the oil, little by little, while whisking vigorously. When the mixture is thick and smooth, season with salt and pepper. Cover the bowl and keep cool.

2 Preheat the oven to 200°C/400°F/Gas 6. Chop the anchovy fillets very finely. Place in a small bowl with the parsley, and add pepper and 45ml/3 tbsp of the oil. Stir to a paste.

3 Place the cod fillets in one layer in an oiled baking dish. Spread the anchovy paste on the top of the cod fillets. Sprinkle with the breadcrumbs and the remaining oil. Bake the dish for 20–25 minutes, or until the breadcrumbs are golden. Serve hot with the garlic mayonnaise.

Cook's Tips

- *The mayonnaise can also be made in a food processor. Process the garlic until very fine then add the egg yolk and mustard. With the motor running, add the oil little by little through the tube until thick and smooth.*
- *Hake can be used instead of cod.*

Baked Salt Cod: *Energy 624kcal/2624kJ; Protein 61g; Carbohydrate 45.6g, of which sugars 12.9g; Fat 23.3g, of which saturates 3.5g; Cholesterol 100mg; Calcium 98mg; Fibre 4.8g; Sodium 918mg.*
Baked Cod: *Energy 637kcal/2642kJ; Protein 37.6g; Carbohydrate 10g, of which sugars 0.6g; Fat 49.8g, of which saturates 6.5g; Cholesterol 139mg; Calcium 71mg; Fibre 0.9g; Sodium 331mg.*

Monkfish with Pimiento and Cream Sauce

This recipe comes from Rioja country, where a special horned red pepper grows and is used to make a spicy sauce. In this version, red peppers are substituted, with a little chilli to add the required heat, while the addition of cream turns the sauce a mellow pink.

Serves 4

2 large red (bell) peppers
1kg/2¼lb monkfish tail or 900g/2lb halibut
plain (all-purpose) flour, for dusting
30ml/2 tbsp olive oil
25g/1oz/2 tbsp butter
120ml/4fl oz/½ cup white Rioja or dry vermouth
½ dried chilli, seeded and chopped
8 raw prawns (shrimp), in the shell
150ml/¼ pint/⅔ cup double (heavy) cream
salt and ground black pepper
fresh flat leaf parsley sprigs, to garnish

1 Preheat the grill (broiler) to high and cook the peppers for 8–12 minutes, turning occasionally, until they are soft, and the skins blackened. Leave, covered, until cool enough to handle. Skin and discard the stalks and seeds. Put the flesh into a blender, strain in the juices and purée.

2 Cut the monkfish or halibut into eight steaks (freeze the bones for stock). Season well and dust with flour.

3 Heat the oil and butter in a large frying pan and fry the fish for 3 minutes on each side. Remove to a warm dish.

4 Add the wine or vermouth and chilli to the pan and stir to deglaze the pan. Add the prawns and cook them briefly, then lift out and reserve.

5 Boil the sauce to reduce by half, then strain into a jug (pitcher). Add the cream to the pan and boil briefly to reduce. Return the sauce to the pan, stir in the puréed peppers and check the seasonings. Pour the sauce over the fish and serve garnished with the cooked prawns and parsley.

Monkfish Medallions with Thyme

Monkfish is found in the Mediterranean as well as the eastern Atlantic and has a sweet flesh that combines well with the distinctive flavours of the region.

Serves 4

500g/1¼lb monkfish fillet, preferably in one piece
45ml/3 tbsp extra virgin olive oil
75g/3oz/½ cup small black olives, pitted
1 large or 2 small tomatoes, seeded and diced
1 sprig fresh thyme, or 1 tsp dried thyme leaves
salt and ground black pepper
1 tbsp very finely chopped fresh parsley, to serve

1 Preheat the oven to 200°C/400°F/Gas 6. Remove the grey membrane from the monkfish, if necessary, and cut the fish into slices about 1.5cm/½in thick.

2 Heat a non-stick frying pan until quite hot, without any oil or fat. Sear the fish quickly on both sides in the hot pan and remove to a plate.

3 Spread 15ml/1 tbsp of the olive oil in the bottom of a shallow baking dish. Arrange the pieces of monkfish in a single layer over the base. Distribute the olives and diced tomato on top of the fish.

4 Sprinkle the dish with thyme, salt and pepper, and the remaining oil. Bake the monkfish for 10–12 minutes, until tender and cooked through.

5 To serve, divide the monkfish medallions between four warmed plates. Spoon on the vegetables and any cooking juices and sprinkle with the chopped parsley.

Cook's Tip
Test that the fish is cooked by parting the flesh of one piece with a sharp knife. It should be opaque all the way through. Don't overcook it.

Monkfish with Cream Sauce: *Energy 500kcal/2087kJ; Protein 49.7g; Carbohydrate 7.2g, of which sugars 6.9g; Fat 27.1g, of which saturates 13.7g; Cholesterol 140mg; Calcium 70mg; Fibre 1.4g; Sodium 113mg.*
Monkfish Medallions: *Energy 211kcal/882kJ; Protein 24.2g; Carbohydrate 1.3g, of which sugars 1.3g; Fat 12.2g, of which saturates 1.9g; Cholesterol 21mg; Calcium 40mg; Fibre 1.4g; Sodium 679mg.*

Monkfish with Tomato and Olive Sauce

This dish comes from the coast of Calabria in southern Italy. Garlic-flavoured mashed potato is delicious with this sauce.

Serves 4

450g/1lb mussels, scrubbed
a few fresh basil sprigs
2 garlic cloves, roughly chopped
300ml/½ pint/1¼ cups dry white wine
30ml/2 tbsp olive oil
15g/½oz/1 tbsp butter
900g/2 b monkfish fillets, skinned and cut into large chunks
1 onion, finely chopped
500g/1¼lb jar tomato sauce or passata
15ml/1tbsp sun-dried tomato paste
115g/4oz/1 cup stoned (pitted) black olives
salt and ground black pepper
extra fresh basil leaves, to garnish

1 Put the mussels in a flameproof casserole with some basil leaves, the garlic and the wine. Cover and bring to the boil. Lower the heat and simmer for 5 minutes, shaking the pan frequently. Remove the mussels, discarding any that fail to open. Strain the cooking liquid and reserve.

2 Heat the oil and butter until foaming, add the monkfish pieces and sauté them over a medium heat until they are just changing colour.

3 Add the onion to the juices in the casserole and cook gently for about 5 minutes, stirring frequently, until softened. Add the tomato sauce or passata, the reserved cooking liquid from the mussels and the tomato paste. Season with salt and pepper to taste. Bring to the boil, stirring, then lower the heat, cover and simmer for 20 minutes, stirring occasionally.

4 Pull off and discard the top shells from the mussels. Add the monkfish pieces to the tomato sauce and cook gently for 5 minutes. Gently stir in the olives and remaining basil, then taste for seasoning. Place the mussels in their half shells on top of the sauce, cover the pan and heat the mussels through for 1–2 minutes. Serve at once, garnished with basil.

Pan-fried Red Mullet with Anchovies, Basil and Citrus

Oranges and lemons grow all over Greece and are incorporated into many dishes. Here, they make a fine marinade and sauce to accompany red mullet.

Serves 4

4 red mullet, about 225g/8oz each, filleted, bones removed
90ml/6 tbsp olive oil
10 peppercorns, crushed
2 oranges, one peeled and sliced and one squeezed
1 lemon
30ml/2 tbsp plain (all-purpose) flour
15g/½ oz/1 tbsp butter
2 drained canned anchovies, chopped
60ml/4 tbsp shredded fresh basil
salt and ground black pepper

1 Place the fish fillets in a shallow dish in a single layer. Pour over the extra virgin olive oil and sprinkle the crushed peppercorns evenly over the top. Lay the orange slices on top, retaining some to garnish the finished dish. Cover the dish, and leave to marinate in the refrigerator for at least 4 hours.

2 Halve the lemon. Remove the skin and pith from one half and slice the flesh thinly. Cover and set aside. Squeeze the juice from the other half and reserve.

3 Lift the fillets out of the marinade and pat dry on kitchen paper. Cover and set aside the marinade and orange slices. Season the fish with salt and pepper. Sprinkle the plain flour on a large plate and coat each fillet, shaking off any excess flour.

4 Heat 45ml/3 tbsp of the marinade in a large pan and fry the fillets for 2 minutes on each side. Remove and keep warm. Wipe out the pan then melt the butter with any remaining marinade. Add the anchovies and cook them until completely softened. Stir in the orange and lemon juice, then check the seasoning, adding salt and freshly ground black pepper as necessary. Simmer until slightly reduced. Stir in the basil. Place the fish on a serving platter and pour over the sauce. Garnish with the reserved orange slices and the lemon slices.

Monkfish: *Energy 357kcal/1505kJ; Protein 42.7g; Carbohydrate 5.4g, of which sugars 5.1g; Fat 13.4g, of which saturates 3.6g; Cholesterol 53mg; Calcium 126mg; Fibre 1.8g; Sodium 1072mg.*
Red Mullet with Anchovies: *Energy 355kcal/1480kJ; Protein 23.4g; Carbohydrate 11g, of which sugars 5.2g; Fat 24.6g, of which saturates 4.4g; Cholesterol 9mg; Calcium 125mg; Fibre 1.3g; Sodium 198mg.*

Baked Red Mullet with Oranges

Oranges are so plentiful in some parts of Greece that they can be picked from trees growing in the streets. The aroma of orange zest pervades many of the Greeks' classic dishes and tempts diners into cafés and restaurants on the mainland and throughout the islands.

Serves 4

a few sprigs of fresh dill
4 large red mullet, total weight 1–1.2kg/2¼–2½lb, gutted and cleaned
2 large oranges, halved
½ lemon
60ml/4 tbsp extra virgin olive oil
30ml/2 tbsp pine nuts
salt

1 Place some fresh dill in the cavity of each fish and lay them in a baking dish, preferably one that can be taken straight to the table. Make sure that the fish are not packed too close together. Sprinkle more dill around the fish.

2 Set half an orange aside and squeeze the rest, along with the lemon. Mix the citrus juices with the olive oil, then pour the mixture over the fish.

3 Turn the fish over so that they are evenly coated in the marinade, then cover the dish and leave in a cool place for the fish to marinate for 1–2 hours, spooning the marinade over the fish occasionally.

4 Preheat the oven to 180°C/350°F/Gas 4. Slice the reserved half orange into thin rounds, then cut each round into quarters. Cover and set aside.

5 Sprinkle a little salt over each fish. Place two or three of the orange wedges over each fish. Bake for 20 minutes, then remove the dish from the oven, baste the fish with the juices and sprinkle the pine nuts over. Return the dish to the oven and bake for 10–15 minutes more.

6 Test the thickest fish to make sure that it is cooked thoroughly, then remove from the oven. You can transfer the fish to a serving platter, garnished with sprigs of fresh dill, or present them in the baking dish.

Grilled Red Mullet with Bay Leaves

Red mullet are called *salmonetes* – little salmon – in Spain because of their delicate, pale pink colour. They are simple to cook on a barbecue, resting them on bay leaves for flavour. Instead of a marinade, a drizzle of tangy dressing is added after cooking.

Serves 4

4 red mullet, about 225–275g/8–10oz each, cleaned and descaled if cooking under a grill (broiler)
olive oil, for brushing
fresh herb sprigs, such as fennel, dill, parsley, or thyme
2–3 dozen fresh or dried bay leaves

For the dressing

90ml/6 tbsp olive oil
6 garlic cloves, finely chopped
½ dried chilli, seeded and chopped
juice of ½ lemon
15ml/1 tbsp parsley

1 Prepare the barbecue or preheat the grill (broiler) with the shelf 15cm/6in from the heat source.

2 Brush each fish with oil and stuff the cavities with the herb sprigs. Brush the grill pan with oil and lay bay leaves across the cooking rack. Place the fish on top and cook for 15–20 minutes until cooked through, turning once.

3 To make the dressing, heat the olive oil in a small pan and fry the chopped garlic with the dried chilli. Add the lemon juice and strain the dressing into a jug (pitcher). Add the chopped parsley and stir to combine.

4 Serve the mullet on warmed plates, with the dressing drizzled over them.

Cook's Tip

Most red mullet are quite small, but the larger fish have a wonderful flavour if you can find them. If you are cooking them on the barbecue, they do not need to be scaled.

Baked Red Mullet: *Energy 344kcal/1434kJ; Protein 30.5g; Carbohydrate 5.4g, of which sugars 5.4g; Fat 22.5g, of which saturates 1.9g; Cholesterol 0mg; Calcium 137mg; Fibre 1.2g; Sodium 153mg.*
Grilled Red Mullet: *Energy 295kcal/1226kJ; Protein 24.3g; Carbohydrate 0.5g, of which sugars 0.1g; Fat 21.8g, of which saturates 2.4g; Cholesterol 0mg; Calcium 98mg; Fibre 0.3g; Sodium 126mg.*

Serrano-Wrapped Trout

Traditionally, the trout cooked in this manner would have been wild, caught in local mountain streams and stuffed and wrapped in locally cured ham. One of the beauties of this method is that the skins come off in one piece, leaving the succulent, moist flesh to be eaten with the crisped, salt ham.

Serves 4

4 brown or rainbow trout, about 250g/9oz each
16 thin slices Serrano ham, about 200g/7oz
50g/2oz/¼ cup melted butter, plus extra for greasing
salt and ground black pepper
buttered potatoes, to serve (optional)

1 Clean the fish and extend the belly cavity of each trout, cutting up one side of the backbone. Slip a knife behind the rib bones to loosen them (sometimes just flexing the fish makes the bones pop up). Snip these off from both sides with scissors, and season the fish well inside with salt and freshly ground black pepper.

2 Preheat the grill (broiler) to high, with a shelf in the top position. Line a baking tray with foil and butter it.

3 Working with the fish on the foil, fold a piece of ham into each belly. Use smaller or broken pieces of ham for this, and reserve the eight best slices.

4 Brush each trout with a little butter, seasoning the outside lightly with salt and pepper. Wrap two ham slices round each one, crossways, tucking the ends into the belly.

5 Grill (broil) the trout for 4 minutes, then carefully turn them over with the help of a metal spatula, rolling them across on their bellies so that the ham doesn't come loose, and grill for a further 4 minutes.

6 Serve the trout very hot, with any spare butter spooned over the top. Diners should open the trout on their plates, and eat them from the inside, pushing the flesh off the skin.

Whole Trout Baked in Paper with Green Olives

Baking fish like this in paper packets keeps in all the flavour and moisture.

Serves 4

4 medium trout, about 275g/10oz each, cleaned
5 tbsp olive oil
4 bay leaves
salt and ground black pepper
4 slices pancetta or bacon
60ml/4 tbsp chopped shallots
60ml/4 tbsp chopped fresh parsley
120ml/4fl oz/½ cup dry white wine
24 green olives, stoned (pitted)

1 Preheat the oven to 200°C/400°F/Gas 6. Wash the trout well inside and out in cold running water. Drain and pat dry with kitchen paper.

2 Lightly brush oil on to 4 pieces of baking parchment (parchment paper) each large enough to enclose a fish. Lay one fish on each piece of oiled paper. Place a bay leaf in each cavity, and sprinkle with salt and pepper.

3 Wrap a slice of pancetta or bacon around each fish. Sprinkle with 15ml/1 tbsp each of chopped shallots and parsley. Drizzle each fish with 15ml/1 tbsp olive oil and 30ml/2 tbsp white wine. Add 6 olives to each packet.

4 Close the paper loosely around the fish, rolling and crimping the edges together to seal them completely. Bake in the hot oven for 25 minutes. Place each parcel on an individual plate and open at the table.

Cook's Tip

This cooking method, known as en papillote *in French and* al cartoccio *in Italian, means that the food steams inside the sealed parcel, and all the delicious flavours are retained. It is especially suitable for delicate fish, but also ideal for meat such as chicken and veal, and vegetables, if a little liquid is added.*

Serrano Trout: *Energy 369kcal/1546kJ; Protein 48g; Carbohydrate 0.6g, of which sugars 0.6g; Fat 19.4g, of which saturates 8.8g; Cholesterol 216mg; Calcium 66mg; Fibre 0g; Sodium 821mg.*
Trout Baked in Paper: *Energy 479kcal/1996kJ; Protein 47.7g; Carbohydrate 1.4g, of which sugars 1g; Fat 29.2g, of which saturates 6.4g; Cholesterol 195mg; Calcium 92mg; Fibre 1.1g; Sodium 1170mg.*

Baked Trout with Rice, Tomatoes and Nuts

Trout is very popular in Spain and this is a modern recipe for *trucha rellena*, baked in foil with a rice stuffing in which sun-dried tomatoes have been used in place of the more traditional chillies.

Serves 4

2 fresh trout, about 500g/1¼lb each, filleted
75g/3oz/¾ cup mixed unsalted almonds, pine nuts or hazelnuts
25ml/1½ tbsp olive oil, plus extra for drizzling
1 small onion, finely chopped
10ml/2 tsp grated fresh root ginger
175g/6oz/1½ cups cooked white long grain rice
4 tomatoes, peeled and very finely chopped
4 sun-dried tomatoes in oil, drained and chopped
30ml/2 tbsp chopped fresh tarragon
2 fresh tarragon sprigs
salt and freshly ground black pepper
dressed green salad leaves, to serve

1 Preheat the oven to 190°C/375°F/Gas 5. Spread out the nuts in a shallow tin (pan) and bake for 3–4 minutes until golden brown, shaking the tin occasionally. Chop the nuts roughly.

2 Heat the olive oil in a small frying pan and fry the onion for 3–4 minutes until soft and translucent. Stir in the grated ginger, cook for a further 1 minute, then spoon into a mixing bowl.

3 Stir the rice, chopped tomatoes, sun-dried tomatoes, toasted nuts and tarragon into the onion mixture. Season the stuffing well with salt and ground black pepper.

4 Place the trout on individual large pieces of oiled foil and spoon the stuffing into the cavities. Add a sprig of tarragon and a little olive oil or oil from the sun-dried tomatoes to each.

5 Fold the foil over to enclose each trout completely, and put the parcels in a large roasting pan. Bake for about 20 minutes or until the fish is just tender. Cut the fish into thick slices. Serve with the salad leaves.

Trout and Prosciutto Risotto Rolls

Risotto is a fine match for the robust flavour of these trout rolls.

Serves 4

4 trout fillets, skinned
4 slices prosciutto
caper berries, to garnish

For the risotto

30ml/2 tbsp olive oil
8 large raw prawns (shrimp), peeled and deveined
1 onion, chopped
225g/8oz/generous 1 cup risotto rice
about 105ml/7 tbsp white wine
about 750ml/1¼ pints/3 cups simmering fish or chicken stock
15g/½oz/¼ cup dried porcini or chanterelle mushrooms, soaked for 10 minutes in warm water to cover
salt and ground black pepper

1 To make the risotto, heat the oil in a heavy pan and cook the prawns very briefly until flecked with pink. Lift out using a slotted spoon and transfer to a plate. Keep warm. Add the chopped onion to the pan and cook gently for 3–4 minutes, or until soft. Add the rice and stir for 3–4 minutes to coat in the oil. Add 75ml/5 tbsp of the wine and then the stock, a little at a time, stirring over a gentle heat and allowing the rice to absorb the liquid before adding more.

2 Drain the mushrooms, reserving the liquid, and cut the larger ones in half. Towards the end of cooking, stir the mushrooms into the risotto with 15ml/1 tbsp of the reserved liquid. Season to taste with salt and pepper. When the rice is *al dente*, remove from the heat and stir in the prawns. Preheat the oven to 190°C/375°F/Gas 5. Grease an ovenproof dish and set aside.

3 Take a trout fillet, place a spoonful of risotto at one end and roll up. Wrap each fillet in a slice of prosciutto and place in the prepared dish. Spoon any remaining risotto around the fish rolls and sprinkle over the remaining wine. Cover loosely with foil and bake for 15–20 minutes, or until the fish is cooked.

4 Spoon the risotto on to a warmed serving platter, arrange the trout rolls on top and garnish the dish with caper berries. Serve immediately.

Baked Trout with Rice: *Energy 501kcal/2094kJ; Protein 46g; Carbohydrate 27.8g, of which sugars 5g; Fat 22.8g, of which saturates 3.3g; Cholesterol 160mg; Calcium 144mg; Fibre 3.2g; Sodium 161mg.*
Risotto Rolls: *Energy 397kcal/1662kJ; Protein 33g; Carbohydrate 43.6g, of which sugars 1.1g; Fat 7.6g, of which saturates 0.3g; Cholesterol 29mg; Calcium 37mg; Fibre 0.2g; Sodium 202mg.*

Marinated Sardines

The Arabs invented marinades as a means of preserving poultry, meat and game. In Spain this method was enthusiastically adopted as a means of preserving fish fresh. The spice gives a delicious lift to the fish.

Serves 2–4

12–16 sardines, cleaned
seasoned plain (all-purpose) flour, for dusting
30ml/2 tbsp olive oil
roasted red onion, green (bell) pepper and tomatoes, to garnish

For the marinade

90ml/6 tbsp olive oil
1 onion, sliced
1 garlic clove, crushed
3–4 bay leaves
2 cloves
1 dried red chilli, seeded and chopped
5ml/1 tsp paprika
120ml/4fl oz/½ cup wine or sherry vinegar
120ml/4fl oz/½ cup white wine
salt and ground black pepper

1 Using a sharp knife, cut the heads off the sardines and split along the belly. Turn the fish over so that the backbone is uppermost. Press down along the backbone to loosen it, then carefully lift it out with as many little bones as possible. Close the sardines up again and dust them with seasoned flour.

2 Heat the olive oil in a frying pan and fry the sardines for 2–3 minutes on each side. Transfer the fish to a plate and allow to cool, then pack them in a single layer in a large shallow dish.

3 To make the marinade, add the olive oil to the oil remaining in the frying pan. Fry the onion with the garlic gently for 5–10 minutes until soft and translucent, stirring occasionally. Add the bay leaves, cloves, chilli and paprika, with pepper to taste. Fry, stirring frequently, for another 1–2 minutes.

4 Stir in the vinegar, wine and a little salt. Allow to bubble up, then pour over the sardines. The marinade should cover the fish completely. When the fish is cool, cover and chill overnight or for up to 3 days. Serve the sardines and their marinade, garnished with the onion, pepper and tomatoes.

Grilled Fresh Sardines

Fresh sardines are quite different in taste and consistency from those canned in oil. They are excellent simply grilled or cooked on the barbecue and served with wedges of zesty lemon.

Serves 4–6

900g/2lb very fresh sardines, gutted and with heads removed
olive oil, for brushing
salt and ground black pepper
3 tbsp chopped fresh parsley, to serve
lemon wedges, to garnish

1 Preheat the grill (broiler) or prepare a barbecue. Rinse the sardines in water and pat dry with kitchen paper.

2 Brush the sardines lightly with olive oil and sprinkle generously with salt and pepper. Place the sardines in one layer on the grill pan or barbecue rack and cook for 3–4 minutes.

3 Turn and cook for 3–4 minutes more, or until the skin begins to brown. Serve immediately, sprinkled with parsley and garnished with lemon wedges.

Cook's Tip

Sardines are ideal for grilling because they contain plenty of oil, which keeps the flesh from drying out. They are also extremely nutritious as they are rich in omega-3 fatty acids.

Marinated Sardines: *Energy 242kcal/1004kJ; Protein 15.8g; Carbohydrate 1.7g, of which sugars 0.9g; Fat 18.1g, of which saturates 3.6g; Cholesterol 0mg; Calcium 70mg; Fibre 0.2g; Sodium 92mg.*
Grilled Sardines: *Energy 214kcal/893kJ; Protein 23.4g; Carbohydrate 0.2g, of which sugars 0.2g; Fat 13.2g, of which saturates 3.2g; Cholesterol 0mg; Calcium 131mg; Fibre 0.4g; Sodium 130mg.*

Pan-Fried Sole with Lemon and Capers

Several species of flat fish are caught in the Mediterranean and they are most commonly simply fried and served with lemon wedges to squeeze over the top. Intensely flavoured capers, which grow extensively in the Balearic Islands, make a pleasant tangy addition to the very simple and quickly made sauce in this recipe.

Serves 2

30–45ml/2–3 tbsp plain (all-purpose) flour
4 sole, plaice or flounder fillets, or 2 whole small flat fish
45ml/3 tbsp olive oil
25g/1oz/2 tbsp butter
60ml/4 tbsp lemon juice
30ml/2 tbsp pickled capers, drained
salt and ground black pepper
fresh flat leaf parsley, to garnish
lemon wedges, to serve

1 Sift the flour on to a plate and season well with salt and ground black pepper. Dip the fish fillets into the flour, to coat evenly on both sides.

2 Heat the oil and butter in a large shallow pan until foaming. Add the fish fillets and fry over a medium heat for 2–3 minutes on each side.

3 Lift out the fillets carefully with a metal spatula and place them on a warmed serving platter. Season with salt and freshly ground black pepper.

4 Add the lemon juice and capers to the pan, heat through and pour over the fish. Garnish with parsley and serve at once with lemon wedges.

Cook's Tip

This is a flavourful, and very quick way to prepare any small flat fish, or fillets of any white fish. The delicate flavour is enhanced by the tangy lemon juice and capers without being overwhelmed by them.

Sole Goujons with Lime Mayonnaise

The sole is a most delicious and highly valued fish. This simple French dish can be rustled up very quickly making an excellent light lunch or supper. If you cannot find a lime, use a lemon instead.

Serves 4

200ml/7fl oz/⅞ cup good-quality mayonnaise
1 small garlic clove, crushed
10ml/2 tsp capers, rinsed and chopped
10ml/2 tsp chopped gherkins
finely grated rind of ½ lime
10ml/2 tsp lime juice
15ml/1 tbsp chopped fresh coriander
675g/1½lb sole fillets, skinned
2 eggs, beaten
115g/4oz/2 cups fresh white breadcrumbs
oil, for deep-frying
salt and ground black pepper
lime wedges, to serve

1 To make the lime mayonnaise, mix together the mayonnaise, garlic, capers, gherkins, lime rind and juice and chopped coriander. Season to taste with salt and pepper. Transfer to a serving bowl and chill until required.

2 Cut the sole fillets into finger-length strips. Dip into the beaten egg, then into the breadcrumbs.

3 Heat the oil in a large pan or deep fryer to 180°C/350°F. Add the fish in batches and fry until golden brown and crisp. Drain on kitchen paper.

4 Pile the goujons on to warmed serving plates and serve them with the lime wedges for squeezing over. Hand round the sauce separately.

Cook's Tip

Fillets of the true sole, known in Britain as Dover sole, make the best goujons. Several other species of flat fish can also be used for the dish, including lemon sole and flounder, and will give a satisfactory result.

__Pan-Fried Sole:__ Energy 425kcal/1773kJ; Protein 34.2g; Carbohydrate 5.9g, of which sugars 0.2g; Fat 29.7g, of which saturates 9.3g; Cholesterol 111mg; Calcium 103mg; Fibre 0.3g; Sodium 316mg.
__Sole Goujons:__ Energy 978kcal/4047kJ; Protein 26.8g; Carbohydrate 25.2g, of which sugars 2.4g; Fat 86.3g, of which saturates 11.1g; Cholesterol 127mg; Calcium 87mg; Fibre 0.1g; Sodium 546mg.

Grilled Swordfish Skewers

Sea-fresh swordfish, often sold in Greek fish markets, is perfect for making these delicious *souvlakia*.

Serves 4

2 red onions, quartered
2 red or green (bell) peppers, quartered
20–24 thick cubes of swordfish, 675–800g/1½–1¾lb in total
75ml/5 tbsp extra virgin olive oil
1 garlic clove, crushed
large pinch of dried oregano
salt and freshly ground black pepper
lemon wedges, to garnish

1 Carefully separate the onion quarters into pieces each composed of two or three layers. Slice each pepper quarter in half widthways, or into thirds if they are very large.

2 Assemble the *souvlakia* by threading five or six pieces of swordfish on to each of four long skewers, alternating with pieces of pepper and onion. Lay them across a grill (broiler) pan or roasting pan.

3 Whisk the olive oil, garlic and oregano together and season to taste. Brush the *souvlakia* on all sides with the sauce.

4 Preheat a hot grill or prepare a barbecue. Cook the *souvlakia* for 8–10 minutes, turning the skewers several times, until the fish is cooked and the peppers and onions have begun to scorch around the edges. Every time you turn the skewers, brush them with the basting sauce to intensify the flavours.

5 Serve the *souvlakia* immediately, garnished with lemon wedges. Serve with a salad of cucumber, red onion and olives.

Cook's Tip

Many fishmongers will prepare and cube the swordfish for you. The cubes should be fairly big, about 5cm/2in square, as they shrink during cooking. If they are larger than this you may need to increase the cooking time slightly to ensure that the fish is cooked through. If in doubt, cut a large cube open to check.

Stuffed Swordfish Rolls

This is a very tasty dish, with strong flavours from the tomato, olive and caper sauce and the salty Pecorino cheese.

Serves 4

30ml/2 tbsp olive oil
1 small onion, finely chopped
1 celery stick, finely chopped
450g/1lb ripe Italian plum tomatoes, chopped
115g/4oz stoned (pitted) green olives, half chopped, half whole
45ml/3 tbsp drained bottled capers
4 large swordfish steaks, each about 1cm/½in thick and 115g/4oz in weight
1 egg
50g/2oz/⅔ cup grated Pecorino cheese
25g/1oz/½ cup fresh white breadcrumbs
salt and ground black pepper
sprigs of fresh parsley, to garnish

1 Heat the oil in a large heavy-based frying pan. Add the onion and celery and cook gently for about 3 minutes, stirring frequently. Stir in the tomatoes, olives and capers, with salt and pepper to taste. Bring to the boil, then lower the heat, cover and simmer for about 15 minutes. Stir occasionally and add a little water if the sauce becomes too thick.

2 Remove the fish skin and place each steak between two sheets of clear film. Pound lightly with a rolling pin until each steak is reduced to about 5mm/¼in thick.

3 Beat the egg in a bowl and add the cheese, breadcrumbs and a few spoonfuls of the sauce. Stir well to mix to a moist stuffing. Spread one-quarter of the stuffing over each swordfish steak, then roll up into a sausage shape. Secure with wooden cocktail sticks (toothpicks).

4 Add the rolls to the sauce in the pan and bring to the boil. Lower the heat, cover and simmer for about 30 minutes, turning once. Add a little water as the sauce reduces.

5 Remove the rolls from the sauce and discard the cocktail sticks. Place on warmed dinner plates and spoon the sauce over and around. Garnish with the parsley and serve hot.

Swordfish Skewers: *Energy 322kcal/1345kJ; Protein 32.5g; Carbohydrate 13.5g, of which sugars 11g; Fat 15.7g, of which saturates 2.8g; Cholesterol 69mg; Calcium 39mg; Fibre 2.8g; Sodium 226mg.*
Swordfish Rolls: *Energy 327kcal/1364kJ; Protein 29.2g; Carbohydrate 9.6g, of which sugars 4.6g; Fat 19.4g, of which saturates 5.4g; Cholesterol 107mg; Calcium 202mg; Fibre 2.4g; Sodium 1013mg.*

Red Snapper with Chilli, Gin and Ginger Sauce

A whole baked fish always looks impressive. Gin transforms the cooking juices into a superb sauce.

Serves 4

1.5kg/3–3½lb red snapper
30ml/2 tbsp sunflower oil
1 onion, chopped
2 garlic cloves, crushed
50g/2oz/¾ cup button (white) mushrooms, sliced
5ml/1 tsp ground coriander
15ml/1 tbsp chopped fresh parsley
30ml/2 tbsp grated fresh ginger
2 fresh red chillies, seeded and sliced
15ml/1 tbsp cornflour (cornstarch)
45ml/3 tbsp gin
300ml/½ pint/1¼ cups chicken or vegetable stock
salt and ground black pepper

For the garnish

15ml/1 tbsp sunflower oil
6 garlic cloves, sliced
1 lettuce heart, finely shredded

1 Preheat the oven to 190°C/375°F/Gas 5. Grease a flameproof dish large enough to hold the fish. Clean the fish and make several diagonal cuts on one side.

2 Heat the oil and fry the onion, garlic and mushrooms for 2–3 minutes. Stir in the ground coriander and chopped parsley. Season with salt and pepper. Stuff the fish with the mushroom mixture and place the dish. Pour in enough cold water to cover the bottom. Sprinkle the ginger and chillies over, then cover with foil and bake for 30–40 minutes, basting occasionally. Remove the foil for the last 10 minutes. Lift the snapper on to a serving dish and keep hot. Tip the cooking juices into a pan.

3 Mix the cornflour with the gin and stir into the juices. Pour in the stock. Bring to the boil, reduce the heat and simmer for 3–4 minutes, stirring, until the sauce thickens. Taste for seasoning, then pour into a sauceboat and keep hot.

4 To make the garnish, heat the oil and stir-fry the garlic and lettuce over a high heat until crisp. Spoon the garnish alongside the snapper and serve with the sauce.

Baked Fish in the Style of Spetses

All kinds of fish are prepared in this way on the tiny Greek island of Spetses. Serve with a fresh salad, or with little boiled potatoes and garlicky green beans.

Serves 4

4 cod or hake steaks
2–3 sprigs of fresh flat leaf parsley
4 slices white bread, toasted, then crumbed in a food processor
salt and ground black pepper

For the sauce

75–90ml/5–6 tbsp extra virgin olive oil
175ml/6fl oz/¾ cup white wine
2 garlic cloves, crushed
60ml/4 tbsp finely chopped flat leaf parsley
1 fresh red or green chilli, seeded and finely chopped
400g/14oz ripe tomatoes, peeled and finely diced

1 Mix all the sauce ingredients in a bowl, and add some salt and pepper. Set the mixture aside.

2 Preheat the oven to 190°C/375°F/Gas 5. Rinse the fish steaks and pat them dry with kitchen paper. Place the steaks in a single layer in an oiled baking dish and sprinkle over the parsley. Season with salt and pepper.

3 Spoon the sauce over the fish, distributing it evenly over each steak. Then sprinkle over half of the breadcrumbs, again evenly covering each steak. Bake for 10 minutes, then baste with the juices in the dish, trying not to disturb the breadcrumbs.

4 Sprinkle with the remaining breadcrumbs, then bake for a further 10–15 minutes.

Variation

If you like, use two whole fish, such as sea bass or grey mullet, total weight about 1kg/2¼lb. Rinse thoroughly inside and out, pat dry, then tuck the parsley sprigs inside. Add the sauce and breadcumbs as above. Bake for 15 minutes, then turn both fish over carefully, and bake for 20–25 minutes more.

Red Snapper: *Energy 409kcal/1706kJ; Protein 31.6g; Carbohydrate 14.5g, of which sugars 12.8g; Fat 25.4g, of which saturates 3.9g; Cholesterol 56mg; Calcium 113mg; Fibre 3.6g; Sodium 973mg.*
Baked Fish: *Energy 362kcal/1510kJ; Protein 31g; Carbohydrate 13.1g, of which sugars 3.7g; Fat 17.9g, of which saturates 2.7g; Cholesterol 36mg; Calcium 49mg; Fibre 1.3g; Sodium 274mg.*

Mediterranean Baked Fish

This fish bake, known as *poisson au souquet*, is said to have originated with the fishermen on the Côte d'Azur, who would cook the last of their catch for their lunch in the still-warm baker's oven.

Serves 4

3 potatoes
2 onions, halved and sliced
30ml/2 tbsp olive oil, plus extra for greasing and drizzling
2 garlic cloves, very finely chopped
675g/1½ lb thick skinless fish fillets, such as turbot or sea bass
1 bay leaf
1 thyme sprig
3 tomatoes, peeled and thinly sliced
30ml/2 tbsp orange juice
60ml/4 tbsp dry white wine
2.5ml/½ tsp saffron strands, steeped in 60ml/4 tbsp boiling water
salt and ground black pepper

1 Cook the potatoes in boiling salted water for 15 minutes, then drain. When the potatoes are cool enough to handle, peel off the skins and slice the potatoes thinly.

2 Meanwhile, in a heavy-based frying pan, fry the onions in the oil over a medium-low heat for about 10 minutes, stirring frequently. Add the garlic and continue cooking for a few minutes until the onions are soft and golden.

3 Preheat the oven to 190°C/375°F/Gas 5. Oil a 2 litre/3⅓ pint/8 cup baking dish and cover the base with a layer of half of the cooked potato slices. Cover with half the onions and season well with salt and black pepper.

4 Place the fish fillets on top of the vegetables and tuck the herbs in between them. Top with the tomato slices and then the remaining onions. Finish with a second layer of potatoes, arranging them neatly.

5 Pour over the orange juice, white wine and saffron liquid, season with salt and black pepper and drizzle a little extra olive oil on top. Bake the fish uncovered for about 30 minutes, until the potatoes are tender and the fish is cooked.

Fish Parcels

All the flavours of the fish and other ingredients are retained when they are sealed in a foil parcel, which also helps to keep the flesh moist and succulent. Sea bass is particularly good for this recipe. Adult fish can be very large, but many smaller fish are now caught and will serve one person. You could also use small whole trout or any firm-textured white fish fillet such as cod or haddock. Serve the dish with chunks of good crusty bread to mop up the juices.

Serves 4

4 pieces sea bass fillet or 4 whole small sea bass, about 450g/1lb each
oil, for brushing
2 shallots, thinly sliced
1 garlic clove, chopped
15ml/1 tbsp capers
6 sun-dried tomatoes, finely chopped
4 black olives, stoned (pitted) and thinly sliced
grated rind and juice of 1 lemon
5ml/1 tsp paprika
salt and ground black pepper
a few sprigs of fresh parsley, to garnish
crusty bread, to serve

1 Preheat the oven to 200°C/400°F/Gas 6. Clean the fish, if whole. Cut four large squares of double-thickness foil, large enough to enclose the fish. Brush each square with a little oil.

2 Place a piece of fish in the centre of each piece of foil and season well with salt and freshly ground black pepper.

3 Sprinkle over the shallots, garlic, capers, tomatoes, olives and grated lemon rind. Sprinkle with the lemon juice and paprika.

4 Fold the foil over loosely, sealing the edges. Bake in the preheated oven for 15–20 minutes. Remove the foil and serve garnished with parsley.

Cook's Tip

If you prefer not to make individual parcels, lay the fish in a well-oiled baking dish, scatter the other ingredients over them and cover the dish tightly with foil.

Baked Fish: *Energy 342kcal/1440kJ; Protein 35.1g; Carbohydrate 33.1g, of which sugars 11.7g; Fat 7.5g, of which saturates 1.2g; Cholesterol 78mg; Calcium 61mg; Fibre 3.8g; Sodium 127mg.*
Fish Parcels: *Energy 343Kcal/1,441kJ; Protein 63.2g; Carbohydrate 2g, of which sugars 1.6g; Fat 9.1g, of which saturates 1.5g; Cholesterol 260mg; Calcium 433mg; Fibre 0.7g; Sodium 396mg.*

Hake with Mussels

With chunky, creamy white flesh, hake is extremely popular in Spain, but cod and haddock cutlets will work just as well in this tasty Spanish-style dish, with its delicious sauce containing both wine and sherry.

Serves

30ml/2 tbsp olive oil
25g/1oz/2 tbsp butter
1 onion, chopped
3 garlic cloves, crushed
15ml/1 tbsp plain (all-purpose) flour
2.5ml/½ tsp paprika
4 hake cutlets, about 175g/6oz each
225g/8oz French beans, cut into 2.5cm/1in lengths
350ml/12fl oz/1½ cups fish stock
150ml/¼ pint/⅔ cup dry white wine
30ml/2 tbsp dry sherry
16–20 mussels, cleaned
45ml/3 tbsp chopped fresh parsley
salt and ground black pepper
crusty bread, to serve

1 Heat the oil and butter in a frying pan, add the onion and cook for 5 minutes, until softened. Add the crushed garlic and cook for a further 1 minute.

2 Mix together the plain flour and paprika, then lightly dust this mixture over the hake cutlets.

3 Push the onion and garlic to one side of the frying pan, then add the hake to the pan and fry until golden on both sides.

4 Stir in the French beans, fish stock, white wine and sherry, and season to taste. Bring to the boil and cook the fish over a low heat for about 2 minutes.

5 Discard any mussels that remain open when tapped. Add the mussels and parsley to the pan, cover and cook for 8 minutes until the mussels have all opened. Discard any shellfish that are not open after cooking.

6 Serve the hake in warmed, shallow soup plates with plenty of crusty bread.

Hake and Clams with Salsa Verde

As the clams in this dish bake, they open and add their delicious juices to the wine and parsley sauce.

Serves 4

4 hake steaks, about 2cm/¾in thick
50g/2oz/½ cup plain (all-purpose) flour, for dusting, plus 30ml/2 tbsp
60ml/4 tbsp olive oil
15ml/1 tbsp lemon juice
1 small onion, finely chopped
4 garlic cloves, finely chopped
150ml/¼ pint/⅔ cup fish stock
150ml/¼ pint/⅔ cup white wine
90ml/6 tbsp chopped fresh parsley
75g/3oz/¾ cup frozen petits pois
16 fresh clams, cleaned
salt and ground black pepper

1 Preheat the oven to 180°C/350°F/Gas 4. Season the fish, then dust with flour. Heat half the oil in a large pan, add the fish and fry for 1 minute on each side. Transfer to an ovenproof dish and sprinkle with the lemon juice.

2 Heat the remaining oil in a clean pan and fry the onion and garlic, stirring, until soft. Stir in the 30ml/2 tbsp flour and cook for about 1 minute.

3 Slowly add the stock and wine to the pan, stirring until thickened. Add 75ml/5 tbsp of the parsley and the petits pois to the sauce and season with plenty of salt and pepper.

4 Pour the sauce over the fish, and bake for 15–20 minutes, adding the clams 3–4 minutes before the end of the cooking time. Discard any clams that do not open once cooked, then sprinkle the fish with with the remaining parsley and serve.

Cook's Tip

To make fish stock, put 450g/1lb fish bones, head and skin in a large pan with 1 sliced onion, 1 sliced carrot, ½ sliced celery stalk, 3–4 thick parsley stalks, 1 bay leaf, 10ml/2 tsp lemon juice or wine vinegar and 175ml/6fl oz/¾ cup dry white wine or vermouth. Bring to the boil, then reduce the heat and simmer for 30 minutes. Strain.

Hake with Mussels: *Energy 1351kcal/5643kJ; Protein 157.3g; Carbohydrate 13.3g, of which sugars 9.9g; Fat 62.2g, of which saturates 19g; Cholesterol 274mg; Calcium 507mg; Fibre 5.8g; Sodium 1176mg.*
Hake and Clams: *Energy 347kcal/1449kJ; Protein 34.2g; Carbohydrate 13.2g, of which sugars 1.4g; Fat 15.2g, of which saturates 2.2g; Cholesterol 51mg; Calcium 109mg; Fibre 2.4g; Sodium 460mg.*

Fish Plaki

Different areas of Greece have distinct versions of this simple dish, which makes the most of the local fresh fish. A whole fish can be used instead of a large fillet, if you prefer. The recipe also works well with sea bass, bream, John Dory, turbot, halibut or brill.

Serves 4

150ml/¼ pint/⅔ cup olive oil
2 large Spanish onions, chopped
2 celery sticks, chopped
4 plump garlic cloves, chopped
4 potatoes, peeled and diced
4 carrots, cut into small dice
15ml/1 tbsp caster (superfine) sugar
2 bay leaves
1 thick middle-cut fillet of grouper or cod, about 1kg/2¼lb
16–20 large black olives
4 large ripe tomatoes, peeled, seeded and chopped
150ml/¼ pint/⅔ cup dry white wine or vermouth
salt and ground black pepper
herb leaves, to garnish
saffron rice, to serve

1 Preheat the oven to 190°C/375°F/Gas 5. Heat the oil in a large frying pan, add the onions and celery and sauté until transparent. Add the garlic and cook for 2 minutes more. Stir in the potatoes and carrots and fry for about 5 minutes, stirring occasionally. Sprinkle with the sugar and season to taste.

2 Grease a large baking dish, slightly larger than the fish. Spoon the vegetable mixture into the dish, and tuck in the bay leaves. Season the fish and lay it on the bed of vegetables, skin-side up. Sprinkle the olives evenly around the edge. Spread the chopped tomatoes over the fish, pour over the wine or vermouth and season with salt and freshly ground black pepper.

3 Bake for 30–40 minutes, until the fish is cooked through. The type of fish you are using and the thickness of the fillet may affect the cooking time, so test the thickest part of the fish to ensure that it is cooked through. If you are using a whole fish, the cooking time will probably be longer.

4 Serve straight from the dish, garnished with herb leaves, such as fresh dill, chives and flat leaf parsley. Saffron rice would be the ideal accompaniment.

Fillets of Sea Bream in Filo Pastry

Each of these little parcels is a meal in itself and can be prepared several hours in advance, which makes the recipe ideal for entertaining. Serve the pastries with fennel braised with orange juice or a mixed leaf salad.

Serves 4

8 small waxy salad potatoes, preferably red-skinned
200g/7oz sorrel, stalks removed
30ml/2 tbsp extra virgin olive oil
16 filo pastry sheets, thawed if frozen
4 sea bream fillets, about 175g/6oz each, scaled but not skinned
50g/2oz/¼ cup butter, melted
120ml/4fl oz/½ cup fish stock
250ml/8fl oz/1 cup whipping cream
salt and ground black pepper
finely diced red (bell) pepper, to garnish

1 Preheat the oven to 200°C/400°F/Gas 6. Cook the potatoes in a pan of lightly salted boiling water for about 15–20 minutes, or until just tender. Drain and leave to cool. Set about half the sorrel leaves aside. Shred the remaining leaves by piling up 6 or 8 at a time, rolling them up like a fat cigar and slicing them with a sharp knife. Thinly slice the potatoes lengthways.

2 Brush a baking sheet with a little of the oil. Lay a sheet of filo pastry on the sheet, brush it with oil, then lay a second sheet crossways over the first. Repeat with two more sheets. Arrange a quarter of the sliced potatoes in the centre, season and add a quarter of the shredded sorrel. Lay a bream fillet on top, skin-side up. Season with salt and ground black pepper.

3 Loosely fold the filo pastry up and over to make a neat parcel, them repeat to make three more. Place the parcels on the baking sheet and brush with half the butter. Bake for about 20 minutes, or until the filo is puffed up and golden brown.

4 Meanwhile, make the sorrel sauce. Heat the remaining butter in a pan, add the reserved sorrel and cook gently for 3 minutes, stirring, until it wilts. Stir in the stock and cream. Heat almost to boiling point, stirring so that the sorrel breaks down. Season to taste and keep hot until the fish parcels are ready. Serve garnished with red pepper. Pass round the sauce separately.

Fish Plaki: Energy 557Kcal/2,322kJ; Protein 48.8g; Carbohydrate 24.3g, of which sugars 10.2g; Fat 27.3g, of which saturates 3.9g; Cholesterol 115mg; Calcium 74mg; Fibre 3.3g; Sodium 179mg.
Sea Bream in Filo Pastry: Energy 651kcal/2710kJ; Protein 35.8g; Carbohydrate 23.2g, of which sugars 3.3g; Fat 46.8g, of which saturates 23.2g; Cholesterol 159mg; Calcium 222mg; Fibre 2g; Sodium 359mg.

Filo-Wrapped Fish

The choice of fish can be varied according to what is freshest on the day of purchase. When working with filo pastry, keep it covered with clear film (plastic wrap) or a damp dish towel as much as possible. Once it is exposed to the air it dries out quickly, making it difficult to handle and cook properly.

Serves 3–4

about 130g/4½oz filo pastry (6–8 large sheets), thawed if frozen
about 30ml/2 tbsp olive oil, for brushing
450g/1lb salmon or cod steaks or fillets
550ml/18fl oz/2½ cups fresh tomato sauce (see Cook's Tip)

1 Preheat the oven to 200°C/400°F/Gas 6. Take a sheet of filo pastry, brush with a little olive oil and cover with a second sheet of pastry. Place a piece of fish on top of the pastry, towards the bottom edge, then top with 1–2 spoonfuls of the tomato sauce, spreading it in an even layer.

2 Roll the fish in the pastry, taking care to enclose the filling completely. Brush with a little olive oil. Arrange on a baking sheet and repeat with the remaining fish and pastry. You should have about half the sauce remaining, to serve with the fish.

3 Bake for 10–15 minutes, or until golden. Avoid opening the oven door before 10 minutes as the drop in temperature can stop the filo pastry from rising. Meanwhile, reheat the remaining sauce gently in a small pan. Serve the wrapped fish immediately with the remaining heated tomato sauce and a lightly dressed green or mixed salad.

Cook's Tip
To make the tomato sauce, fry 1 chopped onion and a crushed garlic clove in 15ml/1 tbsp oil until softened. Add a 400g/14oz can chopped tomatoes, 15ml/1 tbsp tomato purée (paste) and 15ml/1 tbsp chopped fresh herbs. Add a pinch of sugar and season to taste. Simmer for 20 minutes.

Bouillabaisse

Different variations of this French fish stew are found along the coast. Almost any fish can be used.

Serves 8

2.7kg/6lb white fish, such as sea bass, snapper or monkfish, filleted and skinned
45ml/3 tbsp extra virgin olive oil
grated rind of 1 orange
1 garlic clove, very finely chopped
pinch of saffron threads
30ml/2 tbsp pastis
1 small fennel bulb, finely chopped
1 large onion, finely chopped
2.4 litres/4 pints/10 cups well-flavoured fish stock
225g/8oz small new potatoes, sliced
900g/2lb large raw Mediterranean prawns (shrimp), peeled
croûtons, to serve

For the rouille

25g/1oz/⅔ cup soft white breadcrumbs
1–2 garlic cloves, very finely chopped
½ red pepper, roasted
5ml/1 tsp tomato purée (paste)
120ml/4fl oz/½ cup extra virgin olive oil

1 Cut the white fish fillets into serving pieces, place them in a bowl and mix with 30ml/2 tbsp of the olive oil, the orange rind, chopped garlic, saffron threads and pastis. Cover and chill.

2 To make the rouille, soak the breadcrumbs in cold water, then squeeze dry. Place the breadcrumbs in a food processor or blender with the chopped garlic, roasted red pepper and tomato purée and process until smooth. With the motor running, slowly pour the olive oil through the feed tube to make a thick, glossy sauce. Set aside while you cook the fish.

3 Heat the remaining 15ml/1 tbsp oil in a wide flameproof casserole over a medium heat. Cook the fennel and onion for about 5 minutes until the onion just softens, then add the stock. Bring to the boil, add the potatoes and cook for 5–7 minutes. Add the fish, starting with the thickest pieces and adding the thinner ones after 2–3 minutes. Add the prawns and continue to simmer very gently until all the fish and shellfish are cooked.

4 Transfer the fish and potatoes to a heated tureen and ladle the soup over. Serve with croûtons spread with the rouille.

Filo-Wrapped Fish: *Energy 382kcal/1601kJ; Protein 27.1g; Carbohydrate 27.9g, of which sugars 7.8g; Fat 18.8g, of which saturates 3.1g; Cholesterol 56mg; Calcium 103mg; Fibre 3.7g; Sodium 144mg.*
Bouillabaisse: *Energy 321kcal/1344kJ; Protein 46.8g; Carbohydrate 3.2g, of which sugars 2.8g; Fat 13g, of which saturates 1.9g; Cholesterol 115mg; Calcium 38mg; Fibre 1.3g; Sodium 163mg.*

Seafood Stew

"Soups" – really stews – of mixed fish and shellfish are specialities of many parts of the Mediterranean.

Serves 6–8

45ml/3 tbsp olive oil
1 medium onion, sliced
1 carrot, sliced
½ stalk celery, sliced
2 garlic cloves, chopped
400g/14oz can chopped tomatoes
225g/8oz fresh prawns (shrimp), peeled (reserve the shells)
450g/1lb white fish bones and heads, gills removed
1 bay leaf
1 sprig fresh thyme, or ¼ tsp dried thyme leaves
a few peppercorns
675g/1½lb mussels, scrubbed and debearded
450g/1lb small clams, scrubbed
250ml/8fl oz/1 cup white wine
900g/2lb mixed fish fillets, such as cod, monkfish, red snapper or hake, cut into chunks
45ml/3 tbsp finely chopped fresh parsley
salt and freshly ground black pepper
rounds of French bread, toasted, to serve

1 Heat the olive oil in a pan and cook the sliced onion slowly until soft. Stir in the carrot and celery, and cook gently for 5 minutes more. Add the garlic, tomatoes and 1 cup of water. Cook over a moderate heat for about 15 minutes. Purée in a food processor or pass through a food mill, and set aside.

2 Place the prawn shells in a large pan with the fish bones and heads. Add the herbs, peppercorns, and 750ml/1¼ pints/3 cups water. Simmer for 25 minutes, skimming off any scum. Strain and add to the tomato sauce. Season to taste.

3 Place the mussels and clams in a pan with the wine. Cover, and steam until all the shells have opened. (Discard any that do not open.) Lift out and set aside. Filter the cooking liquid through kitchen paper and add to the stock and tomato sauce.

4 Bring the sauce to the boil. Add the fish, and cook for 5 minutes. Add the prawns and boil for 3–4 minutes. Stir in the mussels and clams and cook for 2–3 minutes more. Transfer the stew to a warmed dish. Sprinkle with parsley, and serve with the toasted rounds of French bread.

Chunky Seafood Stew

This is a versatile Spanish stew in which many different combinations of fish and shellfish may be used. Choose whatever looks best on the day and only ever buy fish that is absolutely fresh.

Serves 6

45ml/3 tbsp olive oil
2 large onions, chopped
1 small green pepper, sliced
3 carrots, chopped
3 garlic cloves, crushed
30ml/2 tbsp tomato purée (paste)
2 × 400g/14oz cans chopped tomatoes
45ml/3 tbsp chopped fresh parsley
5ml/1 tsp fresh thyme
15ml/1 tbsp chopped fresh basil, or 5ml/1 tsp dried basil
120ml/4fl oz/½ cup dry white wine
450g/1lb raw prawns (shrimp), peeled and deveined, or cooked peeled prawns
1.5kg/3–3½lb mussels or clams, or a mixture of both, thoroughly cleaned
900g/2lb halibut or other firm, white fish fillets, cut into 5–7.5cm/2–3in pieces
350ml/12fl oz/1½ cups fish stock or water
salt and ground black pepper
chopped fresh herbs, to garnish

1 Heat the oil in a flameproof casserole. Add the chopped onions, green pepper, carrots and garlic and cook, stirring frequently, for about 10 minutes, until the vegetables are softened and beginning to colour.

2 Add the tomato purée, canned tomatoes, herbs and wine and stir well to combine. Bring to the boil then lower the heat and simmer for 20 minutes.

3 Add the raw prawns, if using, the mussels or clams, fish pieces and the stock or water. Season with salt and pepper.

4 Bring back to the boil, then simmer for 5–6 minutes, until the prawns turn pink, the fish flakes easily and the shells open. If using cooked prawns, add these for the last 2 minutes.

5 Ladle into large, warmed soup plates and serve garnished with a sprinkling of chopped fresh herbs.

Seafood Stew: Energy 385kcal/1629kJ; Protein 24g; Carbohydrate 54.4g, of which sugars 8.3g; Fat 5.5g, of which saturates 1.2g; Cholesterol 207mg; Calcium 61mg; Fibre 3.1g; Sodium 322mg.
Chunky Seafood Stew: Energy 2113kcal/8900kJ; Protein 331.4g; Carbohydrate 57.4g, of which sugars 54.5g; Fat 54.9g, of which saturates 8.7g; Cholesterol 1472mg; Calcium 1477mg; Fibre 16.7g; Sodium 2477mg.

Mackerel in Lemon Samfaina

Samfaina is a sauce from the east coast of Spain and the Costa Brava. It shares the same ingredients as ratatouille and is rather like a chunky vegetable stew. This version is particularly lemony, to offset the richness of the mackerel.

Serves 4

2 large mackerel, filleted, or 4 fillets
plain (all-purpose) flour, for dusting
30ml/2 tbsp olive oil
lemon wedges, if serving cold

For the samfaina sauce

1 large aubergine (eggplant)
60ml/4 tbsp olive oil
1 large onion, chopped
2 garlic cloves, finely chopped
1 large courgette (zucchini), sliced
1 red and 1 green (bell) pepper, cut into squares
800g/1¾lb ripe tomatoes, roughly chopped
1 bay leaf
salt and ground black pepper

1 To make the sauce, peel the aubergine, cut the flesh into cubes, sprinkle with salt and leave to stand in a colander for 30 minutes.

2 Heat half the oil in a flameproof casserole large enough to fit the fish. Fry the onion over a medium heat until it colours. Add the garlic, then the courgette and peppers and stir-fry. Add the tomatoes and bay leaf, partially cover and simmer gently, letting the tomatoes just soften.

3 Rinse the salt off the aubergine and squeeze dry in kitchen paper. Heat the remaining oil in a frying pan until smoking. Put in one handful of aubergine cubes, then the next, stirring and cooking over a high heat until the cubes are brown on all sides. Stir into the tomato sauce.

4 Cut each mackerel fillet into three, and dust the filleted side with flour. Heat the oil over a high heat and fry the fish, floured side down, for 3 minutes. Turn and cook for another 1 minute, then slip the fish into the sauce and simmer, covered, for 5 minutes. Serve immediately.

Variation
The fish can also be served cold. Present the mackerel skin-side up, surrounded by the vegetables, with lemon wedges.

Moroccan Fish Tagine

This spicy, aromatic dish proves just how exciting an ingredient fish can be. Serve it with couscous flavoured with chopped fresh mint.

Serves 8

1.3kg/3lb firm fish fillets, skinned and cut into 5cm/2in chunks
30ml/2 tbsp olive oil
4 onions, chopped
1 large aubergine (eggplant), cut into 1cm/½in cubes
2 courgettes (zucchini), cut into 1cm/½in cubes
400g/14oz can chopped tomatoes
400ml/14fl oz/1⅔ cups passata
200ml/7fl oz/scant 1 cup fish stock
1 preserved lemon, chopped
90g/3½oz/scant 1 cup pitted olives
60ml/4 tbsp chopped fresh coriander (cilantro)
salt and freshly ground black pepper
fresh coriander (cilantro) sprigs, to garnish

For the harissa

3 large fresh red chillies, seeded and chopped
3 garlic cloves, peeled
15ml/1 tbsp ground coriander
30ml/2 tbsp ground cumin
5ml/1 tsp ground cinnamon
grated rind of 1 lemon
30ml/2 tbsp sunflower oil

1 To make the harissa, whizz everything together in a blender or food processor to form a smooth paste. Set aside.

2 Put the chunks of fish in a wide bowl and add 30ml/2 tbsp of the harissa. Toss to coat all over, then cover and chill for at least 1 hour, or overnight.

3 Heat 15ml/1 tbsp of the oil in a shallow, heavy pan. Cook the onions gently for 10 minutes, or until golden brown. Stir in the remaining harissa, and cook, stirring occasionally, for 5 minutes.

4 Heat the remaining olive oil in a separate shallow pan. Add the aubergine cubes and cook for about 10 minutes, or until they are golden brown. Add the cubed courgettes and cook for a further 2 minutes.

5 Add the aubergines and courgettes to the onions, then stir in the chopped tomatoes, passata and fish stock. Bring to the boil, then reduce the heat and simmer for about 20 minutes.

Mackerel in Samfaina: Energy 621kcal/2591kJ; Protein 34.3g; Carbohydrate 32.4g, of which sugars 29.4g; Fat 40.6g, of which saturates 7.6g; Cholesterol 66mg; Calcium 134mg; Fibre 19.4g; Sodium 111mg.
Moroccan Fish Tagine: Energy 174kcal/735kJ; Protein 33.7g; Carbohydrate 6.1g, of which sugars 5.9g; Fat 1.8g, of which saturates 0.4g; Cholesterol 81mg; Calcium 32mg; Fibre 2.5g; Sodium 134mg.

Fresh Tuna and Tomato Stew

This is a deliciously simple Italian fish stew that relies on good basic ingredients. To make a complete Italian meal, serve the dish with polenta or pasta.

Serves 4

12 baby onions, peeled
900g/2lb ripe tomatoes
675g/1½lb fresh tuna
45ml/3 tbsp olive oil
2 garlic cloves, crushed
45ml/3 tbsp chopped fresh herbs
2 bay leaves
2.5ml/½tsp caster (superfine) sugar
30ml/2 tbsp sun-dried tomato purée (paste)
150ml/¼ pint/⅔ cup dry white wine
salt and ground black pepper
baby courgettes and fresh herbs, to garnish

1 Leave the onions whole and cook them in a pan of boiling water for 4–5 minutes until softened. Drain.

2 Plunge the tomatoes into boiling water for 30 seconds, then refresh them in cold water. Peel and chop roughly.

3 Cut the tuna into 2.5cm/1in chunks. Heat the olive oil in a large frying pan and quickly fry the tuna until browned. Drain.

4 Add the onions, tomatoes, garlic, chopped herbs, bay leaves, sugar, sun-dried tomato purée and wine and bring the mixture to the boil, breaking up the tomatoes with a wooden spoon as they cook.

5 Reduce the heat and simmer the stew gently for about 5 minutes. Add the cooked tuna chunks to the saucepan and cook for a further 5 minutes. Add salt and black pepper to taste, then serve the stew hot, garnished with baby courgettes and fresh herbs.

Cook's Tips

- *If you can't find very ripe and full-flavoured tomatoes for this dish, substitute two 400g/14oz cans of chopped tomatoes.*
- *Buy a thick piece of tuna to avoid overcooking the chunks.*

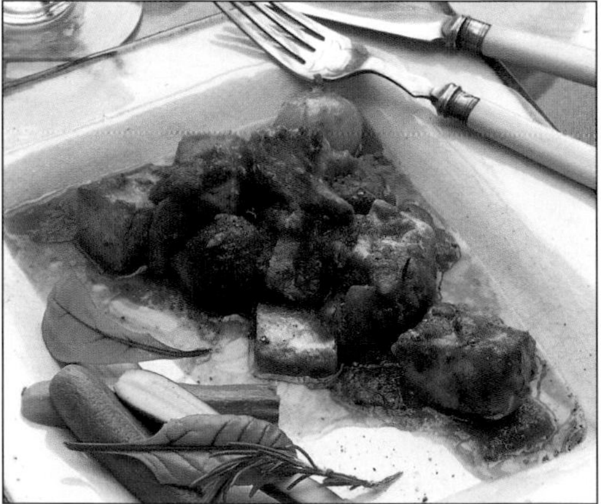

Spanish Seafood Casserole

The Spanish name of this dish, Zarzuela, means 'light musical comedy', reflecting the colour and variety of the stew, which is full of all sorts of fish and shellfish.

Serves 6

250g/9oz monkfish on the bone
1 gurnard, snapper or other whole white fish, about 350g/12oz
1 sole, plaice or flounder, about 500g/1¼lb, cleaned
60ml/4 tbsp olive oil
8 small squid, with tentacles
plain (all-purpose) flour, for dusting
30ml/2 tbsp anis spirit, such as Ricard or Pernod
450g/1lb mussels, cleaned
250ml/8fl oz/1 cup white wine
4 large scampi (extra large shrimp), with heads, uncooked
12 raw king prawns (jumbo shrimp), with heads
115g/4oz prawns (shrimp)
salt and ground black pepper
45ml/3 tbsp chopped fresh parsley, to garnish

For the stock

1 onion, chopped
1 celery stick, chopped
1 bay leaf

For the fish broth

30ml/2 tbsp oil
1 large onion, finely chopped
2 garlic cloves, finely chopped
500g/1¼lb ripe tomatoes, peeled, seeded and chopped
2 bay leaves
1 dried chilli, seeded and chopped
5ml/1 tsp paprika
pinch of saffron threads
salt and ground black pepper

1 Bone the fish, reserving the bones, and cut into portions. You should have about 500g/1¼lb white fish, both firm and soft. Salt the fish and reserve on a plate in the refrigerator. Put the onion, celery, bay leaf and the fish bones and heads in a pan, pour in 600ml/1 pint/2½ cups water, and bring to the boil, then simmer for about 30 minutes.

2 Heat the oil in a large flameproof casserole and fry the onion and garlic gently until soft. Add the tomatoes, bay leaves, dried chilli, paprika and crumbled saffron and cook gently.

3 To cook the fish and shellfish, heat the oil in a large frying pan. Put in the squid tentacles, face down, and cook for 45 seconds. Reserve. Flour and fry the monkfish and white fish for 3 minutes on each side, then the flat fish for 2 minutes on each side. Cut the squid bodies into rings and fry. Pour the anis into a ladle, flame it and pour over the fish in the pan. Remove the fish and reserve.

4 Strain the stock into the casserole and add the wine. Bring to a simmer. Add the mussels in two batches. Cover for 2 minutes to open, then transfer to a plate and remove the upper shells. Add the scampi and cook for about 8 minutes, then lift out. Cut with scissors along the underside from head to tail. Add the raw prawns for 3–4 minutes, then lift out and reserve.

5 About 20 minutes before serving, add the seafood to the broth in the following order, bringing the liquid to simmering each time: firm white fish, soft white fish, squid rings and pan juices, large shellfish, cooked shellfish, any small shelled prawns. Check the seasonings. Rearrange the soup with the best-looking shellfish and squid flowers on top. Scatter over the mussels, cover and leave to steam for 2 minutes. Garnish with parsley. Take the casserole to the table with a plate for shells.

Tuna and Tomato Stew: *Energy 393kcal/1648kJ; Protein 42.8g; Carbohydrate 13.8g, of which sugars 12.4g; Fat 16.8g, of which saturates 3.4g; Cholesterol 47mg; Calcium 64mg; Fibre 3.4g; Sodium 121mg.*
Spanish Seafood Casserole: *Energy 326kcal/1367kJ; Protein 34.8g; Carbohydrate 5.4g, of which sugars 3.4g; Fat 14.4g, of which saturates 2.3g; Cholesterol 248mg; Calcium 79mg; Fibre 1g; Sodium 264mg.*

Seafood Pizza

Here is a pizza that gives you the full flavour of the Mediterranean, ideal for a summer evening supper.

Serves 3-4

1 pizza base, 25–30cm/10–12in diameter
30 ml/2 tbsp olive oil
tomato sauce (see Cook's Tip)
400g/14oz bag frozen mixed cooked seafood (including mussels, prawns and squid), defrosted
3 garlic cloves
30 ml/2 tbsp chopped fresh parsley
30 ml/2 tbsp freshly grated Parmesan, to garnish

1 Preheat the oven to 220°C/425°F/Gas 7. Brush the pizza base with 15ml/l tbsp of the oil.

2 Spread over the tomato sauce. Bake for 10 minutes. Remove from the oven.

3 Pat the seafood dry using kitchen paper, then arrange on top. Chop the garlic and scatter over. Sprinkle over the parsley, then drizzle over the remaining oil.

4 Bake for a further 5–10 minutes until the seafood is warmed through and the base is crisp and golden. Sprinkle with Parmesan and serve immediately.

Cook's Tip

To make the tomato sauce, fry 1 chopped onion and a crushed garlic clove in 15ml/1 tbsp oil until softened. Add a 400g/14oz can chopped tomatoes, 15ml/1 tbsp tomato purée (paste) and 15ml/1 tbsp chopped fresh herbs. Add a pinch of sugar and season to taste. Simmer for 20 minutes.

Variation

If you prefer, this pizza can be made with mussels or prawns on their own, or any combination of your favourite seafood.

Salmon and Avocado Pizza

A mixture of smoked and fresh salmon makes a delicious pizza topping. Capers add piquancy.

Serves 3–4

150g/5oz salmon fillet
120ml/4fl oz/½ cup dry white wine
15ml/1 tbsp olive oil
400g/14oz can chopped tomatoes, drained
115g/4oz mozzarella, grated
1 small avocado, halved, stoned (pitted), peeled and cubed
10ml/2 tsp lemon juice
30ml/2 tbsp crème fraîche or sour cream
75g/3oz smoked salmon, cut into strips
15ml/1 tbsp drained bottled capers
30ml/2 tbsp chopped fresh chives, to garnish
freshly ground black pepper

For the pizza base

175g/6oz/1½ cups strong white (bread) flour
1.5ml/¼ tsp salt
5ml/1 tsp easy-blend (rapid-rise) dried yeast
120–150ml/4–5fl oz/½–⅔ cup lukewarm water
15ml/1 tbsp olive oil

1 To make the base, sift the flour and salt into a bowl, stir in the yeast, then make a well in the centre. Add the lukewarm water, then add the oil. Gradually incorporate the flour to make a soft dough. Knead until elastic, then place in a bowl, cover with clear film (plastic wrap) and leave in a warm place for about 1 hour. Knock back (punch down) the dough, knead it briefly, then roll it out to a 25–30cm/10–12in round and support on a baking sheet. Push up the edges to make a rim.

2 Preheat the oven to 220°C/425°F/Gas 7. Place the salmon in a pan, pour over the wine and season. Bring slowly to the boil, remove from the heat, cover and cool. Skin and flake the salmon, removing any bones.

3 Brush the pizza base with the oil and spread over the tomatoes. Sprinkle over 50g/2oz of the mozzarella. Bake for 10 minutes. Meanwhile, toss the avocado in the lemon juice. Dot teaspoonfuls of the crème fraîche over the pizza. Arrange the salmon, avocado, capers and remaining mozzarella on top. Season and bake for 10 minutes until crisp. Sprinkle with chives.

Seafood Pizza: Energy 343kcal/1444kJ; Protein 25.7g; Carbohydrate 36.2g, of which sugars 2.2g; Fat 11.7g, of which saturates 2.4g; Cholesterol 203mg; Calcium 238mg; Fibre 1.7g; Sodium 444mg.
Salmon and Avocado Pizza: Energy 451kcal/1884kJ; Protein 22g; Carbohydrate 31g, of which sugars 5.3g; Fat 25.3g, of which saturates 8.6g; Cholesterol 53mg; Calcium 193mg; Fibre 3.3g; Sodium 282mg.

Pasta with Fresh Sardine Sauce

In this classic Sicilian dish, sardines are combined with sultanas and pine nuts.

Serves 4

45ml/3 tbsp sultanas (golden raisins)
450g/1lb fresh sardines
90ml/6 tbsp breadcrumbs
1 small fennel bulb
90ml/6 tbsp olive oil
1 medium onion, very thinly sliced
45ml/3 tbsp pine nuts
2.5ml/½ tsp fennel seeds
450g/1lb long hollow pasta such as percatelli, ziti, or bucatini
salt and freshly ground black pepper

1 Soak the sultanas in warm water for 15 minutes. Drain and pat dry.

2 Clean the sardines, then open each fish out flat and remove the backbone and head. Wash well and shake dry. Sprinkle with the breadcrumbs.

3 Trim the fronds off the fennel, chop them coarsely and reserve. Pull off a few outer leaves and wash. Fill a large pan with enough water to cook the pasta. Add the fennel leaves and bring to the boil.

4 Heat the oil in a large frying pan and sauté the onion lightly until soft. Remove with a slotted spoon and reserve on a dish. Add the sardines, a few at a time, and cook over moderate heat until golden on both sides, turning them once carefully. Remove them as they are cooked and reserve.

5 When all the sardines have been cooked, gently return them to the pan. Add the cooked onion, and the sultanas, pine nuts and fennel seeds. Season with salt and pepper.

6 Take about 60ml/4 tbsp of the boiling water for the pasta, and stir it into the pan with the sardines to create a sauce. Add salt to the boiling water, and drop in the pasta. Cook until it is *al dente*. Drain, and remove the fennel leaves. Dress the pasta with the sauce. Divide between individual serving plates, arranging several sardines on each. Sprinkle with the reserved chopped fennel tops before serving.

Saffron and Prawn Pasta

A small amount of saffron in the sauce gives this dish a lovely golden colour.

Serves 4

45ml/3 tbsp olive oil
30ml/2 tbsp butter
2 spring onions (scallions), chopped
150g/5oz/1¼ cups frozen petits pois or peas, thawed
450g/1lb farfalle
350g/12oz fresh or frozen peeled cooked prawns (shrimp)
250ml/8fl oz/1 cup dry white wine
a few whole strands saffron or 1ml/⅛ tsp powdered saffron
salt and freshly ground black pepper
2 tbsp chopped fresh fennel or dill, to serve

1 Bring a large pan of water to a boil. Heat the oil and butter in a large frying pan and sauté the scallions lightly. Add the peas, and cook for 2–3 minutes.

2 Add salt and the pasta to the boiling water. Add the wine and saffron to the peas. Raise the heat and cook until the wine is reduced by about half. Add the prawns and season to taste with salt and pepper. Cover and reduce the heat to low.

3 Drain the pasta when it is *al dente*. Add it to the pan with the sauce. Stir over high heat for 1–2 minutes, coating the pasta evenly with the sauce. Sprinkle with the fresh herbs, and serve at once.

Pasta with Sardine Sauce: *Energy 860kcal/3619kJ; Protein 35.4g; Carbohydrate 110.2g, of which sugars 13.4g; Fat 33.8g, of which saturates 5.1g; Cholesterol 0mg; Calcium 153mg; Fibre 4.4g; Sodium 277mg.*
Saffron and Prawn Pasta: *Energy 624kcal/2629kJ; Protein 29.5g; Carbohydrate 88.1g, of which sugars 5g; Fat 16.5g, of which saturates 4.9g; Cholesterol 160mg; Calcium 102mg; Fibre 5.1g; Sodium 186mg.*

Spaghettini with Vodka and Caviar

This is an elegant yet easy way to serve spaghettini, though here the pasta is definitely not the central attraction of the dish. Obviously, caviar – accompanied by vodka in the traditional way – belongs to Russian cuisine, but it has happily migrated to southern Europe and become a modern tradition in Rome, where it is an after-theatre favourite.

Serves 4

60ml/4 tbsp olive oil
3 spring onions (scallions), thinly sliced
1 garlic clove, finely chopped
120ml/4fl oz/½ cup vodka
150ml/¼ pint/⅔ cup double (heavy) cream
115g/4oz/½ cup black or red caviar
salt and ground black pepper
450g/1lb spaghettini

1 Heat the oil in a small pan. Add the scallions and garlic, and cook gently for 4–5 minutes.

2 Add the vodka and cream, and cook over low heat for about 5–8 minutes more.

3 Remove from the heat and stir in half the caviar. Season with salt and pepper as necessary.

4 Meanwhile, cook the spaghettini in a large pan of rapidly boiling salted water until *al dente*. Drain the pasta, and toss with the sauce. Spoon the remaining caviar on top of the pasta and serve immediately.

Cook's Tip

The finest caviar is the salted eggs or roe of the wild sturgeon, and comes from the Caspian and Black Seas, chiefly from Russian and Iranian producers. Since 2005 it has been illegal to import Beluga caviar into the USA, because the Beluga sturgeon is considered to be a threatened species. Red caviar is salmon roe, which is much cheaper and saltier than sturgeon roe, as is black-dyed lumpfish roe, available in supermarkets.

Baked Seafood Spaghetti

In this dish, each portion is baked and served in an individual packet which is then opened at the table.

Serves 4

450g/1lb mussels
120ml/4fl oz/½ cup dry white wine
4 tbsp olive oil
2 garlic cloves, finely chopped
450g/1lb tomatoes, peeled and finely chopped
450g/1lb spaghetti
30ml/2 tbsp chopped fresh parsley
225g/8oz raw prawns (shrimp), peeled and deveined
salt and ground black pepper

1 Scrub and debeard the mussels under cold running water, cutting. Place them with the wine in a large pan and cook over a high heat, shaking the pan occasionally, until they open. Lift out the mussels and reserve. Strain the cooking liquid and reserve. Preheat the oven to 150°C/300°F/Gas 2.

2 Bring a large pan of salted water to the boil. Meanwhile, heat the olive oil in a medium pan and cook the garlic for 1–2 minutes. Add the tomatoes, and cook over moderate heat until they soften. Stir in 175ml/6fl oz/¾ cup of the mussel liquid. Cook the pasta in the boiling water until it is just *al dente*.

3 Add the parsley and prawns to the tomato sauce and cook for 2 minutes. Season to taste. Remove from the heat.

4 Prepare 4 pieces of baking parchment (parchment paper) or foil about 30 x 45cm/12 × 18in. Place each sheet in a shallow bowl. Turn the drained pasta into a bowl. Add the tomato sauce and mix well. Stir in the mussels.

5 Divide the pasta and seafood between the four pieces of paper, placing a mound in the centre of each, and twisting the paper ends together to make a closed packet. (The bowl under the paper will stop the sauce from spilling while the paper parcels are being closed.) Arrange on a large baking sheet, and place in the centre of the preheated oven. Bake for 10 minutes. Place one unopened packet on each individual serving plate.

Spaghettini and caviar: Energy 668kcal/2798kJ; Protein 14.1g; Carbohydrate 75g, of which sugars 4.2g; Fat 7g of which saturates 14.4g; Cholesterol 87mg; Calcium 48mg; Fibre 3g; Sodium 277mg.
Seafood Spaghetti: Energy 414kcal/1749kJ; Protein 28.3g; Carbohydrate 48.8g, of which sugars 7.8g; Fat 13.2g, of which saturates 3.5g; Cholesterol 198mg; Calcium 131mg; Fibre 2.9g; Sodium 1818mg.

Trenette with Shellfish

Colourful and delicious, this typical Genoese dish is ideal for a dinner party. The sauce is quite runny, so serve it with plenty of bread.

Serves 4

45ml/3 tbsp olive oil
1 small onion, finely chopped
1 garlic clove, crushed
½ fresh red chilli, seeded and chopped
200g/7oz can chopped Italian plum tomatoes
30ml/2 tbsp chopped fresh flat leaf parsley
400g/14oz clams
400g/14oz mussels
60ml/4 tbsp dry white wine
400g/14oz/3½ cups dried trenette or linguine
a few fresh basil leaves
90g/3½oz/⅔ cup peeled cooked prawns (shrimp), thawed and thoroughly dried if frozen
salt and ground black pepper
chopped fresh herbs, to garnish

1 Heat 30ml/2 tbsp of the oil in a pan. Add the onion, garlic and chilli and cook, stirring, over a medium heat for 1–2 minutes. Stir in the tomatoes, half the parsley and pepper to taste. Bring to the boil, cover and simmer for 15 minutes.

2 Meanwhile, scrub the clams and mussels under cold water. Discard any that are open or that do not close when tapped. Heat the remaining oil in a large saucepan, Add the clams and mussels with the rest of the parsley and toss over a high heat for a few seconds. Pour in the wine, then cover tightly. Cook for 5 minutes, shaking the pan frequently, until the shells open. Remove from the heat and transfer the shellfish to a bowl with a slotted spoon, discarding any that have failed to open. Strain the liquid into a measuring jug and set aside. Reserve eight clams and four mussels in their shells and shell the rest.

3 Cook the pasta according to the instructions on the packet. Meanwhile, add 120ml/4fl oz/½ cup of the reserved seafood liquid to the tomato sauce. Bring to the boil, stirring, then add the basil, prawns, clams and mussels. Season to taste.

4 Drain the pasta and tip it into a warmed bowl. Add the sauce and toss well . Serve sprinkled with herbs and garnished with the reserved clams and mussels in their shells.

Tagliatelle with Scallops

Scallops and brandy make this a relatively expensive dish, but it is so delicious that you will find it well worth the cost. Serve it for a lunch party main course.

Serves 4

200g/7oz scallops
30ml/2 tbsp plain (all-purpose) flour
40g/1½oz/3 tbsp butter
2 spring onions (scallions), cut into thin rings
½–1 small fresh red chilli, seeded and very finely chopped
30ml/2 tbsp finely chopped fresh flat leaf parsley
60ml/4 tbsp brandy
105ml/7 tbsp fish stock
275g/10oz fresh spinach-flavoured tagliatelle
salt and ground black pepper

1 Remove the corals from the scallops if they have them, and slice the white part of each one horizontally into 2–3 pieces. Toss the scallops in the flour. Bring a large saucepan of salted water to the boil, ready for cooking the pasta.

2 Meanwhile, melt the butter in a large pan. Add the spring onions, finely chopped chilli and half the parsley and fry, stirring frequently, for 1–2 minutes over a medium heat. Add the scallops and toss over the heat for 1–2 minutes.

3 Pour the brandy over the scallops, then set it alight with a match. As soon as the flames have died down, stir in the fish stock and salt and pepper to taste. Mix well. Simmer for 2–3 minutes, then cover the pan and remove it from the heat.

4 Add the pasta to the boiling water and cook it according to the instructions on the packet. Drain, add to the sauce and toss over a medium heat until mixed. Serve at once, in warmed bowls sprinkled with the remaining parsley.

Cook's Tip

Buy fresh scallops, with their corals if possible. Fresh scallops always have a better texture and flavour than frozen ones, which tend to be watery.

Trenette with Shellfish: Energy 524kcal/2218kJ; Protein 29.9g; Carbohydrate 78.1g, of which sugars 6g; Fat 11.4g, of which saturates 1.7g; Cholesterol 89mg; Calcium 163mg; Fibre 4g; Sodium 717mg.
Tagliatelle with Scallops: Energy 429kcal/1809kJ; Protein 20.7g; Carbohydrate 58.7g, of which sugars 2.6g; Fat 10.3g, of which saturates 5.6g; Cholesterol 45mg; Calcium 46mg; Fibre 2.3g; Sodium 153mg.

Paglia e Fieno with Prawns

The combination of prawns, vodka and pasta is a modern classic in Italy.

Serves 4

30ml/2 tbsp olive oil
¼ large onion, finely chopped
1 garlic clove, crushed
15–30ml/1–2 tbsp sun-dried tomato paste
200ml/7fl oz/scant 1 cup double (heavy) cream
350g/12oz fresh or dried paglia e fieno
12 raw tiger prawns (jumbo shrimp), peeled and chopped
30ml/2 tbsp vodka
salt and ground black pepper

1 Fry the onion and garlic and cook gently, until softened.

2 Add the tomato paste and stir for 1–2 minutes, then add the cream and bring to the boil, stirring. Season with salt and pepper. As the sauce starts to thicken, remove from the heat.

3 Cook the pasta according to the instructions on the packet. When it is almost ready, add the prawns and vodka to the sauce; toss quickly over a medium heat for 2–3 minutes until the prawns turn pink. Tip the drained pasta into a warmed bowl, pour the sauce over and toss well. Serve immediately.

Seafood Lasagne

This makes a luxurious supper dish.

Serves 6

65g/2½oz/5 tbsp butter
450g/1lb monkfish fillets, diced
225g/8oz fresh prawns (shrimp), shelled, deveined and chopped
225g/8oz/3 cups button (white) mushrooms, chopped
40g/1½oz/3 tbsp plain (all-purpose) flour
600ml/1 pint/2½ cups hot milk
300ml/½ pint/1¼ cups double cream
400g/14 oz can chopped tomatoes
30ml/2 tbsp chopped fresh basil
8 sheets non-precook lasagne
75g/3oz/1 cup grated (shredded) Parmesan cheese
salt and ground black pepper
fresh herbs, to garnish

1 Sauté the fish and prawns in 15g/½oz/1tbsp of the butter for 2–3 minutes, until the prawns turn pink. Place in a bowl.

2 Sauté the mushrooms for about 5 minutes until soft. Set aside with the fish. Preheat the oven to 190°C/275°F/Gas 5.

3 Melt the remaining butter in the pan. Stir in the flour for 1–2 minutes. Remove from the heat and whisk in the milk. Next bring to the boil, then simmer and whisk until thick. Add the cream and whisk over a low heat for 2 minutes more. Stir in the mushrooms, fish and any juices. Season well.

4 Spread half the chopped tomatoes at the base of a baking dish. Sprinkle with basil, salt and pepper. Ladle one third of the sauce over and cover with lasagne sheets.Repeat with another tomato, sauce and pasta layer, add the remaining sauce and sprinkle with the cheese. Bake until golden and bubbling.

Cannelloni with Tuna

Children love this pasta dish. Fontina cheese has a sweet, nutty flavour and very good melting qualities. Look for it in large supermarkets and Italian delicatessens.

Serves 4–6

50g/2oz/¼ cup butter
50g/2oz/½ cup plain (all-purpose) flour
about 900ml/1½ pints/3¾ cups hot milk
2 × 200g/7oz cans tuna, drained
115g/4oz/1 cup Fontina cheese, grated
1.5ml/¼ tsp grated nutmeg
12 no-precook cannelloni tubes
50g/2oz/⅔ cup grated Parmesan cheese
salt and ground black pepper
fresh herbs, to garnish

1 Melt the butter in a heavy pan, add the flour and stir over a low heat for 1–2 minutes. Remove the pan from the heat and gradually add 350ml/12fl oz/1½ cups of the milk, beating vigorously after each addition. Return the pan to the heat and whisk for 1–2 minutes until the sauce is very thick and smooth. Remove from the heat.

2 Mix the drained tuna with about 120ml/4fl oz/½ cup of the warm white sauce in a bowl. Add salt and black pepper to taste. Preheat the oven to 180°C/350°F/Gas 4.

3 Gradually whisk the remaining milk into the rest of the sauce, then return to the heat and simmer, whisking constantly, until thickened. Add the grated Fontina and nutmeg, with salt and pepper to taste. Simmer for a few more minutes, stirring frequently. Pour about one-third of the sauce into a baking dish and spread to the corners.

4 Fill the cannelloni tubes with the tuna mixture, pushing it in with the handle of a teaspoon. Place the cannelloni in a single layer in the dish.

5 Thin the remaining sauce with a little more milk if necessary, then pour it over the cannelloni. Sprinkle with Parmesan cheese and bake for 30 minutes or until golden. Serve hot, garnished with herbs.

Paglia e Fieno: Energy 650kcal/2722kJ; Protein 18.3g; Carbohydrate 67.4g, of which sugars 5.1g; Fat 34.2g, of which saturates 17.7g; Cholesterol 142mg; Calcium 81mg; Fibre 2.9g; Sodium 94mg.
Seafood Lasagne: Energy 368kcal/1548kJ; Protein 14.8g; Carbohydrate 47.7g, of which sugars 6.7g; Fat 14.5g, of which saturates 8.2g; Cholesterol 38mg; Calcium 224mg; Fibre 1.5g; Sodium 238mg.
Cannelloni with Tuna: Energy 502kcal/2110kJ; Protein 32.2g; Carbohydrate 44.3g, of which sugars 2.6g; Fat 22.7g, of which saturates 11.4g; Cholesterol 76mg; Calcium 293mg; Fibre 1.7g; Sodium 467mg.

Orecchiette with Anchovies and Broccoli

With its robust flavours, this pasta dish is typical of southern Italian and Sicilian cooking. Anchovies, pine nuts, garlic and Pecorino cheese are all very popular ingredients. Serve with crusty Italian bread for a light lunch or supper.

Serves 4

300g/11oz/2 cups broccoli florets
40g/1½oz/½ cup pine nuts
350g/12oz/3 cups dried orecchiette
60ml/4 tbsp olive oil
1 small red onion, thinly sliced
50g/2oz jar anchovies in olive oil
1 garlic clove, crushed
50g/2oz/⅔ cup freshly grated Pecorino cheese
salt and ground black pepper

1 Break the broccoli florets into small sprigs and cut off the stalks. If the stalks are large, chop or slice them. Cook the broccoli florets and stalks in a saucepan of boiling salted water for 2 minutes, then drain and refresh them under cold running water. Leave to drain on kitchen paper.

2 Put the pine nuts in a dry non-stick frying pan and toss over a low to medium heat for 1–2 minutes or until the nuts are lightly toasted and golden. Remove and set aside.

3 Cook the pasta according to the instructions on the packet.

4 Meanwhile, heat the oil in a pan, add the red onion and fry gently, stirring frequently, for about 5 minutes until softened. Add the anchovies with their oil, then add the garlic and fry over a medium heat, stirring frequently, for 1–2 minutes until the anchovies break down to form a paste. Add the broccoli and plenty of pepper and toss over the heat for a minute or two until the broccoli is hot. Taste for seasoning.

5 Drain the pasta and tip it into a warmed bowl. Add the broccoli mixture and grated Pecorino and toss well to combine. Sprinkle the pine nuts over the top and serve immediately.

Tagliolini with Clams and Mussels

This makes a stunning dish for a dinner party first course. The sauce can be prepared a few hours ahead, then the pasta cooked and the dish assembled at the last minute.

Serves 4

450g/1lb mussels
450g/1lb clams
60ml/4 tbsp olive oil
1 small onion, finely chopped
2 garlic cloves, finely chopped
1 large handful fresh flat leaf parsley, plus extra parsley to garnish
175ml/6fl oz/¾ cup dry white wine
250ml/8fl oz/1 cup fish stock
1 small fresh red chilli, seeded and chopped
350g/12oz squid ink tagliolini or tagliatelle
salt and freshly ground black pepper

1 Scrub the mussels and clams and discard any that are open or damaged, or that do not close when sharply tapped.

2 Heat half the oil in a large pan and cook the onion gently for about 5 minutes until softened. Add the garlic and about half the parsley sprigs, with salt and pepper to taste. Add the mussels and clams and pour in the wine. Cover and bring to the boil over a high heat. Cook for about 5 minutes, shaking the pan frequently, until the shellfish have opened.

3 Tip the mussels and clams into a sieve (strainer) set over a bowl. Discard the aromatics, together with any shells that have failed to open. Return the liquid to the cleaned pan and add the fish stock. Chop the remaining parsley finely and add it to the liquid with the chilli. Bring to the boil, then lower the heat and simmer, stirring, until slightly reduced. Turn off the heat.

4 Remove and discard about half the top shells, then put all the mussels and clams in the sauce, cover tightly and set aside.

5 Cook the pasta according to the instructions on the packet. Drain well and toss with the remaining olive oil. Over a high heat, toss the shellfish quickly to heat through and combine with the sauce. Divide the pasta among four warmed plates, spoon the shellfish mixture over it and sprinkle with parsley.

Orecchiette: *Energy 578kcal/2425kJ; Protein 23.5g; Carbohydrate 67.8g, of which sugars 5.3g; Fat 25.5g, of which saturates 5.1g; Cholesterol 20mg; Calcium 256mg; Fibre 4.9g; Sodium 637mg.*
Tagliolini: *Energy 498kcal/2102kJ; Protein 24.7g; Carbohydrate 66.3g, of which sugars 3.4g; Fat 13.7g, of which saturates 2g; Cholesterol 47mg; Calcium 149mg; Fibre 3g; Sodium 679mg.*

Penne with Cream and Smoked Salmon

This modern way of serving pasta is popular all over Italy. The three essential ingredients combine beautifully, and the dish is very quick and easy to make as the sauce is put together in less time than it takes to cook the pasta.

Serves 4

350g/12oz/3 cups dried penne
115g/4oz thinly sliced smoked salmon
2–3 fresh thyme sprigs
25g/1oz/2 tbsp butter
150ml/¼ pint/⅔ cup extra-thick single (light) cream
salt and ground black pepper

1 Cook the pasta in a large pan of salted boiling water until it is *al dente*, according to the instructions on the packet.

2 Meanwhile, using kitchen scissors, cut the smoked salmon into thin strips, about 5mm/¼in wide. Strip the leaves from the thyme sprigs.

3 Melt the butter in a large saucepan. Stir in the cream with about a quarter of the salmon and thyme leaves, then season with pepper. Heat gently for 3–4 minutes, stirring all the time. Do not allow to boil. Taste the sauce for seasoning.

4 Drain the pasta and toss it in the cream and salmon sauce. Divide among four warmed bowls and top with the remaining salmon and thyme leaves. Serve immediately.

Cook's Tip

Heat the sauce very gently as the salmon strips will cook and their texture will be spoilt if it gets too hot.

Variation

Although penne is traditional, this sauce also goes very well with fresh ravioli stuffed with spinach and ricotta.

Spaghetti with Salmon and Prawns

This is a lovely fresh-tasting pasta dish, perfect for an *al fresco* meal in summer. Serve it for lunch with warm ciabatta or focaccia and a dry white wine.

Serves 4

300g/11oz salmon fillet
200ml/7fl oz/scant 1 cup dry white wine
a few fresh basil sprigs, plus extra basil leaves, to garnish
6 ripe Italian plum tomatoes, peeled and finely chopped
150ml/¼ pint/⅔ cup double (heavy) cream
350g/12oz/3 cups spaghetti
115g/4oz/⅔ cup peeled cooked prawns (shrimp)
salt and freshly ground black pepper

1 Put the salmon skin-side up in a wide shallow pan. Pour the wine over, then add the basil sprigs to the pan and sprinkle the fish with salt and pepper. Bring the wine to the boil, cover the pan and simmer gently for no more than 5 minutes. Using a fish slice, lift the fish out of the pan and set aside to cool a little.

2 Add the cream and tomatoes to the liquid remaining in the pan and bring to the boil. Stir well, then lower the heat and simmer, uncovered, for 10–15 minutes. Meanwhile, cook the pasta according to the instructions on the packet.

3 Flake the fish into large chunks, discarding the skin and any bones. Add the fish to the sauce with the prawns, shaking the pan until the fish and shellfish are well coated. Taste the sauce for seasoning.

4 Drain the pasta and tip it into a warmed bowl. Pour the sauce over the pasta and toss to combine. Serve immediately, garnished with fresh basil leaves.

Cook's Tip

Check the salmon fillet carefully for small bones when you are flaking the flesh. Although the salmon is already filleted, you will always find a few stray "pin" bones. Pick them out carefully using tweezers or your fingertips.

Penne with Salmon: *Energy 573kcal/2403kJ; Protein 18.5g; Carbohydrate 65.5g, of which sugars 3.6g; Fat 28.2g, of which saturates 16.2g; Cholesterol 75mg; Calcium 47mg; Fibre 2.6g; Sodium 589mg.*
Spaghetti with Salmon: *Energy 701kcal/2941kJ; Protein 32.4g; Carbohydrate 70.4g, of which sugars 8.5g; Fat 30.6g, of which saturates 14.3g; Cholesterol 145mg; Calcium 94mg; Fibre 4.1g; Sodium 115mg.*

Shellfish Risotto with Mixed Mushrooms

This is a quick and easy risotto, in which all the liquid is added in one go. The method is well-suited to this shellfish dish, as it means everything cooks together undisturbed.

Serves 6

225g/8oz mussels
225g/8oz Venus or carpet shell clams
45ml/3 tbsp olive oil
1 onion, chopped
450g/1lb/2⅓ cups risotto rice
1.75 litres/3 pints/7½ cups simmering chicken or vegetable stock
150ml/¼ pint/⅔ cup white wine
225g/8oz/2–3 cups assorted wild and cultivated mushrooms, trimmed and sliced
115g/4oz raw peeled prawns (shrimp), deveined
1 medium or 2 small squid, cleaned, trimmed and sliced
3 drops truffle oil (optional)
75ml/5 tbsp chopped mixed fresh parsley and chervil
celery salt and cayenne pepper

1 Scrub and debeard the mussels, clean the clams and discard any broken shellfish and any that are open and do not close when tapped sharply. Set aside.

2 Heat the oil in a large frying pan and fry the onion for 6–8 minutes until soft but not browned.

3 Add the rice, stirring to coat the grains in oil, then pour in the stock and wine and cook for 5 minutes. Add the mushrooms and cook for 5 minutes more, stirring occasionally.

4 Add the prawns, squid, mussels and clams and stir into the rice. Cover the pan and simmer over a low heat for 15 minutes until the prawns have turned pink and the mussels and clams have opened. Discard any shellfish that remain closed.

5 Switch off the heat. Add the truffle oil, if using, and stir in the herbs. Cover the pan tightly and leave to stand for 5–10 minutes to allow all the flavours to blend. Season to taste with celery salt and a pinch of cayenne, pile into a warmed dish, and serve immediately.

Lobster Ravioli

Homemade pasta is essential to obtain the delicacy and thinness this superb filling deserves.

Serves 4 (or 6 as an appetizer)

1 lobster, about 450g/1lb, cooked and taken out of the shell
2 slices soft white bread, about 50g/2oz, crusts removed
200ml/7fl oz/scant 1 cup fish stock, made with the lobster shell and head
1 egg
250ml/8fl oz/1 cup double (heavy) cream
15ml/1 tbsp chopped fresh chives, plus extra to garnish
15ml/1 tbsp finely chopped fresh chervil
salt and ground white pepper
fresh chives, to garnish

For the pasta dough

225g/8oz/2 cups strong flour (Italian tipo 00 if possible)
2 eggs, plus 2 egg yolks

For the mushroom sauce

a large pinch of saffron threads
25g/1oz/2 tbsp butter
2 shallots, finely chopped
200g/7oz/3 cups white button mushrooms, finely chopped
juice of ½ lemon
200ml/7fl oz/scant 1 cup double (heavy) cream

1 To make the pasta, sift the flour with a good pinch of salt. Put into a food processor with the eggs and extra yolks; whizz until the mixture resembles coarse breadcrumbs. Turn out on to a floured surface; knead to make a smooth, dryish dough. Wrap in clear film (plastic wrap) and chill for an hour.

2 Cut the lobster meat into large chunks and place in a bowl. Tear the white bread into pieces and soak them in 45ml/3 tbsp of the fish stock. Place in a food processor with half the egg and 30–45ml/2–3 tbsp of the cream and whizz until smooth. Stir this mixture into the lobster meat, then add the fresh chives and chervil and season to taste with salt and white pepper.

3 Roll the pasta to a thickness of 3mm/⅛in, preferably using a pasta machine. Divide it into four rectangles and dust each lightly with flour.

4 Spoon six equal heaps of filling on to one sheet of pasta, leaving about 3cm/1¼in between each pile. Lightly beat the remaining egg with a little water and brush it over the pasta between the piles of filling. Cover with a second sheet of pasta. Repeat with the other two sheets of pasta and remaining filling.

5 Using your fingertips, press the top layer of dough down well between the piles of filling, making sure each is well sealed. Cut between the heaps with a 7.5cm/3in fluted pastry cutter or a pasta wheel to make 12 ravioli. Place them in a single layer on a baking sheet, cover with clear film or a damp cloth, and refrigerate while you make the mushroom sauce.

6 Soak the saffron in 15ml/1 tbsp warm water. Melt the butter and cook the shallots over a low heat until they are soft but not coloured. Add the chopped mushrooms and lemon juice and continue to cook over a low heat until almost all the liquid has evaporated. Stir in the saffron, with its soaking water, and the cream, then cook gently, stirring, until the sauce has thickened. Keep warm. Cook the ravioli for 2 minutes in a pan of boiling salted water. Drain carefully and serve with the sauce.

Shellfish Risotto: *Energy 423kcal/1768kJ; Protein 21.4g; Carbohydrate 62.5g, of which sugars 0.8g; Fat 7.5g, of which saturates 1.2g; Cholesterol 136mg; Calcium 64mg; Fibre 0.6g; Sodium 335mg.*
Lobster Ravioli: *Energy 652kcal/2722kJ; Protein 23g; Carbohydrate 52.2g, of which sugars 3.1g; Fat 40.5g, of which saturates 22.2g; Cholesterol 361mg; Calcium 186mg; Fibre 2.9g; Sodium 298mg.*

Salmon Risotto with Cucumber and Tarragon

This is another risotto that is cooked all in one go, and is therefore simpler than the classic recipe. If you prefer to cook it the traditional way, add the liquid gradually, adding the salmon about two-thirds of the way through cooking.

Serves 4

25g/1oz/2 tbsp butter
small bunch of spring onions (scallions), white parts only, chopped
½ cucumber, peeled, seeded and chopped
350g/12oz/1¾ cups risotto rice
1.2 litres/2 pints/5 cups hot chicken or fish stock
150ml/¼ pint/⅔ cup dry white wine
450g/1lb salmon fillet, skinned and diced
45ml/3 tbsp chopped fresh tarragon
salt and ground black pepper

1 Heat the butter in a large pan and add the spring onions and cucumber. Cook for 2–3 minutes without letting the spring onions colour.

2 Stir in the rice, then pour in the stock and the wine. Bring to the boil, then lower the heat and simmer, uncovered, for 10 minutes, stirring occasionally.

3 Stir in the diced salmon and season to taste with salt and ground black pepper. Continue cooking for a further 5 minutes, stirring occasionally, then switch off the heat. Cover and leave to stand for 5 minutes.

4 Remove the lid, add the chopped tarragon and mix lightly. Spoon into a warmed bowl and serve.

Variation
Carnaroli risotto rice would be excellent in this risotto, although if it is not available, Arborio can be used instead.

Monkfish Risotto

Monkfish is a versatile, firm-textured fish with a superb flavour, which is accentuated with lemon grass in this sophisticated risotto.

Serves 3–4

30ml/2 tbsp plain (all-purpose) flour, seasoned
about 450g/1lb monkfish, cubed
30ml/2 tbsp olive oil
40g/1½oz/3 tbsp butter
2 shallots, finely chopped
1 lemon grass stalk, finely chopped
275g/10oz/1½ cups risotto rice, preferably Carnaroli
175ml/6fl oz/¾ cup dry white wine
1 litre/1¾ pints/4 cups simmering fish stock
30ml/2 tbsp chopped fresh parsley
salt and ground white pepper
dressed salad leaves, to serve

1 Spoon the seasoned flour over the monkfish cubes in a bowl. Toss the monkfish until coated.

2 Heat 15ml/1 tbsp of the oil with half the butter in a frying pan. Fry the monkfish cubes over a medium to high heat for 3–4 minutes until cooked, turning occasionally. Transfer to a plate and set aside.

3 Heat the remaining oil and butter in a saucepan and fry the shallots over a low heat for about 4 minutes until soft but not brown. Add the lemon grass and cook for 1–2 minutes more.

4 Add the rice. Cook for 2–3 minutes, stirring, until the rice is coated with oil and is slightly translucent. Gradually add the wine and the hot stock, stirring and waiting until each ladleful has been absorbed before adding the next.

5 When the rice is about three-quarters cooked, stir in the monkfish. Continue to cook the risotto, adding the remaining stock and stirring constantly until the grains of rice are tender, but still retain a bit of "bite". Season with salt and white pepper.

6 Remove the pan from the heat, stir in the parsley and cover with a lid. Leave the risotto to stand for a few minutes before serving with a garnish of dressed salad leaves.

Salmon Risotto: *Energy 594kcal/2477kJ; Protein 29.8g; Carbohydrate 70.9g, of which sugars 1g; Fat 18.1g, of which saturates 5.4g; Cholesterol 70mg; Calcium 55mg; Fibre 0.4g; Sodium 92mg.*
Monkfish Risotto: *Energy 431kcal/1802kJ; Protein 23.1g; Carbohydrate 56.4g, of which sugars 1.2g; Fat 9.1g, of which saturates 5.3g; Cholesterol 37mg; Calcium 37mg; Fibre 0.3g; Sodium 84mg.*

Chargrilled Squid with Risotto

Accompany this simple and delicious seafood dish with a plain risotto, made in the classic Milanese way with fresh chicken stock. If you like your food hot, chop some – or all – of the chilli seeds with the flesh. If not, cut the chillies in half lengthways, scrape out the seeds and discard them before chopping the flesh.

Serves 2

2 whole prepared squid, with tentacles
75 ml/5 tbsp olive oil
30 ml/2 tbsp balsamic vinegar
2 fresh red chillies, finely chopped
60 ml/4 tbsp dry white wine
salt and ground black pepper
hot cooked risotto rice, to serve
sprigs of fresh parsley, to garnish

1 Make a lengthways cut down the body of each squid, then open the body out flat. Score the flesh on both sides of the bodies in a criss-cross pattern with the tip of a sharp knife. Chop the tentacles. Place the squid in a china or glass dish. Whisk the oil and vinegar together, add salt and pepper to taste and pour over the squid. Cover and leave to marinate for about 1 hour.

2 Heat a ridged cast-iron pan until hot. Add the body of one of the squid. Cook over a medium heat for 2–3 minutes, pressing the squid with a fish slice to keep it flat. Repeat on the other side. Cook the other squid body in the same way.

3 Cut the squid bodies into diagonal strips. Pile the hot risotto rice in the centre of heated soup plates and top with the strips of squid, arranging them criss-cross fashion. Keep hot.

4 Add the chopped tentacles and chillies to the pan and toss over a medium heat for 2 minutes. Stir in the wine, then drizzle over the squid and rice. Serve garnished with the parsley.

Cook's Tip
Make sure the pan is very hot before cooking the squid bodies briefly, so that they brown but do not overcook.

Calderette of Rice with Aioli

Cooking rice in fish stock gives it such a splendid flavour that in Spain it is often eaten accompanied by allioli, with the fish as a separate course, but if you prefer, the fish can be returned to the casserole while the dish is still liquid.

Serves 6

1.6kg/3½lb mixed fish on the bone, such as snapper, bream, grey or red mullet, or bass
45ml/3 tbsp olive oil
6 garlic cloves, smashed
1 fresh or dried hot chilli, seeded and chopped
250g/9oz ripe tomatoes, peeled, seeded and chopped
pinch of saffron threads
30ml/2 tbsp dry vermouth or white wine
1 tomato, finely diced
30ml/2 tbsp chopped fresh parsley
400g/14oz/2 cups paella rice, washed
115g/4oz tiny unshelled shrimps
salt and freshly ground black pepper

For the stock

1 onion, chopped
2 garlic cloves, chopped
1 celery stick, chopped
1 carrot, chopped
1 litre/1¾ pints/4 cups water

For the aioli

4 garlic cloves, finely chopped
2.5ml/½ tsp salt
5ml/1 tsp lemon juice
2 egg yolks
250ml/8fl oz/1 cup olive oil

1 Remove the heads from the fish. Working from the head end, cut the skin along the back and work the fillets off the bone. Trim the fillets, salt them lightly, cover and place in the refrigerator until required. Put the bones, heads, tails and any other remains into a large pan with the onion, garlic, celery, carrot and water. Bring to the boil, then reduce the heat, cover with a lid and simmer gently for about 30 minutes.

2 To make the aioli, put the chopped garlic in a large mortar (or blender) with the salt and lemon juice and reduce to a purée. Add the egg yolks and mix thoroughly. Gradually work in the oil to make a thick, mayonnaise-like sauce.

3 Put 15ml/1 tbsp of the olive oil in a small pan and add the whole garlic cloves and chilli. Fry for a few minutes until the garlic colours. Add the chopped tomatoes and the saffron and cook to form a sauce. Pour into a blender and purée.

4 Heat the remaining oil in a large pan and fry the fish pieces until they begin to stiffen. Strain the fish stock and add 900ml/1½ pints/3¾ cups stock and the tomato sauce to the fish. Cook the fish gently for a further 3–4 minutes.

5 Remove the fish from the pan with a slotted spoon to a serving dish. Season lightly, sprinkle with the vermouth or wine, diced tomato and parsley. Cover and keep warm.

6 Stir the rice into the stock, season and simmer for 18–20 minutes. Before all the liquid is absorbed, stir in the shrimps, cover and turn off the heat. Stand until the liquid is absorbed: about 5 minutes. Serve the rice from the pan, accompanied by the allioli. When the rice course is almost finished, uncover the fish. Stir the fish juices into the remains of the aioli, then pour over the fish. Eat on the same plates as the rice.

Chargrilled Squid: *Energy 290kcal/1215kJ; Protein 34.7g; Carbohydrate 2.8g, of which sugars 0.1g; Fat 14.8g, of which saturates 2.5g; Cholesterol 506mg; Calcium 31mg; Fibre 0g; Sodium 248mg.*
Calderette of Rice: *Energy 720kcal/2996kJ; Protein 31.3g; Carbohydrate 55g, of which sugars 1.8g; Fat 40.8g, of which saturates 5.6g; Cholesterol 136mg; Calcium 133mg; Fibre 0.5g; Sodium 873mg.*

Truffle and Lobster Risotto

A fresh truffle is a great treat for a very special occasion. To capture its precious qualities if you are lucky enough to obtain one, partner it with lobster and serve in a silky smooth risotto. Both truffle shavings and truffle oil are added towards the end of cooking to preserve their flavour.

Serves 4

50g/2oz/4 tbsp unsalted butter
1 medium onion, chopped
350g/12oz/1¾ cups risotto rice, preferably Carnaroli
1 fresh thyme sprig
150ml/¼ pint/⅔ cup dry white wine
1.2 litres/2 pints/5 cups fresh chicken stock, simmering
1 freshly cooked lobster
45ml/3 tbsp chopped mixed fresh parsley and chervil
3–4 drops truffle oil
2 hard-boiled eggs
1 fresh black or white truffle
salt and ground black pepper

1 Melt the butter, add the onion and fry until soft. Add the rice, stirring well to coat with fat. Add the thyme, then the wine, and cook until it has been absorbed. Add the chicken stock a little at a time, stirring. Let each ladleful be absorbed before adding the next.

2 Twist off the lobster tail, cut along the underside of the shell with scissors and remove the white tail meat. Carefully break open the claws with a small kitchen hammer and remove the flesh. Cut half the lobster meat into big chunks, then roughly chop the remainder.

3 Stir in the chopped lobster meat, half the chopped herbs and the truffle oil. Remove the rice from the heat, cover and leave to stand for 5 minutes.

4 Divide the risotto among warmed plates and centre the lobster chunks on top. Cut the hard-boiled eggs into wedges and arrange them around the lobster meat. Finally, shave fresh truffle over each portion and sprinkle with the remaining herbs. Serve immediately.

Paella Valenciana

Valencia's paella is Spain's best-known dish abroad.

Serves 6–8

90ml/6 tbsp white wine
450g/1lb mussels, scrubbed
115g/4oz/scant 1 cup small shelled broad (fava) beans
150g/5oz green beans, cut into short lengths
90ml/6 tbsp olive oil
6 small skinless, boneless chicken breasts, cut into large pieces
150g/5oz pork fillet, cubed
6–8 large raw prawns (shrimp) tails, deveined, or 12 smaller raw prawns
2 onions, chopped
2–3 garlic cloves, finely chopped
1 red (bell) pepper, sliced
2 ripe tomatoes, peeled, seeded and chopped
60ml/4 tbsp chopped fresh parsley
900ml/1½ pints/3¾ cups chicken stock
pinch of saffron threads, soaked in 30ml/2 tbsp hot water
350g/12oz/1¾ cups paella rice, washed and drained
225g/8oz frying chorizo, sliced
115g/4oz/1 cup peas
6–8 stuffed green olives, sliced
salt, paprika and ground black pepper

1 Heat the wine, add the mussels and steam until opened. Reserve the liquid and mussels separately. Blanch the beans in boiling water, then drain. Pop the broad beans out of their skins.

2 Heat 45ml/3 tbsp oil in a large frying pan (skillet). Season the chicken with salt and paprika, brown on all sides and reserve. Do the same with the pork. Fry the prawns briefly and reserve separately.

3 Heat the remaining oil and fry the onions and garlic for 3–4 minutes. Add the pepper, cook for 2–3 minutes, then stir in the tomatoes and parsley and cook until thick. Stir in the stock, reserved mussel liquid and saffron liquid. Season well and bring to the boil. When it is bubbling, add the rice. Stir once, then add the chicken pieces, pork, shellfish, beans, chorizo and peas.

4 Cook over medium-high heat for 10 minutes. Then lower the heat and cook until the rice is done – another 10–12 minutes. Arrange the mussels and olives on top. Cover and leave to stand for 10 minutes, until all the liquid is absorbed.

Truffle and Lobster Risotto: *Energy 520kcal/2172kJ; Protein 19.9g; Carbohydrate 71.3g, of which sugars 1.2g; Fat 14.3g, of which saturates 7.4g; Cholesterol 172mg; Calcium 68mg; Fibre 0.2g; Sodium 263mg.*
Paella Valenciana: *Energy 504kcal/2108kJ; Protein 36.5g; Carbohydrate 47.7g, of which sugars 6.1g; Fat 17.9g, of which saturates 4.7g; Cholesterol 107mg; Calcium 103mg; Fibre 3.4g; Sodium 352mg.*

Crab Risotto

This is a fresh-flavoured risotto that makes a wonderful main course or starter.

Serves 3–4

2 large cooked crabs
15ml/1 tbsp olive oil
25g/1oz/2 tbsp butter
2 shallots, finely chopped
275g/10oz/1½ cups risotto rice, preferably Carnaroli
75ml/5 tbsp Marsala or brandy
1 litre/1¾ pints/4 cups simmering fish stock
5ml/1 tsp chopped fresh tarragon
5ml/1 tsp chopped fresh parsley
60ml/4 tbsp double (heavy) cream
salt and ground black pepper

1 Hold each crab firmly in one hand and hit the back underside with the heel of your hand to loosen the shell. Using your thumbs, push against the body and pull away from the shell. Remove and discard the intestines and the grey gills (dead man's fingers). Break off the claws and legs from the body, then crack them open and use a pick to remove the meat.

2 Pick the white meat out of the body cavities and reserve with the meat from the claws and legs, selecting some white meat for the garnish. Scoop out the brown meat from inside the shell and set aside with the white meat.

3 Heat the oil and butter in a pan and gently fry the shallots until soft but not browned. Add the rice. Cook for a few minutes, stirring, until the rice is slightly translucent, then add the Marsala or brandy, bring to the boil, and cook, stirring, until the liquid has evaporated.

4 Add a ladleful of hot stock and cook, stirring, until all the stock has been absorbed. Continue cooking in this way until about two-thirds of the stock has been added, then carefully stir in all the crab meat and the herbs.

5 Continue to cook the risotto, adding the remaining stock. When the rice is almost cooked but still has a slight "bite", remove it from the heat, stir in the cream and adjust the seasoning. Cover and leave to stand for 3 minutes to finish cooking. Serve garnished with the reserved white crab meat.

Mussel and Rice Pilaff

This Greek favourite looks and tastes spectacular.

Serves 4 (or 6 as a first course)

1.6kg/3½lb mussels
2 onions, thinly sliced
350ml/12fl oz/1½ cups dry white wine
450ml/¾ pint/scant 2 cups hot water
150ml/¼ pint/⅔ cup olive oil
5–6 spring onions (scallions), chopped
2 garlic cloves, chopped
large pinch of dried oregano
200g/7oz/1 cup long grain rice
45ml/3 tbsp finely chopped fresh flat leaf parsley
45–60ml/3–4 tbsp chopped dill
salt and ground black pepper

1 Scrub and debeard the mussels, discarding any that are broken or open. Place the remainder in a large, heavy pan with one-third of the onion slices, half the wine and 150ml/¼ pint/⅔ cup of the hot water. Cover and cook over a high heat for about 5 minutes, shaking occasionally, until the mussels open. Discard mussels that stay closed. Tip the open mussels into a colander over a large bowl. Shell most of them, but keep a dozen or so whole for garnish. Strain the liquid through a muslin-lined sieve (strainer) and reserve.

2 Heat the oil in a deep, heavy pan, add the remaining onion and spring onions, and sauté over a medium heat until golden. Stir in the garlic and oregano. As soon as the garlic becomes aromatic, add the rice and stir to coat the grains well with oil. After a few minutes, add the remaining wine, stirring until it has been absorbed, then add the remaining 300ml/½ pint/1¼ cups water, the reserved mussel liquid and the chopped parsley. Season with salt and pepper, then cover and cook gently over a low to medium heat for about 5 minutes, stirring occasionally.

3 Add the mussels, including those in their shells. Stir in half the fresh, chopped dill, making sure that you keep the mussels in their shells intact. If necessary, add a little more hot water. Cover and cook gently for 5–6 minutes, or until the rice is cooked but still has a bit of "bite" in the centre of the grains. Sprinkle the remaining dill on top and serve with a green or cabbage salad and black olives.

Crab Risotto: *Energy 496kcal/2060kJ; Protein 14.1g; Carbohydrate 56.4g, of which sugars 1.1g; Fat 18.7g, of which saturates 8.9g; Cholesterol 65mg; Calcium 25mg; Fibre 0.2g; Sodium 229mg.*
Mussel and Rice Pilaff *Energy 405kcal/1686kJ; Protein 15.7g; Carbohydrate 33.3g, of which sugars 3.3g; Fat 19g, of which saturates 2.7g; Cholesterol 43mg; Calcium 93mg; Fibre 1.5g; Sodium 265mg.*

Crumbed Scallops in Pastis Sauce

This sensational dish is as delicious as it is attractive. It is traditionally served in the curved shells of the scallops, but you could serve it with salad or piled on toasts for a new take on bruschetta.

Serves 4

30ml/2 tbsp olive oil
1 onion, finely chopped
2 garlic cloves, finely chopped
200g/7oz can tomatoes
pinch of cayenne pepper
45ml/3 tbsp finely chopped fresh parsley
50ml/2fl oz/¼ cup orange juice
50g/2oz/4 tbsp butter
450g/1lb large shelled scallops, or 8–12 large ones on the shell, detached and cleaned
30ml/2 tbsp pastis, such as Ricard or Pernod
90ml/6 tbsp dry breadcrumbs
salt and ground black pepper

1 Heat the oil in a pan and fry the onion and garlic over a gentle heat. Add the tomatoes and cook for 10–15 minutes, stirring occasionally. Season with a little salt and cayenne pepper. Transfer the mixture to a food processor or blender, add 30ml/2 tbsp of the parsley and the orange juice and blend to form a smooth purée.

2 Preheat the grill (broiler) with the shelf at its highest. Arrange four curved scallop shells, or flameproof ramekin dishes, on a baking tray.

3 Heat 25g/1oz/2 tbsp of the butter in a small frying pan and fry the scallops gently, for about 2 minutes, or until sealed but not totally cooked. Pour the pastis into a ladle and set light to it. Pour over the scallops and shake the pan gently until the flames die down. Divide the scallops among the prepared shells (or ramekin dishes) and salt them very lightly. Add the pan juices to the tomato sauce.

4 Pour the sauce over the scallops. Mix the breadcrumbs with the remaining parsley, season lightly and sprinkle over the top.

5 Melt the remaining butter in a small pan and drizzle over the breadcrumbs. Grill (broil) the scallops for about 1 minute to colour the tops and heat through. Serve immediately.

Scallops with Pastis on Vegetable Rösti

The combination of crisp vegetable cakes and sweet, tender scallops is superb. The flavour of the pastis echoes the taste of the dill used in the sauce of this excellent light main course.

Serves 4

30ml/2 tbsp sunflower oil
2 shallots, chopped
1 green (bell) pepper, chopped
8 large scallops, halved
3 fresh dill sprigs, chopped
15ml/1 tbsp pastis
150ml/¼ pint/⅔ cup fish or chicken stock
2.5ml/½ tsp lemon juice
salt and ground black pepper
fresh dill sprigs, to garnish

For the rösti

2 carrots
1 large courgette (zucchini)
1 parsnip
1 small potato
1 egg, lightly beaten
oil, for frying

1 To make the rösti, coarsely grate the carrots, courgette, parsnip and potato into a bowl. Add the egg and stir to bind.

2 Heat a little oil in a large frying pan. Drop 3–4 heaped spoonfuls of the vegetable mixture into the oil. Flatten slightly with a metal spoon, then cook for 8–10 minutes, or until golden, turning once. Remove from the pan and keep hot.

3 Heat the sunflower oil in a separate frying pan and fry the shallots and green pepper for 6–8 minutes. Add the scallops, chopped dill, pastis, stock and lemon juice and poach for 2 minutes. Season to taste. Spoon the mixture on to the vegetable rösti, garnish with dill and serve.

Cook's Tip

If you can lay your hands on the curved shells of scallops, wash and keep them after use. Fresh scallops are usually sold on the flat shell so the second shell, which can be used as a little dish, is now quite a rarity.

Crumbed Scallops: Energy 394kcal/1652kJ; Protein 29.7g; Carbohydrate 25.5g, of which sugars 4.4g; Fat 18.1g, of which saturates 7.8g; Cholesterol 80mg; Calcium 95mg; Fibre 1.8g; Sodium 459mg.
Scallops with Pastis: Energy 261kcal/1083kJ; Protein 11g; Carbohydrate 14.4g, of which sugars 7.5g; Fat 17.1g, of which saturates 2.6g; Cholesterol 139mg; Calcium 55mg; Fibre 3.2g; Sodium 80mg.

Pan-Fried Squid with Ouzo

This seafood dish takes very little time to cook, so makes a simple lunch or late supper. Ouzo and lemon juice add a piquant note.

Serves 4

500g/1¼lb prepared squid
30ml/2 tbsp olive oil
30ml/2 tbsp sesame seeds
15ml/1 tbsp green peppercorns
2 garlic cloves, crushed
6 spring onions (scallions), sliced
25g/1oz drained canned anchovies, chopped
tender bulb portion of 1 lemon grass stalk, sliced
15ml/1 tbsp chopped fresh parsley
15ml/1 tbsp torn fresh basil leaves
150ml/¼ pint/⅔ cup fish stock
10ml/2 tsp lemon juice
10ml/2 tsp ouzo
75g/3oz/¾ cup mangetouts (snow peas)
salt
fresh basil sprigs and pieces of cooked poppadom, to garnish

1 Cut the squid into strips, rinse under cold water, drain and pat dry with kitchen paper.

2 Heat the oil in a frying pan or wok and toast the sesame seeds with the green peppercorns for a few seconds.

3 Add the garlic, spring onions and squid. Toss to coat in the sesame mixture.

4 Stir in the anchovies, lemon grass, chopped parsley and basil. Pour in the stock, lemon juice and ouzo and simmer for about 12 minutes.

5 Add the mangetouts and cook for 2 minutes more. Season with salt and serve on individual plates. Garnish with basil and pieces of poppadom. Serve immediately.

Cook's Tip

Some canned anchovies can be extremely salty. If you wish to moderate the flavour, soak them in cold milk for 30 minutes. Drain and chop before using.

Squid with Spinach

This dish is sometimes made for special feasts on the island of Crete. It makes a superb meal with crusty bread and crisp, fresh salad.

Serves 4

1kg/2¼lb squid, cleaned
120ml/4fl oz/½ cup extra virgin olive oil
1 large onion, sliced
3 spring onions (scallions), chopped
175ml/6fl oz/¾ cup white wine
150ml/¼ pint/⅔ cup hot water
500g/1¼lb fresh spinach
juice of ½ lemon
45ml/3 tbsp chopped fresh dill
salt and ground black pepper
chunks of fresh white bread, to serve

1 Rinse the squid thoroughly inside and out, and drain well. Slice the body in half vertically, then slice into 1cm/½in strips. Cut each tentacle into smaller pieces.

2 Heat the oil in a wide, heavy pan and sauté the onion slices and spring onions gently until the onion slices are translucent.

3 Increase the heat and add the slices of squid to the pan, including the smaller pieces of tentacles. The process produces some moisture, but keep stirring and this will evaporate. Continue to stir for 10 minutes more, or until the squid starts to turn golden.

4 Pour in the wine and stir in, letting it evaporate slightly. Then add the hot water, with salt and freshly ground black pepper to taste. The flavour will change after further cooking so do not add too much seasoning at this stage. Cover the pan and cook for about 30 minutes, stirring occasionally.

5 Wash the spinach well and drain it carefully, removing any excess moisture with kitchen paper. Remove any stalks and chop it coarsely. Stir into the pan.

6 When the chopped spinach starts to wilt, cover the pan and cook for about 10 minutes. Just before serving, add the lemon juice and dill and mix well. Serve the dish in shallow bowls, accompanied with fresh bread and a salad.

Pan-fried Squid: *Energy 224kcal/937kJ; Protein 23.3g; Carbohydrate 2.9g, of which sugars 1.2g; Fat 12.8g, of which saturates 2g; Cholesterol 285mg; Calcium 107mg; Fibre 1.4g; Sodium 387mg.*
Squid with Spinach: *Energy 462kcal/1931kJ; Protein 42.8g; Carbohydrate 9.5g, of which sugars 5.2g; Fat 25.4g, of which saturates 4g; Cholesterol 563mg; Calcium 264mg; Fibre 3.5g; Sodium 454mg.*

Potato, Mussel and Watercress Salad

A creamy, well-flavoured dressing enhances all the ingredients in this lovely Spanish salad.

Serves 4
675g/1½lb salad potatoes
1kg/2¼lb mussels, scrubbed and debearded
200ml/7fl oz/scant 1 cup dry white wine
15g/½oz fresh flat leaf parsley, chopped
1 bunch of watercress or rocket (arugula)
salt and ground black pepper
chopped fresh chives or spring onion (scallion) tops, to garnish

For the dressing
105ml/7 tbsp olive oil
15–30ml/1–2 tbsp white wine vinegar
5ml/1 tsp strong Dijon mustard
1 large shallot, very finely chopped
15ml/1 tbsp chopped fresh chives
45ml/3 tbsp double (heavy) cream
pinch of caster (superfine) sugar (optional)

1 Cook the potatoes in salted boiling water for 15–20 minutes, or until tender. Drain, cool, then peel. Slice the potatoes and toss with 30ml/2 tbsp of the oil for the dressing.

2 Discard any open mussels. Bring the wine to the boil in a large, heavy pan. Add the mussels and cook vigorously for 3–4 minutes, until they have opened. Discard any that do not open. Drain and shell the mussels, reserving the cooking liquid. Boil this until reduced to about 45ml/3 tbsp. Strain through a fine sieve over the potatoes and toss to mix.

3 To make the dressing, whisk together the remaining oil, 15ml/1 tbsp of the vinegar, the mustard, shallot and chives.

4 Add the cream and whisk again to form a thick dressing. Adjust the seasoning, adding more vinegar and/or a pinch of sugar to taste.

5 Toss the mussels with the potatoes, then gently mix in the dressing and chopped parsley. Arrange the watercress or rocket on a serving platter and top with the salad. Serve sprinkled with extra chives or a little spring onion.

Prawns with Tomatoes and Feta

Greek cooks often use a round earthenware covered pot called a *yiouvetsi*, designed for use in wood-fired ovens and, like the casserole, this pot has given its name to many dishes that are traditionally cooked in it, such as this luxurious and unusual combination.

Serves 4
75ml/5 tbsp extra virgin olive oil
1 onion, chopped
½ red (bell) pepper, cubed
675g/1½lb ripe tomatoes, peeled and roughly chopped
generous pinch of caster (superfine) sugar
2.5ml/½ tsp dried oregano
450g/1lb raw tiger prawns (jumbo shrimp), thawed if frozen and peeled (with the tail shells intact)
30ml/2 tbsp finely chopped fresh flat leaf parsley
75g/3oz feta cheese, cubed
salt and ground black pepper

1 Heat the oil in a frying pan, add the onion and sauté gently for a few minutes until translucent. Add the cubed red pepper and cook, stirring occasionally, for 2–3 minutes more until it begins to soften.

2 Stir in the chopped tomatoes, sugar and oregano, then season with salt and pepper to taste. Cook gently over a low heat for about 15 minutes, stirring occasionally, until the sauce reduces slightly and thickens.

3 Preheat the oven to 180°C/350°F/Gas 4. Stir the prawns and parsley into the tomato sauce, tip into a baking dish and spread evenly. Sprinkle the cheese cubes on top, then bake for 30 minutes. Serve hot with a fresh green salad.

Cook's Tips
- *In Greece, baked dishes of this kind are frequently made in advance of a meal and served warm rather than piping hot, as it is considered that this is how the flavour of the dish can be best appreciated.*
- *Halloumi can be used instead of feta if you prefer.*

Potato and Mussel Salad: *Energy 461kcal/1927kJ; Protein 18.1g; Carbohydrate 28.3g, of which sugars 3.2g; Fat 28g, of which saturates 7.1g; Cholesterol 45mg; Calcium 283mg; Fibre 3.2g; Sodium 210mg.*
Prawns with Tomatoes and Feta: *Energy 183kcal/761kJ; Protein 12.1g; Carbohydrate 5.8g, of which sugars 5.5g; Fat 12.5g, of which saturates 3.2g; Cholesterol 106mg; Calcium 113mg; Fibre 2g; Sodium 289mg.*

Moules Marinière

This is the best and easiest way to serve the small tender mussels, known as *bouchots*, that are farmed along much of the French coastline. Serve this classic dish with plenty of crusty bread to dip in the juices.

Serves 4
1.75kg/4½lb mussels
300ml/½ pint/1¼ cups dry white wine
4–6 large shallots, finely chopped
bouquet garni
freshly ground black pepper

1 Discard any broken mussels and those with open shells that refuse to close when tapped. Under cold running water, scrub the shells, scraping off any barnacles with a knife, and pulling out stringy beards.

2 In a large heavy-based flameproof casserole, combine the wine, shallots, bouquet garni and plenty of black pepper. Bring to a boil over a medium-high heat and cook for 2 minutes.

3 Add the mussels and cook, tightly covered, for about 5 minutes, or until the mussels have opened, shaking the pan occasionally.

4 Using a slotted spoon, divide the cooked mussels among individual warmed soup plates. Discard any mussels that have not opened. Tilt the casserole a little and hold it for a few seconds to allow any sand to settle to the bottom.

5 Spoon or pour the cooking liquid over the mussels, dividing it evenly, then serve immediately.

Cooks Tips
- *Farmed mussels are usually quite clean and the shells do not need very much scrubbing or scraping.*
- *Live mussels can be kept for up to 24 hours in the refrigerator. Always discard any open mussel that will not close when tapped sharply with a knife or on the work surface, as this indicates that it has died.*

Baked Mussels and Potatoes

This dish originates from Puglia, an area in the south-east of Italy that is noted for its imaginative baked casseroles. The cooked mussels, still in their half shells, are baked under a topping of tomato and breadcrumbs on a layer of potatoes that absorb their delicious juices.

Serves 2–3
675g/1½lb large mussels
225g/8oz potatoes, unpeeled
75g/5 tbsp olive oil
2 garlic cloves, finely chopped
8 leaves fresh basil, torn
225g/8oz tomatoes, peeled and thinly sliced
45ml/3 tbsp plain breadcrumbs
freshly ground black pepper

1 Scrub and debeard the mussels under cold running water. Discard any with broken shells and any open shells that do not close when tapped.

2 Place the mussels with a cupful of water in a large pan over a moderate heat. As soon as they have opened, lift them out using a slotted spoon. Discard any mussels that do not open. Remove and discard the empty half shells, leaving the mussels in the other half. Strain the liquid left in the pan through a layer of kitchen paper, and reserve.

3 Boil the potatoes for 12–15 minutes. Remove them from the water when they are still quite firm and leave to cool a little, then peel and slice them.

4 Preheat the oven to 180°C/350°F/Gas 4. Spread 30ml/2 tbsp of the olive oil over the bottom of a shallow ovenproof dish. Cover with the potato slices in a layer. Add the mussels in their half shells in one layer and sprinkle them with chopped garlic and pieces of basil.

5 Cover the mussels with a single layer of the tomato slices. Sprinkle the tomatoes evenly with breadcrumbs and black pepper, then pour over the filtered mussel liquid and the remaining olive oil. Bake for about 20 minutes, or until the tomatoes are soft and the breadcrumbs golden. Serve directly from the baking dish.

Moules Marinière: Energy 189kcal/799kJ; Protein 26.4g; Carbohydrate 2.4g, of which sugars 1.9g; Fat 3.1g, of which saturates 0.5g; Cholesterol 60mg; Calcium 308mg; Fibre 0.4g; Sodium 319mg.
Mussels and Potatoes: Energy 348kcal/1457kJ; Protein 16.7g; Carbohydrate 25.8g, of which sugars 3.4g; Fat 20.5g, of which saturates 3g; Cholesterol 30mg; Calcium 178mg; Fibre 1.7g; Sodium 288mg.

Grilled Garlic Mussels

The crunchy crumb topping provides a good contrast to the succulent mussels in this flavoursome French gratin-style dish.

Serves 4

1.5kg/3–3½lb mussels
120ml/4fl oz/½ cup dry white wine
50g/2oz/4 tbsp butter
2 shallots, finely chopped
2 garlic cloves, crushed
50g/2oz/6 tbsp dried white breadcrumbs
60ml/4 tbsp chopped fresh mixed herbs, such as flat leaf parsley, basil and oregano
30ml/2 tbsp freshly grated Parmesan cheese
salt and ground black pepper
basil leaves, to garnish

1 Scrub and debeard the mussels under cold running water. Discard any that are broken or open. Place in a pan with the wine. Cover and cook over a high heat, shaking the pan occasionally, for 3–4 minutes until the mussels have opened.

2 Strain the mussels and reserve the cooking liquid. Discard any shells that remain closed. Allow to cool slightly, then remove and discard the top half of each shell, leaving the mussels on the remaining halves.

3 Melt the butter in a large frying pan and fry the shallots until softened. Add the garlic and cook for 1–2 minutes.

4 Stir in the breadcrumbs and cook, stirring, until lightly browned. Remove from the heat and stir in the herbs. Moisten with a little of the reserved mussel liquid, then season to taste with salt and pepper. Preheat the grill (broiler).

5 Spoon the breadcrumb mixture over the mussels in their shells and arrange them on baking sheets. Sprinkle with the grated Parmesan.

6 Cook the mussels under the hot grill in batches for about 2 minutes, until the topping is crisp and golden. Keep the cooked mussels warm in a low oven while grilling (broiling) the remainder. Garnish with basil leaves and serve immediately.

Prawns in Spicy Tomato Sauce

The tomato sauce base can be sharpened up by adding hot chillies.

Serves 6

90ml/6 tbsp olive oil
1 medium onion, finely chopped
1 stick celery, finely chopped
1 small red (bell) pepper, chopped
120ml/4fl oz/½ cup red wine
15ml/1 tbsp wine vinegar
400g/14oz can plum tomatoes, chopped, with their juice
900g/2lb raw prawns (shrimp), in their shells
2–3 garlic cloves, finely chopped
45ml/3 tbsp finely chopped fresh parsley
1 piece dried chilli, crumbled or chopped (optional)
salt and ground black pepper

1 In a heavy pan, heat half the olive oil. Add the chopped onion, and cook over low heat until soft. Stir in the chopped celery and pepper, and cook gently for 5 minutes more.

2 Raise the heat to medium high, and add the wine, vinegar and tomatoes. Season with salt and pepper. Bring to a boil and cook for about 5 minutes.

3 Lower the heat, cover the pan, and simmer until the vegetables are soft, about 30 minutes. Purée the sauce through a food mill.

4 Shell the prawns and devein them, either by using a deveiner or by making a shallow incision with a small sharp knife down the centre of the back to disclose the long black vein. Remove and discard.

5 Heat the remaining oil in a clean heavy pan. Stir in the garlic, parsley and chilli, if using. Cook over moderate heat, stirring constantly, until the garlic is golden, but do not let it brown. Add the tomato sauce and bring to the boil. Taste to correct the seasoning.

6 Stir in the prawns and bring the sauce back to the boil. Reduce the heat slightly and simmer until the prawns are pink and firm, 4–6 minutes, depending on their size. Remove from the heat and serve.

Garlic Mussels: *Energy 289kcal/1211kJ; Protein 24g; Carbohydrate 10g, of which sugars 0.6g; Fat 15.2g, of which saturates 8.4g; Cholesterol 79mg; Calcium 333mg; Fibre 0.3g; Sodium 490mg.*
Prawns in Spicy Tomato Sauce: *Energy 191kcal/793kJ; Protein 12.7g; Carbohydrate 4.3g, of which sugars 4g; Fat 12.5g, of which saturates 1.8g; Cholesterol 63mg; Calcium 177mg; Fibre 1.2g; Sodium 1915mg.*

Pork with Marsala and Juniper

Sicilian Marsala gives savoury dishes a rich, fruity and alcoholic tang, but the pork is the most important ingredient, and good quality meat will also enhance the flavour of the sauce. Serve this quickly cooked dish with noodles and steamed green vegetables.

Serves 4
25g/1oz dried ceps
4 lean pork escalopes
10ml/2 tsp balsamic vinegar
8 garlic cloves
15g/½oz/1 tbsp butter
45ml/3 tbsp Marsala
several fresh rosemary sprigs
10 juniper berries, crushed
salt and ground black pepper

1 Put the dried ceps in a small bowl and just cover with hot water. Leave to soak for 15–20 minutes to soften them, then strain, reserving the mushrooms and the soaking water separately. Set aside.

2 Brush the pork with 5ml/1 tsp of the balsamic vinegar and season with salt and pepper. Set aside. Put the garlic cloves in a small pan, cover with boiling water and cook for 10 minutes, or until soft. Drain and set aside.

3 Melt the butter in a large non-stick frying pan. Add the pork and fry quickly until browned on the underside. Turn the meat over and cook for a further 1 minute.

4 Add the Marsala, rosemary sprigs, soaked mushrooms, 60ml/4 tbsp of the mushroom soaking water, the garlic, juniper berries and remaining vinegar.

5 Simmer gently for about 3 minutes, or until the pork is cooked through. Season lightly with salt and pepper and serve immediately.

Cook's Tip
Ceps (Boletus edulis) are known as porcini in Italian. Dried mushrooms can be used to add extra flavour to many sauces, soups and stews made with fresh cultivated mushrooms.

Wild Mushroom and Bacon Rösti

Dried ceps or porcini mushrooms have a wonderful woody, earthy aroma and taste. With salty bacon lardons, they turn potato rösti into a memorable supper.

Serves 4
675g/1½ lb floury potatoes
10g/¼ oz dried ceps or porcini mushrooms
225g/8oz very thick smoked bacon, cut into lardons or thin strips
2 fresh thyme sprigs, chopped
30ml/2 tbsp chopped fresh parsley
30ml/2 tbsp vegetable oil
4 large eggs, to serve
1 bunch watercress, to garnish
crushed black peppercorns, to garnish

1 Cook the potatoes in a saucepan of boiling salted water for 5 minutes and no longer, as they need to remain firm enough to grate at the next stage.

2 Meanwhile cover the mushrooms with boiling water and leave to soften for 5–10 minutes. Drain and chop.

3 Fry the bacon gently in a non-stick pan until all the fat has run out. Remove the bacon using a slotted spoon and reserve the fat.

4 Drain the potatoes and leave to cool. When they are cool enough to handle, grate them coarsely, then pat dry thoroughly on kitchen paper to remove all moisture. Place them in a large bowl and add the mushrooms, thyme, parsley and bacon. Mix together well.

5 Heat the bacon fat with a little of the oil in the frying pan until it is really hot. Spoon in the rösti mixture in heaps and flatten. Fry in batches for about 6 minutes until crisp and golden on both sides, turning once. Drain on kitchen paper and keep warm in a low oven.

6 Heat the remaining oil in the hot pan and fry the eggs as you like them. Serve the rösti at once with the eggs, watercress and crushed peppercorns.

Pork with Marsala: *Energy 184kcal/768kJ; Protein 24.2g; Carbohydrate 1.4g, of which sugars 1.4g; Fat 7.6g, of which saturates 3.5g; Cholesterol 79mg; Calcium 9mg; Fibre 0.1g; Sodium 102mg.*
Rosti: *Energy 387kcal/1616kJ; Protein 18.5g; Carbohydrate 27.2g, of which sugars 2.2g; Fat 23.6g, of which saturates 6.4g; Cholesterol 220mg; Calcium 42mg; Fibre 1.7g; Sodium 955mg.*

Cassoulet

This is a classic French dish in which various meats are baked slowly with root vegetables and tomatoes under a golden crumb crust. It is hearty and rich.

Serves 6–8

675g/1½lb/3¾ cups dried haricot (navy) beans
900g/2lb salt belly pork
4 large duck breast portions
60ml/4 tbsp olive oil
2 onions, chopped
6 garlic cloves, crushed
2 bay leaves
1.5ml/¼ tsp ground cloves
60ml/4 tbsp tomato purée (paste)
8 good quality sausages
12 large tomatoes, peeled
75g/3oz/¾ cup dried breadcrumbs
salt and ground black pepper

1 Put the beans in a large bowl and cover with plenty of cold water. Leave to soak overnight. Put the salt belly pork in a separate bowl of cold water and soak it overnight too.

2 Next day, drain the beans in a colander, rinse under cold water, drain again and put in a pan with fresh water to cover. Bring to the boil and boil the beans hard for 10 minutes. Drain.

3 Drain the pork, then cut it into large pieces, discarding the rind. Halve the duck breasts. Heat 30ml/2 tbsp of the oil in a frying pan and fry the pork in batches, until browned.

4 Put the beans in a large pan with the onions, garlic, bay leaves, ground cloves and tomato purée. Stir in the browned pork and just cover with water. Bring to the boil, then cover and simmer for about 1½ hours until the beans are tender.

5 Preheat the oven to 180°C/350°F/Gas 4. Heat the remaining oil and brown the duck breasts and sausages. Cut the sausages into smaller pieces and quarter the tomatoes.

6 Transfer the bean mixture to a large earthenware pot or ovenproof dish and stir in the fried sausages and duck breasts and the chopped tomatoes, with salt and pepper to taste. Sprinkle with an even layer of breadcrumbs and bake in the oven for 45 minutes to 1 hour until the crust is golden.

Potato, Chorizo and Cheese Tortilla

The classic Spanish tortilla contains only onions and potatoes, gently stewed in olive oil then stirred into eggs to make a thick cake-like omelette fried in a pan, then baked in the oven. Here, the combination of sliced potatoes with chilli and chorizo makes a potato cake with a real kick to it.

Serves 4

15ml/1 tbsp vegetable oil
½ onion, sliced
1 small green pepper, cut into rings
1 garlic clove, finely chopped
1 tomato, chopped
6 stoned (pitted) black olives, chopped
275g/10oz cooked firm, waxy potatoes, sliced
225g/8oz sliced chorizo, in strips
1 fresh green chilli, chopped
50g/2oz/½ cup Cheddar cheese, grated
6 eggs
45ml/3 tbsp milk
1.5ml/¼ tsp ground cumin
1.5ml/¼ tsp dried oregano
1.5ml/¼ tsp paprika
salt and ground black pepper
rocket (arugula) leaves, to garnish

1 Preheat the oven to 190°C/375°F/Gas 5. Line the base of a 23cm/9in round cake tin (pan) with baking parchment (parchment paper).

2 Heat the oil in a large non-stick frying pan. Add the onion, green pepper and garlic and cook over a medium heat for 5–8 minutes until softened.

3 Spoon the onion mixture into the prepared tin with the tomato, olives, potatoes, chorizo and chilli. Mix the ingredients together and sprinkle with cheese.

4 In a small bowl, whisk together the eggs and milk until frothy. Add the cumin, oregano, paprika and salt and pepper to taste. Whisk to blend.

5 Pour the egg mixture on to the vegetables, tilting the tin so that the egg mixture spreads evenly.

6 Bake for 30 minutes until set and lightly golden. Serve in wedges, hot or cold, with rocket leaves.

Cassoulet: *Energy 378kcal/1586kJ; Protein 31.1g; Carbohydrate 28.5g, of which sugars 6.7g; Fat 16.5g, of which saturates 5.6g; Cholesterol 93mg; Calcium 92mg; Fibre 6.6g; Sodium 581mg.*
Tortilla: *Energy 443kcal/1848kJ; Protein 16g; Carbohydrate 32.4g, of which sugars 3.6g; Fat 28.1g, of which saturates 12.3g; Cholesterol 49mg; Calcium 226mg; Fibre 1.9g; Sodium 728mg.*

Spanish Sausage Omelette Rice

This is a really unusual dish, flavoured with garlicky Spanish sausage and topped with beaten egg so that the effect suggests an omelette or even a soufflé. If you cannot get butifarra, use chorizo or any similar Spanish sausage instead.

Serves 6

45ml/3 tbsp sunflower oil
200g/7oz butifarra or other Spanish sausage, sliced
2 tomatoes, peeled, seeded and chopped
175g/6oz lean pork, cut into bitesize pieces
175g/6oz skinless, boneless chicken breast or rabbit, cut into chunks
350g/12oz/1¾ cups Spanish rice or risotto rice
900ml–1 litre/1½–1¾ pints/3¾–4 cups hot chicken stock
pinch of saffron strands, crushed
115g/4oz/⅔ cup cooked chickpeas
6 eggs
salt and ground black pepper

1 Preheat the oven to 190°C/375°F/Gas 5. Heat the oil in a flameproof casserole and fry the sausage for a few minutes. Transfer to a plate.

2 Add the tomatoes and fry for a few minutes until they have thickened slightly. Stir in the pork and chicken or rabbit pieces and cook for 2–3 minutes until the meat has browned lightly, stirring frequently.

3 Add the rice, stir over the heat for about a minute, then pour in the hot stock. Add the saffron, with salt and pepper to taste, and stir well.

4 Bring to the boil, then lower the heat and add the sausage and chickpeas. Cover tightly with a lid and cook over a low heat for about 15 minutes until the rice is tender.

5 Beat the eggs with a little water and a pinch of salt and pour over the rice. Place the casserole, uncovered, in the oven and cook for about 10 minutes, until the eggs have set and browned slightly on top.

Pork-Stuffed Cabbage Leaves

This is a really enticing winter meal, though time-consuming to make. The delicious result makes it well worth the effort.

Serves 4

115g/4oz/generous ½ cup long grain rice
1–2 large green cabbages, total weight 1.6–2kg/3½–4½lb
500g/1¼lb minced (ground) pork, or a mixture of pork and beef
1 large onion, roughly grated
3 eggs
30ml/2 tbsp chopped fresh flat leaf parsley
45–60ml/3–4 tbsp chopped fresh dill
90ml/6 tbsp extra virgin olive oil
25g/1oz/2 tbsp butter
15ml/1 tbsp cornflour (cornstarch)
juice of 1½ lemons
salt and ground black pepper

1 Soak the rice in cold water for 10 minutes, then drain, rinse under cold water and drain again. Core the cabbages and strip off the outer leaves. Rinse and set aside. Peel off the inner leaves until you reach the hard hearts. Set the hearts aside.

2 Rinse the leaves and cabbage hearts in cold water. Bring a large saucepan of water to the boil and blanch the leaves in batches for 1–2 minutes, until just pliable. Remove with a slotted spoon and place in a colander. Put in the cabbage hearts and let them boil for slightly longer. Drain.

3 Prepare the stuffing by combining the meat, rice, onion, one of the eggs and the fresh herbs in a bowl. Mix in half the olive oil and a generous amount of seasoning. Cut the larger leaves of the cabbage in half and trim any hard cores and veins. Place about 15ml/1 tbsp of the stuffing at one end of a leaf, fold the end of the leaf over so it looks like a short fat cigar, then fold in the sides and roll up fairly tightly to make a neat package.

4 Carefully strip as many leaves as possible from the blanched cabbage heart and stuff them individually. Leave the inner heart intact, but open the leaves at the top and stuff it, too.

5 Line a large heavy pan with the uncooked outer leaves. Layer the stuffed rolls in the pan, packing them tightly together. Season each layer as you go, then drizzle the remaining olive oil over the top and dot with butter.

6 Invert a small heatproof plate on top of the last layer. Pour in enough hot water to just cover the top layer. Cover and cook gently for about 50 minutes. As soon as the stuffed cabbage leaves are cooked, tilt the pan, holding the plate down firmly, and empty most of the liquid into a bowl. Let it cool slightly.

7 Mix the cornflour to a cream with a little water. Whisk the two remaining eggs in another bowl, then add the lemon juice and the cornflour mixture and whisk again. Continue to whisk, gradually adding tablespoons of the hot cooking liquid from the stuffed leaves. As soon as the liquid has all been added, pour the sauce over the stuffed cabbage leaves and shake the pan gently to distribute it evenly. Return the pan to a very gentle heat and cook for 3 minutes to thicken the sauce, rotating the pan occasionally, then serve.

Omelette Rice: *Energy 533kcal/2226kJ; Protein 29.1g; Carbohydrate 55.5g, of which sugars 1.7g; Fat 21.7g, of which saturates 6.3g; Cholesterol 242mg; Calcium 72mg; Fibre 1.5g; Sodium 436mg.*
Stuffed Cabbage Leaves: *Energy 697kcal/2902kJ; Protein 37.2g; Carbohydrate 51.5g, of which sugars 23.2g; Fat 38.4g, of which saturates 11.3g; Cholesterol 239mg; Calcium 270mg; Fibre 9.5g; Sodium 172mg.*

Pork with Chickpeas and Orange

This winter speciality is a familiar dish in the Aegean islands, particularly in Crete. Serve it with fresh bread and black olives, or with fluffy white rice.

Serves 4

350g/12oz/1¾ cups dried chickpeas, soaked overnight in water to cover
75–90ml/5–6 tbsp extra virgin olive oil
675g/1½ lb boneless leg of pork, cut into large cubes
1 large onion, sliced
2 garlic cloves, chopped
400g/14oz can chopped tomatoes
grated rind of 1 orange
1 small dried red chilli
salt and ground black pepper

1 Drain the chickpeas, rinse them under cold water and drain them again. Place them in a large, heavy pan. Pour in enough cold water to cover generously, put a lid on the pan and bring to the boil.

2 Skim the surface, replace the lid and cook gently for 1–1½ hours, testing them with a knife tip at intervals, until they are tender. Alternatively, cook them in a pressure cooker for 20 minutes under full pressure. When the chickpeas are soft, drain them, reserving the cooking liquid, and set them aside.

3 Heat the olive oil in the clean pan and brown the meat cubes in batches. As each cube browns, lift it out with a slotted spoon and put it on a plate. When all the meat cubes have been browned, add the onion to the oil remaining in the pan and sauté the slices until golden. Stir in the garlic, then as soon as it becomes aromatic, add the tomatoes and orange rind.

4 Crumble in the chilli. Return the chickpeas and meat to the pan, and pour in enough of the reserved cooking liquid to cover. Add the black pepper, but not salt at this stage.

5 Mix well, cover the pan and simmer for about 1 hour, or until the meat is tender. Stir occasionally and add more of the reserved liquid if needed. The result should be a moist casserole; not soupy, but not dry either. Season with salt before serving.

Spanish Hotpot

This Spanish dish known as cocido is Madrid's most famous stew. The broth makes a soup course and is then followed by the rest.

Serves 8

500–800g/1¼–1¾lb cured brisket or silverside (pot roast)
250g/9oz smoked streaky (fatty) bacon, in one piece
1 knuckle gammon (smoked or cured ham) bone, with some meat still attached
500–750g/1¼–1¾lb beef marrow bone, sawn through
1 pig's trotter (foot), sawn through
1 whole garlic bulb
2 bay leaves
5ml/1 tsp black peppercorns, lightly crushed
250g/9oz/1¼ cups dried chickpeas, soaked overnight and drained
2 quarters corn-fed chicken
1 onion, studded with 2–3 cloves
2 large carrots, cut into big pieces
2 leeks, cut into chunks
500g/1¼lb small new potatoes, scrubbed
2 red chorizo sausages
1 morcilla or 250g/9oz black pudding (blood sausage)
30ml/2 tbsp long grain rice
1 small (bell) pepper, finely diced
salt

1 Put the brisket or silverside, bacon and knuckle into a large pan and cover with water. Bring slowly to the boil, simmer for 5 minutes to remove excess salt, and drain. Pack, with the marrow bone and trotter, into a very large stockpot, skin-side down. Add the garlic bulb, bay leaves and peppercorns, with water to cover. Bring to simmering point and skim off any scum. Add the chickpeas, cover and simmer for 1½ hours, checking occasionally that there is enough liquid. Add the chicken and onion and continue to cook until the chickpeas are done.

2 Put the vegetables in a large pan with the chorizo. Cover with water and bring to the boil. Simmer for 25 minutes. About 5 minutes before the end, add the morcilla or black pudding.

3 Strain off the broth from the meat into a pan. Bring back to the boil, add the rice and cook for 15 minutes. Add the diced pepper and serve as soup. Drain the vegetables and sausages and arrange on a platter. Slice the meats, removing the marrow from the bone and adding it to the chickpeas. Arrange with the meats on another platter, moistening with a little broth.

Pork with Chickpeas: *Energy 654kcal/2743kJ; Protein 56.4g; Carbohydrate 52.4g, of which sugars 9.6g; Fat 25.7g, of which saturates 4.9g; Cholesterol 106mg; Calcium 178mg; Fibre 11.4g; Sodium 164mg.*
Spanish Hotpot: *Energy 593kcal/2478kJ; Protein 46.4g; Carbohydrate 37g, of which sugars 4.5g; Fat 29.6g, of which saturates 10.1g; Cholesterol 138mg; Calcium 116mg; Fibre 5.3g; Sodium 1100mg.*

Pork and Black Bean Stew

This simple stew uses a few robust ingredients to create a deliciously intense flavour: the Spanish equivalent of a French cassoulet.

Serves 5–6

275g/10oz/generous 1½ cups dried black beans
675g/1½lb boneless belly pork rashers (slices)
60ml/4 tbsp olive oil
350g/12oz baby onions
2 celery sticks, thinly sliced
10ml/2 tsp paprika
150g/5oz chorizo sausage, cut into chunks
600ml/1 pint/2½ cups light chicken or vegetable stock
2 green peppers, cut into large pieces
salt and ground black pepper

1 Put the beans in a bowl and cover with plenty of cold water. Leave to soak overnight. Drain the beans, place in a saucepan and cover with fresh water. Bring to the boil and boil rapidly for 10 minutes. Drain through a colander.

2 Preheat the oven to 160°C/325°F/Gas 3. Cut away any rind from the pork and cut the meat into large chunks.

3 Heat the oil in a large frying pan and fry the onions and celery for 3 minutes. Add the pork and fry for 5–10 minutes until the pork is browned all over. Add the paprika and chorizo and fry for a further 2 minutes. Transfer to an ovenproof dish with the black beans and mix together well.

4 Add the stock to the pan and bring to the boil. Season lightly then pour over the meat and beans. Cover and bake in the oven for 1 hour.

5 Stir the green peppers into the stew, then cover and return to the oven for a further 15 minutes. Serve hot.

Cook's Tip
This is the sort of stew to which you can add a variety of winter vegetables such as chunks of leek, turnip, celeriac and even new potatoes.

Pork Empanada

This flat, two-crust pie is famous because it is served at nearly all Spanish special occasions. It is good eaten hot or cold.

Serves 8

75ml/5 tbsp olive oil
2 onions, chopped
4 garlic cloves, finely chopped
1kg/2¼lb boned pork loin, diced
175g/6oz smoked gammon (smoked or cured ham), diced
3 red chorizo or other spicy sausages (about 300g/11oz)
3 (bell) peppers (mixed colours), chopped
175ml/6fl oz/¾ cup white wine
200g/7oz can tomatoes
pinch of saffron threads
5ml/1 tsp paprika
30ml/2 tbsp chopped fresh parsley
salt and ground black pepper

For the corn meal dough

250g/9oz corn meal
7g/2 tsp easy-blend (rapid-rise) dried yeast
5ml/1 tsp caster (superfine) sugar
250g/9oz plain (all-purpose) flour, plus extra for dusting
5ml/1 tsp salt
200ml/7fl oz/scant 1 cup warm water
30ml/2 tbsp oil
2 eggs, beaten, plus 1 for the glaze

1 Heat 60ml/4 tbsp oil and fry the onions, adding the garlic when they begin to colour. Transfer to a flameproof casserole. Fry the pork and gammon until coloured, stirring. Add to the casserole. Add 15ml/1 tbsp oil, fry the sausage and peppers and add to the dish. Deglaze the pan with the wine, and pour into the casserole. Add the tomatoes, saffron, paprika and parsley and season. Cook for 20–30 minutes. Leave to cool.

2 Meanwhile, put the corn meal into a food processor. Add the dried yeast with the sugar. Gradually add the flour, salt, water, oil and 2 eggs and beat to a smooth dough. Put into a bowl, cover with a cloth and leave in a warm place for 40–50 minutes.

3 Preheat the oven to 200°C/400°F/Gas 6. Grease a baking dish 30 × 20cm/12 × 8in and line with half the dough, leaving the border hanging over the edge. Spoon in the filling. Roll out the lid and lay it in place. Fold the outside edge over the lid and seal. Prick and brush with beaten egg. Bake for 30–35 minutes, covering the edges if they brown too much. Cut into squares.

Black Bean Stew: *Energy 625kcal/2599kJ; Protein 31.7g; Carbohydrate 29.7g, of which sugars 7.5g; Fat 42.9g, of which saturates 13.5g; Cholesterol 85mg; Calcium 82mg; Fibre 9g; Sodium 1625mg.*
Pork Empanada: *Energy 704kcal/2944kJ; Protein 35.5g; Carbohydrate 58.6g, of which sugars 6.5g; Fat 35.6g, of which saturates 12.2g; Cholesterol 129mg; Calcium 97mg; Fibre 3.2g; Sodium 592mg.*

Caramelized Onion, Salami and Black Olive Pizza

The flavour of the sweet caramelized onion is offset by the salty black olives and herbs in the pizza base and the sprinkling of Parmesan to finish.

Serves 4

700g/1½lb red onions, sliced
60ml/4 tbsp olive oil
1 quantity pizza dough (see Cook's Tip)
12 pitted black olives, chopped
5ml/1tsp dried herbes de Provence
6–8 slices Italian salami, quartered
30-45ml/2-3tbsp freshly grated Parmesan
ground black pepper

1 Preheat the oven to 220°C/425°F/Gas 7. Heat 30ml/2 tbsp of the oil in a pan and add the onions. Cover and cook gently for 15–20 minutes, stirring occasionally, until they are soft and lightly coloured. Leave to cool.

2 Knead the dough on a lightly floured surface, adding the black olives and dried herbs. Roll out and use to line a 30 × 18cm/12 × 7in shallow tin (pan). Push up the dough edges to make a thin rim and brush with half the remaining oil.

3 Spoon half the onions over the base, top with the salami and the remaining onions.

4 Grind over plenty of black pepper and drizzle over the remaining oil. Bake for 15–20 minutes, or until the dough is crisp and golden. Remove from the oven and sprinkle over the Parmesan to serve.

Cook's Tip
To make a pizza this size, sift 200g/7oz/1¼ cups strong white bread flour with a pinch of salt into a bowl. Add 1.5ml/¼ tsp easy-blend (rapid rise) dried yeast, 50ml/2fl oz/¼ cup olive oil and 75ml/5 tbsp water and mix to a dough. Knead for 10 minutes and leave in a covered, oiled bowl for about 1 hour.

Calzone

Looking like a folded pizza, a calzone consists of bread dough wrapped around a filling. The traditional tomato and garlic can be enlivened with chunks of sweet, melting cheese, olives, crumbled grilled bacon, slices of pepperoni or chorizo or a few chopped anchovy fillets.

Makes 4

30ml/2 tbsp extra virgin olive oil
1 small red onion, thinly sliced
2 garlic cloves, crushed
400g/14oz can chopped tomatoes
50g/2oz sliced chorizo sausage
50g/2oz/½ cup pitted black olives
double quantity pizza dough (see Cook's Tip below left)
200g/7oz mozzarella or other semi-soft cheese, diced
5ml/1 tsp dried oregano
salt and ground black pepper
oregano sprigs, to garnish

1 Heat the oil in a frying pan and sauté the onion and garlic for 5 minutes, until softened. Add the tomatoes and cook for 5 minutes more or until slightly reduced. Add the chorizo and olives. Season well.

2 Make up the pizza dough and put it in an oiled bowl. Cover with a cloth and leave in a warm place for about 1 hour, or until it has doubled in bulk.

3 Knock back the dough and divide it into four portions. Roll out each portion to a 20cm/8in circle. Preheat the oven to 200°C/400°F/Gas 6. Lightly grease two baking sheets.

4 Spread the filling on half of each dough circle, leaving a margin around the edge. Scatter over the cheese.

5 Sprinkle the filling with the dried oregano. Dampen the edges of the dough with cold water. Fold the dough in half and press well to seal.

6 Place two calzones on each baking sheet. Bake for 12–15 minutes until risen and golden. Cool for 2 minutes, then loosen with a palette knife and serve at once garnished with oregano.

Onion Pizza: Energy 462kcal/1928kJ; Protein 14.1g; Carbohydrate 49.8g, of which sugars 11.9g; Fat 24.3g, of which saturates 5.9g; Cholesterol 22mg; Calcium 242mg; Fibre 4.1g; Sodium 804mg.
Calzone: Energy 625kcal/2626kJ; Protein 22.5g; Carbohydrate 75g, of which sugars 7.3g; Fat 28.2g, of which saturates 9.8g; Cholesterol 39mg; Calcium 305mg; Fibre 4g; Sodium 1053mg.

Risotto with Bacon, Baby Courgettes and Peppers

A creamy risotto topped with vegetables and crisp bacon is irresistible and quite easy to make. A well-flavoured home-made stock makes all the difference to the final result. Chicken stock gives the flavour wonderful depth.

Serves 4

30ml/2 tbsp olive oil
115g/4oz rindless streaky (fatty) bacon rashers, cut into thick strips
350g/12oz/1¾ cups risotto rice
1.2 litres/2 pints/5 cups hot vegetable or chicken stock
30ml/2 tbsp single (light) cream
45ml/3 tbsp dry sherry
50g/2oz/⅔ cup freshly grated Parmesan cheese
50g/2oz/⅔ cup chopped fresh parsley
salt and ground black pepper

For the vegetables

1 red (bell) pepper
1 green (bell) pepper
25g/1oz/2 tbsp butter
75g/3oz horse mushrooms, sliced
225g/8oz baby courgettes (zucchini), halved
1 onion, halved and sliced
1 garlic clove, crushed

1 Heat half the oil in a frying pan. Add the bacon and heat gently until the fat runs. Increase the heat and fry until crisp, then drain on kitchen paper and set aside.

2 Heat the remaining oil in a heavy-based saucepan. Add the rice, stir to coat the grains, then ladle in a little of the hot stock. Stir until it has been absorbed. Gradually add the rest of the stock, stirring constantly.

3 Cut the peppers into chunks. Melt the butter in a separate pan and fry the peppers, mushrooms, courgettes, onion and garlic until the onion is just tender. Season well, then stir in the bacon.

4 When all the stock has been absorbed by the rice, stir in the cream, sherry, Parmesan, parsley and seasoning. Spoon the risotto on to individual plates and top each portion with fried vegetables and bacon. Serve immediately.

Leek and Ham Risotto

This risotto makes an easy supper, yet is special enough for a dinner party.

Serves 3–4

7.5ml/1½ tsp olive oil
40g/1½oz/3 tbsp butter
2 leeks, cut in slices
175g/6oz prosciutto, torn into pieces
75g/3oz/generous 1 cup button mushrooms, sliced
275g/10oz/1½ cups risotto rice
1 litre/1¾ pints/4 cups simmering chicken stock
45ml/3 tbsp chopped fresh flat leaf parsley
40g/1½oz/½ cup freshly grated Parmesan cheese
salt and ground black pepper

1 Heat the oil and butter in a pan and fry the leeks until soft. Set aside a few strips of prosciutto for the garnish and add the rest to the pan. Fry for 1 minute, then add the mushrooms and stir-fry for 2–3 minutes until lightly browned.

2 Add the rice. Cook, stirring, for 1–2 minutes until the grains are evenly coated in oil and have become translucent around the edges. Add a ladleful of hot stock. Stir until this has been absorbed completely, then add the next ladleful. Continue in this way until all the stock has been absorbed.

3 When the risotto is creamy and the rice is tender, stir in the parsley and Parmesan. Adjust the seasoning, remove from the heat and cover. Allow to rest for a few minutes. Spoon into a bowl, garnish with the reserved prosciutto and serve.

Risotto with Bacon: *Energy 624kcal/2595kJ; Protein 19g; Carbohydrate 78.4g, of which sugars 7.8g; Fat 24.2g, of which saturates 10g; Cholesterol 49mg; Calcium 228mg; Fibre 3g; Sodium 549mg.*
Leek Risotto: *Energy 444kcal/1853kJ; Protein 18.9g; Carbohydrate 58g, of which sugars 2.5g; Fat 14.8g, of which saturates 8g; Cholesterol 57mg; Calcium 160mg; Fibre 2.1g; Sodium 697mg.*

Roast Lamb with Figs

While there is little land suitable for rearing cattle in the Mediterranean, sheep have always been raised extensively throughout the region, and lamb (and mutton) is the favourite meat, and is invariably chosen for feasts and special occasions. Lamb fillet is an expensive cut of meat, but because it is boneless and very lean, and therefore lower in fat, there is very little waste. Serve it with baked potatoes and steamed green beans.

Serves 6

15ml/1 tbsp olive oil
1kg/2¼lb lamb fillet
9 fresh figs
150ml/¼ pint/⅔ cup ruby port
salt and ground black pepper

1 Preheat the oven to 190°C/375°F/Gas 5. Heat the oil in a flameproof roasting pan over a medium heat. Add the lamb fillet and sear quickly on all sides until evenly browned.

2 Cut the figs in half and arrange them around the lamb. Season the lamb with salt and black pepper and roast for 30 minutes. Pour the port over the figs.

3 Return the lamb to the oven and roast for a further 30–45 minutes. The meat should still be slightly pink in the middle so be careful not to overcook it.

4 Transfer the lamb to a chopping board and leave to rest for about 5 minutes, then carve into slices and serve with the figs and the juices from the pan.

Cook's Tip

In the Mediterranean region, fresh figs are grown mainly in Greece and Turkey and they are at their best from June until the end of September. Ripe figs have plump, soft flesh with a powdery, white bloom on the surface. They are perishable and will only keep fresh for a day or two.

Baked Lamb Yiouvetsi

A lamb *yiouvetsi* is very special in Greece. It is often made for the family lunch on the Feast of the Assumption of the Virgin Mary, on 15 August.

Serves 6

1 shoulder of lamb, most of the fat removed, sliced into serving portions
600g/1lb 6oz ripe tomatoes, peeled and chopped, or 400g/14oz can chopped plum tomatoes
5 ripe garlic cloves, chopped
75ml/5 tbsp extra virgin olive oil
5ml/1 tsp dried oregano
1 litre/1¾ pints/4 cups hot water
400g/14oz/3½ cups orzo pasta, or spaghetti, broken into short lengths
salt and ground black pepper
50g/2oz/½ cup freshly grated Kefalotiri or Parmesan cheese, to serve

1 Preheat the oven to 190°C/375°F/Gas 5. Rinse the meat to remove any obvious bone splinters, and place it in a large roasting pan.

2 Add the fresh or canned tomatoes and the crushed garlic, the olive oil and dried oregano. Season with salt and black pepper and stir in 300ml/½ pint/1¼ cups of the hot water.

3 Bake the lamb for about 1 hour 10 minutes, basting and turning twice.

4 Remove the lamb and reduce the oven temperature to 180°C/350°F/Gas 4. Add the remaining 700ml/scant 1¼ pints/2¾ cups hot water to the roasting pan. Stir in the pasta and add more seasoning.

5 Mix well, return the roasting tin to the oven and bake for 30–40 minutes more, stirring occasionally, until the meat is fully cooked and tender and the pasta is soft. Serve immediately, with a bowl of grated cheese to be sprinkled over the individual portions.

Roast Lamb with Figs: *Energy 517kcal/2170kJ; Protein 35.4g; Carbohydrate 41.1g, of which sugars 41.1g; Fat 23.6g, of which saturates 9.2g; Cholesterol 127mg; Calcium 204mg; Fibre 5.7g; Sodium 191mg.*
Baked Lamb: *Energy 528kcal/2222kJ; Protein 31.8g; Carbohydrate 52.5g, of which sugars 5.3g; Fat 22.7g, of which saturates 7.8g; Cholesterol 100mg; Calcium 131mg; Fibre 2.9g; Sodium 156mg.*

Albanian Liver

This is such a delicious way to eat lamb's liver that it is even possible to convert those who don't usually like offal by serving it to them. It is one of those dishes that was adopted by the Turkish kitchens as the Ottoman Empire consumed vast expanses of eastern Europe. Traditionally served as a hot or cold meze dish with sliced red onion and flat leaf parsley, it is also a wonderful dish for supper, served with a salad and a dollop of creamy yogurt if you like.

Serves 4

500g/1 ¼lb fresh lamb's liver
30ml/2 tbsp plain (all-purpose) flour
5–10ml/1–2 tsp Turkish red pepper or paprika
45–60ml/3–4 tbsp olive oil
2 garlic cloves, finely chopped
5–10ml/1–2 tsp cumin seeds
sea salt
1 large red onion, cut in half lengthways, in half again crossways, and sliced along the grain

To serve

a handful of fresh flat leaf parsley
1 lemon, cut into wedges

1 Using a sharp knife, remove any skin and ducts from the liver, then cut it into thin strips or bitesize cubes.

2 Mix the flour and red pepper or paprika in a shallow bowl and toss the liver in it until well coated.

3 Heat the oil in a heavy pan. Add the garlic and cumin seeds, season with sea salt and cook until the cumin gives off a nutty aroma. Toss in the liver and stir-fry quickly for 2–3 minutes so that it cooks on all sides. Remove and drain on kichen paper.

4 Spread the sliced onion on a serving dish, spoon the the liver in the middle and garnish with parsley leaves. Serve hot or cold, with the lemon wedges for squeezing.

Cook's Tip

Don't overcook the liver as it will quickly become dry and tough. It should still be pink inside, though just cooked through.

Moussaka

The Greeks have a number of cheeses that can be used in cooking. Kefalotiri, a hard cheese made with sheep's or goat's milk, makes the perfect topping for this classic dish.

Serves 6

2 large aubergines (eggplants), thinly sliced
45ml/3 tbsp olive oil
675g/1 ½lb/3 cups lean minced (ground) beef
1 onion, chopped
2 garlic cloves, crushed
2 large fresh tomatoes, chopped, or 200g/7oz canned chopped tomatoes
120ml/4fl oz/½ cup dry white wine
45ml/3 tbsp chopped fresh parsley
45ml/3 tbsp fresh breadcrumbs
2 egg whites
salt and ground black pepper

For the topping

40g/1 ½oz/3 tbsp butter
40g/1 ½oz/⅓ cup plain (all-purpose) flour
400ml/14fl oz/1⅔ cups milk
2.5ml/½ tsp freshly grated nutmeg
150g/5oz/1 ¼ cups grated Kefalotiri cheese
2 egg yolks, plus 1 whole egg

1 Layer the aubergines in a colander, sprinkling each layer with salt. Drain over a sink for 20 minutes, then rinse the salt off thoroughly and pat dry with kitchen paper.

2 Preheat the oven to 190°C/375°F/Gas 5. Spread out the aubergines in a roasting pan. Brush them with olive oil, then bake for 10 minutes, or until just softened. Remove and cool. Leave the oven on.

3 Make the meat sauce. Heat the olive oil in a large pan and brown the minced beef, stirring frequently. When the meat is no longer pink and looks crumbly, add the onion and garlic, and cook for 5 minutes.

4 Add the chopped fresh or canned tomatoes to the pan and stir in the wine. Season with plenty of salt and pepper to taste.

5 Bring to the boil, then lower the heat, cover and simmer for 15 minutes. Remove the pan from the heat, leave to cool for about 10 minutes, then stir in the chopped parsley, fresh breadcrumbs and egg whites.

6 Lightly grease a large baking dish, then spread out half the sliced aubergines, arranging them in an even layer on the base. Spoon over the meat sauce, spreading it evenly, then top with the remaining aubergines.

7 To make the topping, put the butter, flour and milk in a pan. Bring to the boil over a low heat, whisking all the time until the mixture thickens to form a smooth, creamy sauce. Lower the heat and simmer for 2 minutes. Remove the pan from the heat, season, then stir in the nutmeg and half the cheese.

8 Cool the mixture for 5 minutes, then beat in the egg yolks and the whole egg. Pour the sauce over the aubergines and sprinkle with the remaining cheese. Bake for 30–40 minutes, or until golden brown. Allow the dish to stand for 10 minutes before serving.

Albanian Liver: Energy 298Kcal/1245kJ; Protein 27g; Carbohydrate 11.8g, of which sugars 4.3g; Fat 16.3g, of which saturates 3.3g; Cholesterol 538mg; Calcium 37mg; Fibre 1.3g; Sodium 94mg.
Moussaka: Energy 588Kcal/2444kJ; Protein 37.9g; Carbohydrate 14.8g, of which sugars 3.7g; Fat 40.9g, of which saturates 18.2g; Cholesterol 206mg; Calcium 379mg; Fibre 2.4g; Sodium 506mg.

Lamb Cutlets with Tomato Sauce

Although veal is often favoured in Turkey, lamb cutlets are more readily available. The butchers prepare very fine cutlets by bashing them flat with a heavy meat mallet. You can ask your butcher to prepare them in the same way for this elegant dish. The cutlets are then quickly cooked on a griddle in their own fat, or a little butter, and served with a sprinkling of dried oregano and wedges of lemon, or with a piquant tomato sauce.

Serves 4

30ml/2 tbsp olive oil
10ml/2 tsp butter
12 lamb cutlets, trimmed and flattened with a mallet
1 onion, finely chopped
1 fresh green chilli, seeded and finely chopped
2 garlic cloves, finely chopped
5ml/1 tsp sugar
5–10ml/1–2 tsp white wine vinegar
2–3 large tomatoes, skinned and chopped, or 400g/14oz can chopped tomatoes
1 green (bell) pepper, finely chopped
a sprinkling of dried oregano
salt and ground black pepper

1 Heat the oil and butter in a large, heavy pan and quickly brown the cutlets on both sides.

2 Remove the cutlets from the pan, add the onion and fry, stirring frequently, for 6–8 minutes until it softens and begins to brown. Add the garlic and chilli and continue to cook for a few minutes.

3 Stir in the sugar and vinegar, then add the tomatoes and green pepper. Lower the heat, cover and simmer for about 30 minutes, until the mixture is thick and saucy. Season with salt and pepper.

4 Return the cutlets to the pan, covering them in the sauce. Cook for about 15 minutes, until the meat is tender.

5 Transfer the cutlets to a serving dish, arranging them around the edge with the bones sticking outwards. Sprinkle with oregano, spoon the sauce in the middle and serve immediately.

Kidneys in Sherry

Kidneys cooked in this way are extremely popular in Spanish tapas bars, and also make an excellent family supper. If you are serving them as a first course, partner the dish with fried toast triangles or crusty bread. A fino montilla wine could replace the sherry in this dish.

Serves 4

12 plump lambs' kidneys
60ml/4 tbsp olive oil
115g/4oz smoked bacon lardons, or diced pancetta
1 large onion, chopped
2 garlic cloves, finely chopped
30ml/2 tbsp plain (all-purpose) flour
150ml/¼ pint/⅔ cup fino sherry or Montilla wine
15ml/1 tbsp tomato purée (paste)
30ml/2 tbsp chopped fresh parsley
salt and freshly ground black pepper
new potatoes, boiled and buttered, to serve

1 Halve and skin the kidneys, then remove the cores. Cut the kidneys into cubes. Heat half the oil in a large frying pan and fry the bacon or pancetta until the fat starts to run. Add the onion and garlic and fry until softened. Remove to a plate.

2 Add the remaining oil to the pan and divide the kidneys into four batches. Put in one handful, and stir-fry over a high heat until sealed. (They should not give off any juice.) Remove to a plate and repeat with a second handful and remove to the plate. Continue until they are all cooked.

3 Return the onion and bacon mixture to the pan. Sprinkle with flour and cook, stirring gently. Add the sherry or Montilla wine and stir until thickened. Add the tomato purée and parsley. Return the kidneys to the pan, and heat through. Season well and serve hot with new potatoes.

Variation
This traditional dish can also be made with calves' kidneys, or with half lambs' kidneys and half chicken livers.

Lamb Cutlets: *Energy 683kcal/2822kJ; Protein 23.2g; Carbohydrate 7.4g, of which sugars 6.9g; Fat 62.4g, of which saturates 29.2g; Cholesterol 122mg; Calcium 24mg; Fibre 1.7g; Sodium 114mg.*
Kidneys: *Energy 483kcal/2021kJ; Protein 48.2g; Carbohydrate 8.1g, of which sugars 2g; Fat 24.4g, of which saturates 6.2g; Cholesterol 806mg; Calcium 40mg; Fibre 0.6g; Sodium 751mg.*

Lamb Meatballs with Pine Nuts and Cinnamon

A number of different types of meatball are made in the Turkish kitchen. Falling under the generic name *köfte*, they are generally made from lamb or beef, although some recipes are based on chicken, and they are shaped into round balls or plump ovals.

Serves 4–6

250g/9oz/generous 1 cup lean minced (ground) lamb
1 onion, finely chopped
2 garlic cloves, crushed
10–15ml/2–3 tsp ground cinnamon
30ml/2 tbsp pine nuts
30ml/2 tbsp currants, soaked in warm water for 5–10 minutes and drained
5ml/1 tsp Turkish red pepper or paprika
2 slices of day-old white or brown bread, ground into crumbs
1 egg, lightly beaten
15ml/1 tbsp tomato ketchup
1 bunch each of fresh flat leaf parsley and dill
60ml/4 tbsp plain (all-purpose) flour
sunflower oil, for shallow frying
salt and ground black pepper
lemon wedges, to serve

1 In a bowl, pound and mix the lamb with the onion, garlic and cinnamon. Knead with your hands and knock the air out of the mixture, then add the pine nuts with the currants, red pepper or paprika, breadcrumbs, egg and tomato ketchup. Season with salt and pepper.

2 Finely chop the herbs, reserving 1–2 sprigs of parsley for the garnish, and knead into the mixture, making sure all the ingredients are mixed well together.

3 Take apricot-size portions of the mixture in your hands and roll into balls. Flatten each ball so that it resembles a thick disc, then coat lightly in the flour.

4 Heat a thin layer of oil in a heavy pan. Add the meatballs and cook for 8–10 minutes, until browned on all sides. Remove with a slotted spoon and drain on kitchen paper. Serve hot with lemon wedges and garnish with parsley.

Lamb Burgers with Hot, Spicy Red Onion and Tomato Relish

A sharp-sweet red onion relish works really well with burgers based on Middle-Eastern style lamb. Serve them with pitta bread and a green salad.

Serves 4

25g/1oz/3 tbsp bulgur wheat
500g/1¼lb lean minced (ground) lamb
1 small red onion, finely chopped
2 garlic cloves, finely chopped
1 fresh green chilli, seeded and finely chopped
5ml/1 tsp ground toasted cumin seeds
2.5ml/½ tsp ground sumac
15g/½oz fresh parsley, chopped
30ml/2 tbsp chopped fresh mint
olive oil, for frying
salt and ground black pepper

For the relish

2 red onions, cut into 5mm/¼in thick slices
75ml/5 tbsp extra virgin olive oil
2 red (bell) peppers, halved
350g/12oz cherry tomatoes, chopped
1 fresh red or green chilli, seeded and finely chopped
30ml/2 tbsp chopped fresh mint
30ml/2 tbsp chopped fresh parsley
15ml/1 tbsp chopped fresh oregano
2.5–5ml/½–1 tsp ground sumac
15ml/1 tbsp lemon juice
sugar, to taste

1 Pour 150ml/¼ pint/⅔ cup hot water over the bulgur wheat in a bowl and leave to stand for 15 minutes, then tip into a sieve lined with a clean dish towel. Drain, then squeeze out the excess moisture.

2 Place the bulgur wheat in a bowl and add the lamb, onion, garlic, chilli, cumin, sumac, parsley and mint. Mix thoroughly together by hand, then season with 5ml/1 tsp salt and plenty of ground black pepper and mix again.

3 Using your hands, form the mixture into eight burgers and set aside while you make the relish.

4 Brush the onions with 15ml/1 tbsp of the oil and grill (broil) for about 5 minutes on each side, until well browned. Cool, then chop.

5 Grill the peppers, skin-side up, until the skin chars and blisters. Place in a bowl, cover and leave to stand for 10 minutes. Peel off the skin, dice the peppers finely and place in a bowl.

6 Add the onions to the peppers in the bowl, with the tomatoes, chilli, herbs and sumac. Stir in the remaining oil and the lemon juice. Season with salt, pepper and sugar.

7 Heat a heavy frying pan or a ridged, cast-iron grill (broiling) pan over a high heat and grease lightly with olive oil. Cook the burgers for about 5–6 minutes on each side, or until just cooked at the centre.

8 While the burgers are cooking, taste the relish and adjust the seasoning. Serve the burgers as soon as they are cooked, with the relish.

Meatballs: *Energy 261kcal/1088kJ; Protein 11.4g; Carbohydrate 15.4g, of which sugars 5.2g; Fat 17.5g, of which saturates 4g; Cholesterol 64mg; Calcium 40mg; Fibre 0.7g; Sodium 129mg.*
Lamb Burgers: *Energy 537kcal/2228kJ; Protein 27.2g; Carbohydrate 19g, of which sugars 13.4g; Fat 39.6g, of which saturates 11.1g; Cholesterol 96mg; Calcium 83mg; Fibre 4.2g; Sodium 105mg.*

Vine Leaves Stuffed with Lamb and Rice

The best known stuffed vine leaves are the ones filled with aromatic rice and served cold. In Turkey, the meat-filled version is usually served hot as a main course with a dollop of yogurt.

Serves 4–6

350g/12oz/1½ cups finely minced (ground) lamb or beef
2 onions, finely chopped
115g/4oz/generous ½ cup long grain rice, rinsed and drained
1 bunch each of fresh dill, flat leaf parsley and mint, chopped
45–60ml/3–4 tbsp olive oil
25–30 fresh or preserved vine leaves
juice of 1 lemon
salt and ground black pepper

To serve

60–90ml/4–6 tbsp thick natural (plain) yogurt
1 lemon, cut into wedges

1 Put the lamb in a bowl and stir in the onions, rice and herbs. Season, bind with 15ml/1 tbsp of the oil and knead together.

2 Lay a vine leaf on a flat surface and spoon a little of the meat and rice mixture at the top of the leaf. Pull the top over the filling, fold in the sides, then roll the leaf into a tight, stout-shaped log. Repeat with the remaining leaves and filling.

3 Arrange the stuffed vine leaves, seam side down, in a deep, wide, heavy pan. Pack them tightly in circles, making more than one layer if they won't all fit on the bottom of the pan.

4 In a bowl, mix the remaining oil with the lemon juice and 150ml/¼ pint/⅔ cup water, then pour over the vine leaves. The liquid should come at least halfway up the top layer, so you may need to add extra liquid.

5 Put the pan over a medium heat. Once the liquid begins to bubble, place a plate over the leaves to stop them unravelling, followed by a lid or foil. Lower the heat and leave the vine leaves to steam gently for 45 minutes, until the rice and meat are cooked. Serve hot, with the yogurt and lemon wedges.

Turkish Lamb on a Bed of Rice

The juices of the lamb flavour the rice deliciously in this Turkish recipe.

Serves 6

half leg of lamb, about 1.5kg/3–3½lb, boned
bunch of fresh parsley
small bunch of fresh coriander
50g/2oz/½ cup cashew nuts
2 garlic cloves
15ml/1 tbsp sunflower oil
1 small onion, finely chopped
200g/7oz/1¾ cups cooked white long grain rice
75g/3oz/scant ½ cup ready-to-eat dried apricots, finely chopped
salt and ground black pepper
fresh parsley or coriander sprigs, to garnish
tzatziki, black olives and pitta bread, to serve

1 Preheat the oven to 200°C/400°F/Gas 6. Remove the excess fat from the lamb, then trim or cut the joint so that it lies flat.

2 Put the parsley and coriander in a food processor or blender and process until finely chopped. Add the cashew nuts and chop roughly. Crush 1 of the garlic cloves. Heat the oil and fry the onion and garlic for 3–4 minutes until softened.

3 Put the rice in a bowl and add the parsley and cashew nut mixture, the fried onion mixture and the chopped apricots. Season with salt and pepper, stir well, then spoon into the bottom of a roasting pan just large enough to hold the lamb.

4 Cut the remaining garlic clove in half and rub the cut sides over the meat. Season with pepper, then lay the meat on top of the rice, tucking all the rice under the meat.

5 Roast the lamb for 30 minutes, then lower the oven temperature to 180°C/350°F/Gas 4. Cook for 35–45 minutes more or until the meat is cooked to your taste.

6 Cover the lamb and rice with foil and leave to rest for 5 minutes, then lift the lamb on to a board and slice it thickly. Spoon the rice mixture on to a platter, arrange the meat slices on top and garnish with fresh parsley or coriander. Serve at once, with tzatziki, black olives and pitta bread.

Vine Leaves: *Energy 276kcal/1148kJ; Protein 14.6g; Carbohydrate 23.5g, of which sugars 6.6g; Fat 13.8g, of which saturates 4.4g; Cholesterol 45mg; Calcium 88mg; Fibre 2.8g; Sodium 51mg.*
Turkish Lamb: *Energy 644kcal/2706kJ; Protein 77.5g; Carbohydrate 17.2g, of which sugars 5.6g; Fat 30.1g, of which saturates 10.7g; Cholesterol 250mg; Calcium 38mg; Fibre 1.2g; Sodium 184mg.*

Lamb Kebabs

Traditionally, this dish is made with scraps of lamb, chargrilled on swords.

Serves 4–6

2 onions
7.5ml/1½ tsp salt
2 garlic cloves, crushed
10ml/2 tsp cumin seeds, crushed
900g/2lb boneless shoulder of lamb, trimmed and cut into bitesize pieces

For the flat breads

225g/8oz/2 cups strong white bread flour
50g/2oz/¼ cup wholemeal (whole-wheat) flour
5ml/1 tsp salt

To serve

1 large red onion, thinly sliced
1 large bunch of fresh flat leaf parsley, roughly chopped
2–3 lemons, cut into wedges

1 Grate the onions, sprinkle with the salt and leave for about 15 minutes. Place a sieve (strainer) over a large bowl, tip in the onions and press down with a wooden spoon to extract the juice. Discard the onions. Mix the garlic and cumin seeds into the onion juice and toss in the lamb. Cover and leave to marinate for 3–4 hours.

2 To prepare the bread, sift the flours and salt into a bowl. Make a well in the middle and gradually add 200ml/7fl oz/scant 1 cup lukewarm water, drawing in the flour from the sides. Knead the dough until firm and springy – if it is sticky, add more flour. Divide the dough into 24 pieces and knead each one into a ball. Place on a floured surface and cover with a damp cloth. Leave to rest for 45 minutes. Prepare a barbecue.

3 Just before cooking, roll each ball of dough into a wide, thin circle. Dust them with flour and keep them covered with a damp dish towel to prevent them drying out.

4 Thread the meat on to flat skewers and cook on the barbecue for 2–3 minutes on each side. At the same time, cook the flat breads on a hot griddle or other flat pan, flipping them over as they begin to go brown and buckle. Slide the meat off the skewers on to the flat breads. Sprinkle onion and parsley over each pile and squeeze lemon juice over the top. Wrap the breads into parcels and eat with your hands.

Shish Kebab

This is easy and delicious – chargrilled meat served on flat bread with yogurt and tomatoes. Designed to use up day-old Turkish *pide*, for which pitta or plain naan can be substituted, the dish is succulent and tasty and can be devoured on its own.

Serves 4

12 plum tomatoes
30ml/2 tbsp butter
1 large pide, or 4 pitta or small naan, cut into bitesize chunks
5ml/1 tsp ground sumac
5ml/1 tsp dried oregano
225g/8oz/1 cup thick natural (plain) yogurt
salt and ground black pepper
1 bunch of fresh flat leaf parsley, chopped, to garnish

For the kebabs

500g/1¼lb/2¼ cups lean minced (ground) lamb
2 onions, finely chopped
1 fresh green chilli, seeded and finely chopped
4 garlic cloves, crushed
5ml/1 tsp paprika
5ml/1 tsp ground sumac
1 bunch of fresh flat leaf parsley, finely chopped

For the sauce

30ml/2 tbsp olive oil
15ml/1 tbsp butter
1 onion, finely chopped
2 garlic cloves, finely chopped
1 fresh green chilli, seeded and finely chopped
5–10ml/1–2 tsp sugar
400g/14oz can chopped tomatoes

1 To make the kebabs, put the lamb into a bowl with all the other ingredients and knead well to a smooth, sticky paste . Cover and chill for about 15 minutes.

2 Heat the oil and butter in a heavy pan, stir in the onion, garlic and chilli and cook until they begin to colour. Add the sugar and tomatoes and cook, uncovered, for about 30 minutes until quite thick. Season with salt and pepper, remove from the heat and keep warm.

3 Get the barbecue ready for cooking and shape the kebabs. As soon as the kebabs are ready, put them on the barbecue and cook for 6–8 minutes, turning once. Meanwhile, thread the whole plum tomatoes on to four skewers and place them on the barbecue until they are charred.

4 While the kebabs are cooking, melt the butter in a heavy pan and toss in the pide or other bread until golden. Sprinkle with some of the sumac and oregano, then arrange on a serving dish, spreading the pieces out so they form a flat base.

5 Splash a little sauce over the pide and spoon half the yogurt on top.

6 When the kebabs are cooked on both sides, slip the meat off the skewers and cut it into bitesize pieces. Arrange on the pide with the tomatoes, sprinkle with salt and the rest of the sumac and oregano, and garnish with chopped parsley. Serve hot, topped with dollops of the remaining sauce and yogurt.

Cook's Tip

Pide *is a Turkish bread, shaped into flat boat-shaped loaves and often sold filled with mixtures of vegetables or meat.*

Lamb Kebabs: *Energy 433kcal/1821kJ; Protein 34.3g; Carbohydrate 37.1g, of which sugars 4.4g; Fat 17.5g, of which saturates 7.9g; Cholesterol 114mg; Calcium 83mg; Fibre 2.5g; Sodium 460mg.*
Shish Kebab: *Energy 642kcal/2688kJ; Protein 35.2g; Carbohydrate 52.8g, of which sugars 24.1g; Fat 33.9g, of which saturates 15.1g; Cholesterol 121mg; Calcium 253mg; Fibre 6.3g; Sodium 456mg.*

Lamb Shanks with Cannellini Beans

Earthy and substantial, this is the ideal dish for chilly autumn evenings. The beans acquire layers of flavours when slow-cooked in the rich sauce provided by the meat. A clean-tasting, lemon-dressed salad is all it needs as an accompaniment.

Serves 4–6

4 lamb shanks
45ml/3 tbsp plain (all-purpose) flour
45ml/3 tbsp extra virgin olive oil
1 large onion, chopped
2 garlic cloves, sliced
1 celery stick, sliced
1 carrot, sliced
leaves from 2 fresh rosemary sprigs
2 bay leaves
175ml/6fl oz/¾ cup white wine
30ml/2 tbsp tomato purée (paste)
225g/8oz/1¼ cups dried cannellini beans, soaked overnight in water to cover
150ml/¼ pint/⅔ cup hot water
salt and ground black pepper

1 Preheat the oven to 160°C/325°F/Gas 3. Season the lamb shanks and coat them lightly in flour. Heat the oil in a large flameproof casserole over a high heat and brown the meat on all sides. Lift them out and set them aside.

2 Add the onion to the oil remaining in the casserole and sauté gently. As soon as it is light golden, stir in the garlic, celery, carrot, rosemary and bay leaves.

3 Put the meat back in the pan and pour the wine slowly over it. Let it bubble and reduce, then stir in the tomato purée diluted in 450ml/¾ pint/scant 2 cups hot water. Drain the soaked beans and add them to the pan with black pepper to taste. Mix well. Cover the casserole, transfer it to the oven and bake for 1 hour. Stir in salt to taste and add the hot water. Cover and cook for 1 hour more, or until the lamb is tender.

Cook's Tip
Pieces of boned shoulder could be used for this dish, but the bones in the shanks impart extra flavour to the casserole.

Liver and Bacon Casserole

In Spain, liver often means pig's liver because lambs are killed when they are very small so the liver is not much of a meal. However, many people prefer lamb's liver in this succulent recipe.

Serves 3–4

450g/1lb lamb's or pig's liver, trimmed and sliced
60ml/4 tbsp milk (for pig's liver)
30ml/2 tbsp olive oil
225g/8oz rindless smoked lean bacon rashers (strips), cut into pieces
2 onions, halved and sliced
175g/6oz/2¼ cups brown cap (cremini) mushrooms, halved
25g/1oz/2 tbsp butter
30ml/2 tbsp plain (all-purpose) flour
150ml/¼ pint/⅔ cup hot chicken stock
15ml/1 tbsp soy sauce
5ml/1 tsp paprika
salt and ground black pepper

1 If using pig's liver, soak it in the milk for 1 hour for a milder flavour, then blot dry with kitchen paper.

2 Heat the oil in a frying pan and stir-fry the bacon until crisp. Add the onion and cook, stirring, until softened. Add the mushrooms and fry for 1 minute.

3 Using a slotted spoon, remove the bacon and vegetables from the pan and keep warm. Add the liver to the fat left in the pan and cook over a high heat for 3–4 minutes, turning once to seal on both sides. Remove from the pan and keep warm.

4 Melt the butter in the pan, sprinkle the flour over and cook briefly. Stir in the stock, soy sauce and paprika and bring to a simmer. Return the liver and vegetables. Simmer gently for 3–4 minutes. Check the seasoning.

Variation
Bread is the classic accompaniment to this dish, but macaroni or a choice of vegetables also make good partners.

Lamb Shanks: *Energy 588kcal/2465kJ; Protein 43.9g; Carbohydrate 39.9g, of which sugars 6.6g; Fat 26.2g, of which saturates 9.1g; Cholesterol 114mg; Calcium 110mg; Fibre 10.5g; Sodium 161mg.*
Liver and Bacon Casserole: *Energy 386kcal/1610kJ; Protein 35.3g; Carbohydrate 8g, of which sugars 1.4g; Fat 23.9g, of which saturates 8.8g; Cholesterol 336mg; Calcium 29mg; Fibre 0.9g; Sodium 1267mg.*

Spring Lamb Casserole with Fresh Peas

In Greece, milk-fed lamb is at its best in April and May. It is meltingly sweet and tender, and its arrival more or less coincides with the time when fresh peas put in an appearance in the vegetable markets. Young peas play an important role in many traditional Greek spring recipes. Here, peas and lamb are combined to produce one of the most delicious Greek dishes – a real treat.

Serves 4–6

75ml/5 tbsp extra virgin olive oil
4–6 thick shoulder of lamb steaks, with the bone in
1 large onion, thinly sliced
5 or 6 spring onions (scallions), roughly chopped
2 carrots, sliced in rounds
juice of 1 lemon
1.2kg/2½lb fresh peas in pods, shelled (this will yield about 500–675g/1¼–1½lb peas)
60ml/4 tbsp finely chopped fresh dill
salt and ground black pepper

1 Heat the olive oil in a wide, heavy pan. Brown the lamb on both sides. Lift the pieces out, and set them to one side.

2 Sauté the onion slices in the oil remaining in the pan until they are translucent. Add the chopped spring onions and, 1 minute later, the sliced carrots. Sauté for 3–4 minutes, until slightly tender.

3 Return the lamb steaks to the pan, pour the lemon juice over them and let it evaporate for a few seconds. Pour over enough hot water to cover the meat. Add salt and pepper.

4 Cover and simmer for 45–50 minutes, or until the meat is almost tender, turning the steaks over and stirring the vegetables from time to time.

5 Add the peas and half the dill, adding a little more water if the pan is becoming dry. Replace the lid and cook for 20–30 minutes, or until the meat is tender and the vegetables are fully cooked. Sprinkle the remaining dill over the casserole just before serving.

Lamb Sausages with Tomato Sauce

The Greek name for these delicious sausage-shaped meatballs is *soudzoukakia*. Cooked in a thick tomato sauce they make a rich and tasty dish.

Serves 4

50g/2oz/1 cup fresh breadcrumbs
150ml/¼ pint/⅔ cup milk
675g/1½ lb/6 cups minced (ground) lamb
30ml/2 tbsp grated onion
3 garlic cloves, crushed
10ml/2 tsp ground cumin
30ml/2 tbsp chopped fresh parsley
flour, for dusting
60ml/4 tbsp olive oil
salt and ground black pepper
flat leaf parsley, to garnish

For the sauce

600ml/1 pint/2½ cups passata
5ml/1 tsp sugar
2 bay leaves
1 small onion, peeled

1 In a mixing bowl, combine the fresh breadcrumbs and the milk. Then add the minced lamb, onion, garlic, ground cumin and parsley and season with salt and pepper, and mix it all together thoroughly.

2 Shape the lamb mixture with your hands into little fat sausages, about 5cm/2in long, and roll them in flour. Heat the olive oil in a frying pan.

3 Fry the sausages for about 8 minutes, turning them until evenly browned. Drain on kitchen paper.

4 Put the passata, sugar, bay leaves and whole onion in a pan and simmer for 20 minutes. Add the sausages and cook for 10 minutes. Take out the sausages and place on a serving dish, garnished with parsley.

Cook's Tip

Passata is sieved tomatoes, and can be bought in cartons or jars from supermarkets and delicatessens. It is a very useful storecupboard (pantry) standby, handy for making soups and sauces that need to be smooth.

Lamb Casserole: *Energy 858kcal/3551kJ; Protein 40.2g; Carbohydrate 29g, of which sugars 11.8g; Fat 65.6g, of which saturates 26.9g; Cholesterol 119mg; Calcium 79mg; Fibre 10.2g; Sodium 132mg.*
Lamb Sausages: *Energy 477kcal/1990kJ; Protein 35.3g; Carbohydrate 13.8g, of which sugars 3.8g; Fat 31.6g, of which saturates 12.1g; Cholesterol 132mg; Calcium 98mg; Fibre 0.7g; Sodium 229mg.*

Lamb and Cos Lettuce Casserole

A classic Greek dish, this is found on the islands and the mainland, from the Ionian to the Aegean Sea. It is eaten during the period following Easter, when young lambs are at their best and succulent lettuces and fresh dill are abundant.

Serves 4–6

45ml/3 tbsp olive oil
1 onion, chopped
1kg/2¼lb boned leg of lamb, sliced into 4–6 medium steaks
2 cos or romaine lettuces, coarsely shredded
6 spring onions (scallions), sliced
60ml/4 tbsp roughly chopped fresh dill, plus extra to garnish
2 eggs
15ml/1 tbsp cornflour (cornstarch) mixed with 120ml/4fl oz/½ cup water
juice of 1 lemon
salt

1 Heat the olive oil in a large, heavy pan. Add the chopped onion and sauté for 3–5 minutes, until translucent.

2 Increase the heat, add the lamb steaks and cook, turning them over frequently, until all the moisture has been driven off, a process that will take about 15 minutes. Add salt to taste and enough hot water to cover the meat. Cover the pan and simmer for about 1 hour, or until the meat is just tender.

3 Add the lettuces, spring onions and dill. If necessary, pour in a little more hot water so that all the vegetables are almost covered. Replace the pan lid and simmer for 15–20 minutes more. Remove from the heat and leave to stand for 5 minutes.

4 Beat the eggs lightly in a bowl, add the cornflour mixture and beat until smooth. Add the lemon juice and whisk briefly, then continue to whisk while gradually adding 75–90ml/5–6 tbsp of the hot liquid from the pan containing the lamb.

5 Pour the sauce over the meat. Do not stir; instead gently shake and rotate the pan until the sauce is incorporated with the remaining liquid. Return the pan to a gentle heat for 2–3 minutes, just long enough to warm the sauce through. Do not let it boil, or the sauce is likely to curdle. Serve on warmed plates and sprinkle over some extra chopped dill.

Lamb-stuffed Squash

Acorn squash are perfect for baking with fillings. Here, a tasty melange of lamb, rice and feta cheese is topped with a rich and creamy tomato sauce.

Serves 6

6 acorn squash, halved
45ml/3 tbsp lemon juice
25g/1oz/2 tbsp butter
30ml/2 tbsp plain (all-purpose) flour
250ml/8fl oz/1 cup whipping cream
175ml/6fl oz/¾ cup passata (bottled strained tomatoes)
115g/4oz feta cheese, crumbled, and basil leaves, to garnish, plus extra to serve

For the filling

350–450g/12–16oz cooked lean lamb
175g/6oz/1½ cups cooked long grain rice
25g/1oz/2 tbsp butter, melted
25g/1oz/½ cup fresh breadcrumbs
50ml/2fl oz/¼ cup milk
30ml/2 tbsp finely grated onion
30ml/2 tbsp chopped parsley
2 eggs, beaten
salt and ground black pepper

1 Preheat the oven to 180°C/350°F/Gas 4. Trim the bases of the squash, if necessary, so that they will stand up securely. Scoop out the squash with a teaspoon, taking care not to cut the outer skin. Leave about 1cm/½in of flesh at the base.

2 Blanch the squash in boiling water with the lemon juice for 2–3 minutes, then plunge them into cold water. Drain well and leave to cool.

3 Meanwhile, make the filling by combining in a bowl the cooked lamb and rice, the butter, fresh breadcrumbs, milk, onion, parsley, beaten eggs and seasoning. Place the squash in a lightly greased ovenproof dish, and fill with the lamb mixture.

4 To make the sauce, put the butter and flour in a pan. Whisk in the cream and bring to the boil, whisking all the time. Cook for 1–2 minutes, or until thickened, then season. Pour the sauce over the squash, then pour over the passata. Bake for 25–30 minutes. To serve, drizzle with sauce from the pan and sprinkle with cheese and basil. Serve the remaining sauce, feta and basil separately.

Casserole: Energy 598kcal/2497kJ; Protein 53.8g; Carbohydrate 7.1g, of which sugars 3.2g; Fat 39.8g, of which saturates 15.1g; Cholesterol 285mg; Calcium 95mg; Fibre 1.9g; Sodium 260mg.
Stuffed Squash: Energy 583kcal/2,427kJ; Protein 23.3g; Carbohydrate 40g, of which sugars 9.1g; Fat 37g, of which saturates 21.5g; Cholesterol 183mg; Calcium 237mg; Fibre 3.9g; Sodium 513mg.

Lamb Goulash with Tomatoes and Peppers

Goulash is a popular and traditional dish that has travelled from Hungary and makes excellent use of the Mediterranean's wonderful tomatoes, green peppers, marjoram and fresh garlic.

Serves 4–6

30ml/2 tbsp vegetable oil
900g/2lb lean lamb, trimmed and cut into cubes
1 large onion, roughly chopped
2 garlic cloves, crushed
3 green (bell) peppers, diced
30ml/2 tbsp paprika
2 × 400g/14oz cans chopped tomatoes
15ml/1 tbsp chopped fresh flat leaf parsley
5ml/1 tsp chopped fresh marjoram
30ml/2 tbsp plain (all-purpose) flour
salt and ground black pepper
green salad, to serve

1 Heat the oil in a frying pan. Fry the pieces of lamb for 5–8 minutes, stirring frequently with a wooden spoon, or until browned on all sides. Season well.

2 Stir in the chopped onion and crushed garlic, and cook for a further 2 minutes. Add the diced green peppers, then sprinkle over the paprika and stir it in.

3 Pour in the tomatoes and enough water, if needed, to cover the meat in the pan. Stir in the herbs. Bring to the boil, then reduce the heat, cover and simmer very gently for 1½ hours or until the lamb is tender.

4 Blend the flour with 60ml/4 tbsp water and pour into the stew. Bring back to the boil, then reduce the heat and simmer, stirring occasionally, until thickened. Serve with a green salad.

Cook's Tip
Lard (shortening) is traditionally used for frying the lamb cubes, and can be substituted for the vegetable oil.

Lamb with Red Peppers and Rioja

World-famous for its red wine, Rioja in northern Spain also produces excellent red peppers. It even has an annual fair at Lodoso for red peppers. With rioja they give this lamb stew a lovely rich flavour. Boiled potatoes are an ideal accompaniment.

Serves 4

15ml/1 tbsp plain (all-purpose) flour
1kg/2¼lb lean lamb, cubed
60ml/4 tbsp olive oil
2 red onions, sliced
4 garlic cloves, sliced
10ml/2 tsp paprika
1.5ml/¼ tsp ground cloves
400ml/14fl oz/1⅔ cups red Rioja
150ml/¼ pint/⅔ cup lamb stock
2 bay leaves
2 thyme sprigs
3 red (bell) peppers, halved
salt and freshly ground black pepper
bay leaves and thyme sprigs, to garnish (optional)

1 Preheat the oven to 160°C/325°F/Gas 3. Season the flour, add the lamb and toss lightly to coat.

2 Heat the oil in a frying pan and fry the lamb until browned. Transfer to an ovenproof dish. Fry the onions and garlic until soft. Add to the meat.

3 Add the paprika, cloves, Rioja, lamb stock, bay leaves and thyme and bring the mixture to a gentle simmer. Add the halved red peppers.

4 Cover the dish with a lid or foil and cook for about 30 minutes, or until the meat is tender. Garnish with more bay leaves and thyme sprigs, if you like.

Cook's Tip
They are not absolutely essential for this dish, but lamb steaks or chops with bones will provide lots of additional flavour. As the bones cook they will slowly add to the taste. Boiled potatoes with extra virgin olive oil make a delicious accompaniment to the dish.

Lamb Goulash: *Energy 396kcal/1656kJ; Protein 32.6g; Carbohydrate 19.4g, of which sugars 13.8g; Fat 21.5g, of which saturates 8.5g; Cholesterol 114mg; Calcium 53mg; Fibre 4g; Sodium 147mg.*
Lamb with Rioja: *Energy 708kcal/2952kJ; Protein 52.1g; Carbohydrate 20g, of which sugars 14.4g; Fat 39.8g, of which saturates 14.7g; Cholesterol 190mg; Calcium 69mg; Fibre 3.8g; Sodium 231mg.*

Kleftiko

For this traditional Greek classic, the name of which translates as "robbers' lamb", marinated lamb steaks or chops are slow-cooked to develop an unbeatable, meltingly tender flavour. The dish is sealed, like a pie, with a lid of flour and water dough, which traps all the succulence and flavour inside. If you don't have time to make this, a tight-fitting foil cover, if less attractive, will serve almost as well.

Serves 4

juice of 1 lemon
15ml/1 tbsp chopped fresh oregano or mint
4 lamb leg steaks or chump chops with bones
30ml/2 tbsp extra virgin olive oil
2 large onions, thinly sliced
2 bay leaves
150ml/¼ pint/⅔ cup dry white wine
225g/8oz/2 cups plain (all-purpose) flour
salt and ground black pepper

1 Mix the lemon juice, oregano and seasoning, brush over the lamb and marinate for 4 hours. Then drain the lamb, reserving the marinade, and pat dry with kitchen paper.

2 Preheat the oven to 160°C/325°F/Gas 3. Heat the olive oil in a large frying pan and fry the lamb over a high heat until browned on both sides. Transfer the lamb to a shallow pie dish, forming an even layer over the base of the dish.

3 Sprinkle the thinly sliced onions and bay leaves around and over the lamb, then pour over the dry white wine and the reserved marinade.

4 Mix the flour with sufficient water to make a firm dough, kneading it to ensure a good consistency.

5 Moisten the rim of the pie dish. Roll out the dough on a floured surface so that it is large enough to cover the dish, and roughly cut it into the shape of your dish. Place it over the dish and secure so that it is tightly sealed. Bake for 2 hours, then break away the dough crust and serve the lamb hot, with boiled potatoes.

Meatballs in Tomato Sauce

These tasty meatballs in tomato sauce are usually served in tapas bars in individual casserole dishes, accompanied by crusty bread. They make a good supper, too, with a green salad or pasta.

Serves 4

225g/8oz minced (ground) beef
4 spring onions (scallions), thinly sliced
2 garlic cloves, finely chopped
30ml/2 tbsp grated Parmesan cheese
10ml/2 tsp fresh thyme leaves
15ml/1 tbsp olive oil
3 tomatoes, chopped
30ml/2 tbsp red or dry white wine
10ml/2 tsp chopped fresh rosemary
pinch of sugar
salt and ground black pepper
fresh thyme, to garnish

1 Put the minced beef in a bowl. Add the spring onions, garlic, Parmesan and thyme and plenty of salt and pepper.

2 Stir well to combine, then shape the mixture into 12 small firm meatballs.

3 Heat the olive oil in a large, heavy frying pan and cook the meatballs for 5–8 minutes, turning often, until evenly browned.

4 Add the chopped tomatoes, wine, rosemary and sugar to the pan, with salt and ground black pepper to taste.

5 Cover the pan and cook gently for about 15 minutes until the tomatoes are pulpy and the meatballs are cooked through. Check the sauce for seasoning and serve the meatballs hot, garnished with the thyme.

Variation

To make biftek andaluz (the nearest thing Spain has to a beefburger), shape the meat mixture into four wide patties and fry. Serve the patties on a slice of grilled (broiled) beefsteak tomato, or surrounded by tomato sauce. Top with a fried egg, if you like.

Kleftiko: Energy 658kcal/2760kJ; Protein 57.9g; Carbohydrate 53.8g, of which sugars 8.1g; Fat 22.2g, of which saturates 7.2g; Cholesterol 184mg; Calcium 148mg; Fibre 3.5g; Sodium 130mg.
Meatballs: Energy 206kcal/857kJ; Protein 14.7g; Carbohydrate 2.5g, of which sugars 2.5g; Fat 14.6g, of which saturates 5.9g; Cholesterol 41mg; Calcium 105mg; Fibre 0.9g; Sodium 135mg.

Flamenco Eggs

This adaptation of a classic Spanish recipe works very well with Camargue red rice, although any long grain rice – brown or white – could be used.

Serves 4

175g/6oz/scant 1 cup Camargue red rice
chicken or vegetable stock or water
45ml/3 tbsp olive oil
1 Spanish onion, chopped
1 garlic clove, crushed
350g/12oz minced (ground) beef
75g/3oz chorizo sausage, cut into small cubes
5ml/1 tsp paprika, plus extra for dusting
10ml/2 tsp tomato purée (paste)
15–30ml/1–2 tbsp chopped fresh parsley
2 red (bell) peppers, sliced
3 tomatoes, peeled, seeded and chopped
120ml/4fl oz/½ cup passata or tomato juice
4 large eggs
40ml/8 tsp single (light) cream
salt and freshly ground black pepper

1 Preheat the oven to 180°C/350°F/Gas 4. Cook the rice in stock or water, following the instructions on the packet. Heat 30ml/2 tbsp of oil and fry the onion and garlic for 5 minutes until the onion is tinged with brown, stirring occasionally.

2 Add the beef and cook, stirring occasionally, until browned. Stir in the chorizo and paprika and cook over a low heat for 4–5 minutes. Stir in the tomato purée and parsley. Season.

3 Heat the remaining oil and fry the peppers until they begin to sizzle. Cover and cook over a moderate heat, shaking the pan occasionally, for 4–5 minutes until the peppers are browned in places. Add the tomatoes and continue cooking for 3–4 minutes until they are very soft. Remove the pan from the heat, stir in the passata or tomato juice and add salt to taste.

4 Drain the rice, and divide it among four shallow ovenproof dishes. Spread the meat mixture over the rice and top with the peppers and tomatoes. Make a depression in the centre of each portion and break in an egg. Spoon 10ml/2 tsp of the cream over each egg yolk, dust with paprika, and bake for about 12–15 minutes until the whites are set. Serve at once.

Beef Rolls in Tomato Sauce

Thin slices of steak are wrapped around a rich cheese stuffing and baked in a red wine sauce. Delicious with mashed potato.

Serves 4

4 thin slices of rump (round) steak, about 115g/4oz each
4 slices smoked ham
2 eggs, soft-boiled (soft-cooked)
150g/5oz Pecorino cheese, finely grated
2 garlic cloves, finely chopped
75ml/5 tbsp chopped parsley
45ml/3 tbsp extra virgin olive oil, or grapeseed oil
1 large onion, finely chopped
150ml/¼ pint/⅔ cup passata (bottled strained tomatoes)
75ml/5 tbsp red wine
2 bay leaves
150ml/¼ pint/⅔ cup beef stock
salt and ground black pepper
fresh flat leaf parsley sprigs, to garnish

1 Preheat the oven to 160°C/325°F/ Gas 3. Lay the beef slices on a sheet of greaseproof (waxed) paper. Cover with another sheet of paper and beat with a mallet until very thin. Lay a ham slice over each slice of rump steak, trimming it to the same size.

2 Shell the soft-boiled eggs. Place on a plate and use a wooden spoon to mash them. Season to taste and mix well. Put the grated cheese and egg in a bowl. Add the garlic and chopped parsley, and mix well. Spoon this stuffing on to the meat slices. Fold two opposite sides of the meat over the stuffing, then roll up the meat to form neat parcels. Tie with string.

3 Heat the oil in a frying pan. Add the filled beef and ham parcels and fry quickly to brown on all sides, turning frequently with tongs. Transfer to an ovenproof dish.

4 Add the onion to the frying pan and fry for 3 minutes. Stir in the passata, red wine, bay leaves and stock. Season with salt and plenty of ground black pepper. Bring to the boil, then pour the sauce over the meat.

5 Cover the dish and bake in the oven for 1 hour. Lift out the beef rolls and remove the string. Transfer to warmed serving plates. Taste the sauce for seasoning and spoon over the meat. Serve garnished with flat leaf parsley.

Flamenco Eggs: Energy 592kcal/2464kJ; Protein 26.6g; Carbohydrate 30.4g, of which sugars 12g; Fat 41.1g, of which saturates 11.8g; Cholesterol 416mg; Calcium 155mg; Fibre 4.1g; Sodium 1150mg.
Beef Rolls: Energy 488kcal/2036kJ; Protein 51.3g; Carbohydrate 7.8g, of which sugars 6g; Fat 26.8g, of which saturates 11.6g; Cholesterol 219mg; Calcium 532mg; Fibre 2.2g; Sodium 885mg.

Fried Meatballs

No Greek celebration or party is complete without *keftethes*. They are always a must on the meze table, as they are so appetizing. Alternatively, they make a luxurious addition to a simple meal, such as a hot winter soup.

Serves 4
2 medium slices of bread, crusts removed
500g/1¼lb minced (ground) beef or lamb
1 onion, grated
5ml/1 tsp each dried thyme and oregano
45ml/3 tbsp chopped fresh flat leaf parsley, plus extra to garnish
1 egg, lightly beaten
salt and ground black pepper
lemon wedges, to serve (optional)

For frying
25g/1oz/¼ cup plain (all-purpose) flour
30–45ml/2–3 tbsp vegetable oil

1 Soak the slices of bread in a bowl of water for about 10 minutes, then drain. With your hands, squeeze the bread dry before placing it in a large bowl.

2 Add the meat, onion, dried herbs, parsley, egg, salt and pepper to the bread. Mix together, preferably using your hands, until well blended.

3 Shape the meat mixture into walnut-size balls and roll the balls in the flour to coat them lightly, shaking off any excess.

4 Heat the oil in a large frying pan. When it is hot, add the meatballs and fry, turning them frequently, until they are cooked through and look crisp and brown all over. Lift out and drain on a double sheet of kitchen paper, to get rid of the excess oil. Sprinkle with chopped parsley and serve with lemon wedges, if you like.

Cook's Tip
The bread is included both to add bulk to the meatballs and to lighten their texture.

Steak with Blue Cheese Sauce

Well-hung beef is a feature of more luxurious Spanish cuisine. Use good quality meat from your butcher for this recipe. It is served here with Cabrales, the blue cheese from Spain's northern mountains. Roquefort is also extremely popular, because it appeals to the Spanish love of salty flavours. In this recipe the salt and brandy in the sauce are perfectly balanced by the cream.

Serves 4
25g/1oz/2 tbsp butter
30ml/2 tbsp olive oil
4 fillet steaks, cut 5cm/2in thick, about 150g/5oz each
salt and coarsely ground black pepper
fresh flat leaf parsley, to garnish

For the blue cheese sauce
30ml/2 tbsp Spanish brandy
150ml/5fl oz/⅔ cup double (heavy) cream
75g/3oz Cabrales or Roquefort cheese, crumbled

1 Heat the butter and oil together in a heavy frying pan, over a high heat. Season the steaks well with salt and plenty of freshly ground black pepper. Fry them quickly for 2 minutes on each side, to sear them.

2 Lower the heat slightly and cook the steaks for a further 2–3 minutes on each side, or according to your taste. Remove the steaks to a warm plate.

3 Reduce the heat and add the brandy to the pan, stirring to deglaze it and blend with the meat juices. Add the cream and boil to reduce a little.

4 Add the crumbled blue cheese and mash it into the sauce using a spoon. Taste for seasoning. Serve the sauce separately in a small jug (pitcher), or pour it over the steaks. Garnish the steaks with parsley.

Cook's Tip
Cabrales is also known as Picón and Treviso and has a slightly more acidic flavour than Roquefort.

Fried Meatballs: Energy 375kcal/1565kJ; Protein 27.7g; Carbohydrate 13g, of which sugars 1.6g; Fat 24g, of which saturates 8.8g; Cholesterol 144mg; Calcium 78mg; Fibre 1.2g; Sodium 178mg.
Steak with Blue Cheese Sauce: Energy 573kcal/2374kJ; Protein 36.3g; Carbohydrate 0.7g, of which sugars 0.7g; Fat 45.4g, of which saturates 24.4g; Cholesterol 170mg; Calcium 117mg; Fibre 0g; Sodium 341mg.

Spicy Rolled Beef

Slices of tender beef are delicious when rolled around a filling, and often appear in Greek recipes.

Serves 4

4 thin slices of rump (round) steak, about 115g/4oz each
50ml/2fl oz/¼ cup olive oil, plus extra for frying
30ml/2 tbsp black peppercorns, roughly crushed
30ml/2 tbsp coriander seeds
1 onion, finely sliced
300ml/½ pint/1¼ cups red wine
1 egg, beaten
150g/5oz can chopped tomatoes
flat leaf parsley, to garnish
polenta and sour cream, to serve

For the filling

115g/4oz/½ cup minced (ground) ham
40g/1½oz/scant 1 cup fresh breadcrumbs
2 spring onions (scallions), finely sliced
45ml/3 tbsp chopped fresh parsley
1 egg yolk
75g/3oz green (bell) pepper, finely chopped
1.5ml/¼ tsp ground allspice
15–45ml/1–3 tbsp beef stock

1 Place the steaks between two sheets of dampened greaseproof paper. Flatten with a mallet or rolling pin until the meat is evenly thin. Brush the meat with oil, lay it out flat and sprinkle over the crushed peppercorns, coriander seeds and onion. Roll up neatly and place in a shallow glass or china dish. Pour over half the wine, cover and chill for 2 hours.

2 To make the filling, combine the ham, breadcrumbs, spring onions and parsley. Add the egg yolk, green pepper, allspice and a little water or beef stock to moisten the stuffing.

3 Shake the spices and onion off the beef. Spoon 30–45ml/2–3 tbsp of filling into the middle of each piece of meat. Brush the inner surface with egg and roll up well. Secure with a cocktail stick (toothpick) or tie with string.

4 Heat a little oil in a frying pan and brown the rolls on all sides. Reduce the heat and pour over the remaining wine and the canned tomatoes. Simmer for 25–30 minutes, until tender. Season well and serve with the sauce, polenta, sour cream and cracked black pepper. Garnish with flat leaf parsley.

Lasagne al Forno

The classic lasagne is made with good homemade meat sauce and white sauce, layered with freshly grated Parmesan. Keep the layers quite thin – the dish should hold its shape when cut.

Serves 6

about 8–10 lasagne sheets
75g/3oz/1 cup freshly grated Parmesan cheese
salt and ground black pepper
flat leaf parsley, to garnish

For the meat sauce

45ml/3 tbsp olive oil
500g/1¼lb minced (ground) beef
75g/3oz smoked bacon or pancetta, diced
130g/4½oz chicken livers, trimmed and chopped (optional)
1 onion, finely chopped
2 garlic cloves, crushed
150ml/¼ pint/⅔ cup dry white wine (optional)
30–45ml/2–3 tbsp tomato purée (paste)
2 × 400g/14oz cans chopped tomatoes
45ml/3 tbsp single (light) cream

For the white sauce

600ml/1 pint/2½ cups milk
1 bay leaf
1 small onion, sliced
50g/2oz/¼ cup butter
40g/1½oz/⅓ cup plain flour
freshly grated nutmeg

1 Bring a large pan of water to the boil and blanch the pasta sheets, a few at a time, for at least 2 minutes. Stir the pasta during cooking to stop it sticking. Drain the blanched sheets and set them aside in a bowl of cold water.

2 Heat the oil in a large frying pan and brown the minced beef. Add the bacon or pancetta and chicken livers, if using, and cook for 3–4 minutes. Add the onion and garlic, cook for 5 minutes more. Stir in the wine, if using. Cook until well reduced.

3 Stir in the tomato purée and tomatoes, with salt and pepper to taste. Bring to the boil, then lower the heat and simmer for 15–20 minutes until thickened. Stir in the cream and set aside.

4 While the meat sauce is simmering, make the white sauce. Pour the milk into a saucepan and add the bay leaf and sliced onion. Heat gently to just below boiling point, then remove the pan from the heat and leave to infuse for 10 minutes. Strain the milk into a jug and discard the bay leaf and onion.

5 Melt the butter in a saucepan and stir in the flour. Cook for 1 minute, stirring, then gradually whisk in the milk until the mixture boils and thickens to a smooth sauce. Season and add nutmeg to taste. Drain the pasta sheets and pat them dry with kitchen paper.

6 Spread some meat sauce on the base of a rectangular baking dish. Top with a single layer of pasta sheets. Trickle over some white sauce and sprinkle with Parmesan. Repeat the layers until all the ingredients have been used, finishing with a layer made by swirling the last of the two sauces together. Sprinkle liberally with Parmesan.

7 Preheat the oven to 190°C/375°F/Gas 5 and bake the lasagne for about 30 minutes until bubbling and golden brown. Allow to stand for 10 minutes before cutting. Serve garnished with flat leaf parsley.

Spicy Rolled Beef: *Energy 508kcal/2117kJ; Protein 43.7g; Carbohydrate 12g, of which sugars 4.1g; Fat 26.4g, of which saturates 8.1g; Cholesterol 202mg; Calcium 53mg; Fibre 1.3g; Sodium 547mg.*
Lasagne al Forno: *Energy 368kcal/1548kJ; Protein 14.8g; Carbohydrate 47.7g, of which sugars 6.7g; Fat 14.5g, of which saturates 8.2g; Cholesterol 38mg; Calcium 224mg; Fibre 1.5g; Sodium 238mg.*

Beef Casserole with Baby Onions and Red Wine

The warm, rich flavours of this casserole make it an excellent choice for a winter dinner party. It is the kind of easy dish that can be left simmering slowly in the oven for hours without coming to any harm. Serve it with simple rice, pasta, creamy mashed potatoes or fried potatoes.

Serves 4

75ml/5 tbsp olive oil
1kg/2¼lb good stewing or braising steak, cut into large cubes
3 garlic cloves, chopped
5ml/1 tsp ground cumin
5cm/2in piece of cinnamon stick
1 glass red wine, 175ml/6floz/¾ cup
30ml/2 tbsp red wine vinegar
small fresh rosemary sprig
2 bay leaves, crumbled
30ml/2 tbsp tomato purée (paste) diluted in 1 litre/1¾ pints/4 cups hot water
675g/1½lb small pickling-size onions, peeled and left whole
15ml/1 tbsp demerara (raw) sugar
salt and ground black pepper

1 Heat the olive oil in a large heavy pan and brown the meat cubes, in batches if necessary, until pale golden brown all over.

2 Stir in the garlic and cumin. Add the cinnamon stick and cook for a few seconds, then pour the wine and vinegar slowly over the mixture. Let the liquid bubble and reduce for 3–4 minutes.

3 Add the rosemary and bay leaves, with the diluted tomato purée. Stir well, season with salt and pepper, then cover and simmer gently for about 1½ hours or until the meat is tender.

4 Dot the onions over the meat mixture and shake the pan to distribute them evenly. Sprinkle the demerara sugar over the onions, cover the pan and cook very gently for 30 minutes, until the onions are soft but have not begun to disintegrate. If necessary, add a little hot water at this stage. Do not stir once the onions have been added but gently shake the pan instead to coat them in the sauce. Remove the cinnamon stick and sprig of rosemary and serve.

Calf's Liver with Slow-Cooked Onions, Marsala and Sage

Inspired by Italian flavours, this dish is good served with grilled polenta.

Serves 4

45ml/3 tbsp olive oil, plus extra for shallow frying
25g/1oz/2 tbsp butter
500g/1¼lb onions, finely sliced
small bunch of fresh sage leaves
30ml/2 tbsp chopped fresh parsley, plus extra to garnish
2.5ml/½ tsp caster (superfine) sugar
15ml/1 tbsp balsamic vinegar
30ml/2 tbsp plain (all-purpose) flour
675g/1½lb calf's liver, thinly sliced
150ml/¼ pint/⅔ cup Marsala
salt and ground black pepper

1 Heat half the oil with half the butter in a large, heavy-based saucepan and cook the onions, covered, over a very gentle heat for 30 minutes. Stir once or twice.

2 Chop five of the sage leaves and add them to the pan with the parsley, a pinch of salt, the sugar and balsamic vinegar. Cook, uncovered and stirring frequently, until very tender and golden. Taste for seasoning and add salt and pepper as necessary.

3 Heat a shallow layer of oil in a frying pan and fry the remaining sage leaves for 15-30 seconds, then drain them on kitchen paper.

4 Heat the remaining butter and oil in a frying pan over a high heat. Season the flour, then dip the liver in it and fry it quickly for about 2 minutes on each side until browned, but still pink in the middle. Use a draining spoon to transfer the liver to warm plates and keep warm.

5 Immediately add the Marsala to the pan and let it bubble fiercely until reduced to a few tablespoons of sticky glaze.

6 Distribute the onions over the liver and spoon over the Marsala juices. Scatter with the fried sage leaves and extra parsley and serve immediately, ideally with freshly grilled polenta or slices of toasted Italian bread.

Beef Casserole: *Energy 590kcal/2458kJ; Protein 57.6g; Carbohydrate 19.6g, of which sugars 14.6g; Fat 28.4g, of which saturates 8g; Cholesterol 158mg; Calcium 64mg; Fibre 2.9g; Sodium 187mg.*
Calf's Liver: *Energy 429kcal/1788kJ; Protein 33.1g; Carbohydrate 20.2g, of which sugars 11.6g; Fat 19.8g, of which saturates 3.7g; Cholesterol 624mg; Calcium 54mg; Fibre 2g; Sodium 125mg.*

Tagliatelle with Bolognese Sauce

Most people think of bolognese sauce, the famous *ragù* from Bologna, as being served with spaghetti. To be absolutely correct, it should be served with tagliatelle.

Serves 4

30ml/2 tbsp olive oil
1 onion, finely chopped
1 carrot, finely chopped
1 celery stick, finely chopped
1 garlic clove, crushed
350g/12oz lean minced (ground) beef
150ml/¼ pint/⅔ cup red wine
250ml/8fl oz/1 cup milk
400g/14oz can chopped tomatoes
15ml/1 tbsp sun-dried tomato paste
350g/12oz dried tagliatelle
salt and ground black pepper
shredded fresh basil, to garnish
grated Parmesan cheese, to serve

1 Heat the oil in a large saucepan. Add the onion, carrot, celery and garlic and cook gently, stirring frequently, for 10 minutes or until softened. Do not allow the vegetables to colour.

2 Add the minced beef to the pan with the vegetables and cook over a medium heat until the meat changes colour, stirring constantly and breaking up any lumps with a wooden spoon.

3 Pour in the wine. Stir frequently until it has evaporated, then add the milk and continue cooking and stirring until this has evaporated, too. Stir in the tomatoes and tomato paste, with salt and pepper to taste. Simmer the sauce uncovered, over the lowest possible heat for at least 45 minutes.

4 Cook the tagliatelle in a large pan of rapidly boiling salted water for 8–10 minutes or until al *dente*. Drain thoroughly and tip into a warmed large bowl. Pour over the sauce and toss to combine. Garnish with basil and serve at once, with Parmesan cheese handed separately.

Cook's Tip

Don't skimp on the cooking time. Some Italian cooks insist on cooking it for 3–4 hours, so the longer the better.

Mixed Meat Cannelloni

A creamy, rich filling and sauce make this an irresistible cannelloni dish.

Serves 4

60ml/4 tbsp olive oil
1 onion, finely chopped
1 carrot, finely chopped
2 garlic cloves, crushed
2 ripe Italian plum tomatoes, peeled and finely chopped
130g/4½oz minced (ground) beef
130g/4½oz minced (ground) pork
250g/9oz minced (ground) chicken
30ml/2 tbsp brandy
25g/1oz/2 tbsp butter
90ml/6 tbsp double (heavy) cream
16 dried cannelloni tubes
75g/3oz/1 cup freshly grated Parmesan cheese
salt and ground black pepper
green salad, to serve

For the white sauce

50g/2oz/¼ cup butter
50g/2oz/½ cup plain (all-purpose) flour
900ml/1½ pints/3¾ cups milk
nutmeg

1 Heat the oil in a medium pan, add the onion, carrot, garlic and tomatoes and cook over a low heat, stirring, for about 10 minutes or until soft. Add all the meats to the pan and cook gently for about 10 minutes, stirring frequently to break up. Add the brandy, increase the heat and stir until it has reduced, then add the butter and cream and cook gently, stirring occasionally, for about 10 minutes. Allow to cool.

2 Preheat the oven to 190°C/375°F/Gas 5. To make the white sauce, melt the butter in a medium saucepan, add the flour and cook, stirring, for 1–2 minutes. Add the milk a little at a time, whisking vigorously. Bring to the boil and cook, stirring, until smooth and thick. Grate in fresh nutmeg to taste, then season with salt and pepper and whisk well. Remove from the heat.

3 Spoon a little of the white sauce into a baking dish. Fill the cannelloni tubes with the meat mixture and place in a single layer in the dish. Pour the remaining white sauce over them, then sprinkle with the Parmesan. Bake for 35–40 minutes or until the pasta feels tender when pierced with a skewer. Allow to stand for 10 minutes before serving with green salad.

Tagliatelle with Bolognese: Energy 491kcal/2058kJ; Protein 22.6g; Carbohydrate 46.8g, of which sugars 6.7g; Fat 24g, of which saturates 10.9g; Cholesterol 74mg; Calcium 43mg; Fibre 3.1g; Sodium 291mg.
Meat Cannelloni: Energy 1025kcal/4284kJ; Protein 52.5g; Carbohydrate 71.3g, of which sugars 17.1g; Fat 59.1g, of which saturates 28.9g; Cholesterol 188mg; Calcium 563mg; Fibre 3.4g; Sodium 517mg.

Veal Escalopes from Corfu

Corfiot cooking shows an Italian influence derived from the island's Venetian past. Veal is rarely eaten elsewhere in Greece.

Serves 4

675g/1½lb thin veal escalopes (US scallops)
40g/1½oz/⅓ cup plain (all-purpose) flour
90ml/6 tbsp extra virgin olive oil
1 small onion, thinly sliced
3 garlic cloves, finely chopped
2–3 fresh sage leaves, finely chopped
175ml/6fl oz/¾ cup white wine
juice of ½ lemon
450ml/¾ pint/scant 2 cups beef or chicken stock
30ml/2 tbsp finely chopped fresh flat leaf parsley
salt and ground black pepper

1 Sprinkle the veal escalopes with a little salt and pepper, then coat them lightly in the flour. Heat the olive oil in a large frying pan over a medium heat. Add the escalopes and brown lightly on both sides. Transfer them to a wide flameproof casserole.

2 Add the sliced onion to the oil remaining in the frying pan and sauté the slices until translucent, then stir in the chopped garlic and sage. As soon as the garlic becomes aromatic, add the white wine and the lemon juice.

3 Raise the heat to high and cook for 10 minutes, stirring constantly and scraping the base to deglaze the pan.

4 Pour the pan juices over the meat and add the stock. Sprinkle over salt and freshly ground black pepper to taste, then add the finely chopped flat leaf parsley.

5 Bring to the boil, lower the heat, cover and simmer for 45–50 minutes, or until the meat is tender and the sauce is a velvety consistency.

6 Transfer to a serving platter or dish and serve immediately while it is still piping hot. Garnish with salad leaves, such as rocket (arugula), cos or romaine lettuce, and accompany with new potatoes tossed in extra virgin olive oil, or lots of fresh crusty bread.

Veal Casserole with Broad Beans

This delicate Italian stew, which is flavoured with sherry and plenty of garlic, is a spring dish made with new vegetables and known as *menestra de ternera*. For a delicious flavour be sure to add plenty of parsley just before serving. Young spring lamb is equally good cooked in this way, but veal is particularly popular in Italy. If you can find really young and tender broad beans, their skins can be left on.

Serves 6

45ml/3 tbsp olive oil
1.3–1.6kg/3–3½ lb veal, cut into 5cm/2in cubes
1 large onion, chopped
6 large garlic cloves, unpeeled
1 bay leaf
5ml/1 tsp paprika
240ml/8fl oz/1 cup fino sherry
100g/4oz/scant 1 cup shelled, skinned broad (fava) beans
60ml/4 tbsp chopped fresh flat leaf parsley
salt and ground black pepper

1 Heat 30ml/2 tbsp oil in a large flameproof casserole. Add half of the meat and brown well on all sides. Transfer to a plate. Brown the rest of the meat and remove from the pan.

2 Add the remaining oil and cook the onion until soft. Return the meat to the casserole and stir well to mix with the onion.

3 Add the garlic cloves, bay leaf, paprika and sherry. Season with salt and black pepper. Bring to simmering point, then cover and cook very gently for 30–40 minutes.

4 Add the broad beans to the casserole about 10 minutes before the end of the cooking time. Check the seasoning and stir in the chopped parsley just before serving.

Cook's Tip
As with all meat, buy veal from a butcher or supermarket that insists on high standards of animal welfare from its suppliers. Stewing or pie veal is suitable for casseroles and pâtés, and is the type needed for making this recipe.

Veal Escalopes: *Energy 398kcal/1666kJ; Protein 39.7g; Carbohydrate 9.4g, of which sugars 1.4g; Fat 19.6g, of which saturates 3.4g; Cholesterol 88mg; Calcium 44mg; Fibre 0.9g; Sodium 105mg.*
Veal Casserole: *Energy 352kcal/1473kJ; Protein 47.4g; Carbohydrate 3.6g, of which sugars 1.3g; Fat 11.6g, of which saturates 2.8g; Cholesterol 182mg; Calcium 34mg; Fibre 1.2g; Sodium 244mg.*

Roast Chicken with Potatoes and Lemon

This is a lovely, easy dish for a family meal. As with other Greek roasts, everything is baked together so that the potatoes absorb all the different flavours, especially that of the lemon.

Serves 4

1.6kg/3½lb chicken
2 garlic cloves, peeled, but left whole
15ml/1 tbsp chopped fresh thyme or oregano, or 5ml/1 tsp dried, plus 2–3 fresh sprigs of thyme or oregano
800g/1¾lb potatoes
juice of 1 lemon
60ml/4 tbsp extra virgin olive oil
300ml/½ pint/1¼ cups hot water
salt and ground black pepper

1 Preheat the oven to 200°C/400°F/Gas 6. Place the chicken, breast side down, in a large roasting pan, then tuck the garlic cloves and the thyme or oregano sprigs inside the bird.

2 Peel the potatoes and quarter them lengthways. If they are very large, slice them lengthways into thinner pieces. Arrange the potatoes around the chicken, then pour the lemon juice over the chicken and potatoes. Season with salt and pepper, drizzle the olive oil over the top and add about three-quarters of the chopped fresh or dried thyme or oregano. Pour the hot water into the roasting pan.

3 Roast the chicken and potatoes for 30 minutes, then remove the roasting pan from the oven and turn the chicken over.

4 Season the bird with a little more salt and pepper, sprinkle over the remaining fresh or dried herbs, and add a little more hot water, if needed. Reduce the oven temperature to 190°C/375°F/Gas 5.

5 Return the chicken and potatoes to the oven and roast them for another hour, or slightly longer, by which time both the chicken and the potatoes will be a golden colour. Serve with a crisp leafy salad.

Moroccan Spiced Roast Chicken

The spices and fruit in this stuffing give the chicken an unusual flavour and help to keep it moist. Serve with baked potatoes and steamed green beans.

Serves 4

1.3–1.6kg/3–3½lb chicken
15ml/1 tbsp garlic and spice aromatic oil
a few bay leaves
10ml/2 tsp clear honey
10ml/2 tsp tomato purée (paste)
60ml/4 tbsp lemon juice
150ml/¼ pint/⅔ cup chicken stock
2.5–5ml/½–1 tsp harissa

For the stuffing

15g/½oz/1 tbsp butter
1 onion, chopped
1 garlic clove, crushed
7.5ml/1½ tsp ground cinnamon
2.5ml/½ tsp ground cumin
225g/8oz/1⅓ cups mixed dried fruit, soaked overnight
25g/1oz/¼ cup blanched almonds, finely chopped
salt and ground black pepper

1 To make the stuffing, melt the butter in a non-stick pan. Add the onion and garlic and cook gently for 5 minutes, or until soft. Add the cinnamon and cumin and cook, stirring, for 2 minutes. Drain the soaked dried fruit, chop it roughly and add to the stuffing mixture with the almonds; mix well. Season with salt and pepper and cook for a further 2 minutes. Transfer the mixture to a bowl and leave to cool.

2 Preheat the oven to 200°C/400°F/ Gas 6. Stuff the neck of the chicken with the fruit mixture, reserving any excess. Brush aromatic oil all over the chicken and place it in a roasting pan, tuck in the bay leaves, then roast, basting occasionally with the juices, for 1–1¼ hours, or until cooked. Transfer the chicken to a carving board and leave to rest while you make the sauce.

3 Pour or skim off and discard any excess fat from the pan. Stir the honey, tomato purée, lemon juice, stock and harissa into the remaining pan juices. Add salt to taste. Bring to the boil, then reduce the heat and simmer, stirring frequently for 2 minutes.

4 Meanwhile, reheat any excess stuffing. Carve the chicken, pour the sauce into a bowl and serve immediately with the stuffing and chicken.

Roast Chicken: *Energy 767kcal/3195kJ; Protein 53.4g; Carbohydrate 32.5g, of which sugars 2.9g; Fat 47.7g, of which saturates 11.8g; Cholesterol 264mg; Calcium 51mg; Fibre 2.6g; Sodium 206mg.*
Moroccan Spiced Roast Chicken: *Energy 345kcal/1463kJ; Protein 37.4g; Carbohydrate 40.2g, of which sugars 39.9g; Fat 5g, of which saturates 2.4g; Cholesterol 113mg; Calcium 38mg; Fibre 1.3g; Sodium 147mg.*

Crumbed Chicken with Green Mayonnaise

Pechugas de pollo rebozadas are sold ready-prepared in every butcher's in southern Spain. Identical to schnitzel, these crispy, golden chicken breast portions show the Jewish influence on cooking in the region. Lemon wedges are a popular accompaniment.

Serves 4

4 boneless chicken breasts fillets, each weighing about 200g/7oz
juice of 1 lemon
5ml/1 tsp paprika
plain (all-purpose) flour, for dusting
1–2 eggs
dried breadcrumbs, for coating
about 60ml/4 tbsp olive oil
salt and ground black pepper
lemon wedges, to serve

For the mayonnaise

120ml/4fl oz/½ cup mayonnaise
30ml/2 tbsp pickled capers, drained and chopped
30ml/2 tbsp chopped fresh parsley

1 Start a couple of hours ahead, if you can. Skin the chicken breasts. Lay them outer side down and, with a sharp knife, cut horizontally, almost through, from the rounded side and open each piece of chicken up like a book. Press gently, to make a roundish shape, the size of a side plate. Sprinkle with lemon juice and paprika.

2 Set out three plates. Sprinkle flour over one, seasoning it well. Beat the egg with a little salt and pour into the second. Sprinkle the third with dried breadcrumbs. Dip the breasts first into the flour on both sides, then into the egg, then into the breadcrumbs. Chill the crumbed chicken, if you have time.

3 Put all the ingredients for the mayonnaise in a bowl and mix well to combine.

4 Heat the oil in a heavy frying pan over a high heat. Fry the chicken breast portions, two at a time, turning after 3 minutes, until golden on both sides. Add more oil for the second batch if necessary. Serve at once, accompanied by the mayonnaise and lemon wedges.

Chicken Roasted with Mediterranean Vegetables

This is a delicious method of roasting a chicken, which also works well with guinea fowl. Choose a free-range bird, and if it is available, one that has been corn-fed, as this will help give an authentic French flavour.

Serves 4

1.75kg/4–4½lb roasting chicken,
150ml/¼ pint/⅔ cup olive oil
½ lemon
few sprigs of fresh thyme
450g/1lb small new potatoes
1 aubergine (eggplant), cut into 2.5cm/1in cubes
1 red (bell) pepper, quartered
1 fennel bulb, trimmed and quartered
8 large garlic cloves, unpeeled
coarse salt and ground black pepper

1 Preheat the oven to 200°C/400°F/Gas 6. Rub the chicken all over with most of the olive oil and season with pepper. Place the lemon half and the thyme sprigs inside the bird and put the chicken breast-side down in a large roasting pan. Roast for about 30 minutes.

2 Remove the chicken from the oven and season with salt. Turn right-side up and baste with the pan juices. Surround the bird with the potatoes, rolling them in the pan juices, and return to the oven.

3 After 30 minutes, add the remaining vegetables and garlic, and drizzle with the remaining oil. Season with salt and pepper and cook for a further 30–50 minutes, basting and turning the vegetables occasionally.

4 To check that the chicken is cooked, push the tip of a sharp knife between the thigh and breast. If the juices run clear the chicken is done.

5 By the time the chicken is cooked the vegetables should be tender and just beginning to brown. Serve the dish straight from the roasting pan, drizzling some of the delicious juices over each serving.

Crumbed Chicken: *Energy 594kcal/2476kJ; Protein 52g; Carbohydrate 12.5g, of which sugars 1.1g; Fat 37.7g, of which saturates 6g; Cholesterol 210mg; Calcium 64mg; Fibre 1g; Sodium 372mg.*
Chicken with Vegetables: *Energy 798kcal/3310kJ; Protein 43.3g; Carbohydrate 23.7g, of which sugars 6.1g; Fat 59.3g, of which saturates 13.6g; Cholesterol 208mg; Calcium 45mg; Fibre 4.2g; Sodium 183mg.*

Chicken with Lemons and Olives

Preserved lemons are frequently used in Moroccan cooking, where their subtle and interesting flavour enhances all kinds of dishes.

Serves 4

2.5ml/½ tsp ground cinnamon
2.5ml/½ tsp ground turmeric
1.5kg/3¼lb chicken
15ml/1 tbsp olive oil
1 large onion, thinly sliced
5cm/2in piece fresh root ginger, peeled and grated
600ml/1 pint/2½ cups chicken stock
2 preserved or fresh lemons, cut into wedges
75g/3oz/¾ cup pitted brown olives
15ml/1 tbsp clear honey
60ml/4 tbsp chopped fresh coriander (cilantro)
salt and ground black pepper
fresh coriander (cilantro) sprigs, to garnish

1 Preheat the oven to 190°C/375°F/Gas 5. Mix the ground cinnamon and turmeric in a bowl with a little salt and black pepper and rub all over the chicken skin.

2 Heat the oil in a shallow, non-stick frying pan and fry the chicken on all sides until it turns golden. Transfer the chicken to an ovenproof dish.

3 Add the onion to the pan and sauté for 3 minutes. Add the ginger and stock to the pan and bring just to the boil. Then pour the stock mixture over the chicken, cover and bake in the oven for 30 minutes. Remove the chicken from the oven.

4 Add the lemons and the brown olives. Drizzle over the honey, then bake, uncovered, for a further 45 minutes, or until the chicken is cooked. Sprinkle the coriander over the chicken and season. Garnish with coriander. Remove and discard the skin from the chicken, and serve immediately.

Cook's Tip

Lemons are preserved by layering them with salt and lemon juice for about a month. The skin loses its bitterness.

Chargrilled Chicken with Garlic and Peppers

An imaginative marinade can make all the difference to barbecued chicken. Serve it with a large salad and a bowl of tzatsiki.

Serves 4–6

1½ chickens, total weight about 2.25kg/5lb, jointed, or 12 chicken pieces
2–3 red or green (bell) peppers, quartered and seeded
4–5 tomatoes, halved horizontally
lemon wedges, to serve

For the marinade

90ml/6 tbsp extra virgin olive oil
juice of 1 large lemon
5ml/1 tsp French mustard
4 garlic cloves, crushed
2 fresh red or green chillies, seeded and chopped
5ml/1 tsp dried oregano
salt and ground black pepper

1 If you are jointing the chicken yourself, divide the legs into two. Make a couple of slits in the deepest part of the flesh of each piece, so that the marinade is absorbed more efficiently and the chicken cooks thoroughly.

2 Beat together all the marinade ingredients in a large bowl. Add the chicken pieces and turn to coat them thoroughly in the marinade. Cover the bowl with clear film (plastic wrap) and place in the refrigerator for 4–8 hours, turning the chicken pieces over in the marinade a couple of times, if possible.

3 Prepare the barbecue. When the coals are ready, lift the chicken pieces out of the marinade and place them on the grill. Add the pepper pieces and the tomatoes to the marinade and set it aside for 15 minutes. Grill the chicken pieces for 20–25 minutes. Watch them closely and move them away from the area where the heat is most fierce if they start to burn.

4 Turn the chicken pieces over and continue to cook for 20–25 minutes more. Meanwhile, thread the peppers on two long metal skewers. Add them to the barbecue grill, with the tomatoes, for the last 15 minutes of cooking. Remember to keep an eye on them and turn them over at least once. Serve with the lemon wedges.

Chicken with Lemons and Olives: *Energy 146kcal/614kJ; Protein 24.8g; Carbohydrate 4.4g, of which sugars 4g; Fat 3.4g, of which saturates 0.6g; Cholesterol 70mg; Calcium 46mg; Fibre 1.4g; Sodium 487mg.*
Chargrilled Chicken: *Energy 337kcal/1419kJ; Protein 57.6g; Carbohydrate 7.2g, of which sugars 6.9g; Fat 8.7g, of which saturates 1.6g; Cholesterol 163mg; Calcium 48mg; Fibre 2.5g; Sodium 154mg.*

Spanish Chicken

This colourful chicken dish is made throughout Spain in an infinite number of variations. Cubed Serrano ham can replace the bacon if you prefer, but the fat the latter gives off is a constant theme in the Spanish kitchen, and it helps to add to the character of the dish.

Serves 4

5ml/1 tsp paprika
4 chicken portions
45ml/3 tbsp olive oil
150g/5oz smoked bacon lardons, or diced pancetta
1 large onion, chopped
2 garlic cloves, finely chopped
1 green (bell) pepper
1 red (bell) pepper
450g/1lb tomatoes or 400g/14oz canned tomatoes
30ml/2 tbsp chopped fresh parsley
salt and ground black pepper
boiled rice, to serve

1 Rub paprika and salt into the chicken portions. Heat 30ml/2 tbsp oil in a large frying pan. Put in the chicken portions, skin side down, and fry gently.

2 Heat 15ml/1 tbsp oil in a flameproof casserole and add the bacon or pancetta.

3 When the bacon or pancetta starts to give off fat, add the chopped onion and garlic and fry very gently, stirring from time to time, until soft and golden.

4 Remove and discard the stalks and seeds from the peppers and roughly chop the flesh. Spoon off a little fat from the chicken pan, then add the peppers, fitting them into the spaces between the chicken portions, and cook gently.

5 When the onions are soft, stir in the tomatoes and season with salt and pepper. Arrange the chicken pieces in the sauce, and stir in the cooked peppers.

6 Cover the casserole tightly and simmer over a low heat for 15 minutes. Check the seasoning, stir in the chopped parsley and serve with rice.

Chicken with Prawns

In this gorgeous Catalan dish the sauce is thickened with a *picada* of ground toasted almonds and crumbled butter biscuits. Serve with rice and a spinach salad.

Serves 4

1.3kg/3lb chicken
75–90ml/5–6 tbsp olive oil
1 large onion, chopped
2 garlic cloves, finely chopped
400g/14oz tomatoes, peeled, seeded and chopped
1 bay leaf
150ml/¼ pint/⅔ cup white wine
450g/1lb large raw prawns (shrimp), deveined
15g/½oz/1 tbsp butter
30ml/2 tbsp pastis
75ml/2½fl oz/⅓ cup double (heavy) cream
1.5ml/¼ tsp cayenne pepper
salt, paprika and ground black pepper
fresh flat leaf parsley, to garnish

For the picada

25g/1oz/¼ cup blanched almonds
15g/½oz/1 tbsp butter
1 garlic clove, finely chopped
3 Marie, Rich Tea or plain all-butter biscuits (cookies), broken
90ml/6 tbsp chopped fresh parsley

1 Cut the chicken into eight portions and rub them with salt and paprika. Heat 30ml/2 tbsp oil in a casserole. Fry the onion and garlic until soft, then fry the pieces, turning, until golden. Add the tomatoes to the casserole with the bay leaf and cook down to a sauce. Pour in the remaining wine, season and simmer gently for about 30 minutes.

2 Meanwhile, dry-fry the almonds until just coloured and transfer to a blender. Add 15g/½oz/1 tbsp butter to the pan and gently fry the garlic, then add it to the blender, with the biscuits. Add the parsley and blend to a purée with a little of the wine for the casserole.

3 Heat 15ml/1 tbsp oil and 15g/½oz/1 tbsp butter and fry the prawns for 2 minutes on each side. Pour the pastis into a ladle and set light to it. Pour it over the prawns and let it burn off, then add the prawns to the casserole. Stir in the *picada*, then the cream. Add cayenne and other seasonings to taste, heat through gently and serve garnished with parsley.

Spanish Chicken: Energy 513kcal/2152kJ; Protein 68.5g; Carbohydrate 13.9g, of which sugars 12.1g; Fat 20.7g, of which saturates 5.2g; Cholesterol 199mg; Calcium 62mg; Fibre 3.7g; Sodium 640mg.
Chicken with Prawns: Energy 881kcal/3655kJ; Protein 52.5g; Carbohydrate 9.8g, of which sugars 4.1g; Fat 65.8g, of which saturates 22g; Cholesterol 368mg; Calcium 110mg; Fibre 1.7g; Sodium 934mg.

Chicken with Chorizo

The additions of sliced chorizo and sherry give a warm and interesting flavour to this Spanish dish. It can be made with a whole chicken, divided into portions, or with chicken drumsticks and thighs only, as the darker meat stands up well to the other robust flavours in the recipe.

Serves 4

1.5kg/3–3½lb chicken, jointed, or 4 chicken legs, halved and skinned
10ml/2 tsp paprika
60ml/4 tbsp olive oil
2 small onions, sliced
6 garlic cloves, thinly sliced
150g/5oz chorizo sausage, thickly sliced
400g/14oz can chopped tomatoes
2 bay leaves
75ml/3fl oz/⅓ cup medium sherry
salt and ground black pepper
boiled potatoes, to serve

1 Preheat the oven to 190°C/375°F/Gas 5. Coat the chicken pieces in the paprika and season lightly with salt.

2 Heat the olive oil in a frying pan and fry the chicken on all sides to brown. With a slotted spoon, transfer the chicken pieces to an ovenproof dish.

3 Add the onions to the pan and fry quickly until golden. Add the garlic and chorizo and fry for 2 minutes. (Don't burn the garlic, or it will taste bitter.)

4 Add the tomatoes, bay leaves and sherry and bring to the boil. Pour over the chicken and cover with a lid. Bake in the oven for 45 minutes. Remove the lid and season to taste with salt and pepper. Cook for a further 20 minutes until the chicken is tender and golden. Serve with potatoes.

Variation
Use pork chump chops or leg steaks instead of the chicken and reduce the cooking time slightly.

Chicken with Lemon and Garlic

Very easy and quick to cook and delicious to eat, this Spanish dish is usually served with fried potatoes and aioli.

Serves 4

450g/1lb skinless chicken breast fillets
30ml/2 tbsp olive oil
1 shallot, finely chopped
4 garlic cloves, finely chopped
5ml/1 tsp paprika
juice of 1 lemon
30ml/2 tbsp chopped fresh parsley
salt and ground black pepper
flat leaf parsley, to garnish
lemon wedges, to serve

1 Sandwich the chicken breasts between two sheets of baking parchment or clear film (plastic wrap). Pound with the flat side of a meat mallet or roll out with a rolling pin until the fillets are about 5mm/¼in thick.

2 Cut the chicken into strips about 1cm/½in wide. Heat the oil in a large frying pan. Stir-fry the chicken strips with the shallot, garlic and paprika over a high heat for about 6–8 minutes, until lightly browned and cooked through.

3 Add the lemon juice and chopped parsley to the pan and season with salt and pepper to taste. Pile the chicken on to a warmed serving dish and garnish with parsley. Serve hot with lemon wedges.

Variation
For a variation on this dish, try using strips of turkey breast or pork instead of chicken.

Cook's Tips
- *Skinless chicken breasts are available in every butcher's shop and supermarket, but try to buy meat from free-range or corn-fed birds to ensure a really good flavour.*
- *Don't pound the meat so hard that you make holes in it.*

Chicken with Chorizo: *Energy 815kcal/3379kJ; Protein 50.8g; Carbohydrate 7.8g, of which sugars 3.9g; Fat 62.3g, of which saturates 17.6g; Cholesterol 258mg; Calcium 47mg; Fibre 1.2g; Sodium 484mg.*
Chicken with Lemon and Garlic: *Energy 138kcal/579kJ; Protein 18.5g; Carbohydrate 1.5g, of which sugars 1.1g; Fat 6.5g, of which saturates 1g; Cholesterol 53mg; Calcium 30mg; Fibre 0.8g; Sodium 49mg.*

Chicken with Figs and Mint

Grown all over Greece and Turkey, figs are wonderfully fruity when eaten fresh, but are also dried for storage through the winter. The diried fruits are often used in sauces to complement meat and poultry and are very popular in savoury dishes, providing a wonderful hearty sweetness that is usually is balanced out with sharper fruits such as lemon or orange. This recipe also uses marmalade to add an unusual bittersweet note.

Serves 4

500g/1¼lb/3¼ cups dried figs
½ bottle sweet, fruity white wine
4 chicken breast fillets, about 175–225g/6–8oz each, skinned or unskinned
15g/½oz/1 tbsp butter
50g/2oz/2 tbsp dark orange marmalade
10 fresh mint leaves, finely chopped, plus a few more to garnish
juice of ½ lemon
salt and ground black pepper
a few sprigs of fresh mint, to garnish

1 Place the figs in a pan with the wine and bring to the boil, then simmer very gently for about 1 hour. Allow to cool and refrigerate overnight.

2 Fry the chicken breast fillets in the butter over a medium heat until they are cooked through and golden. Remove and keep warm.

3 Drain any fat from the pan and pour in the juice from the figs. Boil and reduce to about 150ml/¼ pint/⅔ cup.

4 Add the marmalade, mint and lemon juice, and simmer for a few minutes. When the sauce is thick and shiny, pour it over the chicken, garnish with mint leaves, and serve.

Cook's Tip
Mint is a characteristic ingredient of eastern Mediterranean cookery. It is often used in combination with lemon to flavour lamb and other meat and poultry dishes.

Tuscan Chicken

This simple peasant casserole has all the flavours of traditional Tuscan ingredients. The dry white wine can be replaced by chicken stock, if you prefer.

Serves

15ml/1 tbsp extra virgin olive oil
8 chicken thighs, skinned
1 onion, thinly sliced
2 red (bell) peppers, sliced
1 garlic clove, crushed
300ml/½ pint/1¼ cups passata (puréed tomatoes)
150ml/¼ pint/⅔ cup dry white wine
1 large oregano sprig, or 5ml/1 tsp dried oregano
400g/14oz can cannellini beans, drained
45ml/3 tbsp fresh white breadcrumbs
salt and ground black pepper
fresh oregano, to garnish

1 Heat the oil in a heavy-based frying pan which can be used under the grill.

2 Cook the chicken until golden. Remove and keep hot. Add the onion and peppers to the pan and sauté gently until softened. Stir in the garlic. Return the chicken to the pan. Add the tomatoes, wine and oregano, and salt and pepper.

3 Bring to the boil. Cover the pan tightly, lower the heat and simmer for 30–35 minutes or until the chicken is tender.

4 When the chicken is thoroughly cooked, stir in the cannellini beans. Cover the pan again and raise the heat slightly. Leave to simmer for about 5 minutes more, stirring once or twice, until the beans are hot. Preheat the grill.

5 Sprinkle the breadcrumbs evenly over the mixture in the pan and grill until the crumb topping is golden brown. Serve immediately, garnished with fresh oregano.

Variation
Stir in a handful of fresh oregano or marjoram leaves just before sprinkling the dish with the breadcrumbs.

Chicken with Figs: *Energy 460kcal/1941kJ; Protein 50.2g; Carbohydrate 38.4g, of which sugars 38.4g; Fat 6.2g, of which saturates 2.6g; Cholesterol 148mg; Calcium 168mg; Fibre 4.4g; Sodium 190mg.*
Tuscan Chicken: *Energy 1354kcal/5716kJ; Protein 144.2g; Carbohydrate 131.2g, of which sugars 46.1g; Fat 21.7g, of which saturates 5.3g; Cholesterol 543mg; Calcium 428mg; Fibre 31.4g; Sodium 750mg.*

Spicy Chicken Casserole with Red Wine

This is a traditional chicken dish of the Greek islands. It is usually served with plain rice or orzo, the small tear-shaped pasta, which is called *kritharaki* in Greek, but it is even better with chunky fried potatoes.

Serves 4

75ml/5 tbsp extra virgin olive oil
1.6kg/3½lb chicken, jointed
1 large onion, peeled and roughly chopped
250ml/8fl oz/1 cup red wine
30ml/2 tbsp tomato purée (paste) diluted in 450ml/¾ pint/scant 2 cups hot water
1 cinnamon stick
3 or 4 whole allspice
2 bay leaves
salt and freshly ground black pepper
boiled rice, orzo or fried potatoes, to serve

1 Heat the olive oil in a large pan or sauté pan and brown the chicken pieces on all sides, ensuring that the skin is cooked and lifts away from the flesh slightly. Lift the chicken pieces out with tongs and set them aside on a plate, cover with another plate or with foil and keep them warm.

2 Add the chopped onion to the hot oil in the same pan and stir it over a medium heat until it becomes translucent.

3 Return the chicken pieces to the pan, pour over the wine and cook for 2–3 minutes, until it has reduced. Add the tomato purée mixture, cinnamon, allspice and bay leaves. Season the dish well with salt and pepper.

4 Cover the pan and cook gently for 1 hour or until the chicken is tender. Serve with rice, orzo or fried potatoes.

Cook's Tip

If you have trouble finding orzo, use a different pasta, but look for a small shape, Long-grained rice can also be used instead of the pasta, if you prefer.

Chicken and Apricot Filo Pie

The filling for this pie includes nuts and spices and has a Middle Eastern flavour.

Serves 6

75g/3oz/½ cup bulgur wheat
50g/2oz/¼ cup butter
1 onion, chopped
450g/1lb minced (ground) chicken breast fillets
50g/2oz/¼ cup ready-to-eat dried apricots, finely chopped
25g/1oz/¼ cup blanched almonds, chopped
5ml/1 tsp ground cinnamon
2.5ml/½ tsp ground allspice
50ml/2fl oz/¼ cup Greek natural (plain) yogurt
15ml/1 tbsp chopped fresh chives
30ml/2 tbsp chopped fresh parsley
6 large sheets filo pastry
salt and ground black pepper
fresh chives, to garnish

1 Preheat the oven to 200°C/400°F/Gas 6. Put the bulgur wheat in a bowl with 120ml/4fl oz/½ cup boiling water. Leave to soak for 5–10 minutes, or until the water is absorbed.

2 Heat 15g/½oz/1 tbsp of the butter in a non-stick pan, add the onion and minced chicken and cook gently, stirring occasionally, until pale golden. Stir in the apricots, almonds and bulgur wheat and cook for a further 2 minutes. Remove from the heat and stir in the cinnamon, allspice, yogurt, chives and parsley. Season to taste with salt and pepper.

3 Melt the remaining butter. Unroll the filo pastry and cut into 25cm/10in rounds. Keep the pastry rounds covered with a clean, damp dish towel to prevent them from drying out.

4 Line a 23cm/9in loose-based flan tin (quiche pan) with three of the pastry rounds, lightly brushing each one with melted butter as you layer them. Spoon in the chicken mixture and cover with three more pastry rounds, lightly brushed with melted butter, as before.

5 Crumple the remaining pastry rounds and place them on top of the pie, then brush over any remaining melted butter. Bake the pie in the oven for about 30 minutes, or until the pastry is golden brown and crisp. Serve hot or cold, cut into wedges and garnished with chives.

Spicy Casserole: *Energy 669kcal/2775kJ; Protein 48.7g; Carbohydrate 5g, of which sugars 3.8g; Fat 45.9g, of which saturates 11.1g; Cholesterol 250mg; Calcium 37mg; Fibre 0.9g; Sodium 196mg.*
Chicken Filo Pie: *Energy 263kcal/1104kJ; Protein 21.9g; Carbohydrate 19.9g, of which sugars 3.8g; Fat 11.3g, of which saturates 5.2g; Cholesterol 70mg; Calcium 69mg; Fibre 1.6g; Sodium 106mg.*

Chicken Tagine

This dish, which is particularly enjoyed in Marrakesh, celebrates two of Morocco's most famous ingredients – cracked green olives and preserved lemons, and takes its name from the traditional Moroccan covered cooking pot. Try this recipe if you want a change from the usual roast chicken and are looking for a new way to cook a whole bird. Serve with plain couscous and a salad or vegetable side dish.

Serves 4

1.3kg/3lb chicken
3 garlic cloves, crushed
small bunch of fresh coriander (cilantro), finely chopped
juice of ½ lemon
5ml/1 tsp coarse salt
45–60ml/3–4 tbsp olive oil
1 large onion, grated
pinch of saffron threads
5ml/1 tsp ground ginger
5ml/1 tsp ground black pepper
1 cinnamon stick
175g/6oz/1½ cups cracked green olives
2 preserved lemons, cut into strips

1 Place the chicken in a deep dish. Rub the garlic, coriander, lemon juice and salt into the body cavity of the chicken. Mix the olive oil with the grated onion, saffron, ginger and pepper and rub this mixture over the outside of the chicken. Cover and leave to stand for about 30 minutes.

2 Transfer the chicken to a tagine or a large, heavy flameproof casserole and pour the marinating juices over it. Pour in enough water to come halfway up the chicken, add the cinnamon stick and bring the water to the boil. Reduce the heat, cover with a lid and simmer gently for about 1 hour, turning the chicken occasionally in the liquid.

3 Preheat the oven to 150°C/300°F/Gas 2. Using two slotted spoons, carefully lift the chicken out of the tagine or casserole and set aside on a plate, covered with foil.

4 Turn up the heat and boil the cooking liquid for 5 minutes to reduce it. Replace the chicken in the liquid and baste it thoroughly. Add the olives and preserved lemon and place the tagine or casserole in the oven for about 15 minutes. Serve the chicken immediately with your chosen accompaniments.

Chicken Liver Risotto

This risotto has a wonderfully rich flavour. It's a great lunch dish, but you could serve smaller portions as an appetizer.

Serves 2–4

175g/6oz chicken livers
about 15ml/1 tbsp olive oil
about 25g/1oz/2 tbsp butter
about 40g/1½oz streaky (fat) bacon, finely chopped
2 shallots, finely chopped
1 garlic clove, crushed
1 celery stick, finely sliced
275g/10oz/1½ cups risotto rice
175ml/6fl oz/¾ cup dry white wine
900ml–1 litre/1½–1¾ pints/3¾–4 cups chicken stock, simmering
5ml/1 tsp chopped fresh thyme
15ml/1 tbsp chopped fresh parsley
salt and ground black pepper
parsley and thyme sprigs to garnish

1 Clean the chicken livers, removing any fat or membrane. Rinse well, dry with kitchen paper and cut into small pieces.

2 Heat the oil and butter in a frying pan and fry the bacon for 2–3 minutes. Add the shallots, garlic and celery and continue frying for 3–4 minutes over a low heat until the vegetables are slightly softened. Increase the heat and add the chicken livers, stir-frying for a few minutes until they are brown all over.

3 Add the rice. Cook, stirring, for a few minutes, then pour over the wine. Allow to boil so that the alcohol is driven off. Stir frequently, taking care not to break up the chicken livers. When all the wine has been absorbed, add the hot stock, a ladleful at a time, stirring constantly.

4 About halfway through cooking, add the thyme and season with salt and pepper. Continue to add the stock as before, making sure that each quantity has been absorbed before adding more.

5 When the risotto is creamy and the rice is tender but still has a bit of "bite", stir in the parsley. Taste and adjust the seasoning. Remove the pan from the heat, cover and leave to rest for a few minutes before serving, garnished with parsley and thyme.

Chicken Tagine: *Energy 585kcal/2422kJ; Protein 40.4g; Carbohydrate 0.4g, of which sugars 0.3g; Fat 46.7g, of which saturates 11.7g; Cholesterol 208mg; Calcium 68mg; Fibre 1.9g; Sodium 1151mg.*
Chicken Liver Risotto: *Energy 627kcal/2614kJ; Protein 22g; Carbohydrate 83.7g, of which sugars 1.1g; Fat 17.5g, of which saturates 7.2g; Cholesterol 279mg; Calcium 42mg; Fibre 0.3g; Sodium 306mg.*

Seville Chicken

Oranges and almonds are favourite ingredients in southern Spain, especially around Seville, where the orange and almond trees, laden with blossom and fruit, are a familiar and wonderful sight.

Serves 4

I orange
8 chicken thighs
plain flour, seasoned with salt and pepper
45ml/3 tbsp olive oil
I large Spanish onion, roughly chopped
2 garlic cloves, crushed
I red (bell) pepper, sliced
I yellow (bell) pepper, sliced
I I5g/4oz chorizo, sliced
50g/2oz/½ cup flaked almonds
225g/8oz/generous I cup brown basmati rice
about 600ml/I pint/2½ cups chicken stock
400g/I4oz can chopped tomatoes
I75ml/6fl oz/¾ cup white wine
generous pinch of dried thyme
salt and ground black pepper
fresh thyme sprigs, to garnish

I Pare a thin strip of peel from the orange and set it aside. Peel the orange, then cut it into segments, working over a bowl to catch the juice. Dust the chicken thighs with seasoned flour.

2 Heat the oil in a large frying pan and fry the chicken pieces on both sides until nicely brown. Transfer to a plate. Add the onion and garlic to the pan and fry for 4–5 minutes until the onion begins to brown. Add the red and yellow peppers and fry, stirring occasionally, until slightly softened.

3 Add the chorizo, stir-fry for a few minutes, then sprinkle over the almonds and rice. Cook, stirring, for I–2 minutes.

4 Pour in the chicken stock, tomatoes and wine and add the orange strip and thyme. Season well. Bring to simmering point, stirring, then return the chicken pieces to the pan.

5 Cover tightly and cook over a very low heat for I–I¼ hours until the rice and chicken are tender. Just before serving, add the orange segments and allow to cook briefly to heat through. Garnish with fresh thyme and serve.

Risotto with Chicken

This is a classic combination of chicken and rice, cooked with Parma ham, white wine and Parmesan cheese. Use Carnaroli rice for a really creamy texture that retains a little "bite".

Serves 6

30ml/2 tbsp olive oil
225g/8oz skinless, boneless chicken breasts, cut into 2.5cm/I in cubes
I onion, finely chopped
I garlic clove, finely chopped
450g/I lb/2⅓ cups risotto rice
I20ml/4fl oz/½ cup dry white wine
pinch saffron threads
I.75 litres/3 pints/7½ cups simmering chicken stock
50g/2oz Parma ham, cut into thin strips
25g/I oz/2 tbsp butter, cubed
25g/I oz/⅓ cup freshly grated Parmesan cheese, plus extra to serve
salt and ground black pepper
flat leaf parsley, to garnish

I Heat the oil in a frying pan over a moderately high heat. Add the cubes of chicken and cook, stirring frequently, until they start to turn white.

2 Reduce the heat to low and add the chopped onion. Cook gently, stirring, until the onion is softened and golden, then add the garlic and cook a few minutes more. Stir in the rice. Sauté for I–2 minutes, stirring constantly, until all the rice grains are coated in oil.

3 Add the wine and cook, stirring, until the wine has been absorbed. Stir the saffron threads into the simmering stock, then add a ladleful of stock to the rice and cook, stirring, until it has been absorbed. Repeat with more stock, allowing each ladleful to be absorbed before adding the next.

4 When the rice is three-quarters cooked, add the Parma ham and continue cooking until the rice is just tender and the risotto creamy.

5 Add the butter and the Parmesan and stir in well. Season with salt and pepper to taste. Serve the risotto hot, sprinkled with a little more Parmesan, and garnish with parsley.

Seville Chicken: *Energy 86 I kcal/3598kJ; Protein 65.3g; Carbohydrate 67.I g, of which sugars I 7.I g; Fat 34g, of which saturates 5.6g; Cholesterol I 55mg; Calcium I 72mg; Fibre 6.3g; Sodium 453mg.*
Risotto with Chicken: *Energy 4 I 8kcal/I 744kJ; Protein I 7.9g; Carbohydrate 60.9g, of which sugars 0.8g; Fat 9.5g, of which saturates 3.8g; Cholesterol 44mg; Calcium 72mg; Fibre 0.I g; Sodium I 94mg.*

Chicken Piri-Piri

This dish came from Portugal, and is based on a hot sauce made from Angolan chillies. It has become widely popular.

Serves 4

4 chicken breast portions
30–45ml/2–3 tbsp olive oil
1 large onion, finely sliced
2 carrots, cut into thin strips
1 large parsnip or 2 small parsnips, cut into thin strips
1 red (bell) pepper, sliced
1 yellow (bell) pepper, sliced
1 litre/1¾ pints/4 cups chicken stock
3 tomatoes, peeled, seeded and chopped
generous dash of piri-piri sauce
15ml/1 tbsp tomato purée (paste)
½ cinnamon stick
1 fresh thyme sprig, plus extra fresh thyme, to garnish
1 bay leaf
275g/10oz/1½ cups white long grain rice
15ml/1 tbsp lime or lemon juice
salt and ground black pepper

1 Preheat the oven to 180°C/350°F/Gas 4 and season the chicken with salt and pepper. Heat 30ml/2 tbsp of the oil in a pan and brown the chicken on all sides. Transfer to a plate.

2 Add some more oil if necessary and fry the onion for 2–3 minutes. Add the carrots, parsnip and peppers, fry for a few minutes then cover and sweat for 4–5 minutes until soft.

3 Pour in the stock, then add the tomatoes, piri-piri sauce, tomato purée and cinnamon stick. Stir in the thyme and bay leaf. Season to taste and bring to the boil. Spoon off 300ml/½ pint/1¼ cups of the liquid and set aside in a small pan.

4 Put the rice in a casserole. Using a slotted spoon, scoop the vegetables out of the pan and spread them over the rice. Arrange the chicken on top. Pour over the spicy stock from the pan, cover tightly and bake for about 45 minutes, until both the rice and chicken are completely tender.

5 Meanwhile, heat the reserved stock, adding a few more drops of piri-piri sauce and the lime or lemon juice. Spoon the piri-piri chicken and rice on to warmed serving plates. Serve the remaining sauce separately or poured over the chicken.

Stuffed Chicken Rolls

In this unusual dish, tender, delicate chicken is perfect with the more robust flavours of Parma ham and wild mushrooms.

Serves 4

25g/1oz/2 tbsp butter
1 garlic clove, chopped
150g/5oz/1¼ cups cooked white long grain rice
45ml/3 tbsp ricotta cheese
10ml/2 tsp chopped fresh flat leaf parsley
5ml/1 tsp chopped fresh tarragon
4 skinless, boneless chicken breasts
3–4 slices Parma ham
15ml/1 tbsp olive oil
120ml/4fl oz/½ cup white wine
salt and ground black pepper
fresh flat leaf parsley sprigs, to garnish
cooked tagliatelle and sautéed blewit or other wild mushrooms, to serve

1 Preheat the oven to 180°C/350°F/Gas 4. Melt about 10g/¼oz/2 tsp of the butter in a small pan and fry the garlic for a few seconds without browning. Spoon into a bowl, add the rice, ricotta, parsley and tarragon and season with salt and pepper. Stir to mix.

2 Place each chicken breast in turn between two sheets of clear film (plastic wrap) and flatten by beating lightly, but firmly, with a rolling pin or steak mallet. Divide the slices of Parma ham between the chicken breasts, trimming them to fit.

3 Place a spoonful of the rice stuffing at the wider end of each ham-topped breast. Roll up carefully and tie in place with string or secure with a cocktail stick (toothpick).

4 Heat the oil and the remaining butter in a frying pan and lightly fry the chicken rolls until browned on all sides. Place side by side in a shallow baking dish and pour over the white wine.

5 Cover the dish with greaseproof (waxed) paper and cook in the oven for 30–35 minutes until the chicken is tender.

6 Cut the rolls into slices and serve on a bed of tagliatelle with sautéed wild mushrooms and a generous grinding of black pepper. Garnish with sprigs of flat leaf parsley.

Chicken Piri-piri: Energy 557kcal/2337kJ; Protein 44.3g; Carbohydrate 75.4g, of which sugars 15.5g; Fat 8.8g, of which saturates 1.5g; Cholesterol 105mg; Calcium 73mg; Fibre 5.8g; Sodium 122mg.
Stuffed Chicken Rolls: Energy 329kcal/1375kJ; Protein 30g; Carbohydrate 21.3g, of which sugars 1.3g; Fat 11.5g, of which saturates 5.1g; Cholesterol 95mg; Calcium 65mg; Fibre 1.3g; Sodium 257mg.

Circassian Chicken

This chicken and walnut dish is Circassian in origin, but was adopted and popularized by Turkish chefs. Sometimes served as a cold meze dish, it is ideal for lunch or supper, or would be lovely as part of a buffet spread.

Serves 6

1 chicken, trimmed of excess fat
3 slices of day-old white bread, crusts removed
150ml/¼ pint/⅔ cup milk
175g/6oz/1½ cup shelled walnuts
4–6 garlic cloves
salt and ground black pepper

For the stock

1 onion, quartered
1 carrot, chopped
2 celery sticks, chopped
4–6 cloves
4–6 allspice berries
4–6 black peppercorns
2 bay leaves
5ml/1 tsp coriander seeds
1 small bunch of fresh flat leaf parsley, stalks bruised and tied together

For the garnish

30ml/2 tbsp butter
5ml/1 tsp Turkish red pepper or paprika
a few fresh coriander (cilantro) leaves

1 Put the chicken into a deep pan with all the ingredients for the stock. Add water to just cover the chicken and bring to the boil. Lower the heat, cover and simmer for about 1 hour.

2 Remove the chicken from the pan and boil the stock with the lid off for about 15 minutes until reduced, then strain and season. When the chicken has cooled a little, discard the skin and tear the flesh into thin strips. Put them into a large bowl.

3 In a shallow dish, soak the bread in the milk for a few minutes until the milk is absorbed. Using a mortar and pestle, pound the walnuts and the garlic to a paste. Beat in the soaked bread, then add to the chicken mixture. Beat in spoonfuls of the warm stock to bind the mixture until it is light and creamy.

4 Spoon the mixture into a mound in a serving dish. Melt the butter and stir in the red pepper or paprika, then pour it in a cross shape over the mound. Garnished with coriander leaves.

Chicken Pilaff

The French lidded cooking pot known as a *marmite* is ideal for this delicious dish.

Serves 3–4

15–20 dried chanterelle mushrooms
15–30ml/1–2 tbsp olive oil
15g/½oz/1 tbsp butter
4 thin rashers (strips) rindless smoked streaky (fatty) bacon, chopped
3 skinless, boneless chicken breasts, cut into thin slices
4 spring onions (scallions), sliced
225g/8oz/generous 1 cup basmati rice, soaked
450ml/¾ pint/scant 2 cups hot chicken stock
salt and ground black pepper

1 Preheat the oven to 180°C/350°F/Gas 4. Soak the dried mushrooms for 10 minutes in warm water. Drain, reserving the soaking liquid. Discard the stalks and slice the caps.

2 Heat the olive oil and butter in a frying pan. Fry the bacon for 2–3 minutes. Add the chicken and fry, stirring constantly, until the pieces are golden brown all over. Transfer the cooked chicken and bacon mixture to a bowl using a slotted spoon.

3 Briefly fry the mushrooms and spring onions in the fat remaining in the pan, then add them to the chicken and bacon.

4 Drain the rice and add it to the pan, with a little olive oil if necessary. Stir-fry for 2–3 minutes. Spoon the rice into an earthenware casserole. Pour the hot chicken stock and liquid from the mushrooms over the rice. Stir in the chicken and mushroom mixture and season.

5 Cover with a double piece of foil and secure with a lid. Cook in the oven for 30–35 minutes until the rice is tender.

Chicken Liver and Herb Conchiglie

Fresh herbs and chicken livers with pasta shells make a perfect supper dish.

Serves 4

50g/2oz/¼ cup butter
115g/4oz pancetta or rindless streaky bacon, diced
250g/9oz chicken livers, diced
2 garlic cloves, crushed
10ml/2 tsp chopped fresh sage
300g/11oz/2¾ cups dried conchiglie pasta
150ml/¼ pint/⅔ cup dry white wine
4 ripe plum tomatoes, diced
15ml/1 tbsp chopped parsley
salt and ground black pepper

1 Fry the bacon or pancetta in half the butter over a medium heat for a few minutes until it is lightly coloured but not crisp.

2 Add the livers, garlic, half the sage and plenty of pepper. Increase the heat and cook for about 5 minutes, until the livers change colour. Meanwhile, cook the pasta according to the packet instructions, drain and reserve in a warmed bowl.

3 Pour the wine over the livers in the pan and let it sizzle, then lower the heat and simmer gently for 5 minutes. Melt in the remaining butter, add the diced tomatoes, mix, then add the rest of the sage and the parsley. Stir well. Taste and add salt if needed. Toss into the warm pasta and serve.

Circassian Chicken: Energy 222kcal/937kJ; Protein 34.1g; Carbohydrate 7.6g, of which sugars 1.6g; Fat 6.4g, of which saturates 3.3g; Cholesterol 105mg; Calcium 53mg; Fibre 0.2g; Sodium 324mg.
Chicken Pilaff: Energy 437kcal/1823kJ; Protein 27.2g; Carbohydrate 45.4g, of which sugars 0.4g; Fat 15.9g, of which saturates 5.1g; Cholesterol 77mg; Calcium 24mg; Fibre 0.7g; Sodium 386mg.
Chicken Liver Conchiglie: Energy 528kcal/2220kJ; Protein 25.4g; Carbohydrate 59g, of which sugars 5.9g; Fat 20.2g, of which saturates 9.6g; Cholesterol 283mg; Calcium 38mg; Fibre 3.2g; Sodium 498mg.

Pappardelle with Chicken and Mushrooms

Rich and creamy, this is a good supper party dish.

Serves 4

15g/½oz dried porcini mushrooms
175ml/6fl oz/¾ cup warm water
25g/1oz/2 tbsp butter
1 garlic clove, crushed
1 small handful fresh flat leaf parsley, roughly chopped
1 small leek, chopped
120ml/4fl oz/½ cup dry white wine
250ml/8fl oz/1 cup chicken stock
400g/14oz fresh or dried pappardelle
2 skinless chicken breast fillets, cut into thin strips
105ml/7 tbsp mascarpone cheese
salt and ground black pepper
fresh basil leaves, shredded, to garnish

1 Put the dried mushrooms in a bowl. Pour in the warm water and leave to soak for 15–20 minutes. Tip into a fine sieve (strainer) set over a bowl and squeeze the mushrooms to release as much liquid as possible. Chop the mushrooms finely and set aside the strained soaking liquid until required.

2 Melt the butter in a medium pan, then add the chopped mushrooms, garlic, parsley and leek, with salt and pepper to taste. Cook over a low heat, stirring frequently, for about 5 minutes, then pour in the wine and stock and bring to the boil. Lower the heat and simmer for about 5 minutes until the liquid has reduced and thickened.

3 Meanwhile, start cooking the pasta in salted boiling water according to the packet instructions, adding the reserved soaking liquid from the mushrooms to the water.

4 Add the chicken to the sauce and simmer for 5 minutes or until just tender. Add the mascarpone a spoonful at a time, stirring well after each addition, then add one or two spoonfuls of the water used for cooking the pasta. Taste for seasoning. Drain the pasta and tip it into a warmed bowl. Add the chicken and sauce and toss well. Serve immediately, topped with shredded basil leaves.

Duck Risotto

This makes an excellent lunch or supper dish with a green salad or mangetouts and sliced, sautéed red (bell) peppers.

Serves 3–4

2 duck breasts
30ml/2 tbsp brandy
30ml/2 tbsp orange juice
1 onion, finely chopped
1 garlic clove, crushed
275g/10oz/1½ cups risotto rice
1–1.2 litres/1¾–2 pints/4–5 cups duck or chicken stock, simmering
5ml/1 tsp chopped fresh thyme
5ml/1 tsp chopped fresh mint
10ml/2 tsp grated orange rind
40g/1½oz/½ cup freshly grated Parmesan cheese
salt and ground black pepper
strips of thinly pared orange rind, to garnish

1 Score the fatty side of the duck breasts and rub them with salt. Put them, fat side down, in a heavy frying pan and dry-fry over a medium heat for 6–8 minutes. Transfer the breasts to a plate. Discard the fat and cut the flesh into 2cm/¾in wide strips.

2 Pour all but 15ml/1 tbsp of the duck fat from the pan into a bowl, then reheat the fat in the pan. Fry the duck slices quickly for 2–3 minutes until evenly brown but not overcooked. Add the brandy, heat to simmering point and then ignite. When the flames have died down, add the orange juice and season with salt and pepper. Remove from the heat and set aside.

3 In a saucepan, heat 15ml/1 tbsp of the remaining duck fat . Fry the onion and garlic over a gentle heat until the onion is soft but not browned. Add the rice and cook, stirring all the time, until the grains are coated in oil and have become slightly translucent around the edges.

4 Add the stock, a ladleful at a time, waiting for each to be absorbed completely before adding the next. Just before adding the final ladleful, stir in the duck, with the thyme and mint. Cook until the risotto is creamy and the rice is tender.

5 Add the orange rind and Parmesan. Season to taste then remove from the heat, cover and leave to stand for a few minutes. Serve garnished with the pared orange rind.

Pappardelle: *Energy 921kcal/3881kJ; Protein 58.2g; Carbohydrate 133.1g, of which sugars 6.9g; Fat 16.9g, of which saturates 6.9g; Cholesterol 161mg; Calcium 206mg; Fibre 4.2g; Sodium 246mg.*
Duck Risotto: *Energy 408kcal/1708kJ; Protein 24g; Carbohydrate 56.7g, of which sugars 1.5g; Fat 8.5g, of which saturates 3g; Cholesterol 93mg; Calcium 147mg; Fibre 0.2g; Sodium 193mg.*

Duck Breasts with a Walnut Sauce

Walnuts and pomegranates, which both grow in the Mediterranean, combine to make an exotic sauce that is perfect with duck. Serve with rice or new potatoes, and a salad.

Serves 6

60ml/4 tbsp olive oil
2 onions, very thinly sliced
2.5ml/½ tsp ground turmeric
400g/14oz/3½ cups walnuts, roughly chopped
1 litre/1¾ pints/4 cups duck or chicken stock
6 pomegranates
30ml/2 tbsp caster (superfine) sugar
60ml/4 tbsp lemon juice
4 duck breasts, about 225g/8oz each
salt and ground black pepper

1 Heat half the olive oil in a frying pan. Add the onions and turmeric, and cook gently until soft. Transfer to a pan, add the walnuts and stock, then season with salt and pepper. Stir well, then bring to the boil and simmer the mixture, uncovered, for 20 minutes, stirring occasionally.

2 Halve the pomegranates and scoop the seeds into a bowl. Reserve the seeds of one pomegranate. Process the remaining seeds in a blender or food processor. Strain through a sieve (strainer), to extract the juice, then stir the sugar and lemon juice into the pomegranate juice.

3 Score the skin of the duck breasts in a lattice pattern with a sharp knife. Heat the remaining oil in a frying pan and place the duck breasts in it, skin down.

4 Cook gently for 10 minutes, pouring off the fat from time to time, until the skin is dark golden and crisp. Turn over and cook for a further 3–4 minutes. Transfer to a plate and leave to rest.

5 Deglaze the frying pan with the pomegranate juice mixture, stirring with a wooden spoon, then add the walnut and stock mixture and simmer for 15 minutes, until the sauce has thickened slightly. Serve the duck breasts sliced, drizzled with a little sauce, and garnished with the reserved pomegranate seeds. Pass the remaining sauce separately.

Braised Quail with Winter Vegetables

Roasting and braising are the two classic techniques for cooking quail. Here, they are cooked and served in a red wine sauce, then elegantly presented on crisp croûtes.

Serves 4

4 quail, cleaned
175g/6oz small carrots, scrubbed
175g/6oz baby turnips
20ml/4 tsp olive oil
4 shallots, halved
450ml/¾ pint/scant 2 cups red wine
30ml/2 tbsp Spanish brandy
salt and ground black pepper
fresh flat leaf parsley, to garnish

For the croûtes

4 slices stale bread, crusts removed
15ml/1 tbsp olive oil

1 Preheat the oven to 220°C/425°F/Gas 7. Season the quail with salt and black pepper. Using a sharp knife, cut the carrots and baby turnips into chunks.

2 Heat half the olive oil in a flameproof casserole and add the quail. Brown the birds all over, then remove from the casserole and set aside.

3 Add the remaining olive oil to the casserole with the carrots, turnips and shallots and cook until just colouring. Return the quail to the casserole, breast-sides down, and pour in the wine. Cover and bake for 30 minutes, or until the quail are tender.

4 Meanwhile, using a 10cm/4in plain cutter, stamp out rounds from the bread. Heat the oil in a non-stick frying pan and cook the bread over a high heat until golden on both sides. Drain on kitchen paper and keep warm.

5 Remove and discard the skin from the quail. Place the croûtes on warmed plates and set a quail on top of each one. Surround with the vegetables, cover and keep hot. Boil the cooking juices rapidly until reduced to a syrupy consistency. Add the brandy and warm through, then season to taste. Drizzle the sauce over the quail, garnish with parsley and serve at once.

Duck Breasts: *Energy 753kcal/3123kJ; Protein 40.2g; Carbohydrate 13.1g, of which sugars 11.5g; Fat 62.9g, of which saturates 6.7g; Cholesterol 165mg; Calcium 105mg; Fibre 3.4g; Sodium 173mg.*
Quail: *Energy 437kcal/1827kJ; Protein 50.5g; Carbohydrate 6.9g, of which sugars 6.3g; Fat 13g, of which saturates 3g, of which polyunsaturates 2.7g; Cholesterol 0mg; Calcium 107mg; Fibre 2.3g; Sodium 161mg.*

Poussins with Grapes in Vermouth

Herbs, vermouth, and grapes are ideal with delicately flavoured poussins.

Serves 4

4 oven-ready poussins, about 450g/1lb each
50g/2oz/4 tbsp butter, softened
2 shallots, chopped
60ml/4 tbsp chopped fresh parsley
225g/8oz white grapes, preferably muscatel, halved and seeded
150ml/¼ pint/⅔ cup dry white vermouth
5ml/1 tsp cornflour (cornstarch)
60ml/4 tbsp double (heavy) cream
salt and ground black pepper
30ml/2 tbsp pine nuts, toasted
watercress sprigs, to garnish

1 Preheat the oven to 200°C/400°F/Gas 6. Wash the poussins inside and out and pat dry with kitchen paper. Spread butter all over the birds and put a hazelnut-size piece in the cavity of each one.

2 Mix the shallots and the parsley. Place a quarter of the mixture inside each bird, then roast them for 40–50 minutes, or until the juices run clear. Keep warm on a platter.

3 Skim off most of the fat from the juices remaining in the roasting pan, then add the grapes and vermouth. Place the pan over a low heat for a few minutes to warm the grapes.

4 Using a slotted spoon, scatter the grapes around the quails. Keep covered. Stir the cornflour into the cream, then add to the pan juices. Cook gently, stirring, until thickened. Adjust the seasoning before pouring the sauce around the poussins. Garnish with pine nuts and watercress. Serve immediately.

Pheasant with Apple Sauce

Olive oil and thyme reveal a Mediterranean influence in this dish from Normandy.

Serves 4

2 oven-ready pheasants
15ml/1 tbsp olive oil
25g/1oz/2 tbsp butter
60ml/4 tbsp Calvados
450ml/¾ pint/1⅞ cups dry (hard) cider
1 bouquet garni
3 eating apples, peeled and sliced
150ml/¼ pint/⅔ cup double (heavy) cream
salt and ground black pepper
thyme sprigs, to garnish

1 Quarter both pheasants. Discard backbones and knuckles.

2 Using a heavy pan, brown the pheasant in the oil and butter in batches. Pour Calvados over the meat and set it alight. As the flames subside, pour in the cider, add the bouquet garni and season.Cover and simmer for 50 minutes.

3 Tuck the apple slices around the pheasant. Cover and cook for 5–10 minutes. Transfer the meat to a warmed serving plate, cover and keep warm. Remove the bouquet garni.

4 Reduce the sauce by half, stir in the cream and simmer for 2–3 minutes until thickened. Spoon over the pheasant and serve at once, garnished with thyme sprigs.

Chargrilled Quails in Pomegranate Marinade

This Turkish recipe is a delicious way of serving small birds, such as quails, on the barbecue. The sharp marinade tenderizes the meat, as well as enhancing the flavour.

Serves 4

4 quails, cleaned and boned (ask your butcher to do this)
Juice of 4 pomegranates
Juice of 1 lemon
30ml/2 tbsp olive oil
5–10ml/1–2 tsp Turksih red pepper, or 5ml/1 tsp chilli powder
30–45ml/2–3 tbsp thick and cream natural (plain) yogurt
salt
1 bunch fresh flat leaf parsley
seeds of ½ pomegranate, to garnish

1 Soak eight wooden skewers in hot water for about 15 minutes, then drain. Thread one skewer throug the wings of each bird and a second skewer through the legs to keep them together.

2 Place the skewered birds in a wide, shallow dish. Beat the pomegranate and lemon juice with the oil and red pepper or chilli powder, pout over the quails and rub it into the skin. Cover with foil and leave to marinate in a cold place of the refrigerator for 2–3 hours, turning the birds from time to time.

3 Get the barbecue ready for cooking. Lift the birds out of the marinade and pour what is left into a bowl. Beat the yogurt into the leftover marinade and add a little salt.

4 Brush some of the yogurt mixture over the birds and place on them on the prepared barbecue.

5 Cook for 4–5 minutes on each side, brushing with the yogurt as they cook to form a crust.

6 Chop some of the parsley and lay the rest on a serving dish. Place the cooked quails on the parsley and garnish with the pomegranate seeds and chopped parsley. Serve hot.

Poussins with Grapes: *Energy 831kcal/3456kJ; Protein 52.1g; Carbohydrate 12.3g, of which sugars 11.1g; Fat 60.2g, of which saturates 21.8g; Cholesterol 308mg; Calcium 62mg; Fibre 1.2g; Sodium 270mg.*
Pheasant with Apple: *Energy 805kcal/3347kJ; Protein 58.8g; Carbohydrate 8.1g, of which sugars 8.1g; Fat 52.9g, of which saturates 24.6g; Cholesterol 525mg; Calcium 91mg; Fibre 0.8g; Sodium 191mg.*
Chargrilled Quail: *Energy 288kcal/1270kJ; Protein 37.4g; Carbohydrate 5.8g, of which sugars 5.8g; Fat 13g, of which saturates 2.7g; Cholesterol 0mg; Calcium 84mg; Fibre 0.5g; Sodium 111mg.*

Marinated Pigeon in Red Wine

Great clouds of migrating pigeons fly over the mountains of Spain, and shooting them is big sport. Here they are marinated in spiced vinegar and red wine, then cooked in the marinade. Cabbage or puréed celeriac goes very well with this.

Serves 4

4 pigeons (squabs), weighing about 225g/8oz each, cleaned and skinned
10ml/2 tsp olive oil
1 onion, roughly chopped
225g/8oz/3 cups brown cap (cremini) mushrooms, sliced
plain (all-purpose) flour, for dusting
300ml/½ pint/1¼ cups beef or game stock
30ml/2 tbsp chopped fresh parsley
salt and ground black pepper
fresh flat leaf parsley, to garnish

For the marinade

10ml/2 tsp olive oil
1 onion, chopped
1 carrot, chopped
1 celery stick, chopped
3 garlic cloves, sliced
6 allspice berries, bruised
2 bay leaves
8 black peppercorns, bruised
120ml/4fl oz/½ cup red wine vinegar
150ml/¼ pint/⅔ cup red wine

1 A day ahead, combine all the ingredients for the marinade in a large, non-metallic dish. Add the pigeons and turn them in the marinade, then cover and chill turning occasionally, for 12 hours.

2 Preheat the oven to 150°C/300°F/Gas 2. Heat the oil in a large flameproof casserole, add the onion and mushrooms and cook for about 5 minutes, or until the onion has softened.

3 Meanwhile, remove the pigeons to a plate with a slotted spoon and strain the marinade, then set both aside separately.

4 Sprinkle the flour over the pigeons, then add them to the casserole, breast sides down. Pour in the marinade and stock, and add the chopped parsley and seasoning. Cover and cook for 1½ hours or until cooked and tender.

5 Adjust the seasoning to taste, then serve the pigeons on warmed plates with the sauce. Garnish with parsley.

Venison Chops with Romesco Sauce

Romesco is the Catalan word for the *ñora* chilli, which lends a spicy roundness to one of Spain's greatest sauces, from Tarragona. It can be served cold as a dip for vegetables, but this spicy version is the ideal partner for game chops.

Serves 4

4 venison chops, cut 2cm/¾in thick and about 175–200g/6–7oz each
30ml/2 tbsp olive oil
50g/2oz/4 tbsp butter
braised Savoy cabbage, to serve

For the sauce

3 ñora chillies
1 hot dried chilli
25g/1oz/¼ cup almonds
150ml/¼ pint/⅔ cup olive oil
1 slice stale bread, crusts removed
3 garlic cloves, chopped
3 tomatoes, peeled, seeded and roughly chopped
60ml/4 tbsp sherry vinegar
60ml/4 tbsp red wine vinegar
salt and ground black pepper

1 To make the sauce, slit and seed the chillies, then leave to soak in warm water for about 30 minutes until soft. Drain the chillies, dry them on kitchen paper and chop finely.

2 Dry-fry the almonds over a medium heat, shaking the pan occasionally, until they are toasted evenly. Transfer the nuts to a food processor. Add 45ml/3 tbsp oil to the frying pan and fry the bread until golden. Drain on kitchen paper. Tear up the bread and add to the processor with the chillies and tomatoes.

3 Fry the garlic in the oil remaining in the pan. Tip the garlic and oil into the processor and blend the mixture to a smooth paste. With the motor running, gradually add the remaining olive oil and then the sherry and wine vinegars. When the sauce is smooth, scrape it into a bowl and season with salt and pepper to taste. Cover and chill for 2 hours.

4 Season the chops with pepper. Heat the olive oil and butter in a heavy frying pan and fry the chops for about 5 minutes each side until golden brown and cooked through. When the chops are almost cooked, heat the sauce gently in a pan adding a little boiling water if it is too thick. Serve the sauce with the chops, accompanied by braised cabbage.

Marinated Pigeon: *Energy 286kcal/1189kJ; Protein 25.6g; Carbohydrate 1.5g, of which sugars 1g; Fat 17.4g, of which saturates 0.9g; Cholesterol 0mg; Calcium 23mg; Fibre 0.8g; Sodium 98mg.*
Venison Chops: *Energy 415kcal/1741kJ; Protein 46.9g; Carbohydrate 6.2g, of which sugars 2.8g; Fat 24g, of which saturates 9.3g; Cholesterol 127mg; Calcium 40mg; Fibre 1.3g; Sodium 229mg.*

Rabbit Salmorejo

Rabbit is a popular meat in Spain. It makes an interesting alternative to chicken in this light, spicy sauté. Serve with a simply dressed salad.

Serves 4

675g/1½lb rabbit pieces
300ml/½ pint/1¼ cups dry white wine
15ml/1 tbsp sherry vinegar
several sprigs of fresh oregano
2 bay leaves
90ml/6 tbsp olive oil
175g/6oz baby onions, peeled and left whole
1 red chilli, seeded and finely chopped
4 garlic cloves, sliced
10ml/2 tsp paprika
150ml/¼ pint/⅔ cup chicken stock
salt and ground black pepper
flat leaf parsley sprigs, to garnish

1 Put the rabbit in a bowl. Add the wine, vinegar and herbs and toss all the ingredients together lightly. Cover and leave to marinate for several hours or overnight.

2 Drain the pieces of rabbit, reserving the marinade, and pat dry on kitchen paper. Heat the oil in a large sauté or frying pan. Add the rabbit and fry over a medium heat on all sides until golden. Drain well. Then lower the heat and fry the onions until just beginning to colour.

3 Remove the onions from the pan and add the chilli, garlic and paprika. Cook, stirring, for 1 minute. Add the reserved marinade, stock and a little seasoning.

4 Return the rabbit to the pan with the onions. Bring to the boil, reduce the heat and cover with a lid. Simmer very gently for about 45 minutes until the rabbit is tender. Serve the salmorejo garnished with sprigs of fresh parsley.

Cook's Tip
If it is more convenient to cook the dish in the oven, transfer the stew to an ovenproof dish and bake at 180°C/350°F/Gas 4 for 50 minutes, or until the meat is tender.

Rabbit with Tomatoes

The Italians have many different ways of serving rabbit. This is a hearty dish with strong and robust flavours.

Serves 4–5

675g/1½lb boned rabbit, cut into chunks
2 garlic cloves, peeled and thinly sliced
75g/3oz/½ cup thinly sliced pancetta or lean bacon
675g/1½lb tomatoes, peeled, seeded and roughly chopped
45ml/3 tbsp chopped fresh basil leaves
salt and ground black pepper
60ml/4 tbsp olive oil

1 Preheat the oven to 200°C/400°F/Gas 6. Pat the rabbit pieces dry with kitchen paper. Place a thin slice of garlic on each piece, then wrap a slice of pancetta or a rasher of bacon around it, making sure the garlic is held in place.

2 Place the tomatoes in a non-stick pan, and cook them for a few minutes until they give up some of their liquid and begin to dry out. Stir in the basil, and season with salt and pepper.

3 Place the tomatoes in a layer in the bottom of a baking dish. Arrange the rabbit pieces on top of the tomatoes. Sprinkle with olive oil and place, uncovered, in the oven. Roast for 40–50 minutes.

4 Baste the rabbit occasionally with any fat in the dish. After the rabbit has cooked for about 25 minutes the dish may be covered with foil for the remaining time if the sauce seems to be too dry.

Cook's Tip
Rabbit is a very lean meat, which means that it is a healthy choice but can be dry. It is very well suited to braises and casseroles in which it is cooked in some liquid. In this dish, wrapping the pieces of rabbit in bacon supplies a little fat as well as flavouring the meat.

Rabbit Salmorejo: *Energy 311kcal/1294kJ; Protein 23.2g; Carbohydrate 9.5g, of which sugars 2.6g; Fat 20.4g, of which saturates 4.1g; Cholesterol 83mg; Calcium 65mg; Fibre 0.9g; Sodium 52mg.*
Rabbit with Tomatoes: *Energy 283kcal/1178kJ; Protein 22.6g; Carbohydrate 4g, of which sugars 4g; Fat 19.7g, of which saturates 5.4g; Cholesterol 105mg; Calcium 18mg; Fibre 1.3g; Sodium 322mg.*

Vegetable Moussaka with Tofu

This Greek dish, traditionally made with lamb, has been ingeniously adapted for vegetarians and vegans. It contains no animal products, but is as rich-tasting and full of flavour as the original.

Serves 8

600g/1lb 5oz aubergines (eggplant), thickly sliced
30ml/2 tbsp olive oil
50ml/3½ tbsp water
paprika and fresh basil leaves, to garnish

For the sauce

30ml/2 tbsp olive oil
2 large onions, coarsely chopped
2 garlic cloves, crushed
2 large carrots, finely chopped
4 courgettes (zucchini), sliced
200g/7oz mushrooms, sliced
2 × 400g/14oz cans chopped tomatoes
30ml/2 tbsp balsamic vinegar
5ml/1 tsp Tabasco sauce
15ml/1 tbsp clear honey
salt and ground black pepper

For the tofu topping

200g/7oz/1¾ cups ground almonds
350g/12oz silken tofu, drained
15ml/1 tbsp soy sauce
15ml/1 tbsp lemon juice
2.5ml/½ tsp English (hot) mustard powder

1 Preheat the grill (broiler) to high and place the aubergine slices in one layer on the grill rack. Drizzle with olive oil and grill (broil) for 2–3 minutes on each side until lightly browned.

2 To make the sauce, heat the oil in a large pan and sauté the onion, garlic and carrots for 5–7 minutes, until softened. Add the remaining ingredients, bring to the boil, then simmer for 20 minutes, stirring occasionally. Season.

3 Meanwhile make the topping. Dry-fry the almonds in a heavy pan for 1–2 minutes, tossing occasionally, until golden. Reserve 75g/3oz/¾ cup. Tip the remainder into a food processor and add the remaining ingredients. Process until smooth.

4 Preheat the oven to 180°C/350°F/Gas 4. Spread half the sauce in the base of a 35 × 23cm/14 × 9in deep-sided ovenproof dish. Arrange the aubergines on top and spread over the remaining sauce. Add the topping, sprinkle with the almonds and bake for 20 minutes. Garnish with paprika and basil.

Roasted Ratatouille Moussaka

Roasting brings out the deep rich flavours of the vegetables, which contrast with the light egg-and-cheese topping.

Serves 4–6

2 red (bell) peppers, cut into large chunks
2 yellow (bell) peppers, cut into large chunks
2 aubergines (eggplant), cut into large chunks
3 courgettes (zucchini), thickly sliced
45ml/3 tbsp olive oil
3 garlic cloves, crushed
400g/14oz can chopped tomatoes
30ml/2 tbsp sun-dried tomato paste
45ml/3 tbsp chopped fresh basil
15ml/1 tbsp balsamic vinegar
1.5ml/¼ tsp soft brown sugar
salt and ground black pepper
basil leaves, to garnish

For the topping

25g/1oz/2 tbsp butter
25g/1oz/¼ cup plain (all-purpose) flour
300ml/½ pint/1¼ cups milk
1.5ml/¼ tsp freshly grated nutmeg
250g/9oz ricotta cheese
3 eggs, beaten
25g/1oz/⅓ cup freshly grated Parmesan cheese

1 Preheat the oven to 230°C/450°F/Gas 8. Arrange the chunks of aubergines and courgettes in an even layer in a large roasting pan. Season well with salt and ground black pepper.

2 Mix together the oil and crushed garlic cloves and pour them over the vegetables. Shake the pan to coat the vegetables thoroughly in the garlic mixture.

3 Roast in the oven for 15–20 minutes, until slightly charred, tossing once during cooking. Remove the pan from the oven and set aside. Reduce the temperature to 200°C/400°F/Gas 6.

4 Put the chopped tomatoes, sun-dried tomato paste, basil, balsamic vinegar and brown sugar in a large, heavy pan and heat gently to boiling point. Reduce the heat and simmer, uncovered, for about 10–15 minutes, until reduced, stirring occasionally. Season with salt and pepper to taste.

5 Carefully tip the roasted vegetables out of their pan and into the tomato sauce. Mix well, coating the vegetables thoroughly. Spoon into an ovenproof dish.

6 To make the topping, melt the butter in a large, heavy pan over a gentle heat. Stir in the flour and cook for 1 minute. Pour in the milk, stirring constantly, then whisk until blended. Add the nutmeg and continue whisking over a gentle heat until thickened. Cook for a further 2 minutes, then remove from the heat and leave to cool slightly.

7 Mix the ricotta cheese and beaten eggs thoroughly into the sauce. Season with salt and plenty of freshly ground black pepper to taste.

8 Level the surface of the roasted vegetable mixture with the back of a spoon. Spoon the moussaka topping over the vegetables and sprinkle with the Parmesan cheese. Bake for 30–35 minutes, until the topping is golden brown. Serve immediately, garnished with basil leaves.

Moussaka: *Energy 768kcal/3255kJ; Protein 60.3g; Carbohydrate 109.6g, of which sugars 10.3g; Fat 13.1g, of which saturates 2.9g; Cholesterol 99mg; Calcium 357mg; Fibre 21.8g; Sodium 320mg.*
Ratatouille Moussaka: *Energy 570kcal/2367kJ; Protein 22.1g; Carbohydrate 27.5g, of which sugars 21.7g; Fat 42.1g, of which saturates 20.3g; Cholesterol 223mg; Calcium 339mg; Fibre 7.1g; Sodium 447mg.*

Polenta with Mushroom Sauce

This is a fine example of just how absolutely delicious soft polenta can be. Polenta is a staple of northern Italian cuisine, and is served as an accompaniment to many savoury dishes. Topped with a robust mushroom and tomato sauce, it tastes quite sublime.

Serves 4

1.2 litres/2 pints/5 cups vegetable stock
350g/12oz/3 cups fine polenta or cornmeal
50g/2oz/ ⅔ cup freshly grated Parmesan cheese
salt and ground black pepper

For the sauce

15g/ ½ oz/ ¼ cup dried porcini mushrooms
150ml/ ¼ pint/ ⅔ cup hot water
15ml/1 tbsp olive oil
50g/2oz/ ¼ cup butter
1 onion, finely chopped
1 carrot, finely chopped
1 celery stick, finely chopped
2 garlic cloves, crushed
450g/1lb/6 cups mixed chestnut and large flat mushrooms, roughly chopped
120ml/4fl oz/ ½ cup red wine
400g/14oz can chopped tomatoes
5ml/1 tsp tomato purée (paste)
15ml/1 tbsp chopped fresh thyme

1 To make the sauce, soak the mushrooms in the hot water for 20 minutes. Drain, reserving the liquid, and chop roughly.

2 Heat the oil and butter in a saucepan and fry the onion, carrot, celery and garlic for 5 minutes, until beginning to soften. Raise the heat and add the both mushrooms. Cook for another 10 minutes. Pour in the wine and cook rapidly for 2–3 minutes, then add the tomatoes and strained, reserved soaking liquid. Stir in the tomato purée and thyme and season with salt and pepper. Lower the heat and simmer for 20 minutes.

3 Meanwhile, heat the stock in a large heavy-based saucepan. Add a pinch of salt. As soon as it simmers, tip in the polenta in a fine stream, whisking until the mixture is smooth. Cook for 30 minutes, stirring constantly, until the polenta comes away from the pan. Stir in half the Parmesan and some pepper.

4 Divide among four heated bowls and top each with sauce. Sprinkle with the remaining Parmesan.

Baked Vegetables with Thyme

Crunchy golden batter surrounds this attractive combination of bright summer vegetables. Flavoured with thyme, the combination is both delicious and filling, and, served with salad, this dish makes an excellent light lunch or supper.

Serves 6

1 small aubergine (eggplant), halved and thickly sliced
1 egg
115g/4oz/1 cup plain (all-purpose) flour
300ml/ ½ pint/1 ¼ cups milk
30ml/2 tbsp fresh thyme leaves, or 10ml/2 tsp dried
1 red onion
2 large courgettes (zucchini)
1 red (bell) pepper
1 yellow (bell) pepper
60–75ml/4–5 tbsp sunflower oil
30ml/2 tbsp freshly grated Parmesan cheese
salt and ground black pepper
fresh herbs, to garnish

1 Place the aubergine in a colander or sieve (strainer), sprinkle generously with salt, and leave for 10 minutes. Drain, rinse well and pat dry on kitchen paper.

2 Meanwhile, beat the egg in a bowl, then gradually beat in the flour and a little milk to make a smooth, thick paste. Gradually blend in the rest of the milk, add the thyme and seasoning to taste, and stir to make a smooth batter. Leave in a cool place until required.

3 Preheat the oven to 220°C/425°F/Gas 7. Quarter the onion, slice the courgettes and quarter the peppers, removing the seeds. Put the oil in a roasting pan and heat in the oven. Add the vegetables, including the aubergines, and toss them in the oil to coat thoroughly. Return the pan to the oven for 20 minutes.

4 When the fat in the pan is really hot, whisk the batter and pour it over the vegetables – it should sizzle as it hits the hot fat. Return the pan to the oven for 30 minutes.

5 When the batter is puffed up and golden, reduce the heat to 190°C/375°F/Gas 5 for 10–15 minutes, or until crisp around the edges. Sprinkle with Parmesan and herbs, and serve.

Polenta with Mushroom Sauce: *Energy 572kcal/2384kJ; Protein 17.2g; Carbohydrate 72.2g, of which sugars 6.1g; Fat 21g, of which saturates 9.7g; Cholesterol 39mg; Calcium 185mg; Fibre 5.4g; Sodium 242mg.*
Baked Vegetables: *Energy 231kcal/966kJ; Protein 8.9g; Carbohydrate 24.1g, of which sugars 8.9g; Fat 11.7g, of which saturates 2.9g; Cholesterol 40mg; Calcium 181mg; Fibre 3.3g; Sodium 93mg.*

Ratatouille

This classic recipe is a combination of the vegetables that grow so abundantly in the South of France.

Serves 6

2 medium aubergines (eggplants) (about 450g/1lb total)
60–75ml/4–5 tbsp olive oil
1 large onion, halved and sliced
2 or 3 garlic cloves, very finely chopped
1 large red or yellow (bell) pepper, cut into thin strips
2 large courgettes (zucchini), cut into 1cm/½in slices
675g/1½lb ripe tomatoes, peeled, seeded and chopped, or 400g/14oz/2 cups canned chopped tomatoes
5ml/1 tsp dried herbes de Provence
salt and ground black pepper

1 Preheat the grill (broiler). Cut the aubergine into 2cm/¾in slices, then brush with olive oil on both sides and grill (broil) until lightly browned, turning once. Cut the slices into cubes.

2 Heat 15ml/1 tbsp of the olive oil in a large heavy pan or flameproof casserole and cook the onion over a medium-low heat for about 10 minutes until lightly golden, stirring frequently. Add the garlic, pepper and courgettes and cook for a further 10 minutes, stirring occasionally.

3 Add the tomatoes and aubergine cubes, dried herbs and salt and pepper and simmer gently, covered, over a low heat for about 20 minutes, stirring occasionally. Uncover and continue cooking for a further 20–25 minutes, stirring occasionally, until all the vegetables are tender and the cooking liquid has thickened slightly. Serve hot or at room temperature.

Variation
To skin the pepper and add flavour to the ratatouille, quarter the pepper and grill (broil), skin-side up, until blackened. Enclose in a plastic bag and set aside until cool. Peel off the skin, then remove the core and seeds and cut into strips. Add to the mixture with the cooked aubergine.

Vegetable Stew with Roasted Tomato and Garlic Sauce

This lightly spiced stew makes a perfect match for couscous, enriched with a little butter or olive oil. Add some chopped coriander (cilantro) leaves and a handful of raisins and toasted pine nuts to make it extra special.

Serves 6

45ml/3 tbsp olive oil
250g/9oz shallots
1 large onion, chopped
2 garlic cloves, chopped
5ml/1 tsp cumin seeds
5ml/1 tsp ground coriander seeds
5ml/1 tsp paprika
5cm/2in piece cinnamon stick
2 fresh bay leaves
300–450ml/½–¾ pint/1¼–scant 2 cups good vegetable stock
good pinch of saffron strands
450g/1lb carrots, thickly sliced
2 green (bell) peppers, thickly sliced
115g/4oz ready-to-eat dried apricots, halved if large
5–7.5ml/1–1½ tsp ground toasted cumin seeds
450g/1lb squash, peeled, and cut into chunks
pinch of sugar, to taste
25g/1oz/2 tbsp butter
salt and ground black pepper
45ml/3 tbsp fresh coriander (cilantro) leaves, to garnish

For the roasted tomato and garlic sauce

1kg/2¼lb tomatoes, halved
5ml/1 tsp sugar
45ml/3 tbsp olive oil
1–2 fresh red chillies, seeded and chopped
2–3 garlic cloves, chopped
5ml/1 tsp fresh thyme leaves

1 Preheat the oven to 180°C/350°F/Gas 4. To make the sauce, place the tomatoes, cut sides uppermost, in a roasting pan. Season well with salt and pepper and sprinkle the sugar over the top, then drizzle with the olive oil. Roast for 30 minutes.

2 Stir the chillies, garlic and thyme into the tomatoes and roast for another 30–45 minutes, until the tomatoes have collapsed but are still a little juicy. Cool, then process in a food processor or blender. Sieve (strain) to remove the seeds.

3 Heat 30ml/2 tbsp of the oil in a large, wide pan and cook the shallots until browned all over. Remove from the pan and set aside. Add the chopped onion to the pan and cook over a low heat for 5–7 minutes, until softened. Stir in the garlic and cumin seeds and cook for a further 3–4 minutes.

4 Add the ground coriander seeds, paprika, cinnamon stick and bay leaves. Cook, stirring constantly, for another 2 minutes, then mix in the vegetable stock, saffron, carrots and green peppers. Season well, cover and simmer gently for 10 minutes.

5 Stir in the apricots, 5ml/1 tsp of the ground toasted cumin, the browned shallots and the squash. Stir in the tomato sauce.

6 Cover the pan and cook for a further 5 minutes. Uncover the pan and continue to cook, stirring occasionally, for 10–15 minutes, until the vegetables are all fully cooked.

7 Adjust the seasoning, adding a little more cumin and a pinch of sugar to taste. Remove and discard the cinnamon stick. Stir in the butter and serve scattered with the fresh coriander leaves.

Ratatouille: *Energy 135kcal/563kJ; Protein 3.6g; Carbohydrate 10.4g, of which sugars 10.1g; Fat 9.1g, of which saturates 1.5g; Cholesterol 0mg; Calcium 41mg; Fibre 4.4g; Sodium 20mg.*
Vegetable Stew: *Energy 204kcal/857kJ; Protein 4.8g; Carbohydrate 32.7g, of which sugars 29.3g; Fat 6.9g, of which saturates 1.2g; Cholesterol 0mg; Calcium 98mg; Fibre 7.9g; Sodium 42mg.*

Spicy Chickpea and Aubergine Stew

This is a Lebanese dish, but similar recipes are found all over the Mediterranean. The vegetables have a warm, smoky flavour, subtly enriched with spices. Crunchy fried onion rings provide a contrast of taste and texture. Serve the stew on a bed of rice.

Serves 4

3 large aubergines (eggplants), cubed
200g/7oz/1 cup chickpeas, soaked overnight
60ml/4 tbsp olive oil
3 garlic cloves, chopped
2 large onions, chopped
2.5ml/½ tsp ground cumin
2.5ml/½ tsp ground cinnamon
2.5ml/½ tsp ground coriander
3 × 400g/14oz cans chopped tomatoes
salt and ground black pepper
cooked rice, to serve

For the garnish

30ml/2 tbsp olive oil
1 onion, sliced
1 garlic clove, sliced
sprigs of coriander (cilantro)

1 Place the aubergines in a colander and sprinkle them with salt. Sit the colander in a bowl and leave for 30 minutes, to allow the bitter juices to escape. Rinse with cold water and dry on kitchen paper.

2 Drain the chickpeas and put in a pan with enough water to cover. Bring to the boil and simmer for 30 minutes, or until tender. Drain.

3 Heat the oil in a large pan. Add the garlic and onion and cook gently until soft. Add the spices and cook, stirring, for a few seconds. Add the aubergine and stir to coat with the spices and onion. Cook for 5 minutes. Add the tomatoes and chickpeas and season with salt and pepper. Cover and simmer for 20 minutes.

4 To make the garnish, heat the oil in a frying pan and, when very hot, add the sliced onion and garlic. Fry until golden and crisp. Serve the stew with rice, topped with the onion and garlic and garnished with coriander.

Mediterranean Vegetables with Chickpeas

The flavours of the Mediterranean are captured in this delicious, healthy vegetable dish, ideal for a light lunch, served with crusty bread.

Serves 6

1 onion, sliced
2 leeks, sliced
2 garlic cloves, crushed
1 red (bell) pepper, sliced
1 green (bell) pepper, sliced
1 yellow (bell) pepper, sliced
350g/12oz courgettes (zucchini), sliced
225g/8oz/3 cups mushrooms, sliced
400g/14oz can chopped tomatoes
30ml/2 tbsp ruby port or red wine
30ml/2 tbsp tomato purée (paste)
15ml/1 tbsp tomato ketchup (optional)
400g/14oz can chickpeas
115g/4oz/1 cup stoned (pitted) black olives
45ml/3 tbsp chopped fresh mixed herbs, including oregano and basil
salt and ground black pepper
chopped fresh mixed herbs, to garnish

1 Put the onion, leeks, garlic, red, yellow and green peppers, courgettes and mushrooms into a large, heavy pan.

2 Add the tomatoes, port or red wine, tomato purée and tomato ketchup, if using, to the pan and mix all the ingredients together well.

3 Rinse and drain the chickpeas and add to the pan. Stir, cover, bring to the boil then reduce the heat and simmer the mixture gently for 20–30 minutes, until the vegetables are cooked and tender but not overcooked, stirring occasionally.

4 Remove the lid of the saucepan and increase the heat slightly for the last 10 minutes of the cooking time, to thicken the sauce, if you like.

5 Stir in the olives, herbs and seasoning. Serve either hot or cold, garnished with chopped mixed herbs.

Spicy Chickpea Stew: *Energy 201kcal/843kJ; Protein 7.1g; Carbohydrate 22.3g, of which sugars 10.4g; Fat 10g, of which saturates 1.4g; Cholesterol 0mg; Calcium 57mg; Fibre 5.9g; Sodium 175mg.*
Mediterranean Vegetables: *Energy 161kcal/678kJ; Protein 7.9g; Carbohydrate 21.7g, of which sugars 13.4g; Fat 4.7g, of which saturates 0.8g; Cholesterol 0mg; Calcium 78mg; Fibre 7g; Sodium 639mg.*

Spiced Turnips with Spinach and Tomatoes

Delicate baby turnips, tender spinach and ripe tomatoes make tempting partners in this simple Eastern Mediterranean vegetable stew, which makes a lovely dish for spring or summer, served warm or cold. Adding a pinch of sugar to the mixture during cooking brings out the natural sweetness of the vegetables.

Serves 6

450g/1lb plum or other well-flavoured tomatoes
60ml/4 tbsp olive oil
2 onions, sliced
450g/1lb baby turnips, peeled
5ml/1 tsp paprika
2.5ml/½ tsp caster (superfine) sugar
60ml/4 tbsp chopped fresh coriander (cilantro)
450g/1lb fresh young spinach
salt and ground black pepper

1 Plunge the tomatoes into a bowl of boiling water for 30 seconds, then refresh in a bowl of cold water. Peel away the tomato skins and chop roughly. Heat the olive oil in a large frying pan or sauté pan and fry the onion slices for about 5 minutes until golden.

2 Add the baby turnips, tomatoes and paprika to the pan with 60ml/4 tbsp water and cook until the tomatoes are pulpy. Cover with a lid and continue cooking until the baby turnips have softened.

3 Stir in the sugar and coriander, then add the spinach and a little salt and pepper and cook for a further 2–3 minutes until the spinach has wilted. Serve warm or cold.

Variations

- *This dish makes a lovely vegetarian main course, but would also be delicious served as a side dish with the new season's roast or barbecued lamb.*
- *For a spicier version of the stew, double the amount of paprika and add a pinch of cayenne.*

Aubergine Parmigiana

This is a classic Italian dish, in which blissfully tender sliced aubergines (eggplants) are layered with melting creamy mozzarella, fresh Parmesan and a good home-made tomato sauce, then baked in a hot oven until appetizingly golden brown.

Serves 4–6

3 medium aubergines (eggplants), thinly sliced
olive oil, for brushing
300g/11oz mozzarella cheese, sliced
115g/4oz/1⅓ cups freshly grated Parmesan cheese
30–45ml/2–3 tbsp dry breadcrumbs
salt and ground black pepper
fresh basil sprigs, to garnish

For the sauce

30ml/2 tbsp olive oil
1 onion, finely chopped
2 garlic cloves, crushed
400g/14oz can chopped tomatoes
5ml/1 tsp granulated sugar
about 6 fresh basil leaves

1 Layer the aubergine slices in a colander, sprinkling each layer with a little salt. Leave to drain over a bowl for about 20 minutes, then rinse thoroughly under cold running water and pat dry with kitchen paper.

2 Preheat the oven to 200°C/400°F/Gas 6. Lay the aubergine slices on non-stick baking sheets, brush the tops with olive oil and bake for 10–15 minutes until softened.

3 Meanwhile, make the sauce. Heat the oil in a pan. Add the onion and garlic and fry over a low heat, stirring occasionally, for 5 minutes. Add the canned tomatoes and sugar and season with salt and pepper to taste. Bring to the boil, then lower the heat and simmer for about 10 minutes, until reduced and thickened. Tear the basil leaves and stir them into the sauce.

4 Layer the aubergines in a greased shallow ovenproof dish with the sliced mozzarella, the tomato sauce and the grated Parmesan, ending with a layer of Parmesan mixed with the breadcrumbs. Bake for 20–25 minutes, until golden brown and bubbling. Allow to stand for 5 minutes before cutting. Serve garnished with basil.

Spiced Turnips: *Energy 363kcal/1519kJ; Protein 326g; Carbohydrate 80g, of which sugars 37g; Fat 2.62g, of which saturates 0.2g; Cholesterol 0mg; Calcium 891mg; Fibre 12.5g; Sodium 1520mg.*
Aubergine Parmigiana: *Energy 819kcal/3417kJ; Protein 51.2g; Carbohydrate 30.9g, of which sugars 14.7g; Fat 55.6g, of which saturates 30.7g; Cholesterol 128mg; Calcium 1169mg; Fibre 7.9g; Sodium 1258mg.*

Stuffed Aubergine

This dish from the Ligurian region of Italy is spiked with paprika and allspice, a legacy of the days when spices came into northern Italy via the port of Genoa.

Serves 4

2 medium aubergines (eggplants), stalks removed
275g/10oz potatoes, peeled and diced
15ml/1 tbsp olive oil
1 small onion, finely chopped
1 garlic clove, finely chopped
good pinch of ground allspice and paprika
30ml/2 tbsp skimmed milk
25g/1oz grated fresh Parmesan cheese
15ml/1 tbsp fresh white breadcrumbs
salt and freshly ground black pepper
fresh mint sprigs, to garnish
salad leaves, to serve

1 Bring a large saucepan of lightly salted water to the boil. Add the whole aubergines and cook for 5 minutes. Remove with a slotted spoon and set aside. Add the diced potatoes to the pan and boil for about 15 minutes or until cooked.

2 Meanwhile, cut the aubergines in half lengthways and scoop out the flesh, leaving 5mm/¼in of the shell intact. Select a baking dish that will hold the aubergine shells snugly in a single layer. Brush it lightly with oil. Put the shells in the dish and chop the aubergine flesh roughly. Set aside.

3 Heat the oil in a frying pan, add the onion and cook gently, stirring, until softened. Add the chopped aubergine flesh and the garlic. Cook, stirring frequently, for 6–8 minutes. Tip into a bowl and set aside. Preheat the oven to 190°C/375°F/Gas 5.

4 Drain and mash the potatoes. Add to the aubergine mixture with the spices and milk. Set aside 15ml/1 tbsp of the Parmesan and add the rest to the aubergine mixture, adding salt and pepper to taste. Spoon the mixture into the aubergine shells.

5 Mix the breadcrumbs with the reserved Parmesan cheese and sprinkle the mixture evenly over the aubergines. Bake in the oven for 30–40 minutes until the topping is crisp. Garnish with mint sprigs and serve with salad leaves.

Onions Stuffed with Goat's Cheese and Sun-dried Tomatoes

Roasted onions and goat's cheese are a winning combination. These stuffed onions make an excellent main course served with a rice or cracked wheat pilaf.

Serves 4

4 large onions
150g/5oz goat's cheese, crumbled or cubed
50g/2oz fresh breadcrumbs
8 sun-dried tomatoes in olive oil, drained and chopped
1–2 garlic cloves, finely chopped
2.5ml/½ tsp chopped fresh thyme
30ml/2 tbsp chopped fresh parsley
1 small egg, beaten
45ml/3 tbsp pine nuts, toasted
30ml/2 tbsp olive oil (use oil from the tomatoes)
salt and ground black pepper

1 Bring a large pan of lightly salted water to the boil. Add the whole onions in their skins and boil for 10 minutes. Drain and cool, then cut each onion in half horizontally and peel. Using a teaspoon, remove the centre of each onion, leaving a thick shell. Reserve the flesh and place the shells in an oiled baking dish. Preheat the oven to 190°C/375°F/Gas 5.

2 Chop the scooped-out onion flesh and place in a bowl. Add the goat's cheese, breadcrumbs, sun-dried tomatoes, garlic, thyme, parsley and egg. Mix well, then season with salt and pepper and add the toasted pine nuts.

3 Divide the stuffing among the onions and cover with foil. Bake for about 25 minutes. Uncover, drizzle with the oil and cook for another 30–40 minutes, until bubbling and well cooked. Baste occasionally during cooking.

Variations

- *Stuff the onions with spinach and rice mixed with some smoked mozzarella and toasted almonds instead of the goat's cheese and sun-dried tomato mixture.*
- *Use peppers preserved in olive oil instead of tomatoes.*

Stuffed Aubergine: *Energy 88kcal/369kJ; Protein 3.3g; Carbohydrate 11.2g, of which sugars 2.2g; Fat 3.6g, of which saturates 1.3g; Cholesterol 4mg; Calcium 68mg; Fibre 1.4g; Sodium 73mg.*
Onions with Goat's Cheese: *Energy 402kcal/1669kJ; Protein 14.8g; Carbohydrate 25.1g, of which sugars 11.7g; Fat 27.7g, of which saturates 8.8g; Cholesterol 82mg; Calcium 120mg; Fibre 3.2g; Sodium 346mg.*

Roasted Peppers with Sweet Cicely

The sweet aniseed flavours of sweet cicely and fennel combine beautifully with succulent peppers and tomatoes and piquant capers. Sweet cicely leaves make an excellent garnish and they taste just like the flowers.

Serves 4

4 red (bell) peppers, halved
8 small or 4 medium tomatoes
15ml/1 tbsp semi-ripe sweet cicely seeds
15ml/1 tbsp fennel seeds
15ml/1 tbsp capers
8 sweet cicely flowers, newly opened, stems removed
60ml/4 tbsp olive oil

For the garnish

a few small sweet cicely leaves
8 more sweet cicely flowers, newly opened

1 Preheat the oven to 180°C/350°F/Gas 4. Place the red pepper halves in a large ovenproof dish and set aside.

2 To skin the tomatoes, cut a cross at the base, then pour over boiling water and leave them to stand for 30 seconds to 1 minute. Cut them in half if they are of medium size.

3 Place a whole small or half a medium tomato in each half of a pepper cavity.

4 Cover with a scattering of semi-ripe sweet cicely seeds, fennel seeds and capers and about half the sweet cicely flowers. Drizzle the olive oil all over.

5 Bake in the top of the oven for 1 hour. Remove from the oven and add the rest of the flowers. Garnish with fresh sweet cicely leaves and flowers, and serve with lots of crusty bread to soak up the juices.

Cook's Tip

Try adding the stems from the sweet cicely to the water in which fruit is stewed. They will add a delightful flavour and reduce the need for sugar.

Pepper Gratin

Serve this simple but delicious Italian dish as a starter or snack with a mixed leaf salad and plenty of good crusty bread to mop up the juices from the peppers.

Serves 4

2 red (bell) peppers
15ml/1 tbsp extra virgin olive oil
1 garlic clove, finely chopped
5ml/1 tsp capers, drained and rinsed
8 stoned (pitted) black olives, roughly chopped
15ml/1 tbsp chopped fresh oregano
15ml/1 tbsp chopped fresh flat leaf parsley
60ml/4 tbsp fresh white breadcrumbs
salt and ground black pepper
fresh herbs, to garnish

1 Preheat the oven to 200°C/400°F/Gas 6. Place the peppers on a grill rack and cook under a hot grill. Turn occasionally until they are blackened and blistered all over. Remove from the heat and place in a plastic bag. Seal and leave to cool.

2 When cool, peel the peppers. (Don't skin them under the tap as the water would wash away some of the delicious smoky flavour.) Halve and remove and discard the seeds, then cut the flesh into large strips.

3 Use a little of the olive oil to grease a small baking dish. Arrange the pepper strips in the dish.

4 Sprinkle the garlic, capers, olives and chopped herbs on top. Season with salt and pepper. Scatter over the fresh white breadcrumbs and drizzle with the remaining olive oil. Bake in the oven for about 20 minutes until the breadcrumbs have browned. Garnish with fresh herbs and serve immediately.

Variation

For non-vegetarians, a few anchovy fillets, drained and chopped can be scattered over the peppers with the other ingredients.

Roasted Peppers with Cicely: *Energy 172kcal/714kJ; Protein 2.5g; Carbohydrate 14.3g, of which sugars 13.8g; Fat 12g, of which saturates 1.9g; Cholesterol 0mg; Calcium 21mg; Fibre 3.8g; Sodium 16mg.*
Pepper Gratin: *Energy 110kcal/460kJ; Protein 2.7g; Carbohydrate 15.5g, of which sugars 5.8g; Fat 4.5g, of which saturates 0.7g; Cholesterol 0mg; Calcium 44mg; Fibre 2.4g; Sodium 326mg.*

Middle-Eastern Stuffed Peppers

Couscous is a form of semolina, and is used extensively in the Middle East – a major influence on Mediterranean cuisine. Choose ripe red peppers for the fullest flavour.

Serves 4

6 red (bell) peppers
25g/1oz/2 tbsp butter
1 medium onion, finely chopped
5ml/1 tsp olive oil
2.5ml/½ tsp salt
175g/6oz/1 cup couscous
25g/1oz/2 tbsp raisins
30ml/2 tbsp chopped fresh mint
1 egg yolk
salt and ground black pepper
mint leaves, to garnish

1 Preheat the oven to 200°C/400°F/Gas 6. Carefully slit each pepper and remove the core and seeds. Melt the butter in a small pan and add the onion. Cook until softened and golden, stirring frequently.

2 To cook the couscous, bring 250ml/8fl oz/1 cup water to the boil. Add the oil and the salt, then remove the pan from the heat and add the couscous. Stir and leave to stand, covered, for 5 minutes.

3 Stir in the cooked onion, raisins and mint, then season well with salt and pepper. Stir in the egg yolk.

4 Using a teaspoon, fill the peppers with the couscous mixture to only about three-quarters full, as the couscous will swell when cooked further.

5 Place in a lightly oiled ovenproof dish and bake, uncovered, for about 20 minutes until tender. Serve hot or cold, garnished with the mint leaves.

Cook's Tip
The couscous sold in supermarkets is pre-cooked and only needs soaking for a brief time and fluffing up with a fork.

Italian Stuffed Peppers

These flavourful Italian stuffed peppers are easy to make for a light and healthy lunch or supper.

Serves 4

10ml/2 tsp olive oil
1 red onion, sliced
1 courgette (zucchini), diced
115g/4oz mushrooms, sliced
1 garlic clove, crushed
400g/14oz can chopped tomatoes
15ml/1 tbsp tomato purée (paste)
25g/1oz pine nuts
30ml/2 tbsp chopped fresh basil
4 large yellow (bell) peppers
25g/1oz/¼ cup finely grated fresh Parmesan or Fontina cheese
salt and freshly ground black pepper
fresh basil leaves, to garnish

1 Preheat the oven to 180°C/350°F/Gas 4. Heat the oil in a saucepan, add the onion, courgette, mushrooms and garlic and cook gently for 3 minutes, stirring the mixture occasionally.

2 Stir in the tomatoes and tomato purée, then bring to the boil and simmer, uncovered, for 10–15 minutes, stirring occasionally, until thickened slightly. Remove the pan from the heat and stir in the pine nuts, if using, chopped basil and seasoning. Set aside.

3 Cut the peppers in half lengthways and deseed them. Blanch the pepper halves in boiling water for about 3 minutes. Drain.

4 Place the peppers cut-side up in a shallow ovenproof dish and fill with the vegetable mixture.

5 Cover the dish with foil and bake in the oven for 20 minutes. Uncover, sprinkle each pepper half with a little grated cheese, if using, and bake, uncovered, for a further 5–10 minutes. Garnish with fresh basil leaves and serve.

Cook's Tip
Red (bell) peppers could be used, but yellow ones look particularly beautiful filled with the vivid red and green stuffing.

Stuffed Peppers: Energy 392kcal/1630kJ; Protein 9.2g; Carbohydrate 25.4g, of which sugars 17.9g; Fat 28.8g, of which saturates 3.2g; Cholesterol 0mg; Calcium 110mg; Fibre 5.5g; Sodium 19mg.
Italian Stuffed Peppers: Energy 108kcal/450kJ; Protein 4.2g; Carbohydrate 17g, of which sugars 16.1g; Fat 2.9g, of which saturates 0.6g; Cholesterol 0mg; Calcium 40mg; Fibre 4.9g; Sodium 28mg.

Stuffed Mushrooms with Spinach

Use fresh ceps, if you can find them, to achieve the traditional flavour of this dish. Large, flat mushrooms work very well too.

Serves 6

12 large flat mushrooms
450g/1lb young spinach leaves
4 large sun-dried tomatoes preserved in oil, cut into 5mm/¼in dice
1 onion, finely chopped
2 egg yolks, beaten
40g/1½ oz/¾ cup fresh breadcrumbs
5ml/1 tsp chopped fresh marjoram
45ml/3 tbsp olive oil or vegetable oil
115g/4oz feta cheese, crumbled
salt and ground black pepper

1 Wipe the mushrooms, peeling them only if necessary. Remove the stalks and chop them finely.

2 Blanch the spinach by dropping it into boiling water for 1–2 minutes, then plunge into cold water. Squeeze dry in kitchen paper, then chop.

3 Dry fry the onion until golden, then add the mushroom stalks. Remove from the heat. Stir in the spinach, egg yolks, tomatoes, breadcrumbs and marjoram, and season to taste.

4 Place the mushrooms, under-sides up, on a baking sheet and brush with a little extra virgin olive oil. Do not add too much olive oil as the mushrooms will produce moisture while they are cooking.

5 Place heaped tablespoons of the spinach mixture on to the mushroom caps. Sprinkle over the cheese and cook the mushrooms under a preheated grill (broiler) for about 10 minutes, or until golden brown.

Cook's Tip

Stuffed mushrooms make a meal in themselves, but are also an excellent accompaniment for barbecued meat or chicken.

Greek Stuffed Vegetables

Colourful peppers and tomatoes make perfect containers for various meat and vegetable stuffings. This rice and herb version uses typically Greek ingredients.

Serves 4

2 large ripe tomatoes
1 green (bell) pepper
1 yellow or orange (bell) pepper
60ml/4 tbsp olive oil, plus extra for sprinkling
2 onions, chopped
2 garlic cloves, crushed
50g/2oz/½ cup blanched almonds, chopped
75g/3oz/scant ½ cup long grain rice, boiled and drained
15g/½oz mint, roughly chopped
15g/½oz fresh parsley, roughly chopped
25g/1oz/2 tbsp sultanas (golden raisins)
45ml/3 tbsp ground almonds
salt and ground black pepper
chopped mixed fresh herbs, to garnish

1 Preheat the oven to 190°C/375°F/Gas 5. Cut the tomatoes in half and scoop out the pulp and seeds using a teaspoon. Leave the tomatoes to drain on kitchen paper with cut sides down. Roughly chop the tomato pulp and seeds.

2 Halve the peppers, leaving the stalks intact. Scoop out the seeds. Brush the peppers with 15ml/1 tbsp of the oil and bake on a baking tray for 15 minutes. Place the peppers and tomatoes in a shallow ovenproof dish and season with salt and pepper.

3 Fry the onions in the remaining oil for 5 minutes. Add the garlic and chopped almonds and fry for a further minute.

Variation

Small aubergines (eggplants) or large courgettes (zucchini) also make good vegetables for stuffing. Halve and scoop out the centres of the vegetables, then oil the vegetable cases and bake for about 15 minutes. Chop the centres, fry for 2–3 minutes to soften and add to the stuffing mixture. Fill the aubergine or courgette cases with the stuffing and bake in the same way as the peppers and tomatoes.

Stuffed Mushrooms: Energy 212kcal/882kJ; Protein 12g; Carbohydrate 8.1g, of which sugars 2.5g; Fat 14.8g, of which saturates 4.8g; Cholesterol 87mg; Calcium 226mg; Fibre 3.7g; Sodium 636mg.
Greek Stuffed Vegetables: Energy 234kcal/981kJ; Protein 5.7g; Carbohydrate 32.5g, of which sugars 14.5g; Fat 9.9g, of which saturates 1.2g; Cholesterol 0mg; Calcium 71mg; Fibre 3.6g; Sodium 14mg.

Leek, Pepper and Spinach Frittata

Unlike Spanish tortilla, Italian frittata does not usually contain potato and is generally slightly softer in texture. The combination of leek, red pepper and spinach is delicious with egg.

Serves 3–4

30ml/2 tbsp olive oil
1 large red (bell) pepper, diced
2.5–5ml/½–1 tsp ground toasted cumin
3 leeks (about 450g/1lb), thinly sliced
150g/5oz small spinach leaves
45ml/3 tbsp pine nuts, toasted
5 large eggs
15ml/1 tbsp chopped fresh basil
15ml/1 tbsp chopped fresh flat leaf parsley
salt and ground black pepper
watercress, to garnish
50g/2oz Parmesan cheese, grated, to serve (optional)

1 Heat a frying pan and add the oil. Add the red pepper and cook over a medium heat, stirring occasionally, for 6–8 minutes, until soft and beginning to brown at the edges. Add 2.5ml/½ tsp of the cumin and cook for another 1–2 minutes, stirring to prevent it burning.

2 Stir in the leeks, then part-cover the pan and cook gently for about 5 minutes, until the leeks have softened and collapsed. Season with salt and ground black pepper.

3 Add the spinach and cover. Allow the spinach to wilt in the steam for 3–4 minutes, then stir to mix it into the vegetables, adding the pine nuts.

4 Beat the eggs with salt, pepper, the remaining cumin, basil and parsley. Add to the pan and cook over a gentle heat until the bottom of the omelette sets and turns golden brown. Pull the edges of the frittata away from the sides of the pan as it cooks and tilt the pan so that the uncooked egg runs underneath and sets.

5 Preheat the grill (broiler). Flash the frittata under the hot grill to set the egg on top, but do not let it become too brown. Cut the frittata into wedges and serve warm, garnished with watercress and sprinkled with Parmesan, if using.

Garlic and Goat's Cheese Soufflé

Balance this rich soufflé with a crisp green salad, including peppery leaves, such as mizuna and watercress.

Serves 3–4

2 large, plump heads of garlic
3 fresh thyme sprigs
15ml/1 tbsp olive oil
250ml/8fl oz/1 cup milk
1 fresh bay leaf
2 × 1cm/½in thick onion slices
2 cloves
50g/2oz/¼ cup butter
40g/1½oz/⅓ cup plain (all-purpose) flour, sifted
cayenne pepper
3 eggs, separated, plus 1 egg white
150g/5oz goat's cheese, crumbled
50g/2oz/⅔ cup freshly grated Parmesan cheese
2.5–5ml/½–1 tsp chopped fresh thyme
2.5ml/½ tsp cream of tartar
salt and freshly ground black pepper

1 Preheat the oven to 180°C/350°F/Gas 4. Place the garlic and thyme sprigs on a piece of foil. Sprinkle with the oil and close the foil around the garlic, then bake for about 1 hour. Leave to cool. Discard the thyme and squeeze the garlic out of its skin and purée the flesh with the oil.

2 Meanwhile, bring the milk to the boil with the bay leaf, onion and cloves, then remove from the heat. Cover and leave to stand for 30 minutes. Melt 40g/1½oz/3 tbsp of the butter in another pan. Stir in the flour and cook gently for 2 minutes, stirring. Reheat and strain the milk, then stir it into the roux. Cook very gently for 10 minutes, stirring frequently. Season with salt, pepper and cayenne. Cool slightly. Preheat the oven to 200°C/400°F/Gas 6.

3 Beat in the egg yolks, one at a time, the goat's cheese, all but 15ml/1 tbsp of the Parmesan and the chopped thyme. Use the remaining butter to grease four 250ml/8fl oz/1 cup ramekins.

4 Whisk the egg whites and cream of tartar until firm but not dry. Stir 45ml/3 tbsp of the whites into the sauce, then fold in the remainder. Pour the mixture into the prepared dishes and scatter with the reserved Parmesan. Place on a baking sheet and cook for 20 minutes until risen and firm to a light touch in the centre. Serve immediately.

Frittata: *Energy 267kcal/1107kJ; Protein 12.7g; Carbohydrate 7.1g, of which sugars 6.2g; Fat 21.2g, of which saturates 3.4g; Cholesterol 238mg; Calcium 131mg; Fibre 4.2g; Sodium 144mg.*
Goat's Cheese Soufflé: *Energy 563kcal/2338kJ; Protein 28.8g; Carbohydrate 16.5g, of which sugars 5.8g; Fat 42.9g, of which saturates 24.1g; Cholesterol 294mg; Calcium 422mg; Fibre 0.7g; Sodium 710mg.*

Moroccan Pancakes

An unusual dish that makes a good main course for an informal dinner party.

Serves 4–6

15ml/1 tbsp olive oil
1 large onion, chopped
250g/9oz fresh spinach
400g/14oz can chickpeas
2 courgettes, grated
30ml/2 tbsp chopped fresh coriander (cilantro)
2 eggs, beaten
salt and ground black pepper
fresh coriander (cilantro) leaves, to garnish

For the pancakes

150g/5oz/1¼ cups plain (all-purpose) flour
1 egg
about 350ml/12fl oz/1½ cups milk
75ml/5 tbsp water
15ml/1 tbsp sunflower oil, plus extra for greasing

For the sauce

25g/1oz/2 tbsp butter
30ml/2 tbsp plain (all-purpose) flour
about 300ml/½ pint/1¼ cups milk

1 Make the batter by blending the flour, egg, milk and water until smooth in a blender. Stir in the oil and a pinch of salt. Heat a lightly greased frying pan and ladle in one-eighth of the batter. Cook for 2–3 minutes, without turning, then slide the pancake out of the pan. Make seven more pancakes.

2 Heat the olive oil in a small pan and fry the onion until soft. Set aside. Wash the spinach, place it in a pan and cook until wilted, shaking the pan occasionally. Chop the spinach roughly.

3 Drain the chickpeas, place in a bowl of cold water and rub them until the skins float to the surface. Drain the chickpeas and mash roughly with a fork. Add the onion, courgettes, spinach and coriander. Stir in the eggs, season and mix well.

4 Preheat the oven to 180°C/350°F/Gas 4. Arrange the pancakes cooked side up and spoon the filling down the centres. Roll up and place in a large oiled ovenproof dish. To make the sauce, melt the butter in a pan, stir in the flour and cook for 1 minute. Gradually whisk in the milk until the mixture boils. Season and pour over the pancakes. Bake for 15 minutes, until golden. Serve garnished with the coriander leaves.

Baked Herb Crêpes

Add fresh herbs to make crêpes something special, then fill them with spinach, pine nuts and ricotta cheese and serve with a garlicky tomato sauce.

Serves 4

25g/1oz/½ cup chopped fresh herbs
15ml/1 tbsp sunflower oil, plus extra for frying
120ml/4fl oz/½ cup milk
3 eggs
25g/1oz/¼ cup plain (all-purpose) flour
pinch of salt
oil, for greasing

For the sauce

30ml/2 tbsp olive oil
1 small onion, chopped
2 garlic cloves, crushed
400g/14oz can chopped tomatoes
pinch of soft light brown sugar

For the filling

450g/1lb fresh spinach, cooked
175g/6oz/¾ cup ricotta cheese
25g/1oz/¼ cup pine nuts, toasted
5 sun-dried tomatoes in olive oil, drained and chopped
30ml/2 tbsp chopped fresh basil
salt, nutmeg and ground black pepper
4 egg whites

1 To make the crêpes, place the herbs and oil in a food processor and blend until smooth. Add the milk, eggs, flour and salt and process again. Leave to rest for 30 minutes. Heat a small frying pan and add a little oil. Add a ladleful of batter. Swirl around to cover the base. Cook for 2 minutes, turn and cook for 2 minutes. Make seven more crêpes.

2 To make the sauce, heat the oil in a pan, add the onion and garlic and cook gently for 5 minutes. Add the tomatoes and sugar and cook for about 10 minutes, or until thickened. Purée in a blender, then sieve and set aside.

3 Preheat the oven to 190°C/375°F/Gas 5. To make the filling, mix the spinach with the ricotta, pine nuts, tomatoes and basil. Season with salt, nutmeg and pepper. Whisk the egg whites until stiff. Fold one-third into the mixture, then gently fold in the rest.

4 Place one crêpe at a time on a lightly oiled baking sheet, add a spoonful of filling and fold into quarters. Bake for 12 minutes until set. Reheat the sauce and serve with the crêpes.

Moroccan Pancakes: *Energy 284kcal/1192kJ; Protein 12.1g; Carbohydrate 32.6g, of which sugars 8.9g; Fat 12.7g, of which saturates 4.7g; Cholesterol 110mg; Calcium 279mg; Fibre 2.7g; Sodium 168mg.*
Herb Crêpes: *Energy 434kcal/1800kJ; Protein 14.9g; Carbohydrate 15.1g, of which sugars 9.8g; Fat 35.4g, of which saturates 8.3g; Cholesterol 161mg; Calcium 251mg; Fibre 5g; Sodium 229mg.*

Roasted Garlic and Aubergine Custards with Red Pepper Dressing

These elegant little moulds make a splendid main course for a special dinner. Serve with good bread and steamed broccoli.

Serves 6

2 large, plump heads of garlic
6–7 fresh thyme sprigs
60ml/4 tbsp extra virgin olive oil, plus extra for greasing
350g/12oz aubergines (eggplants), diced
2 large red (bell) peppers, halved
pinch of saffron strands
300ml/½ pint/1¼ cups whipping cream
2 large eggs
pinch of caster (superfine) sugar
30ml/2 tbsp shredded fresh basil leaves
salt and ground black pepper

For the dressing

90ml/6 tbsp extra virgin oil
15–25ml/1–1½ tbsp balsamic vinegar
pinch of caster (superfine) sugar
115g/4oz tomatoes, peeled, seeded and finely diced
½ small red onion, finely chopped
generous pinch of ground toasted cumin seeds
handful of fresh basil leaves

1 Preheat the oven to 190°C/375°F/Gas 5. Place the garlic on a piece of foil with the thyme and sprinkle with 15ml/1 tbsp oil. Wrap the foil around the garlic and cook for 35–45 minutes, until soft. Cool slightly. Reduce the oven temperature to 180°C/350°F/Gas 4.

2 Meanwhile, heat the remaining olive oil and fry the diced aubergines over a moderate heat, stirring frequently, for 5–8 minutes, until browned and cooked. Grill the peppers, skin-sides uppermost, until charred, then place in a plastic bag and leave for 10 minutes. When cool enough to handle, peel and dice them. Soak the saffron in 15ml/1 tbsp hot water for 10 minutes.

3 Unwrap the roasted garlic and pop it out of its skin into a blender or food processor, discarding the thyme. Add the oil from cooking, the cream and eggs. Process until smooth. Add the saffron with its liquid and season well with salt, pepper and a pinch of sugar. Stir in half the diced red pepper and the basil.

4 Lightly grease 6 large ramekins (about 200–250ml/7–8fl oz/1 cup capacity) and line the base of each with a circle of baking parchment (parchment paper). Grease the parchment.

5 Divide the aubergines among the dishes and pour in the egg mixture, then place them in a roasting pan. Cover each dish with foil, making a little hole in the centre to allow steam to escape. Pour hot water into the pan to come halfway up the ramekins. Bake for 25–30 minutes, until just set in the centre.

6 Meanwhile, make the dressing. Whisk the oil and vinegar with salt, pepper and a pinch of sugar. Stir in the tomatoes, red onion, remaining red pepper and cumin. Set aside some basil leaves, then chop the rest and add to the dressing.

7 Leave the custards to cool for 5 minutes, then turn them out on to warmed serving plates. Spoon the dressing around the custards and garnish each with the reserved fresh basil leaves.

Mediterranean One-Crust Pie

If your pastry cracks when making this free-form pie, just patch it up – it adds to its rustic character.

Serves 4

500g/1¼lb aubergine (eggplant), cubed
1 red (bell) pepper
30ml/2 tbsp olive oil
1 large onion, finely chopped
1 courgette (zucchini), sliced
2 garlic cloves, crushed
15ml/1 tbsp chopped fresh oregano plus extra to garnish
200g/7oz can red kidney beans, rinsed and drained
115g/4oz/1 cup stoned (pitted) black olives, rinsed
350ml/12fl oz/1½ cups passata (bottled strained tomatoes)
1 egg, beaten
30ml/2 tbsp semolina
salt and ground black pepper

For the pastry

75g/3oz/¾ cup plain (all-purpose) flour
75g/3oz/¾ cup wholemeal (whole-wheat) flour
75g/3oz/6 tbsp margarine
50g/2oz/⅔ cup freshly grated Parmesan cheese

1 Preheat the oven to 220°C/425°F/Gas 7. To make the pastry, sift the flours into a bowl. Rub in the margarine then stir in the Parmesan. Mix in enough cold water to form a dough. Wrap in clear film (plastic wrap) and chill for 30 minutes.

2 Place the aubergine in a colander and sprinkle with salt, then leave for about 30 minutes. Rinse and pat dry. Meanwhile, place the pepper on a baking sheet and roast for 20 minutes. Put in a plastic bag and leave for 5 minutes then peel and dice.

3 Heat the oil in a large pan. Fry the onion for 5 minutes until softened, then add the aubergine and fry for 5 minutes. Add the courgette, garlic and oregano, and cook for a further 5 minutes, stirring. Add the kidney beans and olives, then the passata and red pepper. Cook for 5 minutes, then leave to cool.

4 Roll out the pastry to a rough round and place on a lightly oiled baking sheet. Brush with beaten egg, sprinkle over the semolina, leaving a 4cm/1½in border, then spoon over the filling. Gather up the edges to partly cover the filling. Brush with egg and bake for 30–35 minutes until golden. Garnish with oregano.

Garlic and Aubergine Custards: Energy 425kcal/1754kJ; Protein 5.1g; Carbohydrate 9.8g, of which sugars 8.1g; Fat 40.9g, of which saturates 15.9g; Cholesterol 116mg; Calcium 55mg; Fibre 2.8g; Sodium 42mg.
One-Crust Pie: Energy 554kcal/2318kJ; Protein 17.7g; Carbohydrate 56.6g, of which sugars 15.7g; Fat 30.2g, of which saturates 4.2g; Cholesterol 13mg; Calcium 295mg; Fibre 11.6g; Sodium 1353mg.

Spinach and Filo Pie

This popular spinach and filo pastry pie comes from Greece. There are several ways of making it, but feta or Kefalotiri cheese is inevitably included. It is at its best served warm rather than straight from the oven.

Serves 6

1kg/2¼lb fresh spinach
4 spring onions (scallions), chopped
300g/11oz feta or Kefalotiri cheese, crumbled or coarsely grated
2 large eggs, beaten
30ml/2 tbsp chopped fresh parsley
15ml/1 tbsp chopped fresh dill
about 8 filo pastry sheets, each about 30 × 18cm/12 × 7in, thawed if frozen
150ml/¼ pint/⅔ cup olive oil
freshly ground black pepper

1 Preheat the oven to 190°C/375°F/Gas 5. Break off any thick stalks from the spinach, then wash the leaves and cook them in just the water that clings to the leaves in a heavy-based pan. As soon as they have wilted, drain them, refresh under cold water and drain again. Squeeze dry and chop roughly.

2 Place the spinach in a bowl. Add the spring onions and cheese, then pour in the eggs. Mix in the herbs and season the filling with pepper.

3 Brush a filo sheet with oil and fit it into a 23cm/9in pie dish, allowing it to hang over the edge. (Keep the other filo sheets covered with a damp cloth to stop them drying out.) Top with three or four more sheets, placing each one at a different angle and brushing each one with oil.

4 Spoon in the spinach filling, then top the pie with all but one of the remaining filo sheets. Brush each sheet with oil. Fold in the overhanging filo to seal in the filling. Brush the reserved sheet with oil and scrunch it over the top of the pie.

5 Brush the pie with oil. Sprinkle with a little water to stop the filo edges from curling, then place on a baking sheet. Bake for about 40 minutes, until golden and crisp. Cool the pie for 15 minutes before serving.

Vegetable Tarte Tatin

This savoury upside-down tart combines Mediterranean vegetables with a medley of rice, garlic, onions and olives.

Serves 2–3

30ml/2 tbsp sunflower oil
25ml/1½ tbsp olive oil
1 aubergine (eggplant), sliced lengthways
1 large red (bell) pepper, cut into long strips
10 tomatoes
2 red shallots, finely chopped
1–2 garlic cloves, crushed
150ml/¼ pint/⅔ cup white wine
10ml/2 tsp chopped fresh basil
225g/8oz/2 cups cooked white or brown long grain rice
40g/1½oz/scant ½ cup stoned (pitted) black olives, chopped
350g/12oz puff pastry, thawed if frozen
ground black pepper
salad leaves, to serve

1 Preheat the oven to 190°C/375°F/ Gas 5. Heat the sunflower oil with 15ml/1 tbsp of the olive oil in a frying pan and fry the aubergine slices for 4–5 minutes on each side until golden brown. Drain on several sheets of kitchen paper.

2 Add the pepper strips to the pan, turning them to coat in the oil. Cover and sweat the peppers over a medium high heat for 5–6 minutes, stirring occasionally, until soft and browned.

3 Slice two of the tomatoes and set them aside. Plunge the remaining tomatoes into boiling water for 30 seconds, then drain and peel. Remove the core and seeds and chop roughly.

4 Heat the remaining oil and fry the shallots and garlic for 3–4 minutes. Add the tomatoes and cook for a few minutes. Stir in the wine and basil, with black pepper to taste. Bring to the boil, then remove from the heat. Add the rice and olives.

5 Arrange the tomatos, aubergines and peppers in a single layer in a 30cm/12in shallow ovenproof dish. Spread the rice mixture on top. Roll out the pastry slightly larger than the dish and place it on top of the rice, tucking the overlap down inside the dish. Bake for 25–30 minutes, until golden and risen. Cool slightly, then invert the tart on to a large, warmed serving plate. Serve in slices, with a leafy green salad.

Spinach and Filo Pie: *Energy 402kcal/1668kJ; Protein 16.5g; Carbohydrate 16.8g, of which sugars 3.9g; Fat 30.3g, of which saturates 10g; Cholesterol 98mg; Calcium 516mg; Fibre 4.5g; Sodium 980mg.*
Vegetable Tarte Tatin: *Energy 536kcal/2242kJ; Protein 8.3g; Carbohydrate 59.1g, of which sugars 8.8g; Fat 29.5g, of which saturates 1.2g; Cholesterol 0mg; Calcium 89mg; Fibre 2.6g; Sodium 522mg.*

Onion, Fennel and Lavender Tarts

Fragrant lavender combines perfectly with the aromatic flavour of fennel and mild Spanish onion. These unusual tartlets make an appealing light summer meal.

Serves 4

75g/3oz/6 tbsp butter
1 large Spanish onion, finely sliced
1 fennel bulb, trimmed and sliced
30ml/2 tbsp fresh lavender florets or 15ml/1 tbsp chopped dried culinary lavender
2 egg yolks
150ml/¼ pint/⅔ cup crème fraîche
salt and ground black pepper
fresh lavender florets, to garnish

For the pastry

115g/4oz/1 cup plain (all-purpose) flour
pinch of salt
50g/2oz/¼ cup chilled butter, cut into cubes
10ml/2 tsp cold water

1 To make the pastry, sift the flour and salt together. Rub the butter into the flour until the mixture resembles breadcrumbs. Stir in the water and bring the dough together to form a ball.

2 Roll the pastry out on a lightly floured surface to line four 7.5cm/3in round, loose-based flan tins (quiche pans). Prick the bases and chill. Preheat the oven to 200°C/400°F/Gas 6.

3 Melt the butter in a shallow pan and add the sliced onion, fennel and lavender. Reduce the heat, cover the pan and cook gently for 15 minutes, or until golden.

4 Line the pastry cases with greaseproof (waxed) paper and bake blind for 5 minutes. Remove the paper, return to the oven and bake for a further 4 minutes.

5 Reduce the oven temperature to 180°C/350°F/Gas 4. Mix the egg yolks, crème fraîche and seasoning together.

6 Spoon the onion mixture into the pastry cases. Spoon the crème fraîche mixture on top and bake for 10–15 minutes, or until the mixture has set and the filling is puffed up and golden.

7 Sprinkle with a little extra lavender and serve warm or cold.

Tomato and Basil Tart

This is a very simple yet extremely tasty tart made with rich shortcrust pastry, topped with mozzarella cheese and tomatoes, drizzled with olive oil and dotted with fresh basil leaves. It tastes best served while it is hot.

Serves 4

150g/5oz mozzarella cheese, thinly sliced
4 large tomatoes, thickly sliced
about 10 fresh basil leaves
30ml/2 tbsp olive oil
2 garlic cloves, thinly sliced
salt and ground black pepper

For the pastry

115g/4oz/1 cup plain (all-purpose) flour, plus extra for dusting
pinch of salt
50g/2oz/¼ cup butter, at room temperature
1 egg yolk

1 To prepare the pastry, sift the flour and salt into a bowl. Rub in the butter until the mixture resembles fine breadcrumbs. Beat the egg yolk and add to the mixture. Add a little water at a time, and mix together until the dough is smooth. Knead lightly on a floured work surface for a few minutes. Place in a plastic bag and chill for about 1 hour.

2 Preheat the oven to 190°C/375°F/Gas 5. Remove the pastry from the refrigerator, allow about 10 minutes for it to return to room temperature and then roll out into a 20cm/8in round. The pastry should be an even thickness all over.

3 Press the pastry into a 20cm/8in flan tin (quiche pan). Bake in the oven for 10 minutes. Allow to cool. Reduce the oven temperature to 180°C/350°F/Gas 4.

4 Lay the mozzarella slices over the pastry. On top, arrange the sliced tomatoes. Dip the basil leaves in olive oil and scatter them over the tomatoes.

5 Sprinkle the slices of garlic on top, drizzle the surface with the remaining oil and season. Bake the tart for 45 minutes, or until the pastry case is golden brown and the tomatoes are well cooked. Serve hot.

Lavender Tarts: *Energy 539kcal/2233kJ; Protein 6.8g; Carbohydrate 30.7g, of which sugars 6.9g; Fat 44.1g, of which saturates 27.3g; Cholesterol 210mg; Calcium 116mg; Fibre 3.8g; Sodium 214mg.*
Tomato and Basil Tart: *Energy 307kcal/1280kJ; Protein 9.6g; Carbohydrate 19.1g, of which sugars 2.4g; Fat 22g, of which saturates 12.6g; Cholesterol 51mg; Calcium 207mg; Fibre 1.3g; Sodium 262mg.*

Summer Herb Ricotta Flan

Simple to make and infused with aromatic fresh basil, chives and oregano, this delicate flan makes a delightful lunch dish, accompanied by an olive and garlic tapenade.

Serves 4
olive oil, for greasing and glazing
800g/1¾lb/3½ cups ricotta cheese
75g/3oz/1 cup finely grated Parmesan cheese
3 eggs, separated
60ml/4 tbsp torn fresh basil
60ml/4 tbsp chopped fresh chives
45ml/3 tbsp fresh oregano leaves
2.5ml/½ tsp salt
ground black pepper
2.5ml/½ tsp paprika
fresh herb leaves, to garnish

For the tapenade
400g/14oz/3½ cups stoned (pitted) black olives, rinsed and halved, reserving a few whole olives to garnish
5 garlic cloves, crushed
75ml/2½fl oz/⅓ cup olive oil

1 Preheat the oven to 180°C/350°F/Gas 4 and then lightly grease the base and sides of a 23cm/9in springform cake tin (pan) with olive oil.

2 Mix together the ricotta, Parmesan and egg yolks in a food processor. Add all the herbs, and the salt and pepper, and blend until smooth and creamy.

3 Whisk the egg whites in a large bowl until they form soft peaks. Gently fold the egg whites into the ricotta mixture, taking care not to knock out too much air. Spoon the ricotta mixture into the tin and smooth the top.

4 Bake for 1 hour 20 minutes, or until the flan has risen and the top is golden. Remove from the oven and brush lightly with olive oil, then sprinkle with paprika. Leave to cool before removing from the tin.

5 To make the tapenade, place the olives and garlic in a food processor or blender and process until finely chopped. Gradually add the olive oil and blend to a coarse paste, then transfer to a serving bowl. Garnish the flan with fresh herb leaves and serve with the tapenade.

Tomato and Black Olive Tart

This delicious tart has a fresh, rich Mediterranean flavour. Since the flavour of the tomatoes is quite obvious in this dish, it is perfect for trying different tomato varieties.

Serves 4
6 firm plum tomatoes, or other tasty tomatoes
75g/3oz ripe Brie cheese
16 black olives, stoned (pitted)
3 eggs, beaten
300ml/½ pint/1¼ cups milk
30ml/2 tbsp chopped fresh herbs, such as parsley, marjoram or basil
salt and ground black pepper
salad or cooked vegetables, to serve

For the pastry
115g/4oz/½ cup butter
225g/8oz/2 cups plain (all-purpose) flour, plus extra for dusting
1 egg yolk

1 To make the pastry, rub together the butter and flour until it resembles fine breadcrumbs. Blend in the egg yolk and a little cold water, then mix thoroughly to form a smooth dough. Cover and leave for 10 minutes.

2 Preheat the oven to 190°C/375°F/Gas 5. Roll out the pastry thinly on a lightly floured surface. Line a 28 × 18cm/11 × 7in loose-based rectangular flan tin (tart pan), trimming off any overhanging edges with a sharp knife.

3 Line the pastry case with greaseproof (waxed) paper and weigh it down with baking beans, and bake blind for 15 minutes. Remove the paper and beans, and bake for a further 5 minutes until the base is crisp.

4 Meanwhile, slice the tomatoes, cube the cheese, and slice the olives. Mix together the eggs, milk, seasoning and herbs.

5 Place the prepared flan case on a baking tray, arrange the tomatoes, cheese and olives on the base, then pour in the egg mixture.

6 Transfer carefully to the oven and bake for about 40 minutes until just firm and turning golden. Slice hot or cool in the tin and serve with salad or cooked vegetables.

Ricotta Flan: *Energy 730kcal/3021kJ; Protein 32.7g; Carbohydrate 8.6g, of which sugars 6.7g; Fat 63g, of which saturates 26.7g; Cholesterol 245mg; Calcium 335mg; Fibre 4g; Sodium 2512mg.*
Tomato and Olive Tart: *Energy 315kcal/1317kJ; Protein 9.3g; Carbohydrate 26.1g, of which sugars 4.6g; Fat 19.9g, of which saturates 7.2g; Cholesterol 90mg; Calcium 151mg; Fibre 1.7g; Sodium 506mg.*

Red Onion and Goat's Cheese Pastries

Fresh thyme adds a tasty edge to the mellow red onion in these scrumptious pastries, which are topped with luscious goat's cheese. The puff pastry rises around the fillng to create attractive individual tarts.

Serves 4

15ml/1 tbsp olive oil
450g/1lb red onions, sliced
30ml/2 tbsp fresh thyme or 10ml/2 tsp dried
15ml/1 tbsp balsamic vinegar
425g/15oz packet ready-rolled puff pastry, thawed if frozen
115g/4oz goat's cheese, cubed
1 egg, beaten
salt and ground black pepper
fresh oregano sprigs, to garnish (optional)
mixed green salad leaves, to serve

1 Heat the oil in a large, heavy frying pan, add the onions and fry over a gentle heat for 10 minutes, or until softened, stirring occasionally. Add the thyme, seasoning and vinegar, and cook for another 5 minutes. Remove the pan from the heat and leave the onions to cool.

2 Preheat the oven to 220°C/425°F/Gas 7. Unroll the puff pastry and, using a 15cm/6in plate as a guide, cut four rounds. Place the pastry rounds on a dampened baking sheet and, using the point of a knife, score a border, 2cm/¾in inside the edge of each round. (Do not cut through the pastry.)

3 Divide the onions among the pastry rounds and top with the goat's cheese. Brush the edge of each round with beaten egg.

4 Bake the pastries for 25–30 minutes, or until they are golden. Garnish with oregano sprigs, if you like, before serving with mixed salad leaves.

Variation
Ring the changes by spreading the pastry base with pesto or tapenade before you add the filling.

Potato and Leek Filo Pie

This filo pastry pie makes an attractive and unusual centrepiece for a vegetarian buffet. Serve it cool, with a choice of salads.

Serves 8

800g/1¾lb new potatoes, sliced
400g/14oz leeks (trimmed weight), thinly sliced
75g/3oz/6 tbsp butter
15g/½oz parsley, finely chopped
60ml/4 tbsp chopped mixed fresh herbs (such as chervil, chives, a little tarragon and basil)
12 sheets filo pastry
150g/5oz white Cheshire, Lancashire or Cantal cheese, sliced
2 garlic cloves, finely chopped
250ml/8fl oz/1 cup double (heavy) cream
2 large egg yolks
salt and ground black pepper

1 Preheat the oven to 190°C/375°F/Gas 5. Cook the potatoes in boiling, lightly salted water for 3–4 minutes, then drain and set aside.

2 Melt 25g/1oz/2 tbsp of the butter and fry the leeks gently, stirring, until softened. Remove from the heat, season with pepper and stir in half the parsley and half the mixed herbs.

3 Melt the remaining butter. Line a 23cm/9in loose-based metal cake tin (pan) with 6–7 sheets of filo pastry, brushing each sheet with butter. Let the edges of the pastry overhang the tin. Layer the potatoes, leeks and cheese in the tin, scattering a few herbs and the garlic between the layers. Season.

4 Flip the overhanging pastry over the filling and cover with 2 sheets of filo, tucking in the sides to fit and brushing with melted butter. Cover loosely with foil and bake for 35 minutes. (Keep the remaining pastry covered with a damp cloth.)

5 Meanwhile beat the cream, egg yolks and remaining herbs together. Make a hole in the centre of the pie and gradually pour in the eggs and cream. Arrange the remaining pastry on top, teasing it into swirls and folds, then brush with melted butter. Reduce the oven temperature to 180°C/350°F/Gas 4 and bake the pie for another 25–30 minutes, until the top is golden and crisp. Allow to cool before serving.

Onion and Cheese Pastries: *Energy 595kcal/2482kJ; Protein 15.4g; Carbohydrate 50.8g, of which sugars 8.1g; Fat 39.4g, of which saturates 5.9g; Cholesterol 74mg; Calcium 139mg; Fibre 1.6g; Sodium 543mg.*
Potato Filo Pie: *Energy 468kcal/1948kJ; Protein 10.7g; Carbohydrate 33g, of which sugars 3.5g; Fat 33.1g, of which saturates 20g; Cholesterol 137mg; Calcium 225mg; Fibre 3.2g; Sodium 218mg.*

Pissaladière

A Provençal classic, this is a delicious and colourful tart full of punchy flavour. The classic version includes anchovies, but it is just as good without.

Serves 6

225g/8oz/2 cups plain (all-purpose) flour
115g/4oz/ ½ cup butter, chilled and cut into dice
5ml/1 tsp dried mixed herbs
pinch of salt

For the filling

45ml/3 tbsp olive oil
2 large onions, thinly sliced
2 garlic cloves, crushed
400g/14oz can chopped tomatoes
5ml/1 tsp granulated sugar
leaves from small sprig of thyme
freshly grated nutmeg
75g/3oz/ ¾ cup stoned (pitted) black olives, sliced
30ml/2 tbsp capers, rinsed
salt and ground black pepper
chopped fresh parsley, to garnish

1 Preheat the oven to 190°C/375°F/Gas 5. Put the flour in a bowl and rub in the butter until the mixture resembles fine breadcrumbs, then stir in the herbs and salt. Mix to a firm dough with cold water.

2 Roll out the pastry on a lightly floured surface and line a 23cm/9in round flan dish. Line the pastry case with baking parchment and add baking beans. Bake for 20 minutes, then lift out the paper and beans and bake the empty case for 5–7 minutes more. Leave to cool.

3 To make the filling, heat the oil in a frying pan and fry the onions and garlic gently for about 10 minutes, until quite soft. Stir in the tomatoes, sugar, thyme and nutmeg. Season and simmer for 10 minutes.

4 Leave the filling to cool. Mix in the olives and capers, then spoon into the flan case. Sprinkle with parsley and serve.

Variation
To serve Pissaladière hot, top with grated cheese and grill until the cheese is golden and bubbling.

Greek Picnic Pie

Aubergines layered with spinach, feta and rice make a marvellous filling for a pie. It is equally delicious served warm or cool.

Serves 6

375g/13oz shortcrust pastry, thawed if frozen
45–60ml/3–4 tbsp olive oil
1 large aubergine (eggplant), sliced into rounds
1 onion, chopped
1 garlic clove, crushed
175g/6oz spinach
4 eggs
75g/3oz feta cheese
40g/1½oz/ ½ cup freshly grated Parmesan cheese
60ml/4 tbsp natural (plain) yogurt
90ml/6 tbsp creamy milk
225g/8oz/2 cups cooked long grain rice
salt and ground black pepper

1 Preheat the oven to 180°C/350°F/Gas 4. Roll out the pastry thinly and line a 25cm/10in flan ring. Prick the pastry all over and bake the unfilled case in the oven for 10–12 minutes, until the pastry is pale golden.

2 Heat 30–45ml/2–3 tbsp of the oil in a frying pan and fry the aubergine slices for 6–8 minutes on each side, until golden. Lift out and drain on kitchen paper.

3 Add the onion and garlic to the oil remaining in the pan and fry gently until soft, adding a little extra oil if necessary.

4 Chop the spinach finely, by hand or in a food processor. Beat the eggs in a large mixing bowl, then add the spinach, feta, Parmesan, yogurt, milk and the onion mixture. Season well with salt and pepper and stir thoroughly.

5 Spread the rice in an even layer over the base of the partially cooked pastry case. Reserve a few aubergine slices for the top, and arrange the rest in an even layer over the rice.

6 Spoon the spinach and feta mixture over the aubergines and place the remaining aubergine slices on top. Bake for 30–40 minutes, until lightly browned. Serve the pie warm, or cool completely before transferring to a serving plate or wrapping and packing for a picnic.

Pissaladière: *Energy 431kcal/1797kJ; Protein 9.9g; Carbohydrate 51.6g, of which sugars 10g; Fat 21.7g, of which saturates 3.1g; Cholesterol 8mg; Calcium 138mg; Fibre 3.8g; Sodium 825mg.*
Greek Picnic Pie: *Energy 554kcal/2309kJ; Protein 16.6g; Carbohydrate 53.3g, of which sugars 4.3g; Fat 31.4g, of which saturates 15.5g; Cholesterol 185mg; Calcium 299mg; Fibre 2.7g; Sodium 473mg.*

New Potato, Rosemary and Garlic Pizza

New potatoes, smoked mozzarella, rosemary and garlic make the flavour of this pizza unique. For a delicious variation, use sage instead of rosemary.

Serves 2–3

350g/12oz new potatoes
45ml/3 tbsp olive oil
2 garlic cloves, crushed
1 pizza base, 25–30cm/10–12in in diameter
1 red onion, thinly sliced
150g/5oz smoked mozzarella, grated
10ml/2 tsp chopped fresh rosemary
salt and freshly ground black pepper
30ml/2 tbsp freshly grated Parmesan cheese, to garnish

1 Preheat the oven to 200°C/425°F/ Gas 7. Cook the potatoes in boiling salted water for 5 minutes. Drain well. When cool, peel and slice thinly.

2 Heat 30 ml/2 tbsp of the oil in a frying pan. Add the sliced potatoes and garlic and fry for 5–8 minutes until tender.

3 Brush the pizza base with the remaining oil. Scatter over the onion, then arrange the potatoes on top.

4 Sprinkle over the mozzarella and rosemary. Grind over plenty of black pepper and bake for 15–20 minutes until crisp and golden. Remove from the oven and sprinkle over the Parmesan to serve.

Cook's Tip

Rosemary is a common wild shrub in the Mediterranean region. As a flavouring it is particularly popular in Italy, where it appears in both savoury and sweet dishes, and in the South of France. It is most often used to flavour meat, especially lamb, and the woody stems are sometimes burned when smoking cured meat and sausages. It goes very well with garlic and potatoes, as in this pizza topping.

Shallot and Garlic Tarte Tatin with Parmesan Pastry

Savoury versions of the famous apple tarte tatin have been popular for some years. Here, shallots are caramelized in butter, sugar and vinegar before being baked beneath a layer of Parmesan pastry.

Serves 4–6

300g/11oz puff pastry, thawed if frozen
50g/2oz/¼ cup butter
75g/3oz/1 cup freshly grated Parmesan cheese

For the topping

40g/1½oz/3 tbsp butter
500g/1¼lb shallots
12–16 large garlic cloves, peeled but left whole
15ml/1 tbsp golden caster (superfine) sugar
15ml/1 tbsp balsamic or sherry vinegar
45ml/3 tbsp water
5ml/1 tsp chopped fresh thyme, plus a few extra sprigs (optional)
salt and ground black pepper

1 Roll out the pastry into a rectangle. Spread the butter over it, leaving a 2.5cm/1in border. Scatter the Parmesan on top. Fold the bottom third of the pastry up to cover the middle and the top third down. Seal the edges, give a quarter turn and roll out to a rectangle, then fold as before. Chill for 30 minutes.

2 Melt the butter in a 23–25cm/9–10in round heavy pan that will go in the oven. Add the shallots and garlic, and cook until lightly browned. Scatter the sugar over the top and increase the heat a little. Cook until the sugar begins to caramelize, then turn the shallots and garlic in the buttery juices.

3 Add the vinegar, water, thyme and seasoning. Cook, part-covered, for 5–8 minutes, until the garlic is just tender. Cool.

4 Preheat the oven to 190°C/375°F/Gas 5. Roll out the pastry to the diameter of the pan and lay it over the shallots and garlic. Prick the pastry with a sharp knife, then bake for 25–35 minutes, or until the pastry is risen and golden. Set aside to cool for 5–10 minutes, then invert the tart on to a serving platter. Scatter with a few thyme sprigs, if you like, and serve.

Pizza: Energy 690kcal/2899kJ; Protein 24.8g; Carbohydrate 85.2g, of which sugars 6.4g; Fat 30.1g, of which saturates 10.6g; Cholesterol 39mg; Calcium 410mg; Fibre 4.2g; Sodium 620mg.
Tarte Tatin: Energy 618kcal/2567kJ; Protein 12.8g; Carbohydrate 35.5g, of which sugars 9.6g; Fat 48.2g, of which saturates 22.8g; Cholesterol 79mg; Calcium 313mg; Fibre 3g; Sodium 605mg.

Pizza Fiorentina

Spinach is the star ingredient of this pizza. A grating of nutmeg to heighten its flavour gives it a unique character.

Serves 2–3

175g/6oz fresh spinach
45ml/3 tbsp olive oil
1 small red onion, thinly sliced
1 pizza base, 25–30cm/10–12in diameter
175ml/6fl oz/¾ cup tomato sauce (see Cook's Tip)
freshly grated nutmeg
150g/5oz mozzarella
1 egg
25g/1oz Gruyère cheese, grated

1 Preheat the oven to 220°C/425°F/Gas 7. Remove any tough stalks from the spinach and wash the leaves in plenty of cold water. Drain well and pat dry with kitchen paper.

2 Heat 15 ml/1 tbsp of the oil and fry the onion until soft. Add the spinach and continue to fry until just wilted. Drain off any excess liquid.

3 Brush the pizza base with half the remaining oil. Spread over the tomato sauce, then top with the spinach mixture. Grate over some nutmeg. Thinly slice the mozzarella and arrange over the spinach. Drizzle over the remaining oil. Bake for 10 minutes, then remove from the oven.

4 Make a small well in the centre of the filling and break the egg into the depression. Sprinkle over the Gruyère and return to the oven for a further 5–10 minutes until the pizza is crisp and golden and the egg is set. Serve immediately.

Cook's Tip
To make fresh tomato sauce, fry 1 chopped onion and a crushed garlic clove in 15ml/1 tbsp oil until softened. Add a 400g/14oz can chopped tomatoes, 15ml/1 tbsp tomato purée (paste) and 15ml/1 tbsp chopped fresh herbs. Add a pinch of sugar, and season with salt and pepper. Simmer for 20 minutes until reduced and thickened.

Mushroom, Corn and Plum Tomato Wholewheat Pizza

This tasty vegetable pizza, is healthy and easy for children to make. It, can be served hot or cold.

Serves 2

30ml/2 tbsp tomato purée (paste)
10ml/2 tsp dried basil
10ml/2 tsp olive oil
1 onion, sliced
1 garlic clove, crushed or finely chopped
2 courgettes (zucchini), sliced
115g/4oz mushrooms, sliced
115g/4oz/⅔ cup canned or frozen corn kernels
4 plum tomatoes, sliced
50g/2oz/½ cup Red Leicester cheese, finely grated
50g/2oz mozzarella cheese, finely grated
salt and ground black pepper
basil sprigs, to garnish
mixed bean salad and fresh crusty bread or baked potatoes, to serve

For the pizza base

225g/8oz/2 cups plain wholemeal (all-purpose whole-wheat) flour
pinch of salt
10ml/2 tsp baking powder
50g/2oz/4 tbsp margarine
about 150ml/¼ pint/⅔ cup milk

1 Preheat the oven to 220°C/425°F/Gas 7 and oil a baking sheet. Put the flour, salt and baking powder in a bowl and rub the margarine lightly into the flour. Add enough milk to form a soft dough and knead. Roll out to a 25cm/10in circle.

2 Place the dough on the prepared baking sheet and make the edges slightly thicker than the centre. Spread the tomato purée over the base and sprinkle the basil on top.

3 Heat the oil in a pan and gently fry the onion, garlic, courgettes and mushrooms for 10 minutes. Spread them over the pizza base, sprinkle over the corn and season with salt and pepper. Arrange the tomato slices on top.

4 Mix together the Red Leicester and mozzarella cheeses and sprinkle over the pizza. Bake for 25–30 minutes, until crisp and golden. Serve hot or cold in slices, garnished with basil sprigs, with bean salad and crusty bread or baked potatoes.

Fiorentina: *Energy 503kcal/2100kJ; Protein 20.9g; Carbohydrate 40.3g, of which sugars 5.9g; Fat 29.7g, of which saturates 10.9g; Cholesterol 101mg; Calcium 417mg; Fibre 2.8g; Sodium 668mg.*
Mushroom Pizza: *Energy 913kcal/3833kJ; Protein 35.5g; Carbohydrate 102.3g, of which sugars 22.7g; Fat 42.6g, of which saturates 11g; Cholesterol 43mg; Calcium 472mg; Fibre 15.4g; Sodium 729mg.*

Golden Vegetable Paella

Hearty enough for the hungriest guests, this simple vegetarian version of a classic dish takes very little time to prepare and cook.

Serves 4

pinch of saffron strands
750ml/1¼ pints/3 cups hot vegetable stock
90ml/6 tbsp olive oil
2 large onions, sliced
3 garlic cloves, chopped
275g/10oz/1½ cups long grain rice
50g/2oz/⅓ cup wild rice
175g/6oz pumpkin, chopped
1 large carrot, cut into matchstick strips
1 yellow (bell) pepper, sliced
4 tomatoes, peeled, seeded and chopped
115g/4oz/1½ cups oyster mushrooms, quartered
salt and ground black pepper
strips of red, yellow and green pepper, to garnish

1 Place the saffron in a bowl with 60ml/4 tbsp of the hot stock. Leave to stand for 5 minutes.

2 Meanwhile, heat the oil in a paella pan or large, heavy-based frying pan. Add the onions and garlic and fry over a low heat, stirring occasionally, for 3 minutes, until just beginning to soften.

3 Add the long grain rice and wild rice to the pan and toss for 2–3 minutes, until coated in oil. Add the stock to the pan, together with the pumpkin and the saffron strands and liquid. Stir the mixture as it comes to the boil, then reduce the heat to the lowest setting.

4 Cover and cook very gently for 15 minutes, without lifting the lid. Add the carrot strips, yellow pepper and chopped tomatoes and season to taste with salt and pepper. Replace the lid and cook very gently for a further 5 minutes, or until the rice is almost tender.

5 Add the oyster mushrooms, check the seasoning and cook, uncovered, for just enough time to soften the mushrooms without letting the paella stick to the pan. Garnish with the peppers and serve.

Red Pepper Risotto

Several different types of risotto rice are available, and it is worth experimenting to find the one your family prefers. Look out for Arborio, Carnaroli and Vialone Nano.

Serves 6

3 large red (bell) peppers
30ml/2 tbsp olive oil
3 large garlic cloves, thinly sliced
1½ × 400g/14oz cans chopped tomatoes
2 bay leaves
450g/1lb/2½ cups risotto rice
about 1.5 litres/2½ pints/6 cups hot vegetable stock
6 fresh basil leaves, snipped
salt and ground black pepper

1 Put the peppers in a grill (broiler) pan and grill (broil) until the skins are charred and blistered all over. Put them in a bowl, cover with crumpled kitchen paper and leave to steam for 10 minutes to loosen the skin. Peel off the skins, then slice the flesh, discarding the cores and seeds.

2 Heat the oil in a wide, shallow pan. Add the garlic and tomatoes and cook over a low heat, stirring occasionally, for 5 minutes. Stir in the pepper slices and bay leaves and cook for 15 minutes more.

3 Stir the rice into the vegetable mixture and cook, stirring constantly, for 2 minutes, then add a ladleful of the hot stock. Cook, stirring constantly, until it has been absorbed. (Keep the stock simmering in a pan next to the risotto.)

4 Continue to add stock in this way, making sure that each addition has been absorbed before ladling in the next. When the rice is tender, season with salt and pepper to taste. Remove from the heat, cover and leave to stand for 10 minutes before stirring in the basil and serving.

Variation
Both yellow and orange (bell) peppers are also suitable for this recipe, but green peppers are too acerbic.

Vegetable Paella: *Energy 388kcal/1646kJ; Protein 13.5g; Carbohydrate 78.8g, of which sugars 7.5g; Fat 3.6g, of which saturates 0.9g; Cholesterol 0mg; Calcium 57mg; Fibre 8.5g; Sodium 299mg.*
Red Pepper Risotto: *Energy 501kcal/2099kJ; Protein 10.9g; Carbohydrate 103.8g, of which sugars 13.6g; Fat 4.4g, of which saturates 0.7g; Cholesterol 0mg; Calcium 44mg; Fibre 3.9g; Sodium 20mg.*

Tofu Balls with Spaghetti

This dish makes a great family supper, as children and adults alike really love the little tofu balls and the rich vegetable sauce, while pasta never fails to please.

Serves 4

250g/9oz firm tofu, drained
1 onion, coarsely grated
2 garlic cloves, crushed
5ml/1 tsp Dijon mustard
15ml/1 tbsp ground cumin
1 small bunch of parsley, finely chopped
15ml/1 tbsp soy sauce
50g/2oz/½ cup ground almonds
30ml/2 tbsp olive oil
350g/12oz spaghetti
sea salt and ground black pepper

For the sauce

15ml/1 tbsp olive oil
1 large onion, finely chopped
2 garlic cloves, chopped
1 large aubergine (eggplant), diced
2 courgettes (zucchini), diced
1 red (bell) pepper, finely chopped
pinch of sugar
400g/14oz can chopped tomatoes
200ml/7fl oz/scant 1 cup vegetable stock
1 bunch of fresh basil

1 Place the tofu, onion, garlic, mustard, cumin, parsley, soy sauce and ground almonds in a bowl. Season with salt and pepper and mix thoroughly. Roll into about 20 walnut-sized balls.

2 Heat the olive oil in a large frying pan, then cook the balls, turning them gently until brown all over. Remove from the pan and set aside on a plate. Heat the oil for the sauce in the same pan, add the onion and garlic and cook for 5 minutes, until soft.

3 Add the aubergine, courgette, pepper, sugar and seasoning and stir-fry for 10 minutes until the vegetables are beginning to soften and brown. Stir in the tomatoes and stock. Cover and simmer for 20–30 minutes, or until the sauce is thick. Place the tofu balls gently on top of the sauce, replace the lid and heat through for 2–3 minutes.

4 Meanwhile, cook the pasta in a large pan of salted, boiling water according to the manufacturer's instructions, then drain. Sprinkle the sauce with the basil and check the seasoning before serving with the spaghetti.

Spaghetti with Mixed Bean Sauce

Mixed beans are flavoured with fresh chilli and garlic and cooked in a tomato sauce in this quick and easy pasta dish, which makes a warming and substantial winter meal.

Serves 6

1 onion, finely chopped
1–2 garlic cloves, crushed
1 large green chilli, seeded and finely chopped
150ml/¼ pint/⅔ cup vegetable stock
400g/14oz can chopped tomatoes
30ml/2 tbsp tomato purée (paste)
120ml/4fl oz/½ cup red wine
5ml/1 tsp dried oregano
200g/7oz French beans, sliced
400g/14oz can red kidney beans, drained
400g/14oz can cannellini beans, drained
400g/14oz can chickpeas, drained
450g/1lb dried spaghetti
salt and ground black pepper

1 Put the onion, garlic and chilli in a pan with the stock. Bring to the boil and cook for 5 minutes, stirring occasionally.

2 Stir in the tomatoes, tomato purée, wine, oregano and seasoning. Bring to the boil, cover, then reduce the heat and simmer for 20 minutes, stirring the mixture occasionally.

3 Meanwhile, cook the French beans in a saucepan of boiling, salted water for about 5–6 minutes until tender. Drain the beans thoroughly.

4 Add all the beans and the chickpeas to the sauce, stir to mix and simmer for a further 10 minutes. Meanwhile, cook the spaghetti in a large saucepan of boiling salted water, according to the packet instructions, until *al dente*. Drain thoroughly. Transfer the pasta to a serving dish and top with the bean sauce. Serve immediately.

Cook's Tip
Use whatever varieties of canned beans you have in your storecupboard (pantry) for this quick standby recipe.

Tofu Balls with Spaghetti: Energy 576kcal/2422kJ; Protein 22.5g; Carbohydrate 79.4g, of which sugars 15.6g; Fat 21g, of which saturates 2.6g; Cholesterol 0mg; Calcium 425mg; Fibre 8g; Sodium 288mg.
Spaghetti with Bean Sauce: Energy 507kcal/2154kJ; Protein 24.6g; Carbohydrate 94.7g, of which sugars 11.7g; Fat 4.5g, of which saturates 0.6g; Cholesterol 0mg; Calcium 165mg; Fibre 14.9g; Sodium 689mg.

Pasta Primavera

You can use any mixture of fresh, young spring vegetables to make this delicately flavoured seasonal pasta dish. The recipe is simple and ideal for a quick and tasty supper.

Serves 4

225g/8oz thin asparagus spears, trimmed and cut in half
115g/4oz mangetouts (snow peas), topped and tailed
115g/4oz baby corn
225g/8oz whole baby carrots, trimmed
1 small red (bell) pepper, chopped
8 spring onions (scallions), thickly sliced
225g/8oz dried torchietti or other pasta shapes
150ml/¼ pint/⅔ cup low-fat cottage cheese
150ml/¼ pint/⅔ cup low-fat yogurt
15ml/1 tbsp lemon juice
15ml/1 tbsp chopped fresh parsley
15ml/1 tbsp snipped fresh chives
skimmed milk (optional)
salt and ground black pepper
sun-dried tomato bread, to serve

1 Cook the asparagus spears in a pan of boiling, salted water for 3–4 minutes. Add the mangetouts halfway through the cooking time. As soon as the vegetables are al dente, drain them quickly and rinse both under cold water to stop them cooking further. Set aside.

2 Cook the baby corn, carrots, red pepper and spring onions in the same way in a pan of boiling salted water until tender. Drain, rinse and set aside.

3 Meanwhile, cook the pasta in a large pan of boiling salted water, according to the packet instructions, until tender or al dente. Drain thoroughly and keep hot.

4 Put the cottage cheese, yogurt, lemon juice, parsley, chives and seasoning into a blender or food processor and blend until smooth. Thin the sauce with a little skimmed milk, if necessary.

5 Put the sauce into a large pan with the cooked pasta and vegetables, heat gently and toss carefully to mix. Serve at once with sun-dried tomato bread.

Pasta with Pesto, Potatoes and Green Beans

This is a traditional way of serving pesto in Liguria. Although the combination of pasta and potatoes may seem odd, it is delicious.

Serves 4

50g/2oz/½ cup pine nuts
2 large garlic cloves, chopped
90g/3½oz fresh basil leaves, plus a few extra leaves
90ml/6 tbsp extra virgin olive oil
50g/2oz/⅔ cup freshly grated Parmesan cheese
40g/1½oz/½ cup freshly grated Pecorino cheese

For the pasta mixture

275g/10oz waxy potatoes, thickly sliced or cut into 1cm/½in cubes
200g/7oz fine green beans
350g/12oz dried trenette, linguine, tagliatelle or tagliarini
salt and ground black pepper

To serve

extra virgin olive oil
pine nuts, toasted
Parmesan cheese, grated

1 Toast the pine nuts in a dry frying pan until golden. Pound with a pestle and mortar with the garlic and a pinch of salt. Add the basil and continue pounding. Gradually add a little oil to form a paste, then work in the cheeses with the remaining oil. (Alternatively, blend the pine nuts, garlic, basil and oil in a food processor, then stir in the cheeses.)

2 Bring a pan of lightly salted water to the boil and add the potatoes. Cook for 10–12 minutes, until tender. Add the green beans to the pan for the last 5–6 minutes of cooking.

3 Meanwhile, cook the pasta in boiling salted water until al dente, timing the cooking so that both pasta and potatoes are ready at the same time. Drain the pasta, and the potatoes and beans. Place in a large, warmed bowl and toss with two-thirds of the pesto. Season with black pepper and scatter extra basil leaves over the top.

4 Serve immediately with the rest of the pesto, extra olive oil, pine nuts and grated Parmesan.

Pasta Primavera: Energy 324kcal/1369kJ; Protein 18.5g; Carbohydrate 56.8g, of which sugars 16g; Fat 4g, of which saturates 1.4g; Cholesterol 6mg; Calcium 214mg; Fibre 6.7g; Sodium 496mg.

Pasta with Pesto, Potatoes and Beans: Energy 658kcal/2760kJ; Protein 20g; Carbohydrate 78.6g, of which sugars 5.9g; Fat 31.5g, of which saturates 5.8g; Cholesterol 13mg; Calcium 240mg; Fibre 5.7g; Sodium 154mg.

Spinach & Hazelnut Lasagne

Using fromage frais instead of a white sauce makes this a lighter, healthier version of a popular vegetarian dish, and spinach and hazelnuts wonderful colour and crunch to the dish.

Serves 4

900g/2lb fresh spinach
300ml/ ½ pint/1 ¼ cups vegetable stock
1 medium onion, finely chopped
1 garlic clove, crushed
75g/3oz/ ¾ cup hazelnuts
30ml/2 tbsp chopped fresh basil
6 sheets no pre-cook lasagne
400g/14oz can chopped tomatoes
200g/7oz/scant 1 cup low-fat fromage frais
salt and ground black pepper
flaked hazelnuts and chopped fresh parsley, to garnish

1 Preheat the oven to 200°C/400°F/Gas 6. Wash the spinach and place it in a pan with just the water that is still clinging to the leaves. Cover and cook over a fairly high heat for about 2 minutes, until the spinach has wilted. Drain well and set aside until required.

2 Heat 30ml/2 tbsp of the stock in a large pan. Add the onion and garlic, bring to the boil, then simmer until softened. Stir in the spinach, hazelnuts and basil.

3 In a large ovenproof dish, make layers of the spinach, lasagne and tomatoes. Season each layer with salt and pepper to taste. Pour over the remaining stock. Spread the fromage frais evenly over the top.

4 Bake the lasagne for about 45 minutes, or until golden brown. Serve hot, garnished with lines of flaked hazelnuts and chopped fresh parsley.

Cook's Tip

The flavour of hazelnuts is greatly improved if they are roasted. Place them on a baking sheet and bake in a moderate oven or under a hot grill until light golden. Rub off the brown skins, if necessary, in a clean dish towel.

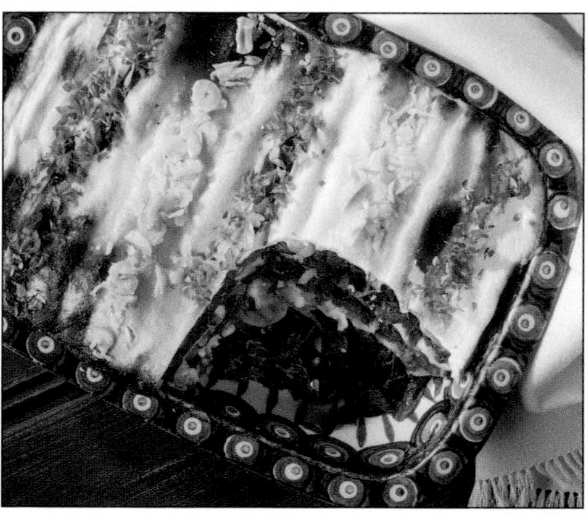

Pappardelle and Summer Vegetable Sauce

A delicious, vibrantly colourful sauce of tomatoes and crisp fresh vegetables, chunkily cut, adds colour and robust flavour to ribbon pasta in this rustic and extremely simple Italian-style supper dish.

Serves 4

2 small red onions, peeled, root left intact
150ml/¼ pint/⅔ cup vegetable stock
1–2 garlic cloves, crushed
60ml/4 tbsp red wine
2 courgettes (zucchini), cut into fingers
1 yellow (bell) pepper, sliced
400g/14oz can tomatoes
10ml/2 tsp chopped fresh thyme
5ml/1 tsp caster (superfine) sugar
350g/12oz dried pappardelle
salt and ground black pepper
fresh thyme and 6 black olives, stoned (pitted) and roughly chopped, to garnish

1 Cut each onion into eight wedges, cutting through the root end so that the layers will hold together during cooking. Put the pieces into a saucepan with the stock and garlic. Bring to the boil, cover then reduce the heat and simmer for 5 minutes, until tender.

2 Add the wine, courgettes, yellow pepper, tomatoes, chopped thyme and sugar. Season with salt and pepper and stir to mix.

3 Bring to the boil and cook gently for 5–7 minutes, shaking the pan occasionally to coat the vegetables with the sauce. (Do not overcook the vegetables as they are much nicer if they are still slightly crunchy.)

4 Meanwhile, cook the pasta in a large saucepan of boiling salted water, according to the packet instructions, until *al dente*. Drain thoroughly.

5 Transfer the pasta to a warmed serving dish and top with the vegetables. Garnish with fresh thyme and chopped black olives and serve immediately.

Spinach Lasagne: *Energy 442kcal/1853kJ; Protein 19.6g; Carbohydrate 48.8g, of which sugars 12.3g; Fat 20g, of which saturates 4.8g; Cholesterol 5mg; Calcium 501mg; Fibre 8.6g; Sodium 350mg.*
Pappardelle: *Energy 424kcal/1792kJ; Protein 15.3g; Carbohydrate 83.6g, of which sugars 18.5g; Fat 4.3g, of which saturates 0.6g; Cholesterol 0mg; Calcium 99mg; Fibre 7.3g; Sodium 51mg.*

Pansotti with Herbs and Cheese

Herb-flavoured pasta with a filling of ricotta, herbs and garlic is served with a rich and satisfying walnut sauce.

Serves 6–8

For the pasta

300g/11oz/2¾ cups pasta flour
3 eggs
5ml/1 tsp salt
3 handfuls chopped fresh herbs
flour, for dusting
50g/2oz/¼ cup butter
freshly grated Parmesan cheese, to serve

For the filling

250g/9oz/generous 1 cup ricotta cheese
150g/5oz/1⅔ cups freshly grated Parmesan cheese
1 large handful fresh basil leaves, finely chopped
1 large handful fresh flat leaf parsley, finely chopped
a few sprigs fresh marjoram or oregano leaves, finely chopped
1 garlic clove, crushed
1 small egg
salt and ground black pepper

For the sauce

90g/3½oz/½ cup shelled walnuts
1 garlic clove
60ml/4 tbsp extra virgin olive oil
120ml/4fl oz/½ cup double (heavy) cream

1 Mound the flour on the work surface and make a deep well in the centre. Crack the eggs into the well, then add the salt and herbs. With a knife, mix the eggs, salt and herbs together, then start incorporating the flour from the sides of the well.

2 As soon as the mixture is no longer liquid use your fingers to work the ingredients into a sticky dough. Press into a ball and knead for 10 minutes until smooth and elastic. Wrap in clear film and leave at room temperature for 20 minutes.

3 To make the filling, mix the ricotta, Parmesan, herbs, garlic and egg with salt and pepper to taste and beat well.

4 To make the sauce, put the walnuts, garlic and oil in a food processor and process, adding up to 120ml/4fl oz/½ cup warm water through the feeder tube to lighten the consistency of the paste. Spoon into a bowl and add the cream. Beat well to mix, then add salt and pepper to taste.

5 Using a pasta machine, roll out one-quarter of the pasta into a 90cm/36in strip. Cut the strip with a sharp knife into two 45cm/18in lengths. Using a 5cm/2in square ravioli cutter, cut eight or nine squares from one of the strips. Using a teaspoon, put a mound of filling in the centre of each square. Wet the edge of each square, then fold diagonally in half over the filling to make a triangular shape. Press the edges gently to seal.

6 Spread out the pansotti on clean, floured dish towels, sprinkle with flour and leave to dry. Repeat with the remaining dough to make 64–80 pansotti altogether. Cook in a large pan of salted boiling water for 4–5 minutes. Meanwhile, put the walnut sauce in a large, warmed bowl and stir a ladleful of the pasta cooking water into it to thin it down. Melt the butter in a small pan until it is sizzling.

7 Drain the pansotti and tip them into the sauce. Drizzle the butter over them, toss well, then sprinkle with Parmesan. Serve immediately, with more Parmesan offered separately.

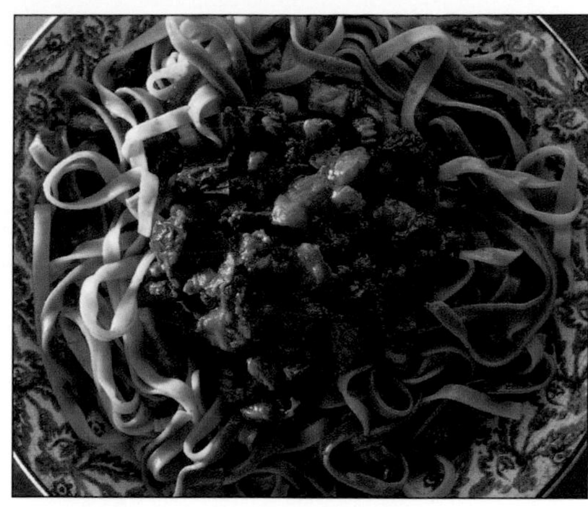

Tagliatelle with Sun-dried Tomatoes

Tagliatelle tossed in a delicious fresh and sun-dried tomato sauce is an ideal main-course meal for all the family to enjoy. Fine flavoured fresh plum tomatoes give the best result, but in seasons when they are not available, substitute canned tomatoes.

Serves 4

1 garlic clove, crushed
1 celery stick, thinly sliced
115g/4oz/1 cup sun-dried tomatoes, finely chopped
90ml/6 tbsp red wine
8 plum tomatoes
350g/12oz dried tagliatelle
salt and ground black pepper

1 Put the garlic, celery, sun-dried tomatoes and wine into a saucepan. Cook gently for 15 minutes, stirring occasionally, until the vegetables are tender and the wine reduced.

2 Meanwhile, slit the skins of the plum tomatoes then plunge them into a pan of boiling water for about 1 minute. Carefully transfer them to a bowl of cold water. Drain, then slip off and discard the skins. Halve the tomatoes, remove and discard the seeds and cores and roughly chop the flesh.

3 Add the chopped tomatoes to the other vegetables, stir to mix and simmer for a further 5 minutes. Season to taste with salt and pepper.

4 Meanwhile, cook the tagliatelle in a large pan of boiling salted water for 8–10 minutes, until tender or *al dente*. Drain well. Toss the cooked pasta with half the tomato sauce and serve on warmed plates, topped with the remaining tomato sauce.

Cook's Tip

It's best to use the sun-dried tomatoes that are sold dry for this sauce, rather than those preserved in oil, which would make the dish rather high in fat. If you need to use the oily type, drain them well on kitchen paper first.

Pansotti: Energy 541kcal/2249kJ; Protein 20.8g; Carbohydrate 31.1g, of which sugars 2.4g; Fat 38.4g, of which saturates 16g; Cholesterol 155mg; Calcium 360mg; Fibre 1.9g; Sodium 421mg.
Tagliatelle with Tomatoes: Energy 346kcal/1471kJ; Protein 11.8g; Carbohydrate 70.5g, of which sugars 8.6g; Fat 2.1g, of which saturates 0.4g; Cholesterol 0mg; Calcium 39mg; Fibre 4.4g; Sodium 25mg.

Turkish Salad

This classic salad is a wonderful combination of textures and flavours. The saltiness of the feta cheese is perfectly balanced by the refreshing sweetness and crunch of the salad vegetables. The salad is the perfect accompaniment for roast or barbecued lamb.

Serves 4

1 cos lettuce heart
1 green (bell) pepper
1 red (bell) pepper
½ cucumber
4 tomatoes
1 red onion
225g/8oz/2 cups feta cheese, crumbled
black olives, to garnish

For the dressing

45ml/3 tbsp olive oil
45ml/3 tbsp lemon juice
1 garlic clove, crushed
15ml/1 tbsp chopped fresh parsley
15ml/1 tbsp chopped fresh mint
salt and ground black pepper

1 Chop the lettuce into bitesize pieces. Seed the peppers, remove the cores and cut the flesh into thin strips. Chop the cucumber and slice or chop the tomatoes. Cut the onion in half, then slice finely.

2 Place the chopped lettuce, peppers, cucumber, tomatoes and onion in a large bowl. Scatter the feta over the top and toss together lightly.

3 To make the dressing, blend together the olive oil, lemon juice and garlic. Stir in the chopped parsley and mint and season with salt and pepper to taste.

4 Pour the dressing over the salad and toss lightly. Garnish with a handful of black olives and serve immediately.

Cook's Tip
Most of the ingredients of this salad will happily sit for a short time in the dressing without deteriorating, so if you need to prepare it a little while before a meal, omit the lettuce.

Spanish Salad

Make this refreshing and substantial salad in the summer when tomatoes are at their sweetest and full of flavour. The distinctively flavoured dressing is spiced with paprika and cumin.

Serves 4

4 tomatoes
½ cucumber
1 bunch spring onions (scallions), trimmed and chopped
1 bunch watercress
8 stuffed olives
30ml/2 tbsp drained capers

For the dressing

30ml/2 tbsp red wine vinegar
5ml/1 tsp paprika
2.5 ml/½ tsp ground cumin
1 garlic clove, crushed
75ml/5 tbsp olive oil
salt and freshly ground black pepper

1 Plunge the tomatoes into a saucepan of boiling water for a minute, then transfer them to a bowl of cold water. Drain, then slip off and discard their skins.

2 Halve the tomatoes, remove and discard the seeds and cores and finely dice the flesh. Put them in a salad bowl.

3 Peel the cucumber, dice it finely and add it to the tomatoes. Add half the spring onions to the salad bowl and mix lightly. Break the watercress into sprigs. Add to the tomato mixture, with the olives and capers.

4 To make the dressing, mix the wine vinegar, paprika, cumin and garlic in a bowl. Whisk in the oil and add salt and pepper to taste. Pour over the salad and toss lightly. Serve immediately with the remaining spring onions.

Variation
Early in the year when tomatoes have yet to reach perfection, add extra flavour to this salad by tossing in the peeled segments of a large, juicy orange.

Turkish Salad: *Energy 273kcal/1133kJ; Protein 11.1g; Carbohydrate 11.2g, of which sugars 10.9g; Fat 20.7g, of which saturates 9.2g; Cholesterol 39mg; Calcium 242mg; Fibre 3.2g; Sodium 826mg.*
Spanish Salad: *Energy 172kcal/712kJ; Protein 2.5g; Carbohydrate 5g, of which sugars 4.3g; Fat 16g, of which saturates 2.4g; Cholesterol 0mg; Calcium 71mg; Fibre 2.2g; Sodium 305mg.*

Greek Salad

Greek tomatoes get plenty of time to ripen in the summer sun and they are always absolutely bursting with flavour. They make the perfect base for a refreshing salad with cucumber and the best-quality feta cheese. Use a good fruity extra virgin olive oil in the dressing for the most successful salad.

Serves 6

1 cos or romaine lettuce, sliced
450g/1lb well-flavoured tomatoes, cut into eighths
1 large cucumber, seeded and chopped
200g/7oz feta cheese, preferably sheep's milk feta, crumbled
4 spring onions (scallions), sliced
50g/2oz/ ½ cup black olives, stoned (pitted) and halved

For the dressing

90ml/6 tbsp extra virgin olive oil
25ml/1½ tbsp lemon juice
salt and ground black pepper

1 Put the sliced lettuce, tomatoes and chopped cucumber into a large serving bowl and add the feta cheese, spring onions and black olives. Mix the ingredients together.

2 To make the dressing, mix together the extra virgin olive oil and lemon juice and season with salt and freshly ground black pepper to taste.

3 Pour the dressing over the salad. Toss the salad well, and serve immediately with crusty bread or hot toasted pitta.

Variations

- *For a more substantial meze-style variation add red (bell) peppers, chopped into bitesize pieces, and sprinkle with pine nuts if you like.*
- *Include a mixture of other salad leaves with, or in place of, the cos lettuce.*
- *Omit the feta and serve the salad with slices of grilled or barbecued halloumi cheese.*

Watermelon and Feta Salad

The combination of soft watermelon with crumbly feta cheese is tangy and refreshing. The salad may be served plain and light, on a leafy base, or with a herbed dressing drizzled over. It is perfect served as an appetizer or a side salad, or taken as part of a meze on a summer picnic.

Serves 4

4 slices watermelon, chilled
130g/4½ oz feta cheese, preferably sheep's milk feta, cut into bitesize pieces
handful of mixed seeds, such as pumpkin seeds and sunflower seeds, lightly toasted
10–15 black olives

1 Cut the rind off the watermelon and remove as many seeds as possible. The sweetest and juiciest part is right in the core, and you may want to cut off any whiter flesh just under the skin.

2 Cut the flesh into triangular chunks. Mix the watermelon, feta cheese, mixed seeds and black olives. Cover and chill the salad for 30 minutes in the refrigerator before serving.

Cook's Tip

The best choice of olives for this recipe are plump black ones, such as kalamata, or dry-cured black olives. Not only does the colour contrast beautifully, but the saltiness is a perfect background to the mellow sweetness of the fruit.

Greek Salad: *Energy 225kcal/935kJ; Protein 11.2g; Carbohydrate 11.8g, of which sugars 11.1g; Fat 15.1g, of which saturates 8.3g; Cholesterol 39mg; Calcium 249mg; Fibre 3.4g; Sodium 827mg.*
Watermelon Salad: *Energy 203Kcal/849kJ; Protein 7.8g; Carbohydrate 16.2g, of which sugars 14.8g; Fat 12.4g, of which saturates 5.2g; Cholesterol 23mg; Calcium 148mg; Fibre 1.1g; Sodium 754mg.*

Sun-ripened Tomato and Feta Salad with Purslane

This tasty salad is a version of a traditional Greek salad, with plenty of purslane added to the usual combination of tomato, pepper, onion, cucumber, feta and olives. This recipe is popular in the rural communities of Greece as purslane is a common grassland plant and grows wild in many Greek gardens and meadows.

Serves 4

225g/8oz tomatoes
1 red onion, thinly sliced
1 green (bell) pepper, cored and sliced in thin ribbons
1 piece of cucumber, about 15cm/6in in length, peeled and sliced in rounds
150g/5oz feta cheese, cubed
a large handful of fresh purslane, trimmed of thick stalks
8–10 black olives
90–105ml/6–7 tbsp extra virgin olive oil
15ml/1 tbsp lemon juice
1.5ml/¼ tsp dried oregano
salt and ground black pepper

1 Quarter the tomatoes and place them in a salad bowl. Add the onion, green pepper, cucumber, feta, purslane and olives.

2 Sprinkle the extra virgin olive oil, lemon juice and oregano on top. Add salt and ground black pepper to taste, then toss to coat everything in the olive oil and lemon, and to amalgamate the flavours.

3 If possible, let the salad stand for 10–15 minutes at room temperature before serving.

Cook's Tip

Purslane is a succulent plant whose paddle-shaped leaves have a mild sweet-sour flavour. It grows wild in many parts of Europe, Asia and America and is easy to grow in the vegetable garden. If it is not available, you can use rocket (arugula) in this salad instead.

Tomato, Mozzarella and Red Onion Salad

Sweet tomatoes and the heady scent of basil make a perfect marriage, and between them capture the essence of summer in this simple but delicious salad. Choose vine-ripened tomatoes as they usually have the best flavour.

Serves 4

5 large ripe tomatoes, peeled
2 buffalo mozzarella cheeses, drained and sliced
1 small red onion, chopped

For the dressing

½ small garlic clove, peeled
15g/½oz fresh basil
30ml/2 tbsp chopped fresh flat leaf parsley
25ml/5 tsp small salted capers, rinsed
2.5ml/½ tsp mustard
75–90ml/5–6 tbsp extra virgin olive oil
5–10ml/1–2 tsp balsamic vinegar
salt and ground black pepper

For the garnish

fresh basil leaves
fresh parsley sprigs

1 First make the dressing. Put the garlic, basil, parsley, half the capers and the mustard in a food processor or blender and process briefly to chop.

2 With the motor of the processor or blender running, gradually pour in the olive oil through the feeder tube until you have a smooth purée with a dressing consistency. Add the balsamic vinegar to taste and season with plenty of freshly ground black pepper

3 Slice the tomatoes. Arrange the tomatoes with the mozzarella slices on a plate. Scatter the onion over and season with a little pepper.

4 Drizzle the dressing over the salad, then scatter a few whole or roughly torn basil leaves, parsley sprigs and the remaining capers on top as a garnish.

5 Leave for 10–15 minutes before serving to allow the flavours to blend.

Tomato and Feta Salad: *Energy 283kcal/1168kJ; Protein 7.2g; Carbohydrate 6.8g, of which sugars 6.3g; Fat 25.4g, of which saturates 7.7g; Cholesterol 26mg; Calcium 158mg; Fibre 1.9g; Sodium 717mg.*
Mozzarella Salad: *Energy 232kcal/960kJ; Protein 10.3g; Carbohydrate 3.6g, of which sugars 3.3g; Fat 19.7g, of which saturates 8.3g; Cholesterol 29mg; Calcium 206mg; Fibre 1.4g; Sodium 208mg.*

Potato and Feta Salad

This lovely salad is full of fresh, herby flavours.

Serves 4

500g/1¼lb small new potatoes
5 spring onions (scallions), green and white parts finely chopped
15ml/1 tbsp bottled capers, rinsed
8–10 black olives
115g/4oz feta cheese, cubed
45ml/3 tbsp finely chopped flat leaf parsley
30ml/2 tbsp finely chopped mint
salt and ground black pepper

For the dressing

90–120ml/6–8 tbsp olive oil
juice of 1 lemon, or to taste
2 salted or preserved anchovies, rinsed and finely chopped
45ml/3 tbsp natural (plain) Greek yogurt
45ml/3 tbsp finely chopped fresh dill, plus a few sprigs, to garnish
5ml/1 tsp French mustard

1 Boil the potatoes in their skins for 25–30 minutes, or until tender. Drain them thoroughly and let them cool a little.

2 Peel the potatoes with your fingers and place them in a large bowl. If they are very small, keep them whole; otherwise cut them into large cubes. Add the chopped spring onions, capers, olives, feta cheese and fresh herbs, and toss gently to mix.

3 Whisk the olive oil in a bowl with the lemon juice and anchovies until the dressing thickens; you may need to add a little more olive oil if it does not. Whisk in the yogurt, dill and mustard, with salt and pepper to taste. Toss into the warm potato mix and leave to sit for an hour before serving.

Lentil, Tomato and Cheese Salad

Small blue-green Puy lentils are perfect in this salad with chunks of crumbly feta.

Serves 6

200g/7oz/scant 1 cup lentils (preferably Puy lentils), soaked for about 3 hours in cold water to cover
1 red onion, chopped
1 bay leaf
60ml/4 tbsp extra virgin olive oil
45ml/3 tbsp chopped fresh flat leaf parsley
30ml/2 tbsp chopped fresh oregano or marjoram
250g/9oz cherry tomatoes, halved
250g/9oz feta, goat's milk cheese or Caerphilly cheese, crumbled
salt and ground black pepper
chicory (Belgian endive) or frisée lettuce leaves and fresh herbs, to garnish
30–45ml/2–3 tbsp lightly toasted pine nuts, to serve

1 Drain the lentils and place them in a large pan with plenty of cold water, the onion and bay leaf. Boil vigorously for 10 minutes, then lower the heat and simmer for 20 minutes or according to the instructions on the packet.

2 Drain the lentils, discard the bay leaf and tip them into a bowl. Add salt and pepper to taste. Toss with the olive oil. Set aside to cool. Mix the lentils with the fresh parsley, oregano or marjoram and cherry tomatoes.

3 Add the cheese. Line a serving dish with chicory or frisée leaves and pile the salad in the centre. Sprinkle over the pine nuts and garnish with fresh herbs.

Panzanella

In this lively salad, a sweet, tangy blend of tomato juice, rich olive oil and red wine vinegar is soaked up by a colourful mixture of roasted peppers, anchovies and toasted ciabatta bread.

Serves 4–6

225g/8oz ciabatta bread (about ⅔ loaf)
150ml/1/4 pint/⅔ cup olive oil
3 red (bell) peppers
3 yellow (bell) peppers
50g/2oz can anchovy fillets, drained
675g/1½ lb ripe plum tomatoes
4 garlic cloves, crushed
60ml/4 tbsp red wine vinegar
50g/2oz capers
115g/4oz/1 cup pitted black olives
salt and ground black pepper
fresh basil leaves to garnish

1 Preheat the oven to 200°C/400°F/Gas 6. Cut the ciabatta into 2cm/¾in chunks and drizzle with 50ml/2fl oz/¼ cup of the oil. Grill (broil) lightly until just golden.

2 Put the peppers on a foil-lined baking sheet and bake for about 45 minutes, until the skins begin to char. Remove the peppers from the oven, place in a strong plastic bag, close the end and leave to cool slightly.

3 Pull the skins off the peppers and cut them into quarters, discarding the stalk ends and seeds. Roughly chop the anchovies and set aside.

4 To make the tomato dressing, score the tomato skins and blanch the tomatoes in a bowl of freshly boiled water for a few minutes. The skins should slip off easily. Halve the tomatoes.

5 Scoop the seeds and pulp into a sieve (strainer) set over a bowl. Using the back of a spoon, press the tomato pulp in the sieve to extract as much juice as possible. Discard the pulp and add the remaining oil, the garlic and vinegar to the juices.

6 Layer the toasted ciabatta, peppers, tomatoes, anchovies, capers and olives in a large salad bowl. Season the tomato dressing with salt and pepper and pour it over the salad. Leave to stand for about 30 minutes. Serve garnished with plenty of basil leaves.

Potato and Feta: Energy 138kcal/566kJ; Protein 1.3g; Carbohydrate 1.2g, of which sugars 1.1g; Fat 14.2g, of which saturates 2g; Cholesterol 0mg; Calcium 75mg; Fibre 1.4g; Sodium 40mg.
Lentil Salad: Energy 324kcal/1352kJ; Protein 15.8g; Carbohydrate 21.9g, of which sugars 3.7g; Fat 19.9g, of which saturates 7.1g; Cholesterol 29mg; Calcium 188mg; Fibre 2.7g; Sodium 619mg.
Panzanella: Energy 239kcal/1003kJ; Protein 5.5g; Carbohydrate 29.6g, of which sugars 7.1g; Fat 11.8g, of which saturates 1.6g; Cholesterol 0mg; Calcium 93mg; Fibre 3.3g; Sodium 905mg.

Salade Niçoise

Served with French bread, this regional classic makes a wonderful summer lunch.

Serves 4–6

225g/8oz French beans
450g/1lb new potatoes, peeled and cut into 2.5cm/1in pieces
white wine vinegar and olive oil, for sprinkling
1 small cos or round lettuce, torn into bitesize pieces
4 ripe plum tomatoes, quartered
1 small cucumber, peeled, seeded and diced
1 green or red (bell) pepper, thinly sliced
4 hard-boiled eggs, quartered
24 black olives
225g/8oz can tuna in brine, drained
50g/2oz can anchovy fillets in olive oil, drained
basil leaves, to garnish
garlic croûtons, to serve

For the anchovy vinaigrette

20ml/4tsp Dijon mustard
50g/2oz can anchovy fillets in olive oil, drained and chopped
1 garlic clove, crushed
60ml/4 tbsp lemon juice
120ml/4fl oz/½ cup sunflower oil
120ml/4fl oz/½ cup extra virgin olive oil
ground black pepper

1 To make the vinaigrette, place the mustard, anchovies and garlic in a bowl and pound together. Season generously with pepper and whisk in the lemon juice. Slowly whisk in the sunflower oil, then the olive oil, in a thin stream, until the dressing is smooth and creamy.

2 Drop the French beans into a large pan of boiling water and boil for 3 minutes until tender, yet crisp. Transfer them to a colander using a slotted spoon, then rinse under cold running water and set aside. Add the potatoes to the same boiling water, reduce the heat and simmer for 10–15 minutes, until just tender, then drain. Sprinkle with a little vinegar and olive oil and a spoonful of the vinaigrette.

3 Arrange the lettuce on a serving platter, top with the tomatoes, cucumber and red or green pepper, then add the French beans and potatoes. Arrange the eggs around the edge. Place the olives, tuna and anchovies on top and garnish with the basil leaves. Drizzle with the remaining vinaigrette and serve with garlic croûtons.

Orange, Chicken and Rice Salad

Orange segments are the perfect partner for tender chicken. To appreciate all the flavours fully, serve the salad at room temperature.

Serves 4

3 large seedless oranges
175g/6oz/scant 1 cup white long grain rice
475ml/16 fl oz/2 cups water
10ml/ 2 tsp Dijon mustard
2.5ml/½ tsp caster (superfine) sugar
175ml/6fl oz/¾ cup vinaigrette dressing
450g/1lb cooked chicken, diced
45ml/3 tbsp snipped fresh chives
75g/3oz/¾ cup cashew nuts, toasted
salt and ground black pepper
salad leaves, to serve

1 Pare one of the oranges finely, taking care to remove only the coloured part of the rind. Put the rind in a saucepan and add the rice. Pour in the water, add a pinch of salt and bring to the boil. Cover and steam over a low heat for about 15 minutes,. until the rice is tender and the water absorbed.

2 Meanwhile, peel all the oranges. Working over a plate to catch the juices, cut them into segments. Add the orange juice, mustard and sugar to the vinaigrette and whisk to combine well. Taste, and add more salt and pepper if needed.

3 When the rice is cooked, discard the orange rind and spoon the rice into a bowl. Let it cool slightly, then add half the dressing. Toss well and cool completely.

4 Add the chicken, chives, cashes nuts and orange segments to the rice. Add the remaining dressing and toss gently. Serve on a bed of salad leaves.

Pan-Fried Chicken Liver Salad

Serve this salad immediately so that the hot dressing does not wilt the leaves.

Serves 4

75g/3oz baby spinach leaves
75g/3oz lollo rosso leaves
75ml/5 tbsp olive oil
15ml/1 tbsp butter
225g/8oz chicken livers, trimmed and thinly sliced
45ml/3 tbsp vin santo or other sweet dessert wine
50–75g/2–3oz fresh Parmesan cheese, shaved into curls
salt and ground black pepper

1 Wash and dry the spinach and lollo rosso. Tear the leaves into a large bowl, season with salt and pepper and toss gently.

2 Heat 30ml/2 tbsp of the oil with the butter in a large heavy-based frying pan. When foaming, add the chicken livers and toss over a medium to high heat for 5 minutes or until the livers are browned on the outside but still pink in the centre.

3 Remove the livers from the pan with a slotted spoon, drain them on kitchen paper, then place on top of the salad leaves.

4 Return the pan to a medium heat, add the remaining oil and the vin santo and stir until sizzling. Pour the hot dressing over the salad, toss to coat and sprinkle over the Parmesan shavings. Serve immediately in a large bowl or on individual plates.

Salade Niçoise: *Energy 542kcal/2260kJ; Protein 46.8g; Carbohydrate 14.3g, of which sugars 9.8g; Fat 33.7g, of which saturates 6.5g; Cholesterol 236mg; Calcium 132mg; Fibre 4.4g; Sodium 671mg.*
Orange Chicken Salad: *Energy 729kcal/3035kJ; Protein 36.3g; Carbohydrate 47.5g, of which sugars 12g; Fat 34g, of which saturates 5.6g; Cholesterol 79mg; Calcium 150mg; Fibre 4.2g; Sodium 561mg.*
Chicken Liver Salad: *Energy 313 kcal/1299kJ; Protein 17g; Carbohydrate 8.3g, of which sugars 8g; Fat 23.7g, of which saturates 4.1g; Cholesterol 333mg; Calcium 42mg; Fibre 2.4g; Sodium 72mg.*

Warm Chicken & Tomato Salad

This simple, warm salad combines pan-fried chicken and spinach with a light, nutty dressing. It's ideal as part of a warm buffet.

Serves 4

45ml/3 tbsp oilice oil
30ml/2 tbsp hazelnut oil
15ml/1 tbsp white wine vinegar
1 garlic clove, crushed
15ml/1 tbsp chopped mixed herbs
225g/8oz baby spinach leaves
250g/9oz cherry tomatoes, halved
1 bunch spring onions (scallions), chopped
2 skinless, boneless chicken breasts, cut into thin strips
salt and ground black pepper

1 First make the dressing; place 30ml/2 tbsp of the olive oil, the hazelnut oil, vinegar, garlic and chopped herbs in a small bowl or jug and whisk together until thoroughly miced. Set aside.

2 Trim any long stalks from the spinach leaves, then place in a large serving bowl with the tomatoes and spring onions, and toss together to mix.

3 Heat the remaining olive oil in a frying pan, and stir-fry the chicken over a high heat for 7-10 minutes until it is cooked, tender and lightly browned.

4 Arrange the cooked chicken pieces over the salad. Give the dressing a quick whisk, then drizzle it over the salad. Add salt and pepper to taste, toss lightly and serve immediately.

Variations

- *Use other meat or fish, such as steak, pork fillet or salmon fillet, in place of the chicken breasts.*
- *Use fried mushrooms instead of meat for a vegan salad.*
- *Use mixed salad leaves rather than the spinach.*
- *Mix a handful of torn basil leaves with the spinach for a really summery flavour.*

Warm Duck Salad with Poached Eggs

Grilled duck cooked on skewers looks and tastes wonderful in this spectacular salad.

Serves 4

3 skinless duck breast portions, thinly sliced
30ml/2 tbsp soy sauce
30ml/2 tbsp balsamic vinegar
30ml/2 tbsp groundnut (peanut) oil
1 shallot, finely chopped
115g/4oz/1½ cups chanterelle mushrooms
4 eggs
50g/2oz mixed salad leaves
salt and ground black pepper
30ml/2 tbsp extra virgin olive oil, to serve

1 Put the duck in a shallow dish and toss with the soy sauce and balsamic vinegar. Cover and chill for 30 minutes. Meanwhile, soak 12 bamboo skewers in water to help prevent them from burning during cooking.

2 Preheat the grill (broiler). Thread the marinated duck slices on to the skewers, pleating them neatly.

3 Place the skewers on a grill pan and cook for 3–5 minutes, then turn the skewers and cook for a further 3 minutes, or until the duck is golden brown.

4 Meanwhile, heat the groundnut oil in a frying pan and cook the chopped shallot until softened. Add the mushrooms and cook over a high heat for 5 minutes, stirring occasionally.

5 While the chanterelles are cooking, half fill a frying pan with water, add a little salt and heat until simmering. Break the eggs one at a time into a cup, then gently tip into the water. Poach the eggs gently for about 3 minutes, or until the whites are set. Use a slotted spoon to transfer the eggs to a warm plate, pat dry with kitchen paper, then trim off any untidy white.

6 Arrange the salad leaves on four plates, then add the chanterelles and duck. Place the eggs on the salad. Drizzle with olive oil and season with pepper, then serve immediately.

Warm Chicken & Tomato Salad: *Energy 260kcal/1081kJ; Protein 20.7g; Carbohydrate 3.7g, of which sugars 3.6g; Fat 18.1g, of which saturates 2.6g; Cholesterol 53mg; Calcium 124mg; Fibre 2.3g; Sodium 140mg.*
Warm Duck Salad: *Energy 271kcal/1132kJ; Protein 29.2g; Carbohydrate 1.5g, of which sugars 1.1g; Fat 18.6g, of which saturates 3.9g; Cholesterol 314mg; Calcium 51mg; Fibre 0.7g; Sodium 196mg.*

Potato Salad With Sausage

This salad is often served in French bistros and cafés as a starter. Sometimes the potatoes are served on their own, simply dressed with vinaigrette and perhaps accompanied by some marinated herrings.

Serves 4

450g/1lb small waxy potatoes
30–45ml/2–3 tbsp dry white wine
2 shallots, finely chopped
15ml/1 tbsp chopped fresh parsley
15ml/1 tbsp chopped fresh tarragon
175g/6oz cooked garlic sausage
a sprig of parsley, to garnish

For the vinaigrette

10ml/2 tsp Dijon mustard
15ml/1 tbsp tarragon vinegar or white wine vinegar
75ml/5 tbsp extra virgin olive oil
salt and ground black pepper

1 In a medium pan, cover the potatoes with cold salted water and bring to the boil. Reduce the heat to medium and simmer for 10–12 minutes until tender. Drain the potatoes and refresh under cold running water.

2 Peel the potatoes if you like or leave in their skins and cut into 6mm/¼ in slices. Sprinkle with the wine and shallots.

3 To make the vinaigrette, mix the mustard and vinegar in a bowl, then whisk in the oil, 15ml/1 tbsp at a time. Season and pour over the potatoes.

4 Add the herbs to the potatoes and toss until well mixed.

5 Slice the sausage thinly and toss with the potatoes. Season with salt and pepper to taste and serve at room temperature, garnished with a parsley sprig.

Cook's Tip

French saucisson à l'ail *is normally used for this salad. It is fully cooked, so is ready to slice and eat, hot or cold. It is often made with wine or brandy and has a spicy, warm flavour.*

Frisée Salad with Bacon

This country-style salad is popular all over France. Frisée and escarole have a slight bitterness that is well complemented by bacon. The salad is sometimes served sprinkled with chopped hard-boiled egg.

Serves 4

225g/8oz/6 cups frisée or escarole leaves
75–90ml/5–6 tbsp extra virgin olive oil
175g/6oz piece of smoked bacon, diced, or 6 thick-cut smoked bacon rashers (slices), cut crossways into thin strips
55g/2oz/1 cup white bread cubes
1 small garlic clove, finely chopped
15ml/1 tbsp red wine vinegar
10ml/2 tsp Dijon mustard
salt and ground black pepper

1 Tear the salad leaves into bitesize pieces and put them in a salad bowl.

2 Heat 15ml/1 tbsp of the oil in a medium non-stick frying pan over a medium-low heat and add the bacon. Fry gently until well browned, stirring occasionally. Remove the bacon with a slotted spoon and drain on kitchen paper.

3 Add another 30ml/2 tbsp of oil to the pan and fry the bread cubes over a medium-high heat, turning frequently, until evenly browned. Remove the bread cubes with a slotted spoon and drain on kitchen paper. Discard any remaining fat.

4 Stir the garlic, vinegar and mustard into the pan with the remaining oil and heat until just warm, whisking to combine. Season to taste, then pour the dressing over the salad and sprinkle with the fried bacon and croûtons.

Cook's Tip

In France, where they are cultivated, dandelion leaves often replace frisée in this salad. They are sometimes forced in order to produce blanched shoots like those of chicory.

Potato Salad: *Energy 315kcal/1313kJ; Protein 8.3g; Carbohydrate 22.3g, of which sugars 3.1g; Fat 21.6g, of which saturates 4.4g; Cholesterol 50mg; Calcium 45mg; Fibre 2.3g; Sodium 372mg.*
Frisée Salad: *Energy 226kcal/940kJ; Protein 10g; Carbohydrate 8.1g, of which sugars 1.5g; Fat 17.3g, of which saturates 3.2g; Cholesterol 14mg; Calcium 38mg; Fibre 0.8g; Sodium 721mg.*

Spinach, Bacon and Prawn Salad

Serve this warm salad with a fresh baguette for an authentic French flavour.

Serves 4
105ml/7 tbsp olive oil
20ml/2 tbsp sherry vinegar
2 garlic cloves, finely chopped
5ml/1 tsp Dijon mustard
12 cooked unshelled king prawns (jumbo shrimp)
115g/4oz streaky (fatty) bacon, rinded and cut into strips
about 115g/4oz young spinach leaves
½ head oak-leaf lettuce, roughly torn
salt and ground black pepper

1 To make the dressing, whisk together 90ml/6 tbsp of olive oil with vinegar, garlic, mustard and seasoning in a small pan. Heat gently until thickened slightly, and keep warm.

2 Pull the heads and shells off the prawns carefully. Remove the legs and leave the tails intact.

3 Heat the remaining oil in a frying pan and fry the bacon until golden and crisp, stirring occasionally.

4 Add the prawns to the bacon and stir-fry for a few minutes until warmed through.

5 Arrange the spinach and torn oak-leaf lettuce on four individual serving plates. Spoon the prawns and bacon over the leaves and pour over the hot dressing. Serve at once with warmed French bread.

French Goat's Cheese Salad

This is a French salad and cheese course all on one plate. It makes a quick and satisfying appetizer or light lunch.

Serves 4
200g/7oz bag of prepared mixed salad leaves
4 rashers (strips) back bacon
115g/4oz full fat goat's cheese
16 thick slices crusty white bread

For the dressing
60ml/4 tsp olive oil
15ml/1 tbsp tarragon vinegar
10ml/1 tsp walnut oil
5ml/1 tsp Dijon mustard
5ml/1 tsp wholegrain mustard

1 Preheat the grill (broiler) to a medium heat. Rinse and dry the salad leaves, then arrange them in four individual bowls. Place the ingredients for the dressing in a screw-topped jar, shake together well, and reserve.

2 Lay the bacon rashers on a board, then stretch them with the back of a knife and cut each into four crosswise. Roll each piece up and grill (broil) for 2–3 minutes.

3 Slice the goat's cheese into eight and halve each slice. Top each slice of bread with a piece of goat's cheese and place under the grill. Turn over the bacon and continue cooking with the toasts until the cheese is golden and bubbling.

4 Arrange the bacon rolls and toasts on top of the prepared salad leaves, shake the dressing well and pour a little of it over each.

Variations
- *If you prefer, just slice the goat's cheese and place it on toasted crusty white bread.*
- *Use wholemeal (whole-wheat) toast for a deliciously nutty flavour that complements the walnut oil in the dressing.*
- *Vegans can replace the bacon rolls with halved, ripe cherry tomatoes, and the goat's cheese with avocado.*

Spinach Bacon & Prawns *Energy 305kcal/1260kJ; Protein 14.6g; Carbohydrate 1.3g, of which sugars 1.3g; Fat 26.8g, of which saturates 5.3g; Cholesterol 116mg; Calcium 104mg; Fibre 1.1g; Sodium 499mg.*
Goat's Cheese Salad: *Energy 667kcal/2806kJ; Protein 24.5g; Carbohydrate 85.6g, of which sugars 5.4g; Fat 27.8g, of which saturates 9g; Cholesterol 40mg; Calcium 240mg; Fibre 4.1g; Sodium 1483mg.*

Figs with Prosciutto and Roquefort

Fresh figs are a delicious treat, whether you choose dark purple, yellowy green or green-skinned varieties. When they are ripe, you can split them open with your fingers to reveal the soft, sweet flesh full of edible seeds. In this easy, stylish dish figs and honey balance the richness of the ham and cheese. Serve with warm bread for a simple appetizer before any main course.

Serves 4

8 fresh figs
75g/3oz prosciutto
45ml/3 tbsp clear honey
75g/3oz Roquefort cheese

1 Preheat the grill (broiler). Quarter the figs and place on a foil-lined grill rack. Tear each slice of prosciutto into two or three pieces and crumple them up on the foil beside the figs.

2 Brush the figs with 15ml/1 tbsp of the clear honey and cook the figs and ham under the grill until lightly browned, watching them all the time.

3 Crumble the Roquefort cheese and divide among four plates, setting it to one side. Add the honey-grilled figs and ham and pour over any cooking juices caught on the foil.

4 Drizzle the remaining honey over the figs, ham and cheese, and season with plenty of freshly ground black pepper. Serve immediately, while still warm.

Variation
When figs are not available, try making a version of this dish with quartered ripe pears.

Cook's Tip
Roquefort is a sheep's milk cheese made in the South of France, and only cheeses ripened in the Cambalou caves near the town of Roquefort may bear its name.

Pasta Salad with Salami

This salad is simple to make and it can be prepared in advance for a perfect appetizer or, served in more generous quantites, to make a satisfying main course.

Serves 4

225g/8oz pasta twists
275g/10oz jar charcoal-roasted peppers in oil
115g/4oz/1 cup stoned (pitted) black olives
4 sun-dried tomatoes, quartered
115g/4oz Roquefort cheese, crumbled
10 slices peppered salami, cut into strips
115g/4oz packet mixed leaf salad
30ml/2 tbsp white wine vinegar
30ml/2 tbsp chopped fresh oregano
salt and ground black pepper

1 Cook the pasta in a large saucepan of boiling salted water for 12 minutes, or according to the instructions on the packet, until tender but not soft. Drain thoroughly and rinse with cold water, then drain again.

2 Drain the peppers and reserve 60ml/4 tbsp of the oil for the dressing. Cut the peppers into long, fine strips and mix them with the olives, sun-dried tomatoes and Roquefort in a large bowl. Stir in the pasta and peppered salami.

3 Divide the salad leaves among four individual bowls and spoon the pasta salad on top, Whisk the reserved oil with the wine vinegar, oregano, garlic and seasoning to taste. Spoon this dressing over the salad and serve at once.

Cook's Tip
If you enjoy a taste of the Mediterranean, grow herbs on your kitchen window sill. Less expensive and longer lasting than those you buy from the supermarket, they are easy to care for and widely available. You could include oregano and basil, thyme and mint. A patio pot-grown rosemary plant provides flavour for many meats, sauces and bakes.

Figs with Proscuitto: *Energy 326kcal/1378kJ; Protein 10.7g; Carbohydrate 57.4g, of which sugars 57.4g; Fat 7.5g, of which saturates 3.8g; Cholesterol 25mg; Calcium 324mg; Fibre 6.9g; Sodium 512mg.*
Pasta Salad: *Energy 429kcal/1797kJ; Protein 17.8g; Carbohydrate 46.7g, of which sugars 6.6g; Fat 20.3g, of which saturates 8.9g; Cholesterol 37mg; Calcium 188mg; Fibre 3.9g; Sodium 1341mg.*

Warm Salad of Bayonne Ham

With a lightly spiced, nutty dressing, this warm salad is as delicious as it is attractive and makes an excellent choice for informal entertaining.

Serves 4

225g/8oz new potatoes, halved if large
50g/2oz green beans
115g/4oz young spinach leaves
2 spring onions (scallions), sliced
4 eggs, hard-boiled and quartered
50g/2oz Bayonne ham, cut into strips
juice of ½ lemon
salt and ground black pepper

For the dressing

60ml/4 tbsp olive oil
5ml/1 tsp ground turmeric
5ml/1 tsp ground cumin
50g/2oz/⅓ cup shelled hazelnuts

1 Cook the potatoes in boiling salted water for 10-15 minutes, or until tender, then drain well. Cook the beans in boiling salted water for 2 minutes, then drain.

2 Toss the potatoes and beans with the spinach and spring onions in a bowl.

3 Arrange the hard-boiled egg quarters on the salad and scatter the stripped ham over the top. Sprinkle with the lemon juice and season with plenty of salt and pepper.

4 Heat the dressing ingredients in a large frying pan and continue to cook, stirring frequently, until the nuts turn golden. Pour the hot, nutty dressing over the salad and serve at once.

Variation

For a lighter dish, replace the potatoes with a 400g/12oz can mixed beans and pulses. Drain and rinse the beans and pulses, then drain again. Toss lightly with the green beans and spring onions.

Bresaola and Onion Salad

Bresaola is an Italian speciality. It is raw beef that has been salted in much the same way as *prosciutto di Parma*, and is served in very thin slices. In this salad, it is combined with sweet, juicy grilled onions.

Serves 4

2 medium onions, peeled
75–90ml/5–6 tbsp olive oil
juice of 1 lemon
12 thin slices bresaola
75g/3oz rocket (arugula)
salt and freshly ground black pepper

1 Slice each onion into eight wedges through the root. Arrange the wedges in a single layer in a flameproof dish. Brush them with a little of the olive oil and season well with salt and black pepper to taste.

2 Place the onion wedges under a hot grill and cook for about 8–10 minutes, turning once, until they are just beginning to soften and turn golden brown at the edges.

3 Meanwhile, to make the dressing, mix together the lemon juice and 60ml/4 tbsp of the olive oil. Add salt and black pepper to taste and whisk until thoroughly blended. Pour the lemon dressing over the hot onions, mix well to coat the onions and leave until cold.

4 Divide the bresaola slices among four individual serving plates and arrange the onions and rocket leaves on top. Spoon over any remaining dressing and serve the salad immediately.

Bayonne Ham Salad: *Energy 323kcal/1341kJ; Protein 12.4g; Carbohydrate 10.9g, of which sugars 2.2g; Fat 25.8g, of which saturates 4.2g; Cholesterol 199mg; Calcium 105mg; Fibre 2.3g; Sodium 270mg*
Bresaola & Onion Salad: *Energy 204kcal/842kJ; Protein 7.4g; Carbohydrate 8.2g, of which sugars 5.9g; Fat 15.9g, of which saturates 2.9g; Cholesterol 15mg; Calcium 58mg; Fibre 1.8g; Sodium 45mg*

Sour Cucumber with Fresh Dill

This is half pickle, half salad, and totally delicious served with rye or other coarse, dark, full-flavoured breads. Cucumbers are widely used for salads in hot regions as they are so refreshing. In summer you may be able to find the small cucumbers that are normally used for pickling, which are ideal for this treatment. It can be served with cold meat or fish, or as part of a mixed hors d'oeuvre.

Serves 4

2 small cucumbers
3 onions
75–90ml/5–6 tbsp cider vinegar
30–45ml/2–3 tbsp chopped fresh dill
salt, to taste

1 Slice the cucumbers and the onions thinly and put them into a large mixing bowl. Season the vegetables with salt and toss together until they are thoroughly combined.

2 Leave the mixture to stand in a cool place for 5–10 minutes.

3 Add the cider vinegar, 30–45ml/2–3 tbsp cold water and the chopped dill to the cucumber and onion mixture.

4 Toss all the ingredients together until they are well combined, then chill in the refrigerator for a few hours, or until ready to serve.

Variation
For a sweet and sour mixture, add 45ml/3 tbsp caster (superfine) sugar to the cucumber and onions with the cider vinegar in step 2.

Cook's Tip
Choose smooth-skinned, smallish cucumbers for this salad, as larger ones tend to be less tender. If you can only buy a large cucumber, peel it before slicing..

Wild Rocket and Cos Lettuce Salad with Herbs

Salads in Greece are clean-tasting and often quite lemony in flavour. There is a national preference for strong-tasting leaves – sometimes quite bitter ones – that is also reflected in fresh salads, especially those that make use of the native cos lettuce. Rocket is another favourite ingredient, added to give salads a sharp edge.

Serves 4

a large handful of rocket (arugula) leaves
2 cos or romaine lettuce hearts
3 or 4 fresh flat leaf parsley sprigs, coarsely chopped
30–45ml/2–3 tbsp finely chopped fresh dill
75ml/5 tbsp extra virgin olive oil
15–30ml/1–2 tbsp lemon juice
salt

1 If the rocket leaves are young and tender they can be left whole, but older ones should be trimmed of thick stalks and then sliced coarsely. Discard any tough stalks.

2 Slice the cos or romaine lettuce hearts into thin ribbons and place these in a bowl, then add the rocket and the chopped fresh parsley and dill.

3 Make a dressing by whisking the extra virgin olive oil and lemon juice with salt to taste in a bowl until the mixture emulsifies and thickens.

4 Just before serving, pour over the dressing and toss lightly to coat everything in the glistening oil. Serve with crusty bread and a cheese or fish dish.

Cook's Tip
It is important to mix the salad leaves in the right proportions to balance the bitterness of the rocket and the sweetness of the cos or romaine lettuce, and the best way to find this out is by taste.

Sour Cucumber: *Energy 59kcal/243kJ; Protein 2.5g; Carbohydrate 11.7g, of which sugars 8.7g; Fat 0.5g, of which saturates 0g; Cholesterol 0mg; Calcium 72mg; Fibre 2.9g; Sodium 11mg.*
Rocket and Cos Salad: *Energy 134kcal/554kJ; Protein 0.6g; Carbohydrate 1.3g, of which sugars 1.3g; Fat 14.1g, of which saturates 2.1g; Cholesterol 0mg; Calcium 21mg; Fibre 0.7g; Sodium 2mg.*

Moroccan Orange, Onion and Olive Salad

This is a refreshing salad, full of sweet, interesting flavours, to follow a rich main dish, such as a Moroccan tagine of lamb, or to lighten any spicy meal. It is also delicious with cold roast duck, and is a very good salad to serve as part of a cold buffet meal.

Serves 6

5 large oranges
90g/3½ oz/scant 1 cup black olives
1 red onion, thinly sliced
1 large fennel bulb, thinly sliced, feathery tops reserved
15ml/1 tbsp chopped fresh mint, plus a few extra sprigs
15ml/1 tbsp chopped fresh coriander (cilantro), plus a few extra sprigs
2.5ml/½ tsp orange flower water

For the dressing

60ml/4 tbsp olive oil
10ml/2 tsp lemon juice
2.5ml/½ tsp ground toasted coriander seeds
salt and freshly ground black pepper

1 Peel the oranges with a knife, removing all the white pith, and cut them into 5mm/¼in slices. Remove any pips and work over a bowl to catch all the orange juice. Set the juice aside.

2 Stone (pit) the olives, if you wish. In a bowl, toss the orange slices, onion and fennel together with the olives, chopped mint and fresh coriander.

3 Make the dressing. In a bowl or jug (pitcher), whisk together the olive oil, 15ml/1 tbsp of the reserved fresh orange juice and the lemon juice. Add the ground toasted coriander seeds and season to taste with a little salt and pepper. Whisk thoroughly to emulsify the dressing.

4 Toss the dressing into the salad and leave to stand for 30–60 minutes for the flavours to mingle.

5 Drain off any excess dressing and place the salad on a serving dish. Scatter with the herbs and fennel tops, and sprinkle with the orange flower water.

Cucumber and Tomato Salad

This salad has been adopted from Bulgaria, where it was traditionally made with the local yogurt. Luxurious Greek yogurt, olive oil and sweet tomatoes lend themselves to this recipe.

Serves 4

450g/1lb firm ripe tomatoes
½ cucumber
1 onion
1 small fresh red or green chilli, seeded and chopped, or fresh chives, chopped into 2.5cm/1in lengths, to garnish
crusty bread or pitta breads, to serve

For the dressing

60ml/4 tbsp olive or vegetable oil
90ml/6 tbsp strained Greek natural (plain) yogurt
30ml/2 tbsp chopped fresh parsley or chives
2.5ml/½ tsp vinegar
salt and freshly ground black pepper

1 Plunge the tomatoes into a saucepan of boiling water for 1 minute, then transfer them to a bowl of cold water. Drain, then slip off and discard their skins. Halve the tomatoes, remove and discard the seeds and cores and chop the flesh into even-sized pieces. Put them into a salad bowl.

2 Chop the cucumber and onion into pieces of similar size to the tomatoes and put them in the bowl.

3 Mix all the dressing ingredients together and season to taste. Pour the dressing over the salad and toss all the ingredients together thoroughly.

4 Sprinkle over black pepper and garnish with the chopped chilli or chives. Serve with chunks of crusty bread or pile into pitta pockets.

Cook's Tip
If you have time, before assembling the salad salt the chopped cucumber lightly and leave it in a colander for about 30 minutes to drain. This will avoid making the salad watery.

Moroccan Salad: *Energy 150kcal/629kJ; Protein 3g; Carbohydrate 18.9g, of which sugars 16.4g; Fat 7.6g, of which saturates 1.1g; Cholesterol 0mg; Calcium 102mg; Fibre 3.8g; Sodium 292mg.*
Cucumber & Tomato Salad: *Energy 156kcal/646kJ; Protein 3g; Carbohydrate 5.8g, of which sugars 5.4g; Fat 13.9g, of which saturates 2.9g; Cholesterol 0mg; Calcium 75mg; Fibre 2.1g; Sodium 32mg.*

Cabbage Salad with Lemon Dressing and Black Olives

In winter, *lahano salata* frequently appears on the Greek table. It is made with compact creamy-coloured "white" cabbage. In more northern climates, this type of tight-headed cabbage can sometimes be a little woody, but in Greece, it always produces a rather sweet-tasting, unusual salad, which has a crisp and refreshing texture.

Serves 4
1 white cabbage
12 black olives

For the dressing
75–90ml/5–6 tbsp extra virgin olive oil
30ml/2 tbsp lemon juice
1 garlic clove, crushed
30ml/2 tbsp finely chopped fresh flat leaf parsley
salt

1 Cut the cabbage in quarters, discard the outer leaves and trim off any thick, hard stems, as well as the hard base.

2 Lay each quarter in turn on its side and cut long, very thin slices until you reach the central core, which should be discarded. Place the shredded cabbage in a bowl and stir in the black olives.

3 Make the dressing by whisking the extra virgin olive oil, lemon juice, garlic, chopped parsley and salt together in a bowl until well blended.

4 Pour the dressing over the cabbage and olives, and toss the salad until everything is evenly coated.

Cook's Tip
The key to a perfect cabbage salad is to shred the cabbage as finely as possible. If you have a slicing blade on your food processor you can use it for cabbage, but be scrupulous about trimming away any woody or fibrous parts before feeding the leaves into the machine.

Mushroom Salad

This refreshing salad is often served as part of a selection of vegetable salads, or crudités, or it could be eaten as a simple first course. Leaving it to stand before serving brings out the inherent sweetness of the mushrooms.

Serves 4
175g/6oz white mushrooms, trimmed
grated rind and juice of ½ lemon
about 30–45ml/2–3 tbsp crème fraîche or sour cream
salt and white pepper
15ml/1 tbsp chopped fresh chives, to garnish

1 Wipe the mushrooms and slice them thinly. Place in a bowl. Add the lemon rind and juice and the cream, adding a little more cream if needed. Stir gently to mix, then season with salt and pepper.

2 Leave the salad to stand for at least 1 hour, stirring occasionally.

3 Sprinkle the salad with chopped chives before serving.

Variation
If you prefer, toss the mushrooms in a little vinaigrette – made by whisking 60ml/4 tbsp walnut oil or extra virgin olive oil into the lemon juice.

***Cabbage Salad:** Energy 208Kcal/861kJ; Protein 4g; Carbohydrate 12.9g, of which sugars 12.5g; Fat 15.8g, of which saturates 2.2g; Cholesterol 0mg; Calcium 155mg; Fibre 6.2g; Sodium 303mg.*
***Mushroom Salad:** Energy 22kcal/93kJ; Protein 1.1g; Carbohydrate 0.6g, of which sugars 0.5g; Fat 1.8g, of which saturates 1g; Cholesterol 5mg; Calcium 17mg; Fibre 0.7g; Sodium 7mg.*

Lemon Carrot Salad

This tangy, colourful and refreshing salad has a wonderfully clear, sweet flavour that balances rich meat or cheese dishes.

Serves 6

450g/1lb small, young carrots
finely grated rind and juice of ½ lemon
15ml/1 tbsp soft light brown sugar
30ml/2 tbsp sunflower oil
5ml/1 tsp hazelnut or sesame oil
5ml/1 tsp chopped fresh oregano
salt and freshly ground black pepper

1 Finely grate the carrots and place them in a large bowl. Stir in the lemon rind and 15–30ml/1–2 tbsp of the lemon juice.

2 Add the sugar, sunflower and hazelnut or sesame oils, and mix well. Add more lemon juice and seasoning to taste, then sprinkle on the oregano and toss lightly to mix.

3 Leave the salad for 1 hour before serving, garnished with a sprig of oregano.

Variation

Experiment with different herbs. Tarragon goes well with carrots, or use a few sprigs of lemon thyme.

Lamb's Lettuce and Beetroot

This salad makes a colourful accompaniment to cold meats. The delicate flavour of the lamb's lettuce is perfect with the tangy beetroot. If you like, sprinkle the salad with chopped walnuts before serving.

Serves 4

150–175g/5–6 oz/3–4 cups lamb's lettuce (corn salad), washed and roots trimmed
250g/½ lb/3 or 4 small beetroot (beets), cooked, peeled and diced
30ml/2 tbsp chopped fresh parsley

For the vinaigrette

30–45ml/2–3 tbsp white wine vinegar or lemon juice
20ml/1 heaped tbsp Dijon mustard
2 garlic cloves, finely chopped
2.5ml/½ tsp sugar
125ml/4fl oz/½ cup sunflower or grapeseed oil
125ml/4fl oz/½ cup crème fraîche or double (heavy) cream
salt and ground black pepper

1 First make the vinaigrette. Mix the vinegar or lemon juice, mustard, garlic, sugar, salt and pepper in a small bowl, then slowly whisk in the oil until the sauce thickens.

2 Lightly beat the crème fraîche or double cream to lighten it slightly, then whisk it into the dressing.

3 Toss the lamb's lettuce with a little of the vinaigrette and arrange on a serving plate or in a bowl.

4 Spoon the beetroot into the centre of the lamb's lettuce and drizzle over the remaining vinaigrette. Sprinkle with chopped parsley and serve immediately.

Cook's Tip

Lamb's lettuce has a mild flavour and a delicate texture. It is known as mâche in France, where it has always been very popular. It is a fairly hardy plant, often found growing wild, so has traditionally been used in winter salads, and can also be steamed and served as a vegetable.

Carrot Salad *Energy 90kcal/372kJ; Protein 1.1g; Carbohydrate 11.8g, of which sugars 8.4g; Fat 4.5g, of which saturates 2.7g; Cholesterol 11mg; Calcium 34mg; Fibre 2.8g; Sodium 59mg.*

Lamb's Lettuce Salad: *Energy 348kcal/1447kJ; Protein 8.7g; Carbohydrate 22.1g, of which sugars 3.4g; Fat 25.7g, of which saturates 7.3g; Cholesterol 20mg; Calcium 199mg; Fibre 3.2g; Sodium 764mg.*

Rocket and Pear Salad

For a sophisticated start to an elaborate meal, try this simple Italian salad of honey-rich pears, fresh Parmesan shavings and aromatic leaves of rocket. Williams or Packhams pears have the right texture for this dish, and should be ripe but not soft. Their slightly gritty texture is perfectly reflected in the shavings of Parmesan cheese.

Serves 4

3 ripe pears
10ml/2 tsp lemon juice
45ml/3 tbsp hazelnut or walnut oil
115g/4oz rocket (arugula), washed and dried
75g/3oz Parmesan cheese, shaved
ground black pepper
open-textured bread, to serve

1 Peel and core the pears and slice thickly lengthways. Moisten the flesh with lemon juice to keep it white.

2 Combine the nut oil with the pears. Add the rocket leaves and toss.

3 Turn the salad out on to four small plates and top with shavings of Parmesan cheese. Season with pepper and serve with the bread.

Cook's Tip

Rocket is fairly easy to find in supermarkets, but if you have a garden you can grow your own from early spring to late summer. The flowers are also edible and tasty.

Variations

- *Crumble a little blue cheese, such as Gorgonzola or Dolcelatte, over the salad instead of the Parmesan.*
- *Scatter a small handful of roasted, roughly chopped hazelnuts into the salad.*
- *Instead of the hazelnuts, try toasted pumpkin seeds.*

Chicory, Carrot and Rocket Salad

This bright and colourful salad combines two of France's most popular vegetables, rocket and chicory. If you don't like rocket, baby spinach leaves or watercress can be used instead, as they have a similarly peppery quality. Use very fresh, juicy carrots to attain the attractive colour and sweetness that will make this salad a firm favourite.

Serves 4–6

3 carrots, coarsely grated
about 50g/2oz fresh rocket (arugula), roughly chopped
1 large head of chicory, separated into leaves

For the dressing

45ml/3 tbsp sunflower oil
15ml/1 tbsp hazelnut or walnut oil (optional)
30ml/2 tbsp cider or white wine vinegar
10ml/2 tsp clear honey
5ml/1 tsp grated lemon rind
15ml/1 tbsp poppy seeds
salt and ground black pepper

1 Mix together the carrots and rocket in a large bowl and season well.

2 Shake the dressing ingredients together in a screw-top jar then pour on to the carrot mixture. Toss the salad thoroughly.

3 Line shallow salad bowls with the chicory leaves and spoon the salad into the centre. Serve lightly chilled.

Rocket and Pear Salad: *Energy 210kcal/875kJ; Protein 8.6g; Carbohydrate 11.4g, of which sugars 11.4g; Fat 14.8g, of which saturates 4.7g; Cholesterol 19mg; Calcium 286mg; Fibre 2.9g; Sodium 222mg.*
Chicory, Carrot and Rocket Salad: *Energy 90kcal/374kJ; Protein 1.2g; Carbohydrate 5.2g, of which sugars 5g; Fat 7.3g, of which saturates 1g; Cholesterol 0mg; Calcium 51mg; Fibre 1.6g; Sodium 16mg*

Radicchio, Artichoke and Walnut Salad

The distinctive, earthy taste of Jerusalem artichokes makes a lovely contrast to the slightly bitter edge of the radicchio and the sharp freshness of the lemony dressing. Serve this unusual grilled salad warm or cold as an accompaniment to grilled steak or barbecued meats. It is perfect for a winter meal.

Serves 4

1 large radicchio or 150g/5oz radicchio leaves
40g/1½oz/⅓ cup walnut pieces
45ml/3 tbsp walnut oil
500g/1¼lb Jerusalem artichokes
thinly pared rind and juice of 1 lemon
coarse sea salt and freshly ground black pepper
fresh flat leaf parsley, to garnish

1 If using a whole radicchio, cut it into 8–10 wedges. Put the wedges or leaves in a flameproof dish. Scatter over the walnuts, then spoon over the oil and season.

2 Peel the Jerusalem artichokes and cut up any large ones so that the pieces are all roughly the same size. Add the artichokes to a pan of boiling salted water with half the lemon juice and cook for 5–7 minutes, until just tender. Drain. Preheat the grill to high.

3 Toss the artichokes into the salad with the remaining lemon juice and the pared rind. Season with coarse salt and pepper. Grill for 2–3 minutes, until beginning to brown. Serve at once garnished with torn pieces of parsley.

Cook's Tip

Jerusalem artichokes, which are not related to globe artichokes but are relatives of the sunflower, are popular in France and are sometimes used raw, grated, in salads. They can be difficult to peel, so choose the least knobbly tubers you can find. Drop them into water with lemon juice as you peel them to stop them discolouring.

Celery and Coconut Salad with Lime

This Turkish salad is unusual in its use of grated coconut, which is mainly reserved in Turkey as a garnish for sweet dishes, or served with shelled pomegranate seeds as a medieval meze. Juicy and refreshing, it is welcome on a hot sunny day as part of a buffet spread outdoors, or as an accompaniment to grilled or barbecued meats and spicy dishes. It looks especially appealing served in coconut shell halves.

Serves 3–4

45–60ml/3–4 tbsp thick natural (plain) yogurt
2 garlic cloves, crushed
5ml/1 tsp grated lime rind
juice of 1 lime
8 long celery sticks, leaves reserved for the garnish
flesh of ½ fresh coconut
salt and ground black pepper
sprigs of fresh flat leaf parsley, to garnish

1 Mix the yogurt and garlic in a bowl, add the lime rind and juice and season with salt and pepper. Set aside.

2 Coarsely grate the celery sticks and the fresh coconut flesh.

3 Fold the grated celery and coconut into the dressing, then leave to sit for 15–20 minutes to let the celery juices mingle with the dressing. Don't leave it for too long or the salad will become watery.

4 To serve, spoon the salad into a bowl and garnish with celery leaves and parsley sprigs.

Cook's Tip

To prepare fresh coconut, pierce the eye at the base of the nut with a nail and drain out the coconut milk. Crack the nut open with a hammer and remove the flesh. The thin brown inner skin can be peeled off using a vegetable peeler or a sharp knife. Grate the flesh coarsely.

Radicchio Salad: *Energy 126kcal/521kJ; Protein 2.1g; Carbohydrate 2.9g, of which sugars 2.9g; Fat 11.9g, of which saturates 10.1g; Cholesterol 0mg; Calcium 63mg; Fibre 3.6g; Sodium 69mg.*
Celery and Coconut Salad: *Energy 126kcal/521kJ; Protein 2.1g; Carbohydrate 2.9g, of which sugars 2.9g; Fat 11.9g, of which saturates 10.1g; Cholesterol 0mg; Calcium 63mg; Fibre 3.6g; Sodium 69mg.*

Halloumi and Grape Salad

In the east Mediterranean, firm salty halloumi cheese is often served fried for breakfast or supper. In this recipe the fried slices of cheese are tossed with sweet, juicy grapes, which really complement the distinctive flavour of halloumi.

Serves 4

For the dressing

60ml/4 tbsp olive oil
2.5ml/½ tsp caster (superfine) sugar
15ml/1 tbsp lemon juice
salt and ground black pepper
15ml/1 tbsp chopped fresh thyme or dill

For the salad

150g/5oz mixed salad leaves
75g/3oz seedless green grapes
75g/3oz seedless black grapes
250g/9oz halloumi cheese
45ml/3 tbsp olive oil
fresh young thyme leaves or dill, to garnish

1 To make the dressing, mix together the olive oil, lemon juice and caster sugar. Season to taste with salt and pepper. Stir in the thyme or dill and set aside.

2 Toss together the salad leaves and the green and black grapes, then transfer to a large serving plate.

3 Thinly slice the halloumi cheese. Heat the oil in a large frying pan. Add the cheese slices and fry briefly until they are turning golden on the underside. Turn the cheese with a fish slice and cook the other side.

4 Arrange the cheese over the salad. Pour over the dressing and garnish with thyme or dill.

Cook's Tip

Halloumi is a sheep's milk cheese that originates in Cyprus and is eaten all over the eastern Mediterranean. It cooks extremely well, without losing its shape, and is often grilled on skewers with vegetables.

Simple Cooked Salad

A version of a North African favourite, this cooked salad is served as a side dish with a main course. Make this one a day in advance to improve the flavours.

Serves 4

2 well-flavoured tomatoes, quartered
2 onions, chopped
½ cucumber, halved lengthways, seeded and sliced
1 green (bell) pepper, chopped
30ml/2 tbsp lemon juice
45ml/3 tbsp olive oil
2 garlic cloves, crushed
30ml/2 tbsp chopped fresh coriander (cilantro)
salt and ground black pepper
sprigs of fresh coriander (cilantro) leaves, to garnish

1 Put the tomatoes, onions, cucumber and green pepper into a pan and add 60ml/4 tbsp water. Heat gently and simmer for 5 minutes. Leave to cool.

2 Mix together the lemon juice, olive oil and garlic. Strain the vegetables, then transfer to a bowl.

3 Pour over the dressing, season with salt and pepper and stir in the chopped coriander.

4 Serve at once or chill overnight so that the flavours develop. Garnish with coriander, if you like.

Halloumi and Grape Salad: *Energy 434Kcal/1811kJ; Protein 16.6g; Carbohydrate 31.4g, of which sugars 2.7g; Fat 27.8g, of which saturates 4g; Cholesterol 0mg; Calcium 149mg; Fibre 12.5g; Sodium 334mg.*
Cooked Salad: *Energy 131kcal/540kJ; Protein 2.2g; Carbohydrate 11g, of which sugars 9.1g; Fat 8.9g, of which saturates 1.3g; Cholesterol 0mg; Calcium 55mg; Fibre 3g; Sodium 13mg.*

Moroccan Braised Chickpeas

This sweet and spicy chickpea salad is a real treat. Serve it warm or cold with couscous to make a perfect barbecue side dish.

Serves 6

250g/9oz/1½ cups dried chickpeas, soaked overnight in cold water
15ml/1 tbsp olive oil
2 onions, cut into wedges
10ml/2 tsp ground cumin
1.5ml/¼ tsp ground turmeric
1.5ml/¼ tsp cayenne pepper
15ml/1 tbsp ground coriander
5ml/1 tsp ground cinnamon
300ml/½ pint/1¼ cups vegetable stock
2 carrots, sliced
115g/4oz/½ cup ready-to-eat dried apricots, halved
50g/2oz/scant ½ cup raisins
25g/1oz/¼ cup flaked (sliced) almonds
30ml/2 tbsp chopped fresh coriander (cilantro)
30ml/2 tbsp chopped fresh flat leaf parsley
salt and ground black pepper

1 Soak a clay pot in cold water for 20 minutes, then drain. Alternatively use a standard casserole dish. Place the chickpeas in a pan with plenty of cold water. Bring to the boil and boil rapidly for 10 minutes, then drain and place the chickpeas in the pot, cover with lukewarm water and cover with the lid.

2 Place in a cold oven and set the temperature to 200°C/400°F/Gas 6. Cook for 1 hour, then reduce the oven temperature to 160°C/325°F/Gas 3. Cook for a further 1 hour, or until the chickpeas are tender.

3 Meanwhile, heat the olive oil in a frying pan, add the onions and cook for about 6 minutes, or until softened. Add the cumin, turmeric, cayenne pepper, coriander and cinnamon and cook for 2–3 minutes. Stir in the stock, carrots, apricots, raisins and almonds and bring to the boil.

4 Drain the chickpeas and return them to the clay pot, add the spicy vegetable mixture and stir to mix. Cover and return to the oven for 30 minutes.

5 Season with salt and pepper, lightly stir in half the chopped coriander and parsley and serve sprinkled with the remainder.

Grilled Aubergine and Couscous Salad

Packets of flavoured couscous are available in most supermarkets – you can use whichever you like, but garlic and coriander is particularly good for this recipe. Together with a crisp green salad, this dish makes a wonderful accompaniment for fish or poultry.

Serves 2

1 large aubergine (eggplant)
30ml/2 tbsp olive oil
115g/4oz packet garlic-and-coriander (cilantro) flavoured couscous
30ml/2 tbsp chopped fresh mint
salt and ground black pepper
fresh mint leaves, to garnish

1 Preheat the grill (broiler) to high. Cut the aubergine into large chunky pieces and toss them with the olive oil. Season with salt and pepper to taste and spread the aubergine pieces on a non-stick baking sheet. Grill (broil) for 5–6 minutes, turning occasionally, until golden brown.

2 Meanwhile, prepare the couscous in boiling water, according to the instructions on the packet.

3 Stir the grilled aubergine and chopped mint into the couscous, toss the salad thoroughly to spread the flavours, and serve immediately.

Variations

- *A similar dish, which is also popular around Greece, uses grilled (broiled) courgettes (zucchini) instead of, or as well as, the aubergine. Slice the courgettes into thin rounds or ovals, brush with olive oil, and place under a hot grill (broiler) for a few minutes on each side.*
- *Make the salad using 115g/4oz/⅔ cup plain couscous, soaked in 175ml/6fl oz/¾ cup boiling water for 5–10 minutes. Add a generous squeeze of lemon juice and a handful of chopped fresh herbs of your choice before tossing the couscous with the aubergine.*

Braised Chickpeas: Energy 630kcal/2639kJ; Protein 51.4g; Carbohydrate 64.1g, of which sugars 16.5g; Fat 20.2g, of which saturates 4.2g; Cholesterol 170mg; Calcium 91mg; Fibre 2.5g; Sodium 169mg.
Aubergines and Couscous: Energy 248Kcal/1,033kJ; Protein 4.4g; Carbohydrate 32.3g, of which sugars 2.5g; Fat 12.1g, of which saturates 1.7g; Cholesterol 0mg; Calcium 24mg; Fibre 2.5g; Sodium 3mg.

Spanish Rice Salad

Rice and a choice of chopped crunchy salad vegetables are served in a well-flavoured dressing. This is a universally popular salad that lends itself to endless variations and is a staple of summer buffet tables.

Serves 6

275g/10oz/1½ cups white long grain rice
1 bunch spring onions (scallions), finely sliced
1 green (bell) pepper, finely diced
1 yellow (bell) pepper, finely diced
225g/8oz tomatoes, peeled, seeded and chopped
30ml/2 tbsp chopped fresh coriander (cilantro)

For the dressing

75ml/5 tbsp mixed sunflower and olive oil
15ml/1 tbsp rice vinegar
5ml/1 tsp Dijon mustard
salt and ground black pepper

1 Cook the rice in plenty of boiling water for 10–12 minutes until it is tender but still *al dente*. Be careful not to overcook it. Drain in a colander, rinse under cold water and drain again. Leave to cool.

2 Place the rice in a large serving bowl. Add the spring onions, peppers, tomatoes and coriander.

3 To make the salad dressing, mix all the ingredients in a jar with a tight-fitting lid and shake vigorously until well mixed. Stir 60–75ml/4–5 tbsp of the dressing into the rice and adjust the seasoning to taste.

4 Cover and chill for about 1 hour before serving. Offer the remaining dressing separately.

Cook's Tips

- *Cooked garden peas, cooked diced carrot and drained, canned sweetcorn can be added to this versatile salad.*
- *Leftover plain boiled rice, either long grain or basmati, can be turned into a salad in this way, provided it is perfectly cooked and not sticky.*

Brown Bean Salad

Brown beans, which are dried broad beans, are widely used in Egyptian cookery, principally to make *ful medames*, which is something of a national dish and is generally eaten for breakfast. The beans can increasingly be found in wholefood shops and supermarkets in other countries.

Serves 6

350g/12oz/1½ cups dried brown beans
3 thyme sprigs
2 bay leaves
1 onion, halved
4 garlic cloves, crushed
7.5ml/1½ tsp cumin seeds, crushed
3 spring onions (scallions), finely chopped
90ml/6 tbsp chopped fresh parsley
20ml/4 tsp lemon juice
90ml/6 tbsp olive oil
3 hard-boiled eggs, shelled and roughly chopped
1 pickled cucumber, roughly chopped
salt and ground black pepper

1 Put the beans in a bowl with plenty of cold water and leave to soak overnight. Drain, transfer to a saucepan and cover with fresh water. Bring to the boil and boil rapidly for 10 minutes.

2 Reduce the heat and add the thyme, bay leaves and onion. Simmer very gently for about 1 hour until tender. Drain and discard the herbs and onion.

3 Mix together the garlic, cumin, spring onions, parsley, lemon juice, oil and add a little salt and pepper. Pour over the beans and toss the ingredients lightly together.

4 Gently stir in the eggs and cucumber and serve immediately.

Cook's Tips

- *The cooking time for dried beans can vary considerably. They may need only 45 minutes, or a lot longer.*
- *If brown beans are not available, dried black or red kidney beans make good substitutes.*

Spanish Rice Salad: *Energy 246kcal/1028kJ; Protein 4.7g; Carbohydrate 42.4g, of which sugars 5.6g; Fat 6.3g, of which saturates 0.8g; Cholesterol 0mg; Calcium 24mg; Fibre 1.7g; Sodium 33mg.*
Brown Bean Salad: *Energy 300kcal/1258kJ; Protein 16.6g; Carbohydrate 27.1g, of which sugars 2.5g; Fat 14.8g, of which saturates 2.5g; Cholesterol 95mg; Calcium 99mg; Fibre 9.9g; Sodium 50mg*

Artichokes with Beans and Aioli

As with the French aioli, there are many recipes for the Spanish equivalent. The one used here is exceptionally garlicky, a perfect partner to freshly cooked vegetables.

Serves 4

For the aioli

6 large garlic cloves, sliced
10ml/2 tsp white wine vinegar
250ml/8fl oz/1 cup olive oil
salt and ground black pepper

For the salad

225g/8oz French beans
3 small globe artichokes
15ml/1 tbsp olive oil
pared rind of 1 lemon
coarse salt and ground black pepper, to sprinkle
lemon wedges, to garnish

1 To make the aioli, put the garlic and vinegar in a blender or mini food processor. With the machine running, gradually pour in the olive oil until the mixture is thickened and very smooth. (Alternatively, crush the garlic to a paste with the vinegar and gradually beat in the oil using a hand whisk.) Season to taste.

2 To make the salad, cook the beans in boiling water for 1–2 minutes until slightly softened. Drain.

3 Trim the artichoke stalks close to the base. Cook the artichokes in a large pan of boiling salted water for about 30 minutes or until you can easily pull away a leaf from the base. Drain well.

4 Halve the cooked artichokes lengthways with a sharp knife and carefully pull out the choke using a teaspoon.

5 Arrange the artichokes and beans on serving plates and drizzle with the oil. Scatter with pared lemon rind and season with coarse salt and pepper. Spoon the aioli into the artichoke hearts and serve warm, garnished with lemon wedges.

Variation

Mediterranean baby artichokes are sometimes available and, unlike the larger ones, can be eaten whole.

Broad Bean and Feta Salad

This recipe is loosely based on a typical medley of fresh-tasting Greek salad ingredients – broad beans, tomatoes and feta cheese. It is lovely served warm or cold as an appetizer or main course accompaniment.

Serves 4–6

900g/2lb broad (fava) beans, shelled, or 350g/12oz shelled frozen beans
60ml/4 tbsp olive oil
175g/6oz plum tomatoes, halved, or quartered if large
4 garlic cloves, crushed
115g/4oz/1 cup firm feta cheese, cut into chunks
45ml/3 tbsp chopped fresh dill
12 black olives
salt and ground black pepper
chopped fresh dill, to garnish

1 Cook the fresh or frozen broad beans in boiling, salted water until just tender. Drain and set aside.

2 Meanwhile, heat the olive oil in a heavy frying pan and add the tomatoes and garlic. Cook until the tomatoes are beginning to colour.

3 Add the feta cheese to the pan and toss the ingredients together for 1 minute. Mix with the drained beans, dill, olives and salt and pepper. Turn into a salad bowl and serve garnished with chopped dill.

Artichokes with Beans & Aioli: *Energy 540kcal/2221kJ; Protein 2.1g; Carbohydrate 3.6g, of which sugars 2.9g; Fat 57.6g, of which saturates 8.2g; Cholesterol 0mg; Calcium 82mg; Fibre 3.1g; Sodium 80mg.*
Broad Bean & Feta Salad: *Energy 175kcal/727kJ; Protein 8.3g; Carbohydrate 8.8g, of which sugars 2.2g; Fat 12g, of which saturates 3.8g; Cholesterol 13mg; Calcium 121mg; Fibre 4.7g; Sodium 342mg.*

Warm Black-Eyed Bean Salad with Rocket

This is an easy dish to make without too much forward planning, as black-eyed beans do not need to be soaked overnight. Adding spring onions and loads of aromatic dill transforms them into a refreshing and healthy meal. The dish can be served hot or at room temperature.

Serves 4

275g/10oz/1½ cups black-eyed beans (peas)
5 spring onions (scallions), sliced into rounds
a large handful of fresh rocket (arugula) leaves, chopped if large
45–60ml/3–4 tbsp chopped fresh dill
150ml/¼ pint/⅔ cup extra virgin olive oil
juice of 1 lemon, or to taste
10–12 black olives
salt and ground black pepper
small cos or romaine lettuce leaves, to serve

1 Thoroughly rinse the beans and drain them well. Tip them into a pan and pour in cold water to just about cover them. Slowly bring them to the boil over a low heat. As soon as the water is boiling, remove the pan from the heat and drain the water off immediately.

2 Put the beans back in the pan with fresh cold water to cover and add a pinch of salt – this will make their skins harder and stop them from disintegrating when they are cooked.

3 Bring the beans to the boil over a medium heat, then lower the heat and cook them until they are soft but not mushy. They will take only 20–30 minutes, so keep an eye on them.

4 Drain the beans, reserving 75–90ml/5–6 tbsp of the cooking liquid. Tip the beans into a large salad bowl. Immediately add the remaining ingredients, including the reserved cooking liquid, and mix well.

5 Serve immediately, piled on the lettuce leaves, or leave to cool slightly before serving.

Baked Vegetables with Rosemary

The Spanish love to scoop up cooked vegetables with bread, and the local name of this dish, mojete, is derived from the word meaning "to dip". Peppers, tomatoes and onions are baked together to make a colourful, soft cooked salad, ideal for barbecues.

Serves 8

2 red (bell) peppers
2 yellow (bell) peppers
1 red onion, sliced
2 garlic cloves, halved
50g/2oz/⅓ cup black olives
6 large ripe tomatoes, quartered
5ml/1 tsp soft light brown sugar
45ml/3 tbsp Amontillado sherry
3–4 fresh rosemary sprigs
25ml/1½ tbsp olive oil
salt and ground black pepper
fresh bread, to serve

1 Halve the peppers lengthways and remove and discard the stalks, cores and seeds. Cut each pepper lengthways into 12 even strips. Preheat the oven to 200°C/400°F/Gas 6.

2 Place the peppers, onion, garlic, olives and tomatoes in a large non-stick roasting pan. Sprinkle the vegetables with the sugar, then pour in the sherry. Season well with salt and pepper, cover with foil and bake in the oven for 45 minutes.

3 Remove the foil from the pan and stir the mixture well. Add the rosemary sprigs and drizzle with the olive oil. Return the pan to the oven and bake, uncovered, for a further 30 minutes, or until the vegetables are very tender.

4 Serve hot or cold with plenty of fresh crusty bread.

Cook's Tip

Spain is the world's chief olive producer, with over 300 million trees. Much of the crop goes into the production of olive oil, and about half the olives sold as fruit are exported. Try to use good quality Spanish olives for this recipe. Choose unpitted ones as they have a better flavour.

Black-eyed Bean Salad: *Energy 238kcal/1007kJ; Protein 16.1g; Carbohydrate 31g, of which sugars 2.4g; Fat 6.4g, of which saturates 0.9g; Cholesterol 0mg; Calcium 114mg; Fibre 12.3g; Sodium 580mg.*
Baked Vegetables: *Energy 75kcal/313kJ; Protein 1.3g; Carbohydrate 7.5g, of which sugars 7.2g; Fat 3.9g, of which saturates 0.6g; Cholesterol 0mg; Calcium 17mg; Fibre 2g; Sodium 151mg.*

Rich Red Salad

This delectable and colourful recipe perfectly combines several red ingredients. Eat the dish at room temperature, accompanied by a leafy green salad and some good, crusty bread.

Serves 4

3 red (bell) peppers
6 large plum tomatoes
2.5 ml/½ tsp dried red chilli flakes
1 red onion, finely sliced
3 garlic cloves, finely chopped
grated rind and juice of 1 lemon
45 ml/3 tbsp chopped fresh flat leaf parsley
30 ml/2 tbsp extra-virgin olive oil
salt and ground black pepper
black and green olives and extra chopped flat leaf parsley, to garnish

1 Preheat the oven to 220°C/425°F/Gas 7. Place the peppers on a baking sheet and roast, turning occasionally, for 10 minutes or until the skins are almost blackened.

2 Add the tomatoes to the baking sheet and return to the oven for a further 5 minutes.

3 Place the peppers in a plastic bag and close the top loosely, trapping in the steam, to loosen the skins. Set aside, with the tomatoes, until they are cool enough to handle.

4 Carefully pull the skins off the peppers. Remove the core and seeds, then chop the peppers roughly and place in a mixing bowl. Chop the tomatoes roughly and add them to the bowl with the peppers.

5 Add the chilli flakes, onion, garlic, lemon rind and juice. Sprinkle over the parsley. Mix well, then transfer to a serving dish. Sprinkle with a little salt and black pepper, drizzle over the olive oil and scatter the olives and extra parsley over the top. Serve at room temperature.

Cook's Tip
Peel the tomatoes as well as the peppers, if you prefer.

Grilled Pepper Salad

Ideally this salad should be made with a combination of red and yellow peppers for the most jewel-like, colourful effect and the sweetest flavour.

Serves 6

4 large (bell) peppers, red or yellow or a combination of the two
30 ml/2 tbsp capers, rinsed
18–20 black or green olives

For the dressing

90 ml/6 tbsp extra-virgin olive oil
2 garlic cloves, finely chopped
30 ml/2 tbsp balsamic or wine vinegar
salt and ground black pepper

1 Place the peppers under a hot grill (broiler) and turn occasionally until they are black and blistered on all sides. Remove from the heat, place in a plastic food bag and close the top loosely to trap the steam and loosen the skins. Set aside until they are cool enough to handle.

2 Carefully peel the peppers, then cut them into quarters. Remove the stems and seeds.

3 Cut the peppers into strips, and arrange them on a serving dish. Distribute the capers and olives evenly over the peppers.

4 To make the dressing, mix the oil and garlic in a small bowl, crushing the garlic with a spoon to release the flavour. Mix in the vinegar and season with salt and pepper. Pour over the salad, mix well and leave to stand for at least 30 minutes before serving to allow the flavours of the dressing to permeate the peppers. Serve at room temperature.

Cook's Tip
- *Grilling (broiling) the peppers until they start to char not only softens and loosens the skins but intensifies their flavour and imparts a lovely smoky flavour to the flesh.*
- *Use any colour (bell) pepper for this salad except green, as green peppers are unripe and their flavour is too sour.*

Rich Red Salad: *Energy 122kcal/510kJ; Protein 2.5g; Carbohydrate 14.3g, of which sugars 13.5g; Fat 6.5g, of which saturates 1.1g; Cholesterol 0mg; Calcium 24mg; Fibre 3.8g; Sodium 18mg.*
Grilled Pepper Salad: *Energy 411kcal/1724kJ; Protein 10.8g; Carbohydrate 52.8g, of which sugars 8.2g; Fat 18.8g, of which saturates 2.8g; Cholesterol 3mg; Calcium 103mg; Fibre 4.6g; Sodium 41mg.*

Roasted Peppers with Tomatoes

This is a Sicilian-style salad, that uses some typical ingredients from the Italian island. The flavour improves if the salad is made about two hours before you plan to eat it.

Serves 4

1 red (bell) pepper
1 yellow (bell) pepper
1 green (bell) pepper
4 sun-dried tomatoes in oil, drained
4 ripe plum tomatoes, sliced
15ml/1 tbsp capers, drained
15ml/1 tbsp pine nuts
1 garlic clove, very thinly sliced
fresh basil sprigs, to garnish

For the dressing

75ml/5 tbsp extra virgin olive oil
15ml/1 tbsp balsamic vinegar
5ml/1 tsp lemon juice
chopped fresh mixed herbs, such as oregano, basil and flat leaf parsley
salt and ground black pepper

1 Preheat the grill (broiler). Cut the peppers in half and remove the seeds and stalks. Cut into quarters and cook, skin-side up, under the hot grill until the skin chars.

2 Put the peppers into a plastic bag and seal loosely to trap the steam and loosen the skin. Leave until cool enough to handle, then peel the pepper halves and cut into strips.

3 Thinly slice the sun-dried tomatoes. Arrange the peppers and fresh tomatoes on a serving dish and scatter over the sun-dried tomatoes, capers, pine nuts and garlic.

4 To make the dressing, mix together the olive oil, balsamic vinegar, lemon juice and chopped fresh herbs and season with salt and pepper to taste. Pour over the salad and leave the bowl in a cool place for the flavours to infuse. Scatter with fresh basil leaves before serving.

Cook's Tip
A little of the flavoured oil from the jar of sun-dried tomatoes can be added to the dressing if you like.

Roasted Peppers with Tomatoes and Artichokes

If you have time, make and dress this salad an hour or two before serving, as this will allow the juices to mingle and create the most mouthwatering salad.

Serves 4

1 red (bell) pepper
1 yellow (bell) pepper
1 green (bell) pepper
4 ripe plum tomatoes, sliced
2 canned or bottled artichokes, drained and quartered
4 sun-dried tomatoes in oil, drained and thinly sliced
15ml/1 tbsp capers, drained
15ml/1 tbsp pine nuts
1 garlic clove, sliced thinly

For the dressing

15ml/1 tbsp balsamic vinegar
5ml/1 tsp lemon juice
75ml/5 tbsp extra virgin olive oil
chopped fresh mixed herbs
salt and freshly ground black pepper

1 Preheat the grill (broiler) to high. Cut the peppers in half, and remove the seeds and stalks. Cut into quarters and place on a grill pan covered with foil. Grill (broil), skin-side up until the skin chars.

2 Put the peppers into a plastic bag and seal loosely to trap the steam and loosen the skin. Leave until cool enough to handle, then peel the peppers and cut into strips.

3 Arrange the peppers, fresh tomatoes and artichokes on a serving dish. Sprinkle over the sun-dried tomatoes, the capers, pine nuts and the garlic.

4 To make the dressing, put the balsamic vinegar and lemon juice in a bowl and whisk in the olive oil, then the chopped herbs. Season with salt and pepper. Pour the dressing over the salad an hour or two before it is served, if possible.

Variation
The flavour of the salad can be varied by using different herbs in the salad dressing.

Roasted Peppers with Tomatoes: *Energy 216kcal/890kJ; Protein 1.5g; Carbohydrate 8.1g, of which sugars 7.9g; Fat 19.9g, of which saturates 2.9g; Cholesterol 0mg; Calcium 22mg; Fibre 2.4g; Sodium 24mg.*
Peppers with Tomatoes and Artichokes: *Energy 218kcal/902kJ; Protein 3.2g; Carbohydrate 12.7g, of which sugars 12.2g; Fat 17.4g, of which saturates 2.4g; Cholesterol 0mg; Calcium 73mg; Fibre 4.6g; Sodium 62mg.*

Spiced Aubergine Salad

The delicate flavours of aubergine, tomatoes and cucumber are lightly spiced with cumin and coriander in this fresh-tasting salad, which is topped with yogurt. It is lovely with grilled kebabs or fried fish, or a rice dish.

Serves 4

2 small aubergines (eggplants), sliced
75ml/5 tbsp extra virgin olive oil
50ml/2fl oz/¼ cup red wine vinegar
2 garlic cloves, crushed
15ml/1 tbsp lemon juice
2.5ml/½ tsp ground cumin
2.5ml/½ tsp ground coriander
½ cucumber, thinly sliced
2 well-flavoured tomatoes, thinly sliced
30ml/2 tbsp natural (plain) yogurt
salt and ground black pepper
chopped fresh flat leaf parsley, to garnish

1 Preheat the grill (broiler). Lightly brush the aubergine slices with olive oil and cook under a high heat, turning once, until golden and tender. Alternatively, cook them on a griddle pan.

2 When they are done, remove the aubergine slices to a chopping board and cut them into quarters.

3 Mix together the remaining oil, the vinegar, garlic, lemon juice, cumin and coriander. Season with salt and pepper and mix thoroughly. Add the warm aubergines, stir well and chill for at least 2 hours.

4 Add the cucumber and tomatoes to the aubergines. Transfer to a serving dish and spoon the yogurt on top. Sprinkle with parsley and serve.

Cook's Tips

The advice is often given to sprinkle sliced aubergines with salt and leave them to disgorge their bitter juices. Most modern varieties of aubergine are not bitter, but this technique is also useful in breaking down the cell walls of the fruit to reduce their capacity to absorb oil.

Marinated Courgettes

This is a simple summer dish served all over Italy when courgettes are in season. It has a light and fresh flavour and can be eaten hot or cold. It is a delicious accompaniment to many meals and would be excellent served with grilled lamb steaks and roasted new potatoes.

Serves 6

4 courgettes (zucchini), sliced
30ml/2 tbsp extra virgin olive oil
30ml/2 tbsp chopped fresh mint, plus whole leaves, to garnish
30ml/2 tbsp white wine vinegar
salt and ground black pepper

1 Fry the courgette slices in 15ml/1 tbsp of the oil in batches, for 4–6 minutes, or until tender and brown around the edges. Transfer to a bowl. Season well with salt and pepper.

2 Heat the remaining oil in the pan, then add the chopped mint and vinegar and let it bubble for a few seconds. Stir into the courgettes. Set aside to marinate for 1 hour, then serve garnished with mint leaves.

Aubergine, Lemon and Caper Salad

Ensure you cook the aubergine until it is meltingly soft and luscious.

Serves 6

1 aubergine (eggplant), about 675g/1½lb, cut into 2.5cm/1in cubes
60ml/4 tbsp olive oil
grated rind and juice of 1 lemon
30ml/2 tbsp capers, rinsed
12 pitted green olives
30ml/2 tbsp chopped fresh flat leaf parsley
salt and ground black pepper

1 Shallow fry the aubergine cubes for about 10 minutes until soft and golden. Drain on kitchen paper, sprinkled with salt.

2 In a large bowl, toss the aubergine with the rest of the ingredients and season well. Serve at room temperature.

Spiced Aubergine Salad: *Energy 161kcal/669kJ; Protein 2.3g; Carbohydrate 5.8g, of which sugars 5.5g; Fat 14.6g, of which saturates 2.2g; Cholesterol 0mg; Calcium 37mg; Fibre 3.7g; Sodium 15mg.*
Marinated Courgettes: *Energy 60kcal/248kJ; Protein 2.7g; Carbohydrate 2.8g, of which sugars 2.3g; Fat 4.3g, of which saturates 0.7g; Cholesterol 0mg; Calcium 49mg; Fibre 1.2g; Sodium 3mg.*
Aubergine, Lemon & Caper: *Energy 141kcal/585kJ; Protein 2g; Carbohydrate 4.1g, of which sugars 3.7g; Fat 13.2g, of which saturates 2g; Cholesterol 0mg; Calcium 50mg; Fibre 4.4g; Sodium 289mg.*

Rosemary Roasties

These tasty Italian-style roast potatoes use far less fat than traditional roast potatoes, and because they still have their skins they not only absorb less oil but also have more flavour.

Serves 4

1kg/2¼lb small red potatoes
10ml/2 tsp walnut or sunflower oil
30ml/2 tbsp fresh rosemary leaves
salt and paprika

1 Preheat the oven to 240°C/475°F/Gas 9. Leave the potatoes whole with the skins on or, if large, cut in half. Place the potatoes in a large pan of cold water and bring to the boil, then remove from the heat. Drain well.

2 Drizzle the walnut or sunflower oil over the potatoes and shake the pan to coat them evenly.

3 Tip the potatoes into a shallow roasting pan. Sprinkle with rosemary, salt and paprika. Roast in the oven for 30 minutes or until cooked and crisp. Serve hot.

Cook's Tip

You can serve these potatoes with roasted meat in the traditional way, but as they cook so quickly they can also accompany many other dishes.

Potato Gnocchi

Gnocchi are little Italian dumplings made either with mashed potato and flour, as in this recipe, or with semolina. They should be light in texture, and must not be overworked while being made. They can be simply dressed with butter and cheese, or served with a variety of sauces.

Serves 6

1kg/2¼lb waxy potatoes, scrubbed
250–300g/9–11oz/2–2½ cups plain (all-purpose) flour
1 egg
pinch of grated nutmeg
25g/1oz/2 tbsp butter
salt
a little grated fresh Parmesan cheese, to serve

1 Place the unpeeled potatoes in a large pan of salted water. Bring to the boil and cook until tender but not falling apart. Drain. Peel as soon as possible, while the potatoes are still hot.

2 Sprinkle the work surface with flour. Pass the hot potatoes through a food mill on to the flour. Sprinkle with about half the remaining flour and mix it very lightly into the potatoes. Break the egg into the mixture, add the nutmeg and knead lightly, drawing in more flour as necessary. When the dough is light to the touch and no longer sticky it is ready to be rolled.

3 Divide the dough into four parts. On a lightly floured board, quickly form each part into a roll about 2cm/¾in in diameter. Cut the rolls crossways into pieces about 2cm/¾in long.

4 Hold a fork with the tips of its tines resting on the board. Roll each piece lightly down the tines towards the points, making ridges on one side.

5 Bring a large pan of water to a fast boil. Add salt and drop in about half the gnocchi. When they rise to the surface, after 3–4 minutes, the gnocchi are done. Scoop them out, allow to drain and place in a warmed serving bowl. Dot with butter. Keep warm while the remaining gnocchi are boiling.

6 As soon as they are cooked, toss the drained gnocchi with the butter, sprinkle with a little grated Parmesan and serve.

__Rosemary Roasties:__ Energy 189kcal/801kJ; Protein 4.3g; Carbohydrate 40.3g, of which sugars 3.3g; Fat 2.3g, of which saturates 0.4g; Cholesterol 0mg; Calcium 15mg; Fibre 2.5g; Sodium 28mg.
__Potato Gnocchi:__ Energy 296kcal/1254kJ; Protein 7.8g; Carbohydrate 59.2g, of which sugars 2.8g; Fat 4.7g, of which saturates 2.3g; Cholesterol 39mg; Calcium 74mg; Fibre 3g; Sodium 52mg.

Patatas Bravas

There are several variations on this Spanish chilli and potato dish, whose name translates literally as "fierce potatoes", but the most important thing is the spicing, which is made even more piquant by adding vinegar. The classic version is made with fresh tomato sauce flavoured with garlic and chilli, and the potatoes are always cut small.

Serves 4

675g/1½lb small new potatoes
25ml/1½ tbsp olive oil
2 garlic cloves, sliced
3 dried chillies, seeded and chopped
2.5ml/½ tsp ground cumin
10ml/2 tsp paprika
30ml/2 tbsp red or white wine vinegar
1 red or green (bell) pepper, sliced
coarse sea salt, for sprinkling

1 Scrub the potatoes and put them into a pan of salted water. Bring to the boil and cook for 10 minutes, or until almost tender. Drain and leave to cool slightly. Peel, if you like, then cut into chunks.

2 Heat the oil in a large non-stick frying or sauté pan and fry the potatoes, turning them frequently, until golden.

3 Meanwhile, crush together the garlic, chillies and cumin using a mortar and pestle. Mix the paste with the paprika and wine vinegar, then add to the potatoes with the sliced pepper and cook, stirring, for 2 minutes. Sprinkle with salt and serve hot as a tapas dish or cold as a side dish.

Potatoes Baked with Tomatoes

This simple, hearty dish from the south of Italy is best when tomatoes are in season and bursting with flavour, but at other times it can be made with canned plum tomatoes.

Serves 6

90ml/6 tbsp olive oil, plus extra for greasing
2 large red or yellow onions, thinly sliced
1kg/2¼lb baking potatoes, thinly sliced
450g/1lb fresh tomatoes, sliced or 400g/14oz can chopped tomatoes
115g/4oz/1–1⅓ cups freshly grated Cheddar or Parmesan cheese
a few fresh basil leaves
60ml/4 tbsp water
salt and ground black pepper

1 Preheat the oven to 180°C/350°F/Gas 4. Brush a large ovenproof dish generously with oil. Arrange some onions in a layer on the base of the dish, followed by a layer of potato and tomato slices, alternating the three.

2 Pour a little of the oil over the surface of the layered ingredients, and sprinkle with some of the cheese. Season with salt and add a generous grinding of black pepper.

3 Continue to layer the ingredients in the dish until they are used up, adding oil, cheese and seasoning as before, and ending with an overlapping layer of potatoes and tomatoes.

4 Tear the basil leaves into small pieces, and add them here and there among the top layer, saving a few for garnish. Sprinkle the top with the remaining grated cheese and oil.

5 Pour the water over the dish. Bake in the oven for 1 hour until the ingredients are tender.

6 Check the potatoes towards the end of the cooking time and if the top is browning too much, place a sheet of foil or greaseproof (waxed) paper, or a flat baking sheet, on top of the dish. Garnish the dish with the remaining fresh basil leaves, and serve hot.

Patatas Bravas: *Energy 256kcal/1070kJ; Protein 3.3g; Carbohydrate 30g, of which sugars 4.9g; Fat 14.4g, of which saturates 2.2g; Cholesterol 0mg; Calcium 14mg; Fibre 2.4g; Sodium 20mg.*

Potatoes with Tomatoes: *Energy 339kcal/1418kJ; Protein 11.7g; Carbohydrate 34.4g, of which sugars 8.2g; Fat 18.1g, of which saturates 5.8g; Cholesterol 19mg; Calcium 262mg; Fibre 3.4g; Sodium 236mg.*

Greek Potato and Tomato Bake

This is an adaptation of a classic Greek dish, which is usually cooked in a pot on the stove. This recipe has a richer flavour as it is stove-cooked first and then baked in the oven, so that the potatoes have time to absorb the flavours of the onion, tomatoes and garlic. The tomatoes provide all the liquid needed in the casserole. It is a lovely accompaniment to plainly cooked meat or fish dishes.

Serves 4

120ml/4fl oz/½ cup extra virgin olive oil
1 large onion, finely chopped
3 garlic cloves, crushed
4 large ripe tomatoes, peeled, seeded and chopped
1kg/2¼lb even-size main-crop waxy potatoes
salt and ground black pepper
a few sprigs of fresh flat leaf parsley, to garnish

1 Preheat the oven to 180°C/350°F/Gas 4.

2 Heat the oil in a flameproof casserole. Fry the chopped onion and garlic for 5 minutes, or until softened and just starting to brown.

3 Add the tomatoes to the pan, season and cook for 1 minute.

4 Cut the potatoes into wedges. Add to the pan, stirring well. Cook for 10 minutes. Season again with salt and pepper, and cover with a tight-fitting lid.

5 Place the covered casserole on the middle shelf of the oven and cook for 45 minutes–1 hour. Garnish with a few sprigs of fresh flat leaf parsley.

Cook's Tips

- *Make sure that the potatoes are evenly sized and completely coated in the olive oil otherwise they will not cook evenly.*
- *Replace the fresh tomatoes with a 400g/14oz can of plum tomatoes.*

Potatoes Baked with Fennel, Onions, Garlic and Saffron

Potatoes, fennel and onions infused with garlic, saffron and spices make a sophisticated and attractive accompaniment for fish or chicken or an egg-based main-course dish.

Serves 4–6

500g/1¼lb small waxy potatoes, cut into chunks or wedges
good pinch of saffron strands (12–15 strands)
1 head of garlic, separated into cloves
12 small red or yellow onions, peeled but left whole
3 fennel bulbs, cut into wedges, feathery tops reserved
4–6 fresh bay leaves
6–9 fresh thyme sprigs
175ml/6fl oz/¾ cup fish, chicken or vegetable stock
30ml/2 tbsp sherry vinegar
2.5ml/½ tsp sugar
5ml/1 tsp fennel seeds, lightly crushed
2.5ml/½ tsp paprika
45ml/3 tbsp olive oil
salt and ground black pepper

1 Boil the potatoes in salted water for 8–10 minutes. Drain. Preheat the oven to 190°C/375°F/Gas 5. Soak the saffron in 30ml/2 tbsp warm water for 10 minutes.

2 Peel and finely chop 2 garlic cloves. Place the potatoes, onions, unpeeled garlic cloves, fennel wedges, bay leaves and thyme sprigs in a roasting dish.

3 Mix together the stock, saffron and its soaking liquid, vinegar and sugar, then pour over the vegetables. Stir in the fennel seeds, paprika, garlic and oil, and season with salt and pepper.

4 Cook in the oven for 1–1¼ hours, stirring occasionally, until the vegetables are tender. Chop the reserved fennel tops, sprinkle over the vegetables and serve.

Cook's Tip

Saffron gives this dish its distinctive colour and flavour, but it is still delicious if made without saffron.

Greek Potato Bake: Energy 399kcal/1670kJ; Protein 5.9g; Carbohydrate 49.3g, of which sugars 10.6g; Fat 21.2g, of which saturates 3.2g; Cholesterol 0mg; Calcium 41mg; Fibre 4.6g; Sodium 39mg.
Potatoes Baked with Fennel: Energy 162kcal/676kJ; Protein 4.4g; Carbohydrate 23.6g, of which sugars 7.1g; Fat 6.2g, of which saturates 0.9g; Cholesterol 0mg; Calcium 49mg; Fibre 4.9g; Sodium 23mg.

French Scalloped Potatoes

These potatoes taste rich even though only a little cream is used. In France they are nearly always served with roast lamb.

Serves 6

1kg/2¼lb potatoes
900ml/1½ pints/3⅔ cups milk
pinch of freshly grated nutmeg
1 bay leaf
15–30ml/1–2 tbsp butter, softened
2 or 3 garlic cloves, very finely chopped
45–60ml/3–4 tbsp crème fraîche or whipping cream
salt and ground black pepper

1 Preheat the oven to 180°C/350°F/Gas 4. Cut the potatoes into fairly thin slices. Put them in a large pan and pour over the milk, adding more to cover if needed. Add the salt and pepper, nutmeg and the bay leaf. Bring slowly to the boil over a medium heat and simmer for about 15 minutes until the potatoes just start to soften, but are not completely cooked, and the milk has thickened.

2 Generously butter a 36cm/14in oval gratin dish and sprinkle the garlic over the base.

3 Using a slotted spoon, transfer the potatoes to the gratin or baking dish. Taste the milk and adjust the seasoning, then pour over enough of the milk to come just to the surface of the potatoes, but not cover them.

4 Spoon a thin layer of cream over the top, or, if you prefer, add more of the thickened milk to cover.

5 Bake the potatoes for about 1 hour until the milk is absorbed and the top is a deep golden brown.

Cook's Tip
If cooked ahead, this dish will keep hot in a low oven for an hour or so without suffering. Moisten the top with a little extra cream, if you like.

Wilted Spinach with Rice and Dill

Spinach is a characterful vegetable that plays a starring role in many recipes and this is a delicious dish that can be made in very little time. In Greece it is particularly popular during periods of fasting, when meat is avoided for religious reasons. As a side dish, it provides a complete accompaniment to meat or fish.

Serves 6

675g/1½lb fresh spinach, trimmed of any hard stalks
105ml/7 tbsp extra virgin olive oil
1 large onion, chopped
juice of ½ lemon
150ml/¼ pint/⅔ cup water
115g/4oz/generous ½ cup long grain rice
45ml/3 tbsp chopped fresh dill, plus extra sprigs to garnish
salt and ground black pepper

1 Thoroughly wash the spinach in cold water and drain. Repeat up to four or five times, until the spinach is completely clean and free of grit, then drain it completely in a colander. Brush off the excess water with kitchen paper and coarsely shred the spinach leaves.

2 Heat the olive oil in a large pan and sauté the onion until translucent. Add the spinach and stir for a few minutes to coat it with the oil.

3 As soon as the spinach looks wilted, add the lemon juice and the measured water and bring to the boil. Add the rice and half of the dill, then cover and cook gently for about 10 minutes or until the rice is cooked to your taste. If it looks too dry, add a little hot water.

4 Spoon the spinach and rice into a serving dish and sprinkle the sprigs of dill over the top. Serve the dish hot or at room temperature.

Cook's Tip
This dish is ideal to accompany fried or barbecued fish or chickpea rissoles. It can also be eaten as a first course.

Scalloped Potatoes: *Energy 204kcal/866kJ; Protein 8g; Carbohydrate 33.9g, of which sugars 9.2g; Fat 5.1g, of which saturates 3.1g; Cholesterol 14mg; Calcium 191mg; Fibre 1.7g; Sodium 98mg.*
Spinach with Rice: *Energy 325kcal/1344kJ; Protein 7.8g; Carbohydrate 29.9g, of which sugars 5.6g; Fat 19.2g, of which saturates 2.7g; Cholesterol 0mg; Calcium 328mg; Fibre 4.8g; Sodium 242mg.*

Artichokes with New Potatoes

Among the first vegetables to appear each year, globe artichokes begin to come into season in Greece in the middle of spring, together with fresh broad (fava) beans and aromatic bunches of dill. All round the eastern Mediterranean artichokes are often served with broad beans in a lemony dressing, but they are also cooked in various combinations with many other spring vegetables. This recipe makes a lovely seasonal first course.

Serves 4

4 globe artichokes
juice of 1½ lemons
150ml/¼ pint/⅔ cup extra virgin olive oil
1 large onion, thinly sliced
3 carrots, peeled and sliced into long batons
300ml/½ pint/1¼ cups hot water
400g/14oz small new potatoes, scrubbed or peeled
4 or 5 spring onions (scallions), chopped
60–75ml/4–5 tbsp chopped fresh dill
salt and ground black pepper

1 Remove and discard the outer leaves of the artichoke until you reach the tender ones. Cut off the top, halfway down. Scoop out the hairy choke. Cut off the stalk, leaving 4cm/1½in, and peel away its outer surface.

2 Drop the prepared artichokes into a bowl of cold water acidulated with about one-third of the lemon juice, which is about half a lemon. Add enough hot water to just about cover the artichokes.

3 Heat the extra virgin olive oil in a pan and sauté the onion slices gently over a low to medium heat until they become translucent. Next add the carrots and sauté for 2–3 minutes. Add the remaining lemon juice and the hot water, stir, and bring to the boil.

4 Drain the artichokes and add them to the pan with the potatoes, spring onions and seasoning. The vegetables should be almost covered with the sauce, so add a little more hot water if needed. Cover and cook gently for 40–45 minutes. Sprinkle the dill over the top and cook for 2–3 minutes more.

Tabbouleh

This classic Lebanese salad, made using large quantities of chopped fresh parsley and mint, is very popular in many Mediterranean countries. It is often served as part of a meze table, accompanied by small leaves from the heart of a cos lettuce, which are used to scoop up the salad, but it also makes an ideal substitute for a rice dish on a buffet table and is excellent served with roasted meats of all kinds.

Serves 4

175g/6oz/1 cup fine bulgur wheat
juice of 1 lemon
45ml/3 tbsp olive oil
60ml/4 tbsp fresh parsley, finely chopped
45ml/3 tbsp fresh mint, chopped
4–5 spring onions (scallions), chopped
1 green pepper, seeded and sliced
salt and freshly ground black pepper
2 large tomatoes, diced, and black olives, to garnish

1 Put the bulgur wheat in a bowl. Add enough cold water to cover the wheat and let it stand for at least 30 minutes and up to 2 hours, until swollen and softened.

2 Drain the bulgur wheat and squeeze it with your hands to remove any excess water. (The wheat will swell to double its original size.) Spread it out on kitchen paper to allow the wheat to dry completely.

3 Place the bulgur wheat in a large mixing bowl, add the lemon juice, olive oil and a little salt and pepper to taste. Allow the mixture to stand for 1–2 hours, if possible, in order for all the flavours in the salad to develop fully.

4 Add the chopped parsley, mint, spring onions and pepper and mix well. Garnish with diced tomatoes and olives.

Cook's tip
Bulgur, also known as burghul and cracked wheat, is whole wheat boiled until just tender, then dried and coarsely ground.

Artichokes with New Potatoes: *Energy 342kcal/1420kJ; Protein 3.2g; Carbohydrate 26.1g, of which sugars 9.8g; Fat 25.7g, of which saturates 3.8g; Cholesterol 0mg; Calcium 60mg; Fibre 4g; Sodium 60mg.*
Tabbouleh: *Energy 204kcal/848kJ; Protein 4.3g; Carbohydrate 24.8g, of which sugars 3.3g; Fat 10.3g, of which saturates 1.4g; Cholesterol 0mg; Calcium 91mg; Fibre 2.6g; Sodium 18mg.*

Rice with Lentils

Lentils are a favourite staple in Greece, especially during periods of fasting in the Orthodox tradition, when meat is not eaten, as they are a nourishing source of protein. In this dish, which is also eaten all over the Middle East, they are combined with rice and spices, making a satisfying side dish to accompany simply fried fish or grilled meat, or a main course to eat with salad.

Serves 6
350g/12oz/1½ cups large brown lentils, soaked overnight in water
2 large onions
45ml/3 tbsp olive oil
15ml/1 tbsp ground cumin
2.5ml/½ tsp ground cinnamon
225g/8oz/generous 1 cup long grain rice
salt and freshly ground black pepper
a few sprigs of fresh flat leaf parsley, to garnish

1 Drain the lentils and put them in a large pan. Add enough cold water to cover the lentils by 5cm/2in. Bring to the boil, cover and simmer for 40 minutes to 1½ hours, or until tender. Drain thoroughly.

2 Finely chop one of the large onions, and finely slice the other. Heat 15ml/1 tbsp olive oil in a large saucepan, add the finely chopped onion and fry until soft. Do not allow to brown.

3 Add the drained lentils and gently stir them in so that they are thoroughly coated in the oil. Then add the cumin and coriander and stir in. Season to taste with salt and freshly ground black pepper.

4 Measure the volume of rice and add it, with the same volume of water, to the lentil mixture. Cover and simmer for about 20 minutes, until the rice is tender.

5 Heat the remaining olive oil in a frying pan, and cook the sliced onion over a medium heat until it has softened and caramelized to a very dark brown. Tip the rice mixture into a serving bowl, sprinkle with the onion rings and serve hot or cold, garnished with flat leaf parsley.

Spicy Roasted Vegetables

Oven roasting brings out and intensifies all the flavours of cherry tomatoes, courgettes (zucchini), onion and red peppers. Serve hot with couscous or rice for a vegetarian meal, or as a side dish with meat or fish.

Serves 4
2–3 courgettes (zucchini)
1 Spanish onion
2 red (bell) peppers
16 cherry tomatoes
2 garlic cloves, chopped
pinch of cumin seeds
5ml/1 tsp fresh thyme or 4–5 torn fresh basil leaves
60ml/4 tbsp olive oil
juice of ½ lemon
5–10ml/1–2 tsp harissa or Tabasco sauce
fresh thyme sprigs, to garnish

1 Preheat the oven to 220°C/425°F/ Gas 7. Trim the courgettes and cut them into long strips. Cut the onion into thin wedges. Cut the peppers into chunks, discarding the seeds and core.

2 Mix these vegetables together and spread them out in a cast-iron dish or roasting pan.

3 Add the cherry tomatoes, chopped garlic, cumin seeds and thyme or torn basil leaves.

4 Sprinkle the vegetables with the olive oil and toss to coat them evenly. Cook the mixture in the oven for 25–30 minutes until the vegetables are very soft and have begun to char slightly at the edges.

5 Meanwhile, mix the lemon juice with the harissa or Tabasco sauce. Stir into the vegetables when they are cooked, garnish with the thyme and serve immediately.

Cook's Tip
Harissa is a chilli paste, popular in North Africa. It can be bought in cans or jars and contains pounded chillies, garlic, coriander, olive oil and seasoning.

Rice with Lentils: *Energy 394Kcal/1,656kJ; Protein 17.5g; Carbohydrate 68g, of which sugars 5.1g; Fat 6.6g, of which saturates 0.9g; Cholesterol 0mg; Calcium 54mg; Fibre 3.8g; Sodium 23mg.*
Spicy Roasted Vegetables: *Energy 117kcal/484kJ; Protein 4.1g; Carbohydrate 14g, of which sugars 11.2g; Fat 5.2g, of which saturates 0.8g; Cholesterol 0mg; Calcium 77mg; Fibre 3.4g; Sodium 9mg.*

Baked Tomatoes with Orange Zest

Cooking tomatoes in the oven intensifies their flavour, and this recipe is given a fruity edge with a hint of orange. For the best results, use Italian plum tomatoes, which have a warm, slightly sweet flavour. They are also fleshier and have fewer seeds than other varieties. Serve this tasty dish with fresh crusty Italian bread or crispbreads.

Serves 4

25g/1oz/2 tbsp unsalted butter
1 large garlic clove, crushed
5ml/1 tsp finely grated orange rind
4 firm plum tomatoes, or 2 large beef tomatoes
salt and ground black pepper
fresh basil leaves, to garnish

1 Soften the butter in a small bowl and blend with the crushed garlic, orange rind, and seasoning. Chill for a few minutes.

2 Preheat the oven to 200°C/400°F/Gas 6. Halve the tomatoes crossways and trim the bases so they stand upright.

3 Place the tomatoes in an ovenproof dish and spread the butter equally over each.

4 Bake the tomatoes in the oven for 15–25 minutes, depending on the size of the tomato halves, until just tender. Serve sprinkled with the fresh basil leaves.

Cook's Tip
Choose a dish in which the tomato halves will fit snugly, without too much space between them. Serve them straight from the dish if possible.

Variation
Sprinkle a few black olives among the tomatoes in the dish or sprinkle the tomatoes with a little Parmesan cheese.

Roasted Garlic with Plum Tomatoes

These are so simple to prepare yet taste absolutely wonderful. Use a large, shallow earthenware dish that will allow the tomatoes to sear and char in a hot oven. The recipe includes a lot of garlic, but the cloves are left whole and the flavour is subtle. Garlic lovers can squeeze the softened cloves out of their skins and eat the sweet flesh with the tomatoes.

Serves 4

8 plum tomatoes, halved
12 garlic cloves
20ml/4 tsp extra virgin olive oil
3 bay leaves
salt and ground black pepper
45ml/3 tbsp fresh oregano leaves, to garnish

1 Preheat the oven to 230°C/450°F/Gas 8. Select an ovenproof dish that will hold all the tomatoes snugly in a single layer. Place the tomatoes in the dish and push the whole, unpeeled garlic cloves between them.

2 Lightly brush the tomatoes with the oil, add the bay leaves and sprinkle black pepper over the top. Bake in the oven for about 45 minutes, until the tomatoes have softened and are sizzling in the dish. They should be charred around the edges. Season with salt and a little more black pepper, if needed. Garnish with oregano leaves and serve immediately.

***Baked Tomatoes:** Energy 65kcal/269kJ; Protein 0.8g; Carbohydrate 3.4g, of which sugars 3.2g; Fat 5.5g, of which saturates 3.4g; Cholesterol 13mg; Calcium 8mg; Fibre 1.1g; Sodium 47mg.*
***Roasted Garlic:** Energy 70kcal/294kJ; Protein 1.8g; Carbohydrate 7.8g, of which sugars 7.8g; Fat 3.8g, of which saturates 0.7g; Cholesterol 0mg; Calcium 18mg; Fibre 2.5g; Sodium 23mg.*

Courgette and Asparagus Parcels

To appreciate their delicate aromas, it's best if these Italian-style vegetable-filled paper parcels are brought to the table sealed, to be broken open by the diners. They are a lovely way to celebrate the unique flavours of early summer vegetables, and make a tasty and low-fat accompaniment to grilled fish or chicken.

Serves 4

2 courgettes (zucchini)
1 leek
225g/8oz young asparagus, trimmed
4 tarragon sprigs
4 whole garlic cloves, unpeeled
1 egg, beaten, to glaze
salt and ground black pepper

1 Preheat the oven to 200°C/400°F/Gas 6. Using a potato peeler, carefully slice the courgettes lengthways into thin strips. (Discard the first and last strips of skin.)

2 Cut the leek into very fine julienne strips and cut the asparagus evenly into 5cm/2in lengths.

3 Cut out four sheets of greaseproof (waxed) paper measuring 30 × 38cm/12 × 15in and fold each one in half. Draw a large curve to make a oval when unfolded. Cut along the inside of the line and open out.

4 Divide the courgettes, leek and asparagus evenly between each sheet of paper, positioning the filling on one side of the fold line, then top each portion with a sprig of tarragon and an unpeeled garlic clove. Season to taste.

5 Brush the edges of the paper lightly with the beaten egg and fold over.

6 Twist the edges of the paper together tightly and firmly so that each parcel is completely sealed. Lay the parcels on a baking sheet.

7 Bake in the preheated oven for 10 minutes. Serve the parcels immediately.

Courgette and Tomato Bake

This dish has been made for centuries in Provence. Its French name is Tian Provençal, from the shallow earthenware casserole, known as a *tian*, in which it is traditionally cooked. In the days before home kitchens had ovens, this kind of dish would have been assembled at home and then carried to the baker's to make use of the heat remaining in the oven after the bread was baked.

Serves 4

15ml/1 tbsp olive oil, plus more for drizzling
1 large onion (about 225g/8oz), sliced
1 garlic clove, finely chopped
450g/1lb tomatoes
450g/1lb courgettes (zucchini)
5ml/1 tsp dried herbes de Provence
30ml/2 tbsp grated Parmesan cheese
salt and ground black pepper

1 Preheat the oven to 180°C/350°F/Gas 4. Heat the oil in a heavy pan over a low heat and cook the sliced onion with the garlic very gently for about 20 minutes until they are soft and golden. Spread the mixture over the base of a 30cm/12in shallow baking dish.

2 Cut the tomatoes crossways into 6mm/¼in thick slices. (If the tomatoes are very large, cut the slices in half.)

3 Trim the courgettes and cut them diagonally into slices about 1cm/½in thick.

4 Arrange alternating rows of courgettes and tomatoes over the onion mixture and sprinkle with the dried herbs and cheese. Season with salt and pepper. Drizzle with olive oil, then bake for 25 minutes until the vegetables are tender. Serve the dish hot or warm.

Cook's Tip
Choose large, ripe tomatoes that have plenty of flavour and slim, evenly sized courgettes for this dish.

Courgette Parcels: Energy 51kcal/211kJ; Protein 4.9g; Carbohydrate 4.2g, of which sugars 3.7g; Fat 1.7g, of which saturates 0.4g; Cholesterol 24mg; Calcium 54mg; Fibre 2.8g; Sodium 11mg.
Courgette and Tomato Bake: Energy 302kcal/1255kJ; Protein 16.4g; Carbohydrate 14.6g, of which sugars 5.2g; Fat 20.2g, of which saturates 6.5g; Cholesterol 120mg; Calcium 249mg; Fibre 2.1g; Sodium 495mg.

Courgettes with Onion and Garlic

Use good-quality olive oil for this dish. Blended with sunflower oil it will give the courgettes a delicious fragrance without overpowering them, making this an ideal vegetable accompaniment for light meat or fish.

Serves 4

10ml/2 tsp olive oil
10ml/2 tsp sunflower oil
1 large onion, chopped
1 garlic clove, crushed
4–5 courgettes (zucchini), cut into 1cm/½ in slices
150ml/¼ pint/⅔ cup vegetable stock
2.5ml/½ tsp chopped fresh oregano
salt and ground black pepper
chopped fresh parsley, to garnish

1 Heat the olive and sunflower oils in a large frying pan and fry the onion with the garlic over a moderate heat for 5–6 minutes, stirring occasionally, until the onion has softened and is beginning to brown.

2 Add the sliced courgettes and fry for about 4 minutes until they begin to be flecked with brown, stirring frequently.

3 Stir in the stock, oregano and seasoning and simmer gently for 8–10 minutes or until the liquid has almost evaporated, stirring occasionally.

4 Spoon the courgettes into a warmed serving dish, sprinkle with chopped parsley and serve immediately.

Cook's Tips

- *This is a fairly robust treatment for courgettes, and is a good way to use them when they are slightly too large to steam. At the end of cooking they will be soft and well flavoured by the stock, but not mushy.*
- *When courgettes are very young and fresh, make the most of their flavour and texture by serving them raw, as crudités and in salads, or very lightly steamed.*

Baked Courgettes in Passata

Sliced courgettes layered with mild red onions and passata, are seasoned with fresh thyme, then baked in the oven to make a delicious, virtually fat-free and trouble-free vegetable dish. Once cooked, it will happily sit, covered, in a warm oven for a while until the rest of the meal is ready.

Serves 4

5ml/1 tsp olive oil
3 large courgettes (zucchini), thinly sliced
½ small red onion, finely chopped
300ml/½ pint/1¼ cups passata (bottled strained tomatoes)
30ml/2 tbsp chopped fresh thyme
garlic salt and freshly ground black pepper
fresh thyme sprigs, to garnish

1 Preheat the oven to 190°C/375°F/Gas 5. Brush an ovenproof dish with the olive oil.

2 Arrange half the courgettes and onion in the dish.

3 Spoon half the passata over the vegetables and sprinkle with some of the fresh thyme, then season to taste with garlic salt and pepper.

4 Arrange the remaining courgettes and onion in the dish on top of the passata, then season to taste with more garlic salt and pepper. Spoon and spread the remaining passata over the vegetables evenly.

5 Cover the dish with foil, then bake for 40–45 minutes, or until the courgettes are tender. Garnish with sprigs of fresh thyme and serve hot.

Cook's Tip

Passata is an Italian storecupboard (pantry) staple, made simply from ripe plum tomatoes, puréed and sieved. The result is a smooth, thick juice. Sometimes called creamed tomato, it is widely available, and can be used in soups and casseroles, or reduced with flavourings such as garlic and herbs to make easy tomato sauces.

Courgettes with Onion and Garlic: *Energy 102kcal/423kJ; Protein 4.4g; Carbohydrate 12.7g, of which sugars 9.6g; Fat 4.1g, of which saturates 0.6g; Cholesterol 0mg; Calcium 69mg; Fibre 3.1g; Sodium 215mg.*
Courgettes in Passata: *Energy 89kcal/370kJ; Protein 4.3g; Carbohydrate 9.2g, of which sugars 8.6g; Fat 4.1g, of which saturates 0.7g; Cholesterol 0mg; Calcium 54mg; Fibre 3.2g; Sodium 235mg.*

Courgettes and Tofu with Tomato Sauce

This dish is great hot or cold, and its flavour improves if it is kept for a day or two, covered, in the refrigerator. It makes the perfect accompaniment to a nut or meat roast.

Serves 4

30ml/2 tbsp olive oil
2 garlic cloves, finely chopped
4 large courgettes (zucchini), thinly sliced on the diagonal
250g/9oz firm tofu, drained and cubed
1 lemon
sea salt and ground black pepper

For the tomato sauce

10ml/2 tsp balsamic vinegar
5ml/1 tsp sugar
300ml/½ pint/1¼ cups passata (bottled strained tomatoes)
small bunch of fresh mint or parsley, chopped

1 First, make the tomato sauce, Place all the ingredients in a small pan and heat through gently, stirring occasionally.

2 Meanwhile, heat the olive oil in a large non-stick wok or frying pan until very hot, then add the garlic and stir-fry for 30 seconds, until golden. Add the courgettes and stir-fry over a high heat for about 5–6 minutes, or until golden around the edges. Remove from the pan.

3 Add the tofu to the pan and brown on one side for a few minutes. Turn gently, then brown again. Grate the rind from half the lemon and reserve for the garnish. Squeeze the lemon juice over the tofu.

4 Season to taste with sea salt and pepper, then leave to sizzle until all the lemon juice has evaporated. Gently stir the courgettes into the tofu until well combined, then remove the wok or pan from the heat.

5 Transfer the courgettes and tofu to a warm serving dish and pour the tomato sauce over the top. Sprinkle with the grated lemon rind, taste and season with more salt and pepper, if necessary, and serve immediately.

Fennel Gratin

With its delicate aniseed flavour, fennel is a popular ingredient in Mediterranean cooking, both as a herb and as a vegetable. The plant grows wild and its feathery leaves are particularly useful as a flavouring for fish, but in 17th-century Italy a cultivated variety was developed with a bulbous, edible root. It is known as Florence fennel, or finocchio, and is often braised or steamed. This gratin is one of the best ways to eat it, either as a light meal or as a vegetable accompaniment to steamed fish or grilled chicken.

Serves 6

2 fennel bulbs, about 675g/1½lb total
300ml/½ pint/1¼ cups semi-skimmed milk
15g/½oz/1 tbsp butter
15ml/1 tbsp plain (all-purpose) flour
25g/1oz/scant ½ cup dry white breadcrumbs
40g/1½oz Gruyère cheese, grated
salt and ground black pepper

1 Preheat the oven to 240°C/475°F/Gas 9. Discard the stalks and root ends from the fennel. Slice the fennel into quarters and place in a large saucepan. Pour over the milk, bring to the boil, then simmer for 10–15 minutes until tender.

2 Grease a small baking dish. Remove the fennel pieces with a slotted spoon, reserving the milk, and arrange in the dish.

3 Melt the butter in a small saucepan and add the flour. Stir well, then gradually whisk in the reserved milk. Cook the sauce until thickened, stirring.

4 Pour the sauce over the fennel pieces, sprinkle with the breadcrumbs and Gruyère. Season and bake in the oven for about 20 minutes until browned. Serve.

Variation
Instead of the Gruyère, Parmesan, Pecorino, mature Cheddar or another similar strong cheese would work perfectly.

Courgettes and Tofu: *:Energy 141kcal/585kJ; Protein 8.8g; Carbohydrate 6.8g, of which sugars 6.3g; Fat 8.9g, of which saturates 1.3g; Cholesterol 0mg; Calcium 389mg; Fibre 2.4g; Sodium 181mg.*
Fennel Gratin: *Energy 101kcal/423kJ; Protein 5.4g; Carbohydrate 9.6g, of which sugars 4.4g; Fat 4.9g, of which saturates 2.9g; Cholesterol 13mg; Calcium 156mg; Fibre 2.9g; Sodium 135mg.*

Baked Fennel

Fennel is widely eaten all over Italy, both raw in salads and cooked in hot vegetable dishes. It is delicious married with the sharpness of Parmesan cheese in this simple recipe.

Serves 4–6

1kg/2¼lb fennel bulbs, washed and halved
50g/2oz/4 tbsp butter
40g/1½oz/⅓ cup freshly grated Parmesan cheese

1 Preheat the oven to 200°C/400°F/Gas 6. Bring a large pan of water to the boil and cook the fennel bulbs until soft but not mushy. Drain thoroughly.

2 Cut the fennel bulbs lengthways into four or six pieces. Place them in a buttered baking dish.

3 Dot with butter, then sprinkle with the grated Parmesan. Bake for 20 minutes until golden brown. Serve at once.

Variation
For a more substantial version of this dish, scatter 75g/3oz chopped ham, bacon or pancetta over the fennel before topping with the grated Parmesan cheese.

Italian Sweet and Sour Onions

Although raw onions are strongly flavoured, like all vegetables they are high in natural sugars, and when they are cooked at a high temperature their sweetness intensifies. Serve these delicious onions with roasted meat or cooked fresh vegetables.

Serves 6

25g/1oz/2 tbsp butter
75ml/5 tbsp sugar
120ml/4fl oz/½ cup white wine vinegar
30ml/2 tbsp balsamic vinegar
675g/1½lb small pickling onions, peeled
salt and ground black pepper

1 Melt the butter in a large saucepan over a gentle heat. Add the sugar and cook until it begins to dissolve, stirring constantly.

2 Add the vinegars to the pan with the onions and heat gently. Season, cover and cook over a moderate heat for 20–25 minutes, stirring occasionally, until the onions are soft when pierced with a knife. Keep an eye on the pan all the time to make sure that the sugar caramelizes but does not burn. Serve hot.

Variation
This recipe also looks good and tastes delicious when made with either yellow or red onions, cut into slices. Cooking times vary, depending on the size of the pieces.

Cook's Tips
- *Balsamic vinegar is a speciality of Modena, in northern Italy, where it has been produced for centuries. It is made from late-harvested grapes with a high sugar content, and is very dark brown, sweet and viscous, with a complex flavour.*
- *Small pickling onions are in season only in the autumn, as they are maincrop onions picked while still small and do not store well. Trim only a very small slice off the root end when preparing them to help them stay intact during cooking.*

__Baked Fennel:__ Energy 149kcal/616kJ; Protein 6.3g; Carbohydrate 2.8g, of which sugars 2.6g; Fat 12.6g, of which saturates 7.8g; Cholesterol 34mg; Calcium 188mg; Fibre 3.6g; Sodium 213mg.
__Sweet and Sour Onions:__ Energy 121kcal/506kJ; Protein 1.4g; Carbohydrate 22g, of which sugars 19.4g; Fat 3.7g, of which saturates 2.2g; Cholesterol 9mg; Calcium 36mg; Fibre 1.6g; Sodium 29mg.

Oven-roasted Red Onions

The wonderful taste of these sweet red onions, gently baked in a clay pot, is enhanced still further with the powerful flavours of fresh rosemary and juniper berries, and the added tangy sweetness of balsamic vinegar.

Serves 4

4 large or 8 small red onions
25ml/1½ tbsp olive oil
6 juniper berries, crushed
8 small fresh rosemary sprigs
30ml/2 tbsp balsamic vinegar
salt and ground black pepper

1 Soak a clay onion baker in cold water for 15 minutes, then drain. (If the base of the baker is glazed, only the lid will need to be soaked.) Alternatively use an ovenproof dish.

2 Trim and discard the roots from the onions and remove the skins, if you like. Cut the onions from the tip to the root, cutting the large onions into quarters and the small onions in half.

3 Rub the onions with olive oil, salt and pepper and the juniper berries. Place the onions in the baker, inserting the rosemary in among the onions. Drizzle the remaining oil and vinegar over.

4 Cover and place in a cold oven. Set the oven to 200°C/400°F/Gas 6 and roast for 40 minutes. Remove the lid and roast for a further 10 minutes.

Variation
Add a similar quantity of long, thin potato wedges to the onion. Use a larger dish so that the vegetables are still in one layer.

Cook's Tip
To help hold back the tears during preparation, chill onions first for at least 30 minutes, and then remove the root end last. The root contains the largest concentration of the sulphuric compounds that make the eyes water.

Italian Aromatic Stewed Mushrooms

Italian cooks use garlic and fresh herbs to transform simple food into great cuisine. In this traditional recipe, a dish of mushrooms becomes something quite memorable.

Serves 6

750g/1½lb fresh mushrooms, a mixture of wild (soaked if necessary) and cultivated
90ml/6 tbsp olive oil
2 garlic cloves, finely chopped
45ml/3 tbsp chopped fresh parsley
salt and ground black pepper

1 Clean the mushrooms carefully by wiping them with a damp cloth or kitchen paper.

2 Cut off the woody tips of the stems and discard. Slice the stems and caps fairly thickly.

3 Heat the oil in a large frying pan. Stir in the garlic and cook for about 1 minute, being careful not to burn it. Add the mushrooms and cook for 8–10 minutes, stirring occasionally.

4 Season with salt and pepper and stir in the parsley. Cook for a further 5 minutes, then transfer to a warmed serving dish and serve immediately.

Variation
You can use this recipe to make a delicious light vegetarian lunch – add the mushrooms to an omelette or serve on toast.

Cook's Tip
Ideally you should use a combination of both wild and cultivated mushrooms for this dish to give a nicely balanced flavour. A good mixture would be chestnut mushrooms and chanterelles, both of which are widely available. Dried mushrooms will need to be rehydrated in warm water before use. These can add an interesting texture to the dish.

Roasted Onions: *Energy 47kcal/194kJ; Protein 1.5g; Carbohydrate 9.9g, of which sugars 7.1g; Fat 0.3g, of which saturates 0g, of which polyunsaturates 0.1g; Cholesterol 0mg; Calcium 32mg; Fibre 1.8g; Sodium 4mg.*
Aromatic Mushrooms: *Energy 122kcal/502kJ; Protein 2.8g; Carbohydrate 1.5g, of which sugars 0.8g; Fat 11.7g, of which saturates 1.7g; Cholesterol 8mg; Calcium 58mg; Fibre 1.9g; Sodium 37mg.*

Marinated Mushrooms

The Spanish are very keen on mushrooms, and wild fungus collecting is a popular pastime. This dish, known as *champiñones en escabeche*, is a good way to serve mushrooms in summer, and makes a refreshing low-fat alternative to the ever-popular mushrooms fried in garlic. Cultivated button mushrooms work well. You could serve it with steak, as a tapas dish or a first course, with crusty bread to mop up the delicious juices.

Serves 4

10ml/2 tsp olive oil
1 small onion, very finely chopped
1 garlic clove, finely chopped
15ml/1 tbsp tomato purée (paste)
50ml/2fl oz/¼ cup amontillado sherry
50ml/2fl oz/¼ cup water
2 cloves
225g/8oz/3 cups button (white) mushrooms, trimmed
salt and ground black pepper
chopped fresh parsley, to garnish

1 Heat the oil in a non-stick pan. Add the onion and garlic and cook until soft.

2 Stir in the tomato purée, sherry, water and cloves and season with salt and black pepper. Bring to the boil, cover and simmer gently for 45 minutes, adding more water if it becomes too dry.

3 Add the mushrooms, then cover and simmer for 5 minutes. Remove from the heat and allow to cool, still covered.

4 Chill in the refrigerator overnight. Serve the mushrooms cold, sprinkled with the chopped parsley, to garnish.

Cook's Tip
A marinade is also a good way to add extra flavour to mushrooms before grilling (broiling) or baking them. Toss them in a little olive oil to which you have added some chopped garlic, crushed chillies or some chopped fresh herbs, and leave to marinate for a couple of hours before cooking.

Cauliflower with Egg and Lemon

Cauliflower is a delicate vegetable, delicious when carefully cooked or crunched raw, but easily ruined by overcooking. In the Mediterranean it is used in many different ways, and is sometimes braised or dipped in batter and fried. In this Greek recipe it is teamed with a lemon sauce, a perfect accompaniment for meatballs.

Serves 6

75–90ml/5–6 tbsp extra virgin olive oil
1 medium cauliflower, divided into large florets
2 eggs
juice of 1 lemon
5ml/1 tsp cornflour (cornstarch), mixed to a cream with a little cold water
30ml/2 tbsp chopped fresh flat leaf parsley
salt

1 Heat the olive oil in a large, heavy pan, add the cauliflower florets and sauté over a medium heat until they start to brown.

2 Pour in enough hot water to almost cover the cauliflower florets, add salt to taste, bring to the boil, then cover the pan and cook for 7–8 minutes until the florets are just soft.

3 Remove the pan from the heat and leave to stand, retaining the hot water and covering the pan tightly to keep in the heat. Meanwhile, make the sauce.

4 Beat the eggs in a bowl, add the lemon juice and cornflour and beat until well mixed. While beating, add a few tablespoons of the hot liquid from the cauliflower. Pour the egg mixture slowly over the cauliflower, then stir gently.

5 Place the pan over a very gentle heat for 2 minutes to thicken the sauce. Spoon into a warmed serving bowl, sprinkle the chopped parsley over the top and serve.

Cook's Tip
This refreshing sauce is also excellent with carefully boiled or steamed broccoli.

Mushrooms: *Energy 44kcal/181kJ; Protein 1.4g; Carbohydrate 2.1g, of which sugars 1.7g; Fat 1.8g, of which saturates 0.3g, of which polyunsaturates 0.3g; Cholesterol 0mg; Calcium 9mg; Fibre 0.9g; Sodium 14mg.*
Cauliflower with Egg: *Energy 211kcal/874kJ; Protein 8g; Carbohydrate 5.2g, of which sugars 3.4g; Fat 17.8g, of which saturates 3g; Cholesterol 95mg; Calcium 63mg; Fibre 2.8g; Sodium 51mg.*

Broccoli with Oil and Garlic

This is a very simple way of transforming steamed or blanched broccoli into a succulent Mediterranean dish. Peeling the broccoli stalks is easy and allows for even cooking.

Serves 6

1kg/2lb fresh broccoil
90ml/6 tbsp olive oil
2–3 garlic cloves, finely chopped
salt and ground black pepper

1 Wash the broccoli. Cut off any woody parts at the base of the stems. Using a small sharp knife, peel the broccoli stems. Cut any very long or wide stalks in half.

2 If steaming the broccoli, place water in the bottom of a pan equipped with a steamer and bring to the boil. Put the broccoli in the steamer, cover tightly and cook for 8–12 minutes, or until the stems are just tender when pierced with the point of a knife. Remove from the heat.

3 If blanching the broccoli, bring a large pan of water to the boil, drop the broccoli into the boiling water and blanch for 5–6 minutes, until just tender. Drain.

4 In a frying pan large enough to hold all the broccoli pieces, gently heat the oil with the garlic. When the garlic is light golden (do not let it brown or it will be bitter) add the broccoli and cook over a medium heat for 3–4 minutes, turning carefully to coat it with the hot oil.

5 Season with salt and pepper. Serve hot or cold.

Variation

To turn the dish into a vegetarian topping for pasta, add about 25g/1oz each of fresh breadcrumbs and pine nuts to the garlic at the beginning of step 4 and cook until golden. The add the broccoli with 25g/1oz sultanas (golden raisins) and some chopped fresh parsley. Toss into cooked pasta and serve with roasted tomatoes.

Grilled Raddichio and Courgettes

Radicchio is often grilled or barbecued in Italian cooking to give it a special flavour. Combined with courgettes, it makes a quick and tasty side dish.

Serves 4

2–3 firm heads radicchio, round or long type, rinsed
4 courgettes (zucchini)
90ml/6 tbsp olive oil
salt and ground black pepper

1 Preheat the grill (broiler) or prepare a barbecue, Using a sharp knife, cut the radicchio in half through the root section or base. Cut the courgettes into 1cm/½in diagonal slices.

2 When ready to cook, brush the vegetables with the olive oil and add salt and pepper. Cook for 4–5 minutes on each side.

Deep-Fried Cauliflower

Deep-frying is a popular form of cooking in Italy and it is used for everything, from cheese to fruit. These cauliflower florets, with their crisp coating, make a good antipasto or side dish.

Serves 4

1 large cauliflower
1 egg
100g/3½oz scant 1 cup flour
175ml/6fl oz/¾ cup white wine
oil, for deep-frying
salt and ground black pepper

1 Soak the cauliflower in a bowl of salted water. Beat the egg in a mixing bowl, then season and beat in the flour to make a thick paste. Add the wine and, if necessary, add more to make a fairly runny batter. Cover and allow to rest for 30 minutes.

2 Steam or boil the cauliflower until just tender – do not overcook. Cut it into small florets when cool.

3 Heat the oil to about 185°C/360°F, or until a small bread cube sizzles as soon as it is dropped in. Dip each floret into the batter before deep-frying until golden. Remove with a slotted spoon and drain on kitchen paper. Serve sprinkled with salt, alongside a cool dip.

Broccoli with Oil and Garlic: Energy 159kcal/657kJ; Protein 3g; Carbohydrate 3.8g, of which sugars 1.4g; Fat 12.5g, of which saturates 1.5g; Cholesterol 0mg; Calcium 40mg; Fibre 3.3g; Sodium 262mg.
Radicchio and Courgettes: Energy 311kcal/1294kJ; Protein 1.5g; Carbohydrate 22.7g, of which sugars 0.6g; Fat 19g, of which saturates 2.6g; Cholesterol 0mg; Calcium 19mg; Fibre 2.6g; Sodium 239mg.
Deep-fried Cauliflower: Energy 189kcal/780kJ; Protein 1.5g; Carbohydrate 4.4g, of which sugars 1g; Fat 17.6g, of which saturates 2.6g; Cholesterol 0mg; Calcium 19mg; Fibre 2g; Sodium 122mg.

Provençal Beans

In the traditional cuisine of Provençe, flavourful tomatoes, ripened in the abundant summer sun, are as important as they are in neighbouring Italy. Here, a tangy sauce based on tomatoes and garlic transform a mixture of green beans into a memorable dish.

Serves 4

5ml/1 tsp olive oil
1 small onion, finely chopped
1 garlic clove, crushed
225g/8oz runner beans, trimmed and sliced
225g/8oz French beans, trimmed and sliced
2 tomatoes, peeled and chopped
salt and ground black pepper

1 Heat the oil in a heavy pan and sauté the onion over a medium heat until softened but not browned.

2 Add the garlic and sauté for 1–2 minutes, then stir in the sliced runner beans, French beans and chopped tomatoes. Season generously with salt and pepper, then cover the pan tightly with a lid.

3 Cook over a fairly low heat, shaking the pan occasionally, for about 30 minutes, or until the beans are tender. Serve hot.

Cook's Tip
When runner beans are not available, just use double the quantity of French beans.

Greek Beans with Tomato Sauce

This is a standard summer dish in Greece, and is made with different kinds of fresh beans according to what is available. When the beans are tender and the tomatoes sweet, the dish, although frugal, can have an astoundingly good flavour, particularly if you use a good quality olive oil, whose flavour will permeate the vegetables. It is usually accompanied by slices of salty feta cheese and good fresh bread.

Serves 4

800g/1¾ lb green beans, trimmed
150ml/¼ pint/⅔ cup extra virgin olive oil
1 large onion, thinly sliced
2 garlic cloves, chopped
2 small potatoes, peeled and cubed
675g/1½lb tomatoes or a 400g/14oz can chopped tomatoes
150ml/¼ pint/⅔ cup hot water
45–60ml/3–4 tbsp chopped fresh parsley
salt and ground black pepper
slices of feta cheese, to garnish

1 If the green beans are very long, cut them in half. Drop them into a bowl of cold water so that they are completely submerged, and leave them for a few minutes to absorb some of the water.

2 Heat the olive oil in a large pan, add the onion and sauté until translucent. Add the garlic, then, when it becomes aromatic, stir in the pieces of potato and sauté the mixture for a few minutes. Do this over a moderate heat, otherwise the garlic may burn.

3 Add the tomatoes and the hot water and cook for 5 minutes. Drain the beans, rinse them and drain again, then add them to the pan with a little salt and pepper to season. Cover and simmer for 30 minutes.

4 Stir in the chopped parsley, with a little more hot water if the mixture looks dry. Cook for 10 minutes more, until the beans are very tender.

5 Serve hot, topped with a few slices of feta cheese or crisply-fried halloumi.

Provençal Beans: *Energy 47kcal/195kJ; Protein 2.5g; Carbohydrate 6.3g, of which sugars 5.3g; Fat 1.4g, of which saturates 0.3g; Cholesterol 0mg; Calcium 46mg; Fibre 3.1g; Sodium 5mg.*
Green Beans: *Energy 350kcal/1448kJ; Protein 6.6g; Carbohydrate 21.9g, of which sugars 13.4g; Fat 26.9g, of which saturates 4g; Cholesterol 0mg; Calcium 121mg; Fibre 7.7g; Sodium 25mg.*

Broad Beans with Bacon

This is a classic combination, given a Spanish twist with the addition of paprika and sherry. Smoky, salty bacon is the perfect foil for the earthy flavour of broad beans. However, for a change, or if you'd like to serve this dish to vegetarians, you can omit the chopped bacon and substitute the same quantity of drained sun-dried tomatoes in oil – it will still be delicious.

Serves 4
10ml/2 tsp olive oil
1 small onion, finely chopped
1 garlic clove, finely chopped
50g/2oz rindless lean smoked back bacon, roughly chopped
225g/8oz broad (fava) beans (shelled weight), thawed if frozen
5ml/1 tsp paprika
15ml/1 tbsp sweet sherry
salt and freshly ground black pepper

1 Heat the oil in a frying pan and cook the onion, garlic and bacon over a fairly high heat for about 5 minutes, or until softened and browned.

2 Add the broad beans and the paprika and stir-fry for 1 minute. Add the sherry, cover the pan and cook until the beans are tender – about 5–10 minutes. Season to taste with salt and pepper, then serve.

Cook's Tip
If you have time, remove the dull grey skins from the broad beans to reveal the bright green beans beneath. This is well worth doing if you are cooking fresh broad beans late in the season, when the skins can become tough.

Variation
Fry the bacon first until crisp, then remove with a slotted spoon and reserve. Cook the onion and garlic in the oil and bacon fat, then complete the dish and top with the reserved bacon.

Spinach with Raisins and Pine Nuts

The pine nut, which is the kernel of the stone pine cone, has a resinous flavour and a unique texture. It is an important ingredient in the Mediterranean, often partnered with raisins. This combination goes into both sweet and savoury dishes, including minced meat stuffings, and is used to spruce up a range of green vegetables to turn them into flavoursome and interesting side dishes. Here, tossed with wilted spinach and croûtons, it makes a tasty snack or main meal accompaniment.

Serves 4
50g/2oz/⅓ cup raisins
1 large thick slice white bread
45ml/3 tbsp olive oil
25g/1oz/¼ cup pine nuts
500g/1¼lb young spinach, stalks removed
2 garlic cloves, crushed
salt and ground black pepper

1 Put the raisins in a small bowl, cover them with boiling water and leave to soak for 10 minutes. Drain and pat dry with kitchen paper.

2 Cut the bread into small cubes and discard the crusts. Heat 30ml/2 tbsp of the olive oil and fry the cubes of bread until golden. Drain.

3 Heat the remaining oil in the pan. Fry the pine nuts, stirring constantly until they begin to turn golden brown. Add the spinach and garlic and cook quickly, turning the spinach until it has just wilted.

4 Toss in the raisins and season lightly. Transfer to a warmed serving dish. Sprinkle with croûtons and serve hot.

Variation
You can also use Swiss chard or spinach beet instead of the spinach in this recipe. They will give a more earthy taste that goes well with red meats. You will need to cook them for a few minutes longer.

Beans with Bacon: *Energy 96kcal/401kJ; Protein 6.7g; Carbohydrate 7.8g, of which sugars 1.6g; Fat 3.9g, of which saturates 1.1g; Cholesterol 7mg; Calcium 36mg; Fibre 3.9g; Sodium 198mg.*
Spinach with Raisins: *Energy 198Kcal/824kJ; Protein 5.2g; Carbohydrate 14.3g, of which sugars 11g; Fat 13.7g, of which saturates 1.6g; Cholesterol 0mg; Calcium 226mg; Fibre 3.1g; Sodium 218mg.*

Eastern Mediterranean Okra

Okra is frequently combined with tomatoes and mild spices in Mediterranean cooking. Look for fresh okra that is soft and velvety, not dry and shrivelled.

Serves 4

450g/1lb fresh tomatoes or 400g/14oz can chopped tomatoes
450g/1lb okra
20ml/4 tsp olive oil
2 onions, thinly sliced
10ml/2 tsp coriander seeds, crushed
3 garlic cloves, crushed
2.5ml/½ tsp sugar
finely grated rind and juice of 1 lemon
salt and freshly ground black pepper

1 If using fresh tomatoes, cut a cross in the base of each tomato, plunge them into a bowl of boiling water for 30 seconds, then refresh them in cold water. Peel off and discard the skins and roughly chop the tomato flesh. Set aside.

2 Trim off and discard any stalks from the okra and leave the pods whole. Heat the oil in a non-stick frying pan and cook the onions and coriander seeds for 3–4 minutes, or until the onions are beginning to colour.

3 Add the okra and garlic to the pan and cook for 1 minute. Gently stir in the chopped fresh or canned tomatoes. Add the sugar, which will bring out the flavour of the tomatoes. Simmer gently for 20–30 minutes, stirring once or twice, or until the okra is tender.

4 Stir in the lemon rind and juice, and add salt and pepper to taste, adding more sugar if necessary. Serve warm or cold.

Cook's Tip
When okra pods are sliced, they ooze a sticky, somewhat mucilaginous liquid which, when cooked, acts as a thickener. It gives dishes a very distinctive texture, which not everyone appreciates. If the pods are left whole, however, as here, all you get is the delicious flavour.

Slow-Cooked Okra with Tomatoes

Okra makes a deliciously sweet casserole and this is one of the best vegetable stews you will taste. Made with fresh tomatoes, at the height of the summer, it is certainly a favourite lunch, especially when served with a fresh-tasting feta cheese and crusty bread. It can be served hot or at room temperature.

Serves 6

675g/1½lb fresh okra
150ml/¼ pint/⅔ cup extra virgin olive oil
1 large onion, sliced
675g/1½lb fresh tomatoes, sliced
2.5ml/½ tsp sugar
30ml/2 tbsp finely chopped flat leaf parsley
salt and ground black pepper

1 Cut off the conical head from each okra pod, removing the stalk without cutting into the body of the okra.

2 Heat the oil in a large, deep pan or sauté pan and fry the onion slices until softened and light golden. Stir in the fresh or canned tomatoes, with the sugar, and salt and pepper to taste. Cook for 5 minutes.

3 Add the okra and shake the pan to distribute them evenly and coat them in the sauce. The okra should be immersed in the sauce, so add a little hot water if necessary.

4 Cook gently for 20–30 minutes, depending on the size of the okra. Shake the pan occasionally, but do not stir. Add the parsley just before serving.

Mediterranean Okra: *Energy 88kcal/370kJ; Protein 4.1g; Carbohydrate 8.6g, of which sugars 7.7g; Fat 4.5g, of which saturates 0.9g; Cholesterol 0mg; Calcium 192mg; Fibre 5.8g; Sodium 20mg.*
Slow-cooked Okra: *Energy 326kcal/1350kJ; Protein 6.5g; Carbohydrate 14.8g, of which sugars 12.8g; Fat 27.3g, of which saturates 4.3g; Cholesterol 0mg; Calcium 295mg; Fibre 9.1g; Sodium 30mg.*

Braised Lettuce and Peas with Mint

Based on the traditional French way of stewing fresh peas in a little butter and stock, this dish is delicious with simply cooked fish or grilled chicken.

Serves 6

25g/1oz/2 tbsp butter
4 Little Gem (Bibb) lettuces, halved lengthways
2 bunches spring onions (scallions)
5ml/1 tsp sugar
1.2kg/2½lb fresh peas in pods, shelled (about 500–675g/1¼–1½lb peas)
4–5 fresh mint sprigs, plus extra to garnish
120ml/4fl oz/½ cup light vegetable or chicken stock
salt and ground black pepper

1 Melt half the butter in a wide, heavy pan over a low heat. Add the lettuces and spring onions and toss in the butter, then sprinkle in the sugar, 2.5ml/½ tsp salt and plenty of pepper. Cover, then cook very gently for 5 minutes, stirring once.

2 Add the peas and mint sprigs to the pan. Toss the peas in the juices, then pour in the stock. Cover the pan and cook over a gentle heat for a further 5 minutes, or until the peas are almost tender, then remove the lid from the pan. Increase the heat to high and cook, stirring occasionally, until the cooking liquid has reduced to a few tablespoons.

3 Stir in the remaining butter and adjust the seasoning. Transfer to a warmed serving dish and garnish with the extra mint. Serve immediately.

Variations

- *Use 1 lettuce, shredding it coarsely, and omit the fresh mint. Towards the end of cooking, stir in about 150g/5oz rocket (arugula) – preferably the slightly stronger-flavoured, wild variety – and cook briefly until just wilted.*
- *Cook 115g/4oz chopped lean smoked back bacon with 1 small chopped red or white onion in the butter. Use 1 bunch of spring onions and omit the mint. Stir in some chopped fresh flat leaf parsley before serving.*

Braised Artichokes with Fresh Peas

This artichoke dish is uniquely delicate. Shelling fresh peas is rather time-consuming but their matchless flavour makes the task very worthwhile. Sit on a step outside in the sunshine, and what at first seemed a chore will become positively pleasurable.

Serves 4

4 medium to large globe artichokes
juice of 1½ lemons
150ml/¼pint/⅔ cup extra virgin olive oil
1 onion, thinly sliced
4–5 spring onions (scallions), roughly chopped
2 carrots, peeled and sliced in rounds
1.2kg/2½lb fresh peas in pods, shelled (about 500–675g/1¼–1½lb peas)
450ml/¾ pint/scant 2 cups hot water
60ml/4 tbsp finely chopped fresh dill
salt and freshly ground black pepper
a few sprigs of fresh dill, to garnish

1 Remove and discard the outer leaves of the artichokes. Trim off the top of the inner leaves, and cut the artichokes in half lengthways. Scoop out the hairy choke and trim the stalk, leaving a length of 4cm/1½in. As you prepare them, drop the artichoke halves into a bowl of water acidulated with about one-third of the lemon juice.

2 Heat the oil in a pan over medium heat and add the onion and spring onions, and then a minute later, add the carrots. Sauté the mixture for a few seconds, then add the peas and stir for 1–2 minutes.

3 Pour in the remaining lemon juice. Let it bubble and evaporate for a few seconds, then add the hot water and bring to the boil. Drain the artichokes and add them to the pan, with salt and pepper to taste.

4 Cover the pan and cook gently for about 40–45 minutes, stirring occasionally. Add the dill and cook for about 5 minutes more, until the vegetables are beautifully tender. Serve the dish hot or at room temperature.

Braised Lettuce: Energy 110kcal/455kJ; Protein 6.2g; Carbohydrate 10.8g, of which sugars 4.3g; Fat 5g, of which saturates 2.5g; Cholesterol 9mg; Calcium 64mg; Fibre 4.2g; Sodium 32mg.
Braised Artichokes: Energy 384kcal/1584kJ; Protein 10.5g; Carbohydrate 25.2g, of which sugars 12.4g; Fat 27.5g, of which saturates 4g; Cholesterol 0mg; Calcium 121mg; Fibre 10g; Sodium 85mg.

Minted Pomegranate Yogurt with Grapefruit Salad

Ruby red or salmon pink, the jewel-like seeds of the pomegranate make any dessert look beautiful. Here they are stirred into luscious Greek yogurt to make a delicate sauce for a fresh-tasting grapefruit salad. This pretty dish is flecked with green thanks to the addition of finely chopped fresh mint, which complements the citrus flavours perfectly. Serve this refreshing combination for breakfast, as a light snack during the day, or as a dessert after a spicy main course.

Serves 3–4

300ml/½ pint/1¼ cups natural (plain) Greek yogurt
2–3 ripe pomegranates
small bunch of fresh mint, finely chopped
clear honey or caster (superfine) sugar, to taste (optional)

For the grapefruit salad

2 red grapefruits
2 pink grapefruits
1 white grapefruit
15–30ml/1–2 tbsp orange flower water

To decorate

handful of pomegranate seeds
fresh mint leaves

1 Put the yogurt in a bowl and beat well. Cut open the pomegranates and scoop out the seeds, removing and discarding all the bitter pith. Fold the pomegranate seeds and chopped mint into the yogurt. Sweeten with a little honey or sugar, if using, then chill until ready to serve.

2 Peel the red, pink and white grapefruits, cutting off and discarding all the pith. Cut between the membranes to remove the segments, holding the fruit over a bowl to catch the juices.

3 Discard the membranes and mix the fruit segments with the reserved juices. Sprinkle with the orange flower water and add a little honey or sugar, if using. Stir gently then decorate with a few pomegranate seeds.

4 Decorate the chilled yogurt with a sprinkling of pomegranate seeds and mint leaves, and serve with the grapefruit salad.

Orange and Date Salad

Dates grow abundantly in the eastern Mediterranean and are now widely available fresh in supermarkets. Fresh dates are best for this sweet, fragrant salad. It is popular throughout the Arab world, and can be served as a dessert, though it also makes an unusual and delicious accompaniment to roasted meats.

Serves 4–6

6 oranges
15–30ml/1–2 tbsp orange flower water or rose water (optional)
lemon juice (optional)
115g/4oz/⅔ cup stoned (pitted) dates
50g/2oz/⅓ cup pistachio nuts
icing (confectioners') sugar, to taste
a few whole or split blanched almonds

1 Peel the oranges with a sharp knife, removing all the pith, and cut into segments, catching the juices in a bowl. Place the orange segments in a serving dish.

2 Stir in the juice caught in the bowl together with a little orange flower or rose water, if using, and sharpen with lemon juice, if necessary.

3 Chop the dates and pistachio nuts and sprinkle over the salad with a little sifted icing sugar. Chill in the refrigerator for about 1 hour.

4 Dry-fry the almonds in a small pan until lightly toasted.

5 Just before serving, sprinkle over the toasted almonds and a little extra icing sugar and serve.

Cook's Tip

Dried dates can be used in this salad, but fresh dates are preferable if available. The fresh fruits are plump and sweet, with a rich, chewy texture, and there are many different varieties. To remove the stones (pits), squeeze each date until the stone appears at one end, then push it through the fruit until it emerges at the other end.

Pomegranate Salad: *Energy 188Kcal/784kJ; Protein 8.8g; Carbohydrate 18g, of which sugars 18g; Fat 10.5g, of which saturates 5.2g; Cholesterol 0mg; Calcium 202mg; Fibre 3.6g; Sodium 82mg.*
Orange and Date Salad: *Energy 343Kcal/1437kJ; Protein 14.3g; Carbohydrate 32.5g, of which sugars 16.8g; Fat 17.9g, of which saturates 3.8g; Cholesterol 13mg; Calcium 327mg; Fibre 2.1g; Sodium 140mg.*

Moroccan Dried Fruit Salad

While fresh fruit ends most Mediterranean meals in summer, in winter assorted dried fruits, together with nuts, are put on the table for guests to enjoy. This fruit salad is a wonderful combination of fresh and dried fruit and makes an excellent light dessert throughout the year. Use frozen raspberries or blackberries in winter.

Serves 4

115g/4oz/½ cup dried apricots
115g/4oz/½ cup dried peaches
1 fresh pear
1 fresh apple
1 fresh orange
115g/4oz/⅔ cup mixed raspberries and blackberries
1 cinnamon stick
50g/2oz/¼ cup caster (superfine) sugar
15ml/1 tbsp clear honey
30ml/2 tbsp lemon juice

1 Soak the apricots and peaches in a bowl of water for 1–2 hours or until plump, then drain and halve or quarter them. Set aside.

2 Peel and core the pear and apple and cut the flesh into cubes. Peel the orange with a sharp knife, removing all the white pith, and cut the flesh into wedges. Place all the fruit in a large pan with the raspberries and blackberries.

3 Add 600ml/1 pint/2½ cups water, the cinnamon stick, sugar and honey and bring to the boil, stirring constantly. Reduce the heat, cover and simmer very gently for 10–12 minutes, then remove the pan from the heat.

4 Stir the lemon juice into the fruit. Allow to cool, then pour the mixture into a bowl and chill in the refrigerator for 1–2 hours before serving.

Variations

- *Omit the soft fruits, or add them to the fruit mixture after cooking and cooling for a fresher tasting salad.*
- *Soak prunes and dried apples and pears and use them instead of the fresh fruit.*

Italian Fruit Salad and Ice Cream

In Italy in the summer, little pavement fruit shops sell dishes of macerated soft fruits, which are delectable on their own, but also make wonderful ice-cream.

Serves 6

900g/2lb mixed summer fruits such as strawberries, raspberries, redcurrants, blueberries, peaches, apricots, plums, melons
juice of 3–4 oranges
juice of 1 lemon
15ml/1 tbsp liquid pear and apple concentrate
60ml/4 tbsp whipping cream
30ml/2 tbsp orange liqueur (optional)
fresh mint sprigs, to decorate

1 Prepare the fruit according to type. Cut it into reasonably small pieces. Put it into a serving bowl and pour over enough orange juice just to cover. Add the lemon juice and chill the fruit for 2 hours.

2 Set half the macerated fruit aside to serve as it is. Purée the remainder in a blender or food processor.

3 Gently warm the pear and apple concentrate and stir into the fruit purée. Whip the cream and fold it in, then add the liqueur, if using.

4 Churn the mixture in an ice cream maker. Alternatively, place it in a suitable container for freezing, freeze until ice crystals form around the edge, then beat the mixture until smooth. Repeat the process once or twice, then freeze until firm.

5 Allow to soften slightly in the refrigerator before serving with the fruit in scoops decorated with sprigs of mint.

Cook's Tip

The macerated fruit also makes a delicious drink. Purée in a blender or food processor, then press through a sieve (strainer).

Moroccan Fruit Salad: Energy 160kcal/682kJ; Protein 2.6g; Carbohydrate 38.9g, of which sugars 38.9g; Fat 0.4g, of which saturates 0g; Cholesterol 0mg; Calcium 57mg; Fibre 4.8g; Sodium 10mg.
Fruit Salad and Ice Cream: Energy 69kcal/289kJ; Protein 2.2g; Carbohydrate 15.2g, of which sugars 15.2g; Fat 0.2g, of which saturates 0g; Cholesterol 0mg; Calcium 38mg; Fibre 1.7g; Sodium 18mg.

Grilled Fruit with Watermelon and Spiced Orange Granitas

For this stunning dessert, fresh pineapple, mango and bananas are caramelized and served with a choice of two fruit granitas.

Serves 6–8
1 pineapple, peeled and sliced
1 mango, peeled and sliced
2 bananas, peeled and halved
45–60ml/3–4 tbsp icing (confectioners') sugar

For the watermelon granita
1kg/2¼lb watermelon, seeds removed
250g/9oz/1¼ cups caster (superfine) sugar
150ml/¼ pint/⅔ cup water
juice of ½ lemon
15ml/1 tbsp orange flower water
2.5ml/½ tsp ground cinnamon

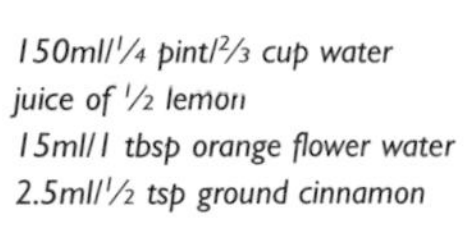

For the spiced orange granita
900ml/1½ pints/3¾ cups water
350g/12oz/1¾ cups caster (superfine) sugar
5–6 whole cloves
5ml/1 tsp ground ginger
2.5ml/½ tsp ground cinnamon
600ml/1 pint/2½ cups fresh orange juice
15ml/1 tbsp orange flower water

1 To make the watermelon granita, purée the watermelon flesh in a blender. Put the sugar and water in a pan and stir until dissolved, then simmer for 5 minutes. Cool. Stir in the lemon juice, orange flower water and cinnamon, then beat in the watermelon purée. Pour into a bowl and freeze, stirring every 15 minutes for 3 hours so that the mixture freezes but is slushy.

2 To make the spiced orange granita, heat the water and sugar together with the cloves, stirring until dissolved, then simmer for 5 minutes and cool. Stir in the ginger, cinnamon, orange juice and orange flower water. Discard the cloves, then pour into a bowl, and freeze in the same way as the watermelon granita.

3 Preheat the grill (broiler). Arrange the pineapple, mango and bananas on a baking sheet. Sprinkle with icing sugar and grill (broil) for 3–4 minutes, until slightly softened and browned. Serve immediately, accompanied by the granitas.

Fresh Orange Granita

Granitas, whch originated in Sicily, are like water ices, but coarser and quite grainy in texture, hence the name. A fruit granita makes a refreshing dessert after a rich main course, or a cooling treat on a hot summer's day.

Serves 6
4 large oranges
1 large lemon
150g/5oz/¾ cup granulated sugar
475ml/16fl oz/2 cups water
blanched pared strips of orange and lemon rind, to decorate
dessert biscuits, to serve

1 Thinly pare the rind from the oranges and lemon, taking care to avoid the bitter white pith, and set aside for the decoration. Cut the fruit in half and squeeze the juice into a jug. Set aside.

2 Heat the sugar and water in a heavy saucepan, stirring over a gentle heat until the sugar dissolves. Bring to the boil, then boil without stirring for about 10 minutes, until a syrup forms.

3 Remove the syrup from the heat, add the pieces of orange and lemon rind and shake the pan. Cover and allow to cool.

4 Strain the sugar syrup into a shallow freezer container and add the fruit juice. Stir well to mix, then freeze, uncovered, for about 4 hours until slushy.

5 Remove the half-frozen mixture from the freezer and stir with a fork, breaking up the ice crystals, then return to the freezer and freeze again for 4 hours more or until frozen hard. To serve, turn into a bowl and allow to soften for about 10 minutes, then break up with a fork again and pile into long-stemmed glasses. Decorate with the strips of orange and lemon rind and serve with dessert biscuits.

Cook's Tip
Granitas vary in texture, from something nearly as smooth as a water ice to extremely grainy and chunky, depending on how much they are stirred during the freezing process.

Grilled Fruit with Granitas: *Energy 434kcal/1854kJ; Protein 2.2g; Carbohydrate 111.7g, of which sugars 111.1g; Fat 0.8g, of which saturates 0.2g; Cholesterol 0mg; Calcium 77mg; Fibre 2.2g; Sodium 17mg.*
Orange Granita: *Energy 606kcal/2585kJ; Protein 2.9g; Carbohydrate 156.2g, of which sugars 155.5g; Fat 1g, of which saturates 0.2g; Cholesterol 0mg; Calcium 107mg; Fibre 2.8g; Sodium 23mg.*

Turkish Delight Sorbet

Serve this superb sorbet instead of sticky Turkish Delight. It has all the flavour and perfumed aroma of the sweetmeat from which it is made, but is refreshing and looks beautiful. Serve it in small portions with a pot of strong coffee.

Serves 4

250g/9oz rosewater-flavoured Turkish delight
30ml/2 tbsp sugar
750ml/1¼ pints/3 cups water
30ml/2 tbsp lemon juice
50g/2oz white chocolate, broken into squares
roughly chopped almonds, to decorate

1 Cut the Turkish delight into small pieces with a pair of scissors. Put half the pieces in a heavy pan with the sugar. Pour in half the water. Heat gently until the Turkish delight has dissolved, stirring. Cool, then stir in the lemon juice with the remaining water and Turkish delight. Chill in the refrigerator for several hours.

2 If you are using an ice cream maker, churn the mixture until it holds its shape. Otherwise, pour the mixture into a shallow freezerproof container and freeze for 3–4 hours, beating twice as it thickens. Return to the freezer until ready to serve.

3 While the sorbet is freezing, dampen eight very small plastic cups or glasses, then line them with clear film (plastic wrap).

4 Spoon the sorbet into the cups and tap them lightly on the surface to compact the mixture. Cover with the overlapping clear film and freeze for at least 3 hours or overnight.

5 Make a paper piping bag. Put the chocolate in a heatproof bowl and melt it over a pan of gently simmering water.

6 Remove the sorbets from the freezer, let them stand for 5 minutes, then pull them out of the cups. Transfer to serving plates and peel off the clear film. Spoon the melted chocolate into the piping bag, snip off the tip and scribble a design over the top of the sorbet and the plate. Sprinkle the almonds over the top and serve.

Rose Petal Sorbet

The ancient Egyptians, Romans, Persians and seafaring Arabs all used the rose for scenting and culinary purposes. By the time it reached the Ottoman palace kitchens, the petals had already been used to make rose water and wine. The palace chefs splashed rose water into their syrupy pastries and milk puddings, and infused the pretty petals in syrup to make fragrant jams and sorbets. This sorbet looks lovely served in frosted glasses or fine glass bowls, decorated with fresh or crystallized rose petals – these are easy to make by brushing the petals with whisked egg white, dipping them in sugar and leaving to dry until crisp.

Serves 3–4

fresh petals of 2 strongly scented red or pink roses, free from pesticides
225g/8oz/generous 1 cup caster (superfine) sugar
juice of 1 lemon
15ml/1 tbsp rose water

1 Wash the petals and cut off the white bases. Place in a pan with 600ml/1 pint/2½ cups water and bring to the boil. Turn off the heat, cover and leave the petals to steep for 10 minutes.

2 Strain off the water and reserve the petals. Pour the water back into the pan, add the sugar and bring to the boil, stirring, until the sugar has dissolved.

3 Boil for 1–2 minutes, then lower the heat and simmer for 5–10 minutes, until the syrup thickens a little.

4 Stir in the lemon juice, rose water and reserved petals; turn off the heat and leave the mixture to cool in the pan.

5 Freeze the mixture in an ice cream maker, or pour into a freezer container and place in the freezer until beginning to set. Take the sorbet out of the freezer at 2–3 hour intervals and whisk to disperse the ice crystals.

6 Before serving, take the sorbet out of the freezer for 5–10 minutes, so that it softens enough to scoop.

Turkish Delight Sorbet: *Energy 280Kcal/1188kJ; Protein 1.4g; Carbohydrate 63.8g, of which sugars 58g; Fat 3.9g, of which saturates 2.3g; Cholesterol 0mg; Calcium 44mg; Fibre 0g; Sodium 34mg.*
Rose Petal Sorbet: *Energy 222kcal/946kJ; Protein 0.3g; Carbohydrate 58.8g, of which sugars 58.8g; Fat 0g, of which saturates 0g; Cholesterol 0mg; Calcium 30mg; Fibre 0g; Sodium 4mg.*

Apricot and Amaretti Ice Cream

Prolong the very short season of fresh apricots by transforming them into this superb and very simple ice cream made with whipped cream. Crushed amaretti biscuits, which are flavoured with apricot kernels, add a contrasting texture.

Serves 4–6

500g/1¼lb fresh apricots, halved and stoned (pitted)
juice of 1 orange
50g/2oz/¼ cup caster (superfine) sugar
300ml/½ pint/1¼ cups whipping cream
50g/2oz amaretti biscuits

1 Put the apricots, orange juice and sugar in a saucepan. Cover and simmer for 5 minutes until the fruit is tender. Leave to cool.

2 Lift out one-third of the fruit and set it aside on a plate. Transfer the remaining contents of the pan into a food processor or blender and process to a smooth purée.

3 Whip the cream until just thick but still soft enough to fall from a spoon. Gradually fold in the fruit purée.

4 Pour into a freezerproof container and freeze for 4 hours, beating once with a fork, electric mixer or in a food processor. Alternatively, use an ice cream maker to churn the apricot purée until it is slushy, then gradually add the whipped cream. Continue to churn until the ice cream is thick, but not yet firm enough to scoop.

5 Beat the ice cream for a second time and crumble in the amaretti biscuits. Add the reserved apricots and gently fold the extra ingredients into the ice cream. (Scrape the ice cream into a tub to do this if you are using an ice cream maker.) Freeze for 2–3 hours or until firm enough to scoop.

Cook's Tip
Chill the fruit purée if you have time; this will speed up the churning or freezing process. If you have some amaretto liqueur, fold in 45ml/3 tbsp with the biscuits.

Istanbul Chewy Ice Cream

There are many delicious ice creams made in Turkey, but this stands out. Pine-scented mastic provides the chewy consistency, while salep, or ground orchid root, acts as a thickening agent. Mastic and salep are both available in Middle Eastern stores.

Serves 4

900ml/1½ pints/3¾ cups full-fat (whole) milk
300ml/½ pint/1¼ cups double (heavy) cream
225g/8oz/generous 1 cup sugar
45ml/3 tbsp ground salep
1–2 pieces of mastic crushed with a little sugar

1 Put the milk, cream and sugar into a heavy pan and bring to the boil, stirring all the time, until the sugar has dissolved. Lower the heat and simmer for 10 minutes.

2 Put the salep into a bowl. Moisten it with a little cold milk, add a spoonful of the hot, sweetened milk, then tip it into the pan, stirring all the time. Beat the mixture gently and stir in the mastic, then continue simmering for 10–15 minutes.

3 Pour the liquid into a freezer container, cover with a dry dish towel and leave to cool.

4 Remove the towel, cover the container with foil and place it in the freezer. Leave to set, beating it at intervals to disperse the ice crystals. Alternatively, churn it in an ice cream maker.

5 Before serving, allow the ice cream to sit out of the freezer for 5–10 minutes so that it becomes soft enough to scoop.

Cook's Tip
Mastic is the aromatic gum from a tree, Pistacia lentiscus, *that grows wild in the Mediterranean. It is sold in clear crystal form, and its aroma indicates the strength of the resinous taste it will impart to the dish, along with a chewy texture. Before using it, the crystals must be pulverized with a little sugar, using a mortar and pestle.*

Apricot Ice Cream: *Energy 289kcal/1202kJ; Protein 2.3g; Carbohydrate 23.4g, of which sugars 19.8g; Fat 21.3g, of which saturates 13.1g; Cholesterol 53mg; Calcium 58mg; Fibre 1.6g; Sodium 43mg.*
Istanbul Ice Cream: *Energy 742kcal/3093kJ; Protein 8.9g; Carbohydrate 70.2g, of which sugars 70.2g; Fat 49.1g, of which saturates 30.7g; Cholesterol 134mg; Calcium 332mg; Fibre 0g; Sodium 117mg.*

Cassata

This irresistible Italian ice cream combines the flavours of pistachio, vanilla and tutti frutti. In this version, it is layered in a terrine.

Serves 8
6 egg yolks
225g/8oz/generous 1 cup caster (superfine) sugar
15ml/1 tbsp cornflour (cornstarch)
600ml/1 pint/2½ cups milk
600ml/1 pint/2½ cups double (heavy) cream
75g/3oz/¾ cup pistachios
2.5ml/½ tsp almond essence
dash each of green and red food colouring
40g/1½oz/¼ cup candied peel, finely chopped
50g/2oz/¼ cup glacé cherries, washed, dried and finely chopped
5ml/1 tsp vanilla extract

1 Whisk the egg yolks, sugar, cornflour and a little of the milk in a bowl until pale and creamy. Bring the remaining milk and the cream to the boil in a large pan. Immediately pour into the egg yolk mixture in a steady stream, whisking well. Pour back into the pan and cook gently, stirring until thickened. Do not let the mixture boil. Remove from the heat and divide into three equal quantities. Cover and leave to cool.

2 Cover the pistachios with boiling water and leave for 1 minute. Drain them and rub off the skins with kitchen paper. Roughly chop and add to one bowl with the almond essence and a drop of green food colouring. Stir the candied peel, cherries and a drop of red food colouring into the second bowl. Stir the vanilla into the third.

3 Pour the mixtures into 3 separate tubs and freeze them until thickened, beating twice. Line a dampened 900g/2lb terrine or loaf tin (pan) with baking parchment (parchment paper). Put the pistachio ice cream into the prepared tin, then the vanilla, then the tutti frutti. Freeze overnight until firm.

4 To serve, dip the tin in very hot water for 2–3 seconds, then place a long serving plate upside down on top of it. Turn them over. Lift off the container. Peel away the lining paper. Serve the cassata in slices.

Almond and Pistachio Ice Creams

Sit at a pavement café in Italy and you can sample some of the most delicious ice creams in the world. There's keen debate about which tastes the best. Cool green pistachio and snowy almond come high on the list, and when presented together, they are truly sensational.

Serves 4
For the almond ice cream
150g/5oz/1¼ cups blanched almonds, finely ground
300ml/½ pint/1¼ cups milk
300ml/½ pint/1¼ cups double (heavy) cream
4 egg yolks
175g/6oz/generous ¾ cup caster (superfine) sugar
30–45ml/2–3 tbsp orange flower water
2–3 drops almond extract

For the pistachio ice cream
150g/5oz/1¼ cups pistachio nuts, blanched and finely ground
300ml/½ pint/1¼ cups milk
300ml/½ pint/1¼ cups double (heavy) cream
4 egg yolks
175g/6oz/generous ¾ cup caster (superfine) sugar
30–45ml/2–3 tbsp rose water
green food colouring (optional)

1 To make the almond ice cream, put the nuts in a pan with the milk and cream, and bring to the boil. In a bowl, beat the egg yolks with the sugar, then pour in the hot milk and cream, beating all the time. Pour the mixture back into the pan and stir over a low heat, until it thickens slightly. Do not overheat or it will curdle. Stir in the orange flower water and almond essence, then leave to cool.

2 Pour into a freezerproof container and chill, then freeze. Whisk the mixture thoroughly after about 1 hour, when it should be icy around the edges. Continue to freeze the ice cream, whisking it two or three more times, until it is smooth and very thick. Freeze for several hours or overnight.

3 Make the pistachio ice cream in the same way as the almond ice cream. Add a little green food colouring, if you like.

4 Remove both batches of ice cream from the freezer 10–15 minutes before serving to allow them to soften slightly.

Cassata: Energy 380kcal/1598kJ; Protein 9.3g; Carbohydrate 50.7g, of which sugars 43.8g; Fat 13.3g, of which saturates 7.3g; Cholesterol 97mg; Calcium 72mg; Fibre 1.9g; Sodium 115mg.
Almond/Pistachio: Energy 1735kcal/7212kJ; Protein 28.4g; Carbohydrate 106.7g, of which sugars 104.8g; Fat 135.8g, of which saturates 59.3g; Cholesterol 618mg; Calcium 478mg; Fibre 5.1g; Sodium 325mg.

Strawberry Semi-freddo

As its name suggests, an Italian *semi-freddo*, like this quickly made strawberry and ricotta dessert, is best served semi-frozen to enjoy the flavour at its best. The addition of a little good-quality strawberry jam sweetens and rounds out the flavour of the fresh fruit. The contrasting texture of crisp dessert biscuits makes them the perfect accompaniment.

Serves 4–6

250g/9oz/generous 2 cups strawberries
115g/4oz/scant ½ cup strawberry jam
250g/9oz/generous 1 cup ricotta cheese
200g/7oz/scant 1 cup natural (plain) Greek yogurt
5ml/1 tsp vanilla extract
40g/1½oz/3 tbsp caster (superfine) sugar
extra strawberries and mint or lemon balm, to decorate

1 Put the strawberries in a bowl and mash them with a fork until broken into small pieces but not completely puréed. Stir in the strawberry jam.

2 Drain off any whey from the ricotta. Tip the ricotta into a bowl and stir in the Greek yogurt, vanilla extract and sugar. Using a dessertspoon, gently fold the mashed strawberries into the ricotta mixture until rippled.

3 Spoon the mixture into individual freezerproof dishes and freeze for at least 2 hours until almost solid. Alternatively freeze until completely solid, then transfer the ice cream to the refrigerator for about 30 minutes to soften before serving. Serve in small bowls with extra strawberries and decorated with mint or lemon balm.

Cook's Tips

- *Don't mash the fresh strawberries too much or they'll become too liquid.*
- *Freeze the dessert in a large freezerproof container if you don't have suitable small dishes. Transfer to the refrigerator to thaw slightly, then scoop into glasses.*

Iced Tiramisú

This favourite Italian combination is usually served chilled, but makes a marvellous, rich ice cream.

Serves 4

150g/5oz/¾ cup caster (superfine) sugar
150ml/¼ pint/⅔ cup water
250g/9oz/generous 1 cup mascarpone
200g/7oz/scant 1 cup virtually fat-free fromage frais
5ml/1 tsp vanilla extract
10ml/2 tsp instant coffee, dissolved in 30ml/2 tbsp boiling water
30ml/2 tbsp coffee liqueur or brandy
75g/3oz sponge finger biscuits
cocoa powder, for dusting
chocolate curls, to decorate

1 Put 115g/4oz/½ cup of the sugar into a small pan. Add the water and bring to the boil, stirring until the sugar has dissolved. Leave the syrup to cool, then chill.

2 Put the mascarpone into a bowl. Beat it with a spoon until it is soft, then stir in the fromage frais. Add the chilled sugar syrup, a little at a time, then stir in the vanilla extract.

3 Spoon the mixture into a freezerproof container and freeze for 4 hours, beating once with a fork, electric mixer or in a food processor to break up the ice crystals. If using an ice-cream maker, churn the mascarpone mixture until it is thick but not yet firm enough to scoop.

4 Meanwhile, put the instant coffee mixture in a small bowl, sweeten with the remaining sugar, then add the liqueur or brandy. Stir well and leave to cool. Crumble the biscuits and toss the pieces in the coffee mixture. If you have made the ice-cream by hand, beat it again.

5 Spoon a third of the ice-cream into a 900ml/1½ pint/3¾ cup freezerproof container, spoon over half the biscuits then top with half the remaining ice-cream. Sprinkle over the last of the coffee-soaked biscuits, then cover with the remaining ice-cream. Freeze for 2–3 hours until firm enough to scoop. Dust with cocoa powder and spoon into glass dishes. Decorate with chocolate curls, and serve.

Strawberry Semi-Freddo: *Energy 181kcal/764kJ; Protein 5.8g; Carbohydrate 29.6g, of which sugars 29.6g; Fat 5.3g, of which saturates 3.2g; Cholesterol 15mg; Calcium 91mg; Fibre 0.9g; Sodium 43mg.*
Iced Tiramisú: *Energy 362kcal/1526kJ; Protein 11.7g; Carbohydrate 54.5g, of which sugars 50.3g; Fat 10.5g, of which saturates 6.1g; Cholesterol 69mg; Calcium 78mg; Fibre 0.2g; Sodium 35mg.*

Honey-Baked Figs with Hazelnut Ice-Cream

In this delectable dessert, figs in a lightly spiced lemon and honey syrup are served with homemade roasted hazelnut ice cream.

Serves 4
finely pared rind of 1 lemon
1 cinnamon stick, roughly broken
60ml/4 tbsp clear honey
8 large figs

For the hazelnut ice cream
450ml/¾ pint/scant 2 cups double (heavy) cream
50g/2oz/¼ cup caster (superfine) sugar
3 large egg yolks
1.5ml/¼ tsp vanilla extract
75g/3oz/¾ cup hazelnuts

1 To make the ice cream, gently heat the cream until almost boiling. Meanwhile, beat the sugar and egg yolks until creamy. Stir a little hot cream into the egg mixture then pour it back into the pan and mix well. Cook over a low heat, stirring constantly, until the mixture thickens slightly and lightly coats the back of the spoon – do not boil. Pour the custard into a bowl, stir in the vanilla extract and leave to cool.

2 Preheat the oven to 180°C/350°F/Gas 4. Place the hazelnuts on a baking sheet and roast for 10–12 minutes, or until golden. Leave the nuts to cool, then grind them in a food processor.

3 Pour the custard into a freezerproof container and freeze for 2 hours. Turn it into a bowl and whisk until smooth. Stir in the nuts and freeze until half set. Beat again, then freeze until firm.

4 Preheat the oven to 200°C/400°F/Gas 6. To make the syrup, put the lemon rind, cinnamon stick, honey and 200ml/7fl oz/scant 1 cup water in a pan and heat slowly. Simmer the mixture for 5 minutes, then leave to stand for 15 minutes. Cut the figs almost into quarters, but leaving them attached at the base. Pack them into a casserole, in a single layer, and pour the syrup over them. Cover with foil and bake for 10 minutes. Serve the figs with the syrup poured round them, accompanied by a scoop or two of the ice cream.

Coffee and Chocolate Bombe

In Italy, commercial ice cream is so good that no one would dream of making their own for this dessert. Assembling this *zuccotto* is impressive enough in itself.

Serves 6–8
15–18 savoiardi (sponge fingers)
about 175 ml/6 fl oz/¾ cup sweet Marsala
75 g/3 oz amaretti biscuits
about 475 ml/16 fl oz/2 cups coffee ice cream, softened
about 475 ml/16 fl oz/2 cups vanilla ice cream, softened
50 g/2 oz dark (bittersweet) chocolate, grated
chocolate curls and sifted cocoa powder or icing (confectioner's) sugar, to decorate

1 Line a 1 litre/1¾ pint/4-cup pudding basin with a large piece of damp muslin (cheesecloth), letting it hang over the edge. Trim the sponge fingers to fit the basin. Pour the Marsala into a shallow dish. Dip in a sponge finger, turning it quickly so that it becomes saturated but does not disintegrate. Stand it against the side of the basin, sugared-side out. Repeat with the remaining sponge fingers to line the basin fully. Fill in the base and any gaps with trimmings cut to fit. Chill for 30 minutes.

2 Put the amaretti biscuits in a large bowl and crush them with a rolling pin. Add the coffee ice cream and any remaining Marsala and mix well. Spoon into the sponge-finger-lined basin. Press the ice cream against the sponge fingers to form an even layer with a central hollow. Freeze for 2 hours.

3 Put the vanilla ice cream and grated chocolate in a bowl and beat together until evenly mixed. Spoon into the hollow in the centre of the mould. Smooth the top, then cover with the overhanging muslin. Place in the freezer overnight.

4 To serve, run a palette knife between the muslin and the basin, then unfold the top of the muslin. Invert a chilled serving plate on top of the zuccotto, then invert the two so that the zuccotto is upside down on the plate. Peel off the muslin.

5 Decorate the zuccotto with the chocolate curls, then sift cocoa powder or icing sugar over. Serve immediately.

Baked Figs: *Energy 433kcal/1816kJ; Protein 1.8g; Carbohydrate 53.6g, of which sugars 52.1g; Fat 21.2g, of which saturates 7g; Cholesterol 24mg; Calcium 227mg; Fibre 4.2g; Sodium 88mg.*
Coffee Bombe: *Energy 433kcal/1810kJ; Protein 8g; Carbohydrate 46.1g, of which sugars 36.3g; Fat 22.6g, of which saturates 12.8g; Cholesterol 57mg; Calcium 154mg; Fibre 0.5g; Sodium 126mg.*

Poached Apricots in Scented Syrup with Buffalo Cream

A legacy of the Ottoman Empire, this Turkish dish is simple yet sophisticated. The apricots are poached in a light syrup scented with orange blossom water, then filled with the Turkish buffalo cream called *kaymak*. Served chilled, it is deliciously sweet and refreshing.

Serves 4
250g/9oz/generous 1 cup dried apricots, soaked in cold water for at least 6 hours or overnight
200g/7oz/1 cup sugar
juice of 1 lemon
30ml/2 tbsp orange blossom water
225g/8oz kaymak (see Cook's Tip)

1 Drain the soaked apricots and measure 250ml/8fl oz/1 cup of the soaking water (if there is not enough, make up the amount with fresh water). Pour the measured liquid into a pan, add the sugar and bring to the boil, stirring all the time.

2 When the sugar has dissolved, boil the syrup vigorously for 2–3 minutes. Lower the heat, stir in the lemon juice and orange blossom water, then slip in the apricots and poach gently for 15–20 minutes. Leave to cool in the syrup.

3 Lift an apricot out of the syrup. Pull it open with your fingers, or slit it with a knife, and fill with the *kaymak*. Place the filled apricot, cream side up, in a shallow serving dish and repeat with the remaining apricots and cream.

4 Carefully spoon the syrup around the filled apricots, so the flesh of the fruit is kept moist but the cream is not submerged. Place the dish in the refrigerator to chill before serving.

Cook's Tip
Made from the milk of water buffalos, kaymak is very thick, almost like clotted cream. If you cannot find it, you can fill the apricots with crème fraîche or clotted cream instead.

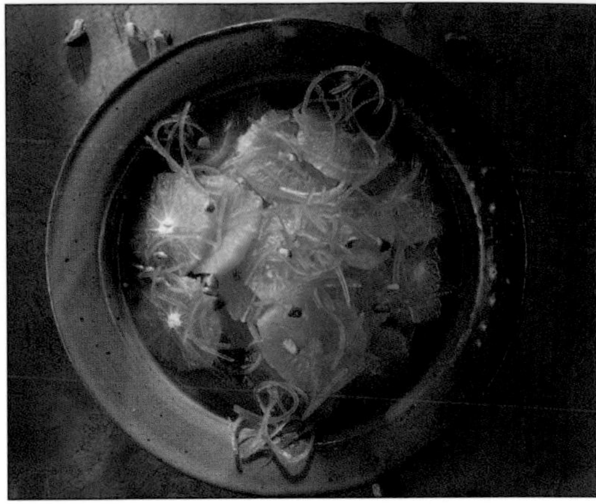

Oranges in Syrup

Both bitter and sweet oranges are extensively cultivated in the Middle East. Of the sweet varieties, Jaffa, which originated in Israel, is probably the best known. This method of serving them, in syrup scented with orange blossom or rose, is very popular.

Serves 4
4 oranges
600ml/1 pint/2½ cups water
350g/12oz/1¾ cups granulated (white) sugar
30ml/2 tbsp lemon juice
30ml/2 tbsp orange flower water or rose water
50g/2oz/½ cup chopped pistachio nuts, to decorate

1 Remove the peel from the oranges with a vegetable peeler, leaving the pith behind.

2 Cut the orange peel into fine strips. Cover with water in a small pan and bring to the boil. Repeat, changing the water several times, to remove the bitterness from the peel. Drain and set aside until required.

3 Place the water, sugar and lemon juice in a pan. Bring to the boil and add the reserved slivers of orange peel. Simmer until the syrup thickens. Stir in the orange flower or rose water, and leave to cool.

4 Using a very sharp knife, completely cut the pith away from the oranges and cut the fruit horizontally into thick slices. Place the slices in a shallow serving dish and pour over the syrup, distributing the strips of peel evenly.

5 Chill the oranges for about 1–2 hours. Decorate with pistachio nuts and serve.

Cook's Tip
This is a perfect dessert to serve after a heavy main course dish. Toasted almonds could be substituted for the pistachio nuts, if you prefer.

Poached Apricots: Energy 333kcal/1416kJ; Protein 4.6g; Carbohydrate 77.6g, of which sugars 77.6g; Fat 2.6g, of which saturates 1.4g; Cholesterol 8mg; Calcium 139mg; Fibre 4g; Sodium 36mg.
Oranges in Syrup: Energy 120kcal/500kJ; Protein 3.6g; Carbohydrate 11.2g, of which sugars 10.9g; Fat 7.1g, of which saturates 0.9g; Cholesterol 0mg; Calcium 70mg; Fibre 2.8g; Sodium 72mg.

Fresh Figs Baked with Honey, Vanilla and Cinnamon

Baking fruit with honey is an ancient cooking method, perhaps devised when local fruit harvests were so abundant there was too much to eat fresh. This is a dish most often made with apricots or figs in rural homes, where it is sometimes served as a sweet snack for everyone to share, with bread to mop up the yogurt and honey. Spices and herbs, such as aniseed, cinnamon, rosemary and lavender, are often used for flavouring. Choose ripe figs with a sweet, pink interior, and an aromatic honey.

Serves 3–4
12 ripe figs
30ml/2 tbsp vanilla sugar
3–4 cinnamon sticks
45–60ml/3–4 tbsp clear honey
225g/8oz/1 cup chilled thick and creamy natural (plain) yogurt, or clotted cream

1 Preheat the oven to 200°C/400°F/Gas 6. Wash the figs and pat them dry. Using a sharp knife, cut a deep cross from the top of each fig to the bottom, keeping the skin at the bottom intact. Fan each fig out, so it looks like a flower, then place them upright in a baking dish, preferably an earthenware one.

2 Sprinkle the vanilla sugar over each fig, tuck in the cinnamon sticks and drizzle with honey. Bake for 15–20 minutes, until the sugar is slightly caramelized but the honey and figs are still moist.

3 Eat the figs straight away. Spoon a dollop of yogurt or cream into the middle of each one and scoop them up with your fingers, or serve them in bowls and let everyone help themselves to the yogurt or cream.

Cook's Tip
To make the vanilla sugar for this recipe, split a vanilla pod (bean) lengthways in half, scrape out the seeds and mix them with 30ml/2 tbsp caster (superfine) sugar.

Poached Pears in Scented Honey Syrup

Mediterranean fruit has been poached in honey-sweetened syrup since ancient times. The Moroccans continue the tradition enjoyed by the Persians, Arabs, Moors and Ottomans in the past. They sometimes add a little orange rind or aniseed, or even a few sprigs of lavender, to give the poaching liquid a subtle flavouring. Delicate and pretty to look at, these scented pears would provide an exquisite finishing touch to any meal with a Middle Eastern or North African theme.

Serves 4
45ml/3 tbsp clear honey
juice of 1 lemon
250ml/8fl oz/1 cup water
pinch of saffron threads
1 cinnamon stick
2–3 dried lavender heads
4 firm pears

1 Heat the honey with the lemon juice in a heavy pan that will hold the pears snugly. Stir the mixture over a gentle heat until the honey has dissolved.

2 Add the water, saffron threads, cinnamon stick and the flowers from 1–2 lavender heads. Bring the mixture to the boil, then reduce the heat and simmer for 5 minutes.

3 Peel the pears, leaving the stalks attached. Add the pears to the syrup in the pan and simmer gently for 20 minutes, turning and basting at regular intervals, until they are tender.

4 Leave the pears to cool in the syrup and serve at room temperature, decorated with a few lavender flowers.

Variations
- *Use whole, peeled nectarines or peaches instead of pears.*
- *Omit the saffron, cinnamon and lavender and flavour the syrup with a split vanilla pod (bean).*

Fresh Figs Baked with Honey: *Energy 198kcal/845kJ; Protein 2.3g; Carbohydrate 48.2g, of which sugars 48.2g; Fat 1g, of which saturates 0g; Cholesterol 0mg; Calcium 155mg; Fibre 4.5g; Sodium 39mg.*
Poached Pears: *Energy 66kcal/278kJ; Protein 0.5g; Carbohydrate 16.5g, of which sugars 16.5g; Fat 0.2g, of which saturates 0g; Cholesterol 0mg; Calcium 17mg; Fibre 3.3g; Sodium 5mg.*

Figs and Pears in Spiced Syrup

Fresh figs picked straight from the tree are so delicious that it seems almost sacrilege to cook them – unless you have so many that you fancy a change, when you can try this superb recipe.

Serves 4
1 lemon
90ml/6 tbsp clear honey
1 cinnamon stick
1 cardamom pod
350ml/12fl oz/1½ cups water
2 pears
8 fresh figs, halved

1 Pare the rind from the lemon using a zester or vegetable peeler and cut the rind into very thin strips.

2 Place the lemon rind, honey, cinnamon stick, cardamom pod and the water in a pan and boil, uncovered, for about 10 minutes, until the liquid is reduced by about half.

3 Cut the pears into eighths, discarding the core. Leave the peel on or discard, as preferred. Place in the syrup, add the figs and simmer for about 5 minutes, until the fruit is tender.

4 Transfer the fruit to a serving bowl with a slotted spoon. Cook the liquid until syrupy, discard the cinnamon stick and pour over the figs and pears. Serve warm or cold.

Figs with Honey and Wine

The best figs come from Greece and Turkey. Any variety can be used in this recipe, but choose figs that are plump and firm, and use them quickly, as they don't store well.

Serves 6
450ml/¾ pint/scant 2 cups dry white wine
75g/3oz/⅓ cup clear honey
50g/2oz/¼ cup caster (superfine) sugar
1 small orange
8 whole cloves
450g/1lb fresh figs
1 cinnamon stick
mint or bay leaves, to decorate

For the cream
300ml/½ pint 1¼ cups double (heavy) cream
1 vanilla pod (bean)
5ml/1 tsp caster (superfine) sugar

1 Put the wine, honey and sugar in a heavy pan and heat gently until the sugar has dissolved.

2 Stud the orange with the cloves and add to the syrup with the figs and cinnamon. Cover and simmer gently for 5–10 minutes, until the figs are softened.

3 Transfer the figs to a serving dish and decorate with bay or mint leaves. Leave to cool.

4 Put 150ml/¼ pint/⅔ cup of the cream in a small pan with the vanilla pod. Bring almost to the boil, then leave to cool and infuse for 30 minutes. If you enjoy a stronger flavour of vanilla, split the pod and scoop some of the seeds into the warm cream.

5 Remove the vanilla pod and mix the vanilla cream with the remaining cream and sugar in a large bowl. Whip lightly to a spooning consistency. Transfer to a serving dish and serve with the figs.

Yogurt with Apricots and Pistachios

If you let plain yogurt drain overnight, it becomes much thicker and more luscious. Add honeyed apricots and nuts and you have a simple dessert with a taste that will transport you to the Mediterranean.

Serves 4
450g/1lb natural (plain) yogurt
115g/4oz/⅔ cup dried apricots, chopped
15ml/1 tbsp honey
orange rind, grated
30ml/2 tbsp unsalted pistachio nuts, shelled and chopped
ground cinnamon

1 Place the yogurt in a fine sieve (strainer) and let it drain overnight in the refrigerator over a bowl.

2 Discard the whey from the yogurt, Place the apricots in a pan, barely cover with water and simmer for just 3 mintues, to soften. Drain and cool, then mix with the honey.

3 Mix the yogurt with the apricots, orange rind and nuts. Spoon into sundae dishes, sprinkle over a little cinnamon and chill thoroughly.

Figs and Pears in Honey: *Energy 143kcal/606kJ; Protein 1.7g; Carbohydrate 34.4g, of which sugars 34.4g; Fat 0.7g, of which saturates 0g; Cholesterol 0mg; Calcium 109mg; Fibre 4.7g; Sodium 28mg.*
Figs, Honey and Wine: *Energy 316kcal/1318kJ; Protein 1.8g; Carbohydrate 29.7g, of which sugars 29.7g; Fat 18.4g, of which saturates 11.1g; Cholesterol 46mg; Calcium 101mg; Fibre 2.3g; Sodium 30mg.*
Yogurt with Apricots: *Energy 255kcal/1064kJ; Protein 10.3g; Carbohydrate 21.7g, of which sugars 21.5g; Fat 15.9g, of which saturates 6.4g; Cholesterol 0mg; Calcium 209mg; Fibre 3.2g; Sodium 126mg.*

Caramelized Apricots with Pain Perdu

Pain perdu is a French invention that literally translates as "lost bread". Americans call it French toast, while a British version is known as Poor Knights.

Serves 4
75g/3oz/6 tbsp unsalted butter, clarified
450g/1lb apricots, stoned (pitted) and thickly sliced
115g/4oz/½ cup caster (superfine) sugar
150ml/¼ pint/⅔ cup double (heavy) cream
30ml/2 tbsp apricot brandy

For the pain perdu
600ml/1 pint/2½ cups milk
1 vanilla pod (bean)
50g/2oz/¼ cup caster (superfine) sugar
4 large eggs, beaten
115g/4oz/½ cup unsalted butter, clarified
6 brioche slices, diagonally halved
2.5ml/½ tsp ground cinnamon

1 Heat a heavy frying pan and melt a quarter of the butter. Add the apricot slices and cook for 2–3 minutes until golden. Using a slotted spoon, transfer them to a bowl. Heat the rest of the butter with the sugar, stirring, until golden.

2 Pour in the cream and brandy and cook gently until the mixture forms a smooth sauce. Boil for 2–3 minutes until thickened, then pour the sauce over the apricots and set aside.

3 To make the pain perdu, pour the milk into a saucepan and add the vanilla pod and half the sugar. Heat gently until almost boiling, then set aside to cool. Remove the vanilla pod and pour the milk into a shallow dish. Whisk in the eggs.

4 Heat a sixth of the butter in the clean frying pan. Dip a slice of brioche into the milk mixture and fry until golden brown on both sides. Add the remaining butter as needed. As the pain perdu is cooked, remove the slices and keep hot.

5 Warm the apricot sauce and spoon it on to the pain perdu. Mix the remaining sugar with the cinnamon and sprinkle a little over each portion.

Stuffed Peaches with Amaretto

Both amaretti biscuits and amaretto liqueur, made with bitter almonds or apricot kernels, have an intense almond flavour, and make good partners for peaches.

Serves 4
4 ripe but firm peaches
50g/2oz amaretti biscuits
25g/1oz/2 tbsp butter, softened
25g/1oz/2 tbsp caster (superfine) sugar
1 egg yolk
60ml/4 tbsp amaretto liqueur
250ml/8fl oz/1 cup dry white wine
8 tiny sprigs of basil, to decorate
ice cream or pouring cream, to serve

1 Preheat the oven to 180°C/350°F/Gas 4. Following the natural indentation line on each peach, cut in half down to the central stone (pit), then twist the halves in opposite directions to separate them. Remove the peach stones, then cut away a little of the central flesh to make a larger hole for the stuffing. Chop this flesh finely and set aside.

2 Put the amaretti biscuits in a bowl and crush them finely with the end of a rolling pin.

3 Cream the butter and sugar together in a separate bowl until smooth. Stir in the reserved chopped peach flesh, the egg yolk and half the amaretto liqueur with the amaretti crumbs.

4 Lightly butter a baking dish that is just large enough to hold the peach halves in a single layer. Spoon the stuffing into the peaches, then stand them in the dish.

5 Mix the remaining liqueur with the wine, pour over the peaches and bake for 25 minutes or until the peaches feel tender when tested with a skewer. Decorate with basil and serve immediately, with ice cream or cream.

Cook's Tip
Amaretto and amaretti get their name from the Italian word amaro, *which means "bitter".*

Caramelized Apricots: Energy 1071kcal/4471kJ; Protein 18.5g; Carbohydrate 92.1g, of which sugars 69.2g; Fat 70.9g, of which saturates 41.6g; Cholesterol 353mg; Calcium 343mg; Fibre 3.3g; Sodium 634mg.
Peaches with Amaretto: Energy 255kcal/1068kJ; Protein 2.6g; Carbohydrate 29.4g, of which sugars 24g; Fat 8.2g, of which saturates 4.4g; Cholesterol 64mg; Calcium 40mg; Fibre 1.7g; Sodium 87mg.

Chocolate Amaretti Peaches

Quick and easy to prepare, this delicious dessert can equally well be made with fresh nectarines or large apricots. Choose fruits that are ripe but not too soft, so that they will retain their shape when cooked. If the stones are small, it's a good idea to enlarge the cavities in the fruit to take a good dollop of filling: add the scooped out flesh to the amaretti mixture before stuffing the peaches.

Serves 4
115g/4oz amaretti biscuits, crushed
50g/2oz dark (bittersweet) chocolate, chopped
grated rind of ½ orange
15ml/1 tbsp clear honey
1.5ml/¼ tsp ground cinnamon
1 egg white, lightly beaten
4 firm ripe peaches
150ml/ ¼ pint/ ⅔ cup white wine
15ml/1 tbsp caster (superfine) sugar
whipped cream, to serve

1 Preheat the oven to 190°C/375°F/Gas 5. Mix together the crushed amaretti biscuits, chocolate, orange rind, honey and cinnamon in a bowl. Add the beaten egg white and stir to bind.

2 Halve and stone the peaches and fill the cavities with the amaretti mixture, mounding it up slightly.

3 Arrange the stuffed peaches in a lightly buttered, shallow ovenproof dish which will just hold them comfortably.

4 Pour the white wine into a measuring jug, then stir in the sugar. Pour the wine mixture around the peaches.

5 Bake for 30–40 minutes, until the peaches are tender. Spoon a little of the cooking juices over the peaches to serve and accompany with whipped cream.

Variation
Omit the chocolate and increase the amount of amaretti. Let the peaches cool, then serve on a bed of vanilla ice cream, accompanied by a raspberry sauce.

Apple-Stuffed Crêpes

Spain's northern coast is apple and cider country, but these apple crêpes are popular all over the region.

Serves 4
115g/4oz/1 cup plain (all-purpose) flour
pinch of salt
2 eggs
175ml/6fl oz/¾ cup milk
120ml/4fl oz/½ cup sweet (hard) cider
butter, for frying
4 eating apples
60ml/4 tbsp caster (superfine) sugar
120ml/8 tbsp clear honey, and 150ml/¼ pint/⅔ cup double (heavy) cream, to serve

1 To make the batter, sift the flour and salt into a large bowl. Add the eggs and milk and beat until smooth. Stir in the cider. Leave to stand for 30 minutes.

2 Heat a small heavy non-stick frying pan. Add a little butter and ladle in enough batter to coat the pan thinly.

3 Cook the crêpe for about 1 minute until it is golden underneath, then flip it over and cook the other side until golden. Slide the crêpe on to a plate, then repeat with the remaining batter to make seven more. Set the crêpes aside and keep warm.

4 To make the apple filling, core the apples and cut them into thick slices. Heat 15g/½oz butter in a large frying pan. Add the apples to the pan and cook until the slices are golden on both sides. Transfer the slices to a bowl with a slotted spoon and sprinkle with sugar.

5 Fold each pancake in half, then fold in half again to form a cone. Fill each with some of the fried apples. Place two filled pancakes on each dessert plate. Drizzle with a little honey and serve at once, accompanied by cream.

Cook's Tip
For the best results, use full-fat (whole) milk in the batter.

Chocolate Amaretti Peaches: Energy 282kcal/1190kJ; Protein 4.1g; Carbohydrate 47g, of which sugars 34.4g; Fat 7.4g, of which saturates 3.8g; Cholesterol 1mg; Calcium 56mg; Fibre 2.4g; Sodium 117mg.
Stuffed Crêpes: Energy 489kcal/2057kJ; Protein 8.2g; Carbohydrate 71.5g, of which sugars 49.6g; Fat 20.1g, of which saturates 11.3g; Cholesterol 139mg; Calcium 137mg; Fibre 2.1g; Sodium 69mg.

Moroccan-style Plum Pudding

There's a strong French influence in Moroccan cooking, as evidenced by this North African version of the French batter pudding known as clafouti, which is usually made with cherries. In this pudding, ground rice and flaked almonds are used instead of eggs, cream and flour to thicken the milk mixture, which is flavoured with orange flower water.

Serves 4

450g/1lb fresh plums or other fruit (see Variation)
600ml/1 pint/2½ cups skimmed or semi-skimmed (low-fat) milk
45ml/3 tbsp ground rice
30–45ml/2–3 tbsp caster (superfine) sugar
75g/3oz/¾ cup flaked almonds
30ml/2 tbsp orange flower water or rose water, to taste
icing (confectioners') sugar, to decorate

1 Preheat the oven to 190°C/375°F/Gas 5. Stone and halve the plums. Bring the milk to the boil in a pan.

2 Blend the ground rice with 30–45ml/2–3 tbsp cold water, beating well to make a smooth paste and avoid lumps.

3 Pour the hot milk over the rice and stir until smooth, then pour the mixture back into the pan. Simmer over a low heat for 5 minutes, until it thickens, stirring all the time.

4 Add the caster sugar and flaked almonds and cook gently for a further 5 minutes. Stir in the orange flower or rose water and simmer for 2 minutes.

5 Butter a shallow ovenproof dish and pour in the almond milk mixture. Arrange the prepared fruit on top and then bake in the oven for about 25–30 minutes, until the fruit has softened. Dust with sifted icing sugar and serve.

Variation
Apricots, cherries or greengages can be used instead of plums for this pudding.

Peach and Apple Compote

Arrope is an old Arab recipe whose name means "syrup". This version of it comes from the Pyrenees. It starts as a lovely fruit compote and becomes a syrupy jam, perfect with soft bread.

Serves 10

3 firm peaches
1kg/2¼lb/5 cups sugar
3 large eating apples
finely grated rind of 1 lemon
3 firm pears
finely grated rind of 1 orange
1 small sweet potato, 150g/5oz prepared weight
200g/7oz butternut squash, peeled, prepared weight
250ml/8fl oz/1 cup dark rum
30ml/2 tbsp clear honey

1 Cut the peaches into eighths, without peeling, and place in a large flameproof casserole. Sprinkle with 15ml/1 tbsp of the sugar. Peel and core the apples and cut into 16 segments, then arrange on top of the peaches. Sprinkle with the lemon rind and 15ml/1 tbsp of the sugar. Prepare the pears in the same way, place in the casserole, then sprinkle over the orange rind, followed by 15ml/1 tbsp of the sugar.

2 Slice the sweet potato into small pieces and spread over the top, followed by the sliced squash. Sprinkle with 15ml/1 tbsp of the sugar. Cover with a plate that fits inside the rim, weight it and leave for 2–12 hours for juice to form.

3 Put the casserole over a fairly low heat and bring to a simmer. Cook for 20 minutes, stirring once or twice. Add the remaining sugar, in three or four batches, stirring to dissolve each time. Bring the mixture up to a rolling boil and boil very steadily for 45 minutes. Stir and lift off any scum.

4 Test the reduced syrup by pouring a spoonful on a plate. It should wrinkle when a spoon is pulled across it. Off the heat, stir in the rum and honey. Return the casserole to a moderate heat and cook for a further 10 minutes, stirring frequently to prevent the fruit sticking. The colour will deepen to russet brown. Remove the pan from the heat and set aside to cool. If the resulting compote is a little too stiff, stir in some more rum before serving.

Moroccan Plum Pudding: Energy 186kcal/790kJ; Protein 1.8g; Carbohydrate 45.9g, of which sugars 45.9g; Fat 0.7g, of which saturates 0g; Cholesterol 0mg; Calcium 110mg; Fibre 4.7g; Sodium 30mg.
Peach and Apple Compote: Energy 308kcal/1291kJ; Protein 1g; Carbohydrate 38.1g, of which sugars 28.6g; Fat 13.2g, of which saturates 2.4g; Cholesterol 9mg; Calcium 246mg; Fibre 2.4g; Sodium 69mg.

Lemon Coeur à la Crème with Cointreau Oranges

This zesty dessert is the ideal choice to follow a rich main course such as roast pork. The little sweetened cream cheese puddings are traditionally made in pierced heart-shaped moulds, hence their name.

Serves 4
225g/8oz/1 cup cottage cheese
250g/9oz/generous 1 cup mascarpone cheese
50g/2oz/¼ cup caster (superfine) sugar
grated rind and juice of 1 lemon
spirals of orange rind, to decorate

For the Cointreau oranges
4 oranges
10ml/2 tsp cornflour (cornstarch)
15ml/1 tbsp icing (confectioner's) sugar
60ml/4 tbsp Cointreau

1 Put the cottage cheese in a food processor or blender and whizz until smooth. Add the mascarpone, caster sugar, lemon rind and juice and process briefly to mix the ingredients.

2 Line four coeur à la crème moulds with muslin, then divide the mixture among them. Level the surface of each, then place all the moulds on a plate to catch any liquid that drains from the cheese. Cover and chill overnight.

3 To make the Cointreau oranges, squeeze the juice from two oranges and pour into a measuring jug. Make the juice up to 250ml/8fl oz/1 cup with water, then pour into a small saucepan. Blend a little of the juice mixture with the cornflour and add to the pan with the icing sugar. Heat the sauce gently, stirring, until it has thickened.

4 Using a sharp knife, peel and segment the remaining oranges. Add the segments to the pan, stir to coat, then set aside. When cool, stir in the Cointreau. Cover and chill overnight.

5 Turn the cream cheese moulds out on to plates and surround with the oranges. Decorate with spirals of orange rind and serve immediately.

Leche Frita with Black Fruit Sauce

The name of this Spanish dessert means "fried milk", but it is really custard squares with a creamy centre and crunchy, golden coating. Here, it is served hot with fruit sauce, but it is also good cold.

Serves 4–6
550ml/18fl oz/2½ cups full-fat (whole) milk
3 finely pared strips of lemon rind
½ cinnamon stick
90g/3½oz/½ cup caster (superfine) sugar, plus extra for sprinkling
60ml/4 tbsp cornflour (cornstarch)
30ml/2 tbsp plain (all-purpose) flour
3 large (US extra large) egg yolks
2 large (US extra large) eggs
90–120ml/6–8 tbsp stale breadcrumbs or dried crumbs
sunflower oil, for frying
ground cinnamon, for dusting

For the sauce
450g/1lb blackcurrants or blackberries
90g/3½oz/½ cup granulated sugar, plus extra for dusting

1 Put the milk, lemon rind, cinnamon stick and sugar in a pan and bring to the boil, stirring gently. Cover and leave to infuse for 20 minutes.

2 Put the cornflour and flour in a bowl and beat in the egg yolks with a wooden spoon. Add a little of the milk and beat to make a smooth batter.

3 Strain the remaining hot milk into the batter, then pour back into the pan. Cook over a low heat, stirring constantly. (The mixture won't curdle, but it will thicken unevenly if you don't stir it.) Cook for a couple of minutes, until it thickens and separates from the side of the pan.

4 Beat the mixture hard to ensure a really smooth consistency. Pour into an 18–20cm/7–8in, 1cm/½in-deep rectangular dish, and smooth the top. Cool, then chill until firm.

5 Meanwhile, make the fruit sauce. Cook the blackcurrants or blackberries with the sugar and a little water for about 10 minutes until soft. Reserve 30–45ml/2–3 tbsp whole currants or berries, then put the rest in a food processor and blend to a smooth purée. Return the purée and the whole berries to the pan and keep warm.

6 Cut the chilled custard into eight or twelve squares. Beat the eggs in a shallow dish and spread the breadcrumbs on a plate. Lift half of the squares with a metal spatula into the egg. Coat on both sides, then lift into the crumbs and cover all over. Repeat with the second batch of squares.

7 Pour about 1cm/½in oil into a deep frying pan and heat until very hot. Lift two or three coated squares with a metal spatula into the oil and fry for a couple of minutes, shaking or spooning the oil over the top, until golden. Reserve on kitchen paper while you fry the other batches.

8 To serve, arrange the custard squares on plates and sprinkle with sugar and cinnamon. Pour a circle of warm fruit sauce round the custard squares, distributing the whole berries evenly.

Lemon Coeur à la Crème: *Energy 333kcal/1400kJ; Protein 14.3g; Carbohydrate 36.8g, of which sugars 34.5g; Fat 11.4g, of which saturates 7g; Cholesterol 35mg; Calcium 137mg; Fibre 2.1g; Sodium 178mg.*
Leche Frita: *Energy 257kcal/1089kJ; Protein 6.9g; Carbohydrate 45.9g, of which sugars 30.6g; Fat 6.4g, of which saturates 2.7g; Cholesterol 133mg; Calcium 159mg; Fibre 2.3g; Sodium 143mg.*

Cold Lemon Soufflé with Caramelized Almond Topping

This refreshing dessert soufflé is terrific to look at and tastes light and luscious.

Serves 6
oil, for greasing
grated rind and juice of 3 large lemons
5 large (US extra large) eggs, separated
115g/4oz/½ cup caster (superfine) sugar
25ml/1½ tbsp powdered gelatine
450ml/¾ pint/scant 2 cups double (heavy) cream
75g/3oz/¾ cup flaked (sliced) almonds
75g/3oz/¾ cup icing (confectioners') sugar
3 physalis, to decorate

1 Cut a strip of baking parchment long enough to fit around a 900ml/1½ pint/3¾ cup soufflé dish and wide enough to extend 7.5cm/3in above the rim. Fit the strip around the dish, tape, then tie it around the top of the dish with string. Brush the inside of the paper lightly with oil.

2 Put the lemon rind and egg yolks in a bowl. Whisk in 75g/3oz/6 tbsp of the caster sugar until light and creamy. Place the lemon juice in a heatproof bowl and sprinkle over the gelatine. Set aside for 5 minutes, then place the bowl in a pan of simmering water. Heat, stirring occasionally, until the gelatine has dissolved. Cool slightly, then stir the gelatine mixture into the egg yolk mixture. In a separate bowl, lightly whip the cream to soft peaks. Fold into the egg yolk mixture and set aside.

3 Whisk the egg whites until stiff peaks form. Gradually whisk in the remaining caster sugar until the mixture is stiff and glossy. Lightly fold the whites into the yolk mixture. Pour into the dish, smooth the surface and chill for 4–5 hours or until set.

4 Preheat the grill (broiler). Scatter the almonds over an oiled baking sheet and sift the icing sugar over. Grill (broil) until the nuts are golden and the sugar has caramelized. Allow to cool, then remove the mixture from the sheet with a knife and break into pieces. When the soufflé has set, carefully peel off the paper. Pile the almonds on top and decorate with the physalis.

Crème Caramel

Of French origin, this creamy, caramel-flavoured custard now enjoys worldwide popularity. The Spanish version, known as *flan*, is practically a national dish. Do not put too much water into the roasting pan or it may bubble over into the ramekins.

Serves 6
90g/3½oz/½ cup granulated (white) sugar
300ml/½ pint/1¼ cups milk
300ml/½ pint/1¼ cups single (light) cream
6 large eggs
90ml/6 tbsp caster (superfine) sugar
2.5ml/½ tsp vanilla extract

1 Preheat the oven to 150°C/300°F/Gas 2 and half fill a large, deep roasting pan with water. Set aside until needed.

2 To make the caramel topping, place the granulated sugar in a small pan with 60ml/4 tbsp water and heat it gently, swirling the pan from time to time, until the sugar has dissolved. Then increase the heat and boil, without stirring, to a good caramel colour.

3 Immediately pour the caramel into six ramekin dishes, dividing it evenly, so that it covers the bases. Place the dishes in the roasting pan and set aside.

4 To make the egg custard, heat the milk and cream together in a pan until almost boiling. Meanwhile, beat together the eggs, caster sugar and vanilla extract.

5 Whisk the hot milk into the eggs and sugar, then pour the liquid through a sieve (strainer) on to the cooled caramel bases.

6 Bake in the oven for 1½–2 hours (topping up the water level after about 1 hour if necessary), or until the custards have set in the centre. Lift out the dishes and leave to cool, then cover and chill overnight.

7 Loosen the sides of the chilled custards with a round-bladed knife and invert on to serving plates, allowing the caramel sauce to run down the sides.

Lemon Soufflé: Energy 647kcal/2686kJ; Protein 10.3g; Carbohydrate 35.2g, of which sugars 34.9g; Fat 52.8g, of which saturates 27.2g; Cholesterol 293mg; Calcium 112mg; Fibre 0.9g; Sodium 90mg.
Crème Caramel: Energy 318kcal/1335kJ; Protein 9.8g; Carbohydrate 36.6g, of which sugars 36.6g; Fat 16g, of which saturates 8.2g; Cholesterol 221mg; Calcium 150mg; Fibre 0g; Sodium 108mg.

Crema Catalana

This delicious pudding from northern Spain is a cross between a crème caramel and a crème brûlée. It is not as rich as a crème brûlée but has a similar caramelized sugar topping. It is usually made and served in individual shallow earthenware dishes.

Serves 4
475ml/16fl oz/2 cups milk
rind of ½ lemon
1 cinnamon stick
4 egg yolks
105ml/7 tbsp caster (superfine) sugar
25ml/1½ tbsp cornflour (cornstarch)
grated nutmeg, for sprinkling

1 Put the milk in a pan with the lemon rind and cinnamon stick. Bring to the boil and simmer for 10 minutes then remove the rind and cinnamon.

2 Whisk the egg yolks and 45ml/3 tbsp of the sugar until pale yellow. Add the cornflour and mix well.

3 Stir in a few tablespoons of the hot milk, then add this mixture to the remaining milk. Return to the heat and cook gently, stirring, for about 5 minutes, until the mixture has thickened and is smooth. Do not let it boil. There should be no cornflour taste.

4 Pour the custard mixture into four shallow ovenproof dishes, about 13cm/5in in diameter. Leave to cool completely, then chill in the fridge, overnight if possible, until firm.

5 Before serving, preheat a grill (broiler). Sprinkle the surface of each custard evenly with 15ml/1 tbsp sugar and a little grated nutmeg. Place the puddings under the grill, on the highest shelf, and grill until the sugar caramelizes. This will only take a few seconds. Leave to cool for a few minutes before serving.

Cook's Tip
The caramelized topping will stay hard and crisp for only about 30 minutes, so leave the final step until shortly before serving.

Zabaglione

This sumptuous warm dessert is very quick and easy to make, but it does need to be served straight away. If you are serving it for a dinner party, assemble all the ingredients and equipment ahead of time so that all you have to do is quickly mix everything together once the main course is over.

Serves 6
4 egg yolks
65g/2½oz/⅓ cup caster (superfine) sugar
120ml/4fl oz/½ cup dry Marsala
savoiardi (Italian sponge fingers), to serve

1 Half fill a pan with water and bring it to simmering point. Put the egg yolks and sugar in a large heatproof bowl and beat with a hand-held electric mixer until pale and creamy.

2 Put the bowl over the pan and gradually pour in the Marsala, whisking the mixture until it is very thick and has increased in volume.

3 Remove the bowl from the water and pour the zabaglione into six heatproof, long-stemmed glasses. Serve immediately, with sponge fingers.

Cook's Tip
When whisking the egg yolks, make sure that the bottom of the bowl does not touch the water or they will scramble.

Crema Catalana: *Energy 244kcal/1030kJ; Protein 7.2g; Carbohydrate 38.8g, of which sugars 33g; Fat 7.8g, of which saturates 2.9g; Cholesterol 217mg; Calcium 182mg; Fibre 0g; Sodium 65mg.*
Zabaglione: *Energy 131kcal/548kJ; Protein 3g; Carbohydrate 14.1g, of which sugars 14.1g; Fat 5.5g, of which saturates 1.6g; Cholesterol 202mg; Calcium 31mg; Fibre 0g; Sodium 12mg.*

Tiramisú

The name of this Italian dessert translates as "pick me up", which is said to derive from the fact that it is so good that it literally makes you swoon as you eat it. It has become popular everywhere in recent years and there are many, many versions of the recipe. It can be adapted to suit your own taste – you can vary the amount of mascarpone, eggs, sponge fingers, coffee and liqueur.

Serves 6–8

3 eggs, separated
450g/1lb/2 cups mascarpone cheese, at room temperature
10ml/2 tsp vanilla sugar
175ml/6fl oz/¾ cup cold, very strong, black coffee
120ml/4fl oz/½ cup Kahlúa or other coffee-flavoured liqueur
18 savoiardi (Italian sponge fingers)
sifted cocoa powder and grated dark (bittersweet) chocolate, to finish

1 Put the egg whites in a grease-free bowl and whisk with an electric mixer until standing in stiff peaks.

2 Mix the mascarpone, vanilla sugar and egg yolks in a separate large bowl and whisk with the electric mixer until evenly combined. Fold in the egg whites.

3 Put a few spoonfuls of the mascarpone mixture in the bottom of a large serving bowl and spread it out evenly.

4 Mix the coffee and liqueur together in a shallow dish. Dip a sponge finger in the mixture, turn it quickly so that it becomes saturated but does not disintegrate, and place it on top of the mascarpone in the bowl. Add five more dipped sponge fingers, placing them side by side.

5 Spoon in about one-third of the remaining mixture and spread it out. Make more layers in the same way, ending with a layer of mascarpone.

6 Level the surface, then sift cocoa powder all over. Cover the dish and chill overnight. Before serving, sprinkle with more cocoa and grated chocolate.

Ricotta Pudding

This creamy, rich dessert, a spongeless version of *cassata Siciliana*, is very easy to make and, as it can be made up to 24 hours ahead, it is an ideal party dish. The combination of ricotta cheese and candied fruits is very popular in Sicily, where the recipe originated. The mixture often includes chocolate and is extremely rich. Fresh raspberries have been added to this version to lighten it.

Serves 4–6

225g/8oz/1 cup ricotta cheese
50g/2oz/⅓ cup candied fruits
60ml/4 tbsp sweet Marsala
250ml/8fl oz/1 cup double (heavy) cream
50g/2oz/¼ cup caster (superfine) sugar, plus extra to serve
finely grated rind of 1 orange
350g/12oz/2 cups fresh raspberries
strips of thinly pared orange rind, to decorate

1 Press the ricotta through a sieve into a bowl. Finely chop the candied fruits and stir into the sieved ricotta, together with half of the Marsala.

2 Put the cream, sugar and orange rind in another bowl and whip until the cream is standing in soft peaks. Fold the whipped cream into the ricotta mixture.

3 Spoon into individual glass serving bowls and top with the raspberries. Chill until serving time. Sprinkle with the remaining Marsala and dust the top of each bowl liberally with caster sugar just before serving. Decorate with the orange rind.

Cook's Tips

- *Buy candied fruits in large pieces from a good delicatessen or wholefood store – the chopped candied peel sold in tubs is too tough to eat raw, and should only be used in baking. The traditional Sicilian pudding includes candied pumpkin and orange peel.*
- *Ricotta needs to be used very fresh: it goes off after only a couple of days.*

Tiramisú: *Energy 215kcal/894kJ; Protein 8.5g; Carbohydrate 12.4g, of which sugars 10.2g; Fat 13.3g, of which saturates 5.9g; Cholesterol 118mg; Calcium 22mg; Fibre 0.1g; Sodium 48mg.*
Ricotta pudding: *Energy 354kcal/1472kJ; Protein 5g; Carbohydrate 18.9g, of which sugars 18.9g; Fat 28.1g, of which saturates 17.4g; Cholesterol 73mg; Calcium 51mg; Fibre 1.9g; Sodium 36mg.*

Festive Semolina Helva with Pine Nuts

In Turkey, this soft semolina helva signifies good fortune and is made for events such as moving house or starting a new job, but it is also traditional for a bereaved family to offer it to friends when someone dies. It is also associated with religious festivals, and makes a regular appearance at holiday celebrations. It is sweet and rich, with a texture rather like that of Italian polenta.

Serves 6–8

225g/8oz/1 cup butter
450g/1lb/scant 2¾cups semolina
45ml/3 tbsp pine nuts
900ml/1½ pints/3¾ cups milk
225g/8oz/generous 1 cup sugar
5–10ml/1–2 tsp ground cinnamon

1 Melt the butter in a heavy pan, stir in the semolina and pine nuts and cook over a medium heat, stirring all the time, until lightly browned.

2 Lower the heat and pour in the milk. Mix well, cover the pan with a dish towel and press the lid down tightly. Pull the flaps of the dish towel up and over the lid and simmer gently for 10–12 minutes, until the milk has been absorbed.

3 Add the sugar and stir until it has dissolved. Cover the pan with the dish towel and lid again, remove from the heat and leave to stand for 1 hour.

4 To serve, mix well with a wooden spoon and spoon into bowls, then dust with cinnamon.

Cook's Tip

Helva, or halva, is a sweet confection made in Greece, Turkey, Bulgaria and the Middle East, as well as in India and Pakistan. There are various forms. The type made with tahini, or sesame paste, is dry and crumbly, usually flavoured with honey, and often contains pistachio nuts.

Chocolate Ravioli

This spectacular Italian dessert is made from sweet pasta. The little packets contain a creamy white chocolate filling.

Serves 4

175g/6oz/1½ cups plain (all-purpose) flour
pinch of salt
25g/1oz/¼ cup cocoa powder
30ml/2 tbsp icing (confectioner's) sugar
2 eggs
single (light) cream and grated dark (bitter sweet) and white chocolate, to serve

For the filling

175g/6oz white chocolate
350g/12oz/3 cups cream cheese
1 egg, plus 1 beaten egg to seal

1 Put the flour, salt, cocoa and icing sugar into a food processor, add the eggs, and process until the dough begins to come together. Tip out the dough and knead until smooth. Wrap in clear film (plastic wrap) and rest for 30 minutes.

2 To make the filling, break up the white chocolate and melt it in a basin over a pan of barely simmering water. Cool slightly, then beat into the cream cheese with the egg. Spoon into a piping bag fitted with a plain nozzle.

3 Cut the dough in half and wrap one portion. Roll out the rest thinly to a rectangle on a lightly floured surface, or use a pasta machine. Cover with a clean, damp dish towel and repeat with the remaining pasta.

4 Pipe small mounds (about 5ml/1 tsp) of filling in even rows, spacing them at 4cm/1½in intervals, across one piece of dough. Brush the dough between the mounds with beaten egg. Using a rolling pin, lift the remaining sheet of pasta over the dough with the filling. Press down firmly between the pockets, pushing out any trapped air. Cut into rounds with a serrated cutter or knife. Transfer to a floured dish towel. Cover and rest for 1 hour.

5 Bring a large pan of water to the boil and add the ravioli a few at a time, stirring to prevent them sticking. Simmer gently for 3–5 minutes, then remove with a slotted spoon. Serve with a generous splash of single cream and some grated chocolate.

Semolina Helva: *Energy 568kcal/2388kJ; Protein 10.2g; Carbohydrate 78.3g, of which sugars 34.7g; Fat 26g, of which saturates 15.9g; Cholesterol 67mg; Calcium 165mg; Fibre 1.2g; Sodium 227mg.*
Chocolate Ravioli: *Energy 894kcal/3722kJ; Protein 16.2g; Carbohydrate 68.1g, of which sugars 34g; Fat 63.9g, of which saturates 36.5g; Cholesterol 226mg; Calcium 299mg; Fibre 2.1g; Sodium 424mg.*

Italian Chocolate Ricotta Tart

This luxurious tart makes a rich afternoon treat.

Serves 6

2 egg yolks
115g/4oz/½ cup caster (superfine) sugar
500g/1¼ lb/2½ cups ricotta cheese
finely grated rind of 1 lemon
90ml/6 tbsp dark (bittersweet) chocolate chips
75ml/5 tbsp chopped mixed peel
45ml/3 tbsp chopped angelica

For the pastry

225g/8oz/2 cups plain (all-purpose) flour
30ml/2 tbsp cocoa powder
60ml/4 tbsp caster (superfine) sugar
115g/4oz/½ cup butter, diced
60ml/4 tbsp dry sherry

1 Preheat the oven to 200°C/400°F/Gas 6. To make the pastry, sift the flour and cocoa into a bowl, then stir in the sugar. Rub in the butter until the mixture resembles fine breadcrumbs, then work in the dry sherry, using your fingertips, until the mixture binds to a firm, smooth dough.

2 Roll out three-quarters of the pastry on a lightly floured surface and use to line a 24cm/9½ in loose-based flan tin (quiche pan). Chill for 20 minutes.

3 Beat the egg yolks and sugar in a bowl, then beat in the ricotta cheese. Stir in the lemon rind, chocolate chips, mixed peel and angelica. Turn the mixture into the pastry case and level the surface. Roll out the remaining pastry thinly and cut into narrow strips, then arrange these in a lattice over the filling.

4 Bake for 15 minutes, then lower the oven temperature to 180°C/350°F/Gas 4 and bake for 30–35 minutes more until golden brown. Leave to cool in the tin.

Cook's Tip

This chocolate tart is best served at room temperature, so if made in advance, chill it when cool, then, when needed, bring to room temperature before serving.

Chocolate Salami

This after-dinner sweetmeat resembles a salami in shape, hence its curious name. It is very rich and will serve a lot of people. Slice it very thinly and serve with espresso coffee and amaretto liqueur.

Serves 8–12

24 Petit Beurre biscuits, broken
350g/12oz dark (bittersweet) chocolate, broken into squares
225g/8oz/1 cup unsalted butter, softened
60ml/4 tbsp amaretto liqueur
2 egg yolks
50g/2oz/½ cup flaked (sliced) almonds, lightly toasted and thinly shredded lengthways
25g/1oz/¼ cup ground almonds

1 Place the biscuits in a food processor fitted with a metal blade and process until coarsely crushed.

2 Place the chocolate in a large heatproof bowl over a saucepan of barely simmering water, add a small chunk of the butter and all the liqueur and heat until the chocolate melts, stirring occasionally. Remove from the heat.

3 Allow the chocolate to cool a little, then stir in the egg yolks followed by the remaining butter, a little at a time. Tip in most of the crushed biscuits, reserving a good handful, and stir well to mix. Stir in the shredded almonds. Leave the mixture in a cold place for about 1 hour until it begins to stiffen.

4 Process the remaining crushed biscuits in the food processor until they are very finely ground. Tip into a bowl and mix with the ground almonds. Cover and set aside until serving time.

5 Turn the chocolate and biscuit mixture on to a sheet of lightly oiled greaseproof (waxed) paper, then shape into a 35cm/14in sausage with a palette knife, tapering the ends slightly so that the roll looks like a salami. Wrap in the paper and freeze for at least 4 hours until solid.

6 To serve, unwrap the "salami". Spread the ground biscuits and almonds out on a clean sheet of greaseproof paper and roll the salami in them until evenly coated. Transfer to a board and leave to stand for about 1 hour before serving in slices.

Chocolate Ricotta Tart: *Energy 701kcal/2938kJ; Protein 14.2g; Carbohydrate 83.4g, of which sugars 54.1g; Fat 35.6g, of which saturates 21.3g; Cholesterol 144mg; Calcium 115mg; Fibre 3g; Sodium 223mg.*
Chocolate Salami: *Energy 453kcal/1885kJ; Protein 4.5g; Carbohydrate 36.6g, of which sugars 26.9g; Fat 32.3g, of which saturates 16.8g; Cholesterol 96mg; Calcium 47mg; Fibre 1.4g; Sodium 173mg.*

Greek Chocolate Mousse Tartlets

These tarts have a dark, rich chocolate pastry and a creamy filling.

Serves 6

200g/7oz white chocolate
120ml/4fl oz/½ cup milk
10ml/2 tsp powdered gelatine
30ml/2 tbsp caster (superfine) sugar
5ml/1 tsp vanilla extract
2 eggs, separated
250g/9oz/generous 1 cup natural (plain) Greek yogurt
melted dark (bittersweet) chocolate, to decorate

For the pastry

115g/4oz/1 cup plain (all-purpose) flour
25g/1oz/¼ cup icing (confectioners') sugar
25g/1oz/¼ cup cocoa powder (unsweetened)
75g/3oz/6 tbsp butter
2 eggs
2.5ml/½ tsp vanilla extract

1 To make the pastry, sift the flour, sugar and cocoa powder and rub in the butter. Mix the eggs with the vanilla extract then add to the dry ingredients and mix to a soft dough. Tip out on to a floured surface and knead lightly until smooth. Wrap in clear film (plastic wrap) and chill for 20 minutes.

2 Roll out the pastry and use to line six deep 10cm/4in loose-based tartlet tins (mini quiche pans). Cover and chill for 20 minutes. Preheat the oven to 190°C/375°F/Gas 5. Prick the base of each case all over using a fork, then line with baking parchment, fill with baking beans and bake blind for 10 minutes. Remove the paper and beans, and bake the cases for a further 15 minutes, until the pastry is firm. Cool completely in the tins.

3 To make the filling, melt the white chocolate in a heatproof bowl over a pan of hot water. Pour the milk into another pan, sprinkle over the gelatine and heat gently, stirring, until it has dissolved. Remove from the heat and stir in the chocolate.

4 Whisk together the sugar, vanilla extract and egg yolks, then beat in the chocolate mixture. Beat in the yogurt until evenly mixed. Chill until beginning to set. Whisk the egg whites until stiff, then gently fold into the mixture. Divide among the pastry cases and leave to set. Drizzle the melted dark chocolate over the tartlets in a random pattern to decorate.

Chocolate Chestnut Roulade

This moist chocolate sponge has a soft, mousse-like texture as it contains no flour. Don't worry if it cracks as you roll it up.

Serves 8

175g/6oz dark (bittersweet) chocolate
30ml/2 tbsp strong black coffee
5 eggs, separated
175g/6oz/¾ cup caster (superfine) sugar
250ml/8fl oz/1 cup double (heavy) cream
225g/8oz unsweetened chestnut purée
45–60ml/3–4 tbsp icing (confectioner's) sugar, plus extra for dusting
single (light) cream, to serve

1 Preheat the oven to 180°C/350°F/Gas 4. Line a 33 x 23cm/13 x 9in Swiss roll tin (jelly roll pan) with baking parchment and brush lightly with oil.

2 Melt the chocolate in a bowl set over a saucepan of barely simmering water. Stir in the coffee and leave to cool slightly. Whisk together the egg yolks and caster sugar until they are thick and light, then stir in the cooled chocolate mixture.

3 Whisk the egg whites in another bowl until they hold stiff peaks. Stir a spoonful into the chocolate mixture to lighten it, then gently fold in the rest. Pour into the prepared tin, and level the surface. Bake for 20 minutes. Remove the roulade from the oven, then cover with a clean dish towel and leave to cool in the tin for several hours or overnight.

4 Put the double cream into a large bowl and whip until it forms soft peaks. In another bowl, mix together the chestnut purée and icing sugar until smooth, then fold into the cream.

5 Lay out a sheet of greaseproof (waxed) paper and dust with icing sugar. Turn the roulade on to the paper and peel off the lining paper. Trim the sides. Spread the chestnut cream evenly all over to within 2.5cm/1in of the edges. Carefully roll up the roulade as tightly and evenly as possible. Chill for 2 hours, then sprinkle liberally with icing sugar. Serve in thick slices with a little single cream.

Chocolate Mousse Tartlets: *Energy 555kcal/2320kJ; Protein 11.9g; Carbohydrate 55g, of which sugars 32.2g; Fat 34g, of which saturates 19.7g; Cholesterol 105mg; Calcium 242mg; Fibre 1.5g; Sodium 263mg.*
Roulade: *Energy 3496kcal/14645kJ; Protein 48g; Carbohydrate 424.1g, of which sugars 355.5g; Fat 187.3g, of which saturates 104.4g; Cholesterol 980mg; Calcium 585mg; Fibre 14.9g; Sodium 416mg.*

Bitter Chocolate Mousse

The Spanish introduced the rest of Europe to chocolate, and chocolate mousse remains a favourite. This one is laced with liqueur.

Serves 8

225g/8oz dark (bittersweet) chocolate, chopped
30ml/2 tbsp orange liqueur or good Spanish brandy
50g/2oz/¼ cup unsalted (sweet) butter, cut into small pieces
4 eggs, separated
90ml/6 tbsp whipping cream
45ml/3 tbsp caster (superfine) sugar

1 Place the chocolate and 60ml/4 tbsp water in a heavy pan. Melt over a low heat, stirring. Off the heat whisk in the orange liqueur or brandy and butter. Beat the egg yolks until thick and creamy, then slowly beat into the melted chocolate.

2 Whip the cream until soft peaks form, then stir a spoonful into the chocolate mixture to lighten it. Gently fold in the remaining whipped cream.

3 In a clean, grease-free bowl, use an electric mixer to slowly whisk the egg whites until frothy. Increase the speed and continue until the egg whites form soft peaks. Gradually sprinkle the sugar over the egg whites and continue beating until the whites are stiff and glossy.

4 Using a rubber spatula or large metal spoon, stir a quarter of the egg whites into the chocolate mixture to lighten it, then gently fold in the remaining whites, cutting down to the bottom of the bowl, along the sides and up to the top in a semicircular motion until they are just combined.

5 Gently spoon the mixture into eight individual dishes or a 2 litre/3½ pint/8 cup bowl. Chill for at least 2 hours until set.

Cook's Tip

The addition of 1.5ml/¼ tsp cream of tartar to the egg whites helps them to stabilize and hold the volume.

Ricotta Cheesecake

In this Sicilian-style dessert, ricotta cheese is enriched with eggs and cream and enlivened with tangy orange and lemon rind.

Serves 8

450g/1lb/2 cups ricotta cheese
120ml/4fl oz/½ cup double (heavy) cream
2 eggs
1 egg yolk
75g/3oz/⅓ cup caster (superfine) sugar
finely grated rind of 1 orange
finely grated rind of 1 lemon

For the pastry

175g/6oz/1½ cups plain (all-purpose) flour
45ml/3 tbsp caster (superfine) sugar
pinch of salt
115g/4oz/8 tbsp chilled butter, diced
1 egg yolk

1 To make the pastry, sift the flour, sugar and salt on to a cold surface. Make a well in the centre, add the diced butter and egg yolk and gradually work in the flour with your fingertips. Gather the dough together, reserve about a quarter for the lattice, then press the rest into a 23cm/9in fluted tart tin (quiche pan) with a removable base. Chill the pastry case for 30 minutes.

2 Meanwhile, preheat the oven to 190°C/375°F/Gas 5 and make the filling. Put the ricotta, cream, eggs, egg yolk, sugar and orange and lemon rinds in a large bowl and beat together.

3 Prick the bottom of the pastry case, then line with foil and fill with baking beans. Bake blind for 15 minutes, then transfer to a wire rack, remove the foil and beans and allow the tart shell to cool in the tin.

4 Spoon the cheese and cream filling into the pastry case and level the surface. Roll out the reserved dough and cut into strips. Arrange the strips on the top of the filling in a lattice pattern, sticking them in place with water.

5 Bake for 30–35 minutes until golden and set. Transfer to a wire rack and leave to cool, then carefully remove the side of the tin, leaving the cheesecake on the base.

Chocolate Mousse: Energy 236kcal/988kJ; Protein 5.5g; Carbohydrate 25.7g, of which sugars 25.4g; Fat 12.2g, of which saturates 6.2g; Cholesterol 121mg; Calcium 31mg; Fibre 0.8g; Sodium 46mg.
Ricotta Cheesecake: Energy 449kcal/1873kJ; Protein 9.9g; Carbohydrate 34.8g, of which sugars 18.1g; Fat 31.1g, of which saturates 18.4g; Cholesterol 173mg; Calcium 62mg; Fibre 0.7g; Sodium 112mg.

Sifnos Cheese and Honey Tart

This Greek cheesecake is an Easter speciality in the Cyclades, particularly on the islands Sifnos and Ios, is made with honey and the fresh, unsalted local cheese called *myzithra*, which is similar to Italian ricotta. Santorini has similar small pastries called *militinia*, flavoured with mastic resin.

Serves 6–8

225g/8oz/2 cups plain (all-purpose) flour sifted with a pinch of salt
30ml/2 tbsp caster (superfine) sugar
115g/4oz/½ cup unsalted butter, cubed
45–60ml/3–4 tbsp cold water

For the filling

4 eggs
50g/2oz/¼ cup caster (superfine) sugar
15ml/1 tbsp plain (all-purpose) flour
500g/1¼lb/2½ cups fresh myzithra or ricotta cheese
60ml/4 tbsp Greek thyme-scented honey
2.5ml/½ tsp ground cinnamon

1 Mix the flour and sugar in a bowl, then rub in the butter until the mixture resembles fine breadcrumbs. Add the water, a little at a time, until the mixture clings together and forms a dough. It should not be too wet. Draw it into a ball, wrap it in clear film (plastic wrap) and chill for 30 minutes.

2 Preheat the oven to 180°C/350°F/Gas 4. Put a baking sheet in the oven to heat. Place the pastry on a lightly floured surface, roll out thinly and use to line a 25cm/10in round springform tin (pan). Carefully trim off any excess pastry.

3 To make the filling, beat the eggs in a bowl, add the sugar and flour and beat until fluffy. Add the cheese, honey and half the cinnamon and beat until well mixed.

4 Pour the cheese mixture into the pastry case and level the surface. Place the tin on the hot baking sheet and cook the tart for 50–60 minutes, until light golden. Remove the tart from the oven and sprinkle with the remaining cinnamon while still hot. Leave to cool before serving.

Honey and Pine Nut Tart

Wonderful tarts of all descriptions are to be found throughout France, and this recipe recalls the flavours of the south, with its sunny Mediterranean influences.

Serves 6

115g/4oz/½ cup butter, diced
115g/4oz/½ cup caster (superfine) sugar
3 eggs, beaten
175g/6oz/⅔ cup sunflower honey
grated rind and juice of 1 lemon
225g/8oz/2⅔ cups pine nuts
pinch of salt
icing (confectioners') sugar, for dusting

For the pastry

225g/8oz/2 cups plain (all-purpose) flour
115g/4oz/½ cup butter, diced
30ml/2 tbsp icing (confectioners') sugar
1 egg
15ml/1 tbsp chilled water

1 Preheat the oven to 180°C/350°F/Gas 4. To make the pastry, sift the flour into a large mixing bowl and rub or cut in the butter until the mixture resembles fine breadcrumbs.

2 Stir in the icing sugar. Add the egg and water and mix to form a soft dough. Knead lightly until smooth.

3 Roll out the pastry on a floured surface and use to line a 23cm/9in flan tin (quiche pan). Prick the base with a fork, then chill for 10 minutes. Line with baking parchment and fill with baking beans. Bake for 10 minutes. Remove the paper and beans and set the pastry case aside.

4 Cream the butter and caster sugar together until light and fluffy. Beat in the eggs one at a time. In a small pan, heat the honey very gently until it melts, then add it to the butter mixture with the lemon rind and juice. Mix well. Stir in the pine nuts and salt, blending well, then pour the filling evenly into the pastry case.

5 Bake the tart for about 45 minutes, or until the filling is lightly browned and set. Leave to cool slightly in the tin, then remove and dust generously with icing sugar. Serve warm, or at room temperature, with crème fraîche or vanilla ice cream, if you like.

Cheese and Honey Tart: *Energy 626kcal/2619kJ; Protein 23.7g; Carbohydrate 53.4g, of which sugars 22.3g; Fat 36.9g, of which saturates 22.6g; Cholesterol 216mg; Calcium 389mg; Fibre 1.3g; Sodium 495mg.*
Honey and Pine Nut Tart: *Energy 899kcal/3750kJ; Protein 13.4g; Carbohydrate 78.4g, of which sugars 49.8g; Fat 61.4g, of which saturates 22.8g; Cholesterol 209mg; Calcium 97mg; Fibre 1.9g; Sodium 285mg.*

Lemon Tart

This classic French tart is one of the most delicious desserts there is. A rich lemon curd is encased in a crisp pastry case. Crème fraîche is an optional – but very nice – extra.

Serves 6

6 eggs, beaten
350g/12oz/1½ cups caster (superfine) sugar
115g/4oz/½ cup butter
grated rind and juice of 4 lemons
icing (confectioners') sugar for dusting

For the pastry

225g/8oz/2 cups plain (all-purpose) flour
115g/4oz/½ cup butter, diced
30ml/2 tbsp icing (confectioners') sugar
1 egg
5ml/1 tsp vanilla extract
15ml/1 tbsp chilled water

1 Preheat the oven to 200°C/400°F/Gas 6. To make the pastry, sift the flour into a mixing bowl and rub or cut in the butter until the mixture resembles fine breadcrumbs. Lightly stir in the icing sugar.

2 Add the egg, vanilla extract and most of the chilled water, then work to a soft dough. Add a few more drops of water if necessary. Knead quickly and lightly until smooth.

3 Roll out the pastry on a floured surface and use to line a 23cm/9in flan tin (quiche pan). Prick the base all over with a fork. Line with baking parchment (parchment paper) and fill with baking beans. Bake the pastry case for 10 minutes. Remove the paper and beans and set the pastry case aside while you make the filling.

4 Put the eggs, sugar and butter into a pan, and stir over a low heat until all the sugar has dissolved. Add the lemon rind and juice, and continue cooking, stirring constantly, until the lemon curd has thickened slightly.

5 Pour the curd mixture into the pastry case. Bake for about 20 minutes, or until the filling is just set. Transfer the tart to a wire rack to cool. Dust the surface generously with icing sugar just before serving.

Fresh Fig Filo Tart

Figs cook wonderfully well and taste superb in this tart – the riper the figs are, the better it will be.

Serves 6–8

five 35 × 25cm/14 × 10in sheets filo pastry, thawed if frozen
25g/1oz/2 tbsp butter, melted, plus extra for greasing
6 fresh figs, cut into wedges
75g/3oz/¾ cup plain (all-purpose) flour
75g/3oz/⅓ cup caster (superfine) sugar
4 eggs
450ml/¾ pint/1¾ cups creamy milk
2.5ml/½ tsp almond extract
15ml/1 tbsp icing (confectioners') sugar, for dusting
whipped cream or Greek yogurt to serve

1 Preheat the oven to 190°C/375°F/Gas 5. Grease a 25 × 16cm/10 × 6¼in baking tin (pan) with butter. Brush each filo sheet in turn with melted butter and use to line the prepared tin.

2 Using scissors, cut off any large pieces of excess pastry, leaving a small amount overhanging the edge of the tin. Arrange the figs in the filo case.

3 Sift the flour into a bowl and stir in the caster sugar. Add the eggs and a little of the milk and whisk until smooth. Gradually whisk in the remaining milk and the almond essence. Pour the mixture over the figs; bake for 1 hour or until the batter has set and is golden.

4 Remove the tart from the oven and allow it to cool in the tin on a wire rack for 10 minutes. Dust with the icing sugar and serve warm with whipped cream or Greek yogurt.

Cook's Tip

Filo pastry dries out extremely quickly before it is brushed with butter. As soon as you have unwrapped the pastry, cover the stack of sheets with a clean, damp dish towel and extract them one at a time to arrange in the tin.

Lemon Tart: *Energy 268kcal/1121kJ; Protein 5.6g; Carbohydrate 27g, of which sugars 10.9g; Fat 16.1g, of which saturates 5.8g; Cholesterol 148mg; Calcium 57mg; Fibre 0.7g; Sodium 173mg.*
Fresh Fig Tart: *Energy 228kcal/964kJ; Protein 7.4g; Carbohydrate 36.9g, of which sugars 22.6g; Fat 6.8g, of which saturates 3g; Cholesterol 105mg; Calcium 152mg; Fibre 1.7g; Sodium 89mg.*

Tarte Tatin

This upside-down tart of caramelized apples is a classic of French cuisine, said to have been devised at the Hotel Tatin in the Sologne region. If you use ready-rolled puff pastry, it is very easily made. You will need a heavy pan with a metal handle that can safely go into the oven.

Serves 6–8

3 large eating apples such as Braeburn or Cox's Orange Pippin
juice of ½ lemon
50g/2oz/¼ cup butter, softened
75g/3oz/⅓ cup caster (superfine) sugar
250g/9oz ready-rolled puff pastry
cream, to serve

1 Preheat the oven to 220°C/425°F/Gas 7. Cut the apples in quarters and remove the cores. Toss the apple quarters in the lemon juice to prevent them discolouring.

2 Spread the butter over the base of a 20cm/8in heavy omelette pan that can safely be used in the oven. Sprinkle the caster sugar over the base of the pan and add the apple wedges, rounded side down.

3 Cook over a medium heat for 15–20 minutes or until the sugar and butter have melted and the apples are golden. Cut the pastry into a 25cm/10in round and place on top of the apples; tuck the edges in with a knife.

4 Place the pan in the oven and bake for 15–20 minutes or until the pastry is golden. Carefully invert the tart on to a plate. Cool slightly before serving with cream.

Cook's Tips

- *Use eating apples rather than cooking apples for the tart, as the pieces need to keep their shape when cooked.*
- *To turn out the tart, place the serving plate upside down on top of it, then, protecting your arms with oven gloves, hold both pan and plate firmly together and deftly turn them over. Lift off the pan.*

Apricot and Almond Jalousie

Jalousie means "shutter" in French, and the slatted puff pastry topping of this fruit pie, traditionally made in a rectangular shape, looks very much like the shutters outside the windows of French houses.

Serves 4

225g/8oz ready-made puff pastry
a little beaten egg
90ml/6 tbsp apricot preserve
30ml/2 tbsp caster (superfine) sugar
30ml/2 tbsp flaked almonds
cream or natural yogurt, to serve

1 Preheat the oven to 220°C/425°F/Gas 7. Roll out the pastry on a lightly floured surface and cut into a 30cm/12in square. Cut in half to make two rectangles.

2 Place one piece of pastry on a wetted baking sheet and brush all round the edges with beaten egg. Spread over the apricot preserve.

3 Fold the remaining rectangle in half lengthways and cut about eight diagonal slits from the centre fold to within about 1cm/½in of the edge all the way along.

4 Unfold the pastry and place it on top of the preserve-covered pastry on the baking sheet, matching each edge carefully to the base. Press the pastry edges together well, to seal, and scallop the edges at close intervals with the back of a small knife.

5 Brush the slashed pastry top with a little water and sprinkle evenly with the sugar and the flaked almonds.

6 Bake in the oven for 25–30 minutes, until well risen and golden brown. Remove the jalousie from the oven and leave to cool on a wire rack. Serve the jalousie sliced, with cream or natural yogurt.

Variation

Make the jalousie using plum preserve instead of apricot.

Tarte Tatin: *Energy 228kcal/955kJ; Protein 1.6g; Carbohydrate 23.8g, of which sugars 15.7g; Fat 15g, of which saturates 6g; Cholesterol 25mg; Calcium 23mg; Fibre 1.1g; Sodium 141mg.*
Apricot Jalousie: *Energy 339kcal/1423kJ; Protein 4.9g; Carbohydrate 43.5g, of which sugars 23.2g; Fat 18g, of which saturates 0.3g; Cholesterol 0mg; Calcium 56mg; Fibre 0.6g; Sodium 186mg.*

Apricot Parcels with Honey Glaze

These parcels can be made with dried apricots that have been poached in syrup before being stuffed with the almond mixture, but fresh fruit is the better option. It has a juicy tartness that cuts through the sweetness of the honey. Roll the filo parcels into any shape, but leave them open so that both fruit and pastry benefit from the glaze.

Serves 6

200g/7oz/1¾ cups blanched almonds, ground
115g/4oz/⅔ cup sugar
30–45ml/2–3 tbsp orange flower water or rose water
12 fresh apricots, slit and stoned (pitted)
3–4 sheets of filo pastry, cut into 12 circles or squares
30ml/2 tbsp clear honey
cream, crème fraîche or Greek yogurt, to serve

1 Preheat the oven to 180°C/350°F/Gas 4. Using your hands or a blender or food processor, bind the almonds, sugar and orange flower or rose water to a soft paste.

2 Take small walnut-size lumps of the paste and roll them into balls. Press a ball of paste into each slit apricot and gently squeeze the fruit closed.

3 Place a stuffed apricot on a piece of filo pastry, fold up the sides to secure the fruit and twist the ends to form an open boat shape. Repeat with the remaining apricots and filo pastry.

4 Place the filo parcels in a shallow ovenproof dish and drizzle the honey over them. Bake for 20–25 minutes, until the pastry is crisp and the fruit has browned on top.

5 Serve hot or cold with cream, crème fraîche or a spoonful of Greek yogurt.

Cook's Tip

Apricots thrive in the Mediterranean climate, and are widely cultivated in the whole region, having been introduced by the Romans from Armenia around the first century BC.

Baked Lattice Peaches

Nectarines can also be used for this recipe, and there's no need to peel them first.

Serves 6

3 peaches
juice of ½ lemon
75g/3oz/scant ½ cup white marzipan
375g/13oz ready-rolled puff pastry, thawed if frozen
a large pinch of ground cinnamon
beaten egg, to glaze
caster (superfine) sugar, for sprinkling

For the caramel sauce

50g/2oz/¼ cup caster (superfine) sugar
30ml/2 tbsp cold water
150ml/¼ pint/⅔ cup double (heavy) cream

1 Preheat the oven to 190°C/375°F/Gas 5. Pour boiling water over the peaches to cover. Leave for 60 seconds, then drain and peel. Toss the fruit in lemon juice to stop them going brown.

2 Divide the marzipan into six balls. Halve and stone the peaches and fill each cavity with marzipan.

3 Unroll the pastry and cut it in half. Set one half aside, then cut out six rounds from the rest, making each slightly larger than a peach half. Sprinkle cinnamon on the pastry rounds, then place a peach half, marzipan side down, on each one.

4 Cut the remaining pastry into a lattice, using a special cutter if you have one. If not, cut small slits in rows all over, starting each row slightly lower than the last. Cut the lattice pastry into six equal squares.

5 Dampen the edges of the pastry rounds, then drape a lattice square over each peach half. Seal the edges, then trim off the excess pastry and decorate with small leaves made from the trimmings. Transfer to a baking sheet, brush with beaten egg and sprinkle with caster sugar. Bake for 20 minutes or until golden.

6 Meanwhile, heat the sugar with the water until it dissolves. Bring to the boil and continue to boil until the syrup turns a dark golden brown. Stand back and add the cream. Heat gently, stirring until smooth. Serve the peach pastries with the sauce.

Apricot Parcels: *Energy 347kcal/1455kJ; Protein 9g; Carbohydrate 37.8g, of which sugars 27.4g; Fat 18.9g, of which saturates 1.5g; Cholesterol 0mg; Calcium 120mg; Fibre 4.2g; Sodium 8mg.*
Lattice Peaches: *Energy 452kcal/1886kJ; Protein 5.1g; Carbohydrate 43.8g, of which sugars 21.4g; Fat 30.4g, of which saturates 8.5g; Cholesterol 34mg; Calcium 64mg; Fibre 0.8g; Sodium 203mg.*

Ladies' Navels

This is a classic Turkish fried pastry, an invention from the Ottoman palace kitchens.

Serves 4–6
50g/2oz/¼ cup butter
2.5ml/½ tsp salt
175g/6oz/1½ cups plain (all-purpose) flour
60g/2oz/⅓ cup semolina
2 eggs
sunflower oil, for deep-frying

For the syrup
450g/1lb/scant 2¼ cups granulated sugar
juice of 1 lemon

1 To make the syrup, put the sugar and 300ml/½ pint/1¼ cups water into a heavy pan and bring to the boil, stirring all the time. When the sugar has dissolved, stir in the lemon juice and lower the heat, then simmer for about 10 minutes, until the syrup has thickened a little. Leave to cool.

2 Put the butter, salt and 250ml/8fl oz/1 cup water in another pan and bring to the boil. Remove from the heat and add the flour and semolina, beating all the time, until the mixture becomes smooth and leaves the side of the pan. Leave to cool. Beat the eggs into the cooled mixture so that it gleams. Add 15ml/1 tbsp of the cooled syrup and beat well.

3 Pour enough oil for deep-frying into a wok or other deep-sided pan. Heat until just warm, then remove the pan from the heat. Wet your hands and take an apricot-sized piece of dough in your fingers. Roll it into a ball, flatten it in the palm of your hand, then use your finger to make an indentation in the middle to resemble a lady's navel.

4 Drop the dough into the pan of warmed oil. Repeat with the rest of the mixture to make about 12 navels.

5 Place the pan back over the heat. As the oil heats up, the pastries will swell, retaining the dip in the middle. Swirl the oil, until the navels turn golden all over. Remove the navels from the oil with a slotted spoon, then toss them in the cooled syrup. Leave to soak for a few minutes, arrange in a serving dish and spoon some of the syrup over.

Semolina and Nut Halva

Hazelnuts and almonds are used to top this soft halva, although other nuts can be used. Pistachio nuts are popular additions to such syrupy dishes, as are walnuts and toasted pine nuts.

Makes 24
115g/4oz/½ cup unsalted (sweet) butter, softened
115g/4oz/generous ½ cup caster (superfine) sugar
finely grated rind of 1 orange, plus 30ml/2 tbsp juice
3 eggs
175g/6oz/1 cup semolina
10ml/2 tsp baking powder
115g/4oz/1 cup ground hazelnuts

To finish
350g/12oz/1¾ cups caster (superfine) sugar
2 cinnamon sticks, halved
juice of 1 lemon
60ml/4 tbsp orange flower water
50g/2oz/½ cup unblanched hazelnuts, toasted and chopped
50g/2oz/½ cup blanched almonds, toasted and chopped
shredded rind of 1 orange

1 Preheat the oven to 220°C/425°F/Gas 7. Grease and line the base of a 23cm/9in square deep solid-based cake tin (pan). Lightly cream the butter in a bowl. Add the sugar, orange rind and juice, eggs, semolina, baking powder and hazelnuts and beat the ingredients together until smooth. Turn into the prepared tin and level the surface. Bake for 20–25 minutes until just firm and golden. Leave to cool in the tin.

2 To make the syrup, put the caster sugar in a small, heavy pan with 575ml/19fl oz/2¼ cups water and the cinnamon sticks. Heat gently over a low heat, stirring frequently, until the sugar has dissolved completely. Bring to the boil and boil fast, without stirring, for 5 minutes. Measure half the syrup and add the lemon juice and orange flower water to it. Pour over the halva. Reserve the remainder of the syrup in the pan.

3 When the halva has absorbed the syrup, turn it out on to a plate and cut diagonally into diamond-shaped portions. Sprinkle with the nuts. Boil the remaining syrup until slightly thickened, then pour it over the halva. Sprinkle the shredded orange rind over the cake. Serve with lightly whipped or clotted cream, or Greek yogurt, if you like.

Ladies Navels: *Energy 517kcal/2190kJ; Protein 6.3g; Carbohydrate 108.8g, of which sugars 78.9g; Fat 9.3g, of which saturates 4.9g; Cholesterol 81mg; Calcium 93mg; Fibre 1.1g; Sodium 80mg.*
Semolina Halva: *Energy 4910kcal/20601kJ; Protein 74.5g; Carbohydrate 638.2g, of which sugars 498g; Fat 247g, of which saturates 74.5g; Cholesterol 816mg; Calcium 738mg; Fibre 18.1g; Sodium 976mg.*

Butter and Almond Shortbreads

Dazzling white *kourabiethes* are traditionally made at Christmas and Easter, but are also an important feature of many other Greek celebrations. They are traditionally crescent-shaped, but here have been cut into stars.

Makes 20–22

225g/8oz/1 cup unsalted butter
150g/5oz/⅔ cup caster (superfine) sugar
2 egg yolks
5ml/1 tsp vanilla extract
2.5ml/½ tsp bicarbonate of soda (baking soda)
45ml/3 tbsp brandy
500g/1¼lb/5 cups plain (all-purpose) flour sifted with a pinch of salt
150g/5oz/1¼ cups blanched almonds, toasted and coarsely chopped
350g/12oz/3 cups icing (confectioners') sugar

1 Cream the butter, beat in the caster sugar gradually, until light and fluffy. Beat in the egg yolks one at a time, then the vanilla. Mix the soda with the brandy and stir into the mixture.

2 Add the flour and salt and mix to a firm dough. Knead lightly, add the almonds and knead again. Cover half the dough with clear film (plastic wrap) and set aside.

3 Preheat the oven to 180°C/350°F/Gas 4. Roll out the remaining dough until about 2.5cm/1in thick. Press out star or half-moon shapes, using pastry cutters. Repeat with the remaining dough.

4 Place the shortbread shapes on baking sheets and bake for 20–25 minutes, or until they are pale golden – do not let them brown.

5 Meanwhile, sift a quarter of the icing sugar on to a platter. As soon as the shortbreads come out of the oven, dust them generously with icing sugar. Let them cool for a few minutes, then place them on the sugar-coated platter.

6 Sift the remaining icing sugar over them. The aim is to give them a generous coating, so they are pure white.

Gazelle's Horns

These pastries filled with orange-scented almond paste are a real sweet treat.

Makes 16

200g/7oz/1¾ cups plain (all-purpose) flour
25g/1oz/2 tbsp butter, melted
about 30ml/2 tbsp orange flower water or water
1 large egg yolk, beaten
pinch of salt
icing (confectioners') sugar, to serve

For the almond paste

200g/7oz/1 cups ground almonds
115g/4oz/1¾ cups icing (confectioners') sugar or caster (superfine) sugar
30ml/2 tbsp orange flower water
25g/1oz/2 tbsp butter, melted
2 egg yolks, beaten
2.5ml/½ tsp ground cinnamon

1 First make the almond paste, mixing together all the ingredients until smooth. Set aside.

2 To make the pastry, mix the flour with a pinch of salt then stir in the melted butter, orange flower water or water, and about three-quarters of the egg yolk. Stir in enough cold water, little by little, to make a fairly soft dough. Knead for about 10 minutes, until smooth and elastic, then roll out very thinly on a floured surface and cut long strips about 7.5cm/3in wide.

3 Preheat the oven to 180°C/350°F/Gas 4. Take small pieces of the almond paste and roll them between your hands into thin "sausages" about 7.5cm/3in long with tapering ends. Place these in a line along one side of the strips of pastry, about 3cm/1¼in apart. Dampen the pastry edges with water and then fold the other half of the strip over the filling and press the edges together firmly to seal.

4 Using a pastry wheel, cut around each "sausage" (as for ravioli) to make a crescent shape. Make sure that the edges are firmly pinched together. Prick the crescents with a fork and place on a buttered baking tray. Brush with the remaining beaten egg yolk and then bake in the oven for 12–16 minutes, until lightly coloured.

5 Remove to a wire rack, cool and then dust with icing sugar.

Almond Shortbreads: *Energy 325kcal/1363kJ; Protein 4.4g; Carbohydrate 46.1g, of which sugars 26.9g; Fat 14.3g, of which saturates 6.4g; Cholesterol 44mg; Calcium 71mg; Fibre 1.3g; Sodium 72mg.*
Gazelle's Horns: *Energy 163kcal/682kJ; Protein 4g; Carbohydrate 18.1g, of which sugars 8.2g; Fat 8.8g, of which saturates 1.5g; Cholesterol 16mg; Calcium 53mg; Fibre 1.3g; Sodium 13mg.*

Baklava

The origins of this recipe lie in Turkey and Greece, where it is traditionally served on religious festival days.

Makes 16

50g/2oz/½cup blanched almonds, chopped
50g/2oz/½ cup pistachio nuts, chopped
75g/3oz/6 tbsp caster (superfine) sugar
75g/3oz/6 tbsp butter, melted
6 sheets of filo pastry, thawed if frozen

For the syrup

115g/4oz/½ cup caster (superfine) sugar
7.5cm/3in piece cinnamon stick
1 whole clove
2 green cardamom pods, crushed
75ml/5 tbsp very strong brewed coffee

1 Preheat the oven to 180°C/350°F/Gas 4. Mix the almonds and pistachios with the sugar. With a little of the melted butter brush a shallow 18 × 28cm/7 × 11in baking tin (pan).

2 Stack the six sheets of filo pastry and cut them to fit the tin exactly. Lay one sheet of pastry in the tin and brush it all over with some of the melted butter. Add two more sheets, brushing each with butter. Sprinkle the filo with half of the nut mixture.

3 Layer three more sheets of filo pastry on top of the nuts, brushing each with butter. Spread the remaining nut mixture evenly over the pastry. Top with the remaining sheets, brushing with butter as before, and liberally brushing the top layer. Gently press down around the edges to seal. Using a very sharp knife, mark the top of the baklava into diamonds. Bake for 20–25 minutes, or until golden and crisp.

4 Meanwhile, make the syrup. Gently heat the sugar, spices and coffee until the sugar has dissolved. Cover the pan and set aside for 20 minutes, to give the spices time to flavour the syrup.

5 When the baklava is cooked, reheat the syrup gently, then strain it evenly over the pastry. Leave to cool in the tin. If you can, set it aside for 6 hours to allow the flavours to mingle. When ready to serve, cut the baklava into diamonds, following the lines scored prior to baking, then remove from the tin.

Almond and Date Pastries

These sweet Moroccan pastries, or briouates, are made with filo or the local equivalent – *ouarka* – and coated in honey and orange flower water.

Makes 30

15ml/1 tbsp sunflower oil
225g/8oz/1⅓ cups blanched almonds
115g/4oz/⅔ cup stoned (pitted) dried dates
25g/1oz/2 tbsp butter, softened
5ml/1 tsp ground cinnamon
1.5ml/¼ tsp almond extract
40g/1½oz/⅓ cup icing (confectioners') sugar
30ml/2 tbsp orange flower water or rose water
10 sheets of filo pastry
50g/2oz/¼ cup butter, melted
120ml/4fl oz/½ cup clear honey
dates, to serve (optional)

1 Heat the oil in a small pan and fry the almonds for a few minutes until golden, stirring all the time. Drain on kitchen paper. When cool, grind the almonds in a coffee or spice mill. Process the dates in a blender or food processor.

2 Spoon the ground almonds into the blender or food processor with the dates, and blend with the softened butter, cinnamon, almond essence, icing sugar and a little flower water to make a soft paste.

3 Preheat the oven to 180°C/350°F/Gas 4. Brush a sheet of filo pastry with melted butter and cut into three equal strips. Place a walnut-size piece of almond paste at the bottom of each strip. Fold one corner over the filling to make a triangle and then fold up, in triangles, to make a neat packet. Brush with melted butter and set aside. Repeat to make 30 pastries. Arrange on baking sheets and bake for 20–25 minutes, until golden and crisp.

4 Meanwhile, pour the honey and a little orange flower or rose water into a pan and heat very gently. When the pastries are cooked, lower them one by one into the pan and turn them in the honey so that they are thoroughly coated all over.

5 Transfer the briouates to a plate and cool a little before serving, with dates if you wish.

Baklava: *Energy 161kcal/675kJ; Protein 2.3g; Carbohydrate 21.3g, of which sugars 16.3g; Fat 8g, of which saturates 2.6g; Cholesterol 8mg; Calcium 27mg; Fibre 0.7g; Sodium 70mg.*
Almond and Date Pastries: *Energy 95kcal/396kJ; Protein 1.8g; Carbohydrate 7.5g, of which sugars 6g; Fat 6.6g, of which saturates 1.7g; Cholesterol 5mg; Calcium 23mg; Fibre 0.7g; Sodium 17mg.*

Crunchy-topped Fresh Apricot Cake

Almonds are perfect partners for fresh apricots as they come from trees of the same family, and this is a great way to use up fruits that are a little too firm to eat raw. In Greece this cake is eaten as a snack at any time of the day.

Serves 8

175g/6oz/1½ cups self-raising (self-rising) flour
175g/6oz/¾ cup butter, softened
175g/6oz/scant 1 cup caster (superfine) sugar
115g/4oz/1 cup ground almonds
3 eggs
5ml/1 tsp almond extract
2.5ml/½ tsp baking powder
8 firm apricots, stoned (pitted) and chopped

For the topping

30ml/2 tbsp demerara (raw) sugar
50g/2oz/½ cup slivered (sliced) almonds

1 Preheat the oven to 160°C/325°F/Gas 3. Grease an 18cm/7in round cake tin (pan) and line the base with baking parchment.

2 Put all the cake ingredients, except the apricots, in a large mixing bowl and whisk until creamy. Fold the chopped apricots into the cake mixture.

3 Spoon the mixture into the prepared tin. Make a hollow in the centre with the back of a spoon. Sprinkle 15ml/1 tbsp of the demerara sugar evenly over the surface, together with the slivered almonds.

4 Bake for about 1½ hours, or until a skewer inserted into the centre of the cake comes out clean. Sprinkle the remaining sugar over the top and cool for 10 minutes in the tin, then remove the cake from the tin and leave on a wire rack to cool completely.

Variation

When fresh apricots are not in season, replace them with 125g/4oz ready-to-eat dried apricots, chopped.

Twelfth Night Bread

This special cake is baked in Spain for Epiphany on 6 January. Traditionally it contains a bean, coin or tiny china doll, and whoever finds it is king of the party.

Serves 12

450g/1lb/4 cups unbleached strong white bread flour
2.5ml/½ tsp salt
25g/1oz fresh yeast
140ml/scant ¼ pint/scant ⅔ cup mixed warm milk and water
75g/3oz/6 tbsp butter
75g/3oz/6 tbsp caster (superfine) sugar
10ml/2 tsp grated lemon rind
10ml/2 tsp grated orange rind
2 eggs
15ml/1 tbsp brandy
15ml/1 tbsp orange flower water
silver coin or dried bean (optional)
1 egg white, lightly beaten

For the decoration

mixed candied fruit slices
flaked (sliced) almonds

1 Lightly grease a large baking sheet. Sift together the flour and salt into a large bowl. Make a well in the centre. Mix the yeast with the milk and water until dissolved. Pour into the well and stir in enough of the flour to make a thick batter. Sprinkle a little of the remaining flour over the top and leave in a warm place, for about 15 minutes or until frothy.

2 Beat the butter and sugar until soft and creamy. Add the citrus rinds, eggs, brandy and orange flower water to the flour mixture and mix to a sticky dough. Gradually add the butter mixture and beat until smooth and elastic. Cover with lightly oiled clear film (plastic wrap) and leave in a warm place, for about 1½ hours, or until doubled in size.

3 Knock back (punch down) the dough and turn on to a floured surface. Knead gently for 2 or 3 minutes, adding the coin or bean, if using, then roll out into a long strip measuring about 65 × 13cm/26 × 5in. Roll up from one long side, join the ends and place seam side down on the baking sheet. Cover and leave in a warm place for 1–1½ hours until doubled in size.

4 Preheat the oven to 180°C/350°F/Gas 4. Brush the ring with lightly beaten egg white and decorate with glacé fruit slices. Sprinkle with flaked almonds and bake for 30–35 minutes.

Apricot Cake: *Energy 414kcal/1734kJ; Protein 6.2g; Carbohydrate 46.8g, of which sugars 30.3g; Fat 23.9g, of which saturates 12.3g; Cholesterol 118mg; Calcium 126mg; Fibre 1.8g; Sodium 241mg.*
Twelth Night Bread: *Energy 217kcal/914kJ; Protein 4.8g; Carbohydrate 36g, of which sugars 7.4g; Fat 6.7g, of which saturates 3.7g; Cholesterol 45mg; Calcium 69mg; Fibre 1.2g; Sodium 54mg.*

Greek Yogurt and Fig Cake

Baked fresh figs, thickly sliced, make a delectable topping for a featherlight sponge, baked upside-down. Figs that are a bit on the firm side work best for this particular recipe, retaining their shape and flavour.

Serves 6–8

6 firm fresh figs, thickly sliced
45ml/3 tbsp clear honey, plus extra for glazing
200g/7oz/scant 1 cup butter, softened
175g/6oz/¾ cup caster (superfine) sugar
grated rind of 1 lemon
grated rind of 1 orange
4 eggs, separated
225g/8oz/2 cups plain (all-purpose) flour
5ml/1 tsp baking powder
5ml/1 tsp bicarbonate of soda
250ml/8fl oz/1 cup natural (plain) Greek yogurt

1 Preheat the oven to 180°C/350°F/Gas 4. Grease a 23cm/9in cake tin (pan) and line the base with baking parchment. Arrange the figs over the base of the tin and drizzle over the honey.

2 In a large mixing bowl, cream the butter and caster sugar with the lemon and orange rinds until the mixture is pale and fluffy, then gradually beat in the egg yolks.

3 Sift the dry ingredients together. Add a little to the creamed mixture, beat well, then beat in a spoonful of Greek yogurt. Repeat this process until all the yogurt and the dry ingredients have been incorporated.

4 Whisk the egg whites in a grease-free bowl until they form stiff peaks. Stir half the whites into the cake mixture to slacken it slightly, then fold in the rest.

5 Pour the mixture over the figs in the tin, then bake for 1¼ hours or until golden and a skewer inserted in the centre of the cake comes out clean.

6 Turn the cake out on to a wire rack, peel off the lining paper carefully, to avoid dislodging the figs, and leave to cool. Drizzle the figs with extra honey before serving.

Pear and Polenta Cake

In this rustic Italian-style cake, the additional of polenta gives the light sponge a slightly nutty texture and a lovely corn flavour that complements the topping of honeyed, sliced pears perfectly. You can serve the cake while still warm as a dessert, accompanied by custard or cream.

Makes 10 slices

175g/6oz/¾ cup golden caster (superfine) sugar
4 ripe pears
juice of ½ lemon
30ml/2 tbsp clear honey
3 eggs
seeds from 1 vanilla pod (bean)
120ml/4fl oz/½ cup sunflower oil
115g/4oz/1 cup self-raising (self-rising) flour
50g/2oz/⅓ cup instant polenta

1 Preheat the oven to 180°C/350°F/Gas 4. Generously grease and line a 21cm/8½in round cake tin (pan). Scatter 30ml/2 tbsp of the golden caster sugar over the base of the prepared tin.

2 Peel and core the pears. Cut them into chunky slices and toss them in the lemon juice. Arrange across the base of the cake tin. Drizzle the honey over the pears and set aside.

3 Mix together the eggs, seeds from the vanilla pod and the remaining golden caster sugar in a bowl.

4 Beat the egg mixture until thick and creamy, then gradually beat in the oil. Sift together the flour and polenta and fold into the egg mixture.

5 Pour the mixture carefully into the tin over the pears. Bake for about 50 minutes or until a skewer inserted into the centre comes out clean. Cool in the tin for 10 minutes, then turn the cake out on to a plate, peel off the lining paper, invert and slice.

Cook's Tip
Use the tip of a small, sharp knife to scrape out the vanilla seeds. If you do not have a vanilla pod, use 5ml/1 tsp pure vanilla extract instead.

Yogurt and Fig Cake: Energy 473kcal/1981kJ; Protein 8.2g; Carbohydrate 59.4g, of which sugars 38g; Fat 24.3g, of which saturates 14g; Cholesterol 149mg; Calcium 167mg; Fibre 2g; Sodium 225mg.
Pear Cake: Energy 205kcal/862kJ; Protein 2.9g; Carbohydrate 31.1g, of which sugars 21.4g; Fat 8.4g, of which saturates 1.2g; Cholesterol 46mg; Calcium 52mg; Fibre 1.4g; Sodium 53mg.

Sicilian Ricotta Cake

Cassata often describes a layered ice cream, but in Sicily it is a traditional cake made of sponge, ricotta and candied peel.

Serves 8–10

675g/1½lb/3 cups ricotta cheese
finely grated rind of 1 orange
20ml/4 tsp vanilla sugar
75ml/5 tbsp orange-flavoured liqueur
115g/4oz candied peel
8 trifle sponge cakes
60ml/4 tbsp freshly squeezed orange juice
extra candied peel, to decorate

1 Push the ricotta through a sieve (strainer) into a bowl, add the orange rind, vanilla sugar and 15ml/1 tbsp of the liqueur and beat to mix. Reserve about one-third of the mixture, covered and chilled. Finely chop the candied peel and beat into the remaining mixture. Set aside.

2 Line the base of a 1.2 litre/2 pint/5 cup loaf tin (pan) with baking parchment. Cut the trifle sponges in half horizontally. Arrange four pieces in the bottom of the tin and sprinkle with 15ml/1 tbsp each of liqueur and orange juice.

3 Spread one-third of the ricotta and fruit mixture evenly over the sponge. Cover with four more pieces of sponge, sprinkled with 15ml/1 tbsp each liqueur and orange juice as before.

4 Repeat the alternate layers of sponge and ricotta mixture until all the ingredients are used, ending with soaked sponge. Cover with a piece of baking parchment. Cut a piece of card to fit inside the tin, place on top of the baking parchment and weight down evenly. Chill for 24 hours.

5 To serve, remove the weights, card and paper and run a palette knife around the sides of the cassata. Invert a serving plate on top of the cassata, then invert the two so that the cassata is upside down on the plate. Peel off the lining paper.

6 Spread the reserved, chilled ricotta mixture over the cassata to cover it completely, then decorate the top with candied peel, cut into fancy shapes. Serve chilled.

Yogurt Cake with Pistachio Nuts, Crème Fraîche and Passion Fruit

One of the Middle East's favourite ingredients, yogurt, is used to make a beautifully moist cake. Use the thick, strained variety sold as Greek yogurt. This cake, with its crunchy pistachio topping, is delicious eaten hot or cold, with a dollop of crème fraîche. Fresh passion fruit pulp adds a tangy note, but this cake would taste just as good with a good apricot compote or a spoonful of Turkish-style sour cherry preserve.

Serves 4–6

3 eggs, separated
75g/3oz/scant ½ cup caster (superfine) sugar
seeds from 2 vanilla pods (beans)
300ml/½ pint/1½ cups natural (plain) Greek yogurt
grated rind and juice of 1 lemon
scant 15ml/1 tbsp plain (all-purpose) flour
handful of pistachio nuts, roughly chopped
60–90ml/4–6 tbsp crème fraîche and 4–6 fresh passion fruit or 50g/2oz/½ cup summer berries, to serve

1 Preheat the oven to 180°C/350°F/Gas 4. Line a 25cm/10in square, ovenproof dish with greaseproof (waxed) paper and grease well.

2 Beat the egg yolks with two-thirds of the sugar in a bowl, until pale and fluffy. Beat in the vanilla seeds and then stir in the yogurt, lemon rind and juice, and the flour. In a separate bowl, whisk the egg whites until stiff, then gradually whisk in the rest of the sugar to form soft peaks. Fold the whisked whites into the yogurt mixture. Turn the mixture into the prepared dish.

3 Place the dish in a roasting pan and pour in enough cold water to come about halfway up the outside of the dish. Bake in the oven for about 20 minutes, until the mixture is risen and just set. Sprinkle the pistachio nuts over the cake and then bake for a further 20 minutes, until browned on top.

4 Serve the cake warm or cooled and chilled, with crème fraîche and a spoonful of passion fruit drizzled over the top. Alternatively, sprinkle with a few summer berries.

Ricotta Cake: *Energy 219kcal/917kJ; Protein 7.3g; Carbohydrate 22.4g, of which sugars 20.2g; Fat 10.6g, of which saturates 6.3g; Cholesterol 51mg; Calcium 26mg; Fibre 0.7g; Sodium 42mg.*
Yogurt Cake: *Energy 474kcal/1987kJ; Protein 13.4g; Carbohydrate 49.4g, of which sugars 46g; Fat 26.3g, of which saturates 10g; Cholesterol 170mg; Calcium 196mg; Fibre 2.2g; Sodium 283mg.*

Lemon and Lime Syrup Cake

This Greek favourite is popular everywhere and is perfect for busy cooks as it can be mixed in moments and needs no icing. The simple tangy lime topping transforms it into a fabulously moist cake.

Serves 8

225g/8oz/2 cups self-raising (self-rising) flour
5ml/1 tsp baking powder
225g/8oz/generous 1 cup caster (superfine) sugar
225g/8oz/1 cup butter, softened
4 eggs, beaten
grated rind of 2 lemons
30ml/2 tbsp lemon juice

For the topping

finely pared rind of 1 lime
juice of 2 limes
150g/5oz/⅔ cup caster (superfine) sugar

1 Preheat the oven to 160°C/325°F/Gas 3. Grease and line a 20cm/8in round cake tin (pan). Sift the flour and baking powder into a bowl.

2 Add the caster sugar, butter and eggs, and beat thoroughly. Then gradually add and beat in the lemon rind and juice.

3 Spoon the mixture into the prepared tin, then smooth the surface and make a shallow indentation in the top with the back of a spoon.

4 Bake in the pre-heated oven for 1¼–1½ hours, or until the top of the cake is golden and a skewer inserted in the centre comes out clean.

5 Meanwhile, mix the topping ingredients together in a small bowl. As soon as the cake is cooked, remove it from the oven and pour the topping evenly over the surface. Allow the cake to cool in the tin.

Variation
Use lemon rind and juice instead of lime for the topping if you prefer. You will need only one large lemon.

Brandy and Almond Cake

The local name of this Spanish dessert, Biscocho Borracho, translates as "tipsy cake", as it is soaked in brandy syrup. Start making it 1–2 days ahead.

Serves 6–8

butter, for greasing
90g/3½oz/¾ cup plain (all-purpose) flour
6 eggs, separated
90g/3½oz/½ cup caster (superfine) sugar
finely grated rind of 1 lemon
90ml/6 tbsp toasted flaked (sliced) almonds
250ml/8fl oz/1 cup whipping cream, whipped, to serve

For the syrup

115g/4oz/generous ½ cup caster (superfine) sugar
120ml/4fl oz/½ cup boiling water
105ml/7 tbsp Spanish brandy

1 Preheat the oven to 200°C/400°F/Gas 6. Butter a shallow 28 × 18cm/11 × 7in tin (pan) and line with baking parchment. Sift the flour into a bowl. Process the egg yolks with the sugar and lemon rind until light. Whisk the whites to soft peaks, then work a little white into the yolk mixture.

2 Dribble a little of the yolk mixture across the whites, sift some flour over and fold in gently. Repeat until all the egg mixture and flour are incorporated. Turn into the tin, smooth the top and bake for 12 minutes. Leave to set for 5 minutes, then turn out on to a wire rack to cool.

3 For the syrup, heat 50g/2oz/¼ cup sugar with 15ml/1 tbsp water until it caramelizes. When it colours, dip the base of the pan into cold water. Add the remaining sugar and the boiling water. Simmer, stirring until the sugar has dissolved. Remove from the heat and add the brandy.

4 Put the cake back into the tin and drizzle half the syrup over it. Cut the cake into scallops with a spoon and layer half into a 700ml/1½ pint/3 cup mould. Scatter 30ml/2 tbsp almonds over the top, pushing them down the cracks. Top with the remaining cake and nuts. Pour the remaining syrup over the cake, cover with foil, weight the top and chill. To serve, turn out, scatter with almonds and serve with whipped cream.

Syrup Cake: *Energy 524kcal/2197kJ; Protein 6g; Carbohydrate 70.4g, of which sugars 49.5g; Fat 26.2g, of which saturates 15.5g; Cholesterol 155mg; Calcium 143mg; Fibre 0.9g; Sodium 310mg.*
Brandy and Almond Cake: *Energy 414kcal/1728kJ; Protein 8.9g; Carbohydrate 37.7g, of which sugars 28.8g; Fat 23.2g, of which saturates 9.6g; Cholesterol 176mg; Calcium 96mg; Fibre 1.2g; Sodium 64mg.*

Individual Brioches

These buttery rolls with their distinctive little topknots are delicious eaten with jam and café au lait.

Makes 8

7g/¼ oz/scant 1 tbsp active dry yeast
15ml/1 tbsp caster (superfine) sugar
30ml/2 tbsp warm milk
2 eggs
about 200g/7oz/1½ cups plain (all-purpose) flour
2.5ml/½ tsp salt
75g/3oz/6 tbsp butter, cut into 6 pieces, at room temperature
1 egg yolk beaten with 10ml/2 tsp water, for glazing

1 Lightly butter eight individual brioche or muffin tins (pans). Put the yeast and sugar in a small bowl, add the milk and stir until dissolved. Leave to stand for about 5 minutes until foamy, then beat in the egg.

2 Put the flour and salt into a food processor fitted with the metal blade, then with the machine running, slowly pour in the yeast mixture. Scrape down the sides and continue processing for about 2–3 minutes, or until the dough forms a ball. Add the butter and pulse the motor about 10 times, or until the butter is incorporated.

3 Transfer the dough to a lightly buttered bowl and cover with a cloth. Set aside to rise in a warm place for about 1 hour until doubled in size, then knock back (punch down).

4 Set aside one-quarter of the dough. Shape the remaining dough into eight balls and put into the prepared tins. Shape the reserved dough into eight smaller balls, then make a depression in the top of each large ball and set a small ball into it.

5 Allow the brioches to rise in a warm place for about 30 minutes until doubled in size. Preheat the oven to 200°C/400°F/Gas 6.

6 Brush the brioches lightly with the egg glaze and bake them for 15–18 minutes until golden brown. Transfer to a wire rack and leave to cool before serving.

Croissants

These croissants are flaky, puffy, light and buttery.

Makes 14

350g/12oz/3 cups unbleached white bread flour
115g/4oz/1 cup fine French plain (all purpose) flour
5ml/1 tsp salt
25g/1oz/2 tbsp caster (superfine) sugar
15g/½ oz fresh yeast
225ml/scant 8fl oz/scant 1 cup lukewarm milk
1 egg, lightly beaten
225g/8oz/1 cup butter

For the glaze

1 egg yolk
15ml/1 tbsp milk

1 Sift the flours and salt together into a large bowl. Stir in the sugar. Make a well in the centre. Cream the yeast with 45ml/3 tbsp of the milk, then stir in the remainder. Add the yeast mixture to the centre of the flour, then add the egg and gradually beat in the flour until it forms a dough.

2 Turn out on to a lightly floured surface and knead for 3–4 minutes. Place in a large lightly oiled bowl, cover with lightly oiled clear film (plastic wrap) and leave in a warm place, for about 45–60 minutes, or until doubled in bulk.

3 Knock back (punch down), re-cover and chill for 1 hour. Flatten the butter into a block about 2cm/¾in thick. Knock back the dough and turn out on to a floured surface. Roll out into a 25cm/10in square, rolling the edges thinner than the centre.

4 Place the butter diagonally in the centre and fold the corners of the dough over it like an envelope, tucking in the edges. Roll the dough into a rectangle about 2cm/¾in thick, approximately twice as long as it is wide. Fold the bottom third up and the top third down and seal the edges with a rolling pin. Wrap in clear film and chill for 20 minutes.

5 Repeat the rolling, folding and chilling twice more, turning the dough by 90 degrees each time. Roll out on a floured surface into a 63 × 33cm/25 × 13in rectangle; trim the edges to leave a 60 × 30cm/24 × 12in rectangle. Cut in half lengthways. Cut crossways into 14 equal triangles with 15cm/6in bases. Place the triangles on two baking sheets, cover with clear film and chill for 10 minutes.

6 To shape the croissants, place each one with the wide end at the top, hold each side and pull gently to stretch the top of the triangle a little, then roll towards the point, finishing with the pointed end tucked underneath. Curve the ends towards the pointed end to make a crescent. Place on two baking sheets, spaced well apart.

7 Mix the egg yolk and milk for the glaze and lightly brush over the croissants, avoiding the cut edges of the dough. Cover loosely with lightly oiled clear film and leave in a warm place for about 30 minutes, or until they are nearly doubled in size.

8 Meanwhile, preheat the oven to 220°C/425°F/Gas 7. Brush the croissants with the remaining glaze and bake for 15–20 minutes, or until crisp and golden. Transfer to a wire rack to cool slightly before serving warm.

Brioches: *Energy 183kcal/765kJ; Protein 4.1g; Carbohydrate 21.6g, of which sugars 2.6g; Fat 9.5g, of which saturates 5.4g; Cholesterol 68mg; Calcium 49mg; Fibre 0.8g; Sodium 77mg.*
Croissants: *Energy 253kcal/1059kJ; Protein 4.3g; Carbohydrate 28.5g, of which sugars 3.2g; Fat 14.4g, of which saturates 8.7g; Cholesterol 50mg; Calcium 72mg; Fibre 1g; Sodium 251mg.*

French Baguettes

Baguettes made by an artisan baker are difficult to reproduce at home, but by using less yeast and triple fermentation you can produce bread far superior to mass-produced loaves.

Makes 3 loaves

500g/1¼lb/5 cups unbleached strong white bread flour
115g/4oz/1 cup fine French plain (all-purpose) flour
10ml/2 tsp salt
15g/½oz fresh yeast

1 Sift the flours and salt into a large bowl. Add the yeast to 550ml/18fl oz/2½ cups lukewarm water in a separate bowl and stir until combined. Gradually beat in half the flour mixture to form a batter. Cover with clear film (plastic wrap) and leave for about 3 hours, or until nearly trebled in size.

2 Add the remaining flour a little at a time, beating with your hand. Turn out on to a lightly floured surface and knead for 8–10 minutes to form a moist dough. Place the dough in a lightly oiled bowl, cover with lightly oiled clear film and leave to rise, in a warm place, for about 1 hour.

3 Knock back (punch down) the dough, turn out on to a floured surface and divide into three equal pieces. Shape each into a ball and then into a 15 × 7.5cm/6 × 3in rectangle. Fold the bottom third up lengthways and the top third down and press down. Seal the edges. Repeat two or three more times until each loaf is an oblong. Leave to rest for a few minutes between foldings.

4 Stretch each piece of dough into a 35cm/14in long loaf. Pleat a floured dish towel on a baking sheet to make three moulds for the loaves. Place the loaves between the pleats, cover with lightly oiled clear film and leave to rise in a warm place for 45–60 minutes.

5 Preheat the oven to maximum. Roll the loaves on to a baking sheet, spaced apart. Slash the top of each diagonally several times. Place at the top of the oven, spray the inside of the oven with water and bake for 20–25 minutes. Spray the oven twice during the first 5 minutes of baking. Allow to cool.

Saffron Focaccia

A dazzling yellow bread that is both light in texture and distinctive in flavour. The olive oil drizzled over the top makes the bread moist and it keeps well.

Makes 1 loaf

a pinch of saffron threads
150ml/¼ pint/⅔ cup boiling water
225g/8oz/2 cups strong white bread flour
2.5ml/½ tsp salt
5ml/1 tsp easy-blend (rapid-rise) dried yeast
15ml/1 tbsp olive oil

For the topping

2 garlic cloves, sliced
1 red onion, cut into thin wedges
rosemary sprigs
12 black olives, stoned (pitted) and coarsely chopped
15ml/1 tbsp olive oil

1 Place the saffron in a heatproof jug (pitcher) and pour in the boiling water. Leave to infuse (steep) until lukewarm.

2 Place the flour, salt, yeast and olive oil in a food processor. Turn on and gradually add the saffron and its liquid. Process until the dough forms a ball. Alternatively, use your hands to incorporate the liquid into the flour.

3 Turn on to a floured surface and knead for 10–15 minutes. Place the dough in a bowl, cover with clear film (plastic wrap) and leave to rise until doubled in size, about 30–40 minutes.

4 Knock back (punch down) the dough and roll into an oval shape about 1cm/½in thick. Place on a lightly greased baking sheet and leave to rise for 30 minutes.

5 Preheat the oven to 200°C/400°F/Gas 6. With your fingers, press indentations over the surface of the bread.

6 To make the topping cover the top of the focaccia evenly with pieces of sliced garlic, onion wedges, rosemary sprigs and chopped olives.

7 Brush lightly with olive oil and bake for 25 minutes, or until the loaf sounds hollow when tapped on the base. Leave to cool on a wire rack.

French Baguettes: *Energy 233kcal/991kJ; Protein 6.4g; Carbohydrate 53.1g, of which sugars 1g; Fat 0.9g, of which saturates 0.1g.; Cholesterol 0mg; Calcium 96mg; Fibre 2.1g; Sodium 439mg.*
Saffron Foccacia: *Energy 1038kcal/4377kJ; Protein 22.3g; Carbohydrate 179.6g, of which sugars 6.7g; Fat 30.5g, of which saturates 4.4g; Cholesterol 0mg; Calcium 360mg; Fibre 9.3g; Sodium 1134mg.*

Polenta Bread

Polenta is widely used in Italian cooking. Here it is combined with pine nuts to make a truly Italian bread with a fantastic flavour.

Makes 1 loaf

50g/2oz/½ cup polenta
300ml/½ pint/1¼ cups lukewarm water
15g/½ oz fresh yeast
2.5ml/½ tsp clear honey
225g/8oz/2 cups unbleached white bread flour
25g/1oz/2 tbsp butter
45ml/3 tbsp pine nuts
7.5ml/1½ tsp salt

For the topping

1 egg yolk
15ml/1 tbsp water
pine nuts, for sprinkling

1 Lightly grease a baking sheet. Mix the polenta and 250ml/8fl oz/1 cup of the water in a pan and slowly bring to the boil, stirring continuously, then simmer for 2–3 minutes, stirring occasionally. Set aside to cool for 10 minutes, or until just warm.

2 Mix the yeast with the remaining water and honey until creamy. Sift 115g/4oz/1 cup of the flour and beat in the yeast mixture, then stir in the polenta mixture. Turn on to a floured surface and knead for 5 minutes until smooth and elastic. Put the dough in a lightly oiled polythene bag and leave in a warm place, for about 2 hours, or until it has doubled in bulk. Meanwhile, melt the butter, add the pine nuts and cook over a medium heat, stirring, until pale golden. Set aside to cool.

3 Add the remaining flour and salt to the dough and mix to a soft dough. Knead in the pine nuts. Turn out on to a floured surface and knead for 5 minutes until smooth and elastic. Place in a lightly oiled bowl, cover and leave in a warm place, for 1 hour, or until doubled in bulk.

4 Knock back (punch down) the dough and turn it out on to a floured surface. Divide into 2 equal pieces and roll each piece into a fat sausage about 38cm/15in long. Plait together and place on the prepared baking sheet. Cover again and leave to rise in a warm place for 45 minutes. Preheat the oven to 200°C/400°F/Gas 6. Mix the egg yolk and water and brush over the loaf. Sprinkle with pine nuts and bake for 30 minutes.

Warm Herby Bread

This Italian-style bread is flavoured with basil, rosemary, olive oil and sun-dried tomatoes.

Makes 3 loaves

5ml/1 tsp caster (superfine) sugar
900ml/1½ pints/3¾ cups warm water
15ml/1 tbsp dried yeast
1.3kg/3lb/12 cups strong white flour, plus extra for dusting
15ml/1 tbsp salt
75ml/5 tbsp mixed fresh chopped basil and rosemary leaves
50g/2oz/1 cup drained sun-dried tomatoes, roughly chopped
150ml/¼ pint/⅔ cup extra virgin olive oil, plus extra for greasing and brushing

To finish

15ml/1 tbsp rosemary leaves
sea salt flakes

1 Put the sugar into a bowl, pour on 150ml/¼ pint/⅔ cup warm water, then sprinkle the dried yeast over the top. Leave in a warm place for 10–15 minutes, or until frothy.

2 Put the flour, salt, chopped basil and rosemary leaves, and sun-dried tomatoes into a large mixing bowl. Add the olive oil together with the yeast mixture, then gradually stir in the remaining warm water. As the mixture becomes stiffer, bring it together with your hands. Mix to a soft but not sticky dough, adding a little extra water if needed.

3 Turn the dough out on to a lightly floured surface and knead for 5 minutes until smooth and elastic. Put back into the bowl, cover loosely with oiled clear film (plastic wrap) and leave in a warm place for 30–40 minutes, or until doubled in size.

4 Knead again until smooth and elastic, then cut into three pieces. Shape each into an oval loaf about 18cm/7in long, and arrange on oiled baking sheets. Slash the top of each loaf with a knife in a criss-cross pattern.

5 Loosely cover and leave in a warm place for 15–20 minutes, or until well risen. Preheat the oven to 220°C/425°F/Gas 7. Brush the loaves with a little olive oil and sprinkle with rosemary leaves and salt flakes. Cook for about 25 minutes. The bases should sound hollow when they are tapped.

Polenta Bread: *Energy 1994kcal/8427kJ; Protein 50.5g; Carbohydrate 366.8g, of which sugars 7.1g; Fat 44.7g, of which saturates 15g; Cholesterol 53mg; Calcium 1085mg; Fibre 14.9g; Sodium 2337mg.*
Warm Herby Bread: *Energy 1789kcal/7563kJ; Protein 41.5g; Carbohydrate 338.2g, of which sugars 7.9g; Fat 39.3g, of which saturates 5.7g; Cholesterol 0mg; Calcium 643mg; Fibre 14.6g; Sodium 1987mg.*

Pane Toscano

This Tuscan bread is made without salt and probably originates from the days when salt was heavily taxed. To compensate for the lack of salt, it is usually served with salty foods, such as anchovies and olives.

Makes 1 loaf

550g/1¼ lb/5 cups unbleached white bread flour
350ml/12fl oz/1½ cups boiling water
15g/½ oz fresh yeast
60ml/4 tbsp lukewarm water

1 To make the starter, sift 175g/6oz/1½ cups of the flour into a large bowl. Pour over the boiling water, leave for a couple of minutes, then mix well. Cover with a damp dish towel and leave for 10 hours.

2 Lightly flour a baking sheet. Cream the yeast with the lukewarm water. Stir into the starter. Gradually add the remaining flour and mix to form a dough. Turn out on to a lightly floured surface and knead for 5–8 minutes until elastic. Place in a lightly oiled bowl, cover with lightly oiled clear film (plastic wrap) and leave in a warm place for 1–1½ hours, or until doubled in bulk.

3 Turn out the dough on to a lightly floured surface, knock back (punch down), and shape into a round. Fold the sides into the centre and seal. Place seam side up on the prepared baking sheet. Cover with lightly oiled clear film and leave in a warm place, for 30–45 minutes, or until doubled in size.

4 Flatten the loaf to about half its height and flip over. Cover again and leave to rise in a warm place for 30 minutes. Meanwhile, preheat the oven to 220°C/425°F/Gas 7. Slash the top of the loaf and bake for 30–35 minutes, or until golden. Transfer to a wire rack to cool.

Cook's Tip
Salt controls the action of yeast so the leavening is more noticeable. Don't let this bread over-rise or it may collapse.

Sicilian Scroll

A wonderful pale yellow, crusty loaf, enhanced with a nutty flavour from the sesame seeds. It's perfect for serving with cheese.

Makes 1 loaf

450g/1lb/4 cups finely ground semolina
115g/4oz/1 cup unbleached white bread flour
10ml/2 tsp salt
20g/¾oz fresh yeast
360ml/12½fl oz/generous 1½ cups lukewarm water
30ml/2 tbsp extra virgin olive oil
sesame seeds, for sprinkling

1 Lightly grease a baking sheet. Mix the semolina, white bread flour and salt in a large bowl and make a well in the centre.

2 Cream the yeast with half the water, then stir in the remainder. Add the creamed yeast to the centre of the semolina mixture with the olive oil and gradually incorporate the semolina and flour to form a firm dough.

3 Turn out the dough on to a lightly floured surface and knead for 8–10 minutes until smooth and elastic. Place in a lightly oiled bowl, cover with lightly oiled clear film and leave to rise, in a warm place, for 1–1½ hours, or until doubled in bulk.

4 Turn out on to a lightly floured surface and knock back (punch down). Knead gently, then shape into a fat roll about 50cm/20in long. Form into an "S" shape.

5 Carefully transfer the dough to the prepared baking sheet, cover with lightly oiled clear film and leave to rise, in a warm place, for 30–45 minutes, or until doubled in size.

6 Meanwhile, preheat the oven to 220°C/425°F/Gas 7. Brush the top of the scroll with water and sprinkle with sesame seeds. Bake for 10 minutes. Spray the inside of the oven with water twice during this time.

7 Reduce the temperature to 200°C/400°F/Gas 6 and bake for a further 25–30 minutes, or until golden. Transfer to a wire rack to cool.

Pane Toscano: *Energy 1876kcal/7975kJ; Protein 51.7g; Carbohydrate 427.4g, of which sugars 8.3g; Fat 7.2g, of which saturates 1.1g; Cholesterol 0mg; Calcium 770mg; Fibre 17.1g; Sodium 17mg*
Sicilian Scroll: *Energy 2344kcal/9922kJ; Protein 64.4g; Carbohydrate 438.4g, of which sugars 1.8g; Fat 49g, of which saturates 5.9g; Cholesterol 0mg; Calcium 443mg; Fibre 15.4g; Sodium 63mg.*

Onion, Parmesan and Olive Bread

This bread is great served warm with olive oil.

Makes 1 large or 2 small loaves

350g/12oz/3 cups unbleached strong bread flour, plus a little extra
115g/4oz/1 cup yellow cornmeal, plus a little extra
rounded 5ml/1 tsp salt
15g/½oz fresh yeast or 10ml/2 tsp active dried yeast
5ml/1 tsp muscovado sugar
270ml/9fl oz/1 cup warm water
5ml/1 tsp chopped fresh thyme
30ml/2 tbsp olive oil
1 onion, finely chopped
75g/3oz/1 cup freshly grated Parmesan cheese
90g/3½oz/scant 1 cup black olives, stoned (pitted)

1 If using fresh yeast, cream it with the sugar and stir in 120ml/4fl oz/½ cup of the warm water. If using dried yeast, stir the sugar into the water, then sprinkle the dried yeast on the surface. Leave in a warm place for 10 minutes, until frothy.

2 Mix the flour, cornmeal and salt, in a warmed bowl. Make a well in the centre and add the yeast liquid and 150ml/ ¼ pint/ ⅔ cup of the remaining warm water. Add the thyme and 15ml/1 tbsp of olive oil and mix thoroughly. Add a dash more warm water, if necessary, to make a soft, but not sticky, dough.

3 Knead the dough on a lightly floured work surface for 5 minutes, until smooth and elastic. Place in a lightly oiled bowl and cover with oiled clear film. Set aside to rise in a warm, not hot place for 1–2 hours or until well risen.

4 Fry the onion until soft, not browned. Once they have cooled, knead them, the Parmesan and olives into the dough.

5 Shape the dough into one or two loaves. Sprinkle cornmeal on the work surface and roll the bread in it, then place on an oiled baking sheet. Make slits across the top. Cover with oiled clear film and leave in a warm place for 1 hour, or until risen.

6 Preheat the oven to 200°C/400°F/Gas 6. Bake for 30–35 minutes, or until the bread sounds hollow when tapped on the base. Cool on a wire rack.

Prosciutto and Parmesan Bread

This delicious bread is bursting with flavour and is great eaten on its own. For lunch or supper, serve it with a selection of Italian cheeses or cooked meats and salads.

Makes 1 loaf

225g/8oz/2 cups self-raising (self-rising) wholemeal (whole-wheat) flour
225g/8oz/2 cups self-raising (self-rising) white flour
5ml/1 tsp baking powder
5ml/1 tsp salt
5ml/1 tsp ground black pepper
75g/3oz prosciutto, chopped
25g/1oz/⅓ cup freshly grated Parmesan cheese
30ml/2 tbsp chopped fresh parsley
45ml/3 tbsp Meaux or wholegrain mustard
350ml/12fl oz/1½ cups buttermilk
skimmed milk, to glaze

1 Preheat the oven to 200°C/400°F/Gas 6. Flour a baking sheet. Place the wholemeal flour in a bowl and sift in the white flour, baking powder and salt. Add the pepper and prosciutto.

2 Set aside about 15ml/1 tbsp of the grated Parmesan and stir the rest into the flour mixture. Stir in the chopped parsley. Make a well in the centre. Mix the mustard and buttermilk together, pour into the flour mixture and quickly mix to form a soft dough.

3 Turn the dough on to a lightly floured surface and knead briefly. Shape into an oval loaf, brush with a little milk and sprinkle with the remaining Parmesan cheese. Place on the prepared baking sheet.

4 Bake the loaf in the oven for 25–30 minutes, or until golden brown. The loaf should sound hollow when tapped on the base. Transfer to a wire rack to cool. Serve in slices.

Cook's Tip
This is a soda bread, made without yeast, and will dry out fairly quickly, so is best eaten on the day it is made.

Onion and Olive Bread: *Energy 571kcal/2402kJ; Protein 18.7g; Carbohydrate 91.3g, of which sugars 3.2g; Fat 16.2g, of which saturates 5.2g; Cholesterol 19mg; Calcium 367mg; Fibre 4.2g; Sodium 714mg.*
Prosciutto and Parmsean Bread: *Energy 226kcal/960kJ; Protein 9.6g; Carbohydrate 44.7g, of which sugars 2.9g; Fat 2.2g, of which saturates 0.9g; Cholesterol 10mg; Calcium 300mg; Fibre 2g; Sodium 616mg.*

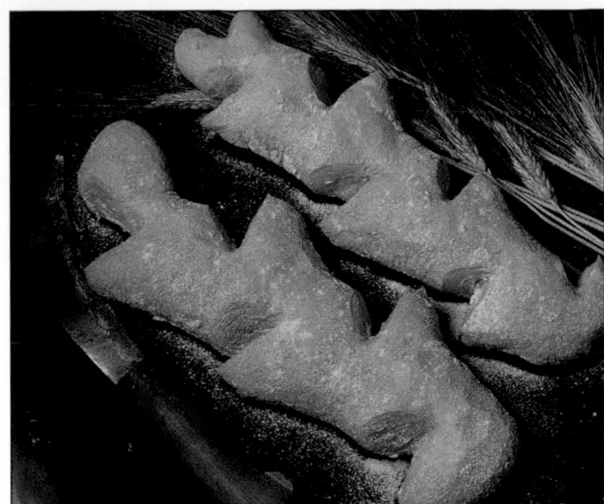

Wheat Ear Loaf

This distinctively-shaped loaf uses fermented French baguette dough as a starter.

Makes 2 loaves
7g/¼ oz fresh yeast
275ml/9fl oz/generous 1 cup lukewarm water
115g/4oz/½ cup French baguette dough 6–10 hours old
225g/8oz/2 cups unbleached white bread flour
75g/3oz/¾ cup fine French plain (all-purpose) flour
5ml/1 tsp salt

1 Sprinkle a baking sheet with flour. Mix the yeast with the water. Place the French bread dough in a large bowl and break up. Add a little of the yeast water to soften the dough. Mix in a little of the bread flour, then yeast water and both flours alternately until fully incorporated. Sprinkle the salt over the dough and knead in. Turn the dough on to a lightly floured surface and knead for about 5 minutes until smooth and elastic.

2 Place in a lightly oiled bowl, cover with lightly oiled clear film (plastic wrap) and leave in a warm place for about 1 hour, or until the dough has doubled in bulk. Knock it back, then cover the bowl again and leave in a warm place, for about 1 hour.

3 Divide the dough into 2 equal pieces, place on a lightly floured surface and stretch each piece into a baguette.

4 Let the dough rest between rolling for a few minutes if necessary to avoid tearing. Pleat a floured dish towel on a baking sheet to make 2 moulds for the loaves. Place them between the pleats of the towel, cover with lightly oiled clear film and leave in a warm place to rise for 30 minutes.

5 Meanwhile, preheat the oven to 230°C/450°F/Gas 8. Using scissors, make diagonal cuts halfway through the dough about 5cm/2in apart, alternating the cuts along the loaf. Gently pull the dough in the opposite direction.

6 Place on the baking sheet and bake for 20 minutes, or until golden. Spray the inside of the oven with water 2–3 times during the first 5 minutes. Transfer to a wire rack to cool.

Rustic Country Bread

This superb country bread is made using a natural French chef starter to produce a rustic flavour and texture. In France, it is often made in huge loaves.

Makes 1 loaf

For the chef
50g/2oz/½ cup wholemeal bread flour
45ml/3 tbsp warm water

For the 1st refreshment
60ml/4 tbsp warm water
75g/3oz/¾ cup wholemeal bread flour

For the 2nd refreshment
120ml/4fl oz/½ cup lukewarm water
115g/4oz/1 cup unbleached white bread flour
25g/1oz/¼ cup wholemeal bread flour

For the dough
150–175ml/5–6fl oz/⅔–¾ cup lukewarm water
350g/12oz/3 cups unbleached white bread flour
10ml/2 tsp salt

1 To make the chef, place the flour in a bowl, add the water and knead for 3–4 minutes to form a dough. Cover with clear film (plastic wrap) and leave in a warm place for 2 days.

2 Pull off the hardened crust and discard, then remove 30ml/2 tbsp of the moist centre. Place in a large bowl and gradually mix in the water for the 1st refreshment. Gradually add the flour and knead for 3–4 minutes to form a dough, then cover with clear film and leave in a warm place for 1 day.

3 Discard the crust and gradually mix in the water for the 2nd refreshment. Add the flours a little at a time, mixing well after each addition to form a firm dough. Cover with lightly oiled clear film and leave in a warm place, for about 10 hours, or until doubled in bulk.

4 Lightly flour a baking sheet. Gradually mix the water into the dough, then gradually mix in the flour, then the salt. Turn out on to a lightly floured surface and knead for about 5 minutes until smooth and elastic. Place the dough in a large lightly oiled bowl, cover with lightly oiled clear film and leave in a warm place for 1½–2 hours, or until almost doubled in bulk.

5 Knock back (punch down) the dough. Cut off 115g/4oz/½ cup and set aside for making the next loaf. Shape the remaining dough into a ball. Line a 10cm/4in high, 23cm/9in round basket or large bowl with a dish towel and dust with flour. Place the dough ball seam side up in the prepared basket or bowl.

6 Cover with lightly oiled clear film and leave to rise, in a warm place, for 2–3 hours, or until almost doubled in bulk.

7 Preheat the oven to 230°C/450°F/Gas 8. Invert the loaf on to the prepared baking sheet and sprinkle with flour. Slash the top of the loaf, using a sharp knife, four times at right angles to each other, to form a square pattern.

8 Sprinkle with a little more flour then bake for 30–35 minutes, or until the loaf has browned and sounds hollow when tapped on the base. Transfer to a rack to cool.

Wheat Ear Loaf: *Energy 705kcal/2996kJ; Protein 19.4g; Carbohydrate 160.5g, of which sugars 3.1g; Fat 2.7g, of which saturates 0.4g; Cholesterol 0mg; Calcium 290mg; Fibre 6.4g; Sodium 1351mg.*
Rustic Country Loaf: *Energy 1632kcal/6940kJ; Protein 50.2g; Carbohydrate 363.5g, of which sugars 8.1g; Fat 7.5g, of which saturates 1.1g; Cholesterol 0mg; Calcium 560mg; Fibre 22.6g; Sodium 3945mg.*

Blue Cheese and Walnut Bread

This lattice-shaped loaf from the South of France can be plain or flavoured with cheese, herbs, nuts or olives.

Makes 2 loaves

450g/1lb/4 cups unbleached white bread flour
5ml/1 tsp salt
20g/¾oz fresh yeast
280ml/9fl oz/generous 1 cup lukewarm water
15ml/1 tbsp extra virgin olive oil

For the filling

50g/2oz/⅓ cup Roquefort cheese, crumbled
40g/1½oz/⅓ cup walnut pieces, chopped
25g/1oz/2 tbsp drained, canned anchovy fillets, soaked in milk and drained again, chopped
olive oil, for brushing

1 Lightly grease 2 baking sheets. Sift the flour and salt and make a well in the centre. Cream the yeast with 60ml/4 tbsp of the water and pour into well with the remaining water and the olive oil. Mix to a soft dough, turn out on to a floured surface and knead for 8–10 minutes until smooth and elastic.

2 Place the dough in a lightly oiled bowl, cover with lightly oiled clear film (plastic wrap) and leave to rise, in a warm place, for about 1 hour, or until doubled in bulk.

3 Knock back (punch down) the dough and divide in half. Flatten one piece, sprinkle with cheese and walnuts and fold over 2–3 times. Repeat with the other piece, using the anchovies. Shape each piece into a ball, flatten and fold the bottom third up and the top third down. Roll the cheese dough into a rectangle and make 4 diagonal cuts almost to the edge. Pull and stretch the dough evenly, so that it resembles a ladder.

4 Shape the anchovy dough into an oval and make 3 diagonal slits on each side. Transfer to the prepared baking sheets, cover with lightly oiled clear film and leave in a warm place for about 30–45 minutes, or until nearly doubled in bulk.

5 Meanwhile, preheat the oven to 220°C/425°F/Gas 7. Brush both loaves with a little olive oil and bake for 25 minutes, or until golden. Transfer to a wire rack to cool.

Walnut Bread

This delicious butter-and-milk-enriched wholemeal bread is filled with walnuts. It is the perfect companion for cheese.

Makes 2 loaves

50g/2oz/¼ cup butter
350g/12oz/3 cups wholemeal bread flour
115g/4oz/1 cup unbleached white bread flour
15ml/1 tbsp light brown muscovado (molasses) sugar
7.5ml/1½ tsp salt
20g/¾oz fresh yeast
275ml/9fl oz/generous 1 cup lukewarm milk
175g/6oz/1½ cups walnut pieces

1 Lightly grease two baking sheets. Heat the butter in a pan until starting to brown, then set aside to cool. Mix the flours, sugar and salt in a large bowl and make a well in the centre. Cream the yeast with half the milk and pour into the well with the remaining milk.

2 Pour the melted butter through a fine strainer into the well with the other liquids. Using your hand, mix the liquids together in the bowl and gradually draw in small amounts of flour to make a batter. Continue until the mixture forms a moist dough. Knead on a lightly floured surface for 6–8 minutes. Place in a lightly oiled bowl, cover with oiled clear film (plastic wrap) and leave in a warm place for 1 hour, or until doubled in bulk.

3 Turn out the dough on to a floured surface and gently knock back (punch down). Flatten and sprinkle with the nuts. Gently press the nuts into the dough, then roll it up. Return to the oiled bowl, re-cover and leave in a warm place for 30 minutes.

4 Turn out on to a lightly floured surface, divide in half and shape each piece into a ball. Place on the baking sheets, cover with lightly oiled clear film and leave in a warm place for 45 minutes or until doubled in bulk.

5 Meanwhile, preheat the oven to 220°C/425°F/Gas 7. Using a sharp knife, slash the top of each loaf 3 times. Bake for about 35 minutes, or until the loaves sound hollow when tapped on the base. Transfer to a wire rack to cool.

Blue Cheese and Walnut: *Energy 1014kcal/4284kJ; Protein 32.4g; Carbohydrate 175.5g, of which sugars 3.9g; Fat 25.1g, of which saturates 6.6g; Cholesterol 27mg; Calcium 494mg; Fibre 7.7g; Sodium 1787mg.*
Walnut Bread: *Energy 1620kcal/6782kJ; Protein 45.4g; Carbohydrate 173.9g, of which sugars 21.3g; Fat 87.4g, of which saturates 20.1g; Cholesterol 61mg; Calcium 403mg; Fibre 20.6g; Sodium 224mg.*

Italian Country Bread

This classic Italian open-textured bread is moistened and flavoured with fruity olive oil. Its floured top gives it a true country feel.

Makes 1 large loaf

For the starter

175g/6oz/1½ cups unbleached white bread flour
7g/¼oz fresh yeast
90ml/6 tbsp lukewarm water

For the dough

225g/8oz/2 cups unbleached white bread flour, plus extra for dusting
225g/8oz/2 cups unbleached wholemeal bread flour
5ml/1 tsp caster (superfine) sugar
10ml/2 tsp salt
15g/½oz fresh yeast
275ml/9fl oz/generous 1 cup lukewarm water
75ml/5 tbsp extra virgin olive oil

1 Sift the flour for the starter into a large bowl. Make a well in the centre. Cream the yeast with the water and pour into the well. Gradually mix in the flour to form a firm dough. Turn out on to a lightly floured surface and knead for 5 minutes until smooth and elastic. Return to the bowl, cover with lightly oiled clear film (plastic wrap) and leave in a warm place for 8–10 hours, or until well risen and starting to collapse.

2 Lightly flour a baking sheet. Mix the flours, sugar and salt for the dough in a large bowl. Cream the yeast and the water in another large bowl, then stir in the starter. Stir in the flour mixture a little at a time, then add the olive oil in the same way, and mix to a soft dough. Turn out on to a lightly floured surface and knead for 8–10 minutes until smooth and elastic. Place in a lightly oiled bowl, cover with lightly oiled clear film and leave in a warm place for 1–1½ hours, or until doubled in bulk.

3 Turn out on to a floured surface and knock back (punch down). Gently pull out the edges and fold under to make a round. Transfer to the baking sheet, cover again and leave in a warm place for 1–1½ hours, or until almost doubled in size.

4 Preheat the oven to 230°C/450°F/Gas 8. Lightly dust the loaf with flour and bake for 15 minutes. Reduce the temperature to 200°C/400°F/Gas 6 and bake for a further 20 minutes, or until the loaf sounds hollow when tapped on the base.

Ciabatta

This irregular-shaped Italian bread is so called because it looks like an old slipper. It is made with a very wet dough flavoured with olive oil, producing a bread full of holes with a chewy crust.

Makes 3 loaves

For the starter

7g/¼oz fresh yeast
175–200ml/6–7fl oz/¾–scant 1 cup lukewarm water
350g/12oz/3 cups unbleached plain (all-purpose) flour, plus extra for dusting

For the dough

15g/½oz fresh yeast
400ml/14fl oz/1⅔ cups lukewarm water
60ml/4 tbsp lukewarm milk
500g/1¼lb/5 cups unbleached strong white bread flour
10ml/2 tsp salt
45ml/3 tbsp extra virgin olive oil

1 Cream the yeast for the starter with a little of the water. Sift the flour into a large bowl. Gradually mix in the yeast mixture and enough of the remaining water to form a firm dough. Turn out on to a floured surface and knead for about 5 minutes, or until smooth and elastic. Return the dough to the bowl, cover with lightly oiled clear film (plastic wrap) and leave in a warm place for 12–15 hours, until risen and starting to collapse.

2 Sprinkle three baking sheets with flour. Mix the yeast for the dough with a little of the water until creamy, then mix in the rest. Add this mixture to the starter and gradually mix in. Mix in the milk, beating thoroughly with a wooden spoon. Using your hand, gradually beat in the flour, lifting the dough as you mix. This will take 15 minutes or more and form a very wet dough.

3 With a spoon, carefully tip one-third of the dough at a time on to the baking sheets without knocking it back in the process. Using floured hands, shape into rough oblong loaves, about 2.5cm/1in thick. Flatten slightly with splayed fingers. Sprinkle with flour; leave to rise in a warm place for 30 minutes.

4 Meanwhile, preheat the oven to 220°C/425°F/Gas 7. Bake the loaves in the oven for 25–30 minutes, or until golden brown and sounding hollow when tapped on the base. Transfer to a wire rack to cool.

Italian Country Bread: *Energy 2502kcal/10567kJ; Protein 71.9g; Carbohydrate 430.4g, of which sugars 11.8g; Fat 66.7g, of which saturates 9.5g; Cholesterol 0mg; Calcium 468mg; Fibre 43g; Sodium 3949mg.*
Ciabatta: *Energy 985kcal/4176kJ; Protein 25g; Carbohydrate 202.8g, of which sugars 4.8g; Fat 13.8g, of which saturates 2.2g; Cholesterol 1mg; Calcium 386mg; Fibre 8.1g; Sodium 1217mg.*

Portuguese Corn Bread

The Portuguese make corn bread with a mixture of cornmeal and white flour. It has a hard crust with a moist crumb.

Makes 1 large loaf

20g/¾oz fresh yeast
250ml/8fl oz/1 cup lukewarm water
225g/8oz/2 cups cornmeal
450g/1lb/4 cups unbleached white bread flour
150ml/¼ pint/⅔ cup lukewarm milk
30ml/2 tbsp olive oil
7.5ml/1½ tsp salt
polenta, for dusting

1 Dust a baking sheet with a little cornmeal. Put the yeast in a large bowl and gradually mix in the lukewarm water until smooth. Stir in half the cornmeal and 50g/2oz/½ cup of the flour and mix to a batter. Cover the bowl with lightly oiled clear film (plastic wrap) and leave in a warm place for about 30 minutes, or until bubbles appear on the surface.

2 Stir the milk into the batter, then stir in the olive oil. Gradually mix in the remaining cornmeal, flour and salt to form a pliable dough. Turn out on to a lightly floured surface and knead for about 10 minutes until smooth and elastic.

3 Place the dough in a lightly oiled bowl, cover with lightly oiled clear film and leave to rise, in a warm place, for 1½–2 hours, or until doubled in bulk.

4 Turn out the dough on to a lightly floured surface and knock back (punch down). Shape into a round ball, flatten slightly and place on the prepared baking sheet. Dust with polenta, cover with a large upturned bowl and leave in a warm place for about 1 hour, or until doubled in size. Meanwhile, preheat the oven to 230°C/450°F/Gas 8.

5 Bake for 10 minutes, spraying the inside of the oven with water 2–3 times. Reduce the oven temperature to 190°C/375°F/Gas 5 and bake for a further 20–25 minutes, or until golden and hollow sounding when tapped on the base. Transfer to a wire rack to cool.

Onion, Chive and Ricotta Bread

Ricotta cheese and chives make a moist, well-flavoured loaf that is excellent for sandwiches. Shape the dough into rolls or one large loaf.

Makes 1 loaf or 16 rolls

5ml/1 tsp caster (superfine) sugar
270ml/9fl oz/generous 1 cup lukewarm water
10ml/2 tsp active dried yeast
450g/1lb unbleached strong white flour, plus a little extra
7.5ml/1½ tsp salt
1 large egg, beaten
115g/4oz/½ cup ricotta cheese
1 bunch spring onions (scallions), thinly sliced
30ml/2 tbsp extra virgin olive oil
45ml/3 tbsp snipped fresh chives
15ml/1 tbsp milk
10ml/2 tsp poppy seeds
coarse sea salt

1 Stir the sugar into 120ml/4fl oz/½ cup of the water, then sprinkle the dried yeast over the surface. Leave in a warm place for 10 minutes. Sift the flour and salt into a bowl. Make a well in the centre and pour in the yeast liquid and the remaining water. Reserve a little beaten egg, then put the rest in the bowl. Add the ricotta and mix to a dough. Add more flour if it is sticky.

2 Knead the dough on a floured work surface until smooth and elastic. Put an oiled bowl covered with lightly oiled clear film (plastic wrap) and leave in a warm place for 1–2 hours, until doubled in size. Meanwhile, cook the spring onions in the oil for 3–4 minutes, until soft. Set aside to cool.

3 Punch down the dough and knead in the onions, with their oil from cooking, and the chives. Shape into rolls or a loaf.

4 Grease a baking sheet or loaf tin (pan) and place the rolls or bread on it. Cover with oiled film and leave in a warm place to rise for about 1 hour. Preheat the oven to 200°C/400°F/Gas 6.

5 Beat the milk into the reserved beaten egg and use to glaze the rolls or loaf. Sprinkle with poppy seeds and a little coarse sea salt, then bake rolls for about 15 minutes or a loaf for 30–40 minutes, or until golden and well risen. When tapped firmly on the base, the bread should feel and sound firm. Cool on a wire rack.

Corn Bread: *Energy 3008kcal/12539kJ; Protein 52.7g; Carbohydrate 303.3g, of which sugars 87.7g; Fat 179.8g, of which saturates 46.1g; Cholesterol 561mg; Calcium 696mg; Fibre 7.4g; Sodium 1672mg.*
Ricotta Bread: *Energy 2042kcal/8626kJ; Protein 61.6g; Carbohydrate 356.9g, of which sugars 13.8g; Fat 50.8g, of which saturates 16.3g; Cholesterol 239mg; Calcium 716mg; Fibre 15.4g; Sodium 97mg.*

Multi-Seed Loaf

This round loaf with a twisted top comes from Spain. The olive oil gives a soft crumb and the millet and seeds provide an interesting mix of textures.

Makes 1 large loaf

350g/12oz/3 cups unbleached white bread flour
115g/4oz/1 cup wholemeal (whole-wheat) bread flour
10ml/2 tsp salt
20g/¾oz fresh yeast
275ml/9fl oz/generous 1 cup lukewarm water
30ml/2 tbsp olive oil
30ml/2 tbsp pumpkin seeds
30ml/2 tbsp sunflower seeds
15ml/1 tbsp millet
cornmeal, for dusting

1 Sprinkle a baking sheet with cornmeal. Mix the flours and salt together in a large bowl and make a well in the centre.

2 Mix the yeast with the water and add to the well with the olive oil or lard and mix to a firm dough. Turn out on to a lightly floured surface and knead for about 10 minutes until smooth and elastic. Place in a lightly oiled bowl, then cover with lightly oiled clear film (plastic wrap) and leave in a warm place, for about 1½–2 hours, or until doubled in bulk.

3 Knock back (punch down) the dough and turn out on to a floured surface. Gently knead in the seeds and millet. Re-cover and leave to rest for 5 minutes, then shape into a ball, twisting the centre to make a cap. Transfer to the prepared baking sheet and dust with cornmeal. Cover with an upturned bowl and leave in a warm place, for 45 minutes, or until doubled in bulk.

4 Meanwhile, place an empty roasting pan in the bottom of the oven. Preheat the oven to 220°C/425°F/Gas 7. Pour about 300ml/½ pint/1¼ cups water into the pan. Lift the bowl off the risen loaf and immediately place the baking sheet in the oven, above the roasting pan. Bake the bread for 10 minutes.

5 Remove the pan of water and bake the bread for a further 25–30 minutes, or until well browned and sounding hollow when tapped on the base. Transfer to a wire rack to cool.

Spanish Country Bread

This Spanish country bread is made with barley and cornmeal. It has a close, heavy texture and is very satisfying.

Makes 1 large loaf
For the starter

175g/6oz/1½ cups cornmeal
560ml/scant 1 pint/scant 2½ cups water
225g/8oz/2 cups wholemeal bread flour
75g/3oz/¾ cup barley flour

For the dough

20g/¾oz fresh yeast
45ml/3 tbsp lukewarm water
225g/8oz/2 cups wholemeal bread flour
15ml/1 tbsp salt
cornmeal, for dusting

1 In a saucepan, mix the cornmeal for the starter with half the water, then blend in the remainder. Cook gently, stirring continuously, until thickened. Transfer to a large bowl and set aside to cool. Mix in the wholemeal and barley flours. Turn out on to a lightly floured surface and knead for 5 minutes. Return to the bowl, cover with lightly oiled clear film (plastic wrap) and leave in a warm place for 36 hours.

2 Dust a baking sheet with cornmeal. In a small bowl, cream the yeast with the water for the dough. Mix the yeast mixture into the starter with the wholemeal flour and salt and work to a dough. Turn out on to a lightly floured surface and knead for 4–5 minutes until smooth and elastic.

3 Transfer the dough to an oiled bowl, cover with oiled clear film and leave in a warm place for 1½–2 hours, until doubled in bulk. Knock back (punch down) and turn out on to a floured surface. Shape into a plump round. Sprinkle with cornmeal.

4 Place the loaf on the prepared baking sheet. Cover with an upturned bowl and leave in a warm place for about 1 hour, or until nearly doubled in bulk. Place a roasting pan in the bottom of the oven. Preheat the oven to 220°C/425°F/Gas 7. Pour 300ml/½ pint/1¼ cups cold water into the pan and immediately place the loaf in the oven. Bake for 10 minutes. Remove the pan, reduce the temperature to 190°C/375°F/Gas 5 and bake for about 20 minutes. Cool on a wire rack.

Multi-Seed Loaf: *Energy 1668kcal/7038kJ; Protein 47g; Carbohydrate 276.1g, of which sugars 6.9g; Fat 49.1g, of which saturates 6g; Cholesterol 0mg; Calcium 443mg; Fibre 20.8g; Sodium 12mg.*
Spanish Country Bread: *Energy 2265kcal/9588kJ; Protein 81.5g; Carbohydrate 463.5g, of which sugars 10.8g; Fat 17.2g, of which saturates 1.4g; Cholesterol 0mg; Calcium 214mg; Fibre 55.4g; Sodium 16mg.*

Olive Bread

Rich olive breads are popular all over the Mediterranean. For this Greek recipe use rich oily olives or those marinated in oil with herbs, rather than canned ones.

Makes 2 loaves

30ml/2 tbsp extra virgin olive oil
2 red onions, thinly sliced
225g/8oz/2 cups stoned (pitted) black or green olives
800g/1¾lb/7 cups strong white bread flour
7.5ml/1½ tsp salt
20ml/4 tsp easy-blend (rapid-rise) dried yeast
45ml/3 tbsp each roughly chopped fresh flat leaf parsley, coriander (cilantro) or mint

1 Heat the olive oil in a frying pan, add the onions and cook gently until soft. Roughly chop the olives.

2 Put the flour, salt, yeast and parsley, coriander or mint in a large bowl with the olives and fried onions and pour in 475ml/16fl oz/2 cups hand-hot water.

3 Mix to a dough using a round-bladed knife, adding a little more water if the mixture feels dry. Turn the dough out on to a lightly floured surface and knead for about 10 minutes until it is smooth and elastic.

4 Put the dough in a clean, lightly oiled bowl, cover with lightly oiled clear film (plastic wrap) and leave in a warm place until doubled in bulk.

5 Preheat the oven to 220°C/425°F/Gas 7. Lightly grease two baking sheets. Turn the dough on to a floured surface and cut in half. Shape each half into a round and place both loaves on the baking sheets. Cover loosely with lightly oiled clear film and leave in a warm place until doubled in size.

6 Slash the tops of the loaves with a knife and then bake in the oven for about 40 minutes, or until the loaves are golden brown and sound hollow when tapped on the bottom. Transfer to a wire rack to cool. Serve with fresh unsalted Greek butter or as part of a meze table with a Greek salad.

Moroccan Holiday Bread

The addition of cornmeal and seeds gives this superb loaf an interesting flavour and texture. Serve it with cooked lean sliced meats.

Makes 1 loaf
Serves 6

275g/10oz/2½ cups unbleached strong white bread flour
50g/2oz/½ cup cornmeal
5ml/1 tsp salt
20g/¾ oz fresh yeast
120ml/4fl oz/½ cup lukewarm water
120ml/4fl oz/½ cup lukewarm semi-skimmed (low-fat) milk
15ml/1 tbsp pumpkin seeds
15ml/1 tbsp sesame seeds
30ml/2 tbsp sunflower seeds

1 Lightly grease a baking sheet and set aside. Mix the flour, cornmeal and salt together in a large bowl and make a well in the centre.

2 Cream the yeast with a little of the water, then stir in the remaining water and the milk. Pour into the well in the flour and mix to form a fairly soft dough.

3 Turn the dough out on to a lightly floured surface and knead for about 5 minutes, or until smooth and elastic. Place the dough in a lightly oiled bowl, cover with lightly oiled clear film (plastic wrap) and leave in a warm place for about 1 hour, or until doubled in bulk.

4 Turn out the dough on to a lightly floured surface and knock back (punch down). Gently knead the pumpkin and sesame seeds into the dough. Shape the dough into a round ball and flatten slightly.

5 Place on the prepared baking sheet, cover with lightly oiled clear film and leave to rise in a warm place for 45 minutes, or until doubled in bulk.

6 Meanwhile, preheat the oven to 200°C/400°F/Gas 6. Brush the top of the loaf with water and sprinkle it evenly with the sunflower seeds. Bake the loaf in the oven for 30–35 minutes, or until it is golden and sounds hollow when tapped on the base. Transfer the loaf to a wire rack to cool. Serve in slices.

Olive Bread: Energy 1546kcal/6538kJ; Protein 38.5g; Carbohydrate 301.9g, of which sugars 13.2g; Fat 28.8g, of which saturates 4.3g; Cholesterol 0mg; Calcium 671mg; Fibre 17.8g; Sodium 4,028mg.
Holiday Bread: Energy 241kcal/1017kJ; Protein 7.1g; Carbohydrate 42.7g, of which sugars 1.7g; Fat 5.6g, of which saturates 0.9g; Cholesterol 1mg; Calcium 139mg; Fibre 2.2g; Sodium 339mg.

Olive Twists

These elaborately shaped rolls are made with dough, enriched with olive oil.

Makes 16 rolls

450g/1lb/4 cups unbleached white bread flour
10ml/2 tsp salt
15g/½oz fresh yeast
250ml/8fl oz/1 cup lukewarm water
60ml/4 tbsp extra virgin olive oil, plus extra for brushing

1 Lightly oil 3 baking sheets. Sift the flour and salt together in a large bowl and make a well in the centre. Cream the yeast with half of the water, then stir in the remainder. Add to the well with the oil and mix to a dough. Turn out on to a lightly floured surface and knead for 8–10 minutes until smooth and elastic. Place in a lightly oiled bowl, cover with lightly oiled clear film (plastic wrap) and leave in a warm place for about 1 hour, or until nearly doubled in bulk. Turn on to a lightly floured surface and knock back (punch down). Divide into 12 equal pieces.

2 For *tavalli* (twisted spiral rolls): roll each piece of dough into a strip about 30cm/12in long and 4cm/1½in wide. Twist into a loose spiral and join the ends together to make a circle.

3 For *filoncini* (finger-shaped rolls): flatten each piece into an oval and roll to about 23cm/9in in length without changing the basic shape. Make it 5cm/2in wide at one end and 10cm/4in wide at the other. Roll up, starting from the wider end. Gently stretch the roll to 20–23cm/8–9in long. Cut in half.

4 For *carciofi* (artichoke-shaped rolls): shape each piece of dough into a ball. Using scissors, snip 4–5 5mm/¼in cuts in a circle on the top of each ball, then make 5 larger horizontal cuts around the sides.

5 Meanwhile, preheat the oven to 200°C/400°F/Gas 6. Place all the rolls on the prepared baking sheets, spaced well apart. Brush lightly with olive oil, cover with lightly oiled clear film and leave to rise, in a warm place, for 20–30 minutes.

6 Bake the rolls for 15 minutes. Transfer to a wire rack to cool.

Olive and Oregano Bread

This tasty Italian bread is highly flavoured with oregano, parsley and olives. Serve warm to enjoy the flavours at their best.

Makes 1 loaf

5ml/1 tsp dried yeast
300ml/½ pint/1¼ cups warm water
pinch of sugar
15ml/1 tbsp olive oil, plus extra for greasing
1 onion, chopped
450g/1lb/4 cups strong white bread flour, plus extra for dusting
5ml/1 tsp salt
1.5ml/¼ tsp ground black pepper
50g/2oz/½ cup stoned (pitted) black olives, roughly chopped
15ml/1 tbsp black olive paste
15ml/1 tbsp chopped fresh oregano
15ml/1 tbsp chopped fresh parsley

1 Sprinkle the dried yeast over half the warm water. Add the sugar, stir well and leave to stand for 10 minutes, or until frothy.

2 Heat the oil in a pan and fry the onion until golden, stirring occasionally. Remove from the heat and set aside.

3 Sift the flour into a bowl with the salt and pepper. Make a well in the centre. Add the yeast mixture, the onions (with the oil), olives, olive paste, oregano, parsley and remaining water. Gradually incorporate the flour, and mix to a soft dough, adding a little extra water if necessary. Turn out on to a lightly floured surface and knead for 5 minutes, or until smooth and elastic.

4 Place in a bowl, cover with a damp dish towel and leave in a warm place for about 2 hours until the dough has doubled in bulk. Lightly grease a baking sheet and set aside. Turn the dough out on to a lightly floured surface and knead again for a few minutes. Shape into a 20cm/8in flat round and place on the baking sheet. Make criss-cross cuts over the top. Cover and leave in a warm place for 30 minutes, or until well risen. Preheat the oven to 220°C/425°F/Gas 7.

5 Dust the loaf with flour. Bake for 10 minutes then lower the temperature to 200°C/400°F/Gas 6. Bake for another 20 minutes, until the loaf sounds hollow when the base is tapped.

Olive Twists: *Energy 121kcal/509kJ; Protein 2.6g; Carbohydrate 21.9g, of which sugars 0.4g; Fat 3.1g, of which saturates 0.5g; Cholesterol 0mg; Calcium 39mg; Fibre 0.9g; Sodium 246mg.*
Olive and Oregano Bread: *Energy 1544kcal/6543kJ; Protein 39.2g; Carbohydrate 319g, of which sugars 9.1g; Fat 21.1g, of which saturates 3.1g; Cholesterol 0mg; Calcium 613mg; Fibre 14.9g; Sodium 1209mg.*

French Dimpled Rolls

A French speciality, these attractive white rolls are distinguished by the split down the centre. They have a crusty finish while remaining soft and light inside thanks to the steaming technique used to bake them – they taste lovely, too.

Makes 10 rolls
400g/14oz/3½ cups unbleached white bread flour
7.5ml/1½ tsp salt
5ml/1 tsp caster (superfine) sugar
15g/½oz fresh yeast
120ml/4fl oz/½ cup lukewarm milk
175ml/6fl oz/¾ cup lukewarm water

1 Lightly grease 2 baking sheets. Sift the flour and salt into a large bowl. Stir in the sugar and make a well in the centre.

2 Cream the yeast with the milk until dissolved, then pour into the centre of the flour mixture. Sprinkle over a little of the flour from around the edge. Leave at room temperature for 15–20 minutes, or until the mixture starts to bubble.

3 Add the water and gradually mix in the flour to form a fairly moist, soft dough. Turn out on to a lightly floured surface and knead for 8–10 minutes until smooth and elastic. Place in a lightly oiled bowl, cover with lightly oiled clear film (plastic wrap) and leave at room temperature for about 1½ hours, or until doubled in bulk.

4 Turn out on to a floured surface and knock back (punch down). Re-cover and leave to rest for 5 minutes. Divide the dough into 10 pieces. Shape into balls, then roll into ovals. Lightly flour the tops. Space well apart on the baking sheets, cover with lightly oiled clear film and leave to rise for about 30 minutes, or until almost doubled in size.

5 Lightly oil the side of your hand and press the centre of each roll to make a deep split. Re-cover and leave to rest for 15 minutes. Meanwhile, place a roasting pan in the bottom of the oven and preheat the oven to 230°C/450°F/Gas 8. Pour 250ml/8fl oz/1 cup water into the pan and bake the rolls for 15 minutes, or until golden. Cool on a wire rack.

Petit Pains au Lait

These classic French round milk rolls have a delicate crust and a sweet crumb. They are great for breakfast and don't last long!

Makes 12 rolls
450g/1lb/4 cups unbleached white bread flour
10ml/2 tsp salt
15ml/1 tbsp caster (superfine) sugar
50g/2oz/¼ cup butter, softened
15g/½oz fresh yeast
280ml/9fl oz/generous 1 cup lukewarm milk, plus 15ml/1 tbsp extra, to glaze

1 Lightly grease 2 baking sheets. Sift the flour and salt together into a bowl. Stir in the sugar. Rub the butter into the flour. Cream the yeast with 60ml/4 tbsp of the milk. Stir in the remaining milk. Pour into the flour and mix to a soft dough.

2 Turn out on to a lightly floured surface and knead for 8–10 minutes until smooth and elastic. Place in a lightly oiled bowl, cover with lightly oiled clear film (plastic wrap) and leave to rise, in a warm place, for 1 hour, or until doubled in bulk.

3 Turn out the dough on to a lightly floured surface and gently knock back (punch down). Divide into 12 equal pieces. Shape into balls and space on the baking sheets.

4 Using a sharp knife, cut a cross in the top of each roll. Cover with lightly oiled clear film and leave to rise, in a warm place, for about 20 minutes, or until doubled in size.

5 Preheat the oven to 200°C/400°F/Gas 6. Brush the rolls with milk and bake for 20–25 minutes. Cool on a wire rack.

Variations
These can also be made into long rolls. To shape, flatten each ball of dough and fold in half. Roll back and forth, using your hand to form a 13cm/5in long roll, tapered at either end. Just before baking, slash the tops horizontally several times.

French Dimpled Rolls: *Energy 145kcal/614kJ; Protein 4.4g; Carbohydrate 31.9g, of which sugars 1.4g; Fat 0.8g, of which saturates 0.3g; Cholesterol 1mg; Calcium 77mg; Fibre 1.2g; Sodium 9mg.*
Petit Pains au Lait: *Energy 169kcal/714kJ; Protein 4.3g; Carbohydrate 30.2g, of which sugars 1.6g; Fat 4.3g, of which saturates 2.5g; Cholesterol 10mg; Calcium 79mg; Fibre 1.2g; Sodium 36mg.*

Ricotta and Oregano Knots

Ricotta adds a wonderful moistness to these rolls, made using a breadmaker. They are best served warm.

Makes 12 rolls

60ml/4 tbsp ricotta cheese
225ml/8fl oz/scant 1 cup water
450g/1lb/4 cups unbleached white bread flour
45ml/3 tbsp skimmed milk powder
10ml/2 tsp dried oregano
5ml/1 tsp salt
10ml/2 tsp caster (superfine) sugar
25g/1oz/ 2 tbsp butter
5ml/1 tsp easy-blend (rapid-rise) dried yeast

For the topping

1 egg yolk
15ml/1 tbsp water
freshly ground black pepper

1 Spoon the cheese into the bread machine pan and add the water. (Reverse the order in which you add the liquid and dry ingredients if the instructions for your machine specify this.)

2 Sprinkle over the flour to cover the cheese and water. Add the skimmed milk powder and oregano. Place the salt, sugar and butter in separate corners of the pan. Make a small indent in the centre of the flour and add the yeast. Set the machine to the basic dough setting (if available). Start.

3 Oil two baking sheets. When the dough cycle has finished, remove the dough and place it on a lightly floured surface. Knock back (punch down) gently, then divide it into 12 pieces and cover these with oiled clear film (plastic wrap).

4 Roll each piece of dough on a floured surface into a rope 25cm/10in long. Lift one end over the other to make a loop. Push the end through the hole in the loop to make a knot.

5 Place the knots on the baking sheets, cover them with oiled clear film and leave in a warm place for about 30 minutes, or until doubled in size. Preheat the oven to 220°C/425°F/Gas 7.

6 Mix the egg yolk and water for the topping and brush over the rolls. Sprinkle some with pepper and leave the rest plain. Bake for about 15–18 minutes, or until golden brown.

Wholemeal and Rye Pistolets

Unless your bread maker has a programme for wholemeal dough, it is worth the extra effort of the double rising, because this gives a better flavour.

Makes 12

300ml/½ pint/1¼ cups water
280g/10oz/2½ cups stoneground wholemeal (whole-wheat) bread flour
50g/2oz/½ cup unbleached white bread flour, plus extra for dusting
115g/4oz/1 cup rye flour
30ml/2 tbsp skimmed milk powder
10ml/2 tsp salt
10ml/2 tsp caster (superfine) sugar
25g/1oz/2 tbsp butter
7.5ml/1½ tsp easy-blend (rapid-rise) dried yeast

For the glaze

5ml/1 tsp salt
15ml/1 tbsp water

1 Pour the water into the bread pan and sprinkle over all three types of flour, covering the water completely. Add the skimmed milk powder. Then add the salt, sugar and buttein separate corners of the pan. Make a small indent in the centre of the flour and add the dried yeast.

2 Set the machine to the dough setting; use wholewheat dough setting (if available), otherwise repeat the programme to allow sufficient rising time. Start. Lightly oil two baking sheets.

3 When the dough cycle has finished, remove the dough and place it on a floured surface Knock back (punch down)gently, then divide it into 12. Cover with oiled clear film (plastic wrap). Shape each piece into a ball and roll into an oval. Place the rolls on the baking sheets. Cover with oiled clear film and leave in a warm place for about 30–45 minutes, or until almost doubled in size. Preheat the oven to 220°C/425°F/Gas 7.

4 Mix the salt and water for the glaze and brush over the rolls. Dust the tops with flour. Using the oiled handle of a wooden spoon held horizontally, split each roll almost in half, along its length. Replace the clear film and leave for 10 minutes. Bake the rolls for 15–20 minutes, until the bases sound hollow when tapped. Turn out on to a wire rack to cool.

Ricotta Knots: *Energy 146kcal/620kJ; Protein 4.7g; Carbohydrate 30g, of which sugars 1.4g; Fat 1.7g, of which saturates 0.7g; Cholesterol 19mg; Calcium 70mg; Fibre 1.2g; Sodium 9mg.*
Wholemeal Pistolets: *Energy 120kcal/511kJ; Protein 4.2g; Carbohydrate 25.3g, of which sugars 0.6g; Fat 0.9g, of which saturates 0.2g; Cholesterol 0mg; Calcium 18mg; Fibre 3.4g; Sodium 330mg.*

Spanish Picos

These small knotted bread shapes, dusted with salt and sesame seeds, are often eaten in Spain with drinks, but can also be served with an appetizer or soup. In this recipe they are made using a breadmaker.

Makes about 70

200ml/7fl oz/⅞ cup water
45ml/3 tbsp extra virgin olive oil
350g/12½oz/3 cups unbleached white bread flour
5ml/1 tsp salt
2.5ml/½ tsp granulated (white) sugar
5ml/1 tsp easy-blend (rapid-rise) dried yeast

For the topping

30ml/2 tbsp water
15ml/1 tbsp sea salt
15ml/1 tbsp sesame seeds

1 Pour the water and oil into the pan and sprinkle over the flour, ensuring that it covers the liquid. (If necessary, reverse the order in which you add the liquid and dry ingredients.) Add the salt and sugar, in separate corners of the pan. Make a small indent in the centre of the flour and add the yeast.

2 Set the machine to the dough setting, using the basic dough setting if available, and start. Lightly oil two baking sheets.

3 When the cycle has finished, place the dough on a floured surface. Knock back (punch down) gently, then roll it out to a rectangle measuring 30 × 23cm/12 × 9in. Cut lengthways into three strips, then cut each strip into 2.5cm/1in wide ribbons.

4 Preheat the oven to 200°C/400°F/Gas 6. Tie each ribbon into a loose knot and space well apart on the prepared baking sheets. Cover with oiled clear film (plastic wrap) and leave in a warm place for 10–15 minutes to rise. Leave the picos plain or brush with water and sprinkle with salt or sesame seeds. Bake for 10–15 minutes, or until golden.

Cook's Tip
Make these tasty nibbles up to a day in advance. Re-heat in a moderate oven for a few minutes, to refresh.

Cashew and Olive Scrolls

These attractively shaped rolls have a crunchy texture and ooze with the flavours of olives and fresh herbs. In this recipe they are made using a breadmaker.

Makes 12 rolls

140ml/5fl oz/⅝ cup milk
120ml/4fl oz/½ cup water
30ml/2 tbsp extra virgin olive oil
450g/1lb/4 cups unbleached white bread flour
5ml/1 tsp salt
2.5ml/½ tsp caster (superfine) sugar
7.5ml/1½ tsp easy-blend (rapid-rise) dried yeast
5ml/1 tsp finely chopped fresh rosemary or thyme
50g/2oz/½ cup salted cashew nuts, finely chopped
50g/2oz/½ cup pitted green olives, finely chopped
45ml/3 tbsp freshly grated Parmesan cheese, for sprinkling

1 Pour the milk, water and oil into the pan. If your bread machine specifies it, reverse the order in which you add the liquid and dry ingredients.

2 Sprinkle over the flour, ensuring that it covers the liquid. Add the salt and sugar, placing them in separate corners of the bread pan. Make a small indent in the centre of the flour (but not down as far as the liquid) and add the yeast.

3 Set the machine to the dough setting; use basic raisin dough setting (if available). Press Start. Add the herbs, cashew nuts and olives when the machine beeps, or five minutes before the end of the kneading period. Lightly oil two baking sheets.

4 When the dough cycle has finished, remove from the machine and place on a lightly floured surface. Knock back (punch down), then divide equally into 12 pieces and cover with oiled clear film (plastic wrap). Take one piece, leaving the rest covered, and roll into a rope about 23cm/9in long, tapering the ends. Shape this into an 's' shape. Repeat with the remaining rolls. Leave to rise in a warm place for 30 minues, until doubled in size.

5 Preheat the oven to 200°C/400°F/Gas 6. Sprinkle the rolls with Parmesan and bake for 18–20 minutes, or until risen and golden. Cool on a wire rack.

Spanish Picos: *Energy 23kcal/95kJ; Protein 0.5g; Carbohydrate 4.2g, of which sugars 0.1g; Fat 0.5g, of which saturates 0.1g; Cholesterol 0mg; Calcium 8mg; Fibre 0.2g; Sodium 28mg.*
Cashew Scrolls: *Energy 196kcal/828kJ; Protein 6.3g; Carbohydrate 30.5g, of which sugars 1.3g; Fat 6.3g, of which saturates 1.7g; Cholesterol 4mg; Calcium 116mg; Fibre 1.4g; Sodium 153mg.*

Mallorcan Sweet Rolls

These spiral- or snail-shaped rolls are a popular Spanish breakfast treat. Traditionally lard (shortening), or *saim*, was used to brush over the sweetened dough; nowadays butter is mainly used.

Makes 16 rolls

225g/8oz/2 cups unbleached white bread flour
2.5ml/½ tsp salt
50g/2oz/¼ cup caster (superfine) sugar
15g/½oz fresh yeast
75ml/5 tbsp lukewarm milk
1 egg
30ml/2 tbsp sunflower oil
50g/2oz/¼ cup butter, melted
icing (confectioner's) sugar, for dusting

1 Grease 2 baking sheets. Sift the flour and salt into a large mixing bowl. Stir in the sugar and make a well in the centre.

2 Cream the yeast with the milk, pour into the well, then sprinkle a little of the flour mixture evenly over the top of the liquid. Leave in a warm place for 15 minutes, or until frothy.

3 Beat the egg and oil together. Add to the flour mixture and mix to a smooth dough. Turn out on to a lightly floured surface and knead for 8–10 minutes until smooth and elastic. Place in a lightly oiled bowl, cover with oiled clear film (plastic wrap) and leave in a warm place for 1 hour, or until doubled in bulk.

4 Turn out the dough on to a lightly floured surface. Knock back (punch down) and divide into 16 equal pieces. Shape each piece into a thin rope about 38cm/15in long. Pour the melted butter on to a plate and dip the ropes into the butter to coat.

5 On the baking sheets, curl each rope into a loose spiral, spacing well apart. Tuck the ends under to seal. Cover with lightly oiled clear film and leave in a warm place for about 45 minutes, or until doubled in size.

6 Meanwhile, preheat the oven to 190°C/375°F/Gas 5. Brush the rolls with water and dust with icing sugar. Bake for 10 minutes, or until light golden brown. Cool on a wire rack. Dust again with icing sugar and serve warm.

Pitta Bread

Soft, slightly bubbly pitta bread is a pleasure to make. It can be eaten in a variety of ways, such as filled with salad or little chunks of barbecued meat. Eat it with a main course or as part of a meze table.

Makes 12

500g/1¼lb/5 cups strong white bread flour, or half white and half wholemeal (whole-wheat)
12.5ml/2½ tsp easy-blend (rapid-rise) dried yeast
15ml/1 tbsp salt
15ml/1 tbsp olive oil

1 Combine the flour, yeast and salt. Combine the olive oil and 250ml/8fl oz/1 cup water, then add the flour mixture, stirring in the same direction, and then working with your hands until the dough is stiff. Place the dough in a clean bowl, cover with a clean damp dish towel and leave in a warm place for at least 30 minutes and up to 2 hours.

2 Knead the dough for 10 minutes, or until smooth. Lightly oil the bowl, place the dough in it, cover again and leave in a warm place for about 1 hour, or until doubled in size.

3 Divide the dough into 12 equal pieces. With lightly floured hands, flatten each piece, then roll out into a round measuring about 20cm/8in and about ½–1cm/¼–½in thick.

4 Heat a heavy frying pan over a medium-high heat. When it is hot, lay one piece of flattened dough in the pan and cook for 15–20 seconds. Turn it over and cook the second side for about 1 minute.

5 When large bubbles start to form on the bread, which should be after about 1–2 minutes, turn it over again. It should puff up. Using a clean dish towel, gently press on the bread where the bubbles have formed. Cook the bread for a total of 3 minutes, then remove the pitta from the pan. Repeat with the remaining dough.

6 Wrap the pitta breads in a clean dish towel, adding each one to the stack as it is cooked. Serve the pittas hot while they are soft and moist.

Mallorcan Sweet Rolls: *Energy 327kcal/1371kJ; Protein 8.7g; Carbohydrate 38.6g, of which sugars 4.3g; Fat 16.1g, of which saturates 9.3g; Cholesterol 117mg; Calcium 172mg; Fibre 1.4g; Sodium 162mg.*
Pitta Bread: *Energy 150kcal/638kJ; Protein 3.9g; Carbohydrate 32.4g, of which sugars 0.6g; Fat 1.5g, of which saturates 0.2g; Cholesterol 0mg; Calcium 58mg; Fibre 1.3g; Sodium 493mg.*

Spring Onion Flatbreads

Use these flatbreads to wrap around barbecue-cooked meat and chunky vegetable salads, or serve with tasty dips such as hummus as part of a buffet or a meze table. They're at their best eaten as soon as they're cooked.

Makes 16

450g/1lb/4 cups strong white bread flour, plus extra for dusting
5ml/1 tsp salt
7g/¼oz packet easy-blend (rapid-rise) dried yeast
4 spring onions (scallions), finely chopped

1 Place the flour in a large mixing bowl and stir in the salt, yeast and spring onions. Make a well in the centre and pour in 300ml/½ pint/1¼ cups hand-hot water. Mix to form a soft, but not sticky, dough.

2 Turn out the dough on to a floured work surface and knead for about 5 minutes, until smooth and elastic.

3 Put the dough back in the bowl, cover with a clean, damp dish towel and leave in a warm place for about 1 hour, or until doubled in size.

4 Knock back (punch down) the dough, and turn it out on to a lightly floured work surface. Divide the dough into 16 equal pieces and roll each piece into a smooth ball. Roll out each ball to flatten it to a 13cm/5in round.

5 Heat a large frying pan or ridged griddle until hot. Dust off any excess flour from the first dough round and lay it in the hot pan. Cook for 1 minute, until the underside is slightly browned in parts, then flip over and cook for 30 seconds. Repeat with the remaining dough rounds. Wrap the completed flatbreads in a dish towel to keep them warm while you cook the rest.

Variation
To make garlic flatbreads, use 2 finely chopped garlic cloves in place of the spring onions (scallions).

Sesame-Studded Grissini

These crisp, pencil-like breadsticks are easy to make and far more delicious than commercially manufactured grissini. Once you start to nibble one, it will be difficult to stop eating them. Serve them with drinks and a variety of creamy dips.

Makes 20

225g/8oz/2 cups unbleached white bread flour
7.5ml/1½ tsp salt
15g/½oz fresh yeast
135ml/4½fl oz/scant ⅔ cup lukewarm water
30ml/2 tbsp extra virgin olive oil, plus extra for brushing
sesame seeds, for coating

1 Lightly oil 2 baking sheets. Sift the flour and salt together into a large bowl and make a well in the centre.

2 Cream the yeast with the water and pour into the well. Add the oil and mix to a soft dough. Turn out on to a lightly floured surface and knead for 8–10 minutes until smooth and elastic.

3 Roll the dough into a rectangle about 15 × 20cm/6 × 8in. Brush with olive oil, cover with lightly oiled clear film (plastic wrap) and leave in a warm place for about 1 hour, or until doubled in bulk.

4 Preheat the oven to 200°C/400°F/Gas 6. Spread out the sesame seeds. Cut the dough into two 7.5 × 10cm/3 × 4in rectangles. Cut each piece into ten 7.5cm/3in strips. Stretch each strip gently until it is about 30cm/12in long.

5 Roll each grissini, as it is made, in the sesame seeds. Place on the prepared baking sheets, spaced well apart. Lightly brush with olive oil. Leave to rise in a warm place for 10 minutes, then bake for 15–20 minutes. Transfer to a wire rack to cool.

Cook's Tip
When baking the grissini turn them over and change the position of the baking sheets halfway through the cooking time, so they brown evenly.

Spring Onion Flatbreads: *Energy 97kcal/410kJ; Protein 2.7g; Carbohydrate 21.9g, of which sugars 0.5g; Fat 0.4g, of which saturates 0.1g; Cholesterol 0mg; Calcium 40mg; Fibre 0.9g; Sodium 124mg.*
Sesame-Studded Grissini: *Energy 53kcal/222kJ; Protein 1.2g; Carbohydrate 8.8g, of which sugars 0.2g; Fat 1.7g, of which saturates 0.2g; Cholesterol 0mg; Calcium 21mg; Fibre 0.4g; Sodium 148mg.*

Index